The Primacy of Movement

Advances in Consciousness Research (AiCR)

Provides a forum for scholars from different scientific disciplines and fields of knowledge who study consciousness in its multifaceted aspects. Thus the Series includes (but is not limited to) the various areas of cognitive science, including cognitive psychology, brain science, philosophy and linguistics. The orientation of the series is toward developing new interdisciplinary and integrative approaches for the investigation, description and theory of consciousness, as well as the practical consequences of this research for the individual in society.

From 1999 the Series consists of two subseries that cover the most important types of contributions to consciousness studies:

Series A: Theory and Method. Contributions to the development of theory and method in the study of consciousness; Series B: Research in Progress. Experimental, descriptive and clinical research in consciousness.

This book is a contribution to Series A.

For an overview of all books published in this series, please see
http://benjamins.com/catalog/aicr

Editor

Maxim I. Stamenov
Bulgarian Academy of Sciences

Editorial Board

Volume 82

The Primacy of Movement. Expanded second edition
by Maxine Sheets-Johnstone

The Primacy of Movement

Expanded second edition

Maxine Sheets-Johnstone

University of Oregon

John Benjamins Publishing Company

Amsterdam / Philadelphia

The paper used in this publication meets the minimum requirements of American National Standard for Information Sciences – Permanence of Paper for Printed Library Materials, ANSI z39.48-1984.

Library of Congress Cataloging-in-Publication Data

Sheets-Johnstone, Maxine.
  The primacy of movement / Maxine Sheets-Johnstone. -- Expanded 2nd ed.
p. cm. (Advances in Consciousness Research, ISSN 1381-589X ; v. 82)
Includes bibliographical references and index.
1. Movement (Philosophy) 2. Movement, Psychology of. I. Title.
B105.M65S44   2011
116--dc22   2011011681
ISBN 978 90 272 5218 0   (Hb ; alk. paper)
ISBN 978 90 272 5219 7   (Pb ; alk. paper)
ISBN 978 90 272 8677 2   (Eb)

John Benjamins Publishing Co. · P.O. Box 36224 · 1020 ME Amsterdam · The Netherlands
John Benjamins North America · P.O. Box 27519 · Philadelphia PA 19118-0519 · USA

To Dmitri and Kevin
with immeasurable love
and with gratitude
for enriching my life immeasurably

Table of contents

Preface to the expanded second edition   XIII

Acknowledgments   XV

Introduction   XVII

    Notes   XXXII

SECTION I

Foundations

CHAPTER 1

Neandertals   3

1. Introduction 3
2. "Remarkable mental adaptations" 5
3. "Symbolic behavior" 7
4. Deepened understandings of the symbolic 12
5. Animate form: Theoretical clarifications 18
6. Animate form: Neandertals 22
    Notes 32

CHAPTER 2 – PART I

Consciousness: A natural history   37

1. Introduction 37
2. Reasons for critically questioning the question 38
3. Life and its definitions: A question of animation and justification 44
4. Corporeal consciousness: A matter of knowing 48
5. To the things themselves: Corporeal matters of fact 55
6. From corporeal matters of fact to corporeal consciousness 62
7. Implications 67
    Glossary 69
    Notes 71

CHAPTER 2 – PART II

Consciousness: An Aristotelian account   77

1. Introduction 77
2. Burnyeat's claim and its initial Aristotelian rejoinder 78
3. Uniformity 84

4.   Receiving the form without the matter   87

5.   Excursus I: On the relationship of form and matter   90

6.   On the way to an understanding of quality:
      Clearing the ground   92

7.   Excursus II: The aesthetics of quality   98

8.   The coincidence of form and quality in everyday life   102

9.   The semantics of quality: A natural history of form   106

      Notes   111

CHAPTER 3

The primacy of movement   113

1.   Introduction   113

2.   Animate organism   115

3.   Kinesthesia   120

4.   Cardinal structures of kinesthetic consciousness   121

5.   A descriptive analysis of movement and a further clarification
      of kinesthesia   126

6.   Kinesthetic consciousness and the primordial
      constitution of time   130

7.   The cardinal structure of time   134

8.   Afterword   140

      Notes   150

SECTION II

Methodology

CHAPTER 4

Husserl and Von Helmholtz — and the possibility of a trans disciplinary
communal task   155

1.   Introduction   155

2.   On the central significance of movement in perception   157

3.   A brief exposition of the phenomenological *epoché*   163

4.   A methodological contrast   164

5.   The central epistemological significance
      of freely-varied movement   167

6.   On factual and essential matters   175

7.   On the epistemological import of the confluences:
      A critical look at cognitivist science and philosophy   181

8.   An alternative approach   187

      Notes   189

CHAPTER 5

On learning to move oneself: A constructive phenomenology   193

1.   Initial remarks   193
2.   A general introduction to the terrain   194
3.   Beginning phenomenological considerations   199
4.   Primal movement and its occlusion by a natural
     attitude view of movement   200
5.   Methodological clarifications for a constructive phenomenology   212
6.   A constructive phenomenology of animation   217
     Notes   234

CHAPTER 6

Merleau-Ponty: A man in search of a method   237

1.   Initial clarification   237
2.   Introduction   238
3.   Pathology   240
4.   Facts   244
5.   A fundamental liability of a fact-based ontological methodology   248
6.   Methodological muddles and opacities   252
7.   Methodology in Merleau-Ponty's earlier and later work   258
8.   The unresolved tension between nature and ontology   266
9.   Tentative conclusions   272
10. Optional epilogue   273
     Notes   276

CHAPTER 7

**Does philosophy begin (and end) in wonder? or what is the nature
of a philosophic act?: A methodological postscript**   279

1.   Introduction and initial gleanings   279
2.   A distinction   288
3.   Freedom and risks   291
     Note   295

SECTION III
Applications

CHAPTER 8

On the significance of animate form   299

1.   Introduction   299
2.   Framing the questions anew   300

3.   The animate is not arbitrary — or the semantic
      specificity of living bodies   302
4.   A sketch of the evil eye as a derived archetypal form   306
5.   The fundamental challenge of animate form and its lexical-conceptual
      consequence as exemplified in two critical analyses   309
      Notes   329

CHAPTER 9
Human speech perception and an evolutionary semantics   321
1.   The motor theory of speech perception   321
2.   Expanding upon the critique   323
3.   Comsigns and tactical deception   330
4.   Challenging counter evidence   336
5.   On the evolution of an evolutionary semantics   339
      Notes   345

CHAPTER 10
Why a mind is not a brain and a brain is not a body   347
1.   Introduction   347
2.   Minds and language   347
3.   The radical doctrine of eliminative materialism   349
4.   Dressing up: The broader eliminative-materialist picture   352
5.   Pause-for-thought problems with neurological mecca   354
6.   From problems with neurological mecca
      to the question "what is it like?"   370
7.   Zeroing in on why a mind is not a brain and a brain is not a body   376
8.   How by exchanging brain technology for history
      we give ourselves the one-two punch   385
      Notes   386

CHAPTER 11
What is it like to be a brain?   391
1.   Introduction   391
2.   Beginning findings   392
3.   Neural firing: A phenomenological inquiry   396
4.   Distinguishing information and ability   402
5.   Animism   406
6.   Reversing materialist charges   411
      Notes   417

CHAPTER 12

Thinking in movement   419

1. The twofold purpose   419
2. Dance improvisation: A paradigm of thinking in movement   420
3. Thinking in movement: Our human developmental background   430
4. Thinking in movement: Our phylogenetic heritage   439
5. Summation   447
    Notes   448

SECTION IV

Twenty-first century reflections on human nature: Foundational
concepts and realities

CHAPTER 13

Animation: The fundamental, essential, and properly descriptive concept   453

1. Introduction   453
2. Basic realities of affectivity   454
3. Primal animation   458
4. Enactive resistances and their biological refutations   460
5. Further reflections on animation   462
6. Animation and current scientific research on *the brain*   465
7. Animate organisms, affectivity, and the challenge of languaging
    experience   466
8. Concluding thoughts on the importance of recognizing and languaging
    the qualitative dynamics of life   470
    Notes   472

CHAPTER 14

Embodied minds or mindful bodies?: A core twenty-first century challenge   477

1. Introduction   477
2. Mind   478
3. The Brain   489
4. Receptivity and responsivity: Reciprocal concepts in phenomenology
    and evolutionary biology   501
5. Afterword on kinesthesia   510
    Notes   521

References   525
Name index   549
Subject index   555

Preface to the expanded second edition

This second edition of *The Primacy of Movement* contains an additional section with two new chapters. The added fourth section, titled "Twenty-First Century Reflections on Human Nature: Foundational Concepts and Realities," takes contemporary research findings in cognitive science and philosophy and in neuroscience into detailed account. Not surprisingly, it sets these findings in the context of movement, most pointedly in the context of the concluding statement in the original edition to the effect that any time we care to turn our attention to movement — and to our fundamental capacity to think in movement — there it is.

The new Chapter 13 provides both a constructive and critical path toward these expanded understandings of movement by showing how animation is the fundamental, essential, and properly descriptive concept for understandings of animate life. It does so by considering affectivity as a staple of animate life, elucidating both its biological and existential foundation, and illuminating its integral dynamic relationship to movement. The chapter originally appeared in 2009 as an article in *Continental Philosophy Review*. Minor changes have been made in the article in adapting it to this book. I thank Springer Publications for their permission to include the article here.

The new Chapter 14 follows up conclusions reached in the chapter on animation. It does so by way of an extended interdisciplinary inquiry into movement from three perspectives: mind, brain, and the conceptually reciprocal realities of receptivity and responsivity as set forth in phenomenology and evolutionary biology, respectively. It follows up these three perspectives with an Afterword on kinesthesia, and this in order to point up the incontrovertible significance of the faculty to cognition and affectivity and its egregious omission in contemporary disquisitions on "embodiment," "motoric functions", an "enactive approach," and the like, in other words, in contemporary research and writings on putatively living — or lived — bodies. The overall inquiry poses — and answers — the question that constitutes the chapter's title: "Embodied Minds or Mindful Bodies? A Core Twenty-First Century Challenge." With respect to each perspective, and as in the preceding chapter, a constructive and critical path is taken in the analysis and discussion of the issues involved, the central issue being a recognition of movement to begin with.

The necessity of recognizing movement should actually be obvious to anyone bent on understanding the nature of animate life and in particular the animate nature of human nature. In a quite literal sense the recognition of movement is a *re-cognition* of what is there and has been there from the phylogenetic and ontogenetic beginnings of life onward: a life-defining animation and its experienced qualitatively-unfolding dynamics. However muted in adult life, the actual experience of movement — both kinesthetic in self-movement and kinetic in the movement of others — is not only correlated with a neurophysiological complexity, but is itself kinetically, affectively, and cognitively complex. In a sense, many present-day cognitivists and neuroscientists seem to think the actual experience of movement is beneath them, and indeed, in a certain sense it commonly is: it is there in their striding legs and swinging arms, in their stoopings to pick up a suitcase, in their bringing a fork to their mouth. But it is just as commonly there at their desk: in their diligent computations of distance and speed, in their logically or causally formulated phenomenal relationships and invariants, in their observationally-tethered assessments of pathologically disturbed individuals, in their laborings through the design of an experiment, in their hesitancy or swiftness to certify a certain conclusion. In short, the complex dynamic dimensions of movement anchor the very so-called "acts" and "actions" of contemporary cognitivists and neuroscientists in ways no different from the way they anchor everyday experiences of humans in the everyday lifeworld.

I thank editors at John Benjamins Publishing for their eagerness to publish an expanded second edition. The book provides a further opportunity not just to prominence movement but to show how much there is still to learn from movement, thus how open-minded our inquiry into movement — real-life animate movement — can be.

Acknowledgments

I thank physical anthropologist John Lukacs and philosopher Jayne Tristan for their respective readings of Chapter 1, philosopher James G. Lennox for his reading of Chapter 2, Part II, philosopher Stephen Crowell for his reading of Chapter 3, philosopher Ronald Bruzina for his reading of Chapters 3 and 4, philosopher Harry Reeder for his reading of Chapter 4, philosopher Kathleen Haney for her reading of Chapter 6, and philosopher Albert A. Johnstone for his generously patient readings of all but a few chapters of the book. I gratefully acknowledge the thoughtful comments of all of these people, none of them being responsible for the final work.

Introduction

This book is about movement. It is about the necessity of incorporating movement in our epistemological and metaphysical investigations of the animate world from the very beginning, and in our scientific and historical investigations of the animate world as well. It is about how this necessity derives from corporeal matters of fact that define our lives from infancy onward and that, in an evolutionary sense, define the lives of all animate forms. It is about learning to move ourselves. It is about how movement is at the root of our sense of agency and how it is the generative source of our notions of space and time. It is about how self-movement structures knowledge of the world — how moving is a way of knowing and how thinking in movement is foundational to the lives of animate forms.

This book is correlatively about recent accounts of knowledge, cognition, and life that ignore or minimize the central importance of movement. In particular, its concern is to examine in a carefully critical manner those cognitivist accounts of mind — or consciousness — that bypass an understanding of actual living bodies — what dynamic systems theorists term "real-time" bodies in "real-time" environments. Not uncommonly, these accounts bypass living bodies for much the same reason that they reduce minds to matter. Indeed, on the one hand, as if the mechanization of our bodies were not enough, we now have a twentieth-century made-in-the-West mechanization of minds; on the other hand, as if the mind/brain problem were not enough, we now have a twentieth-century made-in-the-West body/brain problem, a problem created by an errant reduction of living bodies to the neurophysiological matter located at their head-end. This book spells out basic ways in which such accounts are misguided, how fundamental errors accrue to construals of ourselves that belie our animate heritage. It attempts to reinstate what Thomas Huxley termed "man's place in nature" by recalling that we ourselves are a form of life and that to take ourselves seriously as a form of life is first and foremost to take the evolution of animate forms seriously. When we do so, we see that animation is at the very core of life, and that a deeply reflective study of natural history and a deeply reflective study of infancy are equally mandatory.

This book is furthermore about notable contributions made by philosophers and scientists either directly or indirectly to an understanding of movement — particularly Edmund Husserl, Aristotle, Hermann von Helmholtz, Roger Sperry, Wilder Penfield, and more recently, infant/child psychologists Daniel Stern, Esther Thelen, and Andrew Meltzoff. Husserl and von Helmholtz, for example, came independently to discover a central epistemological dimension of movement. Each came upon the dimension by examining his own everyday experiences of being a body — an "animate organism" as Husserl termed it. Aristotle figures in equally important ways on the basis of his abiding concern with movement, a concern stemming from his observations of the natural world and from his basic insight that motion is the fundamental principle of nature. Given his recognition of this principle, it is not surprising that movement had as sizable a significance for his understanding of *anima* — the soul — as for his understanding of cosmology.

Philosophers and scientists whose writings center on the body but who come up short of a recognition and comprehension of the primacy of movement are of considerable significance too. Critical analyses of the writings of philosopher Maurice Merleau-Ponty and of psychologist J.J. Gibson, for example, bring to light blinders of thought that preclude an appreciation of the foundational phenomenon of animation and the significance of kinesthesia to both a proper ontology and a proper epistemology. The blinders serve as a heuristic in the present endeavor. They alert us to possible conceptual hazards: the hazard of thinking of bodies in the abstract, for example, rather than in the fine sensory-kinetic terms demanded by corporeal analyses; the hazard of instrumentalizing movement to the point that kinesthetic awarenesses are overlooked as a form of knowledge, and in turn, dynamic qualities of movement are left behind and unattended; the hazard of being tradition-bound or skittish rather than neutrally attentive to, and patiently observant of, one's own everyday experiences of movement.

In general, present-day philosophers and scientists begin their studies of mind, consciousness, and related topics from the viewpoint of perception, especially visual perception, movement being seldom accorded equal time or viewed with equal seriousness. "Output," for example, is typically considered simply a response to what is crucial, namely, information. Two commentaries implicitly point up the value of a quite different research strategy. At the Pontifical Academy of Science Study Week meeting held in Italy in 1964, an impressive international group of scientists gathered to discuss topics related to mind-brain matters. Physiological psychologist H.L. Teuber (1966:440–41), remarking on a paper concerning "the controlling function of the brain in voluntary agency" and its relationship to the question of free choice, commented that "[W]e always start at the sensory end and try to come out at the motor side. I very much agree with the late von Holst when he suggests that we start at the other end and work our why (sic) back toward sensation. … It requires some different way of looking." David Bell, in the final chapter of his book on Edmund Husserl's philosophy (1990:215), points out that the reader who has followed his discussion from the beginning is now a long way "from the philosophical vision [anchored in object perception] which predominates in *Ideas* and Husserl's other middle-period works." He goes on to specify that "[t]he pure ego has been transformed into a physical, sentient organism, a human being; the cogito has been replaced by something capable of 'kinaesthesis'; the single perceptible object has made way for an integrated perceptual field, or environment; and the original phenomenological method has been broadened to become something Husserl at one point calls 'the phenomenological-*kinetic* method'" (Bell's italics).[1] A parallel line of thought is evident in these commentaries that is quite remarkable and that follows from the fact that, although a matter of two distinct fields, scientists and philosophers alike have been, and are, commonly disposed to begin their studies from the same perspective. In its own way, each commentary intimates that there is a liability in the approach. As Teuber suggests, when the question of agency is not addressed from the perspective of movement, and as Bell suggests, when perception is not diligently and rigorously pursued to its full dynamic, something crucial is omitted. The liability is in fact clearly visible, one might even say palpable, in the waning years of the twentieth-century Western world and in the burgeoning years of this twenty-first century one. The de-animation of perception and the rise of cognitive science in the past four decades have progressively and strikingly brought the liability to the fore in the form of both information-computational modelings and neurological reductions.

The purpose of *The Primacy of Movement* is essentially to reverse direction, to shift the perspective from which both epistemological and metaphysical — and scientific and historical — studies commonly proceed. It is to demonstrate that movement offers us the possibility not only of formulating an epistemology true to the truths of experience, but of articulating a metaphysics true to the dynamic nature of the world and to the foundationally animated nature of life. The reversal requires not just a corporeal turn, a turn I described in *The Roots of Thinking* (1990) and set forth in multiple perspectives in *The Corporeal Turn: An Interdisciplinary Reader* (2009), but a particular kind of corporeal turn. The basic corporeal/linguistic comparison that I originally drew, however, still holds; that is, like the linguistic turn initiated independently by philosopher Ludwig Wittgenstein and anthropologist Claude Lévi-Strauss, a corporeal turn calls upon us to attend to something long taken for granted. In the present instance, it asks us to be mindful of movement. It thus asks us first of all to be silent, and, in our silence, to witness the phenomenon of movement — our own self-movement and the movement of all that is animate or animated in our surrounding world. It asks us consequent to these experiences of movement, to reflect upon the nature of animation and to discover the epistemological character of the dynamics we find inherent in the qualitative play of forces that constitute our own movement and the movement of all living forms. It asks us to language these experiences and to come to know them in ways that are phenomenologically consonant with the dynamically resonant kinesthetic and kinetic experiences they are; indeed, it confronts us with this task. The enterprise is demanding not only in itself. It is demanding because it asks us to renounce what amounts to received ignorance: biased inattentions to and facile trivializations of movement. In acceding to the demands of a corporeal turn toward movement, we have the possibility of bringing to light an extraordinary terrain. As the linguistic turn in the twentieth century led to profound new insights, so a turn toward the animate will assuredly do no less.

Given the scope of this book, I would hope that the detailed synopsis of each chapter that follows will give the reader not just advance notice, but a solid sense, of the topics covered and the range of their discussion.

The Primacy of Movement begins with a section on Foundations. In particular, it begins with a critical analysis of the controversy over the status of Neandertals vis à vis *Homo sapiens sapiens* — modern-day humans. The purpose of this beginning chapter is certainly not to resolve the controversy, but to show how, by attention to animate form and to corporeal matters of fact, not only deeper but evidentially sound understandings may be had of the hominids in question. Detailed critical analysis of a book on Neandertals and of its estimable review by Stephen Jay Gould shows how paleoanthropological conceptions of Neandertals and modern-day humans are radically skewed by the great Western mind/body dichotomy. Low-life bodies and high-life minds each have, and have had, their appointed and distinctive places in the annals of paleoanthropology. As an alternative to downplaying the mental in Neandertals and elevating the symbolic in modern-day humans in such ways — or more critically put, rather than making attributions that are conceptually muddled because they are projections of one's own biases rather than descriptive of the things themselves — the chapter demonstrates the possibility of questioning the dichotomy that anchors the assessment in the first place. It thereby shows how, through patient analyses of what paleoanthropologists variously term "symbolic behavior" and "mental symbolization," one arrives at patterns of analogical thinking that are rooted in bodily life. In finer terms, it shows the conceptual significance of movement through detailed analyses of kinetic dispositions based on morphology. It shows that thinking is modeled on the body (Sheets-Johnstone 1990) and that what Gould (1994:27) calls "remarkable mental adaptations" are grounded in animate form. It shows that technological differences are readily translated into animate bodily terms, that what is basic to paleoanthropological understandings are understandings of the relationship between bodies and movement, and hence, that our understanding of individuals other than ourselves depends upon our capacity both to imagine ourselves along different corporeal lines, and to trace out what it means to live kinetically and conceptually along those lines. Solid corporeal-kinetic foundations are basic to historical understandings, which is to say to historical reconstructions of our hominid past.

Chapter 2 carries forward the basic theme of elucidating the animate. The chapter has two parts. Part I is devoted to a natural history of consciousness. It lays out this history in terms of animate form, showing consistently from its introductory paragraphs to its concluding ones that the question of "how consciousness arises in matter" (Nagel 1993: 40)[2] is a misconceived question. In particular, it critically assesses reductively materialist renditions of consciousness, notably the renditions of philosophers Paul Churchland and Daniel Dennett; it takes responsivity seriously as "a fundamental and almost universal characteristic" of life (Curtis 1975: 28); it shows in turn how the common practice of using textual markings to differentiate among cognitive capacities in living organisms is without justification; it sets forth at length how the Socratic imperative "know thyself" is a built-in biological matrix that has its evolutionary roots in proprioception; it specifies how the surface recognition sensitivity of protists and bacteria is definitive of a consciousness of something outside oneself — a meta-corporeal consciousness of the chemical constitution of the environment, for example; it specifies how animate forms from the earliest invertebrates are structured in ways that are sensitive to movement, thus how, with respect to the animal kingdom, consciousness is fundamentally a corporeal consciousness and the movement of organisms is fundamentally commensurate with their essentially tactile, proprioceptive, and/or kinesthetic sensitivities; it presents evidence showing that external organs of proprioception were internalized in the course of evolution, thus eventuating in a kinesthetically-tethered corporeal consciousness, and further, how these internally-placed organs constitute an epistemological gateway, a gateway holding open the possibility of more complex affective and cognitive lives; it thus demonstrates how in truth what Dennett (1991: 412–30) calls "The Reality of Selves" has its roots not in words but in corporeal consciousness. Through all of its critical assessments, questionings, and analyses, Part I shows how, by paying attention to corporeal matters of fact as they are articulated in the natural history of life, and by hewing to sensory-kinetic analyses of these corporeal matters of fact, one is led inexorably to understandings of consciousness that are rooted in animate form. It concludes by briefly identifying three implications, the first having to do with received wisdom concerning the chronological relationship of unconsciousness to consciousness; the second with a present-day mesmerization by brains to the exclusion of a serious in-depth attention to natural history; the third with armchair pronouncements — upon consciousness and upon creatures such as lobsters and scallops — that issue from philosophical ivory towers and that lack all semblance of an informed evolutionary backbone.

Part II deepens the understanding of consciousness as arising in animate form by defending the basically Aristotelian propositions that our account of perception should accord with our own essentially qualitative experiences of perception, and in turn, that a proper metaphysics should be consonant with living things in their processes of generation, growth, decay, movement, and rest. It thus questions philosopher Myles Burnyeat's (1992: 26) claim that "To be truly Aristotelian, we would have to stop believing that the emergence of life or mind requires explanation," his general thesis being that twentieth-century humans are inevitably and rightfully "stuck with the mind-body problem as Descartes created it" and by extension, stuck with a conception of matter "as physics and chemistry describe it" (22). The chapter critically examines certain assumptions underlying Burnyeat's claim — the idea that perception is reducible to twentieth-century physics and chemistry, for example, the idea that sense organs are opening conduits to brains — and by this route arrives at a properly Aristotelian understanding of perhaps the most discussed sentence in Aristotle's account of perception; namely, his famous statement (*De Anima* 424a18–21) that "a sense is what has the power of receiving into itself the sensible forms of things without the matter." The critical examination takes seriously the epigraphs from Aristotle's writings quoted at the beginning of Part II. Each epigraph states in unmistakable terms that to understand nature is to understand motion, for nature — by its very nature — everywhere articulates a principle of motion. To understand perception is thus to understand a dynamic event; in particular, it is to understand the kinetic process by which we take in the sensible form of things without the matter and thereby experience qualities such as loud, sharp, soft. In effect, Part II shows that what Aristotle is describing is the process by which we experience a world not of objects *as such*, but a world of varied and changing physiognomies, a qualitatively dynamic world. His essentially experiential, kinetic, and qualitative explication of perception draws on his understanding of perception as sensorially localized: we perceive at the site of our senses. It draws equally on his understanding of sensation as a change of quality, and of change of quality as a matter of movement. In essential respects, his explication adumbrates a process metaphysics, a metaphysics substantively at odds with a metaphysics of matter "as [twentieth-century Western] physics and chemistry describe it," and equally at odds with a metaphysics that is qualitatively opaque and experientially blind. Acknowledging Aristotle's recognition of movement as the foundational principle of nature — a principle confirmed by his astute observation (*Metaphysics* 1071b30) that "Matter will surely not move itself" — we find it cogent to ask which is the more basic metaphysical question: why is there something rather than nothing?; or, why is there movement rather than stillness?

In its phenomenological analysis of kinesthetic consciousness, Chapter 3 sets forth foundational epistemological structures of movement, thus deepening in decisive ways our understanding of consciousness as arising in animate form. The analysis discloses four primary qualities of movement: tensional, linear, amplitudinal, and projectional. The qualities, all of them created by movement, are experienced directly any time we care to pay attention to our own movement — or to the movement of others — and to notice them. The qualities are in fact the source of those kinesthetic regularities and expectations that are foundational to our sense of agency and to our repertoire of "I cans."[3] They are there from the start in our primal kinetic sense-makings and spontaneities. They are there in our first consciousness, a tactile-kinesthetic consciousness of our own bodies in movement. Movement is indeed "the mother of all cognition."[4] It forms the I that moves before the I that moves forms movement. It is the foundation of our conceptual life, that is, the foundation of an ever-growing store of corporeal concepts, concepts such as 'inside', 'heavy', 'light', 'open', 'close', concepts having to do with consequential relationships, and so on. The chapter lays out these rich, subtle, and varied conceptual dimensions of movement and goes on to specify in detail how the challenge of coming to an awareness of the primacy of movement involves us not only in actually moving and becoming kinetically aware of ourselves in everyday happenings such as walking, sneezing, and breathing, but in exemplifying for ourselves — in both Husserlian and von Helmholtzian terms, *bringing to self-evidence* — the cardinal epistemological structures of kinesthetic consciousness. Cardinal structures constitute *qualitative* dimensions of movement. A beginning analysis of the temporal dimension of movement exemplifies the qualitative nature of these cardinal structures and shows specifically how an examination of felt qualitative experiences such as "sudden," "rushed," "fleet," "attenuated," — all temporal qualities of movement — opens up into a phenomenology of the primordial constitution of time. It thereby shows how, as originally experienced, time is not fundamentally akin to the notes of a melody, one note strung out after the other in ordinal before-now-after fashion, but is an unfolding qualitative dynamic.

Appended to Chapter 3 is an Afterword that shows how, in their investigations of qualia, philosophers pay near exclusive attention both to the color red and to pain. Indeed, they use both as paradigms of qualia and disregard the most fundamental qualia of all, the qualia of proprioception and kinesthesia. To virtually all philosophical accounts, the latter are non-existent. The Afterword shows the fatuity of this myopic practice through an analysis of a somewhat classic philosophical thought experiment concerning a person — Mary — who has been brought up in, and is confined to, a wholly black-and-white-world, who is *thoroughly knowledgeable* in every respect about the physical nature of the world, but who, on being let out of her black-and-white room, is confronted with the color red. Philosophers argue contentiously over the proper epistemological interpretation of her being so confronted. Careful critical analysis, however, shows that the thought experiment is incoherent; it is incoherent because Mary is an inconceivable person. Though being putatively able to introspect her own brain states, for example, and to understand propositions such as "the hypothalamus is underneath the thalamus" or "electrical forces push sodium ions inward," Mary is in fact thoroughly dumb to her own body, thus necessarily dumb to what it means to be *underneath*, or what *pushing* or *inward* mean. Lacking kinesthetic experience of her own moving body — being limited to introspection of her brain states on the one hand, and to printed words on a page and images on a television screen on the other — she lacks the requisite foundation for knowledge, let alone for *total* knowledge, about the physical nature of the world. One might say that confrontation with the color red should be the last if not least of philosophers' worries.

The second section of the book is devoted to Methodology. Its first chapter examines in methodological terms the complementary findings of twentieth-century philosopher Edmund Husserl and nineteenth-century physicist-physiologist Hermann von Helmholtz with respect to perception. The examination shows how, though their points of departure are far removed from one another, their accounts of perception overlap and validate each another: both accounts underscore the central role of self-movement in perception, the essential role of introspection, and the importance of self-evidence — consulting one's own experiences as one would consult data gathered in a laboratory. The methodological practice of free variation — imagining the possible — a practice consistently evident in von Helmholtz's extended concerns with the axioms of geometry, and of course an essential step within Husserl's phenomenological methodology, is a further point of confluence, one that has sizable epistemological import. The broader purpose in demonstrating the methodological concordances is to exemplify how a trans-disciplinary communal task is possible, thus how a rich and integral epistemology is possible. The chapter shows how scientific and phenomenological research can complement one another, not only because a phenomenological methodology entails practices familiar to scientists, but because the truths of experience are as proper an aim of science as the truths of behavior. Moreover it shows in detail how fundamental differences in scientific and phenomenological practice enhance the complementarity. Introspection, for example, as practiced in the natural attitude by a scientist is not the same as introspection practiced within the phenomenological reduction. As a result, descriptions of phenomena — perceptual phenomena, for example — are different. The chapter shows how the possibility of a communal task is not thereby jeopardized but on the contrary, epistemologically enriched. The chapter proceeds to exemplify how dominant present-day ideologies militate against the very idea of a trans-disciplinary task by presenting a brief critical analysis of a phenomenologist's inquiry into the relationship between connectionism and phenomenology, specifically into the way in which a connectionist construal of mind might benefit phenomenology. The analysis shows that both the ahistoricity of connectionism and its perseveration of the mind/body dichotomy are obstacles to a salutary relationship. The chapter concludes by suggesting an alternative to a connectionist construal of mind, an alternative that has its roots in dynamic systems theory and is exemplified by the research of neurophysiologist Gerald Edelman and by contemporary researchers in infant/child developmental psychology. The alternative construal is historical in both a phylogenetic and ontogenetic sense; it recognizes the centrality of movement and in consequence leaves neither bodies nor kinesthesia behind; and it holds the promise of carrying forward the trans-disciplinary task adumbrated in the work of both Husserl and von Helmholtz.

The succeeding chapter, "On Learning to Move Oneself," attempts to spell out a methodology in the process of practicing it, namely, a constructive phenomenology of infancy and childhood that, by the very nature of the topic, defines a trans-disciplinary task: an ongoing consolidation of phenomenological and scientific research and findings that elucidate in ever deepening ways how movement is our mother tongue. Taking the fact that we all must learn to move ourselves as a methodological clue, the chapter presents a phenomenological account of what it means to be movement-born, an account of both the phenomenon of primal animation and of our common kinetic apprenticeship. It shows how, by proceeding with a definition of movement as change of position or with a description of movement in terms of an object in motion, one compromises a clear understanding of the kinetic phenomenon itself. It shows that such notions are tied to an unfiltered natural attitude and that, contrary to these notions, movement is first of all the mode by which we make sense of our own bodies and by which we first come to understand the world. It shows, in effect, how we forge a kinetic bond with the world on the basis of an originary kinetic liveliness, how incipient intentionalities play out along the lines of primal animation, and thus how our tactile-kinesthetic bodies are epistemological gateways. In addition to setting forth this account through the method of a constructive phenomenology, the chapter clarifies methodological relationships — in particular, how phenomenology utilizes facts as transcendental clues — and addresses various methodological issues — in particular, how what is commonly referred to as "the background" is not forever hidden away unless or until some untoward happening brings it to light, but that it is accessible through phenomenological analyses. In providing a constructive phenomenology of our originary animation, the chapter shows how psychological findings on infancy complement and support phenomenological ones. Psychological research studies show, for example, that infants respond preeminently not to moving objects but to movement; they show forcefully if indirectly that thinking in movement is an infant's original mode of thinking, that as infants, we come to grasp objects, literally *and* epistemologically, through movement; they validate a resonant tactile-kinesthetic body and kinesthetic consciousness. At the same time, psychological research studies challenge the discipline of phenomenology to articulate a phenomenology of change, a phenomenology that spells out, for example, how changing kinetic possibilities re-define a whole — a whole lively being and way of being. By highlighting how a constructive phenomenology of learning to move oneself requires attention to the phenomenon of emergence — how shifting patterns within a complex dynamic eventuate in new possibilities and how these new possibilities engender new relationships among all constituents of the whole — the chapter shows how an understanding of the phenomenon of learning to move oneself requires a readiness to cross disciplines and to engage oneself not only in a communal task but in an ongoing one whose end is nowhere in sight.

Chapter 6 focuses close and critical attention on the methodologies generating Maurice Merleau-Ponty's philosophy. It does so for multiple reasons, each of considerable import: Merleau-Ponty's philosophy is commonly taken to be a philosophy of our *embodied* humanness, hence a philosophy that should lead us to foundational corporeal-kinetic truths; his philosophy is neither presented as, nor taken to be, a speculative philosophy, hence it is a philosophy we should have a way of both verifying and of carrying forward in further enlightening ways; his philosophy attempts to reconcile philosophic truth with scientific fact, hence it is a philosophy that aims in the direction of a trans-disciplinary task. In view of these reasons, a concern of major significance is whether we can follow along the same methodological paths as Merleau-Ponty. Accordingly, the framing question the chapter asks is the seemingly simple methodological question, "How does Merleau-Ponty do what he does?" What follows is literally an inquiry: question follows upon question; answers are provided only provisionally in the form of further, self-generated questions. The point of the persistent questioning is to trace out the methodological underpinnings of a philosophy that, precisely because it is a philosophy of our humanness, should be methodologically transparent to us. The point of the questioning is thus neither to try the patience of the reader nor to produce a rhetorical exercise. In pursuing answers to the framing question, the chapter attempts to encompass Merleau-Ponty's philosophy, spanning (though not in chronological order) his work from *The Structure of Behavior* to *The Visible and the Invisible*. It begins by examining his use of pathology: Can empirical facts (about pathology) lead to existential facts (about the normal)? The questioning proceeds in the direction of clarifying how the factual enters into the philosophical and continues into an examination of the fundamental liability of a fact-based ontological methodology. It moves on to confront Merleau-Ponty's seeming problematic in distinguishing between fact and experience and between fact and reflection. In this latter context, considerable effort is made to elucidate Merleau-Ponty's statement (1968: 65) that radical reflection "[is] founded on the fact that I am no stranger to myself." Considerable attention too is paid to his denigration of introspection — on the grounds that it is a practice repudiated by science — insofar as introspection appears incontrovertibly to be the source of his radical reflections. In a further attempt to clarify the nature of his methodology, the chapter turns to an investigation of his last writings in the light of his earlier work, asking, for example, whether both "hyper-reflection" and "perceptual faith" as designated in *The Visible and the Invisible* (1968) are not related to his expressed thesis in *Phenomenology of Perception*, i.e. that philosophical analysis of our relationship to the world is futile, that "philosophy can only place [our relationship to the world] once more before our eyes and present it for our ratification" (1962: xviii). The methodological question of a linguistically-attuned philosophy as set forth in *The Visible and the Invisible* (1968: 125) — a philosophy in which words "would combine ... by virtue of a natural intertwining of their meaning," that is, a philosophy in which language speaks the philosopher — is also addressed. Expressly in view of the unresolved tension between nature and ontology in his philosophy, the questioning moves to an interrogation of his specification of a natural bond with the world. The chapter offers two tentative conclusions, one general and one particular, about Merleau-Ponty's methodologies and their implications. It concludes with an optional epilogue that in essence ponders key conceptual correspondences — all of them having to do with the nature of the body and of bodily life — between the ontology of Merleau-Ponty and themes in the writings of poet-prose essayist Paul Valéry.

Chapter 7 is a methodological postscript, an inquiry into both the nature of wonder and the place of wonder in philosophy, specifically, in contemporary American philosophy which, in its strongest and most pervasive guise, seems to have given up all but lip service to wonder. If, on the contrary, wonder is at the heart of philosophy as Plato and Aristotle claimed, then it is of inestimable methodological significance in both generating and fueling the practice of philosophy. In this methodological context, I consider the timelessness of wonder, tying its timelessness to the potential of an individual philosophic act to be part of a communal and infinite task; I consider wonder in the deep sense — the feeling that centers not on wondering what to wear or why the faucet is leaking — but on wondering about death, violence, friendship, memory, and so on; I consider the way in which present-day Western science annihilates wonder by writing promissory notes on its own epistemological and metaphysical behalf and how seductive and beguiling these promissory notes are and how they lead us away from a communal and infinite task; I consider how we lose sight of the fact that to liberate ourselves methodically from ignorance, we must practice philosophy close-up, which means allowing a place for both the fear and longing that are at the heart of the feeling of wonder; I consider how, when we do so, we discover that the professional is personal, and how we are then engaged in a passionate act generated and sustained by a deep and powerful feeling having the possibility of leading us to wisdom.

Five chapters comprise the last section of the book titled Applications. The common thematic underlying each of the chapters is animation: a moving, flesh and bone subject; a moving, acting organism; a moving, sense-making creature; a moving, thinking being. The corollary common thematic is the necessity of taking this subject, organism, creature, and being into epistemological and metaphysical, scientific and historical account.

Chapter 8, "On the Significance of Animate Form," shows how fundamental creaturely meanings derive from animate form, that is, how the animate is not arbitrary. The chapter illustrates concretely the semantic specificity of living bodies, showing in the process how the anatomical organization of our body is not a blank cultural blackboard open for scripting, but a phylogenetically rich and complex density of meanings. It goes on to show in detail how the terms "embodiment" and "lived body" compromise the semantic specificity of living bodies, and correspondingly, how the term "animate form" captures in a more exacting way what we actually experience when we experience our own bodies and the bodies of others: animation, aliveness, dynamically changing conformations and contours, qualitatively meaningful forms — and, by extension, a spatio-temporal world co-terminus with that experienced animation and aliveness, those dynamically changing contours, and so on. The chapter shows further how the term *animate form* brings to the fore elemental facts of our human aliveness, not only that we have a front and back, for example, or that we move more easily forward than backward — aspects of our bodily being that philosopher Hubert Dreyfus and anthropologist Paul Rabinow call attention to as highly significant invariants omitted in the philosophies of Michel Foucault and Maurice Merleau-Ponty — but that we have an evolutionary history. *Animate form* places us rightfully in the context of a natural history, a history that we tend to minimize, ignore, or forget, and that, in proportion as we do so, imperil not merely ourselves but all animate forms, and the planet which is Earth as well.

Chapter 9, "Human Speech Perception and an Evolutionary Semantics," first lays out the motor theory of speech perception as it has been vindicated over the past forty years by the research studies of psychologist Alvin M. Liberman and various associates. The theory (1985:25) states that "the object of [speech] perception is motoric," meaning that gestural rather than acoustic signals are the foundation of speech perception. Liberman et al. originally explained their research findings according to behaviorist tenets; they explain them now according to cognitivist ones, claiming that the brain houses "an internal, innately specified vocal-tract synthesizer ... that incorporates complete information about the anatomical and physiological characteristics of the vocal tract and also about the articulatory and acoustic consequences of linguistically significant gestures" (26). The chapter presents an extended critique of Liberman's "vocal-tract synthesizer" explanation of his research results and offers in its place an explanation grounded in real-life tactile-kinesthetic experiences, experiences that start with babbling, lip-smacking, cooing, and other mouth movement/sound play, and end with a child's mastery of the articulatory gestures of her/his native tongue. In effect, in place of a brain is a living subject. In support of the latter explanation, the chapter goes on to examine a number of relevant topics. It first considers comsigns — primatologist Stuart Altmann's term for communications that are shared by all members of a group or species — and tactical deception — the ability of humans and other primates to deceive by moving in perfectly normal ways for quite other-than-normal ends. Both comsigns and tactical deception raise the question of how a common repertoire of gestures, sounds, visual displays — indeed any form of communication, including verbal language — could possibly have evolved short of living subjects; that is, they raise the question of how interanimate meanings could possibly come to be established short of actual interactions of actual living creatures. Put in the perspective of an evolutionary semantics, the chapter shows that interanimate meanings evolve on the basis of common tactile-kinesthetic bodies, and, on the basis of common tactile-kinesthetic bodies, on the basis of analogical apperception, i.e. apperceiving the movement of other bodies on the basis of one's own tactile-kinesthetic experiences of one's own body. The chapter shows, in effect, that living creatures are sources of meaning and are primed for meaning; meaning is a dimension of both primal animation and primal bodily sensibilities. Interanimate meanings, and in turn species-specific semantics, are from this vantage point grounded in a fundamental and altogether natural propensity toward meaning. Psychologist Jerome Bruner's extensive studies of language development in infants and primatologists' studies of language learning in bonobo chimpanzees indirectly but pointedly validate the propensity.

The chapter that follows — "Why a Mind Is Not a Brain and a Brain Is Not a Body" — examines at length the liabilities of a conspicuously robust but conceptually debilitating theoretical bias in many present-day cognitivist explanations of minds and bodies, a bias that inordinately favors brains to the exclusion of the animated realities of living creatures. The examined liabilities include an undue elevation of language, a radical (eliminative) materialism, and a Meccanized neurology. Each liability is shown to be not only pernicious to an understanding of living creatures — animate forms — but to be internally incoherent, as when language is deemed the beginning of consciousness but the beginning of language, by such a claim, cannot itself be accounted for; or as when one credo is deemed the correct one over all others when in putative truth all credos are neurological equals of each other — all credos being merely neurological events. An extended examination of the conceptual difficulties inherent in brain-in-vat scenarios illustrates in fine detail why a brain can stand neither in place of a living body nor in place of a mind, and why such philosophically-spawned thought experiments are impotent to shed light on the mind/body problem. In this context, some well-known mid-twentieth-century neuroscientific experimental and theoretical literature is cited and discussed, in particular, the work of psychologist Roger Sperry and neuroanatomist Wilder Penfield. Careful study of their research shows that so-called "efferent stimulation" of a vatted brain is a kinetically meaningless locution, both literally were a brain-in-a-vat to exist, and theoretically on behalf of the thought experiment. Close examination of this and other equally vexing problems highlights fundamental difficulties with neurological Mecca that center on the kinetic spontaneity of living subjects. A resolution of the difficulties leads to the possibility of a linkage between philosopher Thomas Nagel's (1979) famous inquiry "What Is It Like To Be a Bat?" and the theoretical formulations of both Sperry and biologist Jakob von Uexküll, in particular, Sperry's conclusion that the brain is an organ of and for movement and von Uexküll's explication (1957: 46–50) of the perceived "functional tone" of an object, a tone created and established through a creature's possible movement in relation to the object, thus its sense of the object in the near Husserlian sense of an object *as meant* (Husserl 1983). When recent twentieth-century scientific literature on the motor system is closely consulted and analyzed, the central significance of self-movement to cognition comes ever more clearly into view. In this context, the chapter presents a range of highly significant findings: that neurological mappings of the motor cortex are as unpredictable as human behavior; that kinetic possibilities are the domain of an intentional subject; that such a subject is not merely goal-directed but meaning-directed; and so on. The chapter concludes with an admonition about the hazards of substituting brain technology for phylogenetic and ontogenetic histories, an admonition tied to the sobriety of adhering to a version of psychologist Lloyd Morgan's famous canon (1930), which would decree that whatever can be explained in terms of animate form should not be explained in terms of mechanical form, not only because animate forms are more commonly distributed than mechanical forms but because only such forms can explain what it is to be a mind and what it is to be a body.

Chapter 11, "What Is It Like To Be a Brain?", is a philosophical inversion of Nagel's (1979) article "What Is It Like To Be a Bat?". The chapter begins by paraphrasing sections in the opening paragraphs of his article in materially reductive cognitivist terms. In drawing out the reverse affinities, the chapter attempts to describe what it is like to be a brain *for the brain itself* — as Nagel would insist it must. It considers first that a brain is commonly described as the site of neurological, electrical, and metabolic happenings, that activity is taken to be a fundamental fact of brain matter, and that neither materialist nor functionalist accounts of brains capture or explain the fundamentally active nature of a brain. The chapter takes up the challenge of this deficiency, inquiring into the active nature of brain matter by focusing on detailed descriptions of neural firing; that is, it examines at length and in exacting terms what it means to say that *an action potential shoots down an axon*. It attempts to specify what it is like *for the neuron itself*, the Nagelian point being that, if we cannot say what it is like for a neuron to fire, i.e. for an action potential to shoot down an axon, then we have not the most elementary notion of what it is like to be a brain. In turn, and in Nagel's terms, we have a belief in the existence of kinetic facts — action potentials shooting down axons — "whose exact nature we cannot possibly conceive" (Nagel 1979: 170). The challenge of reckoning with, and of explaining the elemental animation of brain matter prompts consideration of materialist philosopher David Lewis's (1991) proposed distinction between two forms of knowing: 'to know what it is like' is to possess certain abilities; to know *tout court* is to possess information. By hewing to an informational construal of knowledge, Lewis attempts to save materialist and functionalist doctrine from the taint of qualia (from "phenomenal" or "subjective" experience; 1991: 234). The chapter shows, however, that Lewis's distinction can itself be saved only by de-animating matter, in other words, by conceiving the brain not as the site of kinetic happenings, but as — in Lewis's terms (1991: 234) — "a smart data bank," an information repository. In effect, in order to answer the question, what is it like for a neuron to fire?, the chapter asks whether animism is necessary to materialists' accounts of matter. The question is duly examined. Answers to the general charge of animism show that materialists are committed in spite of themselves — as Nagel inversely notes with respect to bats — to beliefs in the existence of facts beyond their conceptual reach. The last section of the chapter shows how, when we cease pledging allegiance to functionalist and materialist doctrines, and by extension, to *the brain*, we find that the very criticisms materialists lodge against non-reductionists — they are "mysterians" (Flanagan 1991:312–14) or "phenomenologists"(Dennett 1991:55–65) — can be readily lodged against material-ists themselves. It concludes by presenting just such criticisms, specifying how materi-alists are "mysterians" in failing to explain the most basic feature of brain matter — its elemental kinetic activity — and how they are "phenomenologists" in failing to be objective in their methodological procedures and in their conceptions and evaluations of brain activity.

The final chapter, "Thinking in Movement," opens with a descriptive account of a paradigmatic instance of the phenomenon: thinking in movement in improvisational dance. It proceeds to a consideration of two assumptions, each of which might impair an unbiased reading of the descriptive account: the Cartesian assumption that minds think and bodies "do," and the widespread assumption that there is no thinking outside of language — or outside of some kind of symbolic system. Analysis of the paradig-matic experience of thinking in movement in improvisational dance shows that think-ing and moving are not separate happenings but are aspects of a *kinetic bodily logos* attuned to an evolving dynamic situation. It show further that thinking in movement involves no symbolic counters but is tied to an on-going qualitatively experienced dynamic in which movement possibilities arise and dissolve. The analysis accords in fundamental ways with psychological studies showing that an infant's initial concepts are tied to dynamic events, to kinetic happenings, that prior to its passage into a world of language, an infant's initial concepts are tied to experiences of both its own move-ment and movement in its surrounding world. Drawing initially on child psychologist Lois Bloom's (1993) extensive studies of the transition from infancy to language — both because movement is not at the forefront of her research concerns (cognition and affect are) and because movement is nonetheless clearly central in her account of lan-guage development — the chapter shows how studies of infants indirectly affirm that infants think in movement. It points out that psychologist Jerome Bruner's lifelong research and writings on infant/child development indirectly affirm the same thesis, his essential finding being that the principal interest of infants, an interest that carries over into language, centers on agentivity and action (1990). It shows that infant psy-chiatrist/psychologist Daniel Stern similarly affirms the same thesis indirectly, specifi-cally with respect to nonverbal behaviors that never become linguistically encoded but that have variable affective tones and that articulate intercorporeal intentions (1981, 1985). Through such citings of the literature, the chapter makes abundantly clear that rather than speak of the period before language as the *pre-linguistic*, we should speak of the advent of language as the *post-kinetic*. Following an examination of the literature on infant development supporting the thesis that ontogenetically, thinking in movement is our original mode of thinking, the chapter puts the phenomenon of thinking in movement in phylogenetic perspective. It shows that instances of thinking in movement abound in the literature on nonhuman animal life, as when ethologists describe how killdeer move in particular ways to protect their young from particular harms (Griffin 1984; Ristau 1996), when field biologists describe spatially and temporally complex food-supplying behaviors of sand wasps (Tinbergen 1968), and when laboratory biologists describe escape behaviors of creatures such as paramecium and fan worms (Scott 1963; Wells 1968). In each instance, a natural kinetic intelligence, a kinetic bodily logos, is at work. As the chapter demonstrates in some detail, this intelligence cannot be written off as mere instinct, i.e. as robotic and unadulterated biological givens. Neither can it be written off as merely an adaptive mechanism. The intelligence or logos is an elemental biological character of life, a dimension of animate form that, however written between the lines, is confirmed in the writings of zoologists, primatologists, and ethologists. It bears emphasizing that the implicit confirmation is not that animals think in terms of *behavior*, but that they think in terms of kinetically dynamic patterns, in terms of *movement*. Indeed, from this vantage point, behaviors *evolve* only because behaviors are essentially complex dynamic patternings of movement, and movement being the mother tongue of all animate forms, thinking in movement is both a primary fact and a perpetual possibility of animate life.

Notes

1. Although Bell goes on to say (1990:215) that "these changes ... never emerged clearly in Husserl's thought," there is much to say that they did, at the very least to the extent that Husserl recognized them as integral aspects of experience. A clarification is also in order. By the characterization "phenomenological-kinetic method" (Husserl 1980:1, 117), Husserl was not endorsing a peripatetic methodology. His concern was to distinguish ontology from phenomenology, a fixed notion of objects as against an account of their constitution, or in other words, as against genetic understandings of their epistemological origins in experience. The phenomenological method is thus "kinetic" in that it progressively excavates layers of meanings, as those meanings have been laid down over time in experience. But it should be pointed out too that the phenomenological method also elucidates the absolutely pivotal role of "the kinestheses" in the constitution of objects, as Chapter 4 will show, and in this sense might be qualified as "kinetic."

2. The full passage reads "We are still unable to form a conception of *how* consciousness arises in matter."

3. The phrase "I can" comes originally from Edmund Husserl's insightful and seminal descriptive analyses of experience. See especially Husserl 1980:106–12; 1989:13–15, 159–60, 228–31, 266–282, 340–43. See also Husserl 1970a: 106–108, 161, 217, 331–32; 1973:97. The import of this fundamental and eminently significant "faculty," as Husserl termed it, will be apparent many times over, implicitly as well as explicitly, throughout this book.

4. I borrow the phrase from Husserl (and singularize it), who used it not in describing movement but in describing phenomenology. See Husserl 1980:69.

Foundations

CHAPTER 1

Neandertals

> Experience shows the problem of the mind cannot be solved by attacking the citadel itself. — the mind is function of body. — we must bring some *stable* foundation to argue from.   Charles Darwin ([1836–44] 1987: 564)

> We must begin our examination with movement.
>
> Aristotle (*De Anima* 405b: 33)

1. Introduction

I envisage this opening chapter as a contribution to what zooarchaeologist Mary Stiner envisions when she says, "Some new ways of working with archaeological records are needed, as well as new perspectives on the data they yield" (Stiner 1994: 3). With respect to her own work, she says that "The continuity-replacement dialectic [concerning Neandertals and anatomically modern humans] has been useful, but I think that there are other productive ways of visualizing change in human foraging practices, alternatives that merit exploration in light of what we now know from the faunal perspective" (Stiner 1994: 387). Similarly, there are other productive ways of visualizing change in hominid morphology, ways which result in kinetic rather than static understandings of differences between Neandertals and anatomically modern humans and which merit conceptual exploration. Ecological paleoanthropologist Steven Kuhn's critical observation that "Too often, research is framed in terms of 'inherited' questions" (Kuhn 1995: 5) is exactly topical to this endeavor.

There is a way in which the present controversy over the status of Neandertals vis à vis *Homo sapiens sapiens* — modern humans — epitomizes the great Western mind/body dichotomy. When it comes to assessing our capacity for thinking, the terms of the inquiry and subsequent discussion quickly gravitate to language — or to kindred forms of what is designated "symbolic behavior."[1] Bodies are hardly at the forefront of thought about thought; neither for that matter is movement. Not only this but language is not infrequently conceived a solely human phenomenon with no significant historical antecedents, that is, a phenomenon with no substantive evolutionary linkages whatsoever, whether on the basis of deficient anatomies (Lieberman 1983, 1972; Laitman 1983), of a deficiency in linguistic design features (Hockett 1960), of a deficiency in rational behavior (Bennett 1971), of a deficiency in communicative repertoires (Wilson 1972), or of a deficiency with respect to a Center of Narrative Gravity (Dennett 1991). The result is that a certain preeminence is protected. While there is no question but that human language and other so designated forms of "symbolic behavior" such as the creation of art objects are *culturally* unprecedented phenomena and ones that bring with them an untold richness and unending capacity for knowledge, there is every reason to question that such forms arose *de novo*, that they have *no* evolutionary ties, thus that language, for example, sprang full-blown from the mouths of waiting hominids, and that present-day humans are on that account thoroughly unique products of evolution. The concern here is less directly with showing how that preeminence is unfounded and how sustaining it is myopically self-serving (see Sheets-Johnstone 1992b, 1996a, 1996b)[2] than it is with showing how an immediate and thoughtless turn toward language and other so designated "symbolic behaviors" is precipitous: it deflects us from a recognition and understanding of a phylogenetically and ontogenetically more basic phenomenon, the phenomenon of movement. Indeed, those intricate and subtle everyday gestures whose once invented and now learned articulations constitute human speech are consistently taken for granted or ignored.[3]

An airing of the Neandertal controversy appeared in *The New York Review of Books* in an article by the noted zoologist-geologist Stephen Jay Gould. Gould nicely summarizes the controversy, but in marking out his stand on the issue, he straightaway exemplifies the seminally engrained and epistemologically debilitating Western dichotomy that precludes taking movement seriously and giving the body its due. Gould critically considers two 1993 books on Neandertals, each written by "leading experts on Neandertals and on the rise of modern humans" (Gould 1994: 26). The books, according to Gould, "take opposite sides of [the] controversy" (Gould 1994: 26). Christopher Stringer and Clive Gamble, in *In Search of the Neanderthals: Solving the Puzzle of Human Origins*, favor the "Noah's Ark" view, that modern humans arose out of Africa from a small population which migrated first to Europe and then to all parts of the world. Erik Trinkaus and Pat Shipman, in *The Neandertals: Changing the Image of Mankind*, "[take] no 'official' position," Gould says, "but clearly [lean] toward the multi-regionalist approach" (Gould 1994: 26), namely, toward the view that modern humans evolved from populations already spread on three continents (Africa, Europe, and Asia) in the form of *Homo erectus*.[4] Neandertals, on the first view, are not directly related to present-day humans; on the second view, they are our European ancestors. Through a critical examination of Gould's review, we will see first both where and how multiple strands of the engrained Western mind/body dichotomy consistently inform — and skew — research and perspectives on Neandertals. Given this foundation, we will then turn to a detailed critical review of Stringer and Gamble's account of Neandertals. Though plainly severe in its assessment, the purpose of the review is constructive. Its aim is to demonstrate the need for deeper examinations and analyses of "symbolic behavior," and correlatively, to demonstrate the need to expand typical ways of construing "physical" anthropology. The succeeding three sections will carry through the constructive purpose by showing first how symbolic behavior is fundamentally tied to corporeal matters of fact, as evidenced in both the phenomenon of corporeal representation and analogical thinking, and in turn, how understandings of animate form are crucial to comparative studies in paleoanthropology, thus crucial to an understanding of Neandertals.

2.   "Remarkable mental adaptations"

To begin with, a larger question in Gould's article, a question of *theory*, dominates the more immediate question of Neandertals themselves and what they were like. In other words, the question of moment for Gould is not a factual one. As he explains, he does not have "the requisite professional expertise to declare a preference on factual grounds between the two views" (Gould 1994:27–28). His decision in favor of Stringer and Gamble over Trinkaus and Shipman is on the grounds that the Noah's Ark theory is the orthodox evolutionary one. That orthodox theory, Gould says, is defined by its focal emphasis on contingency, chance, unrepeatability, and other such features. Gould has himself enfolded that theory within his theory of punctuated equilibrium — the idea that evolution proceeds not through phyletic gradualism but by relatively sudden change interrupting long periods of stasis. The idea of punctuated equilibrium supports the notion that modern humans replaced Neandertals rather than merged with them genetically over time; it thus supports the Noah's Ark theory. Gould terms the Noah's Ark theory an "entity" theory as opposed to a "tendency" theory, the latter kind of theory defining the kind of view he attributes to Trinkaus and Shipman (Gould 1994:27). He spells out the distinction between the two theories in terms of a difference in the way humans conceive themselves: as creatures evolving everywhere "toward the traditional *summum bonum* of bigger brains … because big brains are so good to have, and natural selection must have favored them in all environments of our diverse geographical spread"; or as creatures whose evolution was a thoroughly fortuitous happening that has no inevitability whatsoever about it (Gould 1994:27).[5] While the global spread of the "entity" that evolved as a small group of hominids "in one small place during one restricted interval in time" might be the result of "remarkable mental adaptations[,]" Gould declares, it was "not an inevitable development arising on a planetary scale" (Gould 1994:27). Clearly, what Gould is at pains to contrast is a view of humans as the inevitable (and even proper) culminating point of eons of evolution with a view of humans as thoroughly contingent and unrepeatable creatures like all others in evolutionary history. The major problem in urging the latter view in this context is that Gould is uncritically seduced both by Stringer and Gamble's characterizations of Neandertals and by their specifications as to what exactly constituted the difference between Neandertals and *Homo sapiens sapiens*. The minor problem is that he casts Trinkaus and Shipman's account into an ill-fitting mould, a problem which we will not examine here.

As his earlier allusion to "remarkable mental adaptations" might indicate, Gould assumes that what distinguishes Neandertals from modern humans lies exclusively in the realm of the mental. Thus, at least to some extent we are forewarned when, in turning to sketch out what Noah's Ark theory might actually mean in terms of a valid understanding of Neandertals and their differences from us, he asks, "Could we possibly define the *mental essence* of these differences, thus helping us to understand the basis of our *uniqueness*?"(Gould 1994:28, italics added). In the simplest and most basic of terms, it is as if minds have categorically nothing to do with bodies. What makes us unique is our mental marrow, pure and unadulterated. Moreover it is as if "the mental" never evolved for, precisely as suggested earlier with respect to the ready gravitation toward language and kindred "symbolic behaviors," when it comes to considering *human* evolution, "remarkable mental adaptations" leave other creatures behind. We will examine this aspect of the issue more fully below. What is of interest to note here is how strongly Darwin affirmed continuities in the evolution of what he called "mental powers" — e.g. attention, memory, reasoning, and so on — and how clearly he did not separate off these powers from living bodies (Darwin [1871] 1981). What is furthermore of interest is how computational cognitivist concerns and practices impel researchers not toward the further study of these powers as they are manifest in such observed and observable behavioral similarities and differences as Darwin noted, but toward specifying and analyzing "rule-governed behaviors," e.g. the rules of syntax, the rules of word use, the rules of object use (e.g. "if B is a container, A belongs inside it" [Clark 1979:159; Clark 1973]), and so on. Indeed, Gould speaks of "general learning rules" that characterize modern humans and of the possibility of "infer[ring] these rules of our uniqueness from differences in the overall patterns of Neandertal and modern life" (Gould 1994:28). With such rules, he says, "we might gain great insight into the biological source of our humanity" (Gould 1994:28). In short, on Gould's account, the rules by which we operate constitute our mental marrow and define us as creatures. Anchoring his thoughts centrally in this fundamental cognitivist notion of rules, Gould then proceeds to pinpoint briefly Stringer and Gamble's three themes that, he says, "strike me as being on the right level of abstraction, in contrast to the overspecificity of most discussions about adaptation" (Gould 1994:28). What Gould wants to avoid through abstraction is an adaptational account on the order of sociobiological analyses that view each and every body part and behavior as "adaptive" in some way. But clearly, in opting for "abstraction," he hazards another liability. To see this, we shall critically examine Stringer and Gamble's three themes directly and in detail.

3. "Symbolic behavior"

In their final chapter, which poses the question "Close Kin or Distant Relatives?" as its title, Stringer and Gamble set forth what they designate a behavioral answer to the question of the relationship of "the Ancients" to "the Moderns," that is, the relationship of Neandertals to modern humans. In particular, they say that the "fate" of the Neandertals is a function of "the enormous changes in behaviour that took place in Europe 40,000 years ago — changes which we believe convincingly *prove* that replacement, rather than continuity, is the best explanation for current evidence" (Stringer & Gamble 1993: 199, italics added). Quite apart from *proving* anything outside of mathematics, the idea that one can prove that a particular historical event took place over a period of time thirty to sixty-or-more thousands of years ago is far-fetched. Precisely where there are no practices to observe first-hand much less any individuals to interview, one can hardly offer anything but an interpretation of the data. If one were to respond that Stringer and Gamble merely over-extended themselves verbally and conceptually muddied the waters inadvertently — that what they meant to say, for example, was that they believe replacement a superior explanation on the basis of current evidence of changes documented in the evolutionary record — one would find oneself hard-pressed to maintain that sympathetic understanding in view of the conceptual muddles in their presentation of, and reasoning about, the "enormous changes" that carry the weight of their explanation. Conceptual over-extension is distressingly evident throughout their discussions.

The three major enormous behavioral changes are linked to the establishment of (1) campsites, (2) settlements, and (3) new habitats. Each of these domains is regarded a social phenomenon and is designated a form of "symbolic behavior." We should note that Stringer and Gamble also discuss tools, "art and symbolism," and burials in their summary yet highly detailed review of the "enormous changes" that took place 40,000 years ago; but as Gould notes, and as Stringer and Gamble themselves document in their remarks in various chapters (Stringer & Gamble 1993: e.g. Chapter 7, p. 146; Chapter 9, pp. 197, 219), the emphasis is on the afore-mentioned three changes. Their emphasis notwithstanding, because the difficulty is basically a conceptual one, the appropriate point of departure for a critical assessment of their account is not with the momentous changes themselves — whichever ones one might single out — but with the concept of "symbolic behavior" or "symbolism" by which they characterize all of the changes.

The introduction of the concept appears first in a chapter titled "The Archaeology of the Ancients" where various references are made to "[the] important debate about the birth of symbolic behaviour" (Stringer & Gamble 1993: 161), but the fuller elaboration occurs in the last chapter "Close Kin or Distant Relatives?" under the section heading "Art and symbolism," where Stringer and Gamble begin by recalling their previous argument that "earlier items [i.e. "art and ornament" *prior* to the

Moderns] are unconvincing as evidence for symbolic behaviour either because they lack a context where symbolism might be required (such as a burial) or because they are unique examples, unrelated to any wider system that used the repetition of design and shape as symbols for action" (Stringer & Gamble 1993: 203). Following this general claim, they state their disagreement with those evolutionists who have argued that symbolic behavior developed slowly; they thus voice their disagreement with those who espouse the idea of *cultural* as well as phyletic gradualism. "We disagree with their insistence," say Stringer and Gamble, "that symbolic behaviour is something that can be turned up and down like a light on a dimmer switch. On the contrary, arranging behaviour according to symbolic codes is an all or nothing situation. The onset of symbolic behaviour can be compared to the flick of a switch" (Stringer & Gamble 1993: 203; cf. Eldredge & Gould 1972 on punctuated equilibrium theory). Spelling out this "arranged-according-to-symbolic-codes" conception of "symbolic behavior," they say that "Symbolism involves making mental substitutions and appreciating associations between people, objects and contexts; once established, symbolism cannot simply be dropped or forgotten." They assert furthermore that "symbolic behaviour requires memory and periodic renewal through repeated ritual" and that "[t]he objects used in such rituals tend to be standardized, leading to the creation of a shared art form." With respect to the objects of "ritual art and ornament" that began appearing in the archaeological record 40,000 years ago, they say that "the symbolic behaviour associated with these objects was … clearly in practice" (Stringer & Gamble 1993: 203).

On the basis of these various claims and statements, one might conclude that what Stringer and Gamble are trying to say is that symbolic behavior is generated by symbolic codes that specify certain mental substitutions. But the question is not only, what exactly does this relational formulation mean? — that is, how does the reputed symbolic process translate concretely into actual life activities? — but how did such behavior — or mental substitutions — originate? Especially if symbolic behavior is "an all or nothing situation," it is difficult to imagine how it could possibly have originated. Indeed, we seem perilously close to affirming the idea that language arose one day full-blown from the mouths of waiting hominids and art one day full-blown from their hands. We seem equally perilously close to affirming the idea not of a "creative explosion," as Stringer and Gamble (borrowing a phrase from John Pfeiffer) characterize "the onset of symbolic behaviour"(Stringer & Gamble 1993: 203), but of an *unconscious* explosion in the sense that forces completely outside of what people ordinarily would call "conscious control" flick the switch in each case. Indeed, if "the huge changes in behaviour that took place in the early Upper Palaeolithic resemble the flick of a switch and *not* the slow upwards movement of a symbolic dimmer," then these hominids must have found themselves doing something entirely new and momentous on the spot, and this could only have happened if unbeknownst to them, symbolic codes — mental substitutions — suddenly arose from an unconscious mental domain and just as suddenly instantiated in them a momentous new behavior. Not only this, but to be effective, the sudden onset would have had to have occurred in *orchestrated concert*. Symbolic codes could only operate *socially* if they were set off in unison.

Stringer and Gamble's discussions and analyses of artifacts readily exemplify the conceptual problem. In a section titled "Campsites as symbols," they contrast "symbolic behaviour" with mere "survival behaviour" (Stringer & Gamble 1993: 204). This distinction notwithstanding — we shall consider it in further detail below — the idea of campsites as symbols and of the architecture of campsites as "symbolic behaviour" is puzzling in the extreme. At the beginning of the section, Stringer and Gamble write that "Having investigated the appearance of symbolic behaviour by examining the changes in art and technology, we will now take a look at the evidence from campsites." They speak of "more formal living spaces" being created at this point in hominid evolution — hearths and huts, for example, and post holes and pits (Stringer & Gamble 1993: 204). The conceptual muddle they generate in the process of describing these new spaces can be put quite simply: what is a campsite a symbol of? An answer to the question is nowhere to be found in the text. Yet clearly, we should have an answer. Indeed, we may ask what a campsite is a symbol of in the same way that we may ask what technology — the crafting of a stone tool — is a symbol of or how its crafting constitutes "symbolic behavior." The latter question may perhaps exemplify the quandary in a more succinct manner because stone tool-making is a more familiar and spatially discrete constructive activity. Recall, for example, that Stringer and Gamble, implicitly contrasting Moderns with Ancients, speak of "repetition of design and shape as symbols for action" (albeit in the context not of tools but of the question, "What is the significance of the appearance of art and ornament?") (Stringer & Gamble 1993: 203). In a patient effort to understand conceptually exactly what they are describing in specifying such repetition, and in thinking back some forty-odd pages to an earlier mention of "repetition" explicitly in reference to hand-axes and other tools of the Ancients, a careful reader might end up piecing together the above suggested formula: symbolic behavior is generated by symbolic codes specified by certain mental substitutions. The formula suggests itself because in their earlier use of the term "repetition," Stringer and Gamble refer to "limited, repetitious forms" that, they declare, were *not* "determined by symbolic codes" (Stringer & Gamble 1993: 161). Thus one assumes that in the crafting of a tool, when the repetition of a particular form is *not* guided by mental substitutions, "symbols of action" are not produced. Validation of the formula by which we should understand what Stringer and Gamble are saying, however, does not ease the strain. The reader remains perplexed. This is because, even with the formula, basic questions go unanswered. Just as Stringer and Gamble nowhere explain what a campsite is a symbol of, they nowhere explain where symbolic codes come from, how certain designs and shapes and not others come to be informed by symbolic codes, or just what a symbolic code might be in the first place. In particular, they nowhere explain how repeating certain designs and shapes (and not others) in the actual crafting of a tool constitutes symbolic behavior and how that symbolic behavior makes particular tool designs and shapes "symbols of action." In some manner or other, mental substitutions are "flicked on," a behavior thereby becomes symbolic, and the symbolic nature of the behavior is somehow transferred such that a completed artifact — a tool — stands for, or "mentally substitutes for" something else, i.e. "action."

Clearly, in spite of efforts to comprehend, a distressing conceptual jumble and consequent muddle of meaning remain. Words or phrases such as "symbolism," "symbolic behavior," and "symbolic codes" have a patently compelling aura about them — they are honorific, they straightaway signify intellectual acumen — and on first glance, we may think we understand what is being said. When we carefully examine what is being said, however, clear, reasonable meaning is nowhere to be found, either in the terms or phrases separately or as a unit. When put to the test — *cashed in for real currency* — the words fail to deliver. This is because campsites themselves are not symbols, nor are items such as tools that are connected with them, nor are "patterns of settlement" nor are "new habitats." These constructions achieve symbolic status only on the basis of *being currently read as symbols*; that is, they are symbols only from the interpretive perspective of Stringer and Gamble — and others — who read them as *symbols of* intelligence. Pits used for the storage of fuel at a campsite, for example, or stacked mammoth bones that form a hut (Stringer & Gamble 1993:204) are not symbolic of anything. They are what they are; they refer to something beyond themselves only in the sense of referring to what Stringer and Gamble (and others) find "intelligent." There is no doubt but that by such a standard, symbols are arbitrarily defined; like proverbial beauty, they exist only in the eye of the beholder. Pits and huts may indisputably be regarded ingenious constructions, extraordinarily clever utilizations of the environment, and so on, but such positive regard does not make them symbols nor can it confer symbolic status upon the behavior of their makers. When Stringer and Gamble write that "architecture now embodies cultural, symbolic behaviour and not purely expedient survival behaviour" (1993:204) they are confusing their own judgments with that which they are judging. Their attributions are conceptually muddled because they are projections of their evaluations and not descriptive of the things themselves.

When we realize this fact, we begin to get a sense of the underlying, fundamental conceptual problem: the mental has been separated off from the physical to effect a rigorous opposition, then is later rejoined to glorifying effect. Although the ostensible concern is with behavior — the fabrication of hearths (thus campsites), the establishment of social networks (thus settlements), the expansion into new habitats (thus colonization) — behavior is conceived as merely a physical happening — a mere survival event. To be something more than a mere survival event, behavior must be regulated by behind the scene mental codes that have somehow arisen and become operative. *Then*, behavior becomes symbolic. But there is nothing actually grounding the epistemological connection; there is only the contiguous placement of two words: symbolic behavior. Moreover, a further difficulty is evident when one tries to bridge the gap between whatever has been established or created — campsite, settlement, new habitat (or tool) — and the symbolic code by which it has purportedly been made, thus a difficulty in identifying the product as a symbol by way of its maker's behavior. The identification might at first seem less difficult in the realm of art, for this kind of product is already a culturally-accepted form of symbol-making activity, at least for us Westerners. But even here, we would hardly attribute "symbolic behavior" to the artist forming the work. Indeed, if we apply the formula to the *making* of a work of art, we find nonsense. To say that the artist fashioning the art object — be it a painting, a dance, or a symphony — is engaging in symbolic behavior is to say that her/his actual behavior at any particular moment in the process of creation — indeed, during the entire process — stands for something else. Thus the actual application of paint, or the actual execution of a series of leaps, or the actual sounding of tones is in each case symbolic, i.e. an act of "mental substitution." The idea that an artist is behaving in this way when she/he is "making art" is clearly absurd. The situation becomes even more absurd when it comes to applying the formula to explain exactly how an art work is symbolic. In particular, how do symbolic codes that exist somewhere in "mental space" come to leave their symbolic mark on objects in the world? Even if the symbolic codes are said to be mediated by "symbolic behavior," it is totally unclear how the thing created by the symbolic behavior comes to have the purported standing-for character of the behavior.

In sum, the terms "symbol" and "symbolic behavior" are in need of fine, painstaking clarification and elucidation. As it stands, they cover a multitude of confusions, the price of playing conceptually loose with language and of attempting to join together lexically not only what has been conceptually rendered asunder but what is being actively maintained asunder by opposing categories of behavior — such as "survival" and "symbolic" — that further harden the familiar three-and-a-half-century-old Western division of "the physical" and "the mental." With such oppositions, the fundamental breach between physical and mental can never be reasonably joined — except by lexical concatenation. In no other way can a mental code suddenly become active, erupt into and substantively inform a behavior, and that behavior, with its substantively informing code, result in and substantively inform a product.

The conceptual muddle thickens when Stringer and Gamble turn to concrete comparisons between "Ancients and Moderns." As we have seen, survival behavior, a physical functioning, aligns itself with Neandertals; symbolic behavior, a mental functioning, with *Homo sapiens sapiens*. The underlying categorical separation remains decisively evident in subsequent epistemic attributions. Not only do Stringer and Gamble cast denigrating doubt on Neandertal burial practices — "whether it was a burial in the modern sense or more akin to rubbish disposal is the point at issue" (1993:159) — they claim that Neandertals "had the capacity for emulation, for change, but not for symbolism." They go on immediately to say, "We explain this as follows: the Neanderthals were under selective pressure, both biological and cultural, to survive" (1993: 207). Their explanation leaves something to be desired, in part because selective pressures to survive are pan-animate: all creatures, modern human lineages included, have been and are "under selective pressure to survive." What Stringer and Gamble perhaps mean to say is that they believe Neandertals were under unusual selective pressures. What these unusual pressures were, however, is not specified except vaguely in the form of "the Moderns": "the Moderns changed the forces of selection on Neanderthal behaviour" (1993: 207). In this context, Stringer and Gamble suggest that since Neandertals were not tied to "millennia-long traditions" and so made "decisions about making tools and building camps … according to expediency and efficiency," they functioned in a thoroughly rote way. Moreover they assert that "the archaeological evidence clearly indicates that the Neanderthals imitated certain aspects of modern behaviour" (1993: 207). The assertion constitutes a bold if not intemperate claim. "Clear indications" are indeed a lot to claim for archaeological evidence, especially when it comes to motivational attributions, i.e. imitation. But Stringer and Gamble press the claim even further in a final judgment. They write that "[W]hile they [Neandertals] could emulate they could not fully understand" (1993: 207).

Now surely this judgment constitutes a form of mind-reading, and especially in the absence of actually observed behavior, mind-reading is not ordinarily countenanced as an empirical tool. To offer an assessment of what another person — let alone another creature, especially one whom one has never seen and whom one discounts as a direct lineal ancestor of humans — understands or does not understand is scientifically risky. Indeed, in primatology, the idea that chimpanzees have a theory of mind ran the gauntlet of critical peer review (Premack & Woodruff 1978). It is surprising, then, that Stringer and Gamble not only exceed the bounds of objectivity in the form of standard scientific practice, but to credit "clear indications" and their ensuing mental attribution, they attempt to solidify their judgment by sharing a suspicion with the reader: "We suspect," they write, "that the structures at Molodova and Arcy-sur-Cure more resembled 'nests' than the symbolic 'homes' of the Moderns at Kostenki or Dolni Vestonice" (1993: 207). With their allusion to nightly nest-making practices of chimpanzees, their downplaying of "the mental" in Neandertals is unmistakable. Their innuendo points to a lapsed, inept, utterly subhuman mind, one incapable of symbolism, and in effect, to what is for them an inarguably deficient hominid.

4.   Deepened understandings of the symbolic

In Stringer and Gamble's view, "the fundamental difference between the Ancients and Moderns is social" (1993: 213) — hence the prominence of "associations between people, objects and contexts" in their definition of symbolism and in what they designate as symbols and as critically significant behavioral changes. This preeminently social understanding of symbolism is not in the least peculiar. Anthropologists and philosophers generally concur that a symbol is a social phenomenon. Cultural anthropologist Raymond Firth, for example, writes that an anthropological approach to symbolism "links the occurrence and interpretations of symbolism to social structures and social events in specific conditions" (Firth 1973:25). Philosopher Susanne Langer, in her earliest work on symbols, differentiates sign and symbol, remarking that "The passage from the sign-function of a word to its symbolic function is … a result of social organization" (Langer 1948:38). There is, however, a further fundamental aspect of a symbol that both Firth and Langer recognize, and that is its representational power. Firth in fact declares the essence of symbolism to lie "in the recognition of one thing as standing for (re-presenting) another" (Firth 1973:15). Symbols, Langer writes, "let us develop a characteristic attitude toward objects *in absentia*, which is called 'thinking of' or 'referring to' what is not here" (Langer 1948:37). The referential aspect is succinctly specified in the definitional statement that a relation is a symbolizing one "if and only if it is a four-term relation of standing for, where in the eyes of a symbolizer something, the symbol, stands for some other thing, the symbolized, within the context of a particular activity — for example, informing, giving orders, entertaining, or playing" (Johnstone 1984:167). What is requisite, especially given Stringer and Gamble's claim that the advent of symbolism was "an all or nothing situation," is an explanation of how *in an evolutionary sense* the idea of "standing for" could have arisen. In particular, the referential and not just the social dimension of symbolization needs to be evidentially grounded. Otherwise, no matter how social the group of creatures in question, there is no reason why all should treat some one thing as standing for some other thing. The referential dimension, in other words, needs to be shown to be anchored in some form of reality as readily perceptible, that is, as open to immediate awareness, as the social reality of other individuals. To that end, we will consider two interlocking ideas: the idea that *symbolization is a form of analogical thinking*, and the idea that *analogical thinking is foundationally structured in corporeal representation*. As might be apparent, such an understanding of symbolization construes mind and body not as two separate entities that are opposed to one another, or indeed, pitted against one another; it construes them to be all of a piece in the form of a living organism, a "persistent whole" (Haldane 1931:13) in the throes and challenges of everyday creaturely life. In the context of eight paleoanthropological case studies ranging from tool-making to burials to sexual signalling behavior to paleolithic cave art, I documented each of the interlocking ideas in detail; I showed how primatological (including hominid) and zoological studies validate both the ideas and their linkage, and exemplified the linkage in analyses of diverse behaviors. To illustrate in an economic manner the relevance of these ideas to the present need to clarify the nature and evolution of symbolism — and the need as well to expand typical conceptions of "physical" anthropology — I will summarize and cite passages from this earlier work (Sheets-Johnstone 1990).

Consider first the descriptive report by primatologist C.R. Carpenter whose research of the 1930s in many ways served to establish the field of nonhuman primate social behavior.

> When approaching a male, [the female howler] will form an oval opening with her lips and her protruding tongue will rapidly oscillate in and out and up and down. It is clear to an observer … that the function of this gesture is to invite copulation…. In a real sense the act is symbolic of sexual desire and readiness for copulation in the female and it stimulates appropriate responses in the male.
>
> (Carpenter 1963: 49–50)

There is no doubt but that Carpenter's description implicitly affirms the tongue to be a readily available spatio-kinetic analogue of the penis and the mouth a readily available spatial analogue of the vagina in the sexual communication of howler monkeys. There is no doubt either that tongue and mouth are sexual analogues in the behavior of other primates as well, as studies of female langurs (Dolhinow 1972) and studies of the tongue-smacking face of some monkey species, especially *Macaca nemestrina* (van Hoof 1969: 52, 58), attest. Genital symbolization is furthermore evident in the sexual tongue-flicking behavior of !Ko Bushmen — present-day hominids (Eibl-Eibesfeldt 1974). Moreover even a ram, in his attempts to interest a ewe in being mounted, flicks his tongue in and out of his mouth as he thrusts his head forward, sidles up to, and nudges the ewe — as any sheep farmer will affirm. In short, there is ample evidence showing that corporeal representation is a biological matrix: in the everyday animal world, there is a fundamental disposition to represent meaning corporeally in the form of tactile-kinetic gestures. By the same token, there is a fundamental disposition to understand meaning corporeally. The quotation from Carpenter documents this fact. Carpenter's untroubled interpretation of the female howler's tongue-flicking behavior shows that Carpenter himself was not puzzled by the behavior nor did he have to analyze the behavior painstakingly to justify to his readers how he arrived at its meaning. On the contrary, his brief verbal description suffices to convey immediately to the reader the same unequivocal meaning the actual behavior embodied for him in the flesh. By the same tactile-kinesthetic/kinetic tokens of experience, the behavior is clear straightaway to the male howler monkey: he too knows "that the function of the gesture is to invite copulation." Were this not so, the gesture would hardly "stimulate appropriate responses in the male."

The fundamental disposition toward corporeal representation in the animate world is a natural disposition toward both iconicity and semanticity; that is, there is an iconic rather than arbitrary relationship between symbol and referent, and a built-in semantic dimension to living bodies that is evident both morphologically and behaviorally. These natural dispositions toward iconicity and semanticity make decisively clear why — and how — animate bodies are semantic templates, or in other words, why corporeal representation is a fundamental biological matrix. It is a primary mode of communication and symbolization. Where meanings are *represented*, animate bodies represent them corporeally. In their form and behavior animate bodies are a primary source of meaning.

Primary modes of human symbolization substantiate the importance of semanticity and iconicity. These primary modes have been variously elucidated — for example, by Sigmund Freud in his psychology of the unconscious, by Susanne Langer in her aesthetics of art objects, by André Leroi-Gourhan in his archaeological analyses of prehistoric artifacts, and by Mary LeCron Foster in her linguistic analysis of primordial language. In each case, great emphasis is placed on the iconicity and semanticity of the symbols. Indeed, this is why a psychology, aesthetics, archaeology, and linguistics of *symbolizing behavior — behavior that produces symbols but is not itself symbolic —* is possible — why pears and mountains can represent female breasts and umbrellas and tree trunks can represent penes; why works of art can be understood as dynamic forms that are logically congruent to the dynamic form of human feeling; why archaeological artifacts in their design features can be interpreted as representations of female and male genitalia; why the articulatory gestures of primordial language can be shown to be tactile-kinesthetic analogues of their referents (Freud 1938, 1953, Vols. 4, 5; Langer 1948, 1953; Leroi-Gourhan 1971; LeCron Foster 1978). What is important to emphasize — and not only in reference to the above specific domains of corporeal representation in human life, but in reference to corporeal representation generally — is that the behavioral disposition toward iconicity, as toward corporeal representation itself, is not a conscious one — or *necessarily* a conscious one. In the most fundamental sense, bodily symbols are structured not in reflective acts but in pre-reflective corporeal experience; that is, they are the spontaneous product of certain species-specific bodily experiences.[6] What Freud said of the dreamer may thus be true of the symbolizing animal: "The dreamer's knowledge of symbolism is unconscious" (Freud 1963: 148). But while the symbolizing animal may be, like the dreamer, unconscious of its symbolizing behavior as such, *unlike the dreamer*, it is not unconscious of its behavior. It is aware of its own actions in a way gradient to that in which a bird, a song sparrow, for instance, is fully and directly aware of its own song in the process of singing it. Both ethologists and sociobiologists have documented this awareness (Marler 1975, 1976; Dawkins & Krebs 1978). Thus, while perhaps unaware of the symbolism *as such*, an animal — human or nonhuman — may well be aware of the dynamic congruency between one behavior (a symbolic one) and another (its referent), for example, aware of the dynamic congruency between in and out movements of the tongue and in and out movements of the penis.

It should be clear from the above consideration of primary modes of symbolization that corporeal representation is a fundamental mode not only of sexual communication

but of multiple kinds of communication. In the *Tanzsprache*, for example, the dancing honeybee represents direction by her orientation to gravity, distance by the spatio-
kinetic contours of her dance, and the richness of the food source by the vigorousness
of her dance (von Frisch 1964, 1967). Whatever the communicative circumstance,
and whichever the creature — whether bees, baboons,[7] bonobos,[8] howler monkeys,
or hominids — a form of behavior is evident in which a gesture or sequence of movements points or refers to something beyond itself. Whatever the particular referent, the
symbolization is conceptually played out corporeally, along the lines of the body.

Given this evolutionary framework for understanding symbols and symbolizing
behavior, two unmistakably major principles emerge: first, *humans (Homo sapiens
sapiens) do not have an exclusive corner on symbolization* — they are not privileged
evolutionary beings who alone are given to symbolizing behaviors; and second, *the
question of the origin of symbolization cannot be reduced to a question of light switches.*
In each case, a good deal more is involved. When symbolization is viewed in evolutionary perspective, a broader array of evidence must be examined and a consequently
fuller and deeper understanding of symbolization must be offered. Consideration of
the origin of hominid tool-making makes both points unequivocally. While a readily
self-evident relationship between teeth and stone tools is consistently and intuitively
recognized by many researchers (Toth: pers. comm.; see also Toth 1987; Foster 1982;
Wolpoff 1980:92, 168; Mann 1972), an empirically demonstrated *conceptual* association between teeth and tools is not shown. In other words, "the idea of a similarity
between teeth and stones is not a new one but neither has it been analyzed to any depth"
(Sheets-Johnstone 1990:26). Thus, to affirm simply that stone tools replaced teeth for
processing food gives no indication of the *experiential* and in effect conceptual basis for
the replacement. Why not a replacement of teeth by knuckles or feet? To answer that
upright posture freed the hands for tool-making does not constitute an explanation of
the connection between tools and teeth and thereby explain the origin of tool-making,
any more than the affirmation "tool-making freed the teeth for sound-making" constitutes an explanation of the connection between sounds and words and thereby explains
the origin of talking. What is needed is a detailed descriptive, i.e. experiential, analysis
that shows a conceptual linkage, even a rational connection, between stone tools and
teeth. Only in this way can one begin to examine and ultimately understand the *origin* of stone tool-making. With this understanding, it becomes immediately clear that
stone tools are not *symbols*; they are stone tools. But they are stone tools that have been
crafted on the model of the body, namely, teeth. They are thus *analogues*. Again, as
with symbols, such analogues are not necessarily structured in reflective acts but are
embedded in pre-reflective corporeal experience. For example, the primary datum of
stones and teeth alike is their resistant hardness. They are not squeezable; they do not
bend. This quintessential resistant hardness is a felt reality, a tactile-kinesthetic lingual
and manual phenomenon. If one knew nothing of stones or teeth but merely saw them,
there would be no reason to posit either as hard — or soft. The binary opposites are

clearly tactile qualities. The primary analogy between stones and teeth is thus one of structural correspondence. Just as the analogy is not necessarily a conscious one, neither is it necessarily an articulated one at all; to think analogically is not necessarily to think in words. On the contrary, as the analogy between teeth and stones demonstrates, the similar quintessential hardness of teeth and stones is an *experienced* fact of life. What the example of the origin of stone tool-making thus demonstrates is that analogical thinking is indeed grounded in the tactile-kinesthetic body. What the example thereby also demonstrates is that corporeal concepts — nonlinguistic concepts such as hardness — are in no way inferior to their linguistic relatives. Most importantly too, the example shows that analogical thinking does not necessarily eventuate in the production of symbols. Analogical thinking is a fundamental form of thinking that generates understandings on the basis of bodily experience, and those understandings may or may not eventuate in the production of symbols.

While the example of stone tool-making shows the original crafting of stone tools neither to constitute in itself "symbolic behavior" nor to eventuate in a symbol, it might nevertheless be claimed that at a later time (the Upper Paleolithic), modern human tools were communally conceived as symbols — symbols of power over others, for example, whether hominids or non-hominids. To be viable, however, the claim must address the question of symbolic reference; it must set forth the analogical basis on which tools come to *stand for* power over others rather than being experienced simply as powerful instruments in and of themselves, instruments that can among other things harm or subjugate others. As one anthropologist has in fact pointedly observed, "stone tools that are regarded as symbolic are generally *not* functional as powerful instruments" (Lukacs, pers. comm.). In this regard, then, it is clearly not sufficient to invoke symbolic codes or theoretical acts on the order of "mental substitutions" as operative in the production of tools. Such invocations merely sanction free-wheeling attributions, ones that in some instances seem to border on unbridled arrogance.[9] This is why conceptual muddles develop. This is also why discontinuities can be easily asserted, not only discontinuities between Modern and Neandertal tool-making behaviors and artifacts (and, ironically, by extension, between Modern and earlier hominid tool-making behaviors and artifacts), but discontinuities with respect to "symbolic behavior." The discontinuities — behavioral, artifactual, and symbolic — go hand in hand. With the advent of modern humans, a definitive break occurs, a Rubicon is crossed. On one side are tools, campsites, burial sites, and so on, which are symbols; on the other side are simply tools, 'nests', "rubbish disposals" and the like. The question of how one gets from one side to the other is answered by incantation, as it were: by calling into being "symbolic codes," "learning rules," "mental substitutions," and certain "associations." An empirically grounded answer, on the contrary, lies in the recognition of a faculty already there. That faculty is the power to think analogically, to perceive similarities in relationships, and to use the body as a semantic template. In short, if corporeal representation is the cornerstone of analogical thinking, and analogical thinking is the cornerstone of symbolization, then it is a leap neither of fancy nor of faith to think that, far from being a matter of newly operating symbolic codes, learning rules, mental substitutions, or associations, symbolization was an extension of an already extant biological matrix. The flick-of-the-switch, light-bulb theory of symbolization, one that basically construes mind and body as antithetical Cartesian substances, fails to recognize this matrix, enshrining intelligence instead in a rarified mental essence belonging to humans alone. As I have elsewhere argued, "intelligence does not reside at such a doubly exclusive address" (Sheets-Johnstone 1986b: 9). It resides in living creatures, "persistent wholes" that are both human and nonhuman.

In sum, symbolization is latent in analogical thinking and analogical thinking is latent in corporeal representation. However revolutionary and strikingly original the practices of Moderns some 40,000 years ago, they are rooted in a mode of thinking that is modelled on the body, that gives rise to corporeal concepts, and that has its origins far back in evolutionary history. When the basic biological matrix of corporeal representation — a clearly apparent evolutionary feature of morphology as well as behavior[10] — is ignored, "the mental" is easily given dominion *über alles* and an entire body of evidence is stifled. Suppressed too is an appreciation of the evolutionary continuities that basically bind hominid to hominid and humans to nonhumans. So also is the fundamental evolutionary principle that there is nothing *de novo* in Nature. This emphasis on continuities does not mean that differences are unimportant — much less non-existent. It means only that difference is not equivalent to a lack of commonalities. In marking out differences, one must take care not to overlook the ties that bind us in a common evolutionary family or in a common creaturehood. These ties may in both a literal and metaphorical sense lie deeper than artifactual and fossilized surfaces, and in turn articulate evolutionary matters of fact not yet examined, discovered, or perhaps even imagined.

5.   Animate form: Theoretical clarifications

The task now is to turn to living creatures themselves and show how deeper understandings of the relationship between bodies and movement — and in consequence deeper understandings of *animate form* — are critical to comparative studies in paleoanthropology. Deeper understandings are critical because the customary leap straight from morphology — fossil bones — to behavior — conjectured lifestyle — lacks a consistently solid empirical foundation. Indeed, "the mere possession of an anatomical part does not guarantee any particular behavior" (Sheets-Johnstone 1983: 205).[11] What it does guarantee, presuming the part and the body as a whole are intact, are certain movement possibilities and not others. To identify and describe these kinetic possibilities is ultimately *to delineate a particular kinetic domain of dispositions*. These movement dispositions exist because, whatever the range of possibilities, certain kinds of movement are more congenial and efficient given the body one is. While kinetic domains among both close and more distantly related species may obviously overlap, dispositions are less likely to do so. In other and broader terms, no group of hominid bodies is kinetically unique through and through, but no group of hominid bodies lacks definitive kinetic distinction. Hence, both kinetic commonalities and differences require attention.

Now if one can differentiate one group of hominids from another on the basis of movement dispositions, then certainly a vocabulary should exist for describing movement in comparative terms, a vocabulary commensurate with the vocabulary specifying relationships among morphologies (e.g. plesiomorphies, synapomorphies, autapomorphies, and so on). The purpose here is not to propose such a vocabulary of relationships, but rather to sketch out what bodily characters might enter into a delineation of movement dispositions, hence to identify features that might basically define a kinetic domain, and by extension, specify the lines along which a distinctive kinetic vocabulary might be drawn. It might be noted that in the same way that, as Trinkaus and Smith observe, "it is possible to make behavioral interpretations [on the basis of morphological evidence] irrespective of the actual phylogenetic relationships between the Neandertals and early modern humans" (Trinkaus & Smith 1985: 330), so it is possible to make kinetic interpretations irrespective of these same phylogenetic concerns.

An important theoretical and methodological distinction attaches to this kind of investigation. It was suggested earlier that in opting for "learning rules" and other such "abstractions" to specify the source of our uniqueness, Gould avoids the necessity of a typical sociobiological adaptationist explanation of the difference between us (Moderns) and them (Ancients). But it was also pointed out that in opting for abstractions, Gould hazards another kind of liability. That other kind of liability is evident in the required separation of "the mental" from "the physical" in order to arrive at an adaptive account at "the right level of abstraction." The important theoretical and methodological distinction hinges on demonstrating an alternative to Gould's "abstraction" strategy. In particular, there is a quite different way of avoiding adaptive catechisms, a way that, in addition, challenges the classic Western metaphysical dichotomy. Moreover this alternative approach has an even further significance. In avoiding the catechisms and in challenging Procrustean received Western wisdom, the alternative approach bridges what is otherwise an empirical void by opening up a new field of study, one that hews to corporeal matters of fact and attempts to do them full justice. Rather than itemizing the body part by part, supplying in turn a specific answer to the question "what is it (the part) good for?" and rather than itemizing conjectured behaviors in the same fashion, one considers the body as a whole and specifies its movement possibilities: *given a particular morphology, certain movement possibilities obtain and not others.* Specifying these possibilities is not the same as specifying the adaptiveness either of a given morphology, part by part, or of given conjectured behaviors. Although, in a kinetic sense, the question "what is it good for?" is still asked — i.e. what does this body allow in terms of movement? — the answer is of a different nature altogether, for what is of moment is both an intact organic whole and a corporeal matter of fact. For example, throwing as a real-life happening is not simply an arm movement; it is a *whole body movement.* By the same token it is not simply a behavior that has a functional significance of some kind or other and is duly fixed within a certain category — e.g. subsistence, sexual signalling, defense. Hence, it is not an act that is already pegged, so to speak, that has already been assigned its place in a creature's behavioral economy. To identify and describe movement possibilities is to ask what such and such a body allows in the way of movement and thereby ultimately define a certain repertoire of "I cans" (see Introduction, Note 3). The end result is thus not catechisms, but potentialities. Being descriptive rather than explanatory, the delineation of kinetic domains leaves open the question of adaptiveness. At the same time, however, *the delineation provides the empirical ground on the basis of which any answer to the question of adaptiveness must be assessed.* Precisely because it is a matter of understanding a living body in its living wholeness, what emerges from an attention to movement is a dynamic sense of how a creature lives or lived, what its repertoire of "I cans" allows or allowed, and what its particular kinetic dispositions are or were likely to have been.

Clarifying movement possibilities in this way (and indirectly, clarifying movement impossibilities and indispositions) results in clarifying corporeal matters of fact such that conjectured behaviors are in the end anchored in corporeally dynamic rather than categorically static facts of life. When it comes to empirically grounding paleoanthropological reconstructions, abstract formulations are clearly no match for corporeal matters of fact. Indeed, one can hardly speak of any *concrete constituents* of once-real evolutionary dramas in a language of abstract formulations. In hewing to corporeal matters of fact, one gains the insight that, in the same way that no body can speak a language for which it is unprepared, no body can move in ways for which it is unprepared; hence, no body can discover tactile-kinetic concepts — *nonlinguistic corporeal meanings* — for which it is unprepared. Corporeal matters of fact from this perspective are not mere items in a catalogue of the physical; they are facts about animate life, creaturely forms having certain potentialities of movement and not others in virtue of being the bodies they are, and in turn, having certain conceptual potentialities and not others. In sum, to bring fossil bones to kinetic life is to show how, given a certain skeletal form, a certain repertoire of "I cans" obtained, how within the compass of those kinetic capacities, certain ways of living were kinetically more congenial and efficient than others, and how, tethered to those fundamental kinetic dispositions, was a specified range of corporeal concepts.

A topical illustration of the morphological-kinetic-conceptual schema is readily available. Neandertal front teeth are consistently described as large and efficient tools used for a variety of "paramasticatory purposes" (Trinkaus & Smith 1985: 330) such as clamping and gripping. C. Loring Brace and Ashley Montagu in fact describe them as "the Lower and Middle Pleistocene equivalent of the Boy Scout knife," stating that "[i]t seems likely that they were used to crack nuts, peel bark, squeeze, scrape, pry, and cut a variety of objects, and also to tan rawhide" (Brace & Montagu 1965: 248). Given their broad utility and on-the-spot availability, we may ask why a Neandertal would spend energy and time making stone equivalents? Such an endeavor would indeed involve not merely time and effort in making the equivalents, but time and effort in looking for proper materials to begin with, in forging a diversity of stone forms specifically tailored to the use each would be put, in carrying such forms about to places they are or might be needed, in devising places to stash them when not being used, and so on. In short, if all the various acts of scraping, peeling, squeezing, and so on, were readily performable *dental* acts — in other words, if the body itself was diversely capable on the spot — then certain ways of living consistent with those diverse capabilities would be more congenial and efficient than other ways, i.e. more congenial than creating a diversified and elaborate stone tool-kit that in many (though not necessarily all) instances would merely duplicate the instrumental proficiencies of one's own teeth. Moreover such a tool-kit would in practice mean *moving* differently from the congenial and efficient ways of moving already practiced; wielding stone tools is different from using one's teeth. Furthermore, if Neandertals used their teeth in such ways as Brace and Montagu describe, then they necessarily had a corporeal concept of cracking, of peeling, of squeezing, and so on.[12] They were thus not at a loss conceptually any more than they were at a loss instrumentally. In effect, the judgment that Neandertals were deficient in their stone tool-making insofar as "they did not elaborate their material culture" (Stringer & Gamble 1993: 199)[13] ignores corporeal matters of fact and their conceptual and technological implications. Indeed, the judgment fastens on the notion of progress — or rather, lack of progress — toward the "*summum bonum* of bigger brains" and pronounces a pejorative verdict accordingly.

Anthropologist William Howells once wrote that "Hands and a big brain would not have made a fish human, they would only have made a fish impossible" (Howells 1959: 341; for a philosophical essay developed along the lines of Howells's remark, see Sheets-Johnstone 1986a). Though speaking about levels of neural organization and not about animate form, Howells's remark rings in the present context with a particular truth. Animate form is the proper starting place for paleoanthropological reconstructions, the central and critical key to understanding the lives of once-living creatures precisely because it does justice to movement possibilities and dispositions, and to the persistent wholeness that is their foundation.

6.   Animate form: Neandertals

Neandertals bodies are consistently described postcranially in terms of their robustic-
ity, their power grip, the shortness of their distal limb segments, and their distinctive
pelves (Rak 1987; Rak 1993; Trinkaus 1983; Trinkaus & Smith 1980). References to
movement in the context of these descriptions are sparse and brief. Indeed, movement
is not an item in any index of any book on Neandertals, any more than it is an item
in indices of books on paleontology or paleoanthropology generally. The subject is
consistently skirted even in places where it appears to be the topic of direct concern.
Stringer and Gamble's sixteen-line section titled "Posture and movement" (in *In Search
of Neanderthals*) is a case in point. Except for a passing reference to "squatting," and a
reference to "strong movement" (the meaning of which is not exemplified), the brief
section concerns itself with anatomy — with the structure of the shoulder blade, for
example, and the way the pelvis "may be related to the different way in which the hip
joint operated" (Stringer & Gamble 1993:93) — and not with either movement or
posture. Indeed, that there is a realm of movement to be explored and understood is
readily attested to by its being nowhere in evidence.

The closest approximation to an awareness of the paleoanthropological significance
of movement, and in particular, the movement style of Neandertals, is to be found in a
1959 article by anthropologist Alice Brues titled "The Spearman and the Archer — An
Essay on Selection in Body Build." In the context of discussing body build in relation
to tool type, Brues focuses attention on specific kinetic acts and gives specific kinetic
definition to precisely such terms as "strong." At one point, for example, she describes
strength in terms of defensive action. She links strength of body build with "static
defense," the creature "stand[ing] its ground instead of fleeing" (Brues 1959:458). She
illustrates how laterality of build that is favorable to static defense is oftentimes linked
to increasing size, citing the gorilla as an example (Brues 1959:458). She notes at a further point, in a discussion of how, in a creature without weapons such as a gorilla, "[the
magnitude of] destructiveness is [proportional] to the amount of squeezing or crushing
force exerted momentarily on the fragile parts of the victim." She astutely points out in
this context that a gorilla's physique "drastically reduces speed of locomotion," with the
effect that, "though he could kill anything he could catch, he cannot catch anything"
(Brues 1959:462). In brief, discussion turns on actual movement, what creatures can
and cannot do. Though Brues does not go on to distill movement dispositions from
these "cans and cannots" — nor indeed speak in terms of a repertoire of "I cans" — it
is clear that such repertoires and dispositions quintessentially characterize the human
and nonhuman animals she describes. In this respect, her analyses readily demonstrate
a seminal attention to animate form. An implicit concern with kinetic and potential
energy undergirds her discussions along with an explicit concern with movement possibilities, possibilities not only of "squeezing or crushing," but of "crashing through"

"leaping," "climbing," "running," "drawing [a bow]," and so on. It should be emphasized that it is not a matter of throwing in a few movement terms here and there in the course of a discussion about body build; the discussion itself is anchored in movement such that a distinct sense emerges of what is kinetically entailed in being a particular kind of body. Furthermore, in the use of words such as "strength," and in descriptions of what are usually simply termed "behaviors" — e.g. "hunting," "striking" — the same distinct kinetic entailments are evident.

It bears emphasizing that Brues was *not* proposing that body build correlates *only* with the disposition to produce and to use a particular type of weapon. In view both of what she writes about body build and of the disclaimers and admonitions with which she concludes her research, anthropologist David Frayer errs in attributing to her such a proposal; Brues never claims that "body size changes are related only to the adoption and use of weapon types" (Frayer 1981:69). Not only does she temper her research conclusions by an awareness of their provisional nature, but she states explicitly both that her suggested correlations "should be critically questioned" and that other factors entering into selection "must be considered jointly" (Brues 1959:469). In this context, she mentions climate. In fact, she has already taken the environment into account — in terms of terrain as well as climate — in describing movement possibilities; for example, in speaking of the kind of place in which "the original specialization of the human leg took place," she speaks of "an open prairie country where continuous running and leaping were possible" (Brues 1959:461).[14] The point is important. Where the focus is on movement, *where one thinks in terms of the movement possibilities of animate forms*, then terrain and climate enter naturally into the discussion. These factors are of indisputable import to an understanding of Neandertals. What one can kinetically do and not do, and similarly, what one is kinetically disposed to do and not to do, are intimately related to environmental conditions, to *circumstances*, as Lamarck would have put it (Lamarck 1963). A study of movement thus necessarily — by its very nature — considers organisms *in situ*, as making their way in the context of a certain topography and climate. It thus joins together causal (selectional) factors that are typically conceived and treated independently of one another. The idea that one must specify *either* thermal regulation *or* biomechanical advantage as causative agent with respect to the morphology of Neandertals is a prime example of typical practice (e.g. Trinkaus 1981). Where movement conceptually anchors the analysis, the idea collapses as a viable working principle.

Thinking in terms of movement one indeed reconstructs in corporeally dynamic terms rather than in categorically static ones. By the same token, one reconstructs holistically, in non-divisionary metaphysical terms. As we have seen, the degree to which the mental and the physical are typically disjoined in paleoanthropological reconstructions is readily exemplified by the cognitivist vocabulary and emphasis with which Neandertals are rendered less than human. Further analysis of Neandertals in terms of animate form will show clearly that paleoanthropological reconstructions can find firmer ground in corporeal matters of fact than in typical divisionary thinking and that the quest to describe "what it was like" (to be such-and-such a hominid) can be far better satisfied.

From virtually the moment of their original discovery, Neandertals have been regularly conceived and are still conceived by many as being mentally deficient in one way or another. They are conceived to have *lacked* something cerebral — something in the way of thoughtfulness — since they did not "improve" in major ways or accede to our 20th century human kind of behavioral capabilities. It is as if, given all the time they had at their disposal — all the time they walked the earth — they stood pat; indeed, we are told that "in terms of hominid colonization, [it was] half a million years or more of inaction" (Stringer & Gamble 1993:215).[15] Considering the esteem in which earlier hominids (*Homo habilis*, *Homo erectus*, not to mention australopithecines) are generally held, the negative judgment is odd,[16] but it is especially odd when coupled with comparative statements concerning the singular abilities of *Homo sapiens sapiens*: their colonization of new areas, for example, their future planning abilities, their sophisticated social networks that insured survival in challenging times, and so on. The negative judgment is especially odd because Neandertals were around for more than 200,000 years (approximately 250,000 to 35,000 BP). That is not a long time in evolutionary terms, but it is a very long time when measured against our own human evolutionary life span of 40,000 years. Indeed, we modern humans have existed less than one quarter of the time that Neandertals existed. In contrast to Neandertals, early *Homo sapiens sapiens* are described in glowing terms that apply still to us since we are their descendants. Thus prized abilities — the ability to plan ahead and to form social networks, for example — are implicitly if not explicitly taken to be features of our own lives, and this in spite of contravening evidence. For example, any quick appraisal of the present global environmental situation readily instructs us that many humans are singularly deficient in planning ahead; they see only as far as their own immediate desires and/or their own lifetime. Moreover rather than building social networks that give them "insurance policies" (as Stringer and Gamble put it; 1993:210) against hard times, humans on the whole appear unkindly disposed if not hostile toward their national and ethnic neighbors, unduly acquisitive, and to have been at war almost incessantly as far back as history records. Furthermore, social networks in the form of treaties between or among nations have proved notoriously unreliable "insurance policies." In short, from a Martian or otherwise more objective viewpoint, modern humans in recorded history appear to be socially and ecologically deficient creatures who are more properly defined as selfishly engaged rather than either future-oriented or socially congenial. However revolutionary, stunning, and undeniably wonderful the practices and inventions of early modern humans, practices and inventions of those latter-day humans who are their descendants arouse — or should arouse — wonder of an altogether different sort. There is every reason to doubt rather than marvel at their so-called "fundamental behavioral capabilities" and "improvements," their "learning rules," and the like. In fact, there is every reason to wonder whether *Homo sapiens sapiens* will match the evolutionary longevity of Neandertals.

The point is not deflective in the least to the topic at issue. What we humans want to claim for ourselves are clearly the *summum bonum* brains of which Gould speaks. We do this by mental comparison — and by a selective perception and amnesia that allow us to identify ourselves only with what we find mentally praiseworthy in the past. Thus it is that *the* significant differences distinguishing modern humans from Neandertals are not *physical* differences but illustrious mental ones that appear *ex nihilo*.[17] This is why *abstract* formulations can be formulated as they are — not only in a mental vacuum and honorifically on behalf of *Homo sapiens sapiens* alone, but as if they specified indelible features of all modern human minds, thus features in whose glory present-day humans may bask since it was "our kind" who mentally distinguished themselves. Clearly, what is at stake and what the comparison secures is "the traditional *summum bonum* of bigger brains … because bigger brains are so good to have" (Gould 1994: 27). In thoroughly supportive fashion, received Western wisdom teaches that quintessentially significant differences are "in the head" and have nothing to do with bodies. This is why Stringer and Gamble can write in answer to their question, "Where did modern behaviour originate?" that "[W]herever new developments took place they did so rapidly (the flick of a switch), *adapting to the anatomy of modern humans that had been around for perhaps 70,000 years*" (Stringer & Gamble 1993: 218; italics added). Great new ideas arose with "the flick of a switch" and adjusted themselves to the corporeal packaging in which they found themselves, the modern human's mind adapting itself swiftly and efficiently to the body in which it happened to be. In this metaphysically divisive way, modern humans find the kind of reasons they seek for cherishing themselves. What they want to cherish is "the mental," the kind of mental that churns out learning rules and mental substitutions, that bequeaths unique and remarkable ingenuities in the form of symbolic behaviors and unique and remarkable abilities such as the ability to plan ahead. They do not seek reasons for cherishing themselves *physically*, except by disdaining what they consider unattractive: prognathous features, no chin, squat build, and so on.

It is ironic that, in his article, "Evolution by Walking" — a review of a newly instituted exhibit of fossil mammals at the American Museum of Natural History — Stephen Jay Gould emphasizes precisely a view of evolution that does *not* give preeminence to modern humans, either "temporally" (they are the latest and thus most intelligent arrivals) or "morally" (i.e. they are "higher" rather than "lower" forms of life). He lauds the cladistic arrangement of the exhibit fossils; they are organized in their chronological order of branching, and not in terms of "their later 'success' or 'advancement'" (Gould 1995: 13). Accordingly, as visitors walk through the exhibit, they do not figuratively climb "a ladder of putative advance" (Gould 1995: 14). They walk through evolutionary time and learn in and by walking, the proper evolutionary place of humans. This seemingly quite novel key idea — that we learn in and by moving — is expressed at the end of the article by the thought that "cogitation and ambulation" go hand in hand (Gould 1995: 15). But Gould has in fact already extolled the idea of "using the visceral to grasp the cerebral." Much earlier in his article, he specifies that "*in order to illustrate a concept*," one moves the body directly through the process or phenomenon of interest (Gould 1995: 10; italics added).

Now if movement can *illustrate* a concept, then might not movement *generate* a concept in the first place, that is, might a concept not have in fact originated in the course of moving or having moved? Not only why but how otherwise would movement possibly be able to illustrate a concept? In a broader sense, might not the most fundamental practices and beliefs of any particular hominid group have been forged in the context of moving and having moved? If so, then in the most basic sense movement possibilities and dispositions delimit one's conceptual possibilities and dispositions. Again, if so, then morphology — whether a matter of living creatures or fossilized specimens — must be ultimately conceived in terms of *animate form*.[18]

Gould's idea of a tight and intimate connection between thinking and moving clearly coincides with the sequence of ideas proposed earlier: in the most fundamental sense, thinking is modelled on the body, in particular, the tactile-kinesthetic body. Animate form is thus at the core of what traditionally passes for strictly cerebral activity. Such an idea is latent not only in Gould's article. It is latent in articles by paleoanthropologists and other researchers. In "Technological Changes across the Middle-Upper Palaeolithic Transition: Economic, Social and Cognitive Perspectives," for example, Paul Mellars notes that "over large areas of Europe, the major changes in both the anatomy of the human populations, and the technology of the associated archaeological assemblages, can be shown to have occurred over at least broadly the same range of time — i.e. broadly between c. 40 000 and 30 000 BP" (Mellars 1989: 338). This idea — that morphology and technology are linked — is actually evident to any perceptive and non-Cartesian-thinking reader who compares two illustrations that Mellars includes in his article. The backed knives (Figure 20.2) representing the tool industry of the Neandertals are squat, bulky, indeed, *robust* tools (Mellars 1989: 344); the points and crescents (Figure 20.3) representing the tool industry of early modern humans are lithe, elongate, indeed, *gracile* tools (Mellars 1989: 346). Tool morphology matches body morphology; the correspondence is palpable.[19] Mellars himself, however, does not make the connection. Instead, he leaps precipitately over the traditional metaphysical chasm to arrive at "symbolic 'meaning'," at the idea that Upper Palaeolithic humans, in contrast to Middle Palaeolithic people, "imposed form" on their raw materials and thus attained to "symbolism and symbolically defined behaviour" (Mellars 1989: 358–60). He attributes the new "cognitive factors" that mark the transition from "'archaic' to 'modern' human populations" to "some kind of fundamental change in the basic structure of human thinking" (Mellars 1989: 357). The idea that thinking could have something to do with the body — or the body with the mind — never surfaces.

The morphological-technological connection is a clear validation of analogical thinking. It is a validation of corporeal representation. Subsistence tools of Neandertals and early modern humans were in the image of their own bodies; their own bodies were semantic templates. When we allow the tools to speak for themselves, they speak unequivocally of this relationship. In this respect, they also speak of distinct differences. Neandertal tools were created not so much in terms of the linear *contours* of the body as in the image of its *bulk*. Moreover they were accessories to rather than extensions of the body; they were, in other words, auxiliaries of a body that was already instrumentally proficient, already by itself a most effective tool. Sheer strength and bulk were at the ever-ready disposal of this body. So also were teeth that could be used in a variety of non-dietary ways. In effect, whatever might be necessary to eking out a living, defending oneself, or dealing with the world, its instrumental point of origin was the body itself. That the tool kit of Neandertals did not change appreciably over 200,000 years is readily understandable in terms of this fact. As pointed out earlier, what need is there to devise ever more sophisticated tools — to take time to look for the proper stone, to take time to flake it in such and such a way, to make the effort to carry it about, and the like — when one has a variety of efficient tools ready-to-hand at the moment one needs or wants them? Moreover why would a labor-saving device in the form of a lever, for example, be thought of if one could immediately pick up the small boulder and move it by oneself? When we think of brawn, we might tend to think of it as antithetical to brains — much like thinking of a linesman in football as compared to a quarterback, for example. But this divisionary thinking misses the point. If one's build and size afford one a reliable effectiveness, if what is there naturally is not only basically sufficient but ever-ready, why would one be disposed to tinker about with the idea of forging something new? What need is there to fashion a complicated tool kit for tasks in which one's own body constitutes tool enough? It is not a matter of brawn versus brains or brains versus brawn. It is a matter of understanding kinetic domains and the movement dispositions of animate forms.

Now the idea of a conceptual linkage between morphology and technology may suggest an absolute synchronization of anatomy with culture, any change in the latter being immediately coincident with a change in the former. The suggestion is erroneous and simplistic on several inter-related counts. To begin with, culture is not reducible to technology. As Stiner (1994) has shown in extended detail, a good deal more is involved in the establishment of, and in the continuity or changes in, cultural practices — specifically those associated with subsistence — than stone tools. Environmental change, land use, and mobility, for example, are highly significant variables. So also are prey focus and prey availability. Absolute synchronization of anatomical and lithic change could occur only in the absence of such fundamental and critical factors. Thus, that anatomically modern humans were present *before* the advent of a modern tool kit, for example, does not contravene the basic idea that hominids made stone tools in the image of their bodies or the ample evidence on which it is based: a palpably visible congruity of bodily and lithic morphologies. Second, recognition of the formal analogy between body morphology and subsistence tools entails no correlative claims about boundaries or watersheds. The typically drawn "boundary" between Middle and Upper Paleolithic is literally set in stone; in other terms, the Neandertal-to-modern human "transition" — be it defined in terms of continuity or replacement — has been evidentially marked primarily on the basis of a difference in stone tool kits. Newer studies question the narrowness of this perspective, not only in terms of there being other highly significant factors to consider as indicated above, but in terms of construing the Neandertal tool industry (the Mousterian) "as a monolithic, static thing" (Kuhn 1995: 171) — not to say a "robotic" thing (Kuhn 1995: 156) — that remained unchanged for thousands of years. In short, the boundary itself is open to question as a readily and exactly delimitable and fixed moment in hominid evolution, a moment that marks both a lithic watershed and a correlative "mental" watershed dividing a "primitive or ineffective" (Kuhn 1995: 171) intelligence from an intelligence that is advanced and powerful. As noted above, recognition of the formal analogy between body morphology and subsistence tools carries with it no temporal claims about stone tool typology as an evolutionary or "mental" boundary marker, hence no claims that a certain kind of tool kit makes its entrance and exit in precise temporal concert with the appearance and disappearance of a certain kind of body. To say that stone tools were modelled on the body in the course of hominid evolution is no more than to acknowledge what is evidentially apparent in paleoanthropological and archaeological data: a basic *formal* analogy between the bodies of anatomically modern humans and *their* tools and between Neandertal bodies and *their* tools. More broadly, it is to say that one designs tools congenial to the body one is, not to the body one is not; equally, one designs them congenial to the use they will be put *and can be put given one's situation*, not to a use that is impossible in virtue of either the environment in which one lives, for example, or of the kind of prey that is available. Third, the relationship between morphology and technology is precisely *not* a "flick of the switch" relationship. Such a relationship would require, *inter alia*, that certain infants at certain times be born as fully formed adults, with bodies radically different from their parents, and correspondingly, with radically different stone tools in their hands. On the contrary, infants are born within a certain lineage, within a certain social tradition, within a certain ecological and climatic environment, and so on. The kind of stone tools made and used by particular groups within a species may certainly vary, but those variations do not suddenly negate the distinctive formal characters that define in a classic way a particular style of stone tool-making any more than morphological variations preclude classic definitions of species. Fourth, radical changes in stone tool-making, at least insofar as they become standardized and are not, for instance, a one-time-and-never-more-pursued accidental discovery, clearly involve conceptual elaborations on a particular pragmatic theme, be it hammering, stripping, grinding, or whatever. Like the pragmatic theme itself, these conceptual elaborations are clearly dependent on lithic resources, on the kind of prey species in the area, and on all those other variables mentioned above. There is, in effect, no reason to think that analogical thinking operates in a vacuum, that the moment a certain kind of body is present, it immediately begins churning out a certain kind of tool kit. The actual is tied to the circumstantially possible. But again, it is also tied in a fundamental sense to the realities of animate form. The tools one makes are the tools one can wield: tools that fit one's grip (however large or small, powerful or weak, for example), that fit one's style of moving (however fleet or heavy, long or short in endurance, for example), that fit one's range of movement (however flexible or constrained, ample or small, for example), and so on. In short, what one conceives and elaborates in the way of a tool is patterned on the animate form one is.

We should perhaps note that the basic formal conjunction is not contravened by the fact that anatomically modern humans were on the scene before their classic tool-kits were *or* that some Neandertals made tools similar to anatomically modern humans. Anthropologist Richard Klein's view that "the modern physical form evolved before the modern capacity for culture" and that "it was culture and not body form that propelled the human species from a relatively rare and insignificant large mammal 35,000 years ago to a geologic force today" (Klein 1989: 397) does not engender a substantive sense of "body form" in the full and detailed sense understood here; in other words, Klein's "body form" is not equivalent to animate form. Moreover although Klein disaffirms a connection between culture and "body form," he actually obliquely supports the idea of corporeal representation — or analogical thinking — when he writes in one instance that "The Upper Paleolithic contrasts with the Mousterian in many ways, of which the most often-cited is the widespread Upper Paleolithic emphasis on stone flakes whose length was at least twice their width" (Klein 1989: 356); and when he writes in another instance of how the "inferior" behavior of Neandertals might be connected with their "distinctive morphology": "the Neanderthals were behaviorally inferior to their modern successors, and, to judge from their distinctive morphology, this behavioral inferiority may well have been rooted in their biological makeup" (Klein 1989: 334). His negative judgment of Neandertals aside — and his implicit idea of a hominid march toward "the *summum bonum* of bigger brains" aside also — Klein obliquely intimates that there is something more to bodies than meets the classic Western eye.[20] Spelled out, this intimation would affirm that "distinctive morphologies" have behavioral implications precisely because they are *animate* morphologies and being animate, they have conceptual implications as well.

When we translate into animate bodily terms assessments of purported "lack" and "inaction," we begin to understand technological differences at their conceptual source. So too when we translate into animate bodily terms assessments of revolutionary new practices. Indeed, the following kind of differences between Middle and Upper Palaeolithic hominids begins to emerge.

A stocky body is not disposed toward ballistic movement.[21] An upright body with short distal limb segments cannot throw in either as easy or as effective a ballistic manner as one with longer distal limb segments. With a greater range of movement comes a greater facility in moving through a ballistic pattern of movement. Moreover more momentum is built up, with the result that the thrown object will release and travel with greater speed. Furthermore, movement of the body as a whole in the direction of the throw can add to the latter's force. Thus if one runs, for example, in the process of throwing, the run will add to the body's momentum and be transferred to the throwing arm and object thrown. Longer distal limb segments are more suited to ballistic movement for just such reasons.

Consider further that in non-ballistic acts such as striking, bludgeoning, or thrusting with a spear rather than throwing it,[22] an upright moving body is consistently in control of the object it utilizes. It wields power directly and firmly; it is always in command of the object with which it hits or batters. A ballistic movement is in contrast self-propelling: an initial thrust of power sends the movement — and the utilized object — on its way, as in throwing or kicking something, or in swinging or hurling an instrument. The fact that movement itself takes over means that one is able to act at a distance. What one relinquishes in the way of continuous control over an object, one gains in the way of power over greater distances, and in the way of a built-in measure of safety with respect to the target toward which the object or implement is aimed.[23] It is of considerable interest in this context to point out that greater bodily injury and trauma are evident on Neandertal fossils than on early modern ones and that the difference is thought to be due to a difference in the material culture of the two hominid species (Klein 1989: 344).

The above minimal distinctions suffice to introduce the possibility of analyzing corporeal concepts in greater detail. The concept of acting in immediate contact with things, for example, of being up against them, and the concept of acting at a distance upon the same things as in throwing something at them, are distinct in several respects. Not only is one's sense of control different in each case, but one's sense of *effort, space,* and of *one's own spatiality* is different. The idea that an object can act effectively on something when it is outside one's own grasp, for instance, is a complicated concept. It engenders a sense of what movement can do on its own, that is, an awareness that an object can do work for a body even when that object is no longer in hand. It engenders a sense of distance, of speed, and of timing with respect to a goal or target. Striking and thrusting have a much narrower compass with respect to effort, space, and one's own spatiality. Distance is measured in terms of the length of one's striking or thrusting arm. The target, whatever it might be, is palpably close. Moreover one's own body movement as a whole may be constrained in the sense that the immediate presence and size of the target may limits one's possibilities of action. What one gains in consistent control of an object may thus be offset by what one risks in the way of safety — of bodily injury or trauma. Range of movement, safety, effort, the spatial immediacy or distance of the target, its comparative size — all such aspects of the tactile-kinetic situation engender distinctive spatial-kinetic concepts. These distinctive concepts, of fundamental significance in and of themselves, may readily contribute to a spatial sense of the world, of where it begins and ends, for example: is it an always close-at-hand, proximate world or an on-going expansive world stretching out beyond actual reach? Clearly, the idea of expanding into new habitats has a certain spatial resonance with the experience of acting at a distance and its attendant concepts, including the concept of possible opportunities in a world not immediately at hand, that is, opportunities in an extended world.

To arrive at such deeper understandings of the conceptual significance of movement, we must necessarily forego the common notion that movement is merely a change of position in conformity with some "mental" directive. That notion is statically focused. Indeed, we must restore to movement its inherent dynamics and in so doing acknowledge the spatio-temporal play of forces that particularizes and situationally defines movement and that potentially generates a particular domain of concepts. This acknowledgment is in large measure an acknowledgment of the fact that *how* one moves is part and parcel of the fact *that* one moves. Like all so-called movement "behaviors," striking and throwing, for example, are inherently distinctive kinetic acts, both experientially and conceptually. They have a different spatiality not only with respect to the object they each utilize and its spatial relationship both to the acting individual and to the target; they have a different spatial dynamic in terms of experienced range of movement and experienced changes in the linear conformations of the body; they have furthermore a different spatiality in terms of experienced corporeal solidity and flexibility. Correlatively, they have a different temporal and tensional structure: the one movement is temporally abrupt and likely repetitive, the other is sequentially articulated; the one is tensionally concentrated, the other is tensionally diffused in a manner coincident with sequential articulation. If one notated in a movement notation system[24] the likely distinctive movement patterns of Neandertals, then one could compare their overall style of movement with the overall movement style of modern humans. Kinetic differences would become evident as would broadly generalized distinctions in animate form: distinctions between strength and agility, for example, between compactness and flexibility, between an ability to stand one's ground, change direction quickly with a ready stability due to a proportionately lower center of gravity and laterally rotated legs, and an ability to run, twist, scamper, change direction quickly but with a lesser stability due to a proportionately higher center of gravity and antero-posterior positioned legs. The primary purpose of charting such distinctions would not be comparison *per se*, especially to the end that an axiological scheme emerges naming a winner and loser or a superior and an inferior. Indeed, if, as Trinkaus and Shipman write of Neandertals, "Tremendous strength, endurance, and fortitude exceeding those of any modern human life-style were required on a daily basis" (Trinkaus & Shipman 1993: 381), then what could — or can — possibly be the purpose of comparing Neandertals to modern humans other than setting in relief the peculiar and unique kinetic possibilities and dispositions of each together with their peculiar and unique conceptual implications? The challenge in articulating kinetic possibilities and dispositions is precisely to show how dynamic elements of movement and the tactile-kinesthetic body play out conceptually, i.e. analogically, in a way similar to the way in which stone tools play out conceptually both the tactile character of teeth and the spatio-kinetic character of animate form.

With deepened understandings of animate form, of corporeal matters of fact, and of the symbolic, the fundamental question concerning Ancients and Moderns shifts to new ground and in consequence is reformed. Rather than a question of whether Neandertals were replaced by or were genetically continuous with early modern humans, the fundamental question is whether we can justly say we know Neandertals if we know them in anything other than "in their own terms" (Trinkaus & Shipman 1993: 380). To know them "in their own terms" means to be able to imagine on the basis of fossil, artifactual, taphonomic, and related kinds of evidence — thus, in a rigorously-tethered empirical way — what it is like to be a body we are not and to draw out the kinetic and conceptual implications of being that body.[25] The quest, in other words, is not merely a factual one in the sense of specifying historical relationships. It is a factual one in the sense of specifying *what it was like*. Accordingly, our capacity to imagine ourselves along different corporeal lines and to fathom in turn what it was like kinetically and conceptually to live along those lines is the beginning ground and measure of our understanding of Neandertals — whether close kin or distant relatives.

Notes

* A shorter and differently focused version of this chapter first appeared in Sheets-Johnstone 1996d under the title "Tribal Lore in Present-day Paleoanthropology: A Case Study" and was also presented as a guest lecture in Social Anthropology at Trondheim University (Norway) in 1996. A still shorter version was presented at the March 1996 meeting of the Society for the Anthropology of Consciousness held in conjunction with the American Philosophical

Association Pacific Division meeting. Another shorter and differently focused version of this chapter appeared in Sheets-Johnstone 1998b.

1.   "Symbolic behavior" is the cardinal term in Stringer and Gamble's thesis concerning the difference between "Moderns" and "Ancients." See Section III below.

2.   See also Sheets-Johnstone 1990 for a detailed examination and vindication of these charges in the context of eight paleoanthropological case studies.

3.   For a notable exception to this practice, see essays of anthropological linguist Mary LeCron Foster, especially 1978, 1990, 1992, 1994a, 1994b, 1996.

4.   Gould's judgment about Trinkaus and Shipman — that their book represents one of the "opposite sides of the controversy" — seems unwarranted since one finds no dogmatic assertions in their book regarding the evolutionary relationship of Neandertals to modern humans. Moreover if, as Gould says, they take no "official position" but merely "lean toward the multi-regionalist approach," then "oppositional sides" are hardly in evidence.

5.   As this chapter will show, *contra* Gould, the pursuit of "the traditional *summum bonum* of bigger brains" is not a pursuit limited to "tendency" multi-regionalist theorists; it is very much a pursuit of "entity" Noah's Ark theorists as well, and this because the pursuit is based not on theory but on an implicit and highly potent mind/body dichotomy.

6.   See Sheets-Johnstone 1990:126–28 for a discussion of primatologist Stuart Altmann's related concept of "comsigns"; see too Chapter 9, this text.

7.   Adult male baboons grind their teeth and display their canines (yawn) as a threat gesture. Iconicity is clearly apparent in these gestures. See Hall and De Vore 1972.

8.   See Savage-Rumbaugh & Bakeman 1977. See also Sheets-Johnstone 1990 for an analysis of bonobo gestural communication as analogical behavior — or corporeal representation.

9.   For example, with respect to the "smaller societies throughout the Ancients' world," Stringer and Gamble write that "It was, in terms of hominid colonization, half a million years or more of inaction" (1993:215); with respect to the absence of the Ancients in eastern Siberia, they write, "Food was always available in these habitats, it was simply high-risk to exploit" (216); with respect to language, after remarking that Neanderthals "no doubt spoke, albeit simply and probably slowly," they write that "Neanderthals lacked complex spoken language because they did not need it (217). All of these judgments are judgments of people Stringer and Gamble *know* only by indirect evidence. The judgments are exceptionally broad and denigrating, considering that first-hand knowledge is in the form of fragmentary, open-ended, and for the most part quite fortuitously discovered evidence. Erik Trinkaus has remarked in the following way on these kinds of limitations: "[O]ur current paleoanthropological record is incomplete and … our interpretations of later Pleistocene human evolution will change as further discoveries are made. Furthermore, the information available at one time to any one researcher or group of researchers is an incomplete set of the potentially available data set. Therefore, all interpretations can be realistically seen as no more than state-of-the-art conclusions, inevitably to fall or be modified as the field progresses" (1992:2).

10.   See, for example, Wickler 1969; Portmann 1967; see also Sheets-Johnstone 1990, Chapter 4, for a discussion of basic male sexual signalling behaviors.

11.   This paper was a very early attempt to show the importance of a consideration of move-ment to paleoanthropological reconstructions.

12.   For detailed paleoanthropological exemplifications and analyses of corporeal concepts, see Sheets-Johnstone 1990.

13.   Note too that rather than attributing any conceptual acumen to Neandertal stone tool-making, Stringer and Gamble observe that "There may be regional variety in the typology of stone tools, … [but] the availability of raw materials and local patterns of land use are prob-ably largely responsible for the variety that did exist" (1993:199).

14.   To be noted is the newer perspective on the environment in which upright hominids emerged. Rather than moving out to "open prairie country where continuous running and leaping were possible," early hominids are thought to have emerged "in the relative safety of the forests while living next to their cousins, the apes" *On the Edge* 1996:3. See also Cowley & Salzhauer 1995.

15.   Cf. Eldredge & Tattersall 1982:3: "The data, or basic observations, of evolutionary biology are full of the message of stability. Change is difficult and rare, rather than inevitable and continual. Once evolved, species with their own peculiar adaptations, behaviors, and genetic systems are remarkably conservative, often remaining unchanged for several millions of years." Eldredge and Tattersall later pointedly equate lack of change with a successful way of life (7).

16.   It is, in fact, inconsistent in an evolutionary sense. For example, how can earlier homi-nids be cherished for their stone tool-making accomplishments, which are not judged by the standard of successive "improvements" over time, and Neandertals disdained for what is deemed their lack of stone tool-making accomplishments on the basis of a lack of successive "improvements" over time? The valuing and de-valuing of our ancestors — be they close kin or distant relatives — personalizes evolutionary history in ways that detract from the history itself.

17.   *The* significant difference is unequivocally clear in Stringer and Gamble's declaration: "[T]he main structural difference distinguishing the Moderns from the Ancients was the practice of symbolically organized behaviour" (1993:207).

18.   The idea of conceiving morphology in terms of animate form coincides obliquely with Freud's notion that "anatomy is destiny." The latter notion obviously requires kinesthetic/ kinetic and in turn conceptual fleshing out. It of course also requires de-sexualization in the sense of being cleansed of its male bias. For related discussions of these matters, see Sheets-Johnstone 1994.

19.   Lest anyone think these are mere "impressions," I should note that while Mellars speaks of the need for more "systematic analyses" of the Middle and Upper-Palaeolithic technolo-gies, he himself relies on what he calls "intuitive impressions." He speaks of such impressions as "pragmatic observations," i.e. intuiting the use of a tool (its type) on the basis of its mor-phology (1989:345).

20.   Such innovative — and liberating — intimations are few and far between in physical anthropology in particular and paleoanthropological literature in general, and they are

quickly put to rest, as, for example, when Klein asks apropos anatomically modern humans, "Why did the evolution of behavior lag behind the evolution of form?" and responds: "Perhaps the answer is that body form was only superficially modern and that some further neurological change was still necessary for full modernity" (1989:410). The implication, of course, is that hominid brains had not yet fully matured, i.e. that while visible bodies were ready "for full modernity," minds were not. Klein suggests as much when he forthrightly declares in an earlier passage that "Plainly, it was culture and not body form that propelled the human species from a relatively rare and insignificant mammal 35,000 years ago to a geologic force today" (1989:397). Although Klein does not raise the question of where that propulsive culture came from, he intimates that it developed as a result of brain maturation. In short, minds beget culture; bodies simply beget more bodies.

As for the notion of "a behavioral lag," one might well be puzzled and ask, *Did* the evolution of behavior lag behind the evolution of form? The implied delay of "*summum bonum* bigger brains" aside, lagging behavior strongly suggests that something was amiss in the creatures in question; their behavior was somehow deficient, less than it should be. In a sense, saying that anatomically modern humans showed a behavioral lag in not acceding sooner to "full modernity" is like saying that lobe-finned fish, since they had bodies that were adaptable to land, were behaviorally deficient in not moving onto land sooner, thus speeding up the process of evolution rather than letting it drag along.

21.   Motor physiologists use the term "ballistic" to refer to movement in which there is no feedback in the period between the initiation and completion of a movement, the hit "target" being the only self-correcting device. But ballistic movement warrants fuller study in terms of animate form.

22.   "Not only were the bones of the Shanidar Neandertals exceptionally stout and robust, … but the locations at which muscles were attached to those bones enhanced the power with which the biceps muscle could bend the elbow or with which the forearm muscles rotated the hand into a supine (palm-up) or prone (palm-down) position — important maneuvers in thrusting with a spear, for example" (Trinkaus & Shipman 1993:381). See also Brues (1959:462) for a discussion of the kinetic technique of bludgeoning.

23.   These ideas concerning ballistic movement were first considered in Sheets-Johnstone 1983.

24.   For sources on Labanotation, see, for example, Laban 1975; Hutchinson 1970. For sources on Effort/Shape notation, see, for example, Bartenieff & Lewis 1980; Bartenieff et al. 1970. For sources on Benesh notation, see Benesh & Benesh 1969. For sources on Eshkol-Wachmann notation, see Eshkol-Wachmann 1958. For a general discussion of movement notation systems, see Youngerman 1984. For interesting ethological applications of movement notation, see Golani 1976, 1981; Moran et al. 1981.

25.   For a detailed analysis of the methodology and the operative criterion for arriving at such paleoanthropological reconstructions, see Sheets-Johnstone 1990, Chapters 13 and 14 which address methodological procedures and issues. For a related perspective on the merits of examining what it is like to be a body one is not and of examining the conceptual implications of being that body, see Sheets-Johnstone 1994:328–330.

Consciousness

A natural history*

> [W]e always start at the sensory end and try to come out at the motor side. I very much agree with the late von Holst when he suggests that we start at the other end and work our why (sic) back toward sensation…. It requires some different way of looking.
> H.L. Teuber (1966: 440–41)[1]

> If any person thinks the examination of the rest of the animal kingdom an unworthy task, he must hold in like disesteem the study of man.
> Aristotle (*Parts of Animals*, 645a: 26–7)

1. Introduction

Thomas Nagel, in a review of John Searle's (1992) book, *The Rediscovery of the Mind*, states that "we do not really understand the claim that mental states are states of the brain." He follows this statement more finely with the remark that "We are still unable to form a conception of *how* consciousness arises in matter" (Nagel 1993: 40). The missing conception is, of course, really a missing answer:

> How *does* consciousness arise in matter?

Nagel implicitly raises the question at the culmination of a discussion of what he categorizes as Searle's first arguments against materialists. He lays out these arguments after summarizing Searle's view of how various theories of mind have attempted to reduce the mental to the physical and of how they all fail to take consciousness into account. Without an account of consciousness, according to Searle, none of the theories can rightfully claim to be a theory of mind. Quoting Searle, Nagel points out that "The crucial question is not 'Under what conditions would we *attribute* mental states to other people?' but rather, 'What is it that people *actually have* when they have mental states?'" (1993: 38). Nagel's agreement with Searle that "the subjective" is precisely the crucial question to address is exemplified in his recognizably-worded statement that "Facts about your external behavior or the electrical activity or functional organization of your brain may be closely connected with your conscious experiences, but they are not facts about *what it's like* for you to hear a police siren" (39; italics added).

The question of "*how* consciousness arises in matter" thus appears absolutely central for both Nagel and Searle.

In this chapter I outline basic reasons for thinking the question spurious. This critical work will allow me to pinpoint troublesome issues within the context of definitions of life and in turn address the properly constructive task of this chapter: to demonstrate how genuine understandings of consciousness demand close and serious study of evolution as a history of animate form. I should note that this demonstration will omit a consideration of botany, though plant life is indisputably part of an evolutionary history of animate form. The omission has nothing to do with importance, but with keeping a manageable focus on the question of consciousness; and it has nothing to do either with a trivialization of the ways in which plants are animate, but with an intentional narrowing of the complexity of an already complex subject. As will be shown in the concluding section, the demonstration has sizable implications for cognitivists generally and for philosophers in particular, notably: (1) a need to re-think the common assumption that unconsciousness historically preceded consciousness; (2) a need to delve as deeply and seriously into natural history as into brains and their computational analogues; (3) a critical stance toward arm-chair judgments about consciousness and a correlative turn toward corporeal matters of fact.

2.   Reasons for critically questioning the question

To begin with, while the question seems to phrase the difficult point in exacting terms, it in fact assumes certain metaphysical distinctions in advance of identifying them, showing them to be the case, and/or justifying them theoretically. To that degree, the question either undermines or precludes any answer that might be proposed.[2] The assumed metaphysical distinctions are actually three in number. Two of them have a relationship to a particular history, the relationship in each case depending upon the interpretational latitude given to the word "arises." In the most general sense, the question assumes a historical distinction between the organic and the inorganic, i.e. an arising of the former from the latter. Thus, in a broad sense, the question assumes a certain placement of consciousness with respect to cosmic history. At closer range, the question assumes a historical distinction between "higher" and "lower" forms of life, i.e. a time at which "higher" capacities arose. In a broad sense, it thus assumes a certain placement of consciousness with respect to the evolution of life, most especially, human life. In still finer perspective, the question assumes a distinction between mind and body, i.e. an arising (development, emergence, issuance) of the mental from the physical. In a broad sense, it thus assumes a certain placement of consciousness with respect to (merely) corporeal being. The first two distinctions are plainly historical; the third distinction has no particular historical character, though some people — for example, philosopher Daniel Dennett — accord it one in ontogenetic terms. Writing of human infants, Dennett says that "[consciousness] arises when there is work for it to do, and the preeminent work of consciousness is dependent on sophisticated language-using activities" (Dennett 1983: 384). To acquire a bona fide historical character rather than being assigned one on the basis of an unsubstantiated ontogenesis, the third distinction would have to address the question of the origin of consciousness within the context of the two earlier distinctions, since it is only in the context of those distinctions that the third distinction actually comes to prominence. In effect, an answer to the question of "*how* consciousness arises in matter" does not reduce to saying how a certain physical or neurological maturity drives consciousness; it must specify how consciousness comes to be in the context of a progressively finer natural history, one that takes into account the actual lives of individual living forms as they are understood within cosmic and animate evolutionary histories. To answer the question in this way, however, necessitates a revision in the question itself, precisely because the historical character of the first two distinctions demands it. In particular, consciousness does not arise in *matter*; it arises in organic forms, forms that are *animate*. What is required is thus an exact rendering of how consciousness is grounded in animate form. How does consciousness come to be in the natural history of living creatures and to inhere in the animate?[3]

Approaching the question of consciousness from an historical perspective is certainly not unique. Neurobiologist Gerald Edelman has emphasized repeatedly the necessity of genetic understandings, genetic not in the sense of genes, but in the sense of origins. As he insists, "There must be ways to put the mind back into nature *that are concordant with how it got there in the first place*" (Edelman 1992: 15; italics added). His approach is to consider morphology and history at all levels: not just at the level of the embryological development of brains, but continuing through to the level of actual life, thus to the level of movement and of experiences of moving, and to a consideration of the effects of these experiences on morphology. Through an attentiveness to an experiential history and its morphological moorings and effects, Edelman conjoins typically separated aspects of creaturely life. He discovers cells, anatomy, and morphologically structured mappings within the brain as undergoing "continuous electrical and chemical change, driving and being driven by animal movement." He furthermore finds animal movement itself to be "conditioned by animal shape and pattern, leading to behavior" (1992: 15). Though he does not term it such, *animate form* is clearly central to his investigations.

Whether or not one is persuaded by Edelman's theory of the origin of consciousness, his focal emphasis upon the need for a proper history of consciousness cannot be dismissed. It articulates from an explicitly evolutionary vantage point the implicit but unexamined historical claims of Nagel and Searle. The essentially evolutionary convergence is not surprising given Searle's insistence on "biological naturalism"[4] and Nagel's famous inquiry about a bat (Nagel 1979); each evinces overtones of a natural history of the animate. Conversely, when Edelman writes, "[I]t is not enough to say that the mind is embodied; one must say how" (1992: 15), he is giving voice to a *how* as pressingly and provocatively "subjective" (e.g. "each consciousness depends on its unique history and embodiment," 1992: 139) as that of Searle and Nagel, but a *how* explicitly tethered to the evolution of life.

Philosophers of mind commonly pursue the same *how* question as Searle and Nagel but many, if not most, take quite other paths and enter at a decisively earlier point. Daniel Dennett and Paul Churchland are notable in this respect and warrant special attention. Both endeavour to offer a historical perspective by placing consciousness first of all in cosmic time. Their respective attempts are not protracted by any means — they do not reflect at any length upon the cosmic beginnings of life — and neither speaks explicitly of *the organic* and *the inorganic*. In what is nonetheless a clearly cosmological answer to the *how* question, both advert straight off to the advent of replicators and of the process of self-replication. Churchland's opening sentence of the first section ("Neuroanatomy: The Evolutionary Background") of a chapter titled "Neuroscience" reads: "Near the surface of the earth's oceans, between three and four billion years ago, the sun-driven process of purely chemical evolution produced some *self-replicating* molecular structures" (Churchland 1984: 121; italics in original).[5] Dennett's opening sentences of the second section ('Early Days') of a chapter titled "The Evolution of Consciousness" reads: "In the beginning, there were no reasons; there were only causes.... The explanation for this is simple. There was nothing that had interests. But after millennia there happened to emerge simple *replicators*" (Dennett 1991: 173; italics in original). Clearly, in both cases there is an attempt to separate out the inchoate creaturely from the "purely chemical," thus to specify the cosmic beginnings of life and thereby the nature of the cross-over from the inorganic to the organic.

Dennett's and Churchland's modest nod in the direction of a natural history is short-lived, as such nods generally tend to be among cognitivist philosophers. Their respective "findings" from studies of the beginnings of life on earth are neither carried forward in a consideration of the evolution of animate forms nor examined in the light of a diversity of intact, actually living bodies. Their respective allusions to self-replication suffice to locate the origin of a natural history of consciousness. In finer terms, self-replication offers for them a fully satisfactory answer to the historical question of "*how* consciousness arises in matter" because self-replication is where it all began and where it all began is where it still is: consciousness is a matter of matter. The molecular explanation of consciousness is succinctly exemplified in Churchland's *Matter and Consciousness*. Whatever Churchland says of the self-replicating beginnings of life at the end of his book is predictably cued in advance by what he has stated at the beginning of his book about human life:

> [T]he important point about the standard evolutionary story is that the human species and all of its features are the wholly physical outcome of a purely physical process.... We are notable only in that our nervous system is more complex and

> powerful than those of our fellow creatures…. We are creatures of matter. And we should learn to live with that fact' (Churchland 1984: 21).

The problem comes not in living with that fact but in living hermetically with that fact. Living hermetically with that fact comes at the expense of a viable natural history, for the fact passes over fundamental understandings of animate corporeal life. These omissions in understanding emerge in a striking way in the metaphysical relationship Churchland proposes between the organic and inorganic (though again, not specifically using these broadly cosmic terms). He insists that "living systems" differ from "nonliving systems" "only by degrees": "There is no metaphysical gap to be bridged" — or as he says a paragraph later with respect to "the same lesson" (i.e. difference "only by degrees") applying to intelligence: "No metaphysical discontinuities emerge here" (1984: 153). This, perhaps at first surprising, viewpoint on the organic and inorganic is not *shown* to be true by Churchland, not even through his "lessons" in how to forge definitions of life that will be opaque to discontinuities, such as claiming that "the glowing teardrop of a candle flame … may just barely meet the conditions of the definition [of life] proposed," i.e. life is "any semiclosed physical system that exploits the order it already possesses, and the energy flux through it, in such a way as to maintain and/or increase its internal order." In brief, Churchland's viewpoint is *of necessity* true in virtue of Churchland theory: if human consciousness is mere matter — relatively "more complex and powerful" matter, (1984: 21) but mere matter nevertheless through and through — then the organic can differ from the inorganic "only by degrees." Metaphysical distinctions are blurred by fiat as only they can be in such a theory.

At least one consequence of the blurring should be singled out in order to demonstrate the questionable propriety of claiming that "No metaphysical discontinuities emerge here." A continuous metaphysics creates a problem for distinguishing in traditional western ways between life and death. However rationally doubtful, on the smudgy face of things, quasi-eternal life ("quasi" insofar as eternal life is apparently punctuated from time to time but not wholly discontinued) suddenly emerges as a viable metaphysical future possibility — if only materialist philosophers can deliver up their stone, aided, of course, by deliveries on promises by western materialist science. Of course, the notion of cosmically differing "only by degrees" is in a metaphysically twisted and thoroughly ironic way also supportive of eastern notions such as reincarnation and of so-called "primitive" notions of life after death, notions exemplified by non-western burial practices in which dead persons are interred along with items they will need in their ongoing journeys. With respect to these latter notions, however, it is rather some form of the mental that is primary; matter is simply contingent stuff for the instantiation of spirit. What differs "only by degrees" is thus not fundamentally matter at all but a principle of life — *spiritus*, *pneuma*, or whatever else might be conceived to constitute invincible and inexhaustible animating vapours.

The consequences and ramifications of holding a "no-gap-here" metaphysical theory about the organic and inorganic aside, the major question is how — and to what extent — such a theory actually clarifies consciousness. In particular, however much information Churchland gives us, whether about self-replication, "energy flux" (1984: 152–54), neurophysiology, or any other material aspects of living systems — and whether in direct terms or in terms of computational networks — and whatever the progressively refined definitions he gives us of life, we never seem to arrive at an elucidation of consciousness. The reductive equation of consciousness to matter is not *in fact* shown. The reductionist programme is at best a matter of correlation; that is, when there is consciousness, there is a certain kind of electrical activity ongoing in a brain; when there is not consciousness, there is not that certain kind of electrical activity ongoing in the brain, but electrical activity of another kind, or no electrical activity at all. No actual identity has ever been shown to exist between a thought, an awareness, a concept, an intention, a meaning, or any other kind of "mental" happening and a particular constellation of material happenings, i.e. neural events in a brain. As physiologist Benjamin Libet has observed, "One can only describe relationships between subjective phenomena and neural events, not how one gets from one to the other" (Libet 1985: 568). The reduction of the mental to the physical — or the identification of the former with the latter — is thus evidentially ungrounded. In effect, without collateral substantiating facts, it is impossible to cash in reductionist or identity theory.

Impediments other than the metaphysical ones discussed above similarly plague accounts of "how consciousness arises in matter." Primary among these is the claim that consciousness is a brain activity exclusive to humans, hence that short of a *human* brain, there is no consciousness, or at least no consciousness worthy of the name. This thesis impedes an understanding of consciousness in a number of ways. Most importantly, it hazards a conceptual break with evolutionary theory. Not that new capacities and/or new modes of living cannot emerge that are discontinuous with previous capacities or modes in the manner specified by punctuated equilibrium theory, but that a disposition to set humans categorically apart from the rest of nature — whether on the basis of language, art, or whatever — goes unexamined and unchecked. Indeed, with such a thesis, one form or another of creationism can easily hold sway. This is because the core concept of evolution in a historical sense — *descent with modification*, to use Darwin's exact phrase — is ignored. Humans may in turn be conceived as special creations, even "Special Creations," as one well-known philosopher affirms (Sellars 1963: 6). A fundamental problem with the view may be stated in the form of a historical truth: while all humans are hominids, not all hominids are human. In particular, with the notion that consciousness is exclusive to *human* brains, aspects of *hominid* evolution become virtually impossible to understand — the beginnings of stone tool-making, for example, by members of the species *Homo habilis* some two and a half million years ago and the development of progressively more complex tool-making techniques by other nonhuman hominid species over the span of those same two and a half million years.[6] Furthermore, nonhuman animal social behaviors, especially those of our nearest extant primate relatives that have unequivocal affinities with our own social behaviors, become virtually impossible to accredit — patting another individual to reassure, for example, or hiding something from another. Grounds vanish for delimiting these social phenomena as behaviors in the first place, which in turn makes grounds for behavioral categorization, much less grounds for warranted human interpretation and assured comprehension of these nonhuman animals, nonexistent. If consciousness is something only human brains produce, then no matter how much a nonhuman brain, even a *hominid* nonhuman brain, might resemble a human one anatomically, creatures that are not human are not conscious but merely robotic pieces of matter. Hence, however much their practices in tool-making or their social interactions might evidence continuities with our own, there are no "mental" connections linking us together. In short, to espouse the notion that consciousness is an exclusively human capacity means that human mental powers are evolutionarily discontinuous with those of other creatures whose behaviors are actually the point of origin of many fundamental human ones and even basically resemble human behaviors. Discontinuity in this instance thus means not an espousal of punctuated equilibrium but an espousal of the view that, however close any particular lineal relationships might be, the connection is purely physical.

It is important to consider this kind of privileging because for all its inconsistencies with evolutionary thought, it is not that disfavored a view. Dennett's conception of consciousness, for example, strongly exemplifies and even urges just this privileging of humankind. Unequivocally tethering his view of consciousness to the having of language, Dennett is loath to find consciousness in any creature that does not speak. He claims specifically that "languageless creature[s]" such as bats and lobsters are severely hampered in having no "Center of Narrative Gravity," and thus have a "dramatically truncated" consciousness "compared to ours." After making this claim, he asks — himself as much as the reader — "Isn't this an awfully anthropocentric prejudice?" He goes about answering the question in an even bolder and more radically separatist way, for he immediately counterposes to himself the question, "[W]hat about deaf-mutes? Aren't they conscious?" His answer: "Of course they are — but let's not jump to extravagant conclusions about their consciousness, out of misguided sympathy." Dennett's criterion is austere and unwavering. No matter a human pedigree, as with bats and lobsters, unless there is language, there is a decidedly impoverished consciousness, if any at all. Dennett concludes that "Many people are afraid to see consciousness explained" because they fear "we will lose our moral bearings"; that is, we might get into bad habits, "treating animals as if they were wind-up toys, babies and deaf-mutes as if they were teddy bears, and — just to add insult to injury — robots as if they were real people" (Dennett 1991: 447, 448).

We are a long way from a natural history of consciousness. Given the ultra- exclusive defining terms Dennett insists on, it is no surprise that that history is hard to come by. By radically privileging language, Dennett pulls the evolutionary rug out from under us.[7] Whatever modest nods made in the direction of an evolutionary history at the beginning of his quest to "explain consciousness," he does not follow through. A consideration of language itself in the terms he conceives it shows his lack of follow-through unequivocally. If, as Dennett explains, human language explains consciousness, then consciousness arose in the form of human language. The question Dennett does not ask himself is how human language itself arose.[8] Clearly, he *should* ask the question. Indeed, he should ask not only how human language could even have been conceived short of an already existing consciousness but how human language in the beginning could even have been standardized short of already intact consciousnesses.[9] Dennett does not seem remotely aware of such questions, much less aware of their needing answers — which is why only linguistic creationism can explain a Dennettian consciousness.

In sum, we cannot arrive at an understanding of "how mind got there in the first place" by espousing biological naturalism but neglecting natural history, by wondering what it is like to be a body other than the one one is but neglecting penetrating studies of other animate forms, by championing a metaphysical theory that shackles inquiry before it even begins, by giving selective definitions of life, by privileging human brains, or by explaining consciousness in narrative terms. In none of these instances do we arrive at an elucidation of consciousness as a dimension of the *animate*. Until such an elucidation is given, a viable answer to the question of "how mind got there in the first place" will be consistently baffled.

3.   Life and its definitions: A question of animation and justification

It is instructive at this point to examine definitions of life more closely — both to exemplify the import of the animate and to highlight in a proper manner the troublesome textual use of quotation marks as a means of apportioning mental credit and distinguishing among mental attributes. Biological texts often devote some pages to definitions of life. Among the constituents of those definitions is self-replication. Order and energy — features Churchland too comes to incorporate in his progressive definitions of life — are also named. Responsivity is specified as a further prime constituent. As one text notes: "Plant seedlings bend toward the light; mealworms congregate in dampness; cats pounce on small moving objects; even certain bacteria move toward or away from particular chemicals… [T]he capacity to respond is a fundamental and almost universal characteristic of life" (Curtis 1975: 28). Oddly enough, this "fundamental and almost universal" dimension of life does not typically figure in definitions of life (living systems, consciousness) offered by cognitivists generally, or by philosophers of mind in particular, especially those in either category who are wedded to information-processing, computational models. Yet responsivity — bending, congregating, pouncing, moving toward or away, in short, *animation* — commonly appears an integral part of phenomena such as cognition, hence part and parcel of consciousness. If queried on the matter, cognitivists and philosophers might respond — in a manner consistent with pervasive present-day western thought — that it depends on what is doing the bending, congregating, pouncing, or moving toward or away, whether the terms "cognitive" or "conscious" apply, that is, whether the terms are proper ascriptions or not. This answer unfortunately skirts the critical point at issue: justifying the cognitive distinctions one makes diacritically. The point is neatly exemplified by Churchland precisely because his account of consciousness, i.e. eliminative materialism, conceptually precludes dia-critical practice to begin with. If the distinction between the organic and the inorganic is blurred, then of course distinctions among the organic are also blurred — just as Churchland in fact says they are blurred with respect to intelligence: there are differ-ences "only by degrees." But the blurring between organic forms is necessarily finer than the blurring between the organic and the inorganic since organic forms are com-paratively more closely related to each other than they are to the inorganic. In effect, to be consistent with Churchland theory, common textual practice should be altered. Quotation marks typically surrounding cognitive functions as they are ascribed to what are termed "lower" forms should be erased. A difference "only by degrees" does not justify them.

To counter that a difference "only by degrees" does not entail that we cannot justly distinguish between degrees of consciousness (cognitive abilities, intelligence) within the organic — that we cannot justly make distinctions on the basis of *who is doing the pouncing*, for example — is a claim difficult to uphold. Proper justification is lacking in the form of wholly objective supporting facts. This is because what basically mat-ters is not who is doing the pouncing; what matters is the ability to provide a wholly unprejudiced rationale for common textual practice. Indeed, the original charge can still be pressed because a fundamental mandate exists; namely, specification of the exact degree(s) at which quotation marks are appropriate. *This mandate exists regard-less of what metaphysical theory one espouses.* It is as necessary to Searle's account of consciousness, for example, as to computational cognitivists' accounts. But as might be evident, the mandate poses an insuperable problem. Whatever might be claimed to constitute a criterion for distinguishing among degrees of consciousness (intelligence, cognitive abilities) is not a matter of fact but a matter of human judgment. While cranial capacities, neuron counts, dendritic branchings, and body size, for example, certainly constitute matters of fact, these matters of fact *do not in themselves* specify anything whatsoever in the way of a standard. One need only recall what Darwin wrote on the basis of his study of Hymenoptera:*"It is certain that there may be extraordinary

---

* For a glossary of biological terms, see end of chapter.

mental activity with an extremely small absolute mass of nervous matter" (Darwin 1981:145).[10] In short, the mandate to show appropriateness appears doomed from the start. Specification — whatever its theoretical context — turns out to be as completely arbitrary as it is absolutely mandatory; a wholly objective supporting base is nowhere to be found. Indeed, in its arbitrariness, specification can only be labelled "subjective"; a standard completely impervious to human bias cannot possibly be identified. In consequence, a cancelling of all quotation marks appears warranted — though as indicated not necessarily on the grounds of Churchland theory at all. The following description of a bacterium moving "toward or away from particular chemicals" is an especially interesting as well as exemplary candidate in this respect.

> Processing in a bacterium may be thought of as a sort of molecular polling: ... the positive "votes" cast by receptors in response, say, to increasing concentrations of a sugar are matched against the negative votes produced by increasing concentrations of noxious compounds. On the basis of this continuous voting process, the bacterium "knows" whether the environment, on the whole, is getting better or worse. The results of this analysis appear to be communicated by electrical signals to the response centers. The final stage, the response, consists of a brief change in the direction of rotation of the several stiff, helical flagella that propel the bacterium. The result is that the bacterium founders briefly and then strikes out in a new direction, once again sampling to see whether the environment is improving or deteriorating (Keeton & Gould 1986:452).

In addition to being an exemplary candidate for diacritical erasure, the descriptive passage demonstrates in an intimately related way why responsivity — the "fundamental and almost universal characteristic of life" — is of critical import. Sampling, foundering, and striking out in a new direction are precisely a matter of animation and animation is precisely in some sense cognitive or mindful — as in assessing propitious and noxious aspects of the environment. Cognitive aspects of organic animation — in this instance, cognitive aspects of a bacterium's animation — cannot thus reasonably be considered mere figurative aspects. More generally, cognitive capacities cannot reasonably be reserved only for what are commonly termed "higher-order" organisms.[11]

The unjustifiable use of diacritical markings to distinguish cognitively among organisms leads to a series of interlinked demands: a cessation of reliance on what is in fact a conceptually lazy, inapt, and/or obfuscating textual practice; a corollary recognition of the import of animation; a consequent investigation of the animate in terms of its natural history; a delineation of what it means cognitively to be animate. In a quite provocative sense, one might say that Churchland's blurring of metaphysical lines itself leads to such a series of interlinked demands. His overarching metaphysical blurring on behalf of an unrelenting materialism — whether one finds the latter credible or not — forces an examination and justification of common textual practice and typical western thinking regarding so-called "higher" and "lower" forms of life. It clearly calls our attention to a fundamental question about where and on what grounds cognitive lines are diacritically drawn in order to distinguish among capacities of various forms of organic life. All the same, it is important to emphasize that in answering to the fourfold demand, we are not charged with the task of *understanding matter*, that is, of making appropriate distinctions in material complexity by taking neuron counts and the like. On the contrary, we are charged with the task of *understanding the animate*, precisely as the bacterium example demonstrates. Accordingly, the quest begins from the other side. We take the phenomena themselves as a point of departure, not theory, and earnestly inquire into what we observe to be living realities. Denying distinctions thus becomes in this instance and in a heuristic sense epistemologically salutary rather than metaphysically catastrophic.

Searle's intense concern with preserving distinctions between kinds of intentionality by maintaining diacritical markings is decidedly topical in this context. After giving examples of what he terms "metaphorical attributions of intentionality," and insisting on the necessity of distinguishing between "intrinsic intentionality" and "as-if intentionality," he states rather hyperbolically that "If you deny the distinction [between the two] it turns out that everything in the universe has intentionality" (Searle 1990b: 587). Because he is concerned not just with the animate world but with carburetors, computers, and such, his broad claim is perhaps less rash than it might at first appear. Understood specifically in terms of present concerns, his point is that when language is used as in the bacterium passage quoted above, intentionality must be read as describing an "as-if" intentionality — not the real "intrinsic" thing. To accede to Searle's line of reasoning and broad warning, however, is precisely to miss the epistemological challenge, and indeed to forego examining what might lead to foundational[12] understandings within "biological naturalism." In this latter respect, it is of course also to miss the challenge of a descriptive metaphysics that would adequately comprehend natural history and on that account offer fundamental understandings of the animate world that are informed by evolutionary thought. While the penalty of blurring distinctions can certainly be confusion, it does not necessarily "turn out" that one reaches "absurdity" if one blurs them, as Searle claims (1990: 587). If the phenomena themselves are taken as a point of departure, it in fact turns out neither that "everything in the universe [is] mental" nor that everything in the universe is material. It turns out only that everything in the *animate* universe needs to be considered as what it is — *animate* — and that in consequence we need to take seriously the historical perspective of evolutionary thought: by examining the lives of living creatures, by determining the corporeal matters of fact that sustain those lives, and by tracing out in an evolutionary sense how consciousness arises in animate form. Only by doing so are we likely to get our conceptual bearings, justify new textual practice, if any, and in the end come to sound understandings of the complexities as well as provenience of consciousness.

The foregoing considerations taken as a whole lead to two interrelated lines of thought relative to carrying forward an understanding of consciousness as arising in animate form. The first strand has to do precisely with what at the level of animate form is describable as the most basic form of consciousness, in other words, with what the "fundamental and almost universal characteristic of life" demonstrates, implies, and/or presupposes in the way of consciousness. The second strand has to do both with Aristotelian thought and with the wrong-headedness of the idea that "To be truly Aristotelian, we would have to stop believing that the emergence of life or mind requires explanation" (Burnyeat 1992:26). The first of these strands will be considered here in Part I of this chapter; the second strand will be considered in Part II.

4.   Corporeal consciousness: A matter of knowing

"Know thyself" is a Socratic imperative. It may also be said to be a built-in biological one in a special and fundamental sense. It is important to set this biological imperative explicitly in the mainstream of general cognitivist trends in current western thought and American philosophy of mind. In so doing, we can show in unequivocal terms how the imperative offers a more exacting evolutionary understanding of consciousness. We can furthermore expose, and in equally unequivocal terms, what is typically omitted in the way of empirical evidence in contemporary theories of consciousness. Accordingly, a longer but proportionally richer and more informative route will be taken to its exposition. We might call this route "The Liabilities of a Paradigmatic Cognitivist Account of the Socratic Imperative." The account is based on descriptive remarks Dennett makes about "The Reality of Selves" in the process of explaining consciousness.

Energetically affirming that "every agent has to know which thing in the world it is!" Dennett begins by specifying what this knowing entails (1991:427). He considers first "simpler organisms" for whom "there is really nothing much to self-knowledge beyond the rudimentary biological wisdom enshrined in such maxims as When Hungry, Don't Eat Yourself! and When There's a Pain, It's Yours!" In this context, he says of a lobster that "[It] might well eat another lobster's claws, but the prospect of eating one of its own claws is conveniently unthinkable to it." He goes on to say that "Its options are limited, and when it 'thinks of' moving a claw, its 'thinker' is directly and appropriately wired to the very claw it thinks of moving.".

The situation is different, Dennett says, when it comes to controlling "the sorts of sophisticated activities human bodies engage in," because "there are more options, and hence more sources of confusion" (1991:427). He states that.

> the body's control system (housed in the brain) has to be able to recognize a wide variety of different sorts of inputs as informing it about itself, and when quandaries arise or scepticism sets in, the only reliable (but not foolproof) way of sorting out and properly assigning this information is to run little experiments: do something and look to see what moves (427–28).

The experimental approach is the same, Dennett says, whether a matter of "external signs of our own bodily movement" or "internal states, tendencies, decisions, strengths and weaknesses": "Do something and look to see what moves." With respect to internal knowledge, he adds that "An advanced agent must build up practices for keeping track of both its bodily and 'mental' circumstances" (428).

Dennett's descriptive passages of course readily offer themselves as candidates for erasure no less than passages in biology, not on cosmic historical grounds — Dennett's materialism does not appear to run so far as to blur the distinction between the organic and the inorganic — but on evolutionary and mind/body ones: Dennett marks "mental" phenomena diacritically both in order to make distinctions between "higher" and "lower" forms of life and in order to maintain a thoroughly materialized consciousness. In short, his theory of consciousness demands that he temper the meaning of "the mental" at both metaphysical levels. What his diacritical markings actually allow is having his material cake and eating it too. However loose his vocabulary (e.g. a *thinking* lobster), and however much it strays from purely materialist theory (e.g. *mental* as well as bodily circumstances), it is diacritically reined in to accord with the theoretical distinctions he wants to maintain and the materialist doctrine he wants to uphold.

What makes both the entailments and elaboration of Dennett's energetic affirmation such a compelling and richly informative point of departure for examining the bio-Socratic imperative is precisely what they overlook in theory, method, and fact. It is as if proprioception in general and kinesthesia in particular[13] did not exist; whatever the talk of movement with respect to humans, for example, it is as if the *sense of movement* were nonexistent. Thus, one has to *look* and *see* what is moving.[14] In such an account, the kinesthetic is more than overridden by the visual; it is not even on the books. Were one to examine Dennett's theory of human agency with respect to infants, one would straightaway discover its error. Were one to examine his theory with respect to blind people, one would do the same. In a word, and *contra* Dennett, we humans learn "which thing we are" by moving and listening to our own movement. We sense our own bodies. Indeed, we humans, along with many other primates, must *learn* to move ourselves. We do so not by *looking* and *seeing* what we're moving; we do so by attending to our bodily feelings of movement, which include a bodily felt sense of the direction of our movement, its speed, its range, its tension, and so on. Our bodily feelings of movement have a certain dynamic. We feel, for example, the swiftness or slowness of our movement, its constrictedness or openness, its tensional tightness or looseness, and more. In short, we perceive the *qualia* of our own movement; our bodily feelings of movement have a certain *qualitative character*.

It is instructive to recall Sherrington's experiential account of proprioception in this context. However inadvertently he excludes kinetic qualia from his account, Sherrington explicitly if briefly affirms them in the course of specifying and describing the nature of our experiential awareness of movement. Underscoring first of all the fact that we have no awareness of neural events, e.g. of nerve fibres "register[ing] the tension at thousands of points they sample in the muscles, tendons, and ligaments of [a] limb," he says "I perceive no trace of all this [neural activity]." With respect to the limb, he states that "I am simply aware of where the limb is, and when it moves." In this context, he also points out that we are not even aware that the limb "possess[es] muscles or tendons" (Sherrington 1953: 248). He goes on to emphasize the lack of this kind of anatomical awareness in actual experience when he describes the experience of moving the limb "to pick up a paper from the table": "I have no awareness of the muscles as such at all" (1953: 248–49).[15] The lack of direct experiential awareness of "muscles as such," however, does not impede an experiential awareness of the movement. As Sherrington affirms,

> [though] I have no awareness of the muscles as such at all, … I execute the movement rightly and without difficulty. It starts *smoothly* as though I had been aware precisely of how tense and how long each muscle and how tense each tendon was, and, thus aware, took them as my starting point for shortening or paying out as may be, each one further (italics added).

Interestingly enough, he then points out that if he had moved "*clumsily*," it would not do much good "*to look at my limb*" (1953: 249; italics added). As he himself says, *looking* provides him no more than an *additional* sense of where his limb is. In effect, with respect to one's own body, he affirms that vision is not a primary but a supplemental spatial sense. Sherrington concludes his experiential account of movement by characterizing "[t]he proprioceptive percept of the limb" as "a mental product," a product "derived from elements which are not experienced as such and yet are mental in the sense that the mind uses them in producing the percept" (249). Insofar as "[s]uch mental products are an intimate accompaniment of our motor acts," he says that "[w] e may suppose therefore there obtains something like them in our animal kith and kin as accompaniment of their intentional motor acts" (249).

Now clearly, if we carefully examine Sherrington's account and reflect both on what he is implicitly affirming and at the same time on what he is inadvertently excluding, we find an open avowal of kinetic qualia. An awareness of *smoothness* is first of all an awareness of something over and above an awareness of *where* a limb is and of *when* it is moving. It is an awareness of *how* a body part or the body as a whole is moving; *how* precisely *not* in the neurophysiological sense Sherrington himself details as impossible, but *how* in the same experiential sense as *where* and *when*. Moreover *smoothness* is not "a mental product," any more than jerky or swift or hesitant or expansive or collapsing or intense or constricted or weak or abrupt are "mental products."[16] Neither is weight "a mental product," the weight one perceives in the felt heaviness or heft of one's body or body parts in moving; neither is mass "a mental product," the mass one perceives in the felt three-dimensionality or volume of one's body and in its felt smallness or largeness. In short, *qualia* are integral to bodily life. They are there in any movement we make. They are differentially there in the bodily life of animate forms. They are not a "mental product," but the product of animation. They are created by movement itself. Accordingly, any time one cares to attend to the felt sense of one's movement, one perceives qualia.

When we learn to move ourselves, we learn to distinguish just such kinetic bodily feelings as smoothness and clumsiness, swiftness and slowness, brusqueness and gentleness, not in so many words, but in so many bodily-felt distinctions. Short of learning to move ourselves and being attentive in this way to the qualia of our movement, we could hardly be effective agents — no more so than a creature who "does something and then looks to see what moves" could be an effective agent. In neither case is there an agent in the true sense of being in command of — or as phenomenological philosopher Edmund Husserl would say, of "holding sway in" — one's own body. An agent who holds sway is a bona fide agent precisely insofar as she/he is aware of her/his own movement, aware not only of initiating it, but aware of its spatio-temporal and energy dynamics, which is to say of its rich and variable qualia.[17] With respect to Dennett's injunctions, were they taken literally to the letter, his agent — so-called — would suffer not only from having to have in sight at all times all parts of his/her body in order to see where they were and what they were doing. His agent, being oblivious of qualia, could in no way build up practices in the manner Dennett suggests, for the build up of such practices depends upon kinesthesia and kinesthetic memory, i.e. upon an awareness of the spatio-temporal and energy dynamics of one's movement. An agent devoid of kinesthesia in fact belongs to no known natural species. Agents — those having the power to act — necessarily have a kinesthetic sense of their own movement.

When Dennett considers "simpler organisms" such as lobsters, the perceptual situation is no different from what it is with humans. Kinesthesia, or its counterpart, is nowhere acknowledged as a feature of these "lower" creatures. The idea that these creatures have a sense of their own body and body movement is alien to the theory of a thoroughly materialized consciousness as well as an alien thought in itself. Whoever "the thinker" might be in Dennett's zoology — a lobster "thinker," a bat "thinker," a lion "thinker" — it appears to get what it wants, if it gets it at all, simply in virtue of its impeccable motor wiring, nothing more. "The thinker" in other words appears not to have — or to need — any proprioceptive connections to its body; its body, in fact, is on Dennett's account no more than a "directly and appropriately wired" mechanical contrivance for getting about in the world. Yet we should ask what it means to say that a lobster will eat another's claws but that *conveniently*, as Dennett puts it, it finds eating one of its own claws unthinkable. Does it mean that there is actually a rule "Don't eat your own claws!" wired into the lobster's neurological circuitry? But it is patently unparsimonious to think that there is such a rule and just as patently absurd to think that every creature comes prepared with an owner's manual, as it were, a rulebook replete with what Dennett calls "maxims." Such a maxim, for example, would be only one of an indefinitely great number of maxims that a lobster (or, in analogous terms, any other "simpler organism") could be said to carry around in the neural machinery that counts as its "Headquarters":[18] "Don't try to go on land!" "Don't try to eat a squid!" "Shovel in new sand grains after molting!" "The large claw is for crushing!" "The small claw is for seizing and tearing!" And so on. What makes eating its own claws "conveniently unthinkable" is clearly something other than a rule of conduct. The putative evolutionary sense of convenience that Dennett invokes is misguided. "Convenience" is not a matter of an opportune adaptation but of an astoundingly varied and intricately detailed biological faculty that allows a creature to know its own body and its own body in movement.

Dennett is not alone either in his omission of the kinesthetic or in his privileging of the visual. Typically, kinesthesia never makes an appearance in discussions of "the senses" — the *five* senses. Any cursory glance at indices of relevant books in biology, psychology, and philosophy discloses either a radically abbreviated treatment of kinesthesia in comparison to vision (and audition), or a complete lack of treatment altogether. One might say with good reason that the mind/body problem is written into the very texts themselves. Moreover the topic of body movement, if making an appearance at all, typically comes on the scene only marginally in these books. The way it does so is through reduction to *the* brain and its efferent pathways. In both typical instances, we come up painfully short of a sense of movement. In one respect it is not surprising that kinesthesia is omitted or slighted and that we believe ourselves to have only five senses. As adults, we have long since forgotten how we learned to move ourselves — in a very real sense, how we learned our bodies. Only if now, as adults, we pay kinesthetic attention — for example, to what it feels like, or rather, *does not feel like* when our arm falls asleep — might we begin to realize how fundamental kinesthesia is. It is fundamental not only to our knowledge of "which thing in the world we are"; it is fundamental both to our ability to make our way in the world — to move knowledgeably in it — and to our knowledge of the world itself. Though we may have forgotten what we first learned of the world through movement and touch, there is no doubt but that we came to know it first by moving and touching our way through it, in a word, through our tactile-kinesthetic bodies.[19]

The astoundingly varied and intricately detailed biological faculty that allows knowing one's own body and body movement and that in the most basic sense allows knowing the world is a dimension of consciousness. Inversely, consciousness is a dimension of living forms that move themselves, that are *animate*, and that, in their animation, are in multiple and complex ways engaged in the world. The earlier description of a bacterium's cognitive capacities is relevant precisely in this context. What the description points to is a chemically-mediated *tactile* discrimination of bodies apart from or outside of the body one is. Given its stereognostic sensitivity, a bacterium's discriminative ability might justifiably be termed a "meta-corporeal" consciousness, a consciousness of something beyond itself. Clearly, the essentially tactile ability to discriminate bodies other than oneself is not the same as a proprioceptive ability to discriminate aspects of oneself as an animate form, though just as clearly tactility is a vital dimension of that proprioceptive ability. Proprioceptively-endowed creatures are not only always in touch with something outside themselves; they tactilely compress and deform themselves bodily in the process of moving. When a creature bends its leg, for example, it brings two surfaces in contact with each other — in mutual deformation. Tactility thus enters into the essentially kinetic cognitional abilities by which a creature discriminates aspects of itself as an animate form. In the most fundamental sense, these kinetic cognitional abilities constitute a *corporeal consciousness*, a consciousness that, as I shall try now to show at some length, is an astoundingly varied and intricately detailed biological faculty. The purpose of the demonstration is to link understandings of consciousness to corporeal matters of fact and thereby to an evolutionary history. In other words, with a recognition of this biological faculty, and with attendant understandings of its rootedness in corporeal matters of fact, we can begin to grasp the possibility of a true evolutionary history of consciousness. It bears emphasizing that *we do this by direct consideration of the topic at issue: consciousness*, and not by appeal to constituents in definitions of life — to self-replication, organization, and so on. The notion of consciousness as fundamentally a corporeal phenomenon in fact already suggests a radical revision of the common evolutionary characterization of consciousness both as "a higher-order" function i.e. a function having nothing to do with bodies, and as a "higher-order" function exclusive to "higher" forms of life, i.e. a preeminently human endowment. Similarly, it already suggests a radical revision of the materialist's characterization of consciousness as identical with neurological brain events. The key to the reconceptualization of consciousness and to the evolutionary import of that reconceptualization is the realization that bodies in the form of living creatures are not mere physical things but animate forms. Consciousness is thus not in *matter*; it is a dimension of living forms, in particular, a dimension of living forms that move. Transposed to this context, Searle's "biological naturalism" — his biological naturalization of consciousness — properly begins with movement. It would show how consciousness is rooted in animate form. Indeed, it would show concretely how, in the evolution of animate forms, consciousness emerged not as a "higher-level" or "intrinsic" stalk that one day sprouted out of a neural blue, but as a dimension that itself evolved along with living, moving creatures themselves.

What is necessary to the task of reconceptualization is a sense of the evolutionary history of proprioception, including a sense of the history of its derivation. It should be clearly evident that a sense of this history does not entail a concern with the evolution of the neural circuitry of proprioception in general, an assessment of the neurology of proprioception in mammals in particular, nor of the neurology of proprioception in humans in singularly fine detail. It entails a concern with the proprioceptive lives of living creatures, invertebrate and vertebrate, insofar as they have been studied and recorded by naturalists, zoologists, and biologists, and insofar as one can discern within such studies what is at times left unsaid with respect to an awareness of movement. However neglected or understated, proprioception is a corporeal matter of fact. Its roots are embedded in the kinetic possibilities of the earliest forms of life. Thus a sense of its evolutionary history means coincidently a concern with organisms such as bacteria and protozoa. In short, understandings of the evolution of proprioception lead precisely to understandings of the provenience of consciousness. With these understandings come a vocabulary consistent with corporeal matters of fact and conceptual clarifications by which one can formulate a standard for linguistic practice that is neither arbitrary nor superficial — a mere diacritical band-aid — but a standard warranted by the evidence from natural history.

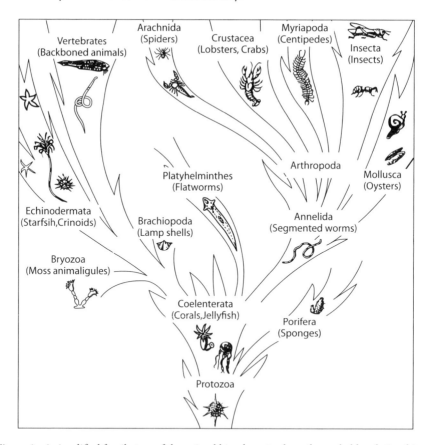

Figure 1. A simplified family tree of the animal kingdom, to show the probable relationships of the vertebrates. (After Romer, *Man and the Vertebrates*, University of Chicago Press. Reproduced by permission.)

5.   To the things themselves: Corporeal matters of fact[20]

Animate forms are built in ways that are sensitive to movement. Their sensitivity can be doubly reflected; they can be sensitive to dynamic modifications in the surrounding world and to dynamic modifications of their own body. They can, in other words, be sensitive to the movement of things in their environment, including the very medium in which they live, and to the movement of their own bodies. A moment's serious reflection on the matter discloses a major reason why this sensitivity to movement is both basic and paramount: no matter what the particular world (*Umwelt*: von Uexküll 1928)[21] in which an animal lives, it is not an unchanging world. Hence, whatever the animal, its movement cannot be absolutely programmed such that, for example, at all times its particular speed and direction of movement, its every impulse and stir-ring, its every pause and stillness, run automatically on something akin to a lifetime tape — as, for example philosopher Peter Carruthers unquestionably indicates when he writes that "brutes" have only "Nonconscious experiences," and so experience "nothing" (Carruthers 1989:268, 259). Consider, for example, an earthworm, its body pressed against the earth as it crawls along, or a beetle walking along the ground. In each case, the immediate environment is tangibly inconsistent; it has topological and textural irregularities — bumps here, smoothness there, moisture here, hardness there, and so on. Both earthworm and beetle must adjust kinetically to what they find in the immediate moment. A prominent invertebrate researcher makes this very point: "Information regarding the absolute disposition of the body is imperative in order that minor adjustments of muscular activity may be made to cope with irregularities in the surface" (Laverack 1976:4–5). Clearly, the world is less than consistent in its conformations and any animal that survives must literally or figuratively bend to its demands. Consider further the very fluid or changing medium in which some animals live. Air and water move, and that movement in the form of currents or winds — cur-rents and winds that themselves shift from gentle to moderate to turbulent — agitates, deforms, or otherwise impinges on the animal's body. In effect, such movement influ-ences how the animal moves from moment to moment; it influences what the animal can do and what it actually does. A locust is proprioceptively sensitive in just this way to air currents. Its face is covered with hairs that respond to the movement of air across their surface: "Each hair responds maximally to wind from a specific direction, with the optimal direction being determined by the angle of curvature of the hair shaft" (Laverack 1976:5–6). Sensitivity to its facial hair displacements facilitates the locust's control of lift during flight and is informative of orientation in flying. The intricate-ness of a spider's external proprioceptive system offers equally impressive testimony to the importance of proprioception. Spiders also have hairs on their body that, when bent, inform them, for example, of the disposition of their body relative to their web (Laverack 1976:27). Far more numerous than their hairs, however, are other surface sensory organs called slit sensilla. These are single or complex proprioceptive organs, the complex ones — lyriform organs — being located on their appendages, pedipalps, and walking legs. A spider's slit sensilla are functionally analogous to an insect's cam-paniform sensilla (see, e.g. Wright 1976: 353–54); both are sensitive to deformation, i.e. cuticular stress through compression. To give an idea of the singular importance of such proprioceptors, consider that the hunting spider *Cupiennius salei* has over 3000 slit organs on its walking legs (Wright: 1976: 351; see also Laverack 1976: 24–25). Given the quantity of such organs, it is no wonder that "the quantity of proprioceptive information … from an appendage at a particular time (e.g. during walking) may be considerable" (Wright 1976: 354).

The above corporeal matters of fact can be put within the purview of a more explicit evolutionary history of animate form by a proportionately broader consider-ation of invertebrates. Broader consideration of these forms of animate life provides an especially edifying evolutionary viewpoint insofar as ninety per cent of animal spe-cies are invertebrates — creatures ranging from sponges and coral to lobster, scallops, mites, centipedes, segmented worms, spiders and hosts of other animals, although most are insects, and of these the largest category comprises species of beetles.[22] Fuller con-sideration will furthermore bring to the fore the immediacy of most creatures' lives with respect to their surrounds. Indeed, it would be erroneous to judge invertebrates by human standards, especially fully-clothed western ones, for external proprioception functions far more as a form of movement detection for them than for humans.

An invertebrate may be soft- or hard-bodied. Hard-bodied invertebrates are so called because they have articulable body parts attached to an exoskeleton. As sug-gested by the above examples, hard-bodied invertebrates have external sensilla of various kinds: hairs, exoskeletal plates, epidermal organs, cilia, spines, pegs, slits, and so on. It is these external sensory organs that make possible an awareness of sur-face events in the double sense noted above: an awareness of the terrain on which and/or the environment through which the animal is moving and an awareness of bodily deformations or stresses occurring coincident with moving on the terrain and/or through the environment. To appreciate in a beginning way the difference in proprioceptive sensitivity between hard- and soft-bodied invertebrates, compare, for example, a beetle and a polyp. A beetle that is walking on the ground has tactile contacts that allow an awareness of the ground's irregularities — bumps, stones, holes, and so on — and tactile contact with the air — breezes, vibrations, and so on — as well as an awareness of itself as topologically deformed or agitated by these contacts. Proprioception is thus distinctively informative of both body and surrounds. A sed-entary hydrozoan polyp has tentacles bearing cilia that are sensitive to vibrations in the surrounding water. When vibrations occur, the polyp bends its tentacles toward their source, thus toward food particles such as barnacle nauplii. Marine biologist, D.A. Dorsett states, "The response is reflexive rather than proprioceptive in that it [the polyp] is not responding to movements generated by or imposed upon the animal itself" (Dorsett 1976: 447). What Dorsett means is that the response is characterized as reflexive because the bending movement is neither generated by the polyp — it is generated by the vibrations — nor imposed upon the polyp — it is not the result of actual surface to surface contact, i.e. contact of animal body with solid object. His point is more broadly made in the context of an analysis by M.S. Laverack, another marine biologist, who distinguishes among four basic modes of external propriocep-tion in invertebrates (Laverack 1976: 3–4). The simplest mode is through distortion of the body, whether through muscle contraction or passive deformation: external proprioceptors are in either case affected. The second mode is tethered to the fact that animals move relative to space; in effect, contact of the surface of an animal's mov-ing body with a solid object results in proprioception concerning its movement and position relative to the object. The third mode is also tethered to the fact that animals move relative to space; it is a reiteration of the second mode of proprioceptive stimu-lation but with reference to a substrate rather than to a solid object. The fourth mode derives from the circumstance in which movement of one body part tactilely stimu-lates another body part through contact of external sensors of one kind or another, e.g. hairs, such contact providing information regarding movement and position of the two body parts. To say that the polyp's bending movement is reflexive is thus to say both that the polyp is not stimulated to move by bodily deformation or stress (the first mode)[23] nor is it stimulated to move because a surface of its body has come into contact with a solid object (the second mode). That the polyp is sedentary means, of course, that it does not budge from its base; hence, the third mode of stimulation is not a possibility. Neither is the fourth mode since the movement of the tentacles does not proprioceptively stimulate another body part.

Polyps belong to a class of animals called coelenterates, "primitive aquatic ani-mals" (Keeton & Gould 1986: 161). It might be tempting to generalize about proprio-ception in coelenterates — and perhaps in other soft-bodied invertebrates such as annelids and molluscs as well — on the basis of the above example and discussion, but given the diversity of coelenterate forms of life, it would be a mistake to write off proprioception altogether in such creatures. Different proprioceptive capacities — or counterparts thereof — are highly suggested by the movement of creatures within the same class and even within the same phylum. The somersaulting hydra, for example, is an exception to what might otherwise be considered "the sedentary hydrozoan polyp rule" with respect to the third possible mode of external proprioception; fighting sea anemones (anthozoans rather than hydrozoans) are sensitive to the touch of an alien form of anemone, thus sensitive in ways consistent with the second possible mode of external proprioception; in moving from one place to another on a rock — one inch per hour — a fighting sea anemone changes contact with a substrate, thus, like the som-ersaulting hydra, it too is open to proprioception through its own movement in space; an anemone belonging to the genus *Actinostola* — a "swimming anemone" — though normally sessile, not only moves to distance itself from chemical substances emitted by starfish but writhes and somersaults in the process (McConnaughey 1978: 270–72). Clearly, there is a diversity of possible proprioceptive acuities commensurate with the diversity of life itself. In spite of the fact that proprioception is less evident in soft-bodied invertebrates and is difficult to document (Dorsett 1976: 479), marine biologists readily affirm a range of proprioceptive possibilities in soft-bodied invertebrates. Laverack, for example, states that "Proprioceptive units in the flexible body wall of soft-bodied animals are probably legion, [although] … few have been shown either anatomically or physiologically" (Laverack 1976: 11); Dorsett states with respect to soft-bodied invertebrates generally that "abundant opportunities for true proprioception occur" (Dorsett 1976: 479). Their affirmation in the face of comparatively slim evidence warrants a moment's reflection as does the related conceptually challenging notion of "true proprioception.".

The best evidence for proprioception in soft-bodied invertebrates comes from studies of gastropods (molluscs). In their complex feeding behavior, a number of species protract and retract a buccal mass in coincidence with whose retraction, a radula rasps against the substrate, taking up bits of plant or animal tissue in the process. The behavior is modulated by proprioception according to load. Given the difference in animate form between a gastropod and a sedentary hydrozoan polyp — which difference of course means a difference in movement possibilities, thus a difference in behavioral possibilities[24] — it is not surprising to find proprioceptive capacities readily evident in the one and not in the other. It is precisely in this context of recognizing differences in animate form that the significance of both the affirmation and the idea of "true proprioception" becomes apparent: What would dispose marine biologists to affirm "proprioceptive units" in the face of slim evidence if not an intuitive sense of the central importance of proprioception to animate life in general, and in particular, of its necessity in carrying through observed complex life-enhancing behaviors such as those of certain gastropod species described above? What if not this intuitive sense generates the idea of such a phenomenon as "true proprioception," thus the idea that there are lesser forms of the same, forms one might historically call proto-proprioception? Consider the following remark that validates just such *evolutionary* notions: "[I]n passing from the coelenterates to the annelids and molluscs, we are looking at some of the earliest stages in the evolution and organization of the nervous system and must ask ourselves at what stage does a true proprioceptive sense arise" (Dorsett 1976: 443). The question is indeed provocative: at what stage *does* "a true proprioceptive sense arise"? Does it arise with molluscs, for example? Or can it be said to have arisen with some of the presumably earlier evolving coelenterates? On the other hand, what is "true proprioception"? And can a "stage" be pinpointed as its inception?; that is, is it possible to say with respect to any particular group of creatures and with respect to any particular evolutionary period, "true proprioception starts here"? In view of the diversity of creaturely life, one might rather say that "true proprioception" arises for each creature according to the animate form it is, and that if "true proprioception" does not arise, the form does not arise either because it is not kinetically viable. In other words, one might want to say that the origin of proprioception is not an historical event as such; it is an event tied to the evolution of *animate* forms. Indeed, the evolution of formal diversity speaks to the evolution of a diversity of proprioceptive capacities because it speaks of the same phenomenon: the evolution of forms of life as forms of animation.

On the basis of the above corporeal matters of fact, we can in fact begin to distill a sense of the evolution of proprioception, from a meta-corporeal consciousness to a corporeal consciousness through the evolution of external sensors. As all of the above examples suggest, the undoubtedly multiple beginnings of proprioception are in each instance tied to *surface recognition sensitivity*. Not only are the cilia of polyps tactilely sensitive to movement, but the surface sensitivity of cilia themselves, organelles that are present in groups of creatures from protozoa (unicellular eukaryotic organisms such as paramecia and amoebas) to mammals, attests to the significance of an original tactile faculty subserving movement and the recognition of something outside of one's own body. Laverack's remark about cilia is in fact highly suggestive in this respect. He writes that "If the cilium may be taken as at least a simple starting point for sense organ structure we may look for receptors even amongst the protozoa. Sensitivity towards physico-chemical events is well known, but specialized receptors much less so" (Laverack 1976: 17). His remark may be glossed in the following way: the evolution of sense organs at the most primitive eukaryotic level heralds a new kind of sensitivity, one mediated by specialized sense organs, i.e. cilia, rather than by physico-chemical events, but still serving the same basic function: movement and the recognition of something outside one's own body. While this surface sensitivity is spoken of in terms of "mechanoreception" (Laverack 1976: 17), it is clearly, and indeed, from the viewpoint of living organisms, more appropriately specified as a form of *tactile*-reception. The protozoan ciliate species *Stentor*, for example, uses its cilia to sweep away noxious particles and the *Stentor* itself bends away from the tactile disturbance.[25] Tactility in the service of movement and of recognizing something outside one's own body similarly describes the cilia-mediated tentacle movement of a sedentary hydrozoan polyp toward a food source. From the viewpoint of cilia as the beginning of specialized sense organ structure, a polyp's movement is not reflexive but proprioceptive (see Note 23). More broadly, the notion of "true proprioception" is definitively recast. It is not a historical attainment; it is a function of animate form.

Specified in animate terms, living forms disclose even broader evolutionary continuities. A bacterium that goes about sampling the environment, as described earlier, shows a related sensitivity. The bacterium — a prokaryotic organism, that is, a single-celled organism without a nucleus and without membrane-enclosed organelles — is environmentally sensitive not to shape or to movement but to the chemical composition of its environment (but see also below on a further mode of bacterial sensitivity). Its sensitivity is all the same similarly mediated by touch, it similarly subserves movement, and it is similarly meta-corporeal. Hence, in both prokaryotic and early unicellular and multicellular eukaryotic forms of life, tactility determines what a particular organism does: a bacterium's surface sensitivity and a ciliated protozoan's and cilia-mediated polyp's sensitivity are founded on contact with something in the environment, a meta-corporeal phenomenon or meta-corporeal event which excites the organism to move in some way. An evolutionary pattern thus begins to emerge with respect to *surface recognition sensitivity*. The pattern is evident in prokaryotic organisms, which are tactilely sensitive to their physico-chemical environment and which move dynamically commensurate with that sensitivity, i.e. sampling, foundering, changing direction; eukaryotic forms of life emerge, which are tactilely sensitive to the environment through specialized sense organs and which move in ways coincident with that sensitivity, protozoan ciliates responding to noxious elements in the environment by bending or sweeping movements, for example, the cilia of sedentary polyps responding to vibrations in the surrounding medium and exciting the polyp to bend a tentacle toward food, mobile forms such as annelids and molluscs moving in strikingly more intricate and varied ways on the basis of more complex external organs sensitive to deformation and stress. In sum, the pattern is a *dynamic* one. Whatever the form of surface sensitivity in prokaryotic and early unicellular and multicellular eukaryotic forms of life, it is ultimately in the service of movement: toward or away from chemicals in the environment, toward sources of food, away from noxious elements or alien creatures, and so on.

A surface sensitivity subserving movement becomes apparent the moment one looks to corporeal matters of fact, analyses them in sensory-kinetic terms, realizes the centrality and significance of movement to creaturely life, and begins thinking in terms of a natural history of *animate forms*. It clearly suggests the basis on which proprioception arises and is clearly suggestive too of its crucial significance. A commonly cited definition of proprioceptors justly acknowledges a prime aspect of this significance: "Sense organs capable of registering continuously deformation (changes in length) and stress (tensions, decompressions) in the body, which can arise from the animal's own movements or may be due to its weight or other external mechanical forces"(Lissman 1950: 35; quoted in Mill 1976: xvi).[26] In a word, proprioceptive sensitivity is *continuous*. Not only is a creature's surface in contact continuously with other surfaces in the environment, whether it is moving or whether it is still, but its own conformations continuously change in the course of moving. Continuous sensitivity is thus doubly indicative of how a moving creature profits from such organs: it is sensitive both to the changing world in which it finds itself and to its own movement and changing bodily form. Moving creatures — animate forms — are, in fact, topological entities, changing shape as they move and moving as they change shape. Proprioception implicitly articulates this truth. Deeper and more detailed study shows it to articulate a further factual truth; namely, that animal movement, however centrally programmed, cannot be considered to be wholly devoid of proprioception.[27]

To understand this further factual truth, we need first to note that understandings of consciousness on the basis of animate form are conceptually revisionary in many respects, perhaps not least in calling into question the practice of bestowing consciousness in miserly and self-serving fashion. The practice flies in the face of corporeal matters of fact, precisely as those detailed above. To those facts may be added the following: Any creature *that moves itself*, i.e. that is not sessile, senses itself moving; by the same token, it senses when it is still. Distinguishing movement from stillness, motion from rest, is indeed a fundamental natural discrimination of living creatures that is vital to survival. The lack of constancy of the everyday world demands such discrimination. As emphasized earlier, whatever the particular *Umwelt* might be for any particular moving creature, that world is not consistent: weather fluctuates; terrains are irregular; surrounds change with growth and decay; the movements and habits of other creatures alter the environment; different creatures themselves appear and disappear each day; sequences of events shift: what occurred progressively yesterday is not what occurs progressively today; and so on. Clearly, no undeviating world presents itself day in and day out for any creature; *Umwelts* repeat themselves neither spatially nor temporally nor dynamically. By the same token, creaturely movement is not the same from one day to the next, "the same" in the sense of an undeviating replication of some master program. Certainly a creature's basic behaviors do not normally change, but they are nonetheless context- dependent in a spatial, temporal, and dynamic sense. A creature does not pursue something that is not actually there for it, for example. What a creature does, that is, how and when it *moves*, is determined at each moment by the situation in which it finds itself. The new and challenging mathematical science of cognition dynamics underscores these very points in its emphasis on "*real*-time." Cognition from a dynamic standpoint is processual, not a static series of representations. It takes place "in the *real* time of ongoing change in the environment, the body, and the nervous system." With respect to these three factors, dynamic analyses show the structure of cognition to be "*mutually and simultaneously influencing change*" (van Gelder & Port 1995: 3; see also, for example, Beer 1995; Giunti 1995, and Schöner [no date].) Accordingly, however rote its basic behaviors might be with respect to its day to day living in the world,[28] a creature is necessarily sensitive in a proprioceptive sense to the present moment; it begins crawling, undulating, flying, stepping, elongating, contracting, or whatever, in the context of a present circumstance. It is *kinetically spontaneous*. Elucidation of this further truth about the nature of animate form will show in

the most concrete way how animate form is the generative source of consciousness —
and how consciousness cannot reasonably be claimed to be the privileged faculty of
humans.

6.   From corporeal matters of fact to corporeal consciousness

A creature's corporeal consciousness is first and foremost a consciousness attuned to
the movement and rest of its own body. When a creature moves, it breaks forth from
whatever resting position it was in; it *initiates* movement, and in ways appropriate
to the situation in which it finds itself. The inherent kinetic spontaneity of animate
forms lies fundamentally in this fact.[29] Kinetic spontaneity may be analysed in terms
of kinesthetic motivations, a species-specific range of movement possibilities, a repertoire of what might be termed "I cans" (see Introduction, Note 3), and — by way of
proprioception and, more particularly, of kinesthesia — a sense of agency. As might be
apparent, these dimensions of spontaneity are keenly inter-related. A creature's initiation of movement is coincident with its kinesthetic motivations, its dispositions to do
this or that — turn, pause, crouch, freeze, run, or constrict; its kinesthetic motivations
fall within the range of its species-specific movement possibilities — an ant is not disposed to pounce any more than a cat is disposed to crawl; these possibilities are the
basis of its particular repertoire of "I cans," a repertoire that may not only change over
the lifetime of the animal as it ages, but that may be selectively distinguished insofar
as the animal can run faster, for example, or conceal itself more effectively than other
members of its group; as enacted, any item within its repertoire of "I cans" is undergirded proprioceptively (kinesthetically) by a sense of agency. A creature's corporeal
consciousness is structurally a composite of these four kinetic dimensions of spontaneity. It is a composite not in a studied analytical comparative sense — e.g. "I, a horse,
cannot fly like a bird" — and certainly *not* in the sense of demanding linguistic formulation, but in an existentially kinetic sense, in the sense of being *animate*. In effect,
creatures know themselves — "they know which thing in the world they are" — in
ways that are fundamentally and quintessentially consistent with the bodies they are.
They know themselves in these ways not by *looking*, i.e. not by way of what is visible to
them of their visual bodies, but proprioceptively, or more finely, kinesthetically, i.e. in
ways specific to movement alone, sensing their bodies as animate forms in movement
and at rest.

This form of creaturely knowing can be spelled out along evolutionary lines,
indeed, along the lines of descent with modification. The evolutionary pattern sketched
above emphasized the basic phenomenon of surface recognition sensitivity — beginning with bacteria and proceeding to ciliated protozoa, to sedentary invertebrates, and
to molluscs and annelids. This beginning sketch can be amplified. Creatures such as

lobsters and spiders are creatures with an articulable skeleton, hence they have not only external sensors but internal ones as well, particularly around their jointed append- ages. Generally termed chordotonal organs in invertebrates, these internal proprio- ceptors are sensitive directly to stresses within the body itself. On the basis of organic analogues and structural homologies, biologists believe these internal proprioceptors to have derived from external sensory organs, that is, to be the result of a migration of certain formerly external proprioceptive bodily structures. Such structural migra- tions are, of course, not unknown in evolution. A quite commonly cited homology concerns three reptilian jaw units that over time came to form the auditory ossicles of the mammalian middle ear: the stapes, malleus, and incus. Using a different example, Laverack makes this very comparison between invertebrate and vertebrate organ deri- vations or homologies. After noting that "Evolutionary trends in several groups [of invertebrates] show a gradual removal of proprioceptors from the surface to a deep or internal placement," he points out that this derivation, while apparent in some inver- tebrates, "is demonstrable in vertebrates," giving as example "the change in position of the acoustico-lateralis system in fish and amphibia" (Laverack 1976:19). Laverack in fact gives various examples of analogous proprioceptive organs in invertebrates: for example, the exoskeletal plates of a hermit crab are analogous to limb proprioceptors in other invertebrates (1976:10). He later gives a specific example of a possible inver- tebrate proprioceptive homology or derivation: "[T]he chordotonal organs of decapod Crustacea [e.g. lobsters] may have originated … from groups of hairs, very similar to hair plates of insects, of which the individual sensilla have shortened, lost their contact with the surface, and finally been incorporated in a connective tissue strand or sheet. The remaining vestiges of hairs are evident as scolopidia [the complex cellular unit of a chordotonal organ]." Further, with respect to the similarity of decapod chordotonal organs to insect hair plates, he adverts to research that, on anatomical and ontogenetic grounds and in consideration of the process of molting, suggests that "the cuticular sheath of sensory hairs and campaniform sensilla [in insects] are homologous to the extracellular cap or tube of scolopidia" (1976:21).

If the thesis is correct that external proprioceptors were modified and internal- ized over time, then a singularly significant consequence obtains: internally-mediated proprioception, however variously accomplished in terms of anatomical structures, remains nonetheless epistemologically consistent in its results, *viz*, a directly move- ment-sensitive corporeal consciousness.[30] Such a proprioceptive consciousness is kinesthetically rather than tactilely rooted. Corporeal consciousness thus evolved from its beginnings in tactility into kinesthesia, into a direct sensitivity to movement through internally mediated systems of corporeal awareness. In effect, through all the intricate and changing pathways of descent with modification, *know thyself* has remained a consistent biological built-in; a kinetic corporeal consciousness informs a diversity of animate forms.

The thesis that internal proprioceptors evolved from external proprioceptive organs may be expanded and in a challenging and perhaps unexpected direction. Laverack writes that external sensors have two major disadvantages: "(1) A lack of discrimination between stimulation generated by movement of the body and that generated by external tactile events. (2) A vulnerability to wear and damage. A superficial placement is bound to expose hairs and pegs to abrasion and other accidents" (1976: 46).[31] He states that these disadvantages "may have placed adaptive significance upon the subsequent development of parallel, internal proprioceptors." His perspective on the disadvantages of external sensors and the adaptive significance of internal ones has certain unexpected affinities with the perspective of molecular biochemist R.M. Macnab who, writing on sensory reception in bacteria, conjoins within a single perspective two otherwise opposed viewpoints on "the sensory apparatus of a unicellular prokaryote" (Macnab 1982: 98). Macnab discusses the sensitivity of a bacterium to surface events or environmental phenomena on the one hand, and to its own kinetic potential or energy level on the other, thus actually calling into question an account of bacterial knowing as only meta-corporeal. Being sensitive to its own kinetic potential, a bacterium can be said to have a rudimentary corporeal consciousness, rudimentary not in the sense of being less than functional — incomplete or underdeveloped, for example — but in the sense of there being no proprioceptive organ other than the organism — the bacterium — itself. Indeed, the source of a bacterium's motility is PMF — "proton motive force, [or] proton electrochemical potential" (Macnab 1982: 78) — and it is described as both the "motor" and "the true sensory input" (1982: 77); "the motor is an autonomous PMF sensing system" (1982: 98). Clearly, movement and the potential for movement are at the heart of a rudimentary corporeal consciousness. The specific contrast in viewpoints that Macnab reconciles bears this out. The contrast concerns a "sensing of the physiological consequences of an environmental parameter [such as light, oxygen, and so on]" and a "sensing of the parameter itself" (1982: 77). In other words, a bacterium can either sense itself with respect to the environment or sense the environment. Macnab points out that "Even in the rudimentary behavioral system of bacteria, both capabilities are present" (1982: 77) — a remark of considerable interest to anyone concerned to provide a bona fide evolutionary account of consciousness. He later specifies explicitly the advantages and disadvantages of each kind of sensibility: in physiological sensing, "the signal can be thought of as: 'For reasons unspecified, your current direction of travel has already resulted in your PMF … falling dangerously low'"; in environmental sensing, "[the signal can be thought of] as: 'Based on the following specific information — increasing aspartate in your external environment — your current direction of travel may offer enhanced opportunities for growth'" (1982: 100). In the first instance, the freely moving bacterium relies on a sense of its own energy to determine the benefits of continuing travel in its present direction. If it senses its energic potential running low, it is not getting what it needs from its immediate environment and moves elsewhere. In this instance, the freely moving bacterium is monitoring its environment *internally* through an electrochemical sensitivity to the effect of the environment on its kinetic potential. In the second instance, the freely moving bacterium relies on specific sensing abilities, i.e. external chemoreceptors for amino acids and sugars, in order to determine whether the path it is following is likely to continue being propitious or not. Macnab points out the value and liability of each mode of sensing in what are actually exacting epistemological terms:

> The physiological consequence of sensory information [i.e. physiologically-derived sensory information] has the advantage that the information is certain, but the disadvantage that it is late; the anticipatory sensory information has the advantage that it is early, but the disadvantage that it is uncertain, because the physiological consequence is presumed, and may in fact never occur'. (1982:100)

The certainty of a bacterium's internally-generated information — as of an animal's internal proprioception — is clearly of moment. As the earlier definition of proprioception implied, continuous sensitivity to one's own bodily condition means knowing with exactitude the nature of that condition — whether one's kinetic potential, one's postural conformation, or the spatio-temporal dynamics of one's movement. An *internally* structured corporeal consciousness is from this viewpoint both kinesthetically indubitable and kinesthetically unambiguous. For a bacterium, this mode of consciousness translates into knowledge that is similarly indubitable and unambiguous. The adaptive significance of a continuous bodily sensitivity in the form of an internally structured corporeal consciousness of movement or of movement potential can thus hardly be minimized. It is the generative source of a creature's immediate kinetic spontaneity. A creature's initiation of movement, including the initiation of a change of direction, is always from a particular corporeal here and now — positionally, energetically, situationally, and so on. Given its particular corporeal here and now, certain species-specific kinetic possibilities exist for it — here and now; other species-specific kinetic possibilities may emerge only when another, different corporeal here and now obtains, the different corporeal here and now that comes with growth, for example, thus with a changed animate form. Similar possibilities and constraints hold with respect to a creature's repertoire of "I cans": given its own particular strengths and liabilities, it has certain corporeal possibilities and not others — here and now. Even a bacterium cannot automatically upgrade its PMF just because the environment is right. For example, while aspartate might be present in its environment, the bacterium's aspartate transport system may be defective. The bacterium may thus be unable to take advantage of the amino acid, precisely as Macnab suggests with respect to physiological consequences being presumed (1982:100).[32] Finally, indubitable and unambiguous knowledge is basic to a creature's sense of agency. Lacking an internally structured corporeal consciousness that is both peculiar to the animate form it is and epistemologically resonant at each moment, a creature could hardly initiate movement — change direction, increase speed, pause, reach out with an appendage, turn itself around, avoid an obstacle or predator, explore, flee, or move purposefully in innumerable other ways — *or stop* — all such movement or cessation of movement being consistent both with the situation in which it finds itself and with its own immediate spatio-temporal corporeality.

Clearly, the corporeal path by which we can trace the evolution of consciousness can be richly elaborated in terms of the inherent kinetic spontaneity of animate forms. Such elaboration decisively challenges the putative evolutionary notion of an agent as something that "does something and then looks to see what moves." Attention to corporeal matters of fact demonstrates that a bona fide evolutionary account of consciousness begins with surface recognition sensitivity. It thereby acknowledges a meta-corporeal consciousness. It furthermore takes into account the emergence of a diversity of animate forms, showing how surface recognition sensitivity, while mediated by touch, is actually in the service of movement for creatures all the way from bacteria to protists to invertebrate forms to vertebrate ones. It strongly suggests how a form of corporeal consciousness is present in bacteria.[33] Indeed, it shows how a bacterium, being an animate form of life, is something first of all that *moves* and is capable of moving on its own power rather than being always impelled to move from without; it shows further how it is something that feeds, that grows, that changes direction, that, in effect, can stop doing what it is doing and begin doing something else. A bona fide evolutionary account shows how, with the evolution of varied and complex external sensors, a different form of corporeal consciousness is present, and how, with the evolution of internal sensors from external ones, a still different form of corporeal consciousness is present. It shows how each of these forms of corporeal consciousness is coincident with the evolution of varied and complex animate forms themselves, and equally, how each form of proprioception that evolved, from the most rudimentary to the most complex of kinesthetic systems, is coincident with particular forms of life. It shows all this by paying attention to corporeal matters of fact and by presenting concrete sensory-kinetic analyses.

There is a final point to be made. For an invertebrate or vertebrate, an internally structured corporeal consciousness is not directly vulnerable to environmental wear and tear and in this sense is protected. As Laverack's second remark suggests, a creature with internal proprioceptors is not at the direct mercy of the surrounding world. For a bacterium, such protection is not of course of moment; being unicellular, it has no sensory or internal organs as such. Some soft-bodied invertebrates such as annelid worms have hydrostatic skeletons, muscles lengthening and shortening the body against semi-fluid body contents that do not compress so that volume remains constant while segments of the animal increase and decrease in diameter. Although internal proprioception has been suggested via studies of stretch response, and although some annelids have very tough outer cuticles which *inter alia* would offer protection for internal proprioceptors, a strong case cannot reasonably be made for protection or the need for protection in the sense Laverack suggests, i.e. the evolution of internal proprioception as a means of protecting sensory organs from environmental wear and tear. The decisive turning point for proprioceptive protection is clearly evidenced in the evolution of an articulable skeleton. Arthropods and vertebrates are notable in this respect. Though their evolutionary lineages are distinct, species within each phylum are similar in having a skeletal structure and in being extremely mobile forms.[34] Although their respective skeletal structure is differently placed, the attaching muscular structure is in each case internal and functions in a similar manner; when a muscle contracts, skeletal joints close, pulling two body segments toward each other. A direct and continuous sensitivity to movement thus appears to have evolved in two distinct but highly mobile forms of life and with the same advantage: an internally-mediated corporeal consciousness of movement that is not dependent on external stimuli, hence on tactility, but that is internally mediated. This kind of corporeal consciousness is not only relatively protected as well as continuous in comparison to an externally-mediated corporeal consciousness. Being internal, its possibilities for elaboration are quite different. In particular, what is being sensed in the case of an internally-mediated corporeal consciousness has the possibility of opening up, of expanding into a richly variable and complex domain of awarenesses. The possibility of such a domain is adumbrated in the question "What is it like to be a bat?" Indeed, the question "What is it like to be a bat?" presumes the existence of an internally-mediated corporeal consciousness that has already opened up into a range of kinetically tied and internally felt phenomena and acts. In other words, it presupposes a range of experiences that a bat has of itself as an animate form. Proprioception is in this sense an *epistemological gateway*, one that, by descent with modification, may clearly be elaborated both affectively and cognitively. In just these ways, corporeal consciousness shows itself to have the possibility of expanding into a sense of self. The evolution of proprioception foundationally explains this possible expansion. "The Reality of Selves" has its roots in corporeal consciousness.

7. Implications

Three implications in particular warrant mention. First, the natural history of consciousness described above demands a re-thinking of the common assumption that historically — particularly with reference to the evolution of nonhuman animals — unconsciousness preceded consciousness. Corporeal matters of fact show this assumption to be unfounded. It has never in fact been shown that nonhuman animals do not think, or choose, or even deliberate with respect to movement,[35] or that they do not have a sense of speed, space, effort, and so on. On the contrary, if the above sensory-kinetic analysis of consciousness is correct, then the evolution of such corporeal capacities and awarenesses is coincident with the evolution of animate forms. Corporeal awareness is a built-in of animate life; as the previous sections have demonstrated, *know thyself* is incontrovertably a fundamental biological built-in.

Second, there is in present-day western society a tendency to be mesmerized by brains, so mesmerized that the larger creaturely world of which humans are a part is forgotten, egregiously slighted, or arrogantly distorted. Cognitivist programmes of research in science and philosophy are at the forefront of this mesmerization. Should researchers in these disciplines find that the subject of nonhuman animals is in general not congenial to their interests, or that the foregoing evolutionary analysis of consciousness is in particular not exciting in the way that computerized study of their own brains is exciting, it may well be because they have lost touch with their own natural history. Indeed, compared with Aristotle's studious forays into the world of animals — human and nonhuman — cognitivists' knowledge of animals appears in many cases painfully limited. One is easily led to think, at least with respect to some of the creatures they write about — lobsters and scallops, for example — that their only encounter with them has been on a plate. Yet serious study of animate forms is required for understandings of consciousness. Included in this requisite study is a study of hominids themselves and for the following reason: any evolutionary understanding of human consciousness — any "naturalistic study of consciousness" (Flanagan 1984: 307) — must acknowledge a historical fact recorded previously, namely, that while all humans are hominids, not all hominids are human. Accordingly, any evolutionary rendition of human consciousness must take into serious account artifactual evidence attesting incontrovertibly to the intellectual acumen of nonhuman animals. Such an account can hardly be rendered in computational brain-state terms. It can, however, be rendered and in fact has been rendered in sensory-kinetic terms demonstrating a corporeal consciousness (cf. Sheets-Johnstone 1990).

The third implication is related to the second. We can hardly hope to understand consciousness if we make authoritative and self-serving evolutionary armchair pronouncements such as "Consciousness did not have to evolve…. Consciousness is not essential to highly evolved intelligent life…. However, from the fact that consciousness is inessential to highly evolved intelligent life, it does not follow that it is inessential to our particular type of intelligent life" (Flanagan 1992: 129; the first sentence also appears in Flanagan 1984: 344); or, if in the course of explaining how it is possible "that some living things are conscious" (Flanagan 1984: 307; 1992: 1), we make claims about creatures whom we have not bothered to study but about whom we feel entitled to make judgments. To affirm, for example, that scallops "are conscious of nothing," that they "get out of the way of potential predators without experiencing them as such, and when they fail to do so, they get eaten alive without (quite possibly) experiencing pain" (Flanagan 1984: 344–45; 1992: 132), is to leap the bounds of rigorous scholarship into a maze of unwarranted assumptions, mistaking human ignorance for human knowledge. As a matter of fact, a well-known introductory biology text shows a picture of a scallop "sensing an approaching starfish," and "leap[ing] to safety." The same book, commenting on the complexity of a scallop's eyes, elsewhere notes that although the lens of its eyes "cannot focus on images," it detects "light and dark and movement" (Curtis 1975: 29, 387).

Evolutionary understandings of consciousness on the basis of animate form are clearly a radical departure from materialist conceptions that, basically identifying consciousness and matter, eschew serious inquiry into the nature of animate life. It is thus not surprising that in offering their reductive programmes, materialists offer a metaphysics in advance of an epistemology and a natural history that support it. Their metaphysics is in advance of a supportive epistemology in that both experience and meticulous study belie theory. Proprioception in general and kinesthesia in particular advert to a knowing subject, a subject that, at minimum, knows when it is moving and knows when it is not. Consciousness can therefore be judged neither "inessential" nor essentially linguistic, a "Center of Narrative Gravity." Consultation of and reflection upon corporeal matters of fact testify to a corporeal consciousness that is epistemic in nature and that can be ignored only at the peril of a degenerate epistemology. Their metaphysics is in advance of a supportive natural history in that it ignores close knowledge of the literature on nonhuman animals, including, as suggested above, those nonhuman animals that were the direct hominid ancestors of modern-day humans. An evolutionary backbone is thus essentially lacking to their metaphysics, which is why it must be propped up by molecular definitions of life and why the life the metaphysics describes, being mere ongoing states of a brain, offers a portrait of life as if life were a series of stills. In sum, serious inquiry into the *nature* of consciousness perforce must take into account its natural history.

Glossary

Although many terms used in the text are defined in the text, a listing is given here for convenience and added reference. (Note: Biological classification is in terms of kingdom, phylum, class, order, family, genus, species.)

Amoeba   A genus of protozoan organisms distinguished by their pseudopodia.

Annelida   a phylum of invertebrate animals that includes earthworms and marine worms, all of which have segmented bodies. (From Latin *anellus*, ring.)

Anthozoa   a class of coelenterates that includes sea anemones and corals. (From Greek *anthos*, flower + *zoion*, animal.)

Arthropoda   a phylum of hard-bodied invertebrate animals — the largest phylum in the animal kingdom — that includes lobsters, spiders, ants, and centipedes, all of which have an external skeleton and thus articulable body parts. (From Greek *arthro*, joint + *podos*, footed.)

buccal   pertaining to the cavity of the mouth.

campaniform sensilla   bell-shaped proprioceptive organs in insects that are sensitive to deformation.

chordotonal organs   internal proprioceptive organs of invertebrates.

cilium (pl. cilia)   a hairlike structure that protrudes from the surface of a cell and is commonly found in rows; it has a characteristic 9 + 2 internal structure, i.e. nine pairs of microtubules surrounding two microtubules at the center.

Coelenterata   a phylum of invertebrate animals that includes polyps, jellyfish, sea anemones, and corals. (From Greek *koilos*, hollow + *enteron*, intestine.)

Crustacea   a class of arthropods that includes barnacles, prawns, crab, water fleas, and crayfish. (From Latin *crusta*, the shell or hard surface of a body.)

decapod Crustacea   crustaceans such as lobsters and crab having five pairs of legs and belonging to the order Decapoda.

eukaryote   a cell that has an outer membrane that separates it from its environment and both a membrane-bound nucleus and membrane-bound organelles. (From Greek *eu*, good + *karyon*, nut, kernel.)

flagellum (pl. flagella)   a hairlike structure that protrudes from the surface of a cell and that is instrumental in locomotion and feeding; it is longer than, but has an internal structure similar to, a cilium.

Gastropoda   A class of mollusks that comprises the largest number of species of mollusks (80,000). The class includes whelks, snails, limpets, conches, and abalones, which have either a univalve shell or no shell at all, and which are more mobile than bivalve mollusks such as the scallop. (From Greek *gastro*, stomach + *podos*, footed.)

Hydrozoa   a class of coelenterates which includes polyps and jellyfish and of which the polyp is the dominant form. (From Greek *hydor*, water + *zoion*, animal.)

Hymenoptera   an order of insects that includes bees, ants, and wasps. (From Greek *hymen*, membrane + *pteron*, wing.)

Mollusca   a phylum of soft-bodied invertebrate animals that includes snails, slugs, oysters, mussels, scallops, octopuses, and squid. (From Latin *molluscus*, soft.)

nauplius (pl. nauplii)   a larval form of crustacean.

Paramecium   a genus of protozoan organisms distinguished by their cilia-mediated movement.

polyp   a coelenterate animal that is usually sessile and that has a vase-shaped or cylindrical body, the mouth of which is surrounded by tentacles.

prokaryote   a cell that has an outer membrane that separates it from its environment. (From Latin *pro*, before + Greek *karyon*, nut kernel.)

Protista   a kingdom of eukaryotic, unicellular organisms.

Protozoa   a phylum of organisms within the kingdom Protista. The animals are character-istically one-celled organisms that are invisible to the naked eye. They are classified accord-ing to their form of locomotion: movement by means of flagella, of cilia, or of pseudopodia. Some protozoa — the sporozoans — are nonmotile forms. (From Greek *protos*, first + *zoion*, animal.)

radula   a feeding organ by which gastropods rasp or scrape off bits of plant or animal tissue. (From Latin *radere*, to scrape.)

scolopidia   complex peg- or spike-like structures comprising the cellular units of chordotonal organs in invertebrates.

sensilla   external proprioceptive organs such as hairs, pegs, slits, and plates.

sessile   stationary, attached to a substrate, not freely moving. (From Latin *sedere*, to sit.)

Stentor   a genus of protozoan organisms distinguished by their cilia-mediated movement.

Notes

* This chapter first appeared in *The Journal of Consciousness Studies* (Sheets-Johnstone 1998a). A shorter version of the article was presented as a guest lecture at the University of Aarhus (Denmark) in November 1996, as an invited paper at an international conference on "The Origin of Cognition" at the University of San Sebastian (Basque Country) in December 1996, and as an invited plenary session address at the March 1997 meeting of the Metaphysical Society of America at Vanderbilt University.

1.   Teuber's remark occurs in the context of discussing D.M. MacKay's paper "Cerebral Organization and the Conscious Control of Action," the theme of which is "the controlling function of the brain in voluntary agency."

2.   Whether it undermines or precludes depends upon the degree to which the assumptions are recognized and acknowledged.

3.   A *Journal of Consciousness Studies* reviewer wrote that "giving an explanation of 'how' if one cannot identify 'what' seems difficult, since the object of the inquiry is not specified." In practice, where the study of consciousness is concerned, the distinction between "how" (consciousness arises) and "what" (consciousness is) is far less straightforward than this remark implies.
    As may be apparent from the discussion thus far, a perusal of current literature on consciousness shows no consideration of the distinction, and thus no apparent inclination on the part of writers to be concerned with it or to think that *what* must be clarified before a consideration of *how*. Indeed, writers on consciousness launch their inquiries straightaway, even sometimes specifying in the beginning what consciousness is in terms that beg the question of saying just what it is — e.g. "we can say that a mental state is conscious if it has a *qualitative feel*.... The problem of explaining these phenomenal qualities is just the problem of explaining consciousness" (Chalmers 1996: 4). The muddle strongly suggests that

clarification of the distinction requires an acknowledgment of what is called "the hermeneutic circle." In classic terms, one already understands that which one is on the way to interpreting; and conversely, one has already interpreted that which one has already understood. In more scientific terms, one already knows *the what* that one is about to investigate; and conversely, one has already investigated *the what* that one already knows. In short, a researcher could hardly investigate anything if there were not already a known delimited subject at hand, a subject that the researcher already knows at least to the extent that s/he wants to investigate it. Moreover the process of investigation is itself a hermeneutic circle: as what is investigated becomes known in more exacting ways, that new knowledge becomes the basis for further investigation. In just this way, *what* consciousness is may be continually elucidated in the process of elucidating *how* it arises. The present paper progressively does just that: it answers the *what* question in the course of specifying *how consciousness arises in animate form*.

4.   "Mental events and processes are as much part of our *biological natural history* as digestion, mitosis, meiosis, or enzyme secretion" (Searle 1992:1; italics added).

5.   It is of interest to point out that Churchland's idea of a natural evolutionary course of events, a kind of biological determinism with respect to life and intelligence, conflicts with prominent ideas and experimental findings in biology. Churchland states that "[G]iven energy enough, and time, the phenomena of both life *and* intelligence are to be expected as among the natural products of planetary evolution" (1984:154). Stephen Jay Gould is a strong proponent of the view that evolution is a thoroughly contingent, non-repeatable historical process (see, e.g. Gould 1989, 1995). See also McDonald 1995. McDonald's article summarizes microbiologist-zoologist Richard E. Lenski's intricate experiments and their results, which show the play of chance in the course of evolution and the unrepeatability of natural history.

6.   The burial practices of nonhuman hominids also become virtually impossible to understand since such practices entail a concept of death. See Sheets-Johnstone (1990), Chapter 8, "On the Conceptual Origin of Death."

7.   He continues to do so in his later writings (1995, 1996). Not only does his consistent use of quotation marks (e.g. "Clever experiments by psychologists and ethologists suggest other ways in which animals can try out actions 'in their heads'" [1996:91]) to make distinctions between "us and them" alert us to the hazards of making simple comparisons among extant creatures over the benefits of examining natural history (cf. Sheets-Johnstone 1992b; 1994 [Chapter 2]; 1996a, 1996b); but his consistent assessment of nonhuman animals in terms of tasks not common to the behavioral repertoire of the species (e.g. 1996:133, 157) alerts us to the hazard of making self-serving prescriptions (e.g. "[W]e must not *assume* that [nonhuman animals think]," 1996:160) over the benefits of examining the presumptions underlying those prescriptions, including the assumption-laden claim that "[T]hose who deplore Artificial Intelligence are also those who deplore evolutionary accounts of human mentality" (1995:370).

8.   Even in his latest book, he takes the invention of language completely for granted: "There is no step more uplifting, more explosive, more momentous in the history of mind design than the invention of language. When *Homo sapiens* became the beneficiary of this invention ..." (Dennett 1996:147).

9.   For a discussion of these matters in detail, see Sheets-Johnstone (1990), Chapter 6, "On the Origin of Language."

10.   Darwin goes on to say: "[T]hus the wonderfully diversified instincts, mental powers, and affections of ants are generally known, yet their cerebral ganglia are not so large as the quarter of a small pin's head. Under this latter point of view, the brain of an ant is one of the most marvellous atoms of matter in the world, perhaps more marvellous than the brain of man."

11.   For an even more impressive indication of a bacterium's cognitive capacities, see Losick and Kaiser (1997).

12.   "Foundational" is a perfectly good English word, as in the sentence, "Evolutionary understandings are foundational to understandings of what consciousness is all about."

13.   Proprioception refers generally to a sense of movement and position. It thus includes an awareness of movement and position through tactility as well as kinesthesia, that is, through surface as well as internal events, including also a sense of gravitational orientation through vestibular sensory organs. Kinesthesia refers specifically to a sense of movement through muscular effort.

14.   Lest it be thought that Dennett is idiosyncratic in his procedure, consider the nineteenth century German philosopher J.J. Engel's criticism of British philosopher David Hume's account of the derivation of the concept of force: "He ought to use his muscles, but instead he uses his eyes; he ought to grasp and struggle, and instead he is content to watch" (Quoted by Scheerer 1987: 176).

15.   It should be noted that Sherrington uses the word *tension* in a purely neuromuscular sense when he says, in tandem with his statement that "I have no awareness of the muscles as such at all," that "I have no awareness of tension in the muscles" (1953: 249). Tension *is* absent in the specified neuromuscular sense, but it is *not* absent in an experiential sense. Sherrington could hardly go on to describe his awareness of his movement as *smooth* if he did not move with a certain tensional quality coincident with smoothness: a certain kinetic tension is integral to smooth movement. That kinetic tension is not a constituent of jagged movement, for example, or of myriad other movements between the two extremes of smooth and jagged. It would thus be an epistemological mistake to think Sherrington's disavowal of an awareness of discrete muscle tensions a disavowal of a direct experiential awareness of the tensional qualities of movement. This would be to conflate neuroscience with experience. On the other hand, it would also be an epistemological mistake to think Sherrington's characterization of proprioception as a "mental product" correct since the *smoothness* Sherrington experiences is not only there, directly evident in his movement; the *smoothness* is created by his movement and exists in virtue of his movement.

16.   One might claim that terms such as swift and weak describe movement directly, while terms such as "hesitant" describe an affective state derivative from movement. The claim is a provocative one, bearing out the etymology of the word "emotion." The term "expansive," for example, describes a generous, open person, one who is affectively sympathetic toward others, a usage clearly tied to movement, i.e. to an expansive — open, generous — spatiality of a body in motion. Observations of infant psychologist and psychiatrist Daniel Stern support the idea of a coincidence, if not a derivation, of affect from movement. In particular, Stern describes what he calls "vitality affects": "qualities [of experience] that do not fit into our existing lexicon or taxonomy of affects [but that] are better captured by dynamic, kinetic terms, such as 'surging', 'fading away', 'fleeting', 'explosive', crescendo', 'decrescendo', 'bursting', 'drawn out', and so on" (Stern 1985:54). Affects may well be "better captured by dynamic, kinetic terms" than special feeling terms because they have their origin in the tactile-kinesthetic body. From this perspective, complexity of affect may be tied to complexity of movement. If this is so, then the evolution of affect might be studied from the viewpoint of the richness and variability of tactile-kinesthetic bodies, and not just from the viewpoint of a social world. A passing remark of anthropologists Sherwood Washburn and Shirley Strum is suggestive in this respect. In their discussion of the evolution of speech, they write that "Attempting to teach a monkey to make more sounds is like trying to teach it to have more emotions" (Washburn & Strum 1972:475). If the emphasis is on the making of sounds and not on the sounds themselves, then a relationship between species-specific possibilities of movement and species-specific possibilities of affect is clearly adumbrated. In turn, however superficial and abbreviated the suggestion, one may well ask, is kinetic complexity the basis of affective complexity?

17.   It might be noted that the degrees-of-freedom problem is intimately related to the fact that movement creates rich and variable qualia.

18.   Dennett (1991: e.g. p. 106): "The brain is Headquarters, the place where the ultimate observer is."

19.   For a detailed account of the tactile-kinesthetic body, see Sheets-Johnstone (1990). In an ontogenetic sense, the priority of movement and tactility is not surprising. The sequence of development of embryonic neural tissue underscores their significance.In particular, there is early beginning development (the fourth week of life) of the semicircular ear canals which, through vestibular sensations, provide a sense of balance or imbalance, and (at the fetal stage) of receptors in the muscles which, through kinesthetic sensations, provide a sense of position and movement. Though rudimentary, the sensory system for balance is in place by the beginning of the fourth month. By the beginning of the fourth month too, reflexive behavior appears, which means that the movement of the fetus is coordinated in response to stimulation. The comparatively early development of neural tissue related to movement is of particular interest in conjunction with physiological studies suggesting that neural development of the motor cortex is stimulated by the body movements of the fetus itself. In other words, form does not develop solely on its own. Movement influences morphology. Myelination studies also show that motor neurons myelinate early and that acoustic-vestibular neurons myelinate next. For a discussion of prenatal development and behavior, see Robeck (1978) and Windle (1971).

20.   Evolutionary studies of proprioception are no longer fashionable. Indeed, attention should be called at the beginning of this descriptive analysis to the fact that contemporary study of proprioception lags so far behind studies of vision and audition that it is barely perceptible in the literature. Moreover most of the journal literature is devoted to proprioceptive injuries to the knee, to knee surgery, and to topics related to the loss of proprioception. Of the 27 articles on proprioception published in scientific journals in 1994 and the first six months of 1995, 14 of them were devoted to such topics. Accordingly, where evolutionary references are pertinent or seem necessary, I use earlier writings, the most comprehensive text being the 686–page volume *Structure and Function of Proprioceptors in the Invertebrates*, edited by P.J. Mill (1976).

21.   Cf. Ernst Cassirer's concise explanation of why there are *Umwelts*: "Every organism ... has a world of its own because it has an experience of its own" (Cassirer 1970:25).

22.   There are approximately 800,000 species of insects of which approximately 275,000 are species of beetles.

23   If one considers that tentacle cilia are passively deformed by vibrations in the surrounding water, then of course a polyp's bending response *is* proprioceptive, not reflexive. See further in the text itself Laverack's remark about cilia as the beginning of specialized sense organ structure.

24.   For an excellent discussion of morphology in relation to movement and of the evolution of arthropods from annelids with respect to that relationship, see Manton (1953). The eminent biologist J.B.S. Haldane spoke laudingly of Manton's work, saying "Manton has done for a phylum what comparative ethologists have done for small vertebrate groups such as the Anatidae." He described her as a "pioneer" with respect to her phylogenetic focus on movement (Haldane 1953: xvi, xvii).

25.   Cf. Curtis (1975: 311): After bending away from a noxious stimulus, and if "the offensive stimulus persists, the *Stentor* will reverse its cilia and try to sweep the particles away. If bending and sweeping are not successful, it contracts and waits. Once it has contracted, it does not bend or sweep again, but it may reach out to sample the water several times before it finally swims away. The length of time it tolerates the noxious stimulus apparently depends on whether or not its site had previously proved a good feeding area. Thus, even ciliates show some flexibility in behavior."

26.   Lissman amends Sir Charles Sherrington's original 1906 coinage and definition of the term "proprioceptors" — sensory organs stimulated by "actions of the body itself" — in that, as Lissman states, Sherrington's definition "does not appear quite adequate, because, clearly, there are few types of sense organs which cannot be stimulated by actions of the body itself" (Lissman 1950: 35).

27.   "[P]roprioceptive information plays a vital part in the control of movements and orientation." It is of interest to note in this context the remarks of zoologist M.J. Wells with respect to the question of the relationship between proprioception and learning: "Because it is normally impossible to eliminate all the proprioceptors and never be quite certain that one has succeeded in eliminating all other sensory cues, it is rarely possible to be certain that an animal is using proprioceptive information when it learns…. One must examine cases where animals learn in circumstances that, *prima facie*, imply that they are taking into account information derived from within their own joints and/or muscles and/or organs of balance and explore these cases rather carefully to see what alternative explanations are possible. It should be emphasized that the object of this exercise is not to establish whether particular sorts of animal can possibly learn from proprioceptive inputs in *any* circumstances (since that question is unanswerable), but rather whether they normally appear to do so" (Wells 1976: 567–68).

28.   We might note that it is only specified behaviors that are chosen for observation and recording, not behaviors outside a set protocol to begin with. Thus the conveniently discardable file called "anecdotal behavior." See, for example, the consternation with which some researchers greet the idea of "tactical deception in primates" as put forth by primatologists Whiten and Byrne (1988).

29.   Kinetic spontaneity describes fundamental dimensions of *animation*. The term is not tied in any way to a centralist doctrine. Hence, the term should not be confused with the

older notions of "innervation sensations," "willing," "volition," or "effort," or in any other way confused with the classic efferent side of the efferent/afferent divide. (For a thoroughgoing criticism of the idea that there is "a consciousness of the motor discharge [from the brain]," see James 1950: Vol. 2, 494).

30.   Cf. Laverack: "If the thesis that many internal receptors may derive from external receptors, (sic) is valid, then it would be anticipated that the properties of all mechanoreceptors will be similar. Variety may be expected as a result largely of anatomical rather than physiological attributes" (1976:48).

31.   We might clarify the first disadvantage by noting that tactility is a reflexive sense, that is, one in which what is touching and what is touched coincide — or blend. Hence, the sense of touch can indeed be ambiguous, precisely as Laverack points out in general rather than sensory-specific terms.

32.   A tangential but critical point might be made with respect to the twofold sensitivities of a bacterium, the one sensitivity being described as immediate, the other as anticipatory, the one informative of the bacterium's present energic state but not of the environmental cause of that state, the other informative of particular aspects of the bacterium's environment but not of what its consequences will be. A caveat might be in order with respect to what amounts to an equipotential weighting of a corporeal consciousness and meta-corporeal consciousness. A bacterium can be conceived profitably attuned to the future only with a certain reserve. If the bacterium has both capabilities, then its sensitivity to its own body is paramount. If there is no guarantee that present environmental munificence will continue and even grow, there is no guarantee either that the bacterium itself will continue and even prosper. If its sensitivity to its own energic level becomes deficient for any reason, it could conceivably exhaust itself in the midst of plenty or in the pursuit of more.

33.   See also Losick's and Kaiser's account of how "[b]acteria converse with one another and with plants and animals" (1997:68).

34.   Cf. Fields (1976), who explicitly draws a parallel between crustaceans and vertebrates with respect to the need for precise control of a multi-jointed, highly mobile body in changing circumstances — e.g. variable load, muscle fatigue, and the like. In particular, Fields draws attention to the fact that the muscle receptor organ of crustaceans is similar to the muscle spindle of vertebrates.

35.   "Animals may constantly be seen to pause, deliberate, and resolve" (Darwin 1981:46).

Consciousness

An Aristotelian account

> Of the things that exist, some exist by nature, some from other causes. By nature the animals and their parts exist, and the plants and the simple bodies (earth, fire air, water) — for we say that these and the like exist by nature.... For each of them has within itself a principle of motion and of stationariness (in respect of place, or of growth and decrease, or by way of alteration).   Aristotle (*Physics* 192b: 9–16)
>
> Nature is a principle of motion and change.... We must therefore see that we understand what motion is; for if it were unknown, nature too would be unknown.
> Aristotle (*Physics* 200b: 12–14)

1. Introduction

In his provocative paper, "Is an Aristotelian Philosophy of Mind Still Credible?" Myles Burnyeat follows up his claim, "To be truly Aristotelian, we would have to stop believing that the emergence of life or mind requires explanation," with two sweeping conclusions: that Descartes has closed off for us the possibility of an Aristotelian philosophy of mind, and that "we are stuck with the mind-body problem as Descartes created it, inevitably and rightly so" (Burnyeat 1992: 26). At more than one point Burnyeat speaks of our unavoidable Cartesian problem, referring to it as "our task" and conceiving it as a "bottom up" approach to mind mandated by modern science. "Aristotle," Burnyeat says, "simply does not have our task of starting from the existence of matter as physics and chemistry describe it and working up to the explanation of the secondary qualities on the one side and animal perceptual capacities on the other" (Burnyeat 1992: 22).

The following inquiry into Burnyeat's claim about the dispensability of Aristotle's philosophy of mind — specifically as it plays out in perception — will clarify in yet further ways an understanding of consciousness as arising not in matter but in animate form.

2.   Burnyeat's claim and its initial Aristotelian rejoinder

At the heart of Burnyeat's dismissal of Aristotle's theory of mind is his critical analysis of Aristotle's claim that in perception, one receives the sensible forms of things without the matter. Many well-known scholars have criticized Burnyeat's analysis and conclusions regarding this statement. My purpose here is neither to review these thoughtful and estimable criticisms nor to elaborate on them directly. It is rather to offer a critique of Burnyeat's notion of dispensability from a different standpoint: namely, that of questioning assumptions undergirding his negative, obviously 20th-century, appraisal of Aristotle's notion of mind in general and explanation of perception in particular. My claim is that these assumptions stand in the way of an appreciation of what Aristotle is affirming about perception and of what evidentially justifies his affirmation.

Burnyeat calls attention to the passage in the *De Anima* in which, speaking specifically of touch, Aristotle states that the organ of perception is potentially that which the sensed object is actually (for example, warm or hard) and that "all sense-perception is a process of being so affected" (*De Anima* 423b29–424a1). On the basis of his examination of the text, Burnyeat concludes "[o]nce again" — i.e. here as elsewhere — that what Aristotle is saying is that "the organ's becoming like the object is not its literally and physiologically becoming hard or warm but a noticing or becoming aware of hardness or warmth" (Burnyeat 1992: 21). Because on his reading, Aristotle's account of the relationship of organ of sense to object of sense is precisely a matter of awareness and not of physiology, i.e. not a bottom-up explanation, Burnyeat finds Aristotle's account useless. As noted, according to Burnyeat, we 20th-century Westerners are bound, by Descartes's legacy, to explain mind and life through an appeal to matter; unlike Aristotle, "*we* are stuck with a more or less Cartesian conception of the physical" (Burnyeat 1992: 26).

Now to begin with, a compound irony permeates Burnyeat's claim: 20th-century Western science is empirical; Aristotle was an empiricist, in fact, the person most Westerners regard as the first empirical scientist; Descartes, in contrast, was a rationalist. Aristotle's investigations into the natural sciences were, in effect, quite unlike Descartes's both in breadth and in fineness of detail. Indeed, Aristotle pursued not a theory-bound, speculative and abstract account of nature; he investigated living things themselves. He observed first-hand in his studies of plants and animals that material nature is intertwined in progressively more complex ways with formal nature as manifest in the singularly animate powers of nutrition, reproduction, sensation, self-movement, and thinking. In short, in his empirically-based inquiries into the natural sciences, Aristotle found matter and form to be of a piece. While Burnyeat implicitly acknowledges the attractiveness of this non-dualistic metaphysics — this "non-Cartesian conception of ⁻he soul" (Burnyeat 1992: 26) — he insists that Aristotle's conception of the physical "is ⁻ us a deeply alien conception" (Burnyeat 1992: 26).

Burnyeat's insistence prompts a two-pronged question: how can there be different metaphysics of the same living systems and their activities?[1] and how, given its rationalist, i.e. Cartesian, rather than empiricist conceptual origins, can the reigning 20th-century Western metaphysics be deemed the correct one? Put more sharply, how, on the one hand, can there ever be a veridical metaphysics of humanness if that metaphysics is merely coincident with what happens to prevail given the epistemological fashion of the times? and how, on the other hand, can a basically rationalist conception take precedence over an empiricist conception — especially in a world in which a thoroughly empirical scientific epistemology reigns over all other possible epistemologies? Clearly there are inconsistencies and unsubstantiated valuations at the core of Burnyeat's claim and conclusions. These problematic aspects can be formulated more sharply still by posing the following questions: Why must we start with the existence of matter "*as physics and chemistry describe it*" and not with our experience of "matter" as it displays itself before us in sight or as it contacts us directly in touch? Why must we give precedence to a matter we have never seen, touched, or smelled, a matter we have never *perceived*, particularly where the concern is to give an account of *perception*? Why, in forging our metaphysics, should we not begin by acknowledging the integral living forms we experience, whether firs, roses, bees, beetles, macaques, or finches — in the manner precisely of Aristotle, not to say of Darwin? Why, indeed, should we not have a metaphysics that is first of all consonant with living things as they are in the changing realities of their lives — in their movement and rest, in their generation, growth, and decay? Why should we have a metaphysics that commences with the inanimate rather than the animate, especially since that metaphysics typically either fails to do justice to, or ignores altogether, a natural history? Moreover why should the mind/body problem in particular be a problem deemed solvable only at the level of a 20th-century conception of matter? Why should it not be a problem solvable at the level of mindbodies themselves, at the level of the "manifestation of persistent wholes" (Haldane 1931:13),[2] of Darwinian bodies (Sheets-Johnstone 1990:Chapter 11), of intact living beings — of individuals like Descartes himself, in the flesh?

Let us take up these questions explicitly with reference to Aristotle's account of perception. In 20th-century Western science and much of 20th-century Western philosophy, a sense organ is considered a particular kind of sensory apparatus that is first of all sensitive to a particular constellation of stimuli from the outside world, and that transmits, by neurological mechanisms, the specific stimuli it receives to the brain, where, as a result of the action of other neurological mechanisms, the specific stimuli are perceived. Aristotle understands sense organs quite differently. Most importantly, a sense organ is not the beginning of *a conduit to a brain*. To acknowledge this fundamental difference is to call attention to the fact that Aristotle entertained not the slightest conception of the brain as the culminating perceptual organ of chordate nervous systems. But it is also to call attention to his notion of perception as the work of *localized bodily senses*: seeing has *its* organ, hearing *its* organ, and so on. This notion of localization, which dovetails superficially with 20th-century scientific accounts, engenders a recognition of physical conformations peculiar to living bodies, that is, a recognition of each sense as having *a particular material nature* and a recognition of the whereabouts of *each such particular arrangement of matter*. But Aristotle's understanding of localization runs much deeper than this. His understanding is patently based on the whereabouts of sensorily sensitive bodily *parts*; but it is thereby also based on the experience of perception itself. In particular, Aristotle's notion of an organ of sense is based on the actual experience of that organ *as an organ of sense* in the process of perceiving. When he writes that, "Generally, about all perception, we can say that a sense is what has the power of receiving into itself the sensible forms of things without the matter" (*De Anima* 424a18–21), he is basing his generalization on what we experience as perceiving when we actually perceive, that is, on what we experience bodily as the locus of sense or as the bodily power to sense. He is describing in general terms *the localized nature of our experience of perceiving* when we are seeing, hearing, or touching something. When we consult actual experiences of perception, "actual" in the sense of setting off our experience of perceiving from 20th-century scientific explanations of perception, *we experience perceiving — sensing — as taking place at the site of the organ itself.* When we discount what we have learned about rods and cones, for example, about the optic chiasm, the occipital lobe and the visual cortex, about parallel distributed processing, about the representational theory of perception, about primary and secondary qualities, and about multiple other anatomical and/or theoretical entities, in other words, when we bracket our science-encumbered natural attitude toward visual perception and simply pay attention to our experience of seeing, *we consistently experience seeing as taking place at the site of our eyes.* Our actual experience of seeing is consistently localized in the same way as our experience of touching is consistently localized and as our experience of smelling, tasting, and hearing is consistently localized: our experience of hearing takes place *in (the area of) our ears*, of smelling *in our noses*, of tasting *in our mouths*, of touching *on our skin*. Everyday experience bears out this localization. When we cannot quite hear something, for example, we draw closer and put our ear to it. We never dream of drawing closer on behalf of our brain and putting our auditory cortex to it. It is thus not surprising that Aristotle affirms that "a sense … has the power of receiving into itself the sensible forms of things without the matter." The *power* to perceive is a power of a located sense organ; "receiving" or "taking in" the form of an object is a site-specific perceptual happening. Thus, when I perceive blue, or loud, or pungent, or sweet, or hard, I take in the thisness or whatness, or, in a broad sense, the qualitative significance of a thing without its matter *at the site of the sensory organ itself.*

An annotative aside is apposite here concerning Aristotle's terms "receiving" and "taking in." The verbs appear to be a consistent source of perplexity for 20th-century

Western scholars. But again we find an irony. It is common for 20th-century Western-ers to learn and speak about sense organs as *receptor* organs, organs that precisely *receive* stimuli. It thus appears that sense organs can receive *stimuli*, but that they can-not receive "the sensible forms of things without the matter"; analogously, they can take in light waves, sound waves, and so on, but they cannot take in "sensible form." The lexical irony strongly suggests that the problem some 20th-century scholars have with an Aristotelian account of perception may not basically be a physiological one at all; that is, the basic problem is not that Aristotle lacks a "bottom-up" account of perception. Indeed, the irony strongly suggests that the problem is not one of explain-ing in a physiological sense what senses *do*, but of explaining what exactly they *get* in doing what they do: stimuli or sensible forms? A proper metaphysics of perception patently hangs in the balance. So also does a proper epistemology of perception.

Given the above initial understanding of the meaningfulness of Aristotle's account of what it is to receive the sensible forms of things without the matter, one might be tempted to agree with Burnyeat that Aristotle is affirming no more than that perception is awareness, a localized awareness, to be sure, but awareness pure and simple, and that he is making no physiological claims at all, at least none that 20th-century Galilean science-bred and -wedded thinkers would or could accept. To agree, however, would be to miss the preeminently experiential perspective from which Aristotle is writing and thereby miss its sizable import. The perspective is mandated by his empirical stance and cannot be summarily dismissed; on the contrary, it must be included in any account of what it is to perceive. If our experience of our sense organs is what it is — if we experience seeing *in (the area of) our eyes*, hearing *in (the area of) our ears*, tasting *in our mouths*, smelling *in our noses*, touching *on our skin* — why, then, is it not of consequence to understand perceiving as such, that is, as a spa-tially localized experienced happening, a basic fact of animate existence? Indeed, on what grounds is existence — life — rejected as legitimate grounds for explaining how (and what) we perceive? If, as Burnyeat writes, "the ultimate thing [for Aristotle] is the existence of life and mind" rather than the physico-chemical elements that 20th-century Western science describes (Burnyeat 1992:25), what ordains a privileging of the latter over the former other than a desire, pure and simple, to reduce life to the microscopic? Why should not a proper metaphysics begin with the eye at the end of the microscope, the eye that is not homonymously an eye but an organic eye, an eye that is animated on behalf of seeing? Why should not a proper metaphysics begin with the person Descartes who is not homonymously Descartes but the Descartes animated on behalf of meditating on the question "what am I?".[3] Not only do we *open* one eye and *close* the other in *peering* through a microscope, for example, but we *focus* things more closely in order to attend to them more finely: we move them further right or left, increase or decrease lighting, etc. Moreover we *adjust* our eyes in numerous ways, moving them to accord with the visual circumstances; and *we move ourselves* toward the same end — going toward things, bending over them, standing back from them, and so on. In short, we do things on behalf of seeing. We do analogous things on behalf of hearing, smelling, tasting, touching. We move spontaneously on behalf of our senses because we are animate creatures. We turn toward things to begin with because we are existentially, by nature — *organ-ically*, if you will — involved with the world.[4]

Conduits to brains are clearly not part of our experiential world. They are in fact "deeply alien" to our everyday ways of making our way in the world and of making sense of it. A further irony is apparent in this very fact. What a thoroughgoing reductive materialization of mind in the end imputes to brains is what formerly belonged — and properly belongs — to living creatures. A thoroughgoing reductive materialism must make such imputations because it must ultimately in some way account for agency, an active experiencer, a subject — if only of a verb since some kind of doing is at stake, and a verb is nothing without a subject. This metaphysical necessity is clearly played out in the writings of present-day scientists and philosophers. For example, molecular biologists Francis Crick and Christof Koch tell us that "the brain infers": "If you see the back of a person's head, the brain infers that there is a face on the front of it" (Crick & Koch 1992:153). This comically eccentric, not to say preposterously homuncular metaphysics is at odds with experience. Statements of neurobiologist Semir Zeki and neurologists Antonio and Hanna Damasio engender a similarly quirky metaphysics: "An object's image varies with distance, yet the brain can ascertain its true size" (Zeki 1992:69); "To obtain its knowledge of what is visible, the brain ... must actively construct a visual world" (Zeki 1992:69); "When stimulated from within the brain, these systems [neural systems in the left cerebral hemisphere that "represent phonemes, phoneme combinations and syntactic rules for combining words"] assemble word-forms and generate sentences to be spoken or written" (Damasio & Damasio 1992:89). A preposterous metaphysics is furthermore implicit in assertions people make with untroubled ease about brain modularity, and equally implicit in the untroubled, easy way in which people seriously take up these assertions. For example, writing about sociobiologist Leda Cosmides and her experiments on a kind of problem-solving that involves cheating, science writer John Horgan states that "One of the most useful [brain] modules, she proposes, is dedicated to detecting 'cheating' by others" (Horgan 1995:177). The leap from experiment to brain modules is, well, extraordinary. So also, of course, is the idea of dedicated circuitry. All such statements plainly impute intentionality to a convoluted mass of nerve tissue all of us carry about inside our heads but never experience, thus confounding otherwise self-sentient, intentional, and intact living creatures with their brains. Indeed, *animism* runs rampant in reductive accounts of mind. Not surprisingly, it runs rampant in eliminative materialist accounts. Patricia Churchland and Terrence Sejnowski, for example, tell us that "If we are to understand how the brain sees, learns, and is aware, we must understand the architecture of the brain itself" (Churchland & Sejnowski 1992: 17). In the context of recognizing that in their "framework" of "activations" and "weights," there is a central problem, that of an absent but absolutely essential dynamics, they write that "After chewing on this question, and taking diametrically opposing views over many weeks, our brains did eventually relax into a stable configuration" (Churchland & Sejnowski 1992: 174). Clearly, what might be called speculative, not to say fabricated, experience should have no place in a properly empirical science. Perhaps the crowning irony embedded in a thoroughgoing materialist science generally, as in Burnyeat's incisive dismissal of Aristotle's philosophy of mind, is precisely this recourse to animism: in starting with matter "as physics and chemistry describe it," one must ultimately, and by one's own hand — and/or mouth — *animate* matter. There is otherwise no inferring, ascertaining, constructing, speaking, writing, cheating, seeing, learning, being aware, chewing on questions, taking opposing views, and relaxing. There is otherwise no explaining either "secondary qualities on the one side" or "animal capacities on the other." By dint of will and word-waving, and whether with blitheful or naive reason aforethought, one must breathe life into matter; one must inspire intentionality — the full richness of experience with all its variable semantic shadings, its active choices and motivated behaviors — into a matter that is only homonymously organic because it is static and piecemeal, and being static and piecemeal is in fact no more than pallid and spiritless tissue. In contrast, Aristotle's empirical rendering of organs of sense tells us something about a *bona fide* subject's experience of perceiving, something about the localized way in which we fundamentally experience our senses in the act of perceiving and about the way in which objects which our senses bring to our attention are experienced, i.e. as *formally* significant phenomena. However much we may question what we consider Aristotle's causal explanation of perception — of which more presently — surely these basic facts of perceptual experience have an import worth examining. In short, surely Aristotle is telling us something not dispensable but of empirical moment.

To get at this something requires an extended examination of Aristotle's descriptive formula of perception. Our initial move in this enterprise will be to examine Aristotle's localized notion of perception in two respects: first, in conjunction with his insistence on uniformity in explanation, hence with his insistence on uniformity in accounting for the senses in perception; second, in conjunction with his account of perception itself, specifically, with his idea of how, in perceiving an object, we receive the sensible form of an object without its matter. However difficult to maintain in their details, both his thesis and his account are extraordinarily relevant to 20th-century epistemology and ontology, and this because their firm experiential grounding is consistently validated by actual everyday perception. There is indeed something basic, universal, enduring about the way in which humans — and all animate creatures for that matter — perceive and have perceived from the very beginning.

3. Uniformity

In the *De Anima*, Aristotle is clearly puzzled at several points as to how to achieve a uniform explanation of the senses. In particular, he views touch as the primary sense and cannot easily accommodate the other senses either to its mode of reception or to its multiple qualities. He judges the sense of touch primary on biological grounds: "no sense is found apart from that of touch, while touch *is* found by itself; many animals have neither sight, hearing, nor smell" (*De Anima* 415a4–6). He makes similar claims on behalf of the uniqueness of touch when he says, for example, that "every body that has soul in it must … be capable of touch," that "the loss of this one sense alone must bring about the death of an animal," and that "it [touch] is the only [sense] which is indispensably necessary to what is an animal" (435114; 435b4–5; 435b6–7). In addition to these uniquenesses, he singles out touch as being a sense that "alone perceives by immediate contact." That the other senses do not come into immediate contact with their object poses a problem, a central and basic problem to which Aristotle responds at one point by stating that these other senses "no doubt … perceive by contact, only [their] contact is mediate" (435a19–20). Moreover while the other senses are composed of one element, touch is composed of more than one element. Being host to a range of tangible qualities, it is composed not only of earth (thus receiving hard and soft), but of fire (thus receiving hot and cold), and of water (thus receiving dry and wet). Clearly, touch is fundamentally different from the other senses; and it is thereby also enigmatic. Aristotle in fact speaks pointedly of the "obscurity" of the organ of touch in contrast to the distinctness of the organs of the other senses, organs whose difference one from another "is too plain to miss" (423a12–13). In this context he voices his unsureness as to whether the organ of touch is flesh or whether the organ of touch lies further inward. In the course of his inquiry on the matter, he asks whether or not "the perception of all objects of sense take place in the same way … e.g. taste and touch requiring contact … while all the other senses perceive over a distance" (423b1–4). He presses for uniformity, emphasizing the indispensability of a medium to each sense. He thus must accommodate the fact that two senses — touch and taste — require contact, thus seemingly no medium, "while all the other senses perceive over a distance." Justifying his claim that a basic "distinction" among the senses is "unsound," he explains their uniformity as follows: "we perceive what is hard or soft, as well as the objects of hearing, sight, and smell, through a 'medium', only that the latter are perceived over a greater distance than the former; that is why the facts escape our notice. For we do perceive everything through a medium; but in these cases the fact escapes us" (423b4–8).

However unconvincing his reasoning — especially with its final escape clause — and inadequate the evidence in support of uniformity, there is no doubt but that Aristotle arrives at a uniform explanation of how the senses perceive. Despite the material uniqueness of each organ of sense and despite the formally unique quality (or qualities) each organ of sense receives, it receives the formal quality in the same manner as the other organs, *viz.*, through a medium which, lying between object and organ, is set in motion by the object and in turn causes movement in the organ. Clearly, Aristotle's explanatory challenge arises from the fact that while touch is primary, it is also deviant: the site of the sense of touch is seemingly in direct contact with the object touched and is, in addition, receptive to multiple qualities. When Aristotle wonders whether touch is one sense or a group of senses, he is wondering precisely about the second deviancy, that is, how to treat the standard set by touch with respect to its receptiveness to multiple qualities. He tells us that unlike sound, tangible qualities do not emanate from a "single subject": wet and moist are a species of tangible quality altogether different from hot and cold, whereas the contraries high and low, and loud and soft, are aural qualities of the single subject, "sound." Being the primary sense which sets the standards, touch in fact creates standards difficult to follow. When Aristotle writes that a solution to the problem of multiple qualities is had in the fact that sound too has "more than one pair of contraries" (*De Anima* 422b28–30), he also confesses that "Nevertheless we are unable clearly to detect in the case of touch what the single subject is which corresponds to sound in the case of hearing" (422b31–32). At later points, trying to distinguish between the medium of touch and the organ of touch in order to resolve the problem that direct contact presents, he considers (through a thought experiment) how, if a membrane enveloped us, the *organ* of touch would not be the membrane, and how, if the enveloping membrane were the *medium* of touch, we would "fancy we can touch objects, nothing coming in between us and them" in the same way that we "fancy" we can touch objects as we do now, being immersed in air or water (423b11–12). When he finally comes to espouse the notion that the organ of touch lies "farther inward" (422b22) and that flesh is the medium of touch, he immediately notes also that a difference remains between touch and the senses of sight and hearing: "in the latter two cases we perceive because the medium [air] produces a certain effect upon us, whereas in the perception of objects of touch we are affected not *by* but *along with* the medium" (423b11–14). In sum, Aristotle achieves uniformity by creating a distance where none exists and by disavowing the possibility of perception without a medium: the organ of touch lies "farther inward" and "flesh is [not the organ but] the medium of touch" because "[o]nly so would there be a complete analogy with all the other senses" (423b24–26).

What propels Aristotle to tether his descriptive analysis of perception to the principle of uniformity? Why is a complete analogy among the senses imperative? Indeed, since sense organs differ, why cannot their mode of affection differ? One might well point to Aristotle's general quest to find lawful order in the nature of things, but what Aristotle tells us in the beginning of his account of sensation suggests a more penetrating and satisfying reason. He states there that "sensation depends … on a process of movement or affection from without, for it is held to be some sort of change of quality" (*De Anima* 416b34–35). Accordingly, Aristotle appears to be claiming that whatever might constitute a change of quality *in specific material terms*, change is dependent upon movement and perceiving is thus fundamentally a dynamic process. In other words, that a particular organ of sense is "being affected" or "acted upon" is fundamentally a matter of movement and not a matter of matter. If this is so, then given that the object of sense, via movement, affects the medium, and the medium, via movement, affects the organ of sense, perception is fundamentally and in all cases precisely the *kinetic process* Aristotle declares it to be. When Nussbaum and Putnam write that Aristotle's "material transition" should remain open rather than be conclusively specified in the manner of Sorabji, who claims that the organ of sense in each case materially takes on the quality in a quite literal sense — when one perceives red, for example, the "eye jelly goes red" (Sorabji 1992: 209ff.) — they implicitly suggest that what is basic to perception is something other than *material* (Nussbaum & Putnam 1992: 36). Aristotle's principle of uniformity is significant in just this context. What he identifies as uniform is precisely what *is* basic. In particular, his abiding concern with contact and lack of contact between object of sense and organ of sense testifies to an abiding concern with what disallows or allows movement, and in turn, with what disallows or allows a dynamic process to occur. In effect, if perceiving is not *a discrete material event* at an organ of sense but a *dynamic process*, then a properly causal account of perception must ultimately explain not a material happening, in the manner, for example, of Sorabji's account, but a central and basic kinetic process. Moreover taking Aristotle's principle of uniformity as the point of departure for understanding his kinetic explanation of perception, we find it understandable why he says that the organ of sense and the sense itself are in fact the same but that their essence is not (*De Anima* 424a: 24–25). The eye is the eye, but the essence of the eye as sense is not the essence of the eye as organ; the ear is the ear, but the essence of the ear as sense is not the essence of the ear as organ; and so on. The essence of the latter is consistently *spatial*; the essence of the former is consistently *qualitative*. The two essences converge in perception, which is to say that, his transposition of the organ of touch aside, everyday sense experience validates Aristotle's account. In perceiving loud, or hard, or moist, or black, or pungent, or sour, we in each case perceive at the site of a certain sense. *Our perceptions of quality are always localized.* Yet however distinct the senses are from one another with respect both to their localization and to the specific qualities they receive, motion consistently effectuates their "change in quality," whatever that change might be in the "*activity* of perceiving."[5] The dynamic process of perception as Aristotle describes it is thus indeed uniform. A particular medium and a particular organ of sense are consistently set in motion. What fundamentally constitutes and explains perception is kinetic in nature.

4. Receiving the form without the matter

Aristotle is telling us something of further empirical moment in his account of perception. This further dimension has to do with his claim that objects of sense — qualities in the world — have the power to affect certain other things, affect them not directly but through a medium, and through the medium to set them in motion. The physiognomic 'whatness' or 'thisness' of an object of sense is thus perceived by an organ of sense. Indeed, Aristotle's account of perception is a *physiognomic* account, not an *object* account. He is not explaining how we come to perceive a house, a melody, an orange, and so on, that is, how we come to perceive objects *as such*. He is thus not explaining what much of 20th-century western science and philosophy generally explain or consider when they explain or consider perception. As earlier citations show, western scientists generally treat perception as an object-recognition or object-production function of the brain — inferring a face, ascertaining an object's true size, constructing a visual world, generating sentences — in essence doing no more than specifying how anatomical features and/or neurological portions of the brain change coincident with a subject's experience of stimuli of various kinds. In marked distinction, Aristotle is explaining how it is that we, phenomenal creatures in the world, perceive color, sound, flavor, odor, warmth, and so on. His concern is with the perception of *qualia*. It would be a mistake, however, to think that he is wrestling with the qualia problem as it arises from the representational theory of perception. The qualia problem for Aristotle is a problem of uniformity; that is, it arises from the fact that, unlike other organs of sense that require distance, some organs of sense seemingly require contact with their respective object(s) of sense — with quality in the flesh, so to speak — and thus seemingly dispense with a medium. Aristotle's qualia problem thus traces ultimately to the fact that we perceive at the site of our senses: in some cases, perceived quality is seemingly in direct contact with the site of the sense; in other cases it is definitely not. As noted above, Aristotle finds this lack of uniformity "unsound": there is not a different perceptual process for each sense; qualities in the world are in each and every case perceived according to the same process. Accordingly, though "the facts escape our notice" with respect to touch (and presumably to taste as well), Aristotle claims that a medium intervenes between the special objects of the sense of touch — e.g. warm, hard, moist — and the organ of sense itself. While one may fault Aristotle's way of harmonizing the process of physiognomic perception — creating distance where none exists and disavowing the possibility of perception without a medium — one may not fault his explanation of qualia. His explanation coincides exactly with everyday sense experience. What we perceive physiognomically is what is actually there in the external world — colors, flavors, sounds, smells, softness, moistness, and so on: "[T]he objects that excite the sensory powers to activity, the seen, the heard, etc., are outside"

(*De Anima* 417b20–21). Clearly, Aristotle does not have an external world problem. As will be shown in a later section, that this problem does not arise for Aristotle is a mark of his thoroughgoing sense of nature and of the natural history approach to perception that that sense of nature dictates. Moreover, as intimated above, Aristotle is not pressed to speak in terms of 'representations'. The sensible form is not something copied in a brain; it is perceived at the site of the sense itself when that sense becomes "identical in character with [an] object without being the object" (*De Anima* 429a16–17). Here again, Aristotle's account coincides with everyday experience. The pungency I smell is identical in character with the pungency of the stew itself; the pungency is *not an object* but a quality; similarly, the smoothness I feel is identical in character with the smoothness of the velvet itself; the smoothness is *not an object* but a quality; and so on. What Aristotle explains is how we are qualitatively affected by what is qualitatively out there in the world. Adherence to his principle of uniformity provides anchorage for this explanation: quality, no matter what its worldly source and what its specific organ of sense, is a *sensible form* whose sensibility is mediated by a medium that both sets in motion and that is itself set in motion.

Because a medium is indispensable to Aristotle's account of perception, it warrants closer examination in the context of both his specification of an object of sense and his explanation of the perception of tangible qualities. As indicated above, Aristotle makes quite clear at the very beginning of his discussion of each of the senses that by the term "object of sense" he means a quality, and in particular, a quality perceived by one sense alone and no others; color is the special object of sight, sound is the special object of hearing, and so on (*De Anima* 418a8–17). Hence, as emphasized, there is no doubt but that in Aristotle's understanding, what perception gives us fundamentally is not an object *per se* but a quality. When perception is understood and analyzed in this qualitative way, the deviancy of the sense of touch becomes flagrantly evident. Were perception of the tangible a matter of direct contact, we would be unable to sense it. Lacking a medium to set in motion, the object of sense — the tangible quality — could not possibly set the organ of touch in motion. Direct contact disallows the perception of quality because it disallows a dynamic process, namely, the object of sense acting upon the organ of sense. The perceptual product of direct contact — were such perception possible — might thus be *per se* rain and not *wet*, *stone* and not *hard*, *ice* and not *cold*. The perceptual product would, in other words, be an object; direct contact, in bringing together two material bodies, would disallow movement and obviate the perception of quality. What Aristotle underscores in the first of his two conclusions on perception bears out this distinction: "the sense is affected by what is coloured or flavoured or sounding *not insofar as each is what it is*, but insofar as it is of such and such a sort and according to its form" (*De Anima* 424a22–24; italics added). In short, were we to perceive by direct contact, we would perceive, in Aristotle's words, *what each is*; we would perceive a *material thing*.[6] In contrast, when we perceive an object's quality — its sensible form — we precisely sense its form, its physiognomy, which is out there in the world and sensible but is not a physical object as such.

Now in order to make the perception of tangible quality possible given the restrictions he himself provides, Aristotle designates — one might even say "invokes" — a medium, "*something* in between" (as he emphatically puts it) the object of sense and the organ of sense (*De Anima* 419a20). As shown earlier, he explains specifically how the medium of touch — flesh — is different from the medium of the other senses: when we perceive objects of touch, we are affected *along with* flesh, not *by* it. Uniformity of process is thereby saved along with appearances: a medium intervenes between every object of sense and its proper organ of sense, including the object and organ of touch; by a special — "along with" — dispensation to the sense of touch, our actual experience of the special objects of touch is preserved. Not only then is the process of reception clearly uniform in that we consistently perceive at the site of our senses; it is clearly uniform in that a medium is integral to every act of perceiving, a medium either through which we are affected by special objects of sense or with which we are conjointly affected by special objects of sense.

While a medium is as problematic to 20th-century Galilean science as it is indispensable to Aristotelian science, it would be a mistake to dismiss — or to "junk," as Burnyeat suggests — Aristotle's philosophy of mind. Rather than being a problem for Aristotle, a medium is what allows the perception of quality; a medium is for Aristotle *a conduit of movement*. Indeed, *media transduce quality*. They in fact transduce quality in a way not altogether unrelated to the way in which light waves or sound waves are considered by 20th-century Western science to instantiate, carry, and/or initially represent quality. All the same, there is a profound difference between the two sciences. The difference is a foundational one, a foundational difference in the way the world is metaphysically conceived: Is the fundamental metaphysical question, "Why is there something rather than nothing?" or, is it rather, "Why is there movement rather than stillness?" As we will presently see in more detail, Aristotle himself raises the metaphysical question when, in one of many contexts in which he examines the origin, nature, and import of movement, he declares, "Matter will surely not move itself" (*Metaphysics* 1071b30).

In sum, if we receive the sensible forms of things without the matter, it is because form, not matter, fundamentally informs perception, which is of course to say once again that we fundamentally sense quality, not objects as such. This is *not* to say that matter is dispensable or irrelevant to the sensing of quality. The psychic power to receive sensible forms without the matter is a power that is itself enmattered and that indeed could not be the power it is without being so enmattered.[7] Moreover not only are spatial magnitudes — *organs* — essential to perception, but as Aristotle points out elsewhere, "[I]f there are causes and principles which constitute natural objects, and from which they primarily are or have come to be … plainly, I say, everything comes to be from both subject [matter] and form" (*Physics* 190b17–20). Moreover speaking elsewhere of a material substratum that underlies the appearance of contrary qualities (precisely the kind of qualities — loud/soft, white/black, dry/wet — that inform perception), Aristotle affirms that "We must reckon as a principle and as primary the matter which underlies, though it is inseparable from, the contrary qualities" (*On Generation and Corruption* 329a29–31). Clearly, while matter *underlies* form and is distinct from it, matter is nonetheless *integral* to form. Matter and form are of a piece.

That a post-Cartesian, Galilean worldview is in general uncongenial to Aristotle's holistic metaphysics, that, in particular, a sovereign conception of matter dominates 20th-century Western science and philosophy and finds such a metaphysics anathema to its materialist program, and that just such a worldview and conception are at issue here in denying any present-day relevance to Aristotle's "philosophy of mind" is all fairly obvious. To bring the foregoing exposition of what is of empirical moment in Aristotle's account of perception to bear explicitly on these matters, and to demonstrate conclusively its specific relevancy to 20th-century Western thought, a brief excursus into Aristotle's compound notion of form and matter is required. This short detour will clarify in pertinent ways basic components of his explanation of perception and provide broader contexts for their understanding.

5.   Excursus I: On the relationship of form and matter

The relationship Aristotle envisions and consistently sets forth between form and matter is keenly and incisively analyzed by James Lennox in the context of his study of Aristotle's biological treatise, *De Partibus Animalium*. Since the same metaphysics pertains to objects as to animals, that is, since for Aristotle, metaphysics is fundamentally a question of an understanding of the relationship between form and matter, and of change in one sense or another, the same metaphysical principles apply. In showing how material nature plays "a more independent and a more central role in Aristotelian science than is typically suggested" (1997:164), Lennox points out specifically how, in contrast to 20th-century functionalist renderings of matter, Aristotle illustrates how matter constrains form, and how form constrains matter. Lennox spells out how this reciprocal relationship is exemplified in Aristotle's explanation of a characteristic of horn-bearing animals: they all lack upper teeth. Aristotle explains the fact materially in the following way: nourishment that would otherwise be in the service of a second set of teeth goes instead toward the growth of horns (Lennox 1997: 175). The explanation has its roots in elemental facts of Nature: a certain amount of "earthen and hard" materials are available for such bodily parts as horns, teeth, claws, hoofs, and so on, parts that provide defense or confer other advantage. As Lennox points out, "[E]ach animal has a fixed quantity of different sorts of basic material ingredients out of which the formal nature constitutes its parts. These 'givens' of an animal's material nature constrain the actions of its formal nature" (176). But as Lennox also points out, the reverse is also true: "[A]n animal's *formal* nature ... determines the placement and structural design of the material" (174). Thus the same elemental material may be differentially utilized in different animals. In particular, when an excess of material is available, what Lennox terms the "Principle of Functional Priority" prevails: "Large viviparous quadrupeds have only a certain amount of 'earthen and bodily' material for hard head appendages, and that means that, should the formal nature be such as to constitute horns, certain teeth will be missing" (176). In just this way, Aristotle gives a formal explanation of the parts of animals being the specific parts that they are.

The mutual constraint that holds relationally between form and matter with respect to the parts of animals holds equally for objects of sense (and of course for organs of sense since organs of sense are parts of animals). In each case, form is materially embodied, and its material embodiment is not arbitrary. While present-day functionalist theory claims that the material way in which any particular function is carried out is not necessarily fixed — the same function can be performed by any number of different materials — Aristotelian theory affirms on the contrary that certain materials are intrinsic to a form's being the form that it is. Accordingly, if, as Lennox puts it in the context of his study of the parts of animals, "Aristotelian formal natures work ... within the bounds of a comprescent material necessity," we may properly ask what the significance of a "comprescent material necessity" is with respect to quality? How, in other words, does material nature constrain quality?

In a quite everyday sense, it appears obvious that sense qualities are constrained by the object in which they inhere or by the object which creates them, and by the organ that they affect. Loud and soft, for example, are materially constrained by the sounding instrument which is their material source — a lyre or a trumpet, for instance, a hammer or a cane. The power to hear loud and soft is materially constrained by ears, the having of them, certainly, but also their acuity or normalcy and their range of sensitivity. A comprescent material necessity is, in effect, integral to *loud* and *soft* being the particular qualitative experience they are. In consequence we may say that the material nature of things necessarily enters into an understanding of how any quality comes to be the particular quality it is. It is important to underscore the fact that material nature does not *explain* quality — whether loud, soft, white, sharp, pungent, bitter, hard, or whatever. It explains it neither causally nor ontologically. In the first instance, quality cannot be materially reduced; such putative reduction ignores the essential (formal) nature of quality, and, in addition, creates problems with respect to its perception and to its aesthetic instantiation, of which more presently. In the second instance, quality cannot be ontologically explicated in an originative sense, any more than, with respect to the world generally, an ontological explication can be given of why there is something rather than nothing. If the point of departure for thinking about quality is that "formal natures work within the bounds of a compresent material necessity," then the material nature of quality is not to be *explained* but *understood*, understood not only in the sense of comprehending how quality shapes and is shaped by matter, but in the sense of comprehending how quality is by nature integral to the life of animate forms, and correlatively, how it is in the variable nature of things for there to be a qualitative world. Aristotle can *explain* the intimate relationship between form and matter with respect to the parts of animals because an ontological explanation in an originative sense — e.g. how horns and/or two sets of teeth come to be in such and such animals — is possible. His explanation derives in large measure from his conception of Nature as a productive but economical source of life. Quality is not amenable to such an explanation because while it is undeniably tied to material aspects of elemental Nature in Aristotle's account of perception — to air, water, earth, and fire — it does not have the material status that a body part has; it is not an object *as such*. With quality, we begin at the other end of the spectrum, so to speak. But the same relationship holds, the same intimate connection of form and matter obtains. Indeed, the challenge is to bring this intimate connection to bear on the seemingly troubled way in which Aristotle describes perception, the process of taking in the sensible forms of things without the matter. Earlier discussion of this problematic elucidated Aristotle's formula in terms of localization — perceiving at the site of the senses — of the necessity of a medium — an in-between that both is set in motion and sets in motion — and, to a limited extent, of the intimate link between form and matter, a link further fleshed out in the foregoing excursus. What we must do now is bring these progressive elucidations to bear on quality, on the perception of *formally* significant phenomena.

6.   On the way to an understanding of quality: Clearing the ground

Aristotle offers no explanation of the passage of quality from object of sense to organ of sense that would count as a physiological explanation today. At the level of what would be recognized as a physiological explanation, he describes only a dynamic process. The activities that define perception, the "*activity* of sound" on the one hand and the "*activity* of hearing" on the other hand, for example, are motion-inducing activities.[8] In effect, perception is basically a kinetic series of happenings, a matter of setting in motion. While Aristotle speaks of sensible qualities as having power — sound qualities have the power to set air in motion, color qualities have the power to set light in motion — and thus implicitly suggests that qualities can influence other things, that is, be a cause of which other things are the effect, his account does not in any way foreshadow what a post-Cartesian, Galilean science would deem a physiological explanation. In particular, he does not begin by specifying *bodily structures as such* — the various facets of the inner ear, for example. Accordingly, no proper sensory *functions* can be structurally assigned. In consequence, no proper physiology can be established. Moreover while Aristotle recognizes *organs of sense* — ears, eyes, and so on — the organs themselves are, on his account, not at all equivalent to the *activity* of hearing, of seeing, of tasting, and so on: "What perceives is, of course, a spatial magnitude, but we must not admit that either the having the power to perceive *or the sense itself* is a magnitude" (*De Anima* 424a25–27; italics added). The activity is in each and every case *motional*, not material *as such*; the activity of seeing, tasting, hearing, touching, smelling coincides directly with the non-material process Aristotle specifies, namely, taking in the sensible forms of things without the matter.

Clearly, there is a difference between movement and objects in motion that is vital to an understanding of what in fact constitutes Aristotle's physiology of perception.[9] Aristotle's focal concern is with the former — movement — not the latter — objects in motion. He does not, for example, say that "the eye jelly goes red" when we see red. More broadly put, he does not say that Nature is a principle of objects in motion. He says that a principle of motion informs all of Nature. In effect, although cosmic bodies are patently part of Aristotle's kinetic account of perception and thus might seem, with some conceptual liberties, to ground his account basically in matter, material nature cannot explain perception. Only a principle of motion can explain perception. Thus, although elemental Nature — air, fire, earth, water — might be said to count *materially* as a physiological explanation of the perception of quality at the finest level, it does not — and cannot — provide an ultimately *material* explanation of the perception of quality, any more than it does or can provide an ultimately *material* explanation of the parts of animals. In short, *contra* present-day Western science, on Aristotle's account, a materially reductive physiological account of perception is *by nature* impossible.

The above brief analysis highlights substantive differences between what Aristotle understands by an explanatory physiology and what present-day Western science understands by an explanatory physiology. In recognizing these differences, however, we are not thereby warranted to "junk" Aristotle's "philosophy of mind," as Burnyeat claims and advises (Burnyeat 1992: 26). On the contrary, we are obliged to recognize that, however closer present-day physiology is to the cultural eidos of our times and to our 20th-century scientific hearts, and however much information it has given us about the unique sensitivities and responsivities of our bodily parts and their proper and deficient functioning, *present-day Western physiology is a physiology that does not and cannot include an explanation of the perception of quality*, except in the quality-effacing reductive sense of a series of localized material happenings all the way to the brain. With respect to color seeing, for example, present-day physiological concern is with the absorption of different wave lengths of light by photoreceptors located in rods and cones of the eye; with the contribution of retinal ganglion cells to the original color coding by the photoreceptors; with the response of the striate cortex to the neural information passed to it; and so on. In other words, if we turn the comparison around with respect to its typical standard, i.e. if we look at what Aristotle's account provides and what present-day physiology lacks rather than vice versa, we find that Aristotle is forthrightly recognizing something with which present-day physiology is unconcerned and about which it is silent. Burnyeat's claim and advice are from this perspective improper if not pointless. Although one might claim on the contrary, and in a manner following Burnyeat, that present-day Western science alone gives the correct account of the physiology of perception, an Aristotelian might justifiably retort that *that* physiology does not and cannot give an account of *perception*; it can only give an account of certain relationships discovered to obtain between particular stimuli in the form of wave-lengths of light and other such phenomena and particular neural pathways to and in a brain. Surely the Aristotelian has a point. Granted that a transposition of intentionality and experience from living person to brain can be carried out without a linguistic hitch, still, an absolutely foundational dimension of perception is lacking to such an account: namely, a credible *subject of perception*, credible in the very sense in which we daily experience ourselves to be subjects of perception, no matter the denigrating categorization of that experience by some as "mere folk psychology."

Radical and far-reaching differences in physiological understandings notwithstanding and the critical necessity of a credible subject as well, a basic commonality actually obtains between the two accounts, a commonality briefly suggested earlier in the context of specifying the essential role of a medium in Aristotle's account of perception. When Aristotle says with respect to the sensing of quality that "The activity of the sensible object and that of the sense is one and the same activity" (*De Anima* 425b27–28), he is telling us something that is basically identical to what present-day Western science tells us in its explanation of perception but tells us in such a way that shrouds the commonality. What Aristotle is saying is that the perception of quality is fundamentally a matter of movement, of "acting" and of "being acted upon" (*De Anima* 426a3). Present-day physiological explanations of perception are in essence no different. Light waves and sound waves on the one hand, and neural impulses and synapses on the other, are similarly a matter basically of movement, not matter; they too are a form of "acting" and of "being acted upon." In contemporary Western thought, however, this movement is itself never thematized; it remains an unacknowledged and unelaborated given of the natural world, animate and inanimate. Yet without movement there would be no perception. Indeed, movement is foundational at every level of perception, from the physiological — whether of an Aristotelian or 20th-century variety — to the experiential, the latter including the perception of objects as well as quality.[10] Given Aristotle's explicit recognition of the essential role of movement in perception, it is not surprising to find him affirming the centrality of movement in the "activities" of perception and an intimate bond between movement and Nature — physiology, of course, being included in the latter. The epigraphs that began this chapter aptly epitomize these affirmations. They furthermore document a closely related observation of Nussbaum in her study of Aristotle's *De Motu Animalium*, namely, that "an essential part of [Aristotle's] search for the best account of animal physiology was an examination of the goal-directed motions of the heavenly spheres" (Nussbaum 1978:163). Animal physiology is, in other words, a matter of motion; and both animal motion and heavenly motion are instances of the principle of motion that constitutes Nature. Accordingly, the two kinds of motion are to be studied and understood together precisely because Nature is fundamentally a principle of motion. From this Aristotelian perspective, a proper epistemology as well as proper ontology of Nature hangs in the balance of a fundamental understanding of movement. Taking light waves, electromagnetic waves, gravitational forces, neurological firings, synapses, vibrations, and other such kinetic phenomena seriously *as movement*, one could readily say the same from the perspective of Galilean science.

We might note that Aristotle's focal concern with movement is not idiosyncratic in the least; movement is frequently at the core of understandings of life and cosmology in ancient Greek writings. The concern with motion permeates virtually all branches of knowledge because it is everywhere apparent that movement *is* the core of life and cosmology — at the very least to people ungroomed in the materialist tradition of a post-Cartesian, Galilean science and/or ontologically and epistemologically unsympathetic to its present-day radical course. Moreover in view of the etymology of the word *physiology*, it is not surprising that Aristotle pinpoints movement as the foundation of his physiological explanation of perception. The word's Greek etymology specifies Nature in a broad sense, not merely the functional nature of the *insides* of living bodies. Aristotle's physiology of perception is cosmologically resonant in just this sense. His basically kinetic explication of perception offers what might be termed a *cosmologically causal explanation*. Because its point of departure is Nature, the explanation is perforce dynamically tethered: one needs simply to live in the natural world to observe and in turn acknowledge "motion and stationariness in respect of place, growth, decrease, and alteration." In calling attention to these cosmological features of the natural world, the epigraphs clearly underscore Aristotle's judgment about the primacy of movement: unless we understand what *motion* is, Aristotle affirms, we will not understand nature. Accordingly, we will not understand the *physiology of perception*. In turn, we will hardly be able to explain it.

The relationship between motion and nature can be amplified in ways that extend Aristotle's thought. In fact, following along his lines of thought we realize that unless we understand motion, we cannot understand the perception of quality, for an understanding of the perception of quality is tied to an understanding of the physiology of perception, which is tied to an understanding of Nature, which is tied to an understanding of movement. To elucidate this complex of understandings, it is instructive to note first that motion is primitive in precisely the sense in which Burnyeat says awareness pure and simple — or as he specifically puts it, "awareness, no more and no less" (Burnyeat 1992:22) — is "primitive" in Aristotle's notion of perception: it is there "from the start," he says (Burnyeat 1992:21). In just this sense, *movement* is primitive in Aristotle's account; it is *movement* that is there in an original sense in that movement is at the very core of nature. Being of the very nature of nature from the start, it cannot be ontologically *explained* in an originative sense, for there is nothing to explain. As we saw earlier with respect to quality, were such an explanation forthcoming, it would be akin to an explanation of why there is something rather than nothing. Its lack of originary explanation, however, does not rule out its *description*. Indeed, movement can be described as it manifests itself in its various forms — of growth, decay, alteration, and so forth. Aristotle's formula for understanding perceived quality derives from just this understanding of movement. Quality too is there "from the start." It too is primitive. It too cannot be ontologically explained in an originative sense. But it can be described as it manifests itself and is perceived in all of its various sensory forms.

Primitiveness is the first point of commonality between movement and quality. In addition to being there from the start, quality, like motion, is objectless. It is not a thing. The perception of quality can thus be readily examined in the terms in which Aristotle describes it: as basically a kinetic process, not a series of material events as such. The most powerful argument against a basically materialist interpretation of Aristotle's account of perception — such as that which Sorabji offers — is that Aristotle himself would have so professed it. Surely it is difficult to believe that Aristotle would have withheld such precise explanatory details as "the eye jelly goes red" when one perceives red if such precise explanatory details were what he had in mind when he said that in perception, one receives the sensible forms of things without the matter. Furthermore, and as was shown earlier, *activity*, as Aristotle speaks of it in the context of perception, is not a designated series of material changes; the activity of giving forth odors, sounds, flavors, moistness, hardness, and so on, and the correlative activity of sensing — hearing, smelling, tasting, and so on — are motional phenomena. They have basically to do with *movement*, with the setting in motion of the medium and of the organ of sense, respectively. It is precisely the power to set in motion — a power natural to objects of sense, i.e. *qualities*, and to media — that generates the perception of quality. Impartial extension of Aristotle's thought leads obviously not to a world conceived fundamentally as matter but to a world conceived fundamentally in kinetic terms. Indeed, impartial extension of Aristotle's thought leads directly to the idea of an already animated world, a world in which motion is not only central but in which that which has the power to set in motion can make things happen. It leads, in short, to the idea of a dynamic world, a world of kinetic powers. The phenomenon of perception is but another instance of this dynamic world.

Now the extremist materialist thesis that recognizes nature — or matter — only "as physics and chemistry describe it" does not and cannot acknowledge or thematize this kinetic power. It can only mark its effects. Consider, for example, the notion of attraction. Just what does this term mean other than that two bodies *move toward each other*. *Why* there is this movement or *that* there is this movement — or more broadly, *that there is movement* — are questions and ideas that seldom surface. Their surfacing would preempt matter pure and simple as the foundation of all of nature, animate and inanimate. Marking the effects of, but not remarking upon movement itself, preserves the rule of matter. More specifically, it preserves the unquestioned hegemony of substance as the ultimate key to explaining the universe by freeing it from what would threaten it most: a recognition of movement, along with its troublesome retinue of cognate notions — animation, animism, teleology, and the like — notions that are anathema to inflexible materialist doctrine. Movement, after all, indicates not only something lively and dynamic; it implies as well an agent or motion-empowering force of some sort or other. In effect, to wonder about movement, that is, to become involved in questions regarding its nature — the forms in which it manifests itself, for example, or its intricate and complex possibilities — is risky in the extreme. Physicist S. Sambursky, whose writings on early Greek science form an otherwise interesting and thoughtful trilogy, makes the hazard of such inquiry quite clear, in particular, the hazard of being unscientific. In the context of his praiseful discussion of the atomists, he speaks beratingly of how Aristotle "severely criticizes the absence of a cause of the movements of the atoms in the doctrine of Leucippus and Democritus" (Sambursky 1956: 112). He quotes passages from Aristotle's *On the Heavens* and *Metaphysics* in illustration. For example, from the latter text he cites the following passage: "They [those such as Leucippus and Plato who "suppose eternal actuality"] say there is always movement. But why and what this movement is they do not say, nor, if the world moves in this way or that, do they tell us the cause of its doing so" (1071b32–34). But Sambursky does not tell us the reason for Aristotle's concern with the nature and cause of movement. That is, he does not give us the context of Aristotle's reproach, which is precisely that "*Matter will surely not move itself*" (*Metaphysics* 1071b30; italics added). In a word, matter must be *animated*. In the final analysis, to make sense of the physical and zoological worlds, animation and animate forms must be accounted for: they are foundational to Nature and to an understanding of Nature. It is because matter must be animated that the atomists (and actually Plato as well, as Aristotle's text shows) suppose eternal movement. Only thus can atomists sustain their doctrine. Aristotle's wrestlings with the cause of movement, with the idea of unceasing or eternal movement, with an unmoved mover, and the like, are straightaway understandable in this context. If "matter will surely not move itself," then surely "a principle of motion" must be found. Understanding a dynamic, animate world is contingent on such a principle. Aristotle's wrestlings are an expression of this necessity. His inquiries into the nature of motion, the cause of movement, and so on, are important in both an explorative and descriptive sense; they are bona fide *wonderings* about the dynamic world in which humans, animals, and plants live. They eventuate in reflective analyses of movement in terms of its actuality and potentiality, its different possible forms — random or regular, for example — its different possible originations — by nature, for instance, or by an outside force — and the effect of these different originations on the way in which the affected things move, and so on. Hence, when Sambursky goes on to say that "It was a sound scientific instinct that saved the founders of the atomic school from this mesh of reasoning in which Aristotle got himself entangled" and when he furthermore commends the founders of the atomic school for not "begin[ning] by raising the problem of the cause of movement, but accept[ing] movement as a given fact" (Sambursky 1956: 112), he is articulating the very paradigm of neglect of movement that characterizes Western science and philosophy. "A given fact" has its price, most obviously in deflecting one from any reflection upon it. To paraphrase anthropologist Daniel Moerman, "A given fact is a social agreement to stop thinking" (pers. comm.). In contrast, reflection upon movement discloses the primitiveness of movement and the objectlessness of movement. Each aspect is a point of departure for further reflection. All such reflections are the very antithesis of "accept[ing] movement as a given fact."

In general terms, we might say that extremist notions of matter — so prevalent in, and so well promulgated culturally by present-day Western science and philosophy, and so mesmerically absorbed too by a material-driven culture — straightaway preclude both thinking about movement and grasping in an empirical as well as theoretical sense how form informs matter and matter, form. This is because they straightaway preclude acknowledging anything that is not an object *as such* (or, if a question of "function," is not a function of an object *as such*), in other words, anything that is not a manipulable material thing that one can pin down, measure, and examine.[11] In these circumstances, the most striking way of bringing home the phenomenon of quality, the way in which its formal and material natures mutually temper one another and the dynamics of its perception, is in the light of aesthetic creation and aesthetic experience. Indeed, perhaps precisely because it is a question of *quality*, the phenomenon of perception, and particularly Aristotle's *physiological*, i.e. kinetic, explanation of perception, is best elucidated in the analogous terms of aesthetic experience.

7.   Excursus II: The aesthetics of quality

In aesthetic experience, we do not see quadriceps, biceps, or gluteals bulging now and again in contraction; we do not hear three 60 decibel G's followed by an 80 decibel E; we do not see a few flecks of greenish paint with a few daubs of red beside them; we do not see a fairly heavy-looking chunk of gray metal sitting on a stand. In aesthetic experience, we perceive the quality of whatever is being presented: a dance, a symphony, a painting, a sculpture. We straightaway perceive quality because it is perceptively there in the art work. It inheres in the presented work and, correlatively, it constitutes the very essence of our aesthetic seeing or hearing. The perception of quality in aesthetic experience is thus fundamentally identical to everyday perception as Aristotle describes it: "the activity of the sensible object and that of the sense is one and the same activity, [even though] the distinction between their being remains" (*De Anima* 425b27–28). The nature of quality of immediate moment here concerns not its dynamic character but its actuality. In other words, just as a qualitative coincidence obtains between what is there qualitatively in a work of art and what is there qualitatively for us in our seeing or hearing it, so a qualitative coincidence obtains between everyday sounding and hearing, between the everyday visibility of things and our seeing them, between the everyday odoriferousness of things and our smelling them, and so on — between what Aristotle identifies basically as "activities"[12] — even though in each case an ontological distinction remains, an ontological distinction between what, in aesthetic experience, we would distinguish as object and subject, and between what, in everyday experience, Aristotle distinguishes as object of sense and organ of sense. Quality is thus dually anchored, in aesthetic as in everyday experience. It is neither free-floating — an ineffable or airy nothing — nor a figment of mind — a purely subjective event, a fantasy, or whatever. It inheres in the object of sense and is sensorily localized for the subject of perception. A range of concrete examples from the world of art will clarify these beginning understandings of quality in further ways and provide the context for a closer examination of how basic facets of Aristotle's philosophy of mind in general and his account of perception in particular accord in fact with the fundamental nature of perception.

To begin with, quality is firmly anchored in the material nature of any particular art object. Consider, for example, Leonardo da Vinci's *Mona Lisa*, Monet's *Water-Lillies*, Beethoven's Fifth Symphony, Pagliaccio's aria "Vesti la giubba," Twyla Tharp's *Push Comes to Shove*, Bill Irwin's *The Regard of Flight*. Each of these art works is uniquely enmattered. Its quality, however, is not reducible to the work's material nature. While the latter can certainly be analyzed, the material features that are in turn examined do not in the end add up to the quality of the work. One may discover how a certain phrase in Beethoven's Fifth, for example, or in Tharp's *Push Comes to Shove* has a certain qualitative character in virtue of its particular tonal or choreographic structure and of the way in which the particular tonal sequence of notes or choreographed sequence of movements is played or executed — at a slow-paced or rapid tempo, with a lilting or driving energy, and so on. Furthermore one may discover how the phrase has a certain qualitative character in virtue of a particular instrumentation (flutes, oboes, violins, for example) or in virtue of particular bodies (tall, short, male, female, for example). Material nature thus constrains form, but the quality of the work is not the sum of such constraints together with each of their qualitative effects. Whatever material feature might be analyzed, it inheres in the global form and has no autonomous power of its own. Hence, whatever the particular qualitative effect of a particular material feature, it cannot be attached to another effect, and another, and another, and so on, so that in the end particular material features can be said to carry certain qualitative parts of the qualitative whole. Aesthetic quality permeates the whole of the presented form and is not materially reducible. Aristotle's conception of an intimate connection between form and matter, and of constraints of the latter upon the former, accords in striking ways with the nature of aesthetic quality.

A further way of bringing out the nature of aesthetic quality — and again, with pointed affinities to Aristotle's understanding of perception — is to consider what is commonly called "the medium" — the material stuff of which each art work is created: sound, color, movement, wood, and so on. Each art medium has certain possibilities inherent in it. These possibilities delimit the formal nature or qualitative possibilities of the work. Consider, for example, the qualitative character of the Mona Lisa and of Pagliaccio's aria. We can in each case examine the qualitative character from the viewpoint of the particular medium in which the art work is created. Numerous aspects of the painting may be analyzed from this perspective: the hues and intensities of its colors, the contours and spatial orientation of its subject, the organization and shape of its volumes, and so on. Analogously, numerous aspects of the aria may be analyzed: its major and minor harmonic modes, its phrasing and accents, the dynamics of its ascending and descending motifs, and so on. The very terms in which we make each analysis testifies to the uniqueness of each medium.[13] They testify to the fact that one cannot put what is qualitatively created in the medium of the Mona Lisa into the medium of Pagliaccio's aria, or vice versa, any more than that one's experience of seeing can be heard, or that one's experience of hearing can be seen. In other words, the qualitative character created by Leonardo da Vinci in his painting of the Mona Lisa is not something that can be rendered musically nor can the qualitative character created by Ruggiero Leoncavallo in his aria, "Vesti la giubba," be rendered visually. When we analyze any art work in terms of the medium in which it is created, we find an intimate relationship between the work's material instantiation and the qualitative nature of the work. We find that quality is constrained by the particular material that is artistically worked. This kind of constraint is coincident with Aristotle's notion of there being qualities peculiar to each sense. At a deeper level, it is coincident with his notion of there being an elemental nature peculiar to the medium which is set in motion by an object of sense and which itself sets in motion an organ of sense. What is elementally *fire*, for instance, cannot be set in motion by hardness. A medium is constrained by its very nature. Just so in the realm of art: media cannot be worked in ways contrary to their nature.

Earlier discussions and examples of the intimate connection between form and matter have shown how material nature is equally and reciprocally constrained by form.

Works of art exemplify this very same kind of constraint. Whether the work is in the process of being created by an artist in a studio, or, being a finished work, is being brought to life by an artist in person in performance, the form of the work bends matter to its will; in the process, material aspects of the work are muted. When Aristotle speaks of matter *underlying* form but being at the same time inseparable from it, he could well be describing this very aspect of art, i.e. the intimate yet constraining relationship of form to matter. The result of this relationship is the creation and experience of quality. Quality literally takes form with the forming of materials, but this literal forming — this literal act of composing, painting, sculpting, or choreographing, or alternatively, this literal act of bringing forth form in performance — is not the forming of an object *as such*. The subtlety of the Mona Lisa's smile is not an *object*; the anguished pathos of Pagliaccio is not an *object*; the sumptuous splendor of Monet's *Water-Lillies* is not an *object*; Bill Irwin's comically impossible descents into a trunk are not *objects*. All such examples attest to the fact that aesthetic quality is a *formal* aspect of an art work that is not itself something an artist shapes directly. It is, after all, *immaterial*: one cannot pick up aesthetic quality, turn it about, or move it from here to there, for example. It is something over and above the medium itself, something over and above the materiality of sound, movement, wood, color, and so on, and their peculiar manipulative possibilities. It is what an artist creates with his or her emerging composition and/or brings to life with the performance of the finished work. Aesthetic quality is thus not only objectless; it is primitive with respect to any particular work of art. It is there from the start and is elaborated to the very end of the work. It comes with the nature of sound, movement, color, wood, metal, and so on, as these media are put in the service of art. All such examples attest equally to the fact that aesthetic quality cannot be materially explained. Like movement, and like quality generally, it can only be analyzed and in turn described. While as we have seen, an analysis of aesthetic quality may lead back to the way in which materials have been worked, reference to materials — or in more general terms, reference to facets of the *medium* of the art — serves merely to evoke the work's aesthetic quality, *not to convert it to matter*. Indeed, and again as we have already seen, aesthetic quality goes beyond the worked materials; it surpasses the material nature of the work and constrains matter in just this sense. It demands of matter that it realize the form being created — the form that the artist is quintessentially attentive to in the process of working and is at pains to achieve in critically questioning the work, standing back from it, editing, augmenting, shading, tightening, and so on. It is in fact the artist who, in the process of creating, demands of matter that it realize the form being created. In the process of creation, matter is of aesthetic moment only — but crucially and centrally — insofar as it adheres or does not adhere to the intent and/or character of the form being created. In sum, artists work materials in virtue of an overriding sense of what they are forming, an overriding sense of the quality of what they are doing or have done with the materials of their art.

A final and quintessential aspect of aesthetic quality emerges from just this consideration. This aspect stems from the fact that quality is dynamic; it is fundamentally kinetic; it moves through a work and — as has been repeatedly emphasized — is neither a thing to be found in the work nor a facet of the work that can in any sense be objectified. Aesthetic quality is quite literally created by movement, not only as in a series of gliding leaps across a stage but as in a cluster of hard brush strokes on a canvas. The gliding leaps are smooth, even, continuous — they skim the surface; the hard brush strokes are stout, firm, strong — they leave a clearly splayed imprint. The series of leaps could have been different; so also the cluster of brush strokes. Obviously, if the manner of execution changes, the quality changes: there might be punctuated rather than gliding leaps, for example, delicate rather than hard brush strokes. It is readily apparent, then, that the manner in which the materials of any art are worked constitutes a kinetic technique of some kind. Movement thus clearly enters into the creation of aesthetic quality from the very beginning. An artist's technique is always in some sense a bodily technique; form is, in turn, always dynamic; and quality is, in turn, always kinetic.

We might conclude, then, by saying that aesthetic form is created by movement which leaves a qualitative trail in its wake. But the nexus of form, quality, and movement runs even deeper. The quality of a work is not simply the formal aspect of a technique, an aspect we can notice and analyze reflectively in terms of the way in which an artist has kinetically engaged and utilized materials. Quality is coincident with the created form itself; it is there, present in the work, and is immediately apparent in genuinely aesthetic experiences of the work. This essential coincidence of form and quality is most readily apparent in the case of dance and music because movement is transparent in these arts: in each case, form itself is in motion. But it is no less so in the other arts — *or* in everyday experience. In fact, the most economical and convincing way of exemplifying the essential coincidence of form and quality at this point — and of bringing to the fore its ubiquity and its depth — is to consider basic facts of life, basic *kinetic* facts of life. Indeed, a consideration of these basic kinetic facts will lead us back full circle to everyday perception and to the enigma of taking in the sensible forms of things without the matter, but enriched now by essential insights into the formal and kinetic nature of aesthetic quality.

8.   The coincidence of form and quality in everyday life

What is naturally organic naturally changes. Aristotle is profoundly and consistently concerned with such change, characterizing the fundamental kinds of change in animals and plants as deriving from "a principle of motion and of stationariness" within the living individual itself. For Aristotle, a principle of motion thus informs organic

life; it is basic, essential; it enunciates the fundamental way in which organic life simply *is*. Now clearly, this principle of motion cannot even now, in the twentieth century,
be explained by appeal to the existence of matter "as physics and chemistry describe
it." It can be neither derived from nor reduced to matter. *The principle is precisely a
principle of movement*. An appeal to matter "as physics and chemistry describe it"
clearly fails from the start to recognize the primitiveness of movement, much less the
need to reflect upon movement and to articulate a principle of motion fundamental
to the whole of Nature. It fails, for example, to recognize that the growth of something
living — whether fish, fowl, flora, or whatever — is more than an increase in physical
size, just as it fails to recognize that the decay of something living is more than a dimi-
nution in physical size. Growth and decay are principles of life, principles of form that
are derivable and reducible neither to matter itself nor to mathematizations of matter — to quantitative equations, statistical probabilities, and the like. The principles
are not thereby esoteric; they are grounded in what is empirically observable. Anyone
can observe quite straightforwardly the growth and decay of living things, just as they
can observe quite straightforwardly a leaf or an apple falling from a tree. Granted,
the observation of the growth and decay of living things is temporally extended in
a way that the observation of the fall of a leaf or an apple is not, the two kinds of
observations are nonetheless empirically analogous: we can experience either kind of
phenomenon first-hand virtually any time we wish because each is a natural phenomenon; each is a dynamic aspect of the organic.[14] Moreover not only are the two phenomena empirically analogous. A metaphysical or cosmological bond unites them.
However much the law of gravity explains in the way of falling leaves and apples, it
does not and cannot basically explain *the fall* of falling bodies, any more than a principle of motion, however much it explains in the way of growth and decay, does or can
basically explain *motion*, specifically, motion in the form of maturation and molder-
ing, development and deterioration. In short, a kinetic metaphysical primitiveness
grounds both phenomena. Both phenomena are not merely *facts* of life, as rules such
as the *law* of gravity might suggest, or as actuarial *tables* or developmental *grids*, or
other mathematically-arrived-at formulae might suggest; they are *kinetic* facts of life.
These facts are plainly as much facts of non-life as of life, precisely as bracing winds,
rippling waters, the revolution of cosmic bodies, continental drift, and more, attest.
Kinetic facts of life and non-life are indeed primitive. The law of gravity to which we
advert in explaining the fall of a leaf or an apple, and which we easily and comfortably
accept as explaining the fall of a leaf or an apple, is indeed basically no more than a
recognition of the fact that in the world in which we live, *forces impel things to move*. If
we ask why we live in a universe in which *forces impel things to move* or why the world
is such that *forces impel things to move*, we cannot answer in terms of mere matter. As
Aristotle points out, "Matter will surely not move itself." We can answer only in terms
of movement, which is to say only by reflecting upon movement, reflecting at length

and in depth upon its ubiquity, its variety, its foundational structure, its physical and metaphysical significance, its organic ties, its qualitative nature, and much more. On the basis of our reflections, grounded as they are in our experience and our observations of the world, we should properly conclude that in order to explain growth or decay or the fall of an apple — or the rushing of rivers, or the attraction of magnets — we need a principle that recognizes a dynamic universe, not a static one. Nature is indeed a principle of motion and change. Indeed, why would forces impel things to move — to fall, to grow, to decay, to revolve, to flow — unless movement were at the heart of the universe, unless *not matter, but motion were primitive.*

Whether forces that impel things to move are essentially from without — as with falling apples — or essentially from within — as with growth and decay — the dynamic they create is qualitative through and through. This is because forces that impel things to move, move them in a certain way. The principle of motion they enunciate is inherently qualitative; it is inherently dynamic. The dynamic might be attenuated, explosive, expansive, discontinuous, volatile, or feeble. The very terms by which we describe — or try to describe — a dynamic straightaway attests to its qualitative kinetic nature. Whatever the created dynamic, it is that dynamic that is imparted to — or, to borrow a term from Aristotle, "received" by — whatever is impelled to move. Organic change is thereby always qualitative. Organic things grow and decay, for example, in remarkably complex ways marked by a variety of dynamic features — by rapidity, oscillation, attrition, continuity, ebullition, dilation, and so on, or in finer descriptive terms, by shriveling, crumbling, inflating, collapsing, vibrating, expanding, congealing, and so on. Organic things — and many inorganic ones as well — furthermore accelerate, open, close, rush forth, spiral, turn, pulsate; they are vitalized — *animated* — in myriad ways. With more pointed reference to everyday creaturely movement, they furthermore saunter, run, skip, slide, pause, fling, pound, clench, twist, circle, pounce, flit, soar, stalk, hover, flee, munch, swallow, chew, peel, suck, and much, much more — each of these motions being imbued with its own peculiar qualitative dynamic. A principle of motion indeed informs animate things themselves. Moreover this principle of motion manifests itself in a complex dynamic in a broader sense. The complex dynamic is apparent not only over the course of a day — as, for example, in the dynamic of an ocean with respect to swelling and receding tides and driving or breezy winds — and over the course of a week — as, for example, in the dynamics of an infant learning and finally mastering the fine art of walking — but over a period of time such as a pregnancy, a journey, an illness, or more generally, a year, or even a lifetime. A complex dynamic is evident with respect to such periods: the pregnancy, the journey, the illness, the year, or the lifetime takes on a certain qualitative shape, a certain dynamic, in a way similar to the way in which a drama takes on a certain qualitative shape when it shifts perspectives, changes scenes or locations, lapses into a still calm, becomes intricately more complicated, builds to a climax, reaches a dénouement, and finally ends.

Shaped by a principle of motion and stationariness, quality courses through life. It is of the essence of movement, and movement is of the essence of dynamic form.

Artists clearly know this. We might indeed recall in this context the common notion of art as "organic form."[15] Not only do musicians and dancers testify to the basically motional, hence organic, character of their art in speaking of its dynamics, but painters, sculptors, dramatists, and other artists do the same. How a monologue is delivered, how a dialogue is paced, how one volume of space opens into the next, how two lines play off one another or converge in the distance — all are of the same qualitative order as how a voice breaks off here and surges forth there, or how a gesture expands into a full-body movement. In short, aesthetic form is *animated* in the same way that organic life is originally *animated*. Movement, thus quality, flows through both. In this respect, what Husserl says of *mind* with respect to *animation* is analogous to what has been said of *quality* with respect to *motion*: "*Animation*," Husserl says, "designates the way in which mind acquires a locality in the spatial world, its spatialization, as it were, and together with its corporal support, acquires *reality*" (1977: 101). Just so, "*Motion* designates the way in which quality acquires a locality in the spatial world, its spatialization, as it were, and together with its corporal support, acquires *reality*." Animation and motion are virtually synonymous in pointing us toward what is primitive. The physical substratum of what is organic — whether identified as material nature or "corporal support" — gains its meaning and its value from movement. In effect, if there is "an alien sense of the physical," it can only be the alien sense of the physical laid down by a post-Cartesian, Galilean science. Kinetic facts of everyday life do not lie any more than do kinetic facts of aesthetic form. However overlayered and ultimately effaced by cultural groomings, what we perceive first and foremost is quality; movement and quality are coincident.

This fundamental form of perceptual experience is confirmed not only through serious and careful reflection upon our own everyday adult experience. It is confirmed by studies of infants and their experiences of quality, experiences that infant psychiatrist and developmental psychologist Daniel Stern describes in detail as "vitality affects." It is of considerable interest to note that Stern introduces his discussion of "vitality affects" with the question, "What do we mean by this, and why is it necessary to add a new term for certain forms of human experience? It is necessary because many qualities of feeling that occur do not fit into our existing lexicon or taxonomy of affects." He goes on to say that "These elusive qualities are better captured by *dynamic, kinetic terms*, such as 'surging', 'fading away', 'fleeting', 'explosive', 'crescendo', 'decrescendo', 'bursting', 'drawn out', and so on. These qualities of experience are most certainly sensible to infants and of great daily, even momentary, importance." (Stern 1985: 54; italics added). In brief, quality is both fundamental and fundamentally kinetic. Before language creeps in and a typically Western adulthood settles us down to a blindered and reductive materialist outlook, we perceive a world abounding in quality and we sense ourselves moving in qualitative ways. A principle of motion precisely on the order of the one Aristotle articulates leads to an elucidation of this foundational level of meaning because the principle is already there at its core.

9. The semantics of quality: A natural history of form

An understanding of quality must finally be elaborated in terms of a natural history. By present-day standards, Aristotle would be said to have had two vocations existing side by side: philosophy and natural history (and/or natural science). But consultation of Aristotle's work shows quite otherwise. As previous observations of his account of perception indicate, Aristotle's philosophy and natural history are intertwined; they are mutually informing and enhancing, both epistemologically and metaphysically. A wider estimation of his philosophy of mind bears out this intimate connection; his philosophy of mind is a bio-zoological philosophy.

Aristotle elucidates a progression of psychic powers: from the nutritive to the appetitive, to sensation, to locomotion, to thinking. Although cultural groomings might dispose one to think this progression an axiological hierarchy, it is not. It is an empirically-based metaphysical one. Food, for example, is on the same footing as any other power; it is "essentially related to what has soul in it" (*De Anima* 416b11–12), just as appetition, sensation, locomotion, and thinking are related — and no more related — to what has soul in it. When Aristotle speaks of food as a power, he is not merely acknowledging its power "to increase the bulk of what is fed by it" (416b12), but acknowledging its power to "[maintain] the being of what is fed," for only "so long as the process of nutrition continues" can the being of what is fed continue (416b13–14). It is thus not surprising that Aristotle explicitly indicates and several times over — not argumentatively but observationally — that plants and animals exist along the same psychic continuum; different forms of life have different arrays of power but are fundamentally related. In particular, plants have the power of nutrition alone; with sensation and appetition come animals, a different form of living thing, but one no less lacking in the power of nutrition (413b1–4). Indeed, as Aristotle points out, "[the] power of self-nutrition can be separated from the other powers mentioned, but not they from it — in mortal beings at least" (413a32–33). In short, Aristotle's analysis of psychic powers shows in essence how mind — *psyche* — and life are of a piece throughout. His philosophy of mind might indeed be characterized as *evolutionary* in that it is based on, and takes into serious account, continuities in forms of life. The import of this integrated perspective, this natural philosophy or philosophical bio-zoology, will become all the more apparent in what follows: an exposition of the semantics of quality.

Quality is quintessential to animate life. It is there from the start in the context of finding food, escaping danger, assessing obstacles or resistances, signalling and recognizing a possible mate, exploring a terrain, and so on. Bees, lizards, bats, sharks, fireflies, dolphins, spiders, locusts, gorillas, wolves, lobster, trout — all animate forms are semantically attuned to what is out there in the world. They are attuned to colorations, patternings, contours, volumes, stridencies, rustlings, currents, breezes, obdurateness, limpness, moistness, scents, pungencies, bitternesses, and so on. Their progenitors were no less so, at least those who survived to reproduce. What is out there in the world in a qualitative sense is of singular moment to life and to survival. Without quality, no distinctions would exist. One could not in fact measure anything because no distinctive thing would exist to measure. What we would otherwise characterize as *things* would be a conglomerate mass: nothing but sheer on-going matter with no inherently distinctive parts. Insofar as no distinctions could be made among things, there would be no possibility of differentiating rotting flesh from a possible meal, a smooth edge from a rough one, a cry from a bellow, softness from hardness, and so on. Moreover without quality, there would be no possibility of differentiating young from old, male from female, a non-aggressive stance from an aggressive one, a nipple from a toe, a head end from a tail end, and so on. In short, the life of animate forms would perish before it was born because it is contingent on quality; it is *structured* in quality, quality that is out there in the world and that is apprehended as such. Indeed, we cannot imagine *Umwelts* short of a qualitative world and qualitatively different senses of that world. The two conditions — objects of sense and organs of sense, in Aristotle's qualitative understanding of those terms — are equally essential. Not only does "every organism … ha[ve] a world of its own because it has an experience of its own," as philosopher Ernst Cassirer has glossed Jakob von Uexküll's basic biological tenet (Cassirer 1970: 25), but every organism has an experience of its own because it has a world of its own. Animate life is at once world-specific and species-specific. Hence, while it is true that we find "only 'fly things'" in the world of a fly (Cassirer 1970: 25), we also find only flies in niches suitable to them; while we find only "sea urchin things" in the world of a sea urchin (Cassirer 1970: 25), we also find only sea urchins in niches suitable to them. An *existential fit* (Sheets-Johnstone 1986a)[16] obtains between animate forms of life and their worlds. This fit is founded upon the presence of quality: certain qualitative worlds exist and correlatively certain animate forms exist having the power to make sense of those qualitative worlds.

Anyone who determinately studies or even spontaneously ponders the phenomenon of *form* in biology — or art — cannot but acknowledge its import to an understanding of what is organically vital to a thing's being both the thing that it is and the viable thing that it is, viable in the sense of livability in face of a particular world. Swiss biologist Adolph Portmann describes just such fundamental formal aspects of creaturely life in terms of what he calls *form values*. He does so in the context of studying highly varied, oftentimes complex and subtle bodily appearances and behaviors of animals, pinpointing in precise ways in each case just how meaning is *formally* generated (Portmann 1967).[17] His concern is basically social, not environmental; he does not consider values that constitute qualitative aspects of a creature's world: deep crevices, jagged terrains, high winds, lush vegetation, irregular stones, meandering rivers, and the like. His richly detailed descriptions of form values in animal morphology and behavior is matched by his equally rich observations of commonalities and differences among animals. For example, he observes that "there is an important, if little-noticed, boundary which divides the large group of molluscs [a phylum comprising soft-bodied, hard-shelled animals such as bivalves and gastropods, although some molluscs, e.g. slugs and octopuses, have lost their hard shell]: the dividing line which separates the organic forms which can see one another and those which are never able to look at each other — a boundary between two stages in the intensity of living" (Portmann 1967:108). What is morphologically and/or behaviorally there to be seen by others is specifically patterned — for example, an ornamental decoration, a deceptive design, bands that appear with the closing of wings, ocelli that appear with the opening of wings, the assumption of a special posture such as a vertical alignment or a crouch, the execution of a special movement such as a baring of teeth, a flattening of the ears, an extension of the hand, a lowering of the head, and so on. Such aspects of animate life are semantically charged; they are formally distinct.

Now clearly what Portmann calls form values defines a *qualitative* morphology and behavior basic to animate forms. A creature is what it is *qualitatively*: it is to begin with a such-and-such — a "this," as Aristotle says — which means that it has these contours, these colorations, these dynamic patterns of movement, these postural possibilities — in a word, *this qualitative character*. But it is furthermore a *young* this, a *male* this, a *sexually signalling* this, an *excited, threatening* this, a *quietly attentive* this, and so on, all in virtue of quality, a formal patterning of one kind or another. Portmann describes the latter two kinds of value under the heading "form as an expression of inwardness," distinguishing such values from those arising through morphology — for example, those having to do with age patternings and behaviors. Whatever the nature of the value, however, form is never equivalent to merely a material marking or material happening of some sort or other — whether a matter of stripes, spots, ocelli, changes in pupillary dilation, spatial positioning, bodily alignment, or whatever. Form values are values attaching to forms of life. They resonate with intra- and inter-specific meaning. Quality is thus not simply a surface feature — mere marks on a piece of skin, for instance. Quality reverberates semantically; it signals a density of being, livingness, an animate form. That it does so means that life is neither an empty shell of markings nor an empty shell of doings, but a qualitatively structured semantic, which, properly understood, demands a natural history of form.

When we compare Portmann's richly detailed empirical study of form values in animate life with "matter as physics and chemistry describe it," we can appreciate how far-fetched it is to take matter as primitive, attempting on its basis to "[work] up to the explanation of the secondary qualities on the one side and animal perceptual capacities on the other." Primitive matter — "matter as physics and chemistry describe it" — is semantically vacuous; it has no inherent value; it is capable neither of generating nor of comprehending quality; it is not in the least dynamic; it is incapable of moving itself. Indeed, if we take matter as primitive, we align ourselves with a Galilean world, an *un*-natural world that cannot possibly give rise either to a *natural* world or to a *natural* history. When Galileo says that "whenever he conceives of "any material or corporeal substance," that he is compelled to think of it "as bounded, and as having this or that shape; as being large or small in relation to other things," and so on; and when he goes on to say that in so conceiving any material or corporeal substance, "my mind does not feel compelled to bring in as necessary accompaniments" any sense of "white or red, bitter or sweet, noisy or silent, and of sweet or foul odor" (Galileo 1957:272), he is clearly thinking outside of a natural history. One might say that, quite fortunately with respect to the realities of his own life, his mindbody knew better. Thinking outside of a natural history, one arrives at matter pure and simple, matter that cannot possibly engender form values, that cannot possibly eventuate in feeding behavior much less social — or anti-social — behavior, that cannot possibly set itself in motion, in a word, *matter that cannot possibly give rise to animate form.* Clearly, animals — humans included — are not static volumes of matter, and neither is the world — or the particular worlds — in which animals live. Animation is vital to an understanding of the organic and the inorganic because both are through and through dynamic, through and through qualitative, and thereby through and through formally distinct. They are in fact in perpetual animation — attracting, repulsing, accelerating, decelerating, joining, splitting, growing, decomposing, bending, twisting, turning, constricting, expanding. They are, in short, moving in myriad ways. They are both foundationally the very antithesis of matter pure and simple because they are both fundamentally *animated.*

To acknowledge the fact that quality is quintessential to life is to realize straightaway that quality is fundamental to an understanding of animate form and of lifeworlds. It is fundamental to the way the world and living things are. In effect, a reinsertion of quality into the natural world of appearances is as mandatory as is a reinstatement of quality into the living world of the senses. A natural science without a natural history is in fact unnatural; it is unable to account for life because it has enshrined matter and left movement behind. A lifeless natural science cannot in fact even properly account for a lifeless world since, in elevating matter in the extreme, it favors a near exclusive attention on what is solid and ignores, or tends to ignore, the basic question, from whence comes all this matter? A lifeless natural science ignores fluidity, dynamics, change, the primordiality of motion. It fastens on the hard materiality of matter, its thingness, its manipulability and management, its operational control; it fastens on what is massively there, however infinitesimal, and hence on what is, if even only metaphorically, amenable to being handled and regulated. Poet-essayist Paul Valéry succinctly captures both the essence and the epistemological-metaphysical liabilities of this reigning vision when, in the context of his simple but penetrating reflections upon a mollusc, he observes first that "*I know only what I know how to handle*," and later that "I observe first of all that living nature is unable to work directly with solids" (Valéry 1964b: 21, 23).[18] His conjoined remarks, lucid and provocative, prompt us to ask whether our epistemological limitations and metaphysical predilections do not bias our epistemology and metaphysics of nature. They prompt us to ask whether matter should not in fact be *problematized* — to use current and highly fashionable jargon — rather than taken for granted. Clearly, matter cannot explain movement. It cannot explain why there is growth or change or attraction or electromagnetic forces or form values or anything else that is dynamic and productive of form. A materialist's material nature, as we have seen, cannot explain quality, not even in an adaptationist sense. This would be to explain why there is skin, eyes, ears, and other bodily parts for sensing quality, for example, but not why quality is in the first place out there in the world and foundational to the very being of animate forms. Matter is indeed not in and of itself an explanatory source of anything. It has no autonomous credentials. It is errantly and aberrantly pretentious to claim that it is the oracular be-all and end-all of the universe.

Aristotle's qualitative account of objects of sense and of organs of sense clearly complements Portmann's notion of a formal semantics. A semantics of quality is a built-in of the world at large and the world of living bodies. The perception of quality — of form values in Portmann's social sense and in the larger natural world as well — is an act of consciousness, a recognition of what is there, of what is physiognomically present. This capacity to distinguish what is physiognomically present is the mark of animate forms, of creatures capable of taking in the forms of things without the matter, creatures attuned to movement. Formal values, both creaturely and worldly, are not after all given once and for all: what is young grows old, what is inert becomes taut, what is calm becomes turbulent, what is smooth becomes bumpy, what is now a quiet attentiveness becomes now an active exploration, what at one time turned one way now turns another way, and so on. *Motion* is at the heart of quality precisely in Aristotle's sense of alteration and change. Moreover it is at the heart of quality in the further sense of animal movement itself, of which more in the next chapter. Clearly, the task of a natural history of consciousness is to trace out the semantics of animation, the qualitative dynamics of both animate form and the animate world.

In sum, the import and value of Aristotle's natural philosophy of mind are unmistakable. His bio-zoological philosophy affords insights into the nature of perception, into the intimate and intricate connection between form and matter, thus into the centrality of quality, movement, form values. Because it takes life seriously, it takes the sensible seriously. Surely we must open ourselves to the way the living world *is*, as Aristotle did, and not turn ourselves myopically to the way a materialist 20th-century Western science and philosophy want metaphysically to compress it.

Notes

1.   I raised this question originally in the context of an essay on Western medicine. See Sheets-Johnstone 1992a.

2.   The text actually reads "manifestations of persistent wholes."

3.   James G. Lennox (personal communication) has offered a perfectly reasonable retort that Burnyeat might give to these questions. He states that Burnyeat might simply respond, "'I am not prescribing the correct approach to science — I am simply saying that the dominant view takes explaining conscious experience from the bottom up as THE serious problem, and it is a problem Aristotle cannot help us with, since for him this is not THE problem at all.'" Lennox continues by remarking, "So [Burnyeat] might agree that nothing in particular 'ordains' this approach. He is simply chastising functionalists and identity theorists for claiming Aristotle as an ally, rather than taking a position on what the correct philosophy of mind actually is."

The problem with this otherwise reasonable retort is that Burnyeat strongly recommends that we *junk* Aristotle's "philosophy of mind" (1992:26). His recommendation obviously harbors a sizable value judgement. More than this, it appears a goad toward doing something active to speed progress toward a bottom-up explanation. In other words, it urges us not simply to turn away from anything not immediately in line with the explanatory goal, but to do away with any such thing. In view of the strong action Burnyeat's recommendation urges, it seems to me that there is "an ordaining" and that the perfectly reasonable retort collapses.

4.   For a phenomenological analysis and understanding of the foundational significance of "turning-toward," see Husserl 1973: especially pp. 71–86.

5.   Aristotle speaks consistently of perception as an activity, both in terms of the object of sense and the organ of sense, e.g. the "activity of sounding" and the "activity of hearing." See further below.

6.   One might be tempted to say *naming* takes precedence over *experience*: that is, when a material *thing* is perceived, sense experience — in adult life, at least — is easily bypassed in favor of linguistic recognition, i.e. labeling.

7.   It is of interest to point out that Aristotle, in specifying in what the psychic power of perception consists, does not say that a sense takes in the sensible forms of things without *their* matter; he consistently says "without the matter." "Matter" may thus refer not only to the

materiality of objects that are objects of sense, but equally to matter that is elemental Nature, i.e. air, fire, earth, water.

8.   See Aristotle *De Anima* 425b26–426a1, for example, where Aristotle speaks of perception as an *activity*. "Actual sensation" "actual sound" (or sight, etc.) and "actual hearing" (or seeing, etc.) are particular aspects of the global *activity* that is perception.

9.   For a discussion of the difference between movement and objects in motion, see Sheets-Johnstone 1979.

10.   As Husserl succinctly put it with respect to the latter, "If perception is to be constitutive of a thing, then there must also pertain to it the possibility of Bodily movements as 'free' movements" (Husserl 1989:323).

11.   The difference between traditional Western medicine and traditional Asian medicine is a classic example. For a discussion of functions with and without structures, see Sheets-Johnstone 1992a.

12.   James Lennox (personal communication) notes that the more traditional translation of the Greek would be rendered 'actuality' rather than 'activity' (the common J.A. Smith translation notwithstanding), a fact that underscores precisely the particular point of moment here, namely, that quality is an actuality with respect to both object of sense and organ of sense.

13.   There are of course overlaps, whether one labels them metaphorical or not, e.g. the *shape* of a musical phrase, the *accents* of color in a painting, and so on.

14.   An apple's falling from a tree is a kinetic fact of life not only in the sense that an unpicked apple will fall from a tree, but precisely in the sense that *circonstances* are part of life. Living things do not live in a vacuum but are quintessentially influenced by their "environment" — i.e. by the very nature of the world in general, and their own surrounding world in particular.

15.   See, for example, the classic art text by Helen Gardner, *Art Through the Ages* (1948:2): "'Form' has many meanings. Here — in fact all through this book — it is used in its widest sense: that of a total *organic* structure." See also noted philosopher of art Susanne K. Langer's *Problems of Art* (1957:44): "Another metaphor of the studio [in addition to "life," "vitality," "livingness,"], borrowed from the biological realm, is the familiar statement that every art work must be organic. Most artists will not even agree with a literal-minded critic that this is a metaphor."

16.   I introduced the concept of existential fit (1986a) originally in terms of the quintessential coherency of 'lived' and 'physical' bodies — not, as here, of the quintessential coherency of creature and world.

17.   For related, paleoanthropologically-based studies showing how the body is a semantic template, see Sheets-Johnstone 1990; see also Sheets-Johnstone 1994:Chapter 2, "An Evolutionary Genealogy."

18.   At the beginning of this same essay, "Man and the Sea Shell" (1964b:5), Valèry opines that "[I]t was child's play for what we call 'living nature' to obtain the relation between form and matter that we [artists or humans] take so much pains to attempt or to make some show of achieving."

CHAPTER 3

The primacy of movement

Animation designates the way in which mind acquires a locality in the spatial world, its spatialization, as it were, and together with its corporal support, acquires *reality*.   Edmund Husserl (1977:101)

It is the special quality of ... animation which accounts for the fact that what is Bodily and ultimately *everything* Bodily from no matter what point of view can assume psychic significance, therefore even where at the outset it is not phenomenally the bearer of a soul.   Edmund Husserl (1989:102)

1. Introduction

Two prefatory comments necessarily begin this chapter, each of them acknowledging the thoughtful writings of others that are in different ways topical to the present endeavor. First, philosopher Algis Mickunas wrote a brief article titled "The Primacy of Movement" that was published in 1974. Although not offering a phenomenological analysis of movement, Mickunas affirmed (9,8) that "kinaesthetic awareness constitutes our basic 'perceptual organ' of space and time" and that kinesthetic consciousness itself is the basis of all perception: it is "a common denominator ... a basic process of knowing, which sub-tends all bodily actions, and synthesizes them." My own research and phenomenological reflections on the primacy of movement were not taken up in conjunction with Mickunas's article (nor did I realize my appropriation of *his* title until after the fact). There is all the same a concurrence of thought about "the primacy of movement."

Second, although perhaps inevitably calling to mind philosopher Maurice Merleau-Ponty's essay, "The Primacy of Perception" (1964b), the title of this chapter does not signal a declaration of war. In fact, there is no question of a contest of any sort between movement and perception, and this for two reasons: creaturely movement is the very condition of all forms of creaturely perception; and creaturely movement, being itself a creature-perceived phenomenon, is in and of itself a source of knowledge. Indeed, as this chapter will attempt to show on the basis of a phenomenology of self-movement, animation is the originating ground of knowledge. Not only is our own perception of the world everywhere and always animated, but our movement is everywhere and always kinesthetically informed. The foundational significance of movement should in consequence be doubly apparent to anyone concerned to investigate the nature of animate life.

Because this significance has been largely ignored in contemporary Western science and philosophy, because perception — most especially visual perception — language, information-processing, computational modelling, and other such topics are at the focal point of contemporary attention, the primacy of movement has in fact gone unrecognized and unexamined. The purpose of this chapter is to correct the omission in the most basic possible way, by going back to actual experience, to the things themselves — or more precisely, to us ourselves — thereby showing first how movement is the generative source of our primal sense of aliveness and of our primal capacity for sense-making, and second how a descriptive account of the phenomenon of self-movement elucidates cardinal epistemological structures inherent in kinesthetic consciousness.[1] To bring these kinetic and kinesthetic understandings and structures historically and resonantly to the fore, I would like to begin by framing them in the context of philosopher Edmund Husserl's notion of animate organism. My purpose is not only to show Husserl's consistent concern with, and insights into, animation, but to call attention to his non-species-specific sense of animation. By his very use of the term "animate organism," Husserl was clearly rendering an account of something not exclusive to humans, that is, something broader and more fundamental than human animate organism. Indeed, as will be apparent, he regarded nonhuman creatures as animate organisms along with humans and included them in an account of reality and nature,[2] never referring to them, for example, in a demeaning way as "brutes" in the manner of Descartes and other philosophers, even present-day ones (e.g. Carruthers 1989). This non-exclusive conception is not the result of a love of animals, or of a particular familial or cultural upbringing. It is the result of regarding the world, and in particular, nature, within the phenomenological attitude; that is, when one brackets one's everyday, natural attitude toward the world, which attitude of course includes a certain attitude toward nonhuman animals, and in turn perceives nonhuman animals in a neutral way without the values — whether social, religious, or even scientific-medical — that one ordinarily brings to one's perception of them, then one of course observes them as *animate organisms*, i.e. live things, beings that move. This is the way they appear; this is the original way in which we experience them. Indeed, this is the way infants and very young children experience them prior to ingesting any particular familial or cultural attitude; they experience them simply as things that move, as *animate forms*. It is noteworthy to point out that perceiving nonhuman animals in the phenomenological attitude is conceptually concordant with an evolutionary viewpoint. In each case, one sees animate organisms *as living, moving things that by their very animate nature are continuous in kind, there being no fundamental break between nonhumans and humans.* Accordingly, although in the phenomenological study that follows, the focus will be on human animation — the necessary starting point of a phenomenology — the most basic findings pertain *mutatis mutandis* to nonhuman animals who, like humans, are animate organisms that move themselves. A notable stipulation applies: having formally distinctive bodies in the same way that earlier hominids — for example, Neandertals, *Homo habilis*, and *Australopithecus afarensis* — had bodies formally distinct from later hominid bodies (in particular, present-day human ones), each species of nonhuman animate organism must ultimately be fleshed out in its own distinctive terms as well. In other words, while an understanding of pan-animate aspects of animate life are required, so also are understandings of animate organisms in their uniqueness. This dual understanding recalls the challenge of knowing Neandertals "in their own terms." What the latter knowing requires is something philosopher Eugen Fink in another but quite pertinent context termed a "constructive phenomenology" (Fink 1995). This dual understanding is implicit in what follows: a fleshing out of the phenomenological distinctiveness of the animate organism that is human against the background of what is phenomenologically pan-animate.

2.   Animate organism

Husserl uses the phrase "animate organism" not only many times over but with a progressively greater and greater range of meaning in referring to living beings. In *Ideas I*, for example, after saying, "let us imagine that … the whole of Nature … is 'annihilated'" (i.e. that our experiences of the world do not add up harmoniously and are in fact totally refractory to harmonization), he goes on to remark that "Then there would be no more animate organisms and therefore no more human beings. I should no longer exist as a human being: and, a fortiori, no fellow human beings would exist for me" (Husserl 1983:127). Clearly, Husserl initially ties the phenomenon 'animate organism' to Nature as a coherent whole. In *Ideas II*, he states that the sensuous and the psychic "are given as *belonging* to the [man or animal] Body in question, and it is precisely because of them that it is called Body or organism, i.e. an '*organ' for a soul* or for a spirit" (Husserl 1989:35–36). Of such bodies, he writes, for example, "I see a playing cat and I regard it now as something of nature, just as is done in zoology. I see it as a physical organism but also as a sensing and animated Body, i.e. I see it precisely as a cat" (Husserl 1989:185). Here, Husserl clearly ties the phenomenon 'animate organism' not only to living nature, but to living creatures in the full sense of their livingness, i.e. of their carrying on activities in the world, of their being dynamically engaged as in playing, and the like. In *Ideas III*, he writes of animate organism from the very beginning, focusing in particular on the way in which we perceive an animate organism and on what he terms the science of "somatology": "We perceive the animate organism," he says, "but along with it also the things that are perceived 'by means of' the animate organism in the modes of their appearance in each case, and along with this we are also conscious of ourselves as human beings and as Egos that perceive such things by means of the animate organism." In short and in sum, 'animate organism' refers in more and more refined ways to living beings whose animateness is the foundation of their perceptual world, including the perceptual world of their own bodies. In implicitly calling attention first and foremost to creaturely movement, the term 'animate organism' underscores the originary significance of movement to creaturely life. What I would like to specify and examine in this Husserlian context are epistemological dimensions of this originariness.[3]

To begin with, Husserl makes the point (as does Ludwig Landgrebe more exten-sively in later commentaries) that "Originally, the 'I move', 'I do', precedes the 'I can do'" (Husserl 1989: 273; Landgrebe 1977). In *The Roots of Thinking*, I elaborated on this precedence noting that "the awareness of corporeal powers [the awareness of "I cans"] does not (and could not) arise *ex nihilo*. It arises from [everyday] tactile-kinesthetic activity: chewing, reaching, grasping, kicking, etc. The awareness of corporeal powers is thus not the result of reflective musings, whether with or without language … [and hence is] not a matter of wondering, What can I do? On the contrary, the sense of corporeal powers is the result either of moving or of already having moved." I gave as example the tactile-kinesthetic act of chewing: in that act, a creature "catches itself in the act of *grinding something to pieces*" (Sheets-Johnstone 1990: 29). In such acts, I said, corporeal powers give rise to corporeal concepts, fundamental human concepts such as grinding, sharpness, hardness, and so on.

Now if we take seriously that the (experience) "I move" precedes the (conceptual realization) "I can do," and if we take with equal seriousness the fact that specific per-ceptual awarenesses of ourselves arising in everyday tactile-kinesthetic acts of doing something are the touchstone and bedrock of our discovery of "I cans" and in turn of corporeal concepts, then it is clear that movement is absolutely foundational not only to perceptual realizations of ourselves as doing or accomplishing certain things or making certain things happen — such as "grinding something to pieces" — and to cor-relative cognitive realizations of ourselves as capable of just such acts or activities, but to perceptual-cognitive realizations of ourselves as alive, i.e. as living creatures, ani-mate organisms, or animate forms. *Aliveness* is thus a concept as grounded in move-ment as the concept "*I can*."[4] Indeed, we intuitively grasp the coincidence of aliveness and animation from the very beginning. With no prior tutoring whatsoever, we take what is living to be that which moves itself and to apprehend what is not moving and has never moved to be precisely inanimate. Experimental studies and observations of infants readily document this intuitive knowledge.[5] They document as well our fasci-nation with movement. What moves straightaway captures our attention; it is consis-tently at the focal point over what is not moving.[6] This focal tethering to movement is no less first-nature to other creatures than it is to ourselves. We are all of us attuned to the animate over the inanimate; we are all alive to movement from the start. Indeed, animation is at the core of every creature's engagement with the world because it is in and through movement that the life of every creature — to borrow Husserl's phrase in the first epigraph — "acquires reality."

Given the fact that we intuitively equate aliveness with movement, it is difficult to explain why philosophers would overlook the primacy of movement in their renditions of what it is to be human, taking instead a textual model which reduces movement to mere visual and/or manual gestures coincident with reading and writing;[7] a computer model which reduces movement to mere "output," the necessary but comparatively dull aftermath of a vastly more interesting and prestigious "input"; an objective model which either typically disregards movement by considering only objects in motion and, in effect, ignores self-movement, or typically instrumentalizes movement by de-cognizing it, making it no more than a means, a necessary but purely serviceable accouterment of perception (or knowledge); or, finally, taking no model at all, simply trivializes it. Most importantly and pointedly in terms of experience — that is, given that we humans all begin life by wiggling, stretching, opening our mouths, swallowing, kicking, crying, and so on — it is odd that philosophers would overlook the *sui generis* character of movement and fail to explore its significance. In the beginning, after all, we do not *try* to move, *think* about movement possibilities, or put ourselves to *the task* of moving. We come straightaway moving into the world; we are precisely not *stillborn*. In this respect, primal movement is like primal sensibility: "it is simply there," Husserl says (Husserl 1989: 346). Moreover in the beginning, we are not surprised by our movements, disappointed by them, or wish that they were different.[8] In the beginning, we are simply infused with movement — not merely with a *propensity* to move, but with the real thing. This primal animateness, this original kinetic spontaneity that infuses our being and defines our aliveness, is our point of departure for living in the world and making sense of it. It is the epistemological foundation of our learning to move ourselves with respect to objects, and thus the foundation of a developing repertoire of "I cans" with respect to both the natural and artifactual array of objects that happen to surround us as individuals in our particular worlds. It is in effect the foundation of our sense of ourselves as agents within a surrounding world. But it is even more basically the epistemological foundation of our sense of who and what we are. *We literally discover ourselves in movement.* We grow kinetically into our bodies. In particular, we grow into those distinctive ways of moving that come with our being the bodies we are.[9] In our spontaneity of movement, we discover arms that extend, spines that bend, knees that flex, mouths that shut, and so on. We make sense of ourselves in the course of moving. We discover ourselves as animate organisms. These kinetic-kinesthetic self-discoveries constitute their own specific repertoire of "I cans"; that is, quite apart from our "I cans" relative to a world of objects, we discover a realm of sheer kinetic "I cans": I can stretch, I can twist, I can reach, I can turn over, and so on. This realm is in truth an open-ended realm of possibilities. That it is so means that our individual repertoires are ultimately a measure of how far we grow into the bodies we are, a measure of both the extent to which we give ourselves over to the spontaneity of movement and the extent to which we explore the kinetic dimensions of our animate nature.

In discovering ourselves in movement and in turn expanding our kinetic repertoire of "I cans," we embark on a lifelong journey of sense-making. Our capacity to make sense of ourselves, to grow kinetically into the bodies we are, is in other words the beginning of cognition. In making sense of the dynamic interplay of forces and configurations inherent in our on-going spontaneity of movement, we arrive at corporeal concepts. On the basis of these concepts, we forge fundamental understandings both of ourselves and of the world. We discover opening and closing in the opening and closing of our eyes, mouths, and hands; we discover that certain things go together such as a certain constellation of buccal movements and certain feelings of warmth — as in the act of nursing; we discover a differential heaviness in lifting our head and lifting our arm and a differential over-all bodily tension in the two movements as well. In making kinetic sense of ourselves, we progressively attain complex conceptual understandings having to do with *containment*, with *consequential relationships*, with *weight*, with *effort*, and with myriad other bodily-anchored happenings and phenomena that in turn anchor our sense of the world and *its* happenings and phenomena. In effect, our first cognitive steps are taken by way of our own movement. With these steps we begin to discover the nature of our being in the double sense of finding a coherency of experiences and of articulating a particular form of life. Correlatively, with these cognitive steps we begin to discover the nature of the world in the double sense of finding a coherency of experiences — "a world progressing harmoniously" (Husserl 1989: 78) — and a particular constellation of objects and events that are not only coincident with our natural surrounds but peculiar to our individual and cultural form of life.

Insofar as our primal animateness is the bedrock of just such kinetically- and kinesthetically-rooted conceptual understandings, our primal animateness is, to borrow (and singularize) a phrase from Husserl, "the mother of all cognition." A remarkable analogy in fact exists between the originariness of movement and the originariness sought by phenomenology, the context in which Husserl actually used the phrase. The analogy is adumbrated in Husserl's remark that "Phenomenology in our sense is the science of 'origins', of the 'mothers' of all cognition; and it is the maternal-ground of all philosophical method: to this ground and to the work in it, everything leads back" (Husserl 1980: 69).

Everything cognitive leads back equally to movement, to animate nature. Clearly, our first consciousness is a tactile-kinesthetic consciousness that arises on the ground of movement that comes to us spontaneously, indeed, on the ground of fundamental and invariant species-specific kinetic acts that we simply "do" in coming into the world, acts such as kicking, stretching, sucking, swallowing, and so on. Such acts happen to us before *we* make them happen. In just this sense, movement is there prior to "I move." Kicking, for example, is there before *I* kick; stretching is there before *I* stretch. In effect, *movement forms the I that moves before the I that moves forms movement.* Spontaneous movement is the constitutive source of agency, of subjecthood, of selfhood, the dynamic core of our sense of ourselves as agents, subjects, selves. Kinesthetic consciousness in turn defines an emergent, progressively expanding consciousness whose structures can be thematized, i.e. analyzed phenomenologically. In particular, kinesthetic consciousness unfolds on the ground of spontaneous movement and in its initial unfolding reveals not only corporeal concepts on the order of those described above, but spatio-temporal concepts that are basically qualitative in nature and that emanate from what we discover to be the creative, i.e. freely variable, character of our movement. I can, for example, lift my head abruptly or in a sustained manner; I can open my mouth minimally or widely; I can kick my legs rhythmically or at random; and so on. Any movement we make has certain degrees of freedom. That it does — that our movement is freely variable — is a measure of the qualitative nature of movement and potential conceptual richness of our unfolding kinesthetic consciousness. It is furthermore suggestive of how spatialities and temporalities are kinetically created — and even of how space and time are fundamentally constituted in and through our experience of self-movement.

In sum, our primal animateness is of profound epistemological significance. In the beginning is movement. Our very emergence as cognizing subjects is grounded in our original kinetic spontaneity. In effect, what is already there — but not by any means already "*all there*" as Merleau-Ponty would have it (Merleau-Ponty 1962:198) — is not the world and the body. What is already there is movement, movement in and through which the perceptible world and acting subject come to be constituted, which is to say movement in and through which we make sense of both the world and ourselves. That "I move" arises on the ground of our primal animateness is of equally profound epistemological significance, for it means that movement is the ground on which transcendental subjectivity — in a broad sense, our sense-making or constituting faculty — arises.[10] Movement awakens transcendental subjectivity in the form of kinesthetic consciousness. To see this relationship is to corroborate and extend Landgrebe's account of "[a] prelinguistic acquaintance with oneself as the center of a spontaneous ability to move." In the context of his account, Landgrebe writes that "kinesthetic *motions* … are the most fundamental dimension of transcendental subjectivity, the genuinely original sphere, so that even the body (*Leib*), as functioning body, is not just something constituted *but is itself constituting as the transcendental condition of the possibility of each higher level of consciousness and of its reflexive character*" (Landgrebe 1977:108; italics added). The kinesthetic correlates of perception — what Husserl calls "the kinestheses" — are hence not simply practical perceptual affordances (to use a Gibsonian term: J.J. Gibson 1979), necessary "*functions of spontaneity* belong[ing] to every perception" (Husserl 1989: 63). They are, in their own right, *perceptual experiences*, the most fundamental of perceptual experiences, and as such are at the very core of the constituting I, that is, of transcendental subjectivity.

If the foregoing beginning analysis is phenomenologically sound, then our common task is to elucidate the kinetic-kinesthetic foundations of fundamental human understandings, tracing out the multiple and complex dynamic structures that lie at the heart of fundamental human cognitions.[11] Before attempting to describe just such cardinal epistemological structures inherent in kinesthetic consciousness, I want briefly to consider Husserl's uncertainty and equivocation about kinesthesia with respect to corporeal localization, especially in contrast to his certainty and specificity about the corporeal localization of touch.

3.   Kinesthesia

In *Ideas II*, Husserl remarks that by comparison with touch, kinesthesia has "a rather indeterminate localization" (Husserl 1989: 158). He says that "The Body as such can be constituted originarily only in tactuality and in everything that is localized with the sensations of touch" (158). He states that "At bottom, it is owing only to their constant interlacing with these primarily localized sensations that the kinetic sensations receive localization" (158). He states further that the reason kinesthetic sensations are parasitic on touch is that "[they] do not spread out in a stratified way over the appearing extension" — i.e. over the appearing object (158). Moreover in affirming that the indeterminate localization of kinesthesia "makes the unity between the Body and the freely moveable thing more intimate" (158), i.e. makes the mysterious nexus that constitutes "the turning point" from causal material body to conditional living Body more intimate (168–69), Husserl appears to give added emphasis to the locative nebulosity of kinesthetic sensations. In *Ideas III*, however, he at one point declares that kinesthetic feelings are among "localized feelings"(Husserl 1980: 107); two pages later, however, he again speaks of the kinesthetic sense as having "vague localization" (109), and a page further, he states that "In general we are convinced that primary localization belongs only to the touch-sensations and the sensations going parallel with them," giving as example "the temperature-sensations that follow the stimulated organismal surfaces with their extension" (110).

What, we may ask, is at the root of this spare and uneven understanding of kinesthesia? Husserl's lack of thoroughness and consistency is in fact odd, out of character one might say. Closer reading shows two things. First and foremost, Husserl does not actually consider self-movement as such; he considers only movement with respect to external perception, that is, with respect to perceived objects in the world. His estimation of kinesthesia is thus clearly restricted. Second, when he speaks of kinesthetic flows, he often does so in terms of a visual object so that kinesthetic flows are aligned rather narrowly with eye movements which, as he himself says, "[do] not come into action as such, i.e. as experienced in this apprehension" (Husserl 1980: 109). He at one point even equates the fundamental constitution of space to "oculomotor" activity (Husserl 1989: 347). In short, Husserl does not turn toward self-movement *tout court*, toward the actual perceptual experience of movement in the phenomenon of kinesthesia. His overriding concern is with external perception. His characterization of a solipsist's experience of the Body "from 'within' — that is, in the 'inner attitude'" — clearly shows his exclusive concern. He describes the solipsist's experience or constitution of the Body only as "a freely moving organ (or system of such organs) by means of which the subject experiences the external world" (Husserl 1989: 168). A descriptive account of the sheer phenomenon of self-movement as it is experienced kinesthetically is distinctly by-passed. Given the earlier insights into the epistemological import of animation, of movement, and of kinesthetic consciousness, it is essential to the task of phenomenology to elucidate self-movement, thereby both amplifying and correcting Husserl's account.

4. Cardinal structures of kinesthetic consciousness

It is in fact appropriate now to ply our trade as practicing phenomenologists, or correlatively, to apply ourselves as humans who, having kinesthetic experiences, can examine them, paying rigorous attention to what is actually there, sensuously present in our experience, and in turn validating or disaffirming what a phenomenological account discloses.[12] In either case, we begin by attending to "the things themselves," meticulously examining what is there, going back again and again in order that we may describe and verify for ourselves what is actually present in our experience and thereby discover and validate aspects of our sense-making that lie sedimented within us. In particular, we ply our trade now in order to elucidate cardinal structures of kinesthetic consciousness. We do this by taking a very simple movement, a movement that is basically familiar — an overhead arm stretch — but slow it down and further heighten our sense of movement by making a formal beginning: we start by closing our eyes, by dropping our head so that our chin falls toward our chest, and by resting our hands in our lap. From this beginning position, we lift our arms from the elbow so that our upper arms move upward and our hands come off our lap. We continue that upward movement without a break by extending our forearms upward and overhead, and finally by extending our fingers upward and overhead. At the same time we do all this, we slowly raise our head from its dropped position to the point that our chin faces upward toward the ceiling. We then reverse the movement, first by letting our elbows flex and our chin begin moving downward, and then by simply continuing the movement of arms and head downward until we come to our original position. We do this sequence of movements three or four times slowly, by ourselves, keeping our eyes closed and sensing the phenomenon of self-movement.

We next perform free variations on this movement theme or sequence of movements, not imaginative free variations as is customary in phenomenological practice, but actual free variations in order to appreciate first-hand, in experience, what is kinetically there. Our purpose is to discover, in Husserl's words, "what holds up amid such free variations of an original … as the invariant, the necessary, … without which something of [this] kind … would be altogether inconceivable." What we want to know is precisely what invariants "[pervade] all the variants" of movement (Husserl 1977: 54).

Let me suggest a variety of possible variations. Rather than moving through the sequence slowly, I can move through the sequence quickly; rather than moving slowly or quickly through the entire sequence, I can move through the first part slowly and the second part rapidly; I can gradually accelerate as I move through the whole pattern, or I can do the reverse, move rapidly in the beginning and progressively decelerate until I come to the end. Clearly, there is a manifold of possibilities with respect to the temporality of my movement. There is similarly a manifold of possibilities with respect to the tensional aspects of my movement. I can move through the pattern with great force, that is, in such a way that I generate a determined and powerful tension; I can move through the pattern weakly, barely expending any energy at all; I can play around with the intensity of my movement, alternating regularly between extremes, for example, shifting gradually into higher and lower gears, spasmodically changing tensions, and so on. I can furthermore vary the manner in which I project force: I can fling my head and arms up and down in a ballistic manner, throwing them upward and downward with a single initial force; I can move them in an even, sustained manner; I can move them suddenly and abruptly such that the movement proceeds as if on an off-and-on switch; I can move them in ways that combine any or all of these projectional possibilities. I can similarly vary the movement spatially, in both a linear and amplitudinal sense. I can emphasize either straight or curved lines in the movement of my arms, for example, or I can accentuate now the one, now the other linear aspect; similarly, I can augment or diminish the magnitude of the movement, bringing the upward movement of my arms to a less than full extension, for example, or making the upward movement broader so that it expands outward as well as upward as it reaches the peak of extension. In sum, I can make seemingly endless dynamic variations.

The question is, what is invariantly there through all these variations — and any further ones anyone could possibly imagine? What is invariantly there is in each case an overall *quality*. Whatever the variation, the movement has a distinctive felt qualitative character coincident with that variation, a felt physiognomic aspect which is in fact a constellation of qualitative aspects. These qualitative aspects — dynamic structures inherent in movement — enter into and define our global qualitative sense of any particular movement variation; they make all of the variations immediately distinctive to us *as variations*.

We notice to begin with, then, that kinesthetic experiences are not equivalent to experiences of a mere change in position, any more than movement itself is a mere change of position. In each case, what is of moment is fundamentally a matter of *change*, not of position. In other words, kinesthetic consciousness is fundamentally a consciousness of an unfolding kinetic dynamic. Moreover we might note that while most of our adult ways of moving are typically habitual and qualitatively apparent to us only at the margins of our awareness, the typically habitual and qualitatively marginal were at one time focal; hence, originally, in assaying or in successfully accomplishing any movement for the first time, we were aware of its felt qualitative character. To get a sense of this originary experience, we need only try different ways of doing something habitual — something like walking, for example, changing not only our leg swings, for instance, by initiating movement from our ankle joints by a spring action rather than from our hip joints, but changing our arm swing, the curvature of our spine, the cadence of our walk, the amplitude of our step, and so on. Calling attention to ourselves in movement in this way, we have the possibility of discovering what is invariantly there in any felt experience of movement. This is because whatever the habitual movement, it now feels strange, even uncomfortable. Just such oddness jars us into an awareness of what we qualitatively marginalize in our habitual ways of doing things. By making the familiar strange, we familiarize ourselves anew with the familiar.

As might be evident, kinetic free variations disclose four primary qualitative structures of movement having to do with force or effort, with space, and with time. These qualitative aspects of movement are of course separable only reflectively, that is, analytically, after the fact; experientially, they are all of a piece in the global qualitatively felt dynamic phenomenon of self-movement. Any movement has a certain felt tensional quality, linear quality, amplitudinal quality, and projectional quality (Sheets-Johnstone 1966).[13] In a very general sense, the felt tensional quality has to do with our sense of effort; the linear quality with both the felt linear contour of our moving body and the linear paths we sense ourselves describing in the process of moving; the amplitudinal quality with both the felt expansiveness or contractiveness of our moving body and the spatial extensiveness or constrictedness of our movement; the felt projectional quality with the way in which we release force or energy. Linear and amplitudinal qualities obviously describe spatial aspects of movement; tensional and projectional qualities obviously describe temporal aspects of movement, what we recognize as the felt intensity of our moving bodily energies and the felt manner in which we project those bodily energies — in a sustained manner, for example, in an explosive manner, in a punctuated manner, in a ballistic manner, and so on. Temporal aspects of movement are the result of the way in which tensional and projectional qualities combine; that is, the temporal quality of any movement derives from the manner in which any particular intensity (or combined intensities) is kinetically expressed.

On the way to spelling out the nature of these qualities more precisely, I should call specific attention to the fact that movement *creates* the qualities that it embodies and that we experience; thus it is erroneous to think that movement simply takes place *in* space, for example. On the contrary, we formally create space in the process of moving; we qualitatively create a certain spatial character by the very nature of our movement — a large, open space, or a tight, resistant space, for example. In effect, particular spatial designs and patterns come into play with self-movement, designs and patterns that have both a linear and amplitudinal quality. The predominant shifting linear designs of our moving bodies may be now curved (as when we bend over), now twisted (as when we turn our heads), now diagonal (as when we lean forward), now vertical (as when we walk), and so on; the predominant linear patterns we create in moving may be now zig-zag (as in a game of tag), now straight (as in marching), now circular (as when we walk around an object or literally 'go in circles'), and so on. The linear contours and linear paths we create in moving are basically *directional* aspects of our body and our movement; the amplitudinal designs and patterns are basically *magnitudinal* aspects. With respect to the latter, both our bodies in the course of moving and our movement itself create a certain spatial expanse and thus have a certain scope or span. For example, when we sit down, we contract ourselves into a progressively smaller shape; in contrast we expand ourselves to the fullest when reaching for something that is almost out of reach. Similarly, when we run, our movement creates an extensive space in contrast to the tight and constricted space it creates when we pace up and down.

We can notice these spatial and other created qualitative aspects of movement quite apart from purposefully changing what is kinetically habitual for us, that is, quite apart from purposefully making the familiar strange. Unexpected moments in everyday experience present opportunities for noticing created aspects of movement, as when we pick up a suitcase lighter than anticipated. Such an experience — which from a phenomenological perspective might be described as "inadvertently making the familiar strange" — highlights in particular the created tensional quality of movement: we prepare ourselves in anticipation of moving in a certain encumbered way and are thrown off guard by the surprising ease we find in lifting and carrying. We thereby become aware of the kinetic energy that drives our movement. What usually passes unnoticed comes to the fore. In turn, we slacken our tension and generate less energy. But in turn too, we subsequently move more fluidly and create a different kinetic temporality in the process. We move not with a jerky cadence as we anticipated, but with a cadence that is rhythmically unbroken. Not only our steps but our whole-body movement is smooth and even. In effect, we not only generate less energy; we generate it in a flowing, steadily continuous manner: one leg swings easily forward, then the other, then the first, and so on. In such ways the temporality of our movement — the temporality of the kinetic energy we create in virtue of the tensional and projectional qualities of movement — is qualitatively different from what it would have been had we actually encountered the weight we expected.

Coincident with the foregoing example, a further point should be made, one that highlights a fundamental aspect of the intimate relationship between kinesthesia and self-agency. Like an infant's differential experience of weight in lifting its head and lifting its arm when lying prone, our own differential experience of weight in lifting a suitcase lighter than expected is grounded in certain kinesthetic regularities. Indeed, imagine what it would be like for us — infant or adult — to experience each time we lifted a particular thing — our head, our arm, the same packed suitcase, or whatever — a different weight from the last. In other words, suppose that we had no reliable expectations of weight because, whether a matter of lifting ourselves — in whole-bodied or partial fashion — or a matter of lifting objects, there were no regularities, no harmonious orderings (as Husserl would say) with respect to our kinesthetic experiences. Were this to happen, self-movement would be a perpetually awkward affair; we would be kinesthetically at a loss to move effectively. In consequence, our sense of ourselves as agents would be compromised. Reliable kinesthetic expectations, like the kinesthetic regularities on which they are based, are foundational to our sense of agency, to our building a repertoire of "I cans," to our ability to move in consistently meaningful ways. Our sensitivities to, and knowledge of, kinesthetic regularities come of course from moving ourselves and experiencing the created force, effort, or energy — and the created spatiality and temporality — that is kinesthetically there each time in any particular overall movement dynamic. It bears emphasizing that these regularities are not simply localized bodily phenomena. Our experience of lifting a suitcase, for example, is not simply "an arm movement," but engenders a whole-body tensional quality that is peculiar to the particular lifting movement we happen to make. Indeed, whatever we do, whether we lift, push, pull, climb, run — or fall — we do so all of a piece. Our whole body is engaged in moving, sometimes engaged simply by being still, as in the preparation to swing at an oncoming ball, or to begin moving a pen upon a blank page, or to speak in response to a question. Moreover parts of us are at times necessarily still while other parts of us move, their stillness being essential to our movement, as in threading a needle or performing surgery or singing an aria — or reading. The *harmoniousness* of our kinesthetic consciousness is harmonious first of all in just this sense: the body moves as an integrated whole. Short of this fundamental kinetic integrity, we could hardly discover regularities. We would be constantly battling an essentially random, fitful, and in consequence, unknowable body.

5.   A descriptive analysis of movement and a further clarification of kinesthesia

A brief descriptive account of each quality of movement as it might appear in an imagined unvarying and ongoing movement sequence one performs oneself will bring into fine focus how created kinetic qualities enter formally into the global qualitative experience of any movement one might make, and how no experience or sense of a spatio-temporal dynamic is possible apart from self-movement. The crucial role of kinesthetic experience to the experience or sense of a spatio-temporal dynamic strongly suggests how the constitution of space and time have their genesis in self-movement, and why the consciousness of animate forms — "flux" as Husserl speaks of consciousness (Husserl 1964) — is in the most fundamental sense just such a spatio-temporal dynamic. The first epigraph prefacing this chapter already points us in the direction of this suggestion: "*Animation* designates the way in which mind acquires a locality in the spatial world … and together with its corporal support, acquires *reality*." The capsulated phenomenological insight into a core significance of movement is, of course, in itself remarkable. As noted earlier, movement — animation — seldom if ever comes into thoughtful philosophical conjunction with cognition, that is, with "mind." The insight becomes even more remarkable and specifically suggestive of the constitution of space and time in the context of philosopher Ronald Bruzina's recent investigations into the phenomenology of time, especially his penetrating studies of Eugen Fink's elaborations of Husserl's internal time consciousness, for in this context, Husserl's insight can be readily and aptly augmented in a spatio-temporal sense. Specifying the way in which Fink's analysis of time is fundamentally coincident with Husserl's, Bruzina writes (in part quoting Fink) that "Fink's formulations … are meant to express in specific ways a point that Husserl insisted upon, namely, 'that original temporality as the meaning of the being of transcendental subjectivity is always spatial'" (Bruzina 1995: 20). The suggestion that self-movement is at the heart of transcendental subjectivity in the form of a spatio-temporal constituting kinesthetic consciousness is virtually transparent the moment one links Husserl's insight to the intent of Fink's formulations. In the following section, we will examine this suggestion specifically. For the present, we note a significant coincidence along the lines of the suggestion: in addition to bringing the created qualities of movement into finer focus, the following descriptive account of movement will alert us to a lexical challenge that kinesthetic consciousness presents, a challenge that coincides with the one Husserl recognizes precisely in the context of describing internal time consciousness.

Let us imagine ourselves walking with resolute step. We find in this way of walking a tensional quality that is taut and hard. We have a sense of our bodies and our moving gait as firm and strong. We find a projectional quality that we might describe in terms of a sharp and even striding, or a flat and heavy clumping; in either case, our projection of force is measured, unhesitant, deliberate. We find linear qualities describable in terms of straight-line bodily contours and straight-line paths of movement, undeviating direct linearities in each instance. We find amplitudinal qualities describable in terms of a controlled but unconstrained bodily spatiality, that is, a controlled but unimpeded range of movement as we carve an unobstructed space. All of these qualities coalesce in the global phenomenon we imagine: "walking with resolute step." Together they articulate an overall spatio-temporal dynamic, a dynamic that coincides with the intended image: "walking with resolute step." Accordingly, the dynamic is there in the imagined movement. Similarly, when we actually walk with resolute step, the dynamic is there in the actual movement. An examination of our own experience thus demonstrates to us that no configuration of qualities exists apart from its creation: there is no firm and strong tensional quality, no sharp and even striding, no straight-line designs and patterns, no controlled but unimpeded amplitudes short of their imaginary or perceptual instantiation in movement. In actually walking with resolute step, we can sense ourselves creating this spatio-temporal dynamic and attend specifically to any of its qualities; any time we care to turn our attention to them, there they are. We find, then, that in moving, we bring a certain play of forces to life and spatialize and temporalize them in the process. An overall dynamic with distinctive qualities is created by our movement and experienced in our kinesthetic consciousness of movement.

Now it is one thing to attend to movement kinesthetically and to discover experientially the distinctive play of qualities that are there in our movement, and quite another to try to put that kinesthetic experience into words. It is not only difficult to find adequate adjectives or nouns by which to describe the different qualities we experience in moving, but difficult to avoid unwanted associations along the way. The terms force, effort, and even energy, for example, have a somewhat static ring — they may well conjure up a contained amount of "muscle contraction," an amount one supposedly dissipates in the process of moving. On the contrary, the tensional quality of any movement is not a power package which one progressively unwraps. Force, effort, or energy is continuously created in the process of moving; it is part of the global kinetic dynamic, the changing, shifting interplay of created spatialities and temporalities. Clearly, the gap between the experiential and the linguistic is not easily bridged, but kinetic experience is not on that account doubtful in the least. While fine-grained kinetic terms to describe the created qualities of movement are hard to come by — if not at times seemingly altogether lacking — the qualitative experience itself is kinetically unmistakable. When we pay attention to our own movement, we find that that nonverbal experience has a distinctive spatio-temporal dynamic coincident with the manner in which we are moving. Appreciated in this perspective, what Husserl says with respect to "the temporally constitutive flux" that is "absolute subjectivity" — "For all this, names are lacking" — is not unlike what may be said of kinesthetic consciousness.

More than this, given the crucial role of kinesthetic experience to the experience of a spatio-temporal dynamic, the similarity in verbal difficulties strongly suggests that kinesthetic consciousness is the prototype of world-constituting consciousness, the prototype, that is, of our dynamic sense-makings of the world. As pointed out and discussed earlier in section two, we make sense of our bodies first and foremost. We make sense of them in and through movement, in and through *animation*. Moreover we do so without words. This primordial sense-making is the standard upon which our sense-making of the world unfolds. Indeed, short of this corporeal sense-making, our sense-makings of the world would be virtually impossible, mere registerings of whatever happens to come along — something passing through our visual field, for example, or coming within hearing range, or touching our shoulder. Indeed, we would be not unlike the statue Condillac describes, a statue that has first this sense then that sense given to it, but that, lacking movement, is powerless to know the world except in a purely happenstance way (Condillac [1754] 1982). Indeed, the world would reduce to random events which, in the absence of active exploration, could hardly give rise to the idea of full-fledged objects, let alone full-fledged subjects. Landgrebe's earlier-cited emphasis upon the foundational significance of kinesthesia is particularly noteworthy in this context. The body is not merely a thing of which we make sense as a functioning unit. Our bodies, *through movement*, through what Landgrebe calls "kinesthetic motions," are the very source of our being in the world — "the center of a spontaneous ability to move" — and the very condition of our constituting the world — "the transcendental condition of the possibility of each higher level of consciousness and of its reflexive character." Clearly, by "kinesthetic motions" Landgrebe means not simply movement, but self-movement, movement which, by its very nature, is experienced kinesthetically, that is, by a moving subject him/herself. It is precisely in this sense that animation is at the very origin of consciousness; kinesthetic motions are, precisely as Landgrebe describes them, "the genuinely original sphere." From this vantage point, a similarity in lexical difficulties is not surprising. The lexical challenges kinesthetic consciousness presents are reflected in what flows from it with respect to "each higher level of consciousness" because kinesthesia is at the core of consciousness. Its dynamic spatio-temporal nature is part of the "fundamental dimension of transcendental subjectivity"; its nature thus informs "the temporally constitutive flux" that is consciousness.

Phenomenological grounds for affirming kinesthetic consciousness to be the core of transcendental subjectivity, transcendental in the sense of specifying originary epistemological structures and ones common to all subjects, are plainly evident. When our primal kinetic spontaneity and kinetic sense-making are taken into account, they leave no doubt but that in the most fundamental sense, "movement is the mother of all cognition." Further, when kinesthetic consciousness is phenomenologically analyzed, there is no doubt but that it is foundationally a temporalizing and spatializing consciousness. Indeed, however marginalized in our everyday awareness, there is no doubt but that self-movement is a spatio-temporal phenomenon, a phenomenon in which distinctive spatio-temporal dynamics are consistently created, that kinesthesia gives us direct and immediate awareness of these created dynamics, and that, in turn, kinesthesia leads us to the experiential core of constituting consciousness.

Clearly, when we turn our attention away from the everyday world — from external perception — and toward the movement of our own bodies, we experience ourselves kinetically; we perceive our own movement. This very experience, however, confronts us with an enigma of sizable phenomenological import and proportions. We have not always been the adult bodies that we now perceive ourselves to be. In other words, we have a history to account for. Two facets of the enigma should in particular claim our attention. In the beginning, we were *all* challenged to learn our bodies. None of us came into the world thoroughly knowledgeable in the ways of being the bodies we are. Not only did we all learn to walk and to speak, but prior to these fundamental "I cans," we all *discovered* ourselves in the acts of sucking, swallowing, crying, kicking, turning, stretching, reaching, smiling, babbling, and much, much more. In the process of discovering ourselves in all these ways, we expanded our repertoire of "I cans"; we learned possibilities of movement and became progressively aware of our capacity to move effectively with respect to these possibilities — by moving ourselves. It is important to emphasize that in these situations, we were precisely *discovering* our bodies, not *controlling* them. In attending to and exploring our primal animateness, and in thereby learning the myriad ways in which our bodily movement related us, and could relate us, to a surrounding world, we were apprentices, not would-be masters, of our bodies. In effect, a dichotomous mind/body rendition of infancy is an unfounded adult projection. An infant is not a mind trying to control a body nor is it an out-of-control body waiting for a mind to catch up with it. Any close observation of infants and young children — not to mention developmental and clinical literature of the past 20 years and more — shows unequivocally that these conceptions are unfounded. One facet of the enigma is thus to know as adults what it is like to learn one's body *by being it*, in particular by being it in movement, and more particularly to know what it is like to experience this self-movement as something other than the attainment of mind over matter.

Fink's call for a "constructive phenomenology" (see also Husserl 1973a: 79, 141) decisively affirms the need to account for our originary experiences of movement and in fact leads us precisely to the second facet of the enigma. Fink writes that "[I]t is not only the worldly facts of birth and death through which transcendental questions about a genesis are to be 'constructed', but also the world phenomena of *early childhood development*, insofar as precisely this early period lies beyond the reach of our memory…. The *transcendental* response to [this question of a period beyond the reach of our memory]… cannot proceed in intuitive fashion, i.e. it cannot bring the archaic building processes actually to a present or recollective self-givenness, it can only 'construct' them" (Fink 1995: 63; italics in original).[14] The question is: how does one proceed to construct what is not only "beyond the reach of our memory" but *what is before language*? In particular, how does one proceed to construct our originary experiences of movement, thus our beginning kinesthetic consciousness? The most direct answer is perhaps obvious: to move, and in moving, challenge ourselves anew to learn our bodies. Such a challenge does not properly turn us toward wielding a new tool, toward manoeuvering with new gear or garb, or toward any other like kind of novel kinetic manipulations or constraints. It properly turns us toward self-movement *tout court*. In effect, it turns us to purely kinetic, natural everyday movements such as walking, stretching, reaching, chewing, bending, and perhaps beyond these, to more complex purely kinetic experiences such as movement improvisation and T'ai Chi. Purely kinetic experiences have no goal or purpose beyond themselves. Walking in this sense is not getting us someplace; stretching in this sense is not exercising; reaching in this sense is not an effective way of getting a book off the shelf; and so on. In each case, *the meaning of the kinetic experience is in the movement itself*. Through such experience, we approximate to what is beyond memory and before language. But the challenge of learning our bodies in motion anew turns us toward something even more. It turns us toward walking, stretching, reaching, chewing, bending, and the like, with what Buddhists would call "bare attention," and what phenomenologists would call a bracketed attitude. In other words, it calls upon us methodologically. (See Chapter 4, this text; see also Sheets-Johnstone 1990.) We are challenged to examine natural, everyday kinetic experiences outside the natural attitude, apart from the retinue of meanings and values the experiences have and have had for us in the course of our normal everyday adult lives. Through such an examination, we arrive at the possibility of rediscovering our kinesthetic consciousness in the most pristine sense, and in turn rediscovering at the most fundamental level what it is to be animate.

Taking the two facets of the enigma seriously, I would like to attempt a beginning descriptive sketch of how a phenomenology of kinesthetic consciousness opens up a phenomenology of the primordial constitution of time. By doing so, I hope to exemplify and to flesh out more deeply the nature of those cardinal epistemological structures specified but not wholly analyzed earlier.

6.   Kinesthetic consciousness and the primordial constitution of time

Kinesthetic consciousness is fundamentally a "streaming present." The descriptive phrase comes from Husserl, who describes consciousness generally in just such terms, but the phrase has obvious affinities with William James's "stream of thought, of consciousness, or of subjective life" (James 1950, vol. 1: 239). The point of emphasis here is that, with respect to kinesthetic consciousness, the streaming present is a dynamic flux that we originally experience *qualitatively*. To bring to self-evidence the originary qualitative nature of kinesthetic consciousness, we move in everyday or more complex ways, as suggested earlier, and examine our experience in a methodical phenomenological manner. In doing so, we discover first-hand and from the beginning that self-movement is not an *object* of consciousness in the way that a chair or a melody or even a flight of birds across the sky is an object of consciousness.[15] From the start, what we find primordially there in self-movement is a felt unfolding dynamic and in virtue of that dynamic, a felt overall kinetic quality — a fleet swiftness, perhaps, or a sluggish heaviness, or a relaxed jauntiness, or an erratic intensity — or a constellation of qualities generated by a more intricate interplay of forces, an interplay that we might describe preeminently in terms of rhythmic complexity and abrupt directional changes, or in terms of constricted, jagged spatialities and alternately violent and fragile energies, for example. Whatever the unfolding dynamic, kinesthetic protentions and retentions[16] are not protentions and retentions of *things* — objects of one kind or another, as with tonal, olfactory, visual, or tactile phenomena in which one note, smell, sight, or texture follows another. Protentions and retentions are not moments of time but temporal dilations that foreshadow and reverberate — "protend" and "retend" — *qualitatively*. Because they are temporally constituted not in terms of momentary successions as such — in other words, in terms of befores, nows, and afters — but qualitatively in terms of an ongoing global dynamic, kinetic expectations and what we might call kinetic lingering auras are not reducible to past and future *nows*. Fleetness, gnarledness, liveliness, determinateness, and so on, have no kinetic "parts" as such. Certainly the streaming present of movement may be accentuated or even suddenly quiescent; it may fluctuate and change in delicate, restless, or even smoothly repetitive and monotonous ways, and in that sense be marked successively, but that marking is constituted in a wholly qualitative manner, not a quantitative, i.e. additive, one. In short, kinetic quality is indivisible. It inheres in the unfolding movement pattern or dynamic as a whole.

Whether movement happens to us or whether we make it happen, when we attend purely to the experience of self-movement, we find precisely an unfolding qualitative dynamic, a dynamic in which a certain temporality is apparent. In the former instance — when we sneeze, for example — we are kinesthetically aware of unfolding suddennesses and suspensions of movement whose lingering aura reverberates qualitatively throughout our bodies. We can conceptually reduce these suddennesses to "quick intakes of breath" and these suspensions to "waiting at the edge of the sneeze proper," but in doing so, we are attending less to a descriptive account of the temporal dynamics of the movement that is happening to us than to a specification of the defining features of a sneeze — to a specification of sneeze parts, so to speak. When we make movement happen — as when we intentionally breathe in deeply, for example — we are kinesthetically aware of a smooth, protracted temporality whose ongoing smoothness and protraction we anticipate from the beginning; we anticipate what we already experientially know the temporal feel of such a breath to be. Similarly, the lingering aura of the deep breath has the same even, drawn-out temporal quality. In both kinds of kinetic situation, our movement creates a certain temporality, and that temporality is qualitatively constituted. In effect, we experience a particular temporal dynamic any time we attend purely to the experience of self-movement.

In originary self-movement, *what is created and what is constituted are one and the same*. A further way of putting this fundamental character of self-movement is to say that self-movement is originarily not only *not* an object in the usual sense — a *thing* that appears; it is by the same token not a phenomenon that endures across different perceptions of it or that has different profiles to begin with. We can approach visual, auditory, or olfactory phenomena more closely, for example, we can perceive them from now this, now that perspective, and so on. We cannot do the same with self-movement. Self-movement precisely does not show itself in ways other than the way it is. And that way is moreover ephemeral, not enduring. Obviously, something quite different is going on in the perception and constitution of self-movement than in the perception and constitution of objects in the world. In self-movement, a particular unfolding dynamic is kinesthetically present that cannot be otherwise kinesthetically present except by our moving differently and thereby creating a different qualitative dynamic. We can immediately discover and appreciate this uniqueness, this coincidence of creation and constitution, by going back to an experience of self-movement *tout court* and examining what is there. Whatever the movement might be — walking, stretching, reaching, or whatever — we can, temporally speaking, soften or accentuate the flow of the movement — its ebbings, surges, uniformities, punctuations, explosions, attentuations, accelerations, brakings, and so forth. Temporal aspects of movement are malleable and indeed, can be so quintessentially subtle that exact repetition of a particular temporal dynamic can be challenging. In this sense, like everyday object-targeted or goal-oriented kinetic intentions, sheer kinetic intentions *tout court* can be unfulfilled. In other words, even though I am walking simply for the sake of walking, for example, and not walking to the bus stop or to the refrigerator or to meet a friend, I can unexpectedly, and even unaccountably, shift my weight in a peculiar manner from heel to toe, perhaps even turn my ankle or stumble. In such ways, I can fall short of the sheer experience of walking that is the meaning of my movement. Moreover temporal aspects of movement are fleeting and their impermanence makes their recapture an equal challenge. All that endures of self-movement is a reverberating felt sense of its dynamics. There is nothing tangible to inspect, nothing audible to which to draw nearer, nothing to hold up to the light, and so on.[17] In a word, *kinestheses are correlated only with other kinestheses*. In any attempt to recapture a temporal quality, the point of return is always a kinetic process that is exquisitely fragile.

The ephemerality of self-movement might be said to mirror the ephemerality of time. Indeed, we say that time and movement both *flow*. But if the *flow* of time, as Fink indicates, is a metaphorical flow (Fink 1978: 61), we may rightfully wonder whether it is not the ephemerality of time that mirrors the ephemerality of self-movement. Hence, while Fink also speaks at an earlier point of a "vicious circle" insofar as "On the basis of time, we understand movement, and on the basis of movement, time" (Fink 1978: 61), we might ask if there is not rather a priority; namely, whether we do not have grounds for thinking that our sense of *time itself*, as distinguished from our awareness of *something in time*, is not epistemologically generated in primordial self-movement. In other words, we may ask whether the very eidos of time does not originate in primordial self-movement, and correlatively, whether our everyday *verbal* concept of time, as evidenced in our speaking of time as *flowing*, does not have its origin in that nonlinguistic eidetic intuition.

To explore this possibility, we need first to call attention in a broader way to the notion of quality, particularly from the viewpoint of a constructive phenomenology. We can do this initially by recalling that insofar as what is created and what is constituted coincide in the phenomenon of originary self-movement, and insofar as quality is the very pith of that creation and constitution, quality is properly part of the study of the constitution of time. Quality is thus not only properly a subject fundamental to "investigations concerning the constitution of a *world*" (Husserl 1973a: 154; italics added). It is — one might even say, *antecedentally* it is — properly a subject fundamental to investigations concerning the constitution of self-movement and the process of constitution itself. In particular, what Husserl describes as "*the beginning of a radical clarification of the sense and origin* (or of the sense in consequence of the origin) *of the concepts: world, Nature, space, time, psychophysical being, man, psyche, animate organism, social community, culture*, and so forth"(Husserl 1973a: 154) requires a phenomenological study of quality as a basic structure of animation and of kinesthetic consciousness as the ground of sense-making or constituting consciousness. Indeed, in keeping with the notion of quality as antecedent, one would want precisely to speak of the beginning of a radical clarification of sense *in consequence of the origin* with respect to most of the named concepts. Quality is what Galileo left behind. It is what Western science leaves behind, quality not only in the sense of kinetic quality, of course, but in the sense of sensory qualities generally. Quality is obviously less substantial than *objects*. Moreover kinetic quality in particular is processual rather than substantive. The studied neglect of quality in the Western scientific world is ironic since it is a structure that is there from the very beginning of our lives — indeed, very likely our prenatal lives insofar as we open and close our lips, wrinkle our forehead, turn our head, and more, even as eleven-week-old fetuses (Furuhjelm et al. 1976: 91). Clearly, a phenomenology of quality as primordially present in self-movement is rich in possibilities, both conceptual and eidetic. As earlier analyses of originary movement and of the awareness of corporeal powers show, such a phenomenology discloses an extensive conceptual field that is foundational to the way in which we come to constitute the world, that is, foundational to our sense-makings. We come to know the world and make our way through it by way of fundamental kinetically-forged concepts that are in the beginning nonlinguistic and that may, for lack of a subtle, fine-grained vocabulary that captures dynamic contours and shadings, even remain nonlinguistic. Where we are not wholly at a loss for words, we have broad ways of qualifying movement, by terms such as swift, sudden, sustained, slow, bursting, rushed, weak, resolute, expansive, constrained, erratic, quick, meandering, and so on. In short, a phenomenology of the qualitative dynamics of originary self-movement leads us to the origin of concepts foundational to our lives as animate organisms and to our knowledge of ourselves as animate — *moving* — organisms to begin with.

With respect to eidetic understandings of a phenomenology of quality, our task is to make explicit in a beginning way how the qualitative nature of primordial movement relates to cardinal epistemological structures inherent in kinesthetic consciousness. These cardinal structures are the very constituents of quality: they are the temporal, spatial, and energic elements of originary self-movement that we have been describing from the beginning. These constituents of quality are cardinal in the sense of their being invariant — eidetic — structures of kinesthetic consciousness, and ones whose nature is clearly distinguishable from ordinal structures. Through a consideration of time and temporality, we will be able to exemplify these cardinal qualitative structures in finer detail.

7.   The cardinal structure of time

In a recent paper on the phenomenology of time, Ronald Bruzina cautions that we must not confuse felt time with phenomenal world time, the latter understood as "the phenomenology of 'the consciousness of internal time.'" It is phenomenal world time that is the focus of his paper. In the context of distinguishing between the two kinds of time, Bruzina raises the question of how there is in felt organic living "an awareness of its time" and of whether such time could in fact be "characterized in terms of noetic-noematic structure," that is, in terms of acts of meaning (perceiving, judging, remembering, and so on) and meaning structures (aspectival, historical, and other dimensions of *the meant*). An answer to his question is succinctly if unwittingly illustrated by Aristotle in his discussion of "how many ways we speak of the 'now'" (*Physics* 222b: 27–30). The Aristotelian answer highlights in a decisively striking way the nature of "felt time." It highlights as well a constitutive distinction between ordinal time — what I earlier characterized as "quantitative" or "additive" time — and cardinal time. Aristotle states that "The 'now' is the link of time" and that it is spoken of in terms of "at some time," "lately," "just now," "long ago," and "suddenly" (*Physics* 222a: 10ff.). Clearly, there is something jarringly odd about the last of Aristotle's examples. "Suddenly" has a decisive temporal character wholly distinct from the other terms. It has in fact a *qualitative* temporal character that is nowhere evident in a "just now," for example, or a now in relation to "long ago." Aristotle says simply that "'Suddenly' refers to what has departed from its former condition in a time imperceptible because of its smallness" (and goes on from there to speak of change, destruction, and coming into being) (*Physics* 222b: 15–16). By his definition, he is obviously taking "suddenly" as a quantitative term parallel to the other quantitative terms or phrases he gives. In the context of self-movement, how-ever, "suddenly" is something quite other than an interval of time "imperceptible because of its smallness." It is a *qualitatively* experienced temporality, just as rushed, prolonged, or creeping are *qualitatively* experienced temporalities.[18] All such "felt time" experiences are cardinal by their very nature.

Two arithmetical comparisons will help clarify that nature further. Cardinal temporality is akin to recognition counting: one *sees* two dots on a blank page or two sheep in the field, one does not count them; one *feels* one's two legs or two shoulders or two hands, one does not count them. In recognition counting, a certain qualitative spatial gestalt presents itself; it is immediately apparent in the percep-tion. Cardinal temporality is similarly akin to original kinetic bodily pairings — of inhalation and exhalation, for example, of opening and closing (eyes, mouths, or fist), of walking on one foot then the other, and so on. In such kinetic bodily pairings, it is the feel of the movements, *not their numerical ordering* — which indeed is in many instances an arbitrary ordering since the phenomenon is cycli-cal and each member of the pair is dependent on the other for its appearance — that is paramount. In brief, cardinal temporality, like recognition counting and original kinetic bodily pairings, is experienced *physiognomically*. For any particular temporality to be the temporality it is — as for any number in recognition counting or for any kinetic bodily pairing to be, respectively, the number or pairing it is — a certain temporal quality is essential to it: an ongoing evenness as when we walk normally or an ongoing unevenness as when we walk with a limp; a jaggedness as when we move in fits and starts, a swiftness as when we punch an oncoming ball; a suddenness as when we duck, a hesitant slowness as when we move warily with apprehension and stealth; and so on.

In our approximations to primordial kinesthetic consciousness via self-movement *tout court*, we experience precisely the cardinality of time, not its ordinality. We do not experience kinetic *befores, nows, and afters*. This tripartite *ordinal ordering* of time is a sophisticated, reflective attainment that, in terms of the originary temporal structures of self-movement, imposes divisions where none exist, divisions that if present would in fact disrupt what is experienced as a global qualitative dynamic. Empirically-based

psychological-psychiatric studies of infants corroborate this constructive phenomenological finding. In particular, infant psychiatrist-psychologist Daniel Stern's
descriptive account of "vitality affects" attests to the physiognomic character both of
originary self-movement and of our original perceptions of others (Stern 1985, 1990).
In explaining vitality affects, he writes to begin with that the category is necessary
"because many qualities of feeling that occur do not fit into our existing lexicon or taxonomy of affects." He goes on to say that "These elusive qualities are better captured by
*dynamic, kinetic terms, such as 'surging', 'fading away', 'fleeting', 'explosive', 'crescendo',
'decrescendo', 'bursting', 'drawn out', and so on*" (italics added). He states further that
"These qualities of experience are most certainly sensible to infants and of great daily,
even momentary, importance" and that we ourselves as adults "are never without their
presence, whether or not we are conscious of them" (Stern 1985: 54). Moreover he
explicitly affirms that infants experience these qualities both "from within" and "in the
behavior of other persons" (Stern 1985: 54). In short, originary temporal structures
of experience are cardinal in nature; vitality affects — surgings, fadings, and all such
qualitative features of experience — are primary with respect to our experiences of
ourselves and our experiences of others.

Now to say that there are no befores, nows, and afters in originary self-movement
experiences — or in vitality affects more generally — does not mean that there are no
if/then relationships. The latter dual ordinal-ordering is not only distinctly different
numerically from a tripartite ordering of befores, nows, and afters; its intentional structure is different. If/thens — what Stern in fact describes under the term "consequential
relationships" (Stern 1985: 80–81) — are essentially causal in nature, essentially causal
in the sense of a subject actually doing something and thereby bringing something else
about. In the context Husserl speaks of them, if/then relationships refer specifically
to the correlation between certain movements I make and certain perceptions I have
in consequence of those movements — drawing closer to something, for example, or
turning something about in my hand. What my movement does is bring about different aspects, or in Husserl's terms, different *profiles* of things. My movement is in this
sense causally efficacious or informing in particular ways. If/then relationships are
thus certainly temporal by nature, but not apart from my movement, that is, *not apart
from the particular dynamics of the kinetic acts* which bring about the essentially causal
if/then sequence. In this sense, if/then relationships have a central qualitative aspect,
an aspect that in fact may be pivotal to the way in which a particular if/then relationship actually plays out. Consider, for example, head-turning in relation to seeing a
mosquito that a friend tells me is on my bare arm. If I turn my head slowly, then I
may well see the mosquito; if I turn my head quickly, then I may well see nothing
at all because the mosquito will have flown away, my too abrupt movement having
disturbed it.

Phenomenological studies of time are commonly riveted on its ordinality. The sequence before-now-after is consistently the principal concern for Sartre and Merleau-Ponty as well as for Husserl, for example. But temporality clearly has another more basic and global dimension, a dimension which, although Husserl did not explicitly recognize it, is adumbrated in his allusions to *style* — as in, for example, "Every man has his character, we can say, his style of life in affection and action" (Husserl 1989: 283).[19] The term *style* unquestionably specifies a *qualitative* character. In temporal terms, this qualitative character might be spelled out as hurried, relaxed, or abrupt, for example. It might also, of course, be spelled out in spatial and tensional terms — e.g. expansive, intense, lethargic, and so on. It is significant that Husserl's concern is with the style of things in the world as well as with the style of animate organisms. In this regard he speaks specifically of "qualitative change" (Husserl 1981a: 239). Although he describes qualitative change broadly, notably, in terms of the alteration or nonalteration of things and not in detailed descriptive terms that attempt to grasp the physiognomic dynamics of a thing's change, he is nonetheless aware of the fundamental importance of quality. He in fact makes pointed reference to the fundamental importance when, after introducing the notion of the world as constituting a singular perspectival style — "a totality of perspectives for me" (Husserl 1981a: 238) — where things progress harmoniously or disharmoniously, i.e. where things may run "counter to the [singular] style" by being illusions, for example, (239) he subsequently notes that what he has said thus far falls short of being a full description of "the concrete style of appearance ... [f]or there was no discussion of quality" (239). In short, Husserl's consistent references to qualitative change within his discussions of style implicitly acknowledge the intimate connection between style and quality. Moreover when he speaks in the same essay of two kinds of style, the style of appearances and the causal style "experienced within the temporality of immanent life," he notes with respect to the latter that "The style of change [of something in the world], in its 'rest' (in its momentary nonalteration) and 'motion', is inseparably connected to my possible resting or moving" (239). By the latter remark, he is, of course, clearly tying the changing character of things in the world to causal if/then relationships, that is, to a moving subject. But a basic concern, as indicated, is with normal and abnormal "styles of appearance," that is, with the possibility of things developing anomalies that intrude on what we otherwise perceive to be a "harmonious style of change" (239). The point of moment here with respect to these two styles is that the temporality of appearances — the temporality of things as they are experienced — has a certain cardinal temporal aspect that is tied both to alterations or nonalterations of a thing in itself and to a subject's movement with respect to the thing. In other words, the "*style of change*" of any appearance is coincident with a certain kinetic dynamic — a certain vitality affect, to borrow Stern's term — realized by changes in the thing itself and by the movement of a subject in relation to the thing. A thing explodes, sags, breaks, swells, recedes, quivers, flutters. Alternatively, it endures unaltered across perceived changes as we move (run, reach, recoil, pause, embrace, stumble …) in relation to it, experiencing different profiles of it. Each and every appearance has a distinctive temporal character.

Similar remarks may be made about Merleau-Ponty's Husserlian-derived elaborations of *style*. Like Husserl, Merleau-Ponty does not explicitly elucidate the qualitative dimensions of style, though clearly these dimensions are just as latent in his allusions — as, for example, when he writes that "[Movement and time] bring about the patterning of tactile phenomena…. The style of these modulations particularizes so many modes of appearance of the tactile phenomenon…." (Merleau-Ponty 1962: 315). Recognition and elucidation of the qualitative character of style would show here too that, with respect to animate organisms, *style* is originarily a matter of the qualitative structures of movement. It would show precisely the way in which cardinal structures of animation coalesce and kinetically articulate a certain qualitative dynamic that we intuit and that we linguistically identify by the word *style*. Indeed, we may ask, what is *style* in such instances if not an affirmation of a certain kinetic character, a *certain manner of doing things*? And what is a certain manner of doing things in a temporal sense if not moving with a distinctive *qualitative dynamic*, that is, not just proceeding actively in a certain *order*, but actively creating a quite particular temporal quality? Anything that we call a "behavior" has in fact a generic temporal quality in just this cardinal sense. Throwing has a certain temporal character that is distinct from reaching, for example, just as kicking has a certain temporal character that is distinct from stamping, or that walking has from running, and so on. Certainly there are and/or can be variations within these separate "behaviors," but each behavior is distinctively what it is precisely in virtue of its temporal — spatial and energic — quality.

Brief amplification of earlier descriptions of qualitative protentions and retentions is informative in this context. These temporal aspects of kinesthetic consciousness are, in an originary sense, precisely not ordinal in nature. The originary experience of time in self-movement, what we might call the qualitative nature of primordial time, does not run off like notes of a melody. (A melody is the example Husserl uses in analyzing internal time consciousness and in articulating the nature of protentions and retentions [Husserl 1964].) Protentions and retentions in originary self-movement do not adhere to discrete objects; they do not in fact adhere to any-*thing* at all. Rather, temporal expectations and lingering auras are embedded in the kinetic flux and flow of self-movement as it is created and constituted; that is, they permeate the global kinetic dynamic — the distinctive style of movement — as it unfolds. While one might object that such a descriptive account of protentions and retentions verges on a rendition of life as a dance[20] and thus distorts understandings of the temporality of everyday immanent life, such an objection misses the point. When we pay attention to self-movement *tout court*, whether for the purpose of developing a constructive phenomenology and thereby gaining insight into what we as adults all once experienced but cannot now remember, or for the purpose of grasping what is actually there, sensuously present in self-movement and thereby gaining direct insight into the cardinal structures of self-movement, what we discover is *quality*. Quality is built into our moving bodies; it is a built-in of the animate world. It is the basic staff of life that in various ways literally informs the life of all animate organisms, both as the style of appearance of an organism's own moving body as it experiences itself in the process of moving, and as a "style of appearance" of something in the world. Given its pervasive reality, it is indeed odd that quality is commonly conceived as something foreign to everyday life, something that is in fact regularly thought to pertain only to a properly "aesthetic" domain of experience. That kinetic protentions and retentions are qualitative, that we find them phenomenologically to be so, and that they can be described as embedded in the kinetic flux and flow of their own creation and constitution clearly refutes the common conception. When we examine our experience of self-movement, we find kinetic protentions and retentions to be consistently part and parcel of a qualitative dynamic in process.

In sum, we learn our bodies by moving and in moving both create and constitute our movement as a spatio-temporal dynamic. If we look more deeply into the matter, we discover that movement is the originating ground of our sense-makings, in phenomenological terms, the originating ground of transcendental subjectivity; we constitute space and time originally in our kinesthetic consciousness of movement. Flux, flow, a streaming present, a stream of thought, consciousness, or subjective life, a style of change — all such descriptive terms are in both a temporal and spatial sense rooted in originary self-movement: they are all primordially present not in the constitution of objects but in our original spontaneity of self-movement, in our original experience and sense of our dynamically moving bodies. To think the reverse is to overlook precisely that in the beginning was movement: we all of us came into the world moving and at the same time had to learn our bodies and to move ourselves. In effect, to think the reverse is to overlook *animation*, the spatio-temporal dynamic that is the foundational structure of that animation, and the fact that that animation is the very bedrock of our coming to know the world. It is ultimately to ignore the transcendental clues Husserl himself provides in his consistent references to, and descriptions of, both animation and animate organism. His phenomenological insights into the fundamental meanings of animation and of animate organism are in fact a validation of his methodological use of intentional objects as "transcendental clues" (Husserl 1973a: 50–53).[21] In particular, Husserl took animation and animate organism as transcendental clues to understanding how we come to make sense of the world. However incomplete his phenomenological analyses of animation and animate organism, his insights are springboards to understanding how, in self-movement, we come to constitute ourselves as spatio-temporal forms of life — how, in a broad sense, we make sense of ourselves — and how we derive our very concept of a spatio-temporal world on the basis of our own moving bodies. In this respect, his insights are themselves clearly transcendental clues to the cardinal epistemological structures of kinesthetic consciousness.

8. Afterword

Philosophers regularly examine the phenomenon of pain, conceiving it prototypical of that class of things known as *qualia*, in this instance, qualia in the form of sensations. They look at the phenomenon of pain prototypically also to raise questions about knowledge of other minds, to specify experiences that separate humans from "animals," and so on. Philosopher David Chalmers, in considering a range of conscious experiences, rightly remarks that "Pain is a paradigm example of conscious experience, beloved by philosophers" (Chalmers 1996: 9).

Philosophers also regularly examine qualia as a feature of what is typically called "subjective" experience. They most frequently examine the subjective experience of the color red, other sensory qualities such as loud and bitter being much further from the center of their attention. Given their preeminent concern with visual qualia, it is not surprising to find that Chalmers's "catalog of conscious experiences" (which he says "[should not be] taken too seriously as philosophy, but ... should help focus attention on the subject matter at hand," namely, consciousness), begins straight off with "Visual experiences" (32 lines). His catalog then proceeds to "Auditory experiences" (21 lines), "Tactile experiences" (5 lines), "Olfactory experiences" (16 lines), "Taste experiences" (5 lines), "Experiences of hot and cold" (4 lines), "Pain" (where the opening sentence in his 7–line entry is the sentence quoted above), "Other bodily sensations" (8 lines), "Mental imagery" (11 lines), "Conscious thought" (12 lines), "Emotions" (12 lines), and "The sense of self" (8 lines). Under the category "Other bodily sensations," Chalmers lists pain, headaches, "hunger pangs, itches, tickles, and the experience associated with the need to urinate," orgasms, and "hitting one's funny bone." His last sentence detailing this particular category of conscious experiences reads: "There are also experiences associated with proprioception, the sense of where one's body is in space."

Described in this utterly negligible, wayward, and offhand way, proprioception is clearly as misidentified as it is misunderstood. Moreover categorically conceived in company with a highly diverse assortment of "Other bodily sensations," proprioception is clearly misplaced. The very idea of kinetic qualia can hardly surface in such surrounds. Chalmers's deficient conception of proprioception is not of course atypical in the least. Over the long history of Western philosophy, philosophers have consistently omitted a certain type of qualia in their investigative studies of subjective phenomena, and they continue consistently to omit a certain type of qualia, precisely as Chalmers's own "catalog of conscious experiences" so well shows. In a word, Western philosophers not only commonly disregard proprioception and kinesthesia; they appear to know next to nothing of such kinds of experience. They tend to think of both proprioception and kinesthesia, if they think of both — or either — at all, as piddling, inferior experiences. They certainly do not think of either in terms of qualia. And they certainly do not think of either in the insistently bodily terms demanded. On the contrary, qualia for philosophers are mental states or mental objects or brain events. To see red, for example, is to be in a certain mental state or to entertain a certain mental object or to have certain spiking frequencies in a certain area of the brain. Were kinetic qualia mentalized or reductively cerebralized in this way, their living reality would be compromised and their foundational significance to the very enterprise of life would be ignored.

Careful critical reflection on a well-known scenario — a somewhat classic philosophical thought experiment concerning qualia — supports the above claims. Careful critical reflection in fact aptly brings to the fore the price of neglect and trivialization: a lack of empirical credibility. While notable philosophers may argue vehemently about what the thought experiment shows or does not show — i.e. the eliminability or non-eliminability of everything that is not physical — and thus take sides with respect to the reducibility of qualia to propositional statements about brain events, their arguments thoughtlessly pass over something absolutely pivotal to taking the thought experiment itself seriously, indeed, something that the thought experiment both as it is spelled out and discussed overlooks, namely, corporeal matters of fact. In effect, philosophers on neither side can possibly win the argument because in spite of their intense analytically-riveted and analytically-detailed discussions, like the thought experiment itself, they omit consideration of something essential to a credible realization of the scenario.

Philosopher Frank Jackson first presented his thought-experiment in an essay titled "Epiphenomenal Qualia" (1982). Philosopher Paul Churchland subsequently criticized Jackson's analysis of the experiment in an article titled "Reduction, Qualia, and the Direct Introspection of Brain States" (1985). Jackson answered to Churchland's criticisms in his article "What Mary Didn't Know." The following precis of the thought experiment is taken directly from the latter essay (Jackson 1991: 392).

> Mary is confined to a black-and-white room, is educated through black-and-white books and through lectures relayed on black-and-white television. In this way she learns everything there is to know about the physical nature of the world. She knows all the physical facts about us and our environment, in a wide sense of 'physical' which includes everything in completed physics, chemistry, and neurophysiology, and all there is to know about the causal and relational facts consequent upon all this, including of course functional roles. If physicalism is

true, she knows all there is to know. For to suppose otherwise is to suppose that there is more to know than every physical fact, and that is just what physicalism denies…. It seems, however, that Mary does not know all there is to know. For when she is let out of the black-and-white room or given a color television, she will learn what it is like to see something red, say. This is rightly described as learning — she will not say 'ho hum.' Hence, physicalism is false.

What is the matter with this thought experiment?

The matter with this thought experiment is Mary herself. She is not taken into account as a flesh and bone creature, a living body, an animate form. On the one hand, she is no more than a word-processing device. As such, she belongs to no known natural species. On the other hand, she is no more than a neuroscientific concept factory, indeed, "a trading station where [neurological] factors reside and transact business" (definition of "factory" in Webster's New College Dictionary 1965). In this sense too, she belongs to no known natural species.[22] To flesh out "the matter with Mary" in finer detail, we will first consider a range of corporeal matters of fact commencing with the more obvious. These matters of fact will show in beginning but decisive ways how fundamental defects contaminate the thought experiment, making it ultimately incoherent and thus, along with Mary herself, inconceivable.

Mary herself has certain skin tones that are neither black nor white. When she sees her hands that hold her book, she cannot fail to see that they match neither her black-and-white book nor her black-and-white television screen, for her hands are neither black nor white.

When Mary "is educated through black-and-white books" (as with books of any color, for that matter), she must first of all learn how to read, which means she must not only learn to use her eyes in a certain oculo-motor fashion that is different from, say, looking from one black and white wall to another black and white wall, but she must engage herself bodily in the world, by turning the book's pages, for example. In fact, even prior to learning how to turn a book's pages, she must learn that a book is a certain kind of object in the world that needs to be opened in a certain way, treated in a certain way, and so on. Moreover she must learn that in order to read a book, she must position herself in certain ways in order to read efficiently and effectively. In short, she must learn certain bodily comportments in relation to books and to the reading of books. If we ask how she learns these comportments, we find only one answer. Mary can learn the proper comportments only if she has already learned her body and has thus learned to move herself.

With respect to Mary's learning to read, her education cannot be breezily assumed as taking place through television lectures on black-and-white television screens and thus involve no persons with skin tones that are neither black nor white. Someone must actually *teach* Mary to read. Such an education is complicated, as any primary grade teacher and attentive parent will attest. Neither can Mary's education be breezily assumed as a purely physical phenomenon since to understand written words, Mary must come to understand that certain configurations of lines and squiggles have certain meanings, i.e. they signify something that has no sensuous presence anywhere in the physical world, not only small configurations like the word "and," for example, but larger configurations comprising sentences. Equally, *concepts* that Mary learns in the course of her education have no actual physical instantiation. Thus it matters not whether Mary, in her "*completed*" physical education, recognizes something in its physical presence or as a constellation of neural firings. In either case, her *concept* — say, of a television screen — is nowhere to be found either in her room or in her brain. Hence "the relevant neuroscientific concepts" that philosopher Paul Churchland claims Mary has learned in the course of her education and that pertain to sensations — including sensations such as *red* that have no corollary in Mary's actual experience, but that on Churchland's account Mary can nevertheless identify as a particular spiking frequency in her brain — have actually no physical instantiation whatsoever, any more than the concept *red* has any physical instantiation when Mary looks at a real tomato upon being let out of her room and senses redness. Whether Mary knows a certain spiking frequency as *red*, or whether she knows *red* experientially in the presence of an actual tomato, the concept *red* is itself unaccounted for physically and unaccountable physically. In brief, Mary's "*completed*" physical education may tell her "everything there is to know about the physical nature of the world," but it does not provision her with a *completed epistemology*.

When Mary is educated through television lectures, she must make sense of sounds she hears being articulated by persons on the screen in front of her, which means she must have knowledge of *speech* — speech production as well as speech perception (Liberman & Mattingly 1985) — and hence must have a sense of what it is to be an articulator of sounds, i.e. a sound-maker. Such a sense would in fact be part and parcel of her instruction about, and knowledge of, the physical nature of the world — part of all of those "physical facts about us and our environment" — but it would likewise be part and parcel of her immediate and unstudied knowledge of herself since, at the very least — i.e. even if somehow she herself never speaks — she can feel and hear herself cough, burp, sneeze, and breathe. Whenever she coughs, for example, she feels not only certain pressures in her chest, but feels herself moving in ways that are quite spontaneous and that have a quite particular dynamic. Now it might be argued that such knowledge of herself does not mean that "sensations are beyond the reach of physical science," as Churchland puts it (1985: 24), that is, that sensations are not representable in the neurophysiology of the brain. As Churchland asserts, *the brain uses more modes and media of representation than the simple storage of sentences*" (24; italics in original). Churchland would thus undoubtedly claim that while Mary's experiential knowledge of herself as a sound-maker and her linguistic knowledge of others as sound-makers are differently represented in the brain, the two knowledges amount to the same thing. Indeed, as he explicitly affirms and urges with respect to sensational knowledge of red and brain state knowledge of red, there are "different *type[s]* of knowledge … of exactly the same thing" (24; italics in original). But Mary's self-knowledge of herself as a sound-maker is not knowledge "of exactly the same thing" as her knowledge of others as sound-makers. Indeed, Mary's experience of herself as a sound-maker remains problematic. Her knowledge of herself as a sound-maker is from the inside in a quite different way from the way that her knowledge of others as sound-makers is from the inside. That is, Mary's actual experience of her own living body affords knowledge that is *qualitatively incommensurate* with her knowledge of what is happening in a brain, whether her own brain or that of another person. Indeed, if Mary is an astute person, someone capable of learning "everything there is to know about the physical nature of the world," then she necessarily knows that her perceptual knowledge of herself as sound-maker is quite different from her perceptual knowledge of others as sound-makers. It is precisely not a question of "different *types* of knowledge … *of exactly the same thing,*" but a question of something Churchland tries to silence, namely, the question of "*what* is respectively known" in each instance, the question of "the nature of the thing(s) known" (24). It is in fact implausible that a purportedly intelligent person like Mary, a person capable of learning "everything there is to know about the physical nature of the world," would disregard differences between knowledge of herself and knowledge of others.

A related dimension of Mary's television education makes a similarly significant point. In spite of their black-and-white appearances, lecturers appearing on Mary's television screen would appear to Mary to be in certain respects like herself. Quite apart from her *physical education*, Mary would be spontaneously aware of physical commonalities between the arms and legs that she sees on the television screen and the arms and legs that she sees *and feels* as her own. When a lecturer turns toward a blackboard and begins drawing on it, for example, Mary, being justifiably presumed as intelligent an observer as she is an intelligent learner, is aware of a physical commonality between the lecturer's leg and arm movements and her own possible leg and arm movements. This knowledge that she has of bodies does not come to her through instruction about brain events but is constituted spontaneously by Mary herself. Even were only lecturers' faces to appear on the television screen, Mary would still be aware of physical correspondences. In particular, without any prior experiences with mirrors, Mary would spontaneously match her own felt face with a face she sees — just like any normal human infant (Meltzoff & Moore 1983). In effect, she would be aware of the correspondence between the visual face of a lecturer and her tactile-kinesthetically felt face, and correlatively aware of the difference between the two perceptions without the aid of instruction from others. In fact, it is only after her spontaneously originating knowledge of faces that she would later learn in the course of her mastery of "physical facts about us and our environment" about such things as the cross-modal competencies of infants. In just such spontaneous ways as these, Mary would of necessity be aware of her own body as well as the bodies of others. She would be aware of her own body not in a merely physical sense, i.e. her body is an object of particular parts that move in particular ways and not others, and not in a reductive neurophysiological sense, i.e. aware of her body in terms of spiking frequencies in certain parts of her brain, but in an *animated* sense, a directly living proprioceptive-kinesthetic sense, which would include a felt sense of her own movement, of her own movement in relation to the room and the items within it, and of her motivations, as in, for example, her desire to hear another lecture, and hence to move in certain ways coincident with that desire by reaching for the remote, or her inclination to read a book instead of listening to lectures, hence to move in ways coincident with that inclination by leaning forward to pick up a book.

The above critical considerations consistently show that for the thought experiment to be a viable thought experiment, Mary herself has to be a viable person. In fact, she must be a viable person in an even broader sense. She has to do such things as sleep from time to time. Thus, she has to lie down. In effect, she has to get up from the chair or couch on which she sits when she reads a book or hears a television lecture, walk over to her bed, take her clothes off, put on her pajamas, turn the covers back, climb into bed, lie down, and close her eyes. Were she consistently to read and to listen to lectures lying in bed, i.e. were the thought experiment to stipulate that she be in bed from the beginning of her life and continuously until the time that she is let out of the room, and this in order that she might lead a bodily-undistracted life, her life would be short-lived: her muscles would atrophy, she would develop bed sores, and so on; she would not be able to continue her education, let alone actually stand and walk at the time she is "let out" of the room. Moreover not only would Mary have to move about in order to prepare herself for, and position herself to sleep, she would also have to move about in order to eat her meals and to go to the bathroom.[23] Clearly, however hypothetical, if Mary is to be a believable person, she cannot live by books and lectures alone. She has to learn to move herself. She has first and foremost to learn her body. She has to become aware of herself as an animate form, and coincidentally as an agent in the world, even her small world. No instructional books or television lectures can teach Mary her body in this crucial sense. She necessarily learns her body on her own. In fact, were Mary actually to learn a "*completed* physics" and thereby actually to come to know "all the physical facts about us and our environment," then in the very process of having mastered this wealth of physical information, she would have realized that there is something epistemologically missing. Being the observant, intelligent woman that she is, she would have readily realized that "all the physical facts" in fact omit basic facts of life. In short, by her very nature as an animate form, Mary would know herself to be something both more and other than a mere physical fact. She would know herself in immediate tactile-kinesthetic ways having nothing to do either with bare sensations or with brains. She would know herself in these ways because she would necessarily learn — and in fact have to learn — about herself as a living body before she could possibly even begin mastering all the physical information. Precisely in virtue of knowing herself as an animate form, she would know such things as that, if she moves the graph closer to her, she can read its inscriptions more easily. Indeed, before she could possibly come to conceive of herself as a physical specimen — to know herself as a set of "physical facts" — she would have to have experiences relevant to those "physical facts." Consider, for example, what is involved in Mary's getting up from her chair and moving across her room to the television set. Mary knows herself as a "here" with respect to every "there" in her room, and she furthermore knows herself as an agent with respect to everything in her room. More than this, in navigating in her enclosed space, Mary is both proprioceptively and kinesthetically attuned. She is aware of herself moving slowly or quickly away from her chair; she is aware of herself reaching out a certain distance for a book on the television set; she is aware of herself turning around and pausing before walking back to her chair; and so on. If Mary is a plausible hypothetical Mary, Mary is hypothetically *alive*.

Now when Mary learns to move herself, she knows there are qualia. As indicated above, she knows there are qualia because she experiences kinetic qualities directly, not only such qualities as slowness or quickness when she walks across her room, but qualities such as suddenness when, for example, after reading something in one book, she is impelled suddenly to reach for another book which contains something relevant to the passage she has just read. In a similarly qualitative way, she experiences directly the attenuated manner in which she turns a page or the heaviness of her body as she gets up from her chair. It is her own experiences of kinetic qualities that allow her to recognize kinetic qualities in her world — for example, the slowness of speech of one lecturer in contrast to another. More pointedly still, it is her own qualitative kinetic experiences that allow her to understand physical facts: the idea of an action potential shooting down an axon when she is studying neurology, or the idea that one thing can collide with another when she is studying quantum physics. Were Mary lacking in tactile-kinesthetic experience and were she to see one thing collide with another on her television screen, she would have no understanding of the collision *as such* because understanding the physicality of the event on a two-dimensional screen is contingent on understanding the physicality of the event in a three-dimensional world, which means having colliding or bumping experiences of one's own. If Mary is to be a plausible person in a plausible thought experiment, she cannot be simply a word-processor and information repository; she must be a hypothetically real *living body*.

Even were the above objections discounted and the second half of the scenario allowed to unfold as it does — Mary's being let out of the black-and-white room and seeing something red; Mary consequently finding that there is something she does not know — other objections would readily expose the same major devastating flaw:

a complete and utter neglect of the living body known as Mary, the result both of an empirically defective thought experiment that conceptually reduces a person to a word-processing information repository and of a consistent opacity of philosophers to recognize flesh and bone moving bodies and give them their living due. However putatively complete Mary's *physical* education, however putatively conclusive her knowledge of "physical facts about us and our environment," Mary has been educationally raised on no other standard than language; she has been educated in an exclusively verbal manner. Thus, whatever she might perceive in the normal everyday world when she is let out of the room, she has no basis for understanding it. As the thought experiment itself specifies, the limited world in which Mary has lived has consisted of two colors, whose only interest for Mary has been the words they form, and two objects, whose only interest for Mary has been the words they contain or spew forth. Accordingly, Mary's knowledge is verbal from beginning to end. It is not tangibly, kinesthetically, visually, or in any other *immediate* sensory way connected to the world, neither the larger everyday world into which she is let out and finally enters, nor the confined and limited world in which she has lived. Thus, while Jackson states that Mary learns "what it is like to see something red" when she is let out of her room, Mary in fact has no basis for comprehending "*what it is like* to see something red, or *what it is like* to see — or hear, or feel, or smell, or taste — anything for that matter, for she has no experience whatsoever of *what it is like* to perceive anything. Her concentrated diet of wholly verbal physical facts has omitted consideration of any such concerns and experiences. The consequences of such a diet are strikingly apparent the moment one considers experiences of kinesthesia and proprioception. Whatever Mary's experiences of movement might have been while confined to the black-and-white room — supposing proper and due attention had been paid to them — the experiences would have been transformed in conformity with her education into propositional statements about physical facts. Self-movement would thus have been for Mary nothing more than statements about lever action, efferent pathways, neuronal tracts, joint angles, and the like. By the very terms of Jackson's scenario, her experience of movement would pointedly lack qualia — expansiveness, zig-zagness, flaccidness, heaviness, and so on. Indeed, according to Jackson, qualia enter into the thought experiment only when Mary is let out of the black-and-white room and sees the color red.

Churchland's objections to Jackson's explanatory "what it is like" construal of Mary's post-confinement situation concern what he calls Jackson's "shortcomings" about various distinctions with respect to the term "knowledge" (Churchland 1985: 23). But shortcomings plague Churchland's own objections, shortcomings that coincide with the very ones shown above to plague Jackson: a blindered tethering to language and a correlative blindered neglect of proprioception and kinesthesia. In the context of specifying his first objection, for example, Churchland distinguishes sharply between verbal knowledge and non-verbal knowledge, or, as he terms the latter, "prelinguistic" knowledge. Sensations are exemplary of the latter kind of knowledge and they have a decidedly lesser status. Thus when Churchland speaks of Mary's seeing the color red, he does not accord the sensation an epistemic value on par with propositional statements regarding physical facts. Indeed, he quite noticeably demonstrates the deficient epistemic value of sensations in his diacritical markings: he speaks not of knowledge of one's sensations but of "'knowledge' of one's sensations," diacritically calling the reader's attention to a form of knowledge distinctly inferior to propositionally-stated knowledge about physical facts (24). In effect, when Churchland affirms that there are "different *types* of knowledge," neuroscientific knowledge and sensation knowledge, it is clear that only the person who "has mastered the complete set of true propositions about people's brain states" is the person who has accurate and proper knowledge (24). It is in this context that Churchland explicitly claims that the important difference between neuroscientific or brain state knowledge and sensational or qualia knowledge is "the manner of knowing" and not "*what* is respectively known" because knowledge in each case is "*of exactly the same thing*," i.e. knowledge of exactly the same brain event. Clearly, what Churchland overlooks completely in maintaining the identity of the known is that red *as it is experienced* is epistemically different in essential ways from red neuroscientifically rendered in the form of propositional knowledge about a certain state of the brain. A neuroscientifically verbalized red is not red in person — any more than brain neurology is equivalent to actual experience. Hence, whatever the known might be — red, black, Beethoven's Fifth Symphony, a botanical specimen, a hamburger, a plush pillow, Washington's monument, a rare Burgundy wine, the novel *War and Peace* — the *what* that is known is in each case crucially different according to whether it is known as a brain state or an actual experience. When Churchland affirms identity of the *what* and thus denies it any significance, he is in truth affirming that only brain events matter, be they in the form of "prelinguistic" brain representations or linguistic ones. This tunnel-brain vision of knowledge explains why he can urge that Mary, in spite of her limited black-and-white life, can have knowledge of qualia. If Mary "has learned to conceptualize her inner life, *even in introspection*, in terms of the completed neuroscience," then Mary is capable of identifying "various spiking frequencies" in her brain in spite of never having had sensations corresponding to them (25–26; italics added).

On Churchland's account, Mary's knowledge is in fact definitively and narrowly circumscribed: she is capable of knowing nothing other than events in brains, brains in general and her own brain in particular. Insofar as she is capable of formulating everything there is to know in the form of propositional statements about neurophysiological happenings in brains, then whatever her knowledge might be knowledge of — whatever the known at any particular time and place might be — Mary knows it only in a canonical brain language. She does not know anything of the living world because she has never effectively entered into it, not even the small living world that was the black-and-white room in which she presumably lived for many years. Indeed, the words she read and heard inside the room had neither any actual context of utterance nor actual point of reference. Learning one's body and learning to move oneself are crucial in this respect. One has to learn one's body and to move oneself before one can come to have knowledge of a physical world. In short, *if one were really to know "everything there is to know about the physical nature of the world"* (Jackson 1991: 392), *then one would have first of all to experience oneself as a moving, kinesthetically sentient creature.* This requisite is as binding hypothetically as it is binding actually; that is, it is as binding to thought-experiment knowledge as to real-life knowledge. Acquisition of the basic physical notion of three-dimensionality makes the point unequivocally. Only by learning her body and learning to move herself could Mary possibly come to know what it means in a physically exact sense to say, for example, that the hypothalamus is *underneath* the thalamus, or that an electrical force *pushes* positive sodium ions *inward*. Such spatial understandings derive ultimately from a felt sense of her own three-dimensional body, which is to say from proprioceptive and kinesthetic experiences of qualia having to do not just with movement generally, but with weight, force, alignment, mass, and so on. Mary cannot possibly learn the three-dimensionality of objects in the world, even the three-dimensionality of her own brain, short of directly experiencing the three-dimensionality of her own living body. Since according to Churchland, Mary's direct experiential knowledge of her own body and body movement can provide no accurate and proper knowledge of its three-dimensionality — her direct knowledge of her body is mere 'knowledge' — we can justifiably ask how Mary obtains the "relevant neuroscientific concept" of three-dimensionality. We can furthermore justifiably ask other fundamental questions, such as how Mary can possibly navigate in the world if all the time she is moving she is fixated on identifying spiking frequencies in her brain and rendering those frequencies in canonical propositional form. Ultimately, we can justifiably ask, Who is this Mary, this thoroughly enlightened paragon of knowing whose knowledge amounts to nothing more than knowledge of events in her brain? Who is this person who is able to introspect her own brain states but who has no deep and exemplary sense of her own movement? Who is this putative *complete knower* whose life consists solely of words?

In sum, the semi-classic thought experiment fails to provide a coherent and therefore conceivable scenario. One cannot imagine Mary learning all the physical facts there are to learn because, being consummately and exclusively tied to propositional language, she cannot understand in any concrete and full sense the physical facts to which any particular proposition refers. Indeed, being herself nothing more than a neuro-linguistic repository of knowledge, Mary is in fact an inconceivable person. There is, in effect, no hypothetical knower of the knowledge about which philosophers such as Jackson and Churchland are arguing.

Notes

* A considerably shorter version of this chapter was presented at the Husserl Circle meeting in June 1996 in Arlington, TX and at an all-University guest lecture at Trondheim University (Norway) in December 1996. Without in any way wishing to suggest his concordance with the substance of this chapter, I would like to acknowledge Ronald Bruzina for the central idea that was its genesis. In particular, I found his expositions of philosopher Eugen Fink's elaborations of the work of Edmund Husserl — along the lines of the originating and the originated — to be extraordinarily provocative.

1.   Claesges (1964) enumerates six moments of kinesthetic consciousness: time, space, horizon, world (which he says subsumes the previous three moments), body, and self. He identifies these moments without reference to the originariness of movement — its "before-hand givenness" in primal animation — thus without reference to the originating ground of our sense-making. His broad equation of kinesthetic consciousness with these moments and his concern to show that *the world* is pregiven (thus, by his definition, kinesthetic consciousness is pregiven) contain no reference to movement itself.

2.   See, for example, Husserl 1989:351: "But the animal and, in the first place, human beings can also be regarded as reality or nature, and we can here distinguish again between the animal as intuitive unity and the animal as unity of modes of behavior"; and Husserl 1989:142: "Without the soul, it [the psychic subject] is unable to stand alone; and yet again, it is a unity which in a certain sense encompasses the soul and which is at the same time so prominent that it dominates the general way of speaking about human and animal subjects."

3.   What I want tangentially to suggest is that the ontological ground Ronald Bruzina has uncovered in the context of his elucidation of Fink's emendations to Husserl has its epistemological corollary in the primacy of movement: the ontological temporal is coterminous with the epistemological kinetic: the latter too is the grounding ground that defies constitutional explication insofar as it is already there prior to and refusing constitution, but is at the same integrated with it.

4.   Cf. Sokolowski (1972:76): "[A]ll these motions of joints [i.e. the kinestheses] [are] preceded by the activity of motion. And [they are preceded] first of all [by] being awake. There is no basic consciousness without being awake and being awake is one of the basic data. We have to thank our bodies for it." The experience of motion, of course, is not *preceded* by the "activity of motion" but coincident with it. Sokolowski's point, however, about being first of all *awake* is suggestive of being first of all *alive*.

5.   See, for example, Spitz (1983), in particular, the essays, "Life and the Dialogue" and "The Evolution of Dialogue."

6.   This empirical fact is strongly if indirectly supportive of Husserl's analysis of empathy (1973: Fifth Meditation) in its suggestion that an attentiveness to the movement and actions of what is living is central to our existence.

7.   This textual model is well exemplified by Derrida (1976 and in other writings of his as well). For a critique of this textual model, see Sheets-Johnstone 1994, Chapter 4: "Corporeal Archetypes and Postmodern Theory."

8.   Obviously, this description of infant experience is not phenomenological. There is nevertheless good — even excellent — reason, to think that, like phenomenologically derived insights, it is true to the truths of experience.

9.   By "distinctive" ways of moving, I do not necessarily mean thoroughly unique. Species-overlapping patterns — including bipedality (higher primates other than humans are bipedal but not *consistently* bipedal) — are apparent in many everyday human movement behaviors.

10.   For a more detailed clarification of *constitution*, see pages 187–91.

11.   Clearly, to allow ourselves to be beguiled by the visual and the lingual is to succumb to a less than fully human assessment of our creaturehood. More than this, a tendency to devalue movement appears to coincide with a basic mind/body split, movement, in effect, being conceived through and through body rather than mind, in turn natural rather than cultural, and so on. In this dichotomous vein, movement is equally aligned with the trivial, perhaps even with what is feminine, particularly if there is no hammer in hand, thus nothing being wielded or manipulated. From this perspective, the mind/body split must be cured, rooted out at its source, before movement can be, or will ever be, given its due. "Animate form" or "animate organism" go a long way toward the cure because they describe what is there first and foremost in our experience: the animate; not "the lived" and not the "embodied," but the unity itself. Indeed, what is "lived" or what is "embodied" join over a gaping conceptual chasm what is still being rendered asunder. (See this text, Chapter Eight.)

12.   There are differences, of course, between examining experience in the phenomenological attitude and in the natural attitude. The differences, however, should not in this instance prevent validation or disaffirmation. But see Chapter 4 for differences between introspection in the natural attitude and introspection within the phenomenological *epoché*.

13.   I have changed the original descriptive term "areal quality" (Sheets-Johnstone 1966) to "amplitudinal quality."

14.   Note that "the world phenomena of *early childhood development*" is, in light of the concern here, the "world phenomenon" of self-movement.

15.   A melody — and less centrally a flight of birds and galloping cavalry — is the core of Husserl's phenomenological analysis of internal time consciousness (Husserl 1964).

16.   The terms "protention" and "retention" come from Husserl's (1964) analysis of internal time consciousness. They refer to expectations and memories with respect to an ongoing present.

17.   This is why Merce Cunningham can write (1968, unpaginated): "you have to love dancing to stick to it. it gives you nothing back, no manuscripts to store away, no paintings to show on walls and maybe hang in museums, no poems to be printed and sold, nothing but that single fleeting moment when you feel alive. it is not for unsteady souls."

18.   We could elaborate this "something other" of a qualitatively experienced temporality by saying that "felt organic living time" has a certain physiognomy and that, appropriating musical terms, we might describe it in any number of ways such as largo, andante, allegretto, allegro, presto, staccato, legato, gradamente, ritardando, accelerando, and so on. Because we have a felt *kinetic* sense of the particular way a piece of music or phrase of music unfolds

temporally, the terms might seem to us to confer an objective reality upon felt organic living time, to concretize what we might otherwise think of as rather vague and "subjective." But this would be to miss the origin of such terms; it would be to forget the corporeal source from which they spring, namely, the phenomenon of self-movement: walking, breathing, blinking, coughing, sneezing, crying, laughing, running, sauntering, shoving, pulling, pounding, and so on. All such movements are clearly familiar to us as dynamically lived-through realities. The felt temporality of these realities, however, is not something of which we are ordinarily mindful as adults. Indeed, it may well be that a vocabulary attuned to the dynamics of movement is lacking because adults do not attend to self-movement in the way they attend to the dynamics of sound in the form of music. Hence it is not surprising that what Husserl said in his attempt to pinpoint descriptively "the temporally constitutive flux" — "For all this, names are lacking" — can be said of the lived temporal experience of movement, and in particular for our considerations here, the lived temporal experience of *self*-movement.

19.   See also further on the same page: "one can to a certain extent expect how a man will behave in a given case if one has correctly apperceived him in his person, *in his style*" (italics added).

20.   Steven Crowell's comment on the shorter version of this chapter at the 1996 Husserl Circle meeting.

21.   For a more detailed clarification of a *transcendental clue*, see pages 212–13, 231.

22.   Indeed, on the one hand, Mary is reminiscent of Chalmers's conscious thermostat (Chalmers 1996), and on the other hand, reminiscent of his equivocation concerning the need for a veritable biological tethering of consciousness. While he states at the beginning of his book that "we would like the theory [of consciousness] to enable us to see consciousness as an integral part of the natural world" (1996: 5), he is quite content to claim some 290 pages later that "the fact that a thermostat is not made up of *biological* components makes no difference, in principle" (1996: 296).

23.   Lesser but still critical problems afflict the thought experiment in this respect. Were the thought experiment a truly credible thought experiment and Mary herself a truly credible person, then both Mary's food and Mary's toilet eliminations would have to be taken into account and accommodated in some way. Both otherwise present problems with respect to Mary's being kept in a putatively all black-and-white world. Fruits and vegetables, for example, come in a wide variety of colors; toilet eliminations are yellow and brown. Moreover if Mary is a normal woman, then in spite of her confinement, she menstruates. Hence, however black-and-white her room, books, and television screen, the philosophically favored and much-discussed color red is something Mary cannot avoid experiencing, unless, of course, she is fitted with some kind of glasses which she is instructed never to remove and which turn all colors into either black or white.

Methodology

Husserl and Von Helmholtz — and the possibility of a trans disciplinary communal task*

The laws of thought, after all, are the same for the scientist as for the philosopher.
Hermann von Helmholtz (1971: 369)

We put out of action the general positing which belongs to the essence of the natural attitude…. The epoché in question here is not to be mistaken for the one which positivism requires… It is not now a matter of excluding all prejudices that cloud the pure objectivity of research, not a matter of constituting a science 'free of theories', 'free of metaphysics' … [T]he interest governing these meditations concerns a new eidetics …
Edmund Husserl (1983: 61, 62, 63)

1.   Introduction

What I would like to do first in this opening chapter on methodology is to give a synopsis of the striking confluence in thought between 20th-century philosopher Edmund Husserl (1859–1938) and 19th-century physicist-physiologist Hermann von Helmholtz (1821–1894), specifically with respect to their common emphasis upon the central significance of movement in perception and their common use of the procedure of free variation. The purpose of showing the confluences is not basically to show historical connections; the aim is to show methodological connections, ones that ultimately subserve epistemological ends. Von Helmholtz and Husserl both had a background in and a mutual concern with arithmetic and/or geometry, a mutual *un*concern with metaphysics, a mutual estimation of the preeminence of epistemological undertakings, and, von Helmholtz's strong Kantian ties notwithstanding, a mutual emphasis upon experience with respect to these undertakings. Accordingly, what I want to draw out is the methodological and ultimately the epistemological import of the confluences for phenomenology and science alike, in particular, for the experimental scientist and for the phenomenologist engaged in the actual doing of phenomenology, in its actual practice as a rigorous science, which means, as Husserl envisaged it, the production of concrete analyses of the experiential origin of concepts, meanings, and values. In this context of praxis, a further confluence is not only relevant but critically coincident

with the aim of the chapter. Both Husserl and von Helmholtz envisioned epistemological undertakings to be a communal task — a shared and on-going labor rather
than the isolated and dispersed effort of single individuals.[1] Their singular vision has
strong implications. An active and confederated practice of phenomenology should
result in an active and confederated foundational epistemology. With its implicit call
back to experience — "to the things themselves" — a foundational epistemology holds
the promise of drawing together people whose work, though in as disparate fields of
study as that of Husserl and von Helmholtz, is basically intertwined. In other words, if
in and through the actual practice of phenomenology phenomenologists themselves
begin taking phenomenology seriously as the ultimate ground of diverse and multiple epistemological endeavors, then the sense of a communal and on-going trans-
disciplinary task has the potential of taking hold in earnest. Correlatively, a sound and
complete science requires sound and complete grounding. Objective scientific findings take for granted that strata of concepts, meanings, and values that phenomenological analyses expose. Indeed, Western science simply appropriates concepts such as
space, nature, force, and so on, without explicating where those concepts come from,
how we come to think in such terms, and why those terms are so central to our lives.
A communal and on-going trans-disciplinary task has the potential to enlighten and
deepen scientific knowledge by exposing the roots of its self-defined objective epistemology, providing it with foundations otherwise outside its purview of the world.
Insofar as the intentional infrastructure of scientific thought needs just such elucidation, the ultimate epistemological project is more immediately a methodological one.
In particular, a certain scientific practice is demanded beyond the typical laboratory
one that presently constitutes the hub of scientific work. Alternatively stated, what is
demanded is that the very concept of a laboratory be expanded, that a laboratory cease
to be necessarily a realm sequestered from the lifeworld, that laboratories enter the
everyday marketplace, so to speak, that experimental work in turn be anchored in the
experiential rather than exclusively in the behavioral, and that, coincident with this
locative and experimental expansion, persons become, with proper training, laboratories unto themselves. As will be evident, the epistemologically separate but concordant practices of von Helmholtz and Husserl accord with this larger conception. They
thereby demonstrate how the larger conception makes possible the idea of an on-going
trans-disciplinary task.

    After drawing out the epistemological import of the methodological points of
confluence between von Helmholtz and Husserl, I hope to show how dominant ideo
logical practices in current Western philosophy and science militate against the very
idea of a common task. The ideological practices are epitomized by two intimately
related phenomena: the de-animation of perception and the rise of cognitivist science. The immediate result is a science and a philosophy of mind that are opaque to
experience. But there is also a more extended consequence. The two intimately related
phenomena — both late twentieth-century epistemological moves — effectively

foreclose the possibility of a trans-disciplinary communal task. To elucidate the two phenomena and show the foreclosure in action, I will critically examine a phenomenologist's claim that points of confluence obtain between phenomenology and connectionism. I will then briefly contrast this account with a more promising scientific approach that takes movement seriously, and that therefore both conceptually and practically engages the rich and complex phenomenon of animation. By exemplifying obstacles to the very idea of a trans-disciplinary communal task, I hope to join methodological concerns with practical and epistemologically critical ones.

2. On the central significance of movement in perception

The most concise way of bringing out the extraordinary affinity in thought between Husserl and von Helmholtz with respect to the central significance of movement in perception is by direct quotation. The following exemplary observations from von Helmholtz's various research studies document his consistent concern with, and diverse insights into, the significance of movement.

1. After describing aspects of infant-child behaviors beginning with hand-play, von Helmholtz concludes by stating that "the child learns to recognize the different views which the same object can afford in correlation with the movements which he is constantly giving it" (von Helmholtz 1971b: 214).[2]

2. "Once we have acquired an accurate conception of the form of any object, we can deduce from it ... the various movements we should have to impress upon it in order to obtain ... successive images" (von Helmholtz 1971b: 214).

3. "As soon as we have gained a correct notion of the shape of an object, we have the rule for the movements of the eyes which are necessary for seeing it. In carrying out these movements and thus receiving the visual impressions we expect, we retranslate the notion we have formed into reality; and finding that this retranslation agrees with the original, we become convinced of the accuracy of our conception" (von Helmholtz 1971b: 215).[3]

4. "[O]ur body's movement sets us in varying spatial relations to the objects we perceive, so that the impressions which these objects make upon us change as we move" (von Helmholtz: 1971a: 373).[4]

Von Helmholtz draws on a variety of sources in compiling his evidence: observations of infants, children, and himself in the normal course of living; experimental laboratory studies he and others have performed; a variety of experimental situations that he devises for himself. Bringing an observational and descriptive perspicuity to everyday experience, von Helmholtz notes, for example, that "In walking along, the objects that are at rest by the wayside stay behind us; that is, they appear to glide past us in our field of view in the opposite direction to that in which we are advancing. More distant objects do the same way, only more slowly, while very remote bodies like the stars maintain their permanent positions in the field of view, provided the direction of the head and body keep in the same directions" (von Helmholtz 1962:295). He brings the same observational and descriptive perspicuity to the experimental situations he devises for himself. The latter studies are of particular interest insofar as they validate the idea of a personal laboratory, a movable experimental workshop in the form of one's own moving body. One of the most extraordinary everyday experiments von Helmholtz conducts is in quest of understanding what he calls "judgment[s] of relief in the floor-plane." He tells us that

> This [judgment] can be tested by standing in a level meadow and first observing the relief of the ground in the ordinary way. There may be little irregularities here and there, but still the surface appears to be distinctly horizontal for a long way off. Then bend the head over and look at it from underneath the arm; or stand on a stump or a little elevation in the ground, and stoop down and look between the legs, without changing much the vertical distance of the head above the level ground. The farther portions of the meadow will then cease to appear level and will look more like a wall painted on the sky. I have frequently made observations of this kind as I was walking along the road between Heidelberg and Mannheim.
> (von Helmholtz 1962:433–34)

Clearly, experience is not discounted but meticulously examined and just as meticulously varied; it is the source of scientific discoveries. The relationship between the spatiality of one's own body and the spatiality of the world is, in particular, both observationally and experimentally fleshed out in various ways by von Helmholtz. What is of further moment are two terms von Helmholtz uses with respect both to the nature of the relationship between movement and perception and to the pivotal place of experience in epistemologically grounding that relationship. These important terms are precisely ones Husserl uses to similar but deeper and broader epistemological ends, as we shall presently see. The terms are *correlation* and *self-evidence*, respectively. In the first of the above citations, von Helmholtz speaks explicitly of correlations between movement and perception; he observes that, on the basis of hand-play, a child comes to recognize fundamental relationships between certain bodily movements and certain perceptions of a given object. To exemplify the relationship for ourselves in an everyday way, consider that the cup we perceive when we run our fingers over its top edge is different from that same cup we perceive when we run our fingers along its sides or its handle; and that similarly, the cup we perceive visually in the course of bringing it to our mouth is different from that same cup we perceive when it is resting on the table. What we perceive of an object at any moment is not only *correlated* with the movements we make and the bodily postures we assume in reference to it; it is *consistently correlated* with our movement and bodily postures.

Von Helmholtz's meadow-laboratory observations implicitly affirm this fact. Though not specified as *invariant* relationships in the above cited passages, there is no doubt but that invariant correlations — lawful regularities — are at the epistemological center of von Helmholtz's observations and insights concerning movement and the perception of objects.

Clearly, movement in a quite literal sense informs perception. But von Helmholtz offers a further insight into the relationship. This further insight turns on the fact that the sensory-kinetic relationship itself can be brought to self-evidence any time we care to notice; that is, we can at any time turn our attention to *it* and not to the object in sight, in hand, or whatever. Von Helmholtz affirms this possibility when, in the third citation above, he speaks of our ability to "retranslate the notion we have formed [of the shape of an object] into reality." What our retranslation consists in is a reiteration of the movements necessary to recapturing the object's shape. What our retranslation provides is precisely *a bringing to self-evidence* the genesis of our sense of the shape of the object. Through retranslation, as von Helmholtz affirms, "we become convinced of the accuracy our conception," and this because through a recreation of our original experience(s), we bring to attention the rule or invariant governing the kinetic-perceptual situation.

The concept of *self-evidence* surfaces in an extended and critically important sense when von Helmholtz ponders the question of whether the axioms of geometry derive from experience or not, that is, whether as, according to Kant, the axioms are a form of transcendental intuition or not. Von Helmholtz's concern is to weigh — or perhaps better, re-weigh — the place of experience in the provenience of our mathematical spatial intuitions and thus to question Kant's claim. In the process of doing so, he contrasts our non-mediated intuitions of everyday space with our mediated intuitions of meta-mathematical space; as examples of the latter, he mentions Gauss's notion of surface curvature, Riemann's geometry, and other mathematical innovations. In the former case our spatial intuitions are straightaway self-evident, that is, they are immediately given "without reflection or effort, ... [and] above all cannot be reduced to other mental processes" (von Helmholtz 1971a: 377). In the latter case, our spatial intuitions are not straightaway self-evident but require previous analytical training and effort to achieve. With respect to the difference, von Helmholtz writes that "our attempts to represent [meta-]mathematical spaces indeed do not have the ease, rapidity and striking self-evidence with which we for example perceive the form of a room which we enter for the first time, together with the arrangement and forms of the objects contained in it, the materials of which these consist, and much else as well. Thus if this kind of self-evidence were an originally given and necessary peculiarity of all intuition, we could not [rightly claim the conceivability of meta-mathematical spaces]" (von Helmholtz 1977: 130–31).[5] Von Helmholtz is clearly unsettled by the fact that meta-mathematical spatial intuitions straggle behind everyday spatial ones and that, given their non-conformance with everyday spatial experience, they could be judged inconceivable. The question of where the axioms of geometry come from must be answered in a way that somehow accords with everyday sensory experience. Confronted with the challenge, von Helmholtz consults experience and finds "upon further consideration ... that there are a large number of experiences which show that we can develop speed and certainty in forming specific ideas after receiving specific sense impressions, even in cases where there are no natural connections between the ideas and the impressions" (von Helmholtz 1971a: 380). He gives as examples a child's learning of language, an adult's later facility with language, an artist's original vision, and an attentive observer's artistic understanding of that vision. He thereby tries to demonstrate that the axioms of geometry *are* tied to experience — to sense impressions — and that the relative slowness of our mathematical spatial intuitions is not the result of a deficiency in experience. On the contrary, he says, "investigation of the facts of experience shows that the axioms of geometry, taken in the only sense in which they can be applied to the external world, are subject to proof or disproof by experience" (1971: 381). He thus concludes that although meta-mathematical space is not immediately conceivable but requires training in analytical concepts for its introduction, the spatial relations it posits are tied to experience and are not transcendental in nature.

Von Helmholtz's central and continuing concern with the origin and meaning of the axioms of geometry together with his attempt to repudiate a Kantian transcendental origin is of fundamental methodological significance. Husserl is similarly concerned with the origin and meaning, as the title of his well-known essay "The Origin of Geometry" attests. Husserl's concern, however, has considerably broader and deeper roots, and this because it is conceptually linked to a methodology that provides access to origins, and because Husserl, in addition, has a fundamental and all-encompassing notion of self-evidence. In particular, Husserl speaks of how geometrical concepts may be "reactivated," that is, brought back to self-evidence. He asks, "Now what about the possibility of complete and genuine reactivation in full originality, through going back to the primal self-evidences[?]" He says that "Here the fundamental law [is] ... if the premises can actually be reactivated back to the most original self-evidence, then their self-evident consequences can be also" (Husserl 1970: 365). His point is that geometry has a history, that it developed from an original meaning into an internally coherent system of thought, and that its origin and historical progression can be systematically recovered. In other words, rather than being a compilation of ready made truths, geometry developed through "lively, productively advancing formation[s] of meaning" (365). Accordingly, when Husserl speaks of self-evidence at one point as being "nothing more than grasping an entity with the consciousness of its original being-itself-there [*Selbst-da*]" (356), he does not mean simply going back to a single point in time and recuperating, with respect to a consciousness of the primitive meaning of geometry, "some undiscoverable Thales of geometry" (369). On the contrary, to bring to self-evidence is to reactivate the whole of a history of meanings, not only an original, but further and successive acquisitions. Thus he says that "every new proposition can by itself be 'cashed in' for self-evidence" (363). In effect, the whole *"inner structure of meaning"* of geometry can be made self-evident by reactivating everything from its "primal beginnings" onward (371, 367).

Now what makes this epistemological journey possible is a genetic methodology, a specific procedure that, in the end, allows one to see how invariants of human experience, invariants that are not "time-bound" but stretch across civilizations, are the foundation of human thought (Husserl 1970: 377). Von Helmholtz's notion of *retranslation* hints at this possibility with its notion of going back to experience and bringing lawful regularities to self-evidence, but his notion of self-evidence stops short of history and of a correlatively elaborated methodology. There is in fact no methodology for "getting back"; there is only a broad-based scientific introspectional, experimental, and observational methodology used to gather evidence from everyday experience. In finer terms, *retranslation* pertains only to verifying the epistemological relationship between movement and perception; *reactivation* pertains to the whole of human epistemology in the sense of recovering its foundations and doing so through the practice of a rigorous methodology. Thus, where von Helmholtz turns to analogies with language and with art in his quest to anchor the axioms of geometry in experience, Husserl turns to the history of geometry itself. Von Helmholtz's notion of *retranslation* is nonetheless strongly suggestive of Husserl's notion of *reactivation*: both affirm the possibility of a return to the self-evidence of experience and the discovery of invariants. The notion of retranslation is in this sense latent in the notion of reactivation: in the same way that one can retranslate the notion of the shape of an object back into the movements that are its rule, so one can retranslate the progression of geometric meanings into their original: one can bring them again to self-evidence. Rather than seeing the possibility of this history, von Helmholtz sees "training in the understanding of analytical methods, perspective constructions, and optical phenomena" (von Helmholtz 1971a: 379). In general terms, self-evidence remains tied for von Helmholtz to an everyday perceptual present. Husserl's insight into the possibilities of self-evidence has a further, historical dimension. By investigating perceptual experience phenomenologically in the everyday world, one can discover invariants, regularities that can be brought to light any time one cares to "find out how matters actually are" (Husserl 1969: 278–79). But one can equally bring the same method to bear in a historical sense: one can recover origins by the practice of a genetic phenomenology.

In the several quoted passages that follow, we shall see that *correlation* is an equally key notion in Husserl's analyses of perceptual experience and that, as with the notion of self-evidence, there is a striking conjunction with von Helmholtz's thought.

1. "*[I]f* the eye turns in a certain way, *then* so does the 'image'; if it turns differently in some definite fashion, then so does the image alter differently, in correspondence. We constantly find here this two-fold articulation: kinesthetic sensations on the one side, the motivating; and the sensations of features on the other, the motivated" (Husserl 1989: 63).
2. "'[E]xhibitings of' are related back to correlative multiplicities of kinesthetic processes having the peculiar character of the 'I do', 'I move' (to which even the 'I hold still' must be added).... [A] hidden intentional 'if-then' relation is at work here.... [I]t is in this way that [the exhibitings] are indicated in advance, in expectation, in the course of a harmonious perception. The actual kinestheses here lie within the system of kinesthetic capacity, which is correlated with the system of possible following events harmoniously belonging to it" (Husserl 1970a: 161–62).
3. "Clearly the aspect-exhibitions of whatever body [i.e. object] is appearing in perception, and the kinestheses, are not processes [simply running] alongside each other; rather, they work together in such a way that the aspects have the ontic meaning of, or the validity of, aspects of the body [i.e. object] only through the fact that they are those aspects continually required by the kinestheses ... and they correspondingly fulfill the requirement" (Husserl 1970a: 106).
4. "Only [the living body] is given to me originally and meaningfully as 'organ'..., such that I can hold sway in a particular perception in just the ways peculiar to these [kinesthetic] functions. Obviously it is only in this way that I have perceptions" (Husserl 1970a: 217).

The above quotations demonstrate the remarkably similar findings of von Helmholtz and Husserl. There is in fact a notable highlighting by both von Helmholtz and Husserl of visual perception, thus of the correlation between eye movement and object seen. Moreover both make reference to expectations: "exhibitings," Husserl says, "are indicated in advance"; we receive "the visual impressions we expect," says von Helmholtz. From a methodological viewpoint, the beginning point of interest is that concordant observations are possible between science and phenomenology. In particular, correlations and expectations alike may be observed by a practicing scientist who is an attentive introspectionist. As von Helmholtz shows, careful reflection upon one's own perceptual experiences discloses certain regular features of experience. It bears emphasis that neither correlations nor expectations require a phenomenological methodology for their discovery; both are readily apparent to a careful observer. In the second passage cited, however, Husserl mentions that expectations are the result of a hidden intentional 'if-then' relation, and that this relation itself derives from an "I do," "I move"; and in the third passage, he speaks of "aspect-exhibitions" and of kinesthetic and perceptual "processes"; and in the fourth passage, he speaks of the living body as a kinesthetic 'organ'. In light of these intricate elaborations, we may ask what makes a phenomenologist's observations different from a scientist's observations, in particular, a scientist's introspective observations of his perceptual experience? What does Husserl, a phenomenologist, bring to an analysis of perception over and above what an introspectively attuned scientist brings and what is the value of this different knowledge? The questions are basically methodological ones. To answer them, let us first briefly spell out the initial phenomenological move: bracketing.

3.   A brief exposition of the phenomenological *epoché*

We live in what Husserl terms "the natural attitude." We take the world as it presents itself, *and go from there* with our investigations and inquiries. In the natural attitude, we perceive other animate beings; they are immediately there for us as are objects such as tables, cars, and pianos. In the natural attitude, we take the world and everything we find in it as factually existing. We carry on in this factually existing world of objects and of other animate beings with our likings and judgings and valuings and seeings and touchings and attentions and memories, and so on. This factually existing world — of which we ourselves are members — is continually as well as immediately there for us. As Husserl remarks, "The *natural* world ... is, and has been, *there for me continuously* as long as I go on living naturally" (Husserl 1983:54). It is this immediate and continuous natural world that we explore, travel in, and ask questions about. It is this same factually existing world that is the world of science, the world that, with proper care and study, yields data. Scientists pursue the practice of science within the natural attitude. They gather facts about the immediate and continuously existing factual world, implementing procedures to secure an objective stance toward it. Their aim is, as Husserl has so well expressed it, "[t]o cognize 'the' world more comprehensively, more reliably, more perfectly in every respect than naive experiential cognizance can" (Husserl 1983:57).

Bracketing both nullifies the natural attitude and puts the factually existing world in parentheses. Making this move does not mean that we no longer like and dislike, see and touch, and so on, nor that we doubt the factuality of the natural world. On the contrary, everything is as it has been all along; we live in the very same world, only it no longer has the force, especially the epistemological force, it immediately and continuously had. By bracketing we effect a suspension, an *epoché*: judgments and beliefs no longer have the potency they have in the natural attitude. Their modification frees us from epistemological constraints of the natural attitude such that we perceive things afresh. The sky, another human, a symphony, a siren, an ant, an infant, a piece of chocolate, a glass of water — whatever the object of our attention, we perceive it in a new light. It is stripped of its usual ontological, epistemological, and axiological baggage. Precisely because it is, we perceive it as strange and at the same time become aware of the presuppositions we ordinarily bring to its perception. By effecting such a move we have the possibility of elucidating how it is the thing comes to have the meaning and value it does for us *in the natural attitude*. In other words, we expose our own assumptions and prejudices such that we meet the object as if for the first time, on its own ground. The natural attitude that has bound the object naively to a certain way of thinking, believing, judging — in short, to a certain domain of meanings — is lifted. But bracketing expands our possibilities for knowledge in further ways. With particular attention to perception, it allows us the possibility of gaining insight into the epistemological structures of perception itself. This is because through bracketing, the act itself of perception becomes a phenomenological object. It does so precisely because bracketing nullifies our natural attitude, an attitude that in perception commonly rivets our attention wholly on the perceived world. That perceived world, however, is in actuality not only a world of perceived objects but includes us as perceivers. What is of particular moment in the present context of attempting to pinpoint essential differences between the observations of a phenomenologist and of an attentive introspective scientist and to specify the peculiar value of the former's analyses, centers on the very question of how an object is perceived, thus on the perceiver in his/her acts of perception. In consequence, the method of phenomenology discloses a notion of perception radically different from that obtaining in the natural attitude. Rather than being a camera-ready take on the world, and one particularly construed as a copy of the world in the form of a representation in a brain, phenomenological investigations show the perception of an object to be an epistemological process; objects are *constituted*. They are constituted not in an ontological sense — we do not *create* the objects we perceive — but in an epistemological sense. We put the world together. We make sense of it — precisely as Husserl's descriptions indicate with respect to correlations. Moreover we can bring the process of constitution to the fore, in part by bringing correlations back to originary evidence, as Husserl implicitly indicates in the passages cited. What phenomenological analyses bring to our understanding of perception are decisively deeper understandings of the process of constitution, including deeper understandings of both the relationship between movement and perception as indicated by if-then relations, by an "I move," and so on, and the possibility of self-evidence. A finer look at the citations from both von Helmholtz and Husserl will bring aspects of these deeper understandings to light. It will do so by highlighting methodological differences between the scientific approach of von Helmholtz and the phenomenological approach of Husserl.

4.   A methodological contrast

In the passages cited, von Helmholtz describes the perception of an object as a *fait accompli* that one can analyze in retrospect. In passages (2) and (3), he says, respectively, "Once we have acquired an accurate conception of the form of any object …"; "As soon as we have gained a correct notion of the shape of an object …". In contexts such as these, correlations constitute the empirical means by which we can justify our conception of an object: by rehearsing our movements in relation to the perceptions of any object, we may go back and check for ourselves the *correctness* of our conception. Indeed, von Helmholtz writes explicitly at one point that "Each movement we make by which we alter the appearance of objects should be thought of as an experiment designed to test whether we have understood correctly the invariant relations of the phenomena before us, that is, their existence in definite spatial relations" (von Helmholtz 1971a: 384). In the passages cited, Husserl describes the perception of an object as a process of putting together, a process in which we can catch ourselves in the act. As noted above, he speaks in this context of an "I move," of if-then relations, of "aspect-exhibitions," and of a kinesthetic 'organ'. In just this sense, his concern is with the *constitution* of objects. It is precisely the constitution of objects that constitutes perception. Thus, for example, "aspect-exhibitions" — what Husserl elsewhere and more consistently describes as *profiles* of an object — are linked with "the kinestheses." Aspect-exhibitions have ontic meanings for us — we perceive an edge, for example, or hardness, or roundness — in virtue, and only in virtue, of particular movements we make that bring these meanings to perceptual life for us. Each particular perspective brings with it certain meanings and not others. Our concept of an object is the result of multiple perspectives and multiple correlations; it is an achievement that can be spelled out in terms of if-then relations, of the moving body as an organ of perception, of the experience of oneself as an agent of doings and movings, and so on. What phenomenology affords is thus ultimately a deeper and more comprehensive account of perception because its methodology affords, from the beginning, access to experience outside the natural attitude. While the focal point of attention is experience in both von Helmholtz's science and Husserl's phenomenology, and while introspection is the pivotal mode of access in each practice, the actual introspective methodology is in each practice substantively different: *in phenomenology, introspection takes place not within the natural attitude but within the epoché.* Accordingly, introspective findings are different and the language of the descriptive account is different. In phenomenology, the object of perception is traced out as it comes to be constituted, that is, as it is synthesized in the process of multiple perceptual consciousnesses of it; in science, the object of perception is taken as already there and it is introspectively inspected from that vantage point, a given part of the natural world, a factually existing something about which we can gather facts and form fact-based conceptions. Although the correlation between movement and perception is introspectively discovered in both instances — and recognized as fundamental in both instances — and although, as we shall see, on the basis of these correlations other seminal aspects of perception are discovered and recognized as fundamental in both instances, the epistemological import of introspective findings for von Helmholtz and for Husserl is ultimately different.

It is ultimately different because the fundamental difference in methodology results in the perceived object and the perceiver being differently experienced in each instance. The above citations bear out these experiential, and ultimately, conceptual, differences. They show that the interest of correlation for von Helmholtz is how, with respect to the form or shape of an object, certain movements we have already made have brought about a certain concept of the object's shape, and how, by retranslating our concept of the shape of the object back "into reality," i.e. into those movements, we can "become convinced of the accuracy of our conception." The focal point of von Helmholtz's concern in these passages is most certainly on how the perception of objects is tied to movement, but the perception of objects *already formed*, that is, the perception of what we take to be fully-fledged objects of which we have come to a fully-fledged conception; and, most importantly, on the possibility of verifying the correctness of our fully-fledged conception. From the vantage point of these passages, introspection in the natural attitude clearly takes the object as factually existing and does not disclose how, beyond certain factual correlations, it comes to be an already formed object for us. It does not, for example, disclose how the very concept of shape takes form for us — how the concept arises, on the basis of what experiences it derives.[6]

The above remarks are certainly not a denigration of the practice of introspection in general or of von Helmholtz's introspective technique and findings in particular. On the contrary, they indicate a remarkable validation of an introspective methodology. Through introspection in the natural attitude, detailed aspects of experience come to light such that, as with von Helmholtz, we can verify the presence of certain spatial relationships between movement and object perceived. Moreover, as will be shown in the following section, we can follow von Helmholtz's introspective methodology and make further seminal empirical discoveries on the basis of these spatial correlations. Von Helmholtz's particular discoveries aside, introspection in the natural attitude is a practice of everyday life. We specify such things as the exact nature of a headache — its intensity(ies), its duration, its localization(s) — through introspection; we examine such things as bodily tensions in learning a new piece of music, a new sport, or even a surgical technique. Introspection in the natural attitude typically involves reflecting upon some dimension of ourselves in a just-past experience — thus it has been called "retrospection" (see Lyons 1986) — but it may also typically be an observation of ourselves through a sequence of events, a past or future sequence on the order either of an introspective replay of a progression of thought just prior to a present impasse, for example, or an imaginative forecast of experience in answer to the question, "how might such and such an individual react in such and such a circumstance?" a question whose answer is based upon introspective imaginings of our own possible actions in such a situation, and a question that, incidentally, arises in the design stage of experimental science. Clearly, a rich and varied knowledge of experience is possible through introspection in the natural attitude. What introspection in the natural attitude does not provide is an exacting and comprehensive knowledge of the process of cognition, including knowledge of the origin of fundamental concepts and how things come to have the meaning and value they do. The latter knowledge cannot be systematically and substantively gained through a methodology in the natural attitude. The interest of correlation for Husserl bears out this epistemological distinction. His interest is precisely in the latter kind of knowledge, thus in the complex constitutional dimensions of movement-perception correlations. Like our concept of every other aspect of an object, our concept of the shape of an object — to use von Helmholtz's example — is built up; it is never given all at once but constituted across the system of "kinesthetic sensations on the one side" and "sensations of features on the other." With respect to its multiple profiles, no one profile of the object is sufficient by itself, i.e. no one by itself encompasses the shape of the object. The unity of the object indeed exists in the synthesis of acts of perception. This is in broad terms what is meant by *constitution*. What introspection discloses within a bracketed world is the way in which any object is synthesized in acts of perception, any object not in an ontological but an epistemological sense, i.e. in Husserl's term, any object *as meant*. This epistemological object is not out there in the world such that it can be taken as it presents itself, factually given, for it is not only never altogether there to be taken as such, but, as indicated, it exists across the acts of perception through which we come to constitute it.

In sum, and coincident with the passages quoted, just as basic and striking commonalities are apparent, so basic and striking differences are apparent. The differences are differences in introspective methodologies. While facts gathered through introspection in the natural attitude clearly can — *and do* — accord with descriptive accounts in phenomenology, they are not equivalent to the deeper and more comprehensive findings afforded through phenomenological introspection and requiring an intensive attention to an accurate and adequate languaging of the phenomenon. With respect to the methodological difference, we might say that what is wanted by an introspective scientist is a definitive and correct account of an object, not an exhaustive and thoroughgoing account of how one perceives and comes to know it. But we can say this only provisionally, because there are other passages to consult.

5. The central epistemological significance of freely-varied movement

Von Helmholtz brings notable insights to his account of perception that are based upon his discovery of the correlation between perception and movement but go beyond it. Before proceeding to specify and examine these insights, we should note that it is not just that self-movement enables us to perceive, affording us now this, now that profile of an object. It is that in this very correlation, we move and are clearly empowered to move. As Husserl puts it in passage (4) above: "I can hold sway." Thus it is not simply movement but freely chosen ways of moving that "require" certain perceptual results; they require these results according to the particular spatio-temporal structures they themselves articulate. These two insights, the one into the central significance of movement to perception, the other into self-agency with respect to movement, together lead to a profound understanding of the role of volition in perception. In this respect von Helmholtz's notion of *presentabilia* — possible perceptions by way of volitional movement — is of considerable significance as is his notion of "unconscious inference" — other perceptions of the same object are possible; we have only to choose them, i.e. move in certain ways so as to produce them. These notions, both of them emanating from his basic insight into the correlation of movement with perception, accord in fundamental ways with phenomenological analyses of perception, in particular, with the epistemological principle of constitution, and with the second methodological procedure, i.e. the method of free variation. What conceptually underlies the latter method is the realization that, in an attempt to reach fundamental epistemological understandings of perception, one may utilize *possible* experiences. Thus, in Husserl's terms, I can perform free variations on any perceptual theme: I can imagine possible instances of holding sway with respect to any particular perceptual circumstance, and in so doing generate possible if-then relationships in which specific possible kinestheses give rise to specific possible aspect-exhibitings. Similarly, of course, in so doing, I generate possibilities of agency and thereby have the possibility of gaining insight into fundamental structures of "I move" and "I do," and into multiple dimensions of my *organ*-ic body. Clearly, neither von Helmholtz nor Husserl is alone in realizing the epistemological value of imagining the possible. Von Helmholtz did not develop his procedural use of imagination into the method of free variation as did Husserl, but, as we will see, he clearly utilized the method, and not just in a cursory or happenstance fashion, but in ways that substantively informed his epistemological investigations and carried them forward. In the process, he clearly realized that possible movement is of considerable significance, indeed, that "potential volition," as we might term it, is primary in forming the concept "object."

Passages in two of von Helmholtz's essays — "The Facts of Perception" and "The Origin and Meaning of the Axioms of Geometry" — are especially topical and informative in this respect. In the first passages we will consider, von Helmholtz is grappling with the question of whether it is only from movement that the data of perception arise. The question is somewhat akin to the formation of a null hypothesis in science: the question is formulated negatively rather than positively since the latter would require investigation of every instance of perception. Von Helmholtz sets about answering the question by way of a thought experiment:

> Let us try to set ourselves back to the state or condition of man without any experience at all. In order to begin without any intuition of space, we must assume that such an individual no longer recognizes the effects of his own innervations, except to the extent that he has now learned how, by means of his memory of a first innervation or by the execution of a second one contrary to the first, to return to the state out of which he originally moved.... Let us assume that the man at first finds himself to be just one object in a region of stationary objects. As long as he initiates no motor impulses, his sensations will remain unchanged. However, if he makes some movement (if he moves his eyes or his hands, for example, or moves forward), his sensations will change. And if he returns (in memory or by another movement) to his initial state, all his sensations will again be the same as they were earlier (von Helmholtz 1971a: 374–75).[7]

In the discussion of the thought experiment that ensues, Von Helmholtz's explicitly recognizes the epistemological significance of potential as well as actual freely-varied movement. His descriptive language in fact has a strikingly familiar Husserlian cast:

> If we call the entire group of sensation aggregates which can potentially be brought to consciousness during a certain period of time by a specific limited group of volitions the temporary *presentabilia* — in contrast to the *present,* that is, the sensation aggregate within this group which is the object of immediate awareness — then our hypothetical individual is limited at any one time to a specific circle of *presentabilia,* out of which, however, he can make any aggregate present at any given moment by executing the proper movement [i.e. he can freely vary his movement and thereby perceive a different aggregate]. Every individual member of this group of *presentabilia,* therefore, appears to him to exist at every moment of the period of time, regardless of his immediate present, for he has been able to observe any of them at any moment he wished to do so. This conclusion — that he could have observed them at any other moment of the period if he had wished — should be regarded as a kind of inductive inference, since from any moment a successful inference can easily be made to any other moment of the given period of time (von Helmholtz 1971a: 375).[8]

Von Helmholtz's *presentabilia* are in essence Husserl's *presentiations* — possible perceptions. *Presentabilia* are tied to *volition* just as *presentiations* are. They are the equivalent of "free variations" arrived at through modified kinestheses. In phenomenology, free variations are a means of arriving at eidetic truths, that is, truths about the essential nature of the thing in question — perception, memory, willing, disliking, or whatever. One performs free variations by running through possible instances of whatever it is one is investigating. One thereby discovers what is essential to it. Helmholtz was not a phenomenologist, yet he arrived at just such essential insights. The important methodological question of how he did so will be addressed subsequent to the discussion of his two essays. The significant point of interest here is von Helmholtz's recognition that a certain range of possible volitions — what Husserl would term possible

"I cans" — specifies a certain "circle of *presentabilia*." In particular, insofar as "every individual member" of any group of presentabilia "exist[s] at every moment" during the period of time considered — since it could be observed "at any moment" the perceiver wished to turn attention to it — then the epistemological *object* (again, in Husserl's terms, the object *as meant*) clearly resides in the unity of acts of correlation; it is *constituted*. Von Helmholtz implies just this when he writes that "In this way [i.e. "by executing the proper movement"] *presentabilia*, along with their individual members, come to be something given to us, that is, they come to be *objects*" (1971: 376; italics in original).[9] However brief and passing his insight into how objects come to be objects for us, there is no doubt but that von Helmholtz recognizes self-movement as the epistemological backbone of — to use the phenomenological term — the constitution of objects; that is, his realization that perceptual possibilities are in essence kinetic possibilities leads him to the further insight that objects come to be objects for us only in virtue of the series of movements we make in relation to them, only in virtue of the series of movements we make in relation to "circles of *presentabilia*."

A further aspect of the remarkable confluence in epistemological understandings concerns what translators of von Helmholtz's writings term "unconscious judgments" (1912:, vol. 1: 269), "unconscious inferences" (1971: 217, 381), "unconscious conclusions" (1962: 4), "inductive conclusions" (1962: 556), and in the instance cited above, an "inductive inference." Although there are fundamental differences, all of these terms conceptually converge in a fundamental way with Husserl's idea of "passive synthesis." Von Helmholtz expressly states that

> In some of my earlier works I called *the connections of ideas* [italics added] which take place in these [psychic] processes unconscious inferences. These inferences are unconscious insofar as their major premise is not necessarily expressed in the form of a proposition; it is formed from a series of experiences whose individual members have entered consciousness only in the form of sense impressions which have long since disappeared from memory .... *Obviously we are concerned here with the elementary processes which are the real basis of all thought.*
> (von Helmholtz 1971a: 381, italics added; cf. von Helmholtz 1977: 132)

Compare this decisive grounding of knowledge in "elementary processes" with Husserl's notion of passive synthesis:

> [So long as the unity of experience and the harmony of the world are maintained,] then we are constantly guided by that passive synthesis in which precisely the multiplicity of experience yields a unity of an experiential object as something consistently existing. Passive synthesis which itself belongs in its various forms to experience and which is fundamentally its unity, *is everywhere our support for putting into play the activities of relating and of constituting logically universalizing universal concepts and propositions ... in such a way that the concepts ... become intuitive knowledge* (Husserl 1977: 75).

Clearly, von Helmholtz and Husserl both find that knowledge is a process of putting together, a process accounted for only in the recognition of passively accomplished, nonlinguistic integrations of experience. In effect, knowledge of an object as such is neither a ready-made fact nor a matter of language; it is an epistemological achievement. Cognition, in turn, is thus not an instant take on the world but a complex epistemological process.

Now as the earlier quotation shows, von Helmholtz ties elementary inductive inference specifically to potential observations, thus ultimately to what may be termed "potential volitions." He thus not only anchors perception in volitional movement; he anchors passively formed inductive conclusions in volitional movement. In particular, he states that his hypothetical individual has a sense of all other possible impressions in the given group of *presentabilia* in the given period of time because "he has been able to observe any of them at any moment he wished to do so." In effect, his hypothetical individual concludes — not in a reasoned but in an elementary way — that he can instantiate any "sensation aggregate" at will by moving accordingly. While von Helmholtz does not mention an "I move," his hypothetical individual clearly forms the inductive inference *only because he can move and is free to move*. The notion of an "I move" or "I do" is thus an implicit and unexplicated dimension of von Helmholtz's notion of volition. On the other hand, while Husserl recognizes an "I move" and an "I do" in conjunction with the fundamental correlation of movement and perception, he does not elucidate the connection between kinetic powers and inductive processes. Indeed, since induction is commonly conceived and spoken of as deriving from, or pertaining to, factual evidence, a form of reasoning in the natural attitude, it is not a form of thinking central to Husserl's basic phenomenological concerns. Consideration of the connection is, however, topical to present concerns with volitional movement. At one level, consideration of the connection will illustrate how phenomenological analyses can deepen epistemological findings of science, indeed, how the process of induction can be analyzed phenomenologically. An article elaborating the connection is instructive in this respect. The article will furthermore allow us to see how, though beginning their investigations into perception from quite different perspectives and with decidedly different aims altogether, von Helmholtz and Husserl both affirm the fundamental role of freely-varied movement in perception.

In his article, "The Role of 'Ich Kann' in Husserl's Answer to Humean Skepticism," philosopher Albert Johnstone shows both how spontaneity — what Husserl speaks of as the "ego's free potentiality" — is experientially joined to randomization, and how randomization is necessary to warranted inductive inferences. Focusing on Husserl's elucidation of "I can" — *Ich Kann* — Johnstone points out that "[The] facultative possibility of moving or not moving, of observing or not observing, yields something further than mere concomitantly perceived series of kinesthetic and sensuous data; it yields facultative or optional observations any of which could have not been made, or could have been made at some other time…. As a consequence any uniformity displayed in the observed set of phenomena provides grounds for an extrapolation of the uniformity to the phenomena which were not, but could have been, observed" (Johnstone 1986: 592–93). Johnstone in turn concludes that implicit in Husserl's "I cans" is the possibility of random movement, and that it is the possibility of random movement that grounds inductive procedures: "Spontaneity … provides the randomizer which allows a valid inductive conclusion to be drawn" (594). Its deeper notion of randomization notwithstanding, Johnstone's analysis accords in basic ways with von Helmholtz's: both affirm the seminal importance of a freedom to move, a freedom that is "spontaneous," that may be exercised "at any moment." Keeping Johnstone's Husserlian elaborations in mind, we see in effect an extraordinary concordance of thought about the fundamental role of freely-varied movement in both von Helmholtz and Husserl: on the one side, freely-varied movement is the basis for elementary inductive inferences basic to our perceptual experiences of objects; on the other side, freely-varied movement is an essential dimension of the power to perceive.

In this context of Husserlian elaborations, a crucially significant aspect of free variation demands clarification. Husserl's privileging of the possible over the actual is in the service of the eidetic. To attain to what is essential demands a methodology proper to the task. But an imaginative free variation of self-movement can only be a *spectated* imaginative free variation of movement. In other words, *the kinestheses*, the very stuff of an "I move," of an "I do," of an *organ* body, and so on, can be freely varied *imaginatively* only as a *visual* phenomenon. What appears in such an imaginative free variation is the visual phenomenon of oneself — or, as it turns out on close scrutiny, some body or other — moving. The resultant phenomenology of movement is a phenomenology of movement seen. This in no way invalidates the phenomenology; it does not mean, for example, that such a phenomenology fails to include energy dynamics and appears as a purely spatio-temporal form. It means only that the peculiar kinesthetic character of movement — movement as it is kinesthetically experienced — is not a structure to be found in any of the imaginative free variations. A concerted attempt to run through *imaginative kinesthetic* variations consistently involves the *actual tactile-kinesthetic* body. To imagine oneself slamming a door, for example, or swaying, or running, or doing whatever, involves incipient kinesthetic feelings of slamming, swaying, running, and so on. Accordingly, when Husserl writes that "There are reasons by virtue of which in phenomenology, as in all other eidetic sciences, presentations and, more precisely, *free phantasies acquire a position of primacy over perceptions* and do so *even in the phenomenology of perception itself, excluding, to be sure, the phenomenology of the Data of sensation*" (Husserl 1983: 158–59; italics in original), he is affirming, but does not concretely specify, a domain of study demanding a methodology other than that of *imaginative* free variation. Clearly, though Husserl himself does not so specify, the phenomenology of kinesthesia presents itself as just such an exception to imaginative free phantasy. In effect, *active self-experimentation* is essential to understanding *the kinestheses.* In this respect, it is in fact doubtful that Husserl could possibly have arrived at his rich (if less than fully explicated notion) of the kinestheses by way of imaginative free variation; he undoubtedly would have arrived at it through first-hand active self-experimentations, precisely of the kind von Helmholtz carried out. In effect, active self-experimentations were the point of departure for phenomenological analysis; they were what Husserl elsewhere calls "the transcendental clue" grounding an investigation outside the natural attitude (Husserl 1973: Second Meditation). Given this clarification of free variation with respect to freely-varied movement, we can appreciate the peculiar challenge that movement presents: phantasized movement can enlighten us only so far. To get at the essentials of movement, and, in turn, to arrive at fully fleshed out understandings of an "I move," of an "I do," of an *organ* body — structures into which Husserl gained initial insight but which he did not fully explore — it is essential to move.

In passages from the second essay of interest with respect to the practice of free variation, von Helmholtz is concerned with the question of whether axioms of geometry are "necessities of thought" (von Helmholtz 1971c: 247). He presents a flatland thought experiment to determine if they are.[10] He introduces the experiment in the following way:

> Let us, as we logically may, suppose reasoning beings of only two dimensions to live and move on the surface of some solid body. We shall assume that they have not the power of perceiving anything outside this surface, but that upon it they have perceptions similar to ours. If such beings worked out a geometry, they would of course assign only two dimensions to their space. They would ascertain that a point in moving describes a line and that a line in moving describes a surface. But they could as little represent to themselves what further spatial construction would be generated by a surface moving, as we can represent what would be generated by a solid moving out of the space we know. By the much abused expression to represent or to be able to think how something happens I understand — and I do not see how anything else can be understood by it without loss of all meaning — *the power of imagining the whole series of sensible impressions that would be had in such a case* (1971c: 248; italics added).

On the basis of this *"power of imagining,"* von Helmholtz goes on to describe just what the "surface-beings" would be able to do and not do in a variety of surface-living situations: for example, he imagines these "reasoning beings existing on the surface of an egg-shaped body" rather than on an infinite plane or on the surface of a sphere, in which case "not even such a simple figure as a triangle could be moved on [the] surface without change of form" (250); he imagines them living on a flat plane, in which case they could draw the shortest lines between two points, lines that "would not necessarily be straight lines in our sense, but ... [ones] technically called geodesic lines of the surface on which they live" (248–49); he imagines them living on a pseudospherical surface, in which case "the axiom of parallels does not hold

good" (250); and so on. In his concluding remarks he makes the interesting methodological point that

> inhabiting a space of three dimensions and endowed with organs of sense for
> their perception, we can represent to ourselves the various cases in which surface-
> beings might have developed their perception of space, for we have only to limit
> our own perceptions to a narrower field. It is easy to think away the perceptions
> we have, but it is very difficult to image perceptions to which there is nothing
> analogous in experience. When, therefore, we pass to space of three dimensions
> we are stopped in our power of representation by the structure of our organs and
> the experiences obtained through them, which correspond only to the space in
> which we live (252–53).[11]

What von Helmholtz is affirming here is that what we cannot imagine cannot enter
into our epistemology. This principle is equivalent to the principle that *where we cannot imagine ourselves bodily, we cannot know.* The etymology of the word *can* (*Kennen*)
is of considerable interest in this respect, conjoining as it does "I can" with knowledge.
Von Helmholtz himself draws explicit attention to the connection when he writes that
"This kind of knowledge (*Kennen*) we also call being able to do a thing (*konnen*) and
understanding how to do it (*verstehen*), as, "I know how to ride," "I am able to ride,"
and "I understand how to ride." Earlier, he affirms that "[T]his kind of knowledge
(*Kennen*) may attain the highest possible degree of precision and certainty. In this
respect it is not inferior to any knowledge (*Wissen*) which can be expressed in words"
(von Helmholtz: 1971b: 218).[12]

   The imaginative technique of free variation is a consistent procedure within von
Helmholtz's methodological practice, a nonverbal procedure. His thought experiments are imaginative free variations on a particular spatial theme. They are an exploration of the theme from the vantage point of *possibilities of experience.* We see this in
the flatlander thought experiment as in the earlier-cited thought experiment featuring
a hypothetical individual who, from no experience at all comes to grasp an *object*. We
see this exploration of possible experience furthermore in *active* free variations, in von
Helmholtz's own self-designed, introspectively examined meadow-laboratory experiments. Indeed, his remarks upon the central epistemological significance of *active* free
variation — what might be called "active self-experimentations" — are unequivocal.
Remarking precisely upon the correlation between movement and perception and the
possibility of retranslation, von Helmholtz states,

> This last point [regarding retranslation] is, I believe, of great importance. The
> meaning we assign to our sensations depends upon experiment, not upon
> mere observation of what takes place around us. We learn by experiment that
> the correspondence between [the] two processes takes place at any moment
> which we choose, and under conditions which we can alter as we choose. Mere
> observation would not give us the same certainty, even though often repeated

under different conditions, for we should thus learn only that the processes in question appear together frequently (or even always, as far as our experience goes). Mere observation would not teach us that they appear together at any moment we select (von Helmholtz 1971b: 215).

What makes von Helmholtz's studies in perception something more than a compilation of factual truths about perception — though such works as his formidable *Physiological Optics* remain classic texts in traditional 20th-century science — is the openness and precision of his methodological practices. His crediting of the technique of free variation in his thought experiments and correlative utilization of "*the power of imagining*," and his crediting of the technique of active self-experimentation in extended laboratory settings and correlative utilization of what may be termed "the power of meticulous introspective probings," are each a validation of the range and rigor of his methodological practices. The techniques in each case afford him insights into invariant relationships, regularities in the structure of experience. The techniques are not fully developed phenomenological techniques, but they are definitively phenomenological in character. Indeed, we have seen through a thoughtful examination of von Helmholtz's work how, especially combined with the meticulousness of his introspective studies, the imaginative technique of free variation sets the stage for eidetic intuitions. Through the process of free variation, von Helmholtz moves from an everyday world of observed facts to a world of possible experience. Investigation of possible experience in the form of imaginative variations — and of active self-experimentations as well — allows him essential insights into *how we come to perceive*.

6. On factual and essential matters

One might well ask how it is that von Helmholtz, a scientist, arrives at the door of "eidetic intuitions" or "*essential* insights," especially since the idea of a phenomenological methodology was not even born at the time he lived. The question is ultimately a question of fact and essence, or perhaps better, of the relationship between factual matters and essential ones. The most promising place to begin an inquiry is with von Helmholtz's conception of *intuition* and his use of *introspection*, the former as a particular kind of knowledge, the latter as a particular kind of methodology.

Von Helmholtz conceives *intuition* as a form of knowledge that is effortless and immediate; it involves no deliberate reflection or thought, but simply happens. Von Helmholtz is, of course, not alone in this understanding. A clue to an actual working sense of this important form of knowledge is given in the context of his writings about an experiential over an a priori origin of the axioms of geometry. By examining the relevant passage, we can tease out a more exacting notion of this effortless and immediate form of knowing. Von Helmholtz writes that

> I do not, of course, suppose that mankind first arrived at space intuitions in agreement with the axioms of Euclid by any carefully executed system of exact measurement. It was rather a succession of everyday experiences — especially the perception of the geometric similarity of great and small bodies, possible only in flat space — that led to the rejection as impossible of every geometric representation at variance with this fact. For this no knowledge of the necessary logical connection between the observed fact of geometric similarity was needed, *but only an intuitive apprehension of the typical relations among lines, planes, angles, etc., obtained by numerous, attentive observations.*
>
> (von Helmholtz 1971c: 264; italics added)

The intuitive apprehension of which von Helmholtz speaks is clearly not equivalent to the "numerous, attentive observations" themselves. Intuitive apprehensions of the kind are not apprehensions of fact; they are apprehensions of a regularity — whether a regularity in the relationship of one thing to another, or a regularity in the character of the thing itself. Intuitive apprehensions of the kind are fundamental to mathematics. Indeed, there could be no mathematics without such apprehensions. They are the basis of mathematics as an eidetic science, a science not of the everyday world but of an idealized world. The mathematical backgrounds of von Helmholtz and Husserl are of methodological moment in this respect. Not only does Husserl speak at length of the eidetic truths of mathematics and indeed comprehend mathematics as a methodological blueprint for a phenomenological science of the eidetic, but von Helmholtz, in answering objections to his espousal of an experiential over an a priori origin of the axioms of geometry, unequivocally affirms the importance of a geometrician's power to form "imaginative representations," i.e. ideal objects (von Helmholtz 1971d: 360–65). Mathematical valuings aside, two points claim our attention: the practice of imaginative free variation is natural to mathematical thinking and yields insights into invariant relationships; the same kind of insights obtain in the course of phenomenological free-variation, that is, in the course of following through on Husserl's eidetic methodology. Phenomenological free variations also exist in an idealized world in which, by the very play of imaginative possibilities — by the very envisioning of the possible — one is led to invariants, to eidetic insights into the nature of the thing investigated.

Viewed within this methodological perspective, what von Helmholtz terms "an intuitive apprehension of typical relations" might be judged to fall as short of an eidetic insight as it falls beyond a strictly factual account. Indeed, although based on "numerous and attentive observations," an "intuitive apprehension of typical relations" is certainly not an empirical generalization, for what is *intuited* is intuited straightaway; there is no reasoning process involved. On the other hand "an intuitive apprehension of *typical* relations" is not an apprehension of *essential* relations; hence it is not a question of a *bona fide* eidetic insight. In effect, von Helmholtz's intuitive apprehension appears to hang in an epistemological limbo between factual and eidetic knowledge.

Given the specifically mathematical context of his affirmation, however, and given as well his more general validation of imaginative free variation, and, in addition, his very notion of intuition as an effortless, non-deliberative process, it is not unreasonable to place "an intuitive apprehension of typical relations" on the side of an eidetics. While one could, in further support of this placement, hypothesize that, subsequent to making numerous and attentive observations, the individual(s) who discovered the axioms of geometry ran through possible experiences of "lines, planes, angles, etc." and thereby arrived at an intuitive apprehension of the typical relations forming the basis of the axioms, a less speculative explanation of the discovery is possible.

An intuitive apprehension clearly specifies something over and above "numerous and attentive observations." Indeed, it specifies an effortless and immediate form of knowing on the order of a flash of insight. In exactly this sense, an intuitive apprehension just happens; it comes on its own. *It is a personally prompted but personally unbidden epistemological moment.* It is personally prompted in the sense that its epistemological ground is prepared beforehand — *precisely as with numerous and attentive observations.* It is thus a short-lived moment with a history, one that is the result of a process of informed thinking and doing. Hence, although the moment of apprehension arrives on its own, it is not a pristine epistemological bolt out the blue. When Picasso says he does not seek but finds, for example, he is not saying that his findings are willy-nilly anything, i.e. aesthetically uninformed. On the contrary, there is a ground on which his findings rest and that ground is prepared. In a similar way, when Nobel prize-winning cytogeneticist Barbara McClintock remarks with respect to scientific knowledge that "You get lots of correlations, but you don't get the truth" (quoted in Keller 1983: 203), she is not saying that there is no merit in conventional scientific knowledge. On the contrary, her capacity to see outside the facts and procedures ordained by traditional scientific methodology is in part the result of a thoroughly studied knowledge of those facts and procedures. Yet however prepared the ground, an autonomous, unbidden insight — a sudden flash of meaning — *is* out of the blue. Although the culminating moment of a process of thinking and doing — a process of *active* reflection of some kind or other — the flash of insight is an utterly spontaneous happening that arrives on its own. Moreover *the flash of insight appears apart from any method.* It is not the product of any particular approach; it is not bound exclusively to any particular practice. Neither is it an esoteric or exotic happening. It is a quite natural if extraordinary epistemological event. An intuitive apprehension is indeed akin to a "click": a sudden grasp of meaning, a sudden putting together of things one has been reflecting upon or laboring over; it is akin to an epiphany: an awakening to meaning in an otherwise prosaic situation; it is akin to a "eureka" moment: an unexpected discovery of how something works; and so on. Clearly, an intuitive apprehension is a thoroughly and utterly spontaneous event that comes unbidden, though not unprepared.

In this context, it is instructive to point out that although Husserl speaks of *seeing*, *grasping*, and *apprehending* essences, he does not account for the moment of insight itself as a structure of consciousness, or rather, he accounts for it only in the important sense of recognizing it as an *object* of consciousness (see Husserl 1983). Yet clearly, from a phenomenological viewpoint, a moment of insight — whether a grasping of essence or an intuitive apprehension — is a structure of consciousness itself, a specific and clearly recognized experienced happening within the flow. As such, it can be described phenomenologically: a flash of insight is *invariantly* a spontaneously unifying thought, for example, *invariantly* a spontaneous putting together. Hence, a flash of insight does not just reveal an essential relationship or an invariant structure; it itself has an invariant structure. Moreover, precisely in the sense of being a spontaneous putting together, and invariantly so, a flash of insight is a vindication of passive synthesis: it marks a passively accomplished integration of experience that brings together, crystallizes, and carries forward. What the phenomenological method of free variation provides is an epistemological framework for the realization of this moment. Yet however deliberately cultivated, here too the moment of insight *just comes*. All the same, something finer and deeper is realized precisely for its being discovered in the context of a deliberate process of free variation. By drawing on the possible rather than the actual, on imaginative rather than observed instances, the phenomenological method provides an epistemological framework for the realization of relationships that are invariant rather than typical, that, in effect, go beyond intuitive apprehensions to eidetic intuitions. In just this sense, phenomenology has the possibility of grounding scientific knowledge arising from matters of fact. It has the possibility of grounding the factual in the eidetic through a specific methodology based upon "the power of imagining."

The relationship between the factual and the essential can be specified in further methodological ways that tie von Helmholtz's central notion of intuition to his central use of introspection and that highlight the signal importance of introspection to his scientific work on perception. To spell out the relationship in these further ways will validate a basic methodological claim of this chapter; namely, that the findings of science can be epistemologically grounded in experience through the practice of a phenomenological methodology that is in striking ways concordant with methodological practices already familiar to scientists, indeed, already exemplified by a well-known and particularly venerated man of science, and that remain open still to all scientists.

Observed facts are there, present in the natural attitude in the natural world. Rain is wet; I cut my finger and it bleeds; I hear the dogs' barking.[13] Observed facts need not be formulated propositionally in order to be recognized; they need only be there, experientially present to an attentive observer. An observed fact might concern the character of a thing or its relation to another thing: an orange is orange; a roll of thunder precedes a flash of lightning. Each and every factual instance of an observed thing has essential aspects: it is of the nature of an orange to be orange; it is of the nature of thunder to precede lightning, and to be heard and not seen. It is of the very nature of every factual existent in the world, *of everything contingent*, to have a specific or composite essential nature that belongs to it and marks it as the thing it is. The phenomenon of perception may be studied as just such a factual event: however different the modalities of perception, perception itself has an essential character. As the earlier passages from von Helmholtz show, it is of the very nature of perception to entail a certain range of possible volitions that specify a certain range of *presentabilia*. The volition-perception relationship that von Helmholtz discovers is patently something over and above the facts; the relationship pertains to all perceptions and affords one a procedure for validating the accuracy of one's conception of any perceived object. The relationship is thus not presented as an empirical generalization; it is presented as an intuitively apprehended insight, in fact an insight precisely of the kind had by individuals who discovered "typical relations" with respect to "lines, planes, angles, etc.," but with a distinctive and crucial difference as well. The intuitive apprehension in the former instance is obtained by numerous and attentive *self*-observations, that is, it is obtained on the basis of *introspection*: by numerous and meticulous introspective self-reflections. From this perspective, the role of introspection in von Helmholtz's active self-experimentations on behalf of perception — thus in his overall scientific legacy on perception — can hardly be minimized, let alone ignored. What the scientific practice of introspection allows is not merely an awareness of the particular character of present feelings or thoughts, of a past sequence of feelings or thoughts, or the possible character of future ones, as noted earlier. Numerous and attentive *self*-observations allow insight into *experience*. In this respect, introspection is as vital a scientific as phenomenological methodology; the truths of experience are as proper an aim of science as the truths of behavior. Their denial can only result in an emaciated and incomplete epistemology. Indeed, without introspective knowledge, the truths of perception are at best half-known. A final methodological clarification of introspection will highlight this point and in the process demonstrate the natural methodological connections underpinning the significance of a trans-disciplinary communal task.

The role that introspection plays in a phenomenological methodology is succinctly exemplified by Husserl's layered insights into the correlation of perception and movement. As noted earlier, in the context of discussing the correlation, Husserl speaks of if-then relationships, of an "I do," I move," of aspect-exhibitions, and of a kinesthetic 'organ'. Each of these findings enunciates a finer and deeper truth about perception, a finer and deeper truth arrived at first of all through the process of bracketing. Introspection in the phenomenological attitude, i.e. introspection outside the natural attitude, discloses a world divested of its customary assessments and meanings. The everyday facts of perception are transformed into sheer experiences. The practice of free variation in the phenomenological attitude discloses invariant structures of perception. It thus becomes clear how factual matters — functioning as transcendental clues in the actual practice of phenomenology — are related to essential ones, how self-experience is potentially a common meeting ground in the practice of science and phenomenology through a basic confluence in the methodological practices of introspection and free variation. It is of considerable interest to note in this respect Husserl's own realization of the confluence in his very discovery of phenomenology. He writes that "*descriptive psychology offers a genuine and natural point of departure for the working out of the idea of phenomenology. This was in fact the way which led me to phenomenology*" (Husserl 1989:326; italics in original). What Husserl found was that paying attention to one's own psychic life through the process of introspection and the practice of self-experimentation discloses "so-called 'inner experience' (more precisely, self-experience as well as 'empathy' [i.e. intersubjective experience]" (Husserl 1989:411).[14] Hewing faithfully to descriptions of these experiences, Husserl in turn found — by "a mere 'nuance,'" as he terms it — the possibility of a change in attitude, a turn away from the immanent to the transcendental, that is, a turn away from the mundane and empirical to the *purely subjective*, to *pure consciousness* (Husserl 1989:414). What he discovered was a parallelism between a descriptive psychology and a phenomenology, in other words, a parallelism between a science of the psyche and a transcendental phenomenology. "To every eidetic," he declares, "as well as to every empirical … a parallel must correspond on the other side" (414). His 'must' is far from an obligatory flourish; it enunciates an experientially verifiable relationship. By "attending to the nuance that conducts one from a pure inner psychology to transcendental phenomenology," and in reverse, from the latter to the former, one is aware of the possible move in either direction (Husserl 1989:415). It thus becomes clear how a rigorously demanding and consummate epistemology may be forged through phenomenological practice. The practice has the possibility of grounding scientific knowledge in finer and deeper truths about sense-making precisely because it carries forward what is already there in descriptive psychology and because, in the first place, there is a confluence between science and phenomenology, a confluence not only in findings — e.g. the correlation between movement and perception — but in methodology. If the methodologies of self-experimentation and introspection were in fact reclaimed by science, then the facts of perception — and more generally, the facts of conception, memory, attention, and so on — would be the point of departure for a bold and vigorous trans-disciplinary epistemology. Equally, if phenomenologists would reclaim and carry forward Husserl's detailed and ever-renewed investigations, the first philosophical science he envisioned and labored to realize would be duly launched. If-then relationships, an "I do," "I move," a kinesthetic 'organ', "aspect exhibitions" — these are, after all, not fancy embellishments of perception and ones that have no place in science, but structures inherent in the sense-making processes of animate organisms.

7.   On the epistemological import of the confluences: A critical look at cognitivist science and philosophy

What I would like to do now is draw out the epistemological import of the extraordinary confluences in thought and methodology in terms of late twentieth-century Western science and philosophy. In both historical and visionary terms, the import is subsumable in the observation that if there is a basic concordance between a particularly renown philosopher and a particularly renown scientist on the self-evidential primacy of movement in perception, on the significance of free variation and introspective self-experimentations, on the workings of passive synthesis or unconscious conclusions in arriving at understandings of an object, then the dream of which Husserl spoke is not over; it has just been prematurely broken off. Moreover, not only is it not over, but with respect to confederated phenomenological practice and the promise of a trans-disciplinary communal task, it is far richer than Husserl imagined. Before that richness can be realized, however, the rupture must be examined; and not only causally but in a prognostic sense as well so that precipitating conceptual factors that continue to foreclose the dream can be exposed and in turn positively recast. In the most general terms, causal examination on the phenomenological side reveals internal strife and fragmentation, and metaphysical diversions; on a broader philosophic front, specifically with respect to analytic American philosophy, it reveals an infatuation with scientifically-rendered humans — or *models* of humans — over everyday experiencing ones. On the scientific side it reveals an infatuation with a materialist program, an infatuation currently expressed computationally in terms of adept information-processing machines over dynamically living animate organisms. I would like to elaborate the epistemological import first along the general lines of the two infatuations, showing how their fundamental allegiances preclude a trans-disciplinary communal task from coming into view much less being realized. I will then turn to a more specific analysis of major conceptual obstacles that lie in the way of restoring the dream.

Both infatuations are transparent in present-day cognitivist accounts of consciousness, intelligence, minds, and so on. In such accounts, all attention is riveted on brains, mental representations, computational renderings of intelligence, and the like; actual experience counts for naught. Indeed, by a surgically deft *legerdemain* (or alternatively, a conceptually deft *legerdetête*) cognition is dissected out of perception and studied *ex situ*, an event unto itself divorced from real-life. It is no longer tied either to that dynamic living reality that both Husserl and von Helmholtz discovered at the heart of human knowledge — namely, movement — or to crucially related underlying dimensions of thought which both Husserl and von Helmholtz realized structured the possibility of knowledge — namely, passive syntheses or unconscious conclusions. Clearly, the de-animation of perception and the rise of cognitive science go hand in hand. Short of a suspension of animation, perception could never have been reduced to mere afferent stimuli and cognitivists, in turn, could never establish a sovereign domain of cognition in the form of brain happenings, mental representations, or computational functions. Not surprisingly, models of mind that cognitivists proffer are thoroughly object-oriented ones, static and lacking all reference to movement. They are wholly and utterly geared to answering the question of how we know or name a world of ready-made objects. Knower or namer are not *fundamentally* accounted for in this model; only a generic, disconnected, one-size-fits-all "mental life" is accounted for, and this in terms of hypothesized events happening inside a wholly unnatural (because severed) head.

To refine this very general critical sketch, it will be instructive to consider phenomenological philosopher Thomas Nenon's highly intriguing essay, "Connectionism and Phenomenology."[15] We will consider it from two points of view: first, and most positively, from the perspective of Nenon's implicit general proposal that points of confluence obtain between science and phenomenology; and then more critically from the perspective of Nenon's explicit claims regarding points of confluence between connectionism and phenomenology. We will hope to show why connectionism for two very basic reasons — its perseveration of the classical mind/body dichotomy and its ahistoricity — does not lead to confluence and hence cannot contribute to the realization of a trans-disciplinary communal task.

Nenon strongly suggests that phenomenologists might learn from connectionist models of mind and vice versa. He finds that "there is indeed interesting and significant work to be done at the intersection between these two approaches, work from which each could benefit" (Nenon 1994: 133). His general view that findings in science and phenomenology can complement and/or inform one another is clearly a vindication of the idea that the confluence of Husserl's and von Helmholtz's epistemological understandings and methodology is not a historical fluke but a bona fide conjunction of thought that can be carried forward. In other words, there are ways in which, rather than being at epistemological odds with one another, science and phenomenology can work together and shed mutually illuminating light. Indeed, as Nenon affirms, "[E]ven if one grants what Husserl says about the conditions necessary to establish Phenomenology as a rigorous science and about the immunity of the results of phenomenological research from challenges that originate in the empirical sciences, then it still does not necessarily follow that *the concrete practice of Phenomenology* will not and cannot be strongly influenced by what we think we have learned from other spheres" (124; italics added). Though Nenon gives no such examples of this influence, we could readily cite the tacit incorporation of evolutionary thought in Husserl's enfoldment of *all* animate life, nonhuman as well as human, in his phenomenological investigations, analyses, and understandings of "animate organism," for example, and in his idea of earth as "original ark" (Husserl 1981b; see also Kersten 1981). We could on these grounds amplify Nenon's unequivocal affirmation of outside influences, that is, influences from "non-phenomenological science … upon the practice of Phenomenology," strongly insisting that findings in the empirical sciences can not only "have a profound effect" on phenomenological findings, as Nenon avers (125); they can coincide with phenomenological findings, precisely in the way that Husserl's and von Helmholtz's research findings coincide. In sum, Nenon's implicit general proposal that there are ways in which science and phenomenology can come together and mutually benefit one another is a salutary one.

Let us turn now to an examination of Nenon's specific claims with respect to connectionism. The first point at issue can be marked out in a general way by Nenon's idea that we can learn something about "the mental," "mental states," or "mental life" (126, 127) by hewing entirely to the cognitive, including the "proto-cognitive," and without reference to "biology" or "the merely physical" (128, Note 17). There is no doubt but that the classical mind/body dichotomy lurks unexamined at the base of this conception of cognition. To show this concretely, I would like to put the conception in the context of Nenon's own cautionary comments with respect to models of mind in general. He points out specifically that working phenomenologists may make mistakes, and this because, for example, they have allowed themselves "to be misled by models that have been imported from another sphere" (125). Thus, he says, "the kind of paradigmatic examples we use in (*sic*) when reflecting upon mental life can have a great effect upon what the results of our investigation will be, and these examples will most often be strongly affected by what we think we know about the nonmental sphere and intimately, perhaps even unavoidably related to questions concerning the physical basis or instantiation of mental events" (125). In such terms he suggests that biological reductionism can influence us. What I want to suggest is that, as working phenomenologists, we need not turn *only* to biological reductionism for an understanding of how we might be led to make mistakes. We can turn to our own model of mind; that is, we can — and indeed should — uncover and examine the classical philosophical model we ourselves may be implicitly using with respect to minds and bodies. "The mental" and "the physical" are indeed simplistic, categorically oppositional terms that do not do justice to Husserl's rich analyses of animate nature.[16]

Now in this very same context of trying to hew entirely to a lean and rarified cognitive, Nenon points out that Husserl recognized that "human beings as persons, as centers of motivation, are founded in bodies, and thus … the mental will depend for its existence on a non-mental, natural stratum in human beings" (126). He points out that this recognition "does not involves (*sic*) a reduction of the mental to the physical, but it does mean that a truly plausible account of the mental must at least be compatible with what we think we know about bodies and brains" (126). The question is, What *do* we know — or "think we know" — about bodies? I would suggest that in light of what we *do* know about the fundamental significance of movement and the kinestheses, we might very well want to "go back and reexamine what we think we know" (126) — not about "bodies and brains," as Nenon suggests should our views about the mental and the physical not "square up" (126), but about bodies. For rather than conclude as Nenon does on the basis of the dependence of the mental on the physical, that there is a close connection "between theories about cognition as processes in machines and brains, on the one hand, and the theories about mental life, on the other" (126), I would conclude that there is a basic inadequacy underlying such a model of mind, that it is based on an underdeveloped examination and knowledge of bodies, and that this basic inadequacy gives rise to two basic and inter-related conceptual errors. First, a brain is not a body. Thus to collapse "the physical" into brains is an epistemological mistake of the first order. Living bodies, "animate organisms," to use Husserl's phrase, are neither equiva- lent to nor condensable into sulci and gyri, neural nets and processes, silicon chips or brains in vats. Living bodies, in fact, include brains in the same way that they include hearts and knees, livers and toes. Indeed, a brain *tout court* — a brain without a spinal cord, for example — is not a functioning laboratory specimen, let alone a function- ing living being. Second, to affirm a close connection between computational theories about brains or machines and philosophical theories about mental life is essentially to model the mind on *statics*, on a *receiving* set, the internal parts of which may change in their hypothetical *weightings*, as connectionist theory stipulates they do, but a set which in itself is in a stationary spatio-temporal sense both what it is and where it is. In this respect, what is being modelled is more akin to a fungal specimen or at most a sessile animate form, though here too, the model is altogether ahistorical. What con- nectionism forgets, and what cognitivists in general forget, is "the movement we are constantly giving things"; it forgets "the kinestheses." It more accurately captures pas- sive life than the life of mobile animate forms.

A brain *mechanics* of cognition based on *weightings* — suggesting precisely *sub- stance* heavinesses rather than *openly-evolving dynamical processes* — is categorically removed both from the realities of morphogenesis and from formatively related strata of actual experience. It is in fact categorically removed from life both as it develops and has developed over time and as it is lived. To model the mind on a static mechanics is to conceive the mind not as a developmental faculty in either an ontogenetic or phylo- genetic historical sense but as a thoroughly complete, consummately formed, mechan- ical device that hypothetically stoops now to this point, now to that point, according to its weight gains and losses. This mechanical model, because it is wholly divorced from living histories and from the complex experiential layers of meaning that inform those histories, compounds the epistemological mistake. Where bodies are collapsed into brains and where minds in turn are linked to ahistorical mechanical devices, there is clearly a lack of understanding of living bodies. In addition, when the point of depar- ture for understanding mind or cognition is, as Nenon envisages it, to "divide up the world into the mental as that which is directly accessible to consciousness and the non-mental as that which is not" (128), then fundamental categories being already set, everything to begin with must be just so identified and lined up accordingly. Indeed, everything must be made to conform to a preconceived and everywhere binding binary oppositional scheme. As Nenon himself points out, however, the scheme presents something of a problem for dispositions: "we would have to assign dispositions to the realm of the non-mental" (128). It is this problematic placement in particular that precipitates his turn toward connectionism and explains his claim that "Connectionism can indeed help phenomenologists better conceive of one phenomenon, namely dispositions or — to use Husserl's term — 'habitualities.'" His idea, in brief, is that *weightings* give phenomenologists a way of thinking about dispositions insofar as weightings specify "tendencies" toward certain kinds of "representations" under certain conditions (130). In effect, "[t]he 'experience' of a cognitive system then would consist not in a practically infinite number of stored beliefs, but in the weightings it has adopted to bring about appropriate beliefs under the specific conditions" (130). Presumably, taking "the 'experience' of a cognitive system" as a standard, one can make an analogy either to the actual 'experience' of an actual brain, or, more radically, and with appropriate diacritical erasure, to the actual experience of an actual person. But connectionism can in truth be of help in this way only because the divisionary scheme is instituted and sanctioned in the first place, and because problematic assignment of dispositions to the realm of the nonmental is, by an ontologically discrete conceptual twist, a short-lived problem if any problem at all for a connectionist or for cognitivists generally. In particular, given a properly conceived cognitive system, e.g. a properly conceived brain, the divisionary scheme dissolves: a properly conceived brain encompasses both "the mental" and "the nonmental." The mental and the nonmental co-exist because connectionism can play the cognitive system — the brain — on both sides of the ontological divide. It can construe "the mental" an all lucid realm of a consummate brain and "the nonmental" the covert realm of the same consummate brain, a consummate brain that can thus indeed have, as Nenon states, "a tendency to process new information in certain ways," that is, have "dispositions" or "habitualities" that "[function] within mental life" (130). Clearly, the connectionist model lets a fully-formed generic brain in through the back door and gives it full run of the house. Located in such a cognitive system, dispositions can be saved from the taint of the non-mental.[17]

Now apart from being an odd way of going about solving a phenomenologically challenging problem, and apart from dissolving the problematic oppositional scheme by adopting a non-categorical model, the suggestion of thinking in terms of weightings is oddly ironic. If weightings are conceived not as *mechanical* additions and subtractions but as changeable *bodily* proclivities, and not changeable proclivities of a purely physical body but of a dynamically involved living body, then a quite striking connectionist connection emerges. Construed in this way, weightings are indeed heavinesses; they indeed suggest bodily leanings in one direction or another, shifts in bodily alignment; they indeed suggest inclinations, *felt bodily dispositions* toward doing this rather than that. In short, to be conceived as dispositions or habitualities, one has to transpose weightings to a body, which, in connectionist thought, is precisely something they are not. Although Nenon speaks of dispositions as neither neatly mental, physical, or ideal entities, and wants to think of them "as functions within mental life," rather than, as with Husserl, as either "sedimented beliefs" or as "spontaneous tendencies," it is only as bodily felt weightings that the connectionist model makes sense phenomenologically. If a habituality or disposition to do something is closely examined phenomenologically, it discloses a certain bodily readiness toward some kind of action. If taken as a mode of thought, i.e. a habitual form of thinking, certainly sedimented beliefs are involved, but those beliefs are contextually realized in some way, precisely in a disposition to do this or that. In short, a disposition is an inclination to instantiate a certain meaning or meanings. The same may be said for habitualities and for tendencies; they are all context-specific leanings of a tactile-kinesthetic body that clearly cut across the artificially instituted ontological divide of "the mental" and "the nonmental." Taken in this sense, dispositions, habitualities, and tendencies are not *residual* things nor things to begin with. They are neither entities lurking about at the bottom of some kind of mental well, nor entities that must be categorized and given a place in some ontological system. They are complex facets of intentionality needing elucidation (Johnstone, unpublished essay).

The connectionist concept of weightings is of course far from embracing this sense. In fact, though not concerned with brains explicitly, a familiar axiology obtains in the connectionist-spawned conception. Insofar as brains are typically treasured in a manner parallel to minds, the primary uneven valorization explicit in the classical mind/body dichotomy transfers implicitly to a brain/body dichotomy. Bodies are, in effect, disposable both in typical models of mind and in typical models of brain. Developmental histories are forgotten in these models because bodies are forgotten; movement is forgotten for the same reason. Clearly, cognitivists in general run off with the brain and leave living bodies behind; they take cognition out of perception and hie it away to heady climes where weightings, unit processings, and the like, take the place of those actual living encounters that inform the life of animate forms. They forget that "at the basis of all judgment, decision, and action," as Nenon, ultimately quoting Husserl, reminds us, "lies the *experience* of something 'that is a substrate with simple *sensually graspable qualities*'" (127–28; italics added). To start with such *facts of experience* in the fundamental animate sense in which Husserl and von Helmholtz grasped them is to start at a place quite different with respect to understandings of mind and to arrive at a place quite different with respect to understandings of both brains and mind/brain connections. Indeed, what is wanted first and foremost are methodological understandings. The coming together of science and phenomenology lies not by way of helping each other think about things, though there is certainly room for conceptual spin-offs as the brief discussion of weighting suggests. The truly trans-disciplinary task lies concretely by way of methodological practices, basic epistemological procedures, such that actual findings that emerge in science and phenomenology are mutually supportive and enlightening because they come from similar methodological roots. Correlatively, this means that movement figures centrally in an experiential sense, precisely as von Helmholtz's and Husserl's studies demonstrate. Introspection, active self-experimentation, and imaginative free variation are in this sense vital methodological techniques. They each afford insight into self-movement. Life is neither a series of stills nor is it something conclusively known through the observation of others. Accordingly, animation, in particular self-animation, is not a disposable dimension of creaturely life. It is neither a mere output on the way to more information consumption and processing nor a negligible dimension from the viewpoint of experience. It is the centerpin of life because to move is to be alive.

8. An alternative approach

I would like quite briefly to sketch out both a radically different understanding of minds in order to show how present-day infatuations need not begin — or end — with a disposal of bodies. At least one extensive and complex line of brain research demonstrates the centrality of living bodies to knowledge — in precisely ways that coincide with Husserl's and von Helmholtz's respective insights into, and understandings of, the constitution of objects.

In his neurobiological research over the last decade and more, Nobel prize-winning neurophysiologist Gerald Edelman[18] has worked to put mind back into nature. His guiding principle is that "There must be ways to put the mind back into nature that are concordant with how it got there in the first place" (Edelman 1992: 15). It is because of his preeminently *historical* perspective — both embryological-ontogenetic and phylogenetic — that, rather than sacrificing living creatures to theory, he grasps the utter necessity of taking living creatures into account in any reliable and legitimate rendition of mind. In this respect he might be considered an unorthodox present-day human scientist: he neither disdains minds in the austerely blindered ways of a behaviorist, does away with them in the reductively genetical ways of a sociobiologist, nor, most topical to the point here, disjoins brains from bodies in the blithefully trivializing ways of a cognitive scientist. It is clear from his work that he does not separate mind and body along traditional Cartesian lines such that movement and perception are categorically sundered nor does he conceptually sunder brains from bodies leaving animate organisms behind. As a result, his research program does not suffer from the distortions wrought by the categorical cleaver that cognitivists typically bring down on the subject of their studies. The evolutionary perspective that informs Edelman's approach to mind allows him to see that animate form — dynamic morphology, down to the level of the brain — is at the basis of mind; in particular, it allows him to see that perceptual categorization — what he comprehends as the basic link between psychology and physiology — is a matter of experience, that brain structure is in turn a matter of experience, that there is thus not only a reciprocal but developmental link between form (morphology) and experience — thus making what we are in brain terms not something divorced from experience — and that, more generally, there is an ongoing history of form at all levels throughout life in both an embryological-ontogenetic and phylogenetic sense. What is furthermore of particular moment — and perhaps not surprising given the historical perspective — is the fleeting suggestion that freely-varied self-movement is significant with respect to perceptual categorization. On the basis of his research with automata, Edelman writes that "[P]erceptual categorization occurs only … after disjunctive sampling of [visual, tactile, and kinesthetic] signals" (Edelman 1992:93). In more concrete terms, only "as a result of explorations with its 'hand-arm' and 'eye'" does the automaton Darwin III "decide," for example, "that something is an object, that the object is striped, and that the object is bumpy" (93).[19] The suggestion is that through active exploration — freely-varied movement that is not programmed in any way and is hence, truly random — Darwin III arrives at perceptual categorizations. The suggestion is epitomized in Edelman's statement that Darwin III "categorizes only on the basis of experience" (93), experience that clearly involves not merely looking with a movable eye, but moving with a movable body. In sum, animate form, movement, and experience are all, in Edelman's view, fundamental to the evolution of mind.

Edelman's work dovetails in important complementary ways with the work of developmental psychologists whose studies of infants, children, and nonhuman animals are anchored in a dynamic systems approach. The theoretical infrastructure of the latter approach is characterized by a concern with "real-time" in the sense of mapping maturational and behavioral events in the fullness of their actual dynamics; thus, by extension, it is characterized by a concern with "real-life." This concern is at striking odds with studies wedded to connectionist or cognitivist models which treat the environment, for example, as a "probability function" and a leg as a "[part of] the environment of a controller within the body of [an] agent."[20] A dynamic systems approach takes a holistic view of intelligence (consciousness, behavior, etc.) with the result that cognition is not separated from perception, perception is not separated from movement, and movement is not separated from an environment nor from a larger category designated as a behavior; on the contrary, the movement-perceptual system *is* behavior in the sense that it is the actual "real-time," "real-life" event as it unfolds. Indeed, it is what is mapped, as in ethologist John Fentress's intricate studies of "how mice scratch their faces," for example, or, in his and other's combined study of ritualized fighting in wolves (Fentress 1989:45–46; Moran, Fentress, and Golani 1981). As with Edelman's work, movement is given its due.

It is fitting to conclude this brief sketch of an alternative approach, especially with its historical, developmental concerns, with Darwin's provocative thought about "the problem of the mind." In one of his metaphysical notebooks, Darwin wrote — undoubtedly on the basis of his years of observations of creaturely life — that: "experience shows the problem of the mind cannot be solved by attacking the citadel itself. — the mind is function of body. — we must bring some *stable* foundation to argue from" (Darwin [1836–1844] 1987: 564). The work of Husserl and of von Helmholtz, and the work of Edelman and many of those engaged in a dynamic systems approach to infancy and childhood, being anchored in distinctive ways in animate form, in experience, in movement, in bodily life, *and*, being anchored too in distinctive ways in a *historical* approach, bring just that kind of foundation. (See also Sheets-Johnstone 1984, 1986a, 1986b, 1990, 1992, 1994a, 1994b, 1996a, 1996b, 1996c.) In singular but convergent ways they provide the foundation for restoring the dream, awakening us both to confederated practice and to the rich possibilities of a trans-disciplinary communal task.

Notes

* A shorter version of this chapter was presented at the Husserl Circle meeting in June 1995 in Loveland, CO.

1.   See, for example, Husserl (1970c: 287): "[I]f the general idea of truth-in-itself becomes the universal norm of all the relative truths that arise in human life, then … there develops a communal activity of a particular sort, that of working with one another and for one another, offering one another helpful criticism, through which there arises a pure and unconditioned truth-validity as common property"; von Helmholtz (1971e: 142): "Let each of us think of himself, not as a man seeking to gratify his own thirst for knowledge, or to promote his own private advantage, or to shine by his own abilities, but rather as a fellow laborer on one great common work, upon which the highest interests of humanity rest."

2.   (Note: I use two different translations of this article — the second one by E. Atkinson in von Helmholtz 1912 — depending on the clarity of the translation with respect to the point under consideration.) Cf. also von Helmholtz (1971f: 505): "How young children first acquire an acquaintance with or knowledge of the meaning of their visual images is easily understood if we observe them while they busy themselves with playthings. Notice how they handle them, consider them by the hour from all sides, turn them around, put them into their mouths, and so on, and finally throw them down or try to break them. This is repeated every day. There can be no doubt that this is the school in which the natural relations among the objects around us are learned, along with the understanding of perspective images and the use of the hands."

3.   Von Helmholtz makes this affirmation on the basis of his own experiences of looking at stereoscopic pictures.

4.   (Note: I have used two different translations of this article — the second one by M.F. Lowe in von Helmholtz 1977— depending on the clarity of the translation with respect to the point

under consideration.) Elsewhere, von Helmholtz calls attention to the experimental evidence of others as well: "[E]xperiments by Fechner, Volkmann, and myself … prove that even the fully developed eye of an adult can only compare accurately the size of those lines or angles in the field of vision whose images can be thrown one after another upon precisely the same spot of the retina by the ordinary movements of the eye" (von Helmholtz 1971b: 199). He goes on to say that "[w]e may convince ourselves by a simple experiment that the correspondence of the perceptions of touch and sight depend, even in an adult, upon a continuous comparison of the two by means of the retinal images of our hands *as they move*" (italics added).

5.   The bracketed end of the last sentence actually comes from Kahl's translation of the same essay. The Lowe translation is less clear. (See von Helmholtz 1971a: 380.) (Note: Kahl uses the terms "immediate evidence" and "immediate clarity" rather than "self-evidence.")

6.   Such an analysis would of course require investigation of the tactile-kinesthetic body. For an exposition of the methodology involved in such an investigation, see Sheets-Johnstone 1990.

7.   Von Helmholtz's thought experiment is reminiscent of Condillac's thought experiment involving a statue that is progressively given different forms of sensation (Condillac 1982 [1754]). Attention might also be called to von Helmholtz's primary concern with *innervation sensations*. For an informative history of interest in and research on this topic, see Scheerer 1987.

8.   Cf. Lowe's translation of this same passage; Lowe speaks, for example, of *presentables* rather than *presentabilia*.

9.   With respect to his question, von Helmholtz thus concludes that only on the basis of freely- varied movement — from "motor volitions" (1971a: 374) — do the data of perception arise.

10.   I have not been successful in ascertaining the original date of publication of E. Abbott's book *Flatland*, only the date of its second edition, which is 1884. Von Helmholtz's "The Origin and Meaning of Geometric Axioms (I)" was originally published in English in *Mind* 1/3 (July 1876): 301–21.

11.   Von Helmholtz goes on to say, however, that there is a further methodological route open, namely, measuring. He concludes that "space, considered as a region of measurable quantities, does not correspond at all with the most general conception of an aggregate of three dimensions. It involves special conditions, depending, not only on the perfectly free mobility of solid bodies without change of form to all parts of it and with all possible changes of direction, but also on the special value of the measure of curvature, which for our actual space equals, or at least is not distinguishable from, zero. This latter definition is given in the axioms of straight lines and parallels" (1971c: 255).

12.   There is no doubt but that, as in the previous example, von Helmholtz has used the method of free variation in pursuit of epistemological truth. (With respect to his original query, it might be noted that on the basis of his various imaginings, von Helmholtz concludes that the axioms of geometry are *not* necessities of thought [and thus not the "necessary consequences of an *a priori* transcendental form of intuition as Kant thought"]. It is on the basis of these findings that he goes on to say, "Let us then examine the opposite assumption — that

their origin is empirical — and see whether they can be inferred from facts of experience" [von Helmholtz 1971c: 258].)

13. Someone might at first think that *hearing* dogs barking is not an observed fact, that is, unless the dogs are simultaneously *seen*. Based on a hypervisualist notion of evidence, such skepticism would have cost our ancestors dearly. Moreover *seeing* a dog barking is, after all, itself a cause for skepticism.

14. Husserl's path to phenomenology, as he himself describes it, strongly supports the earlier suggestion regarding his active self-experimentations in arriving at essential insights into "the kinestheses."

15. I would like to note at the outset that several pages into his essay (1994: 123), Nenon asks the question, "[W]hat could cognitive science have to offer to Phenomenology?" He answers: "My first response would be that Connectionism is above all a way of thinking about things." His answer resonates with my response to Gerald Edelman's work and the work of dynamic systems theorists in the area of infant/child development. I would urge only that some models and some approaches are for very good reasons better to think with than others.

16. Neither do they accord with more recent elaborations of the quintessential coherence of "the physical" and "the mental" or of the ways in which, with respect to fundamental human beliefs and practices, thinking is modelled on the body. See Sheets-Johnstone 1986a and 1990, respectively.

17. We might note that some connectionist researchers believe that the model sheds light on postural reflexes. See Olson & Hanson 1990. We might note too that to use a connectionist model to explain what goes on *epistemologically* outside of immediate experience is to make such non-experienced phenomena something other than what they basically are. The model turns astoundingly complex, subtly varied neurophysiological phenomena into modes of action in a living world. In this sense, the rise of cognitive science is coincident not only with a de-animation of perception; it is coincident more generally with a de-animation of life.

18. I should specify at the outset that in moving from his theory of neuronal group selection (TNGS) and his research experiments substantiating that theory to questions of consciousness — "primary consciousness" and "higher-order consciousness" — concepts, memory, thoughts, judgments, and emotions, Edelman travels quickly over vast territories in an attempt to embrace facets of mind in a phylogenetic sense. Taking a cue from Darwin, one might find it more prudent to proceed on the basis of "mental powers." While certainly not the last word, Darwin's approach appears more singularly tied to life as it is actually lived — in the same way that Edelman's own TNGS and its experiential underpinnings is tethered to life as it is lived. In his examination of mind in *The Descent of Man and Selection in Relation to Sex*, Darwin devotes a chapter to "Mental Powers" in which he considers in turn: instincts, emotions, curiosity, imitation, attention, memory, imagination, reason, and then moves on to consider progressive improvement (in a broad sense, "learning"), the use and making of tools, language, and self-consciousness. (He also examines a sense of beauty and spiritual beliefs, but these not necessarily concern us here.) It should be noted with respect to this list that Darwin wrote an entire book on emotions: *The Expression of the Emotions in Man and Animals*. The point is that, while drawing the larger picture is certainly not without value — at the very least, it makes us think — it passes too quickly over homely things, precisely such things as instincts, curiosity, attention, imagination, and the like. Such mental powers are in many ways presupposed in Edelman's research. They appear difficult to program into an automaton, yet they are fundamental to grasping the nature of mind and its basic somaticity.

19.   Darwin III is a "recognition automaton ... that has a single movable eye, a four-jointed arm with touch at the last joint, and kinesthesia (joint sense) signaled by neurons in its joints as they move." It seems telling that Edelman, assumably because his readers might be unfamiliar with the term, must specify what kinesthesia means. That this most fundamental sense needs a lexical introduction speaks volubly of how much we know or "think we know" about bodies. Note that Edelman puts scare quotes around *hand-arm* and *eye*, thus signalling that these automaton parts are only — to borrow a word from Aristotle — homonymously a hand-arm and an eye. But note too that he makes no comparable distinction when speaking of touch and kinesthesia. He takes these capacities as real accomplishments. In effect, and in physiological terms, although structure is recognized as something other than the real thing, function is not. This lack of consistency of course generates a fundamental problem: are robots and automata sensorily and motorically continuous with actually living creatures?

20.   Regarding models which treat the environment as a "probability function," see as an example Rumelhart 1989:141–142. Regarding models which treat a leg as a part of the environment, see Smithers 1993. Smithers criticizes the conception as it is set forth by John C. Gallagher and Randall D. Beer in their article titled "A Qualitative Dynamical Analysis of Evolved Locomotion Controllers." Smithers comments that "The analysis they present is ... of the performance of the controller, not of the behavior of the agent interacting with its environment. This is good controller design practice, but it is not analysis of agent-environment system behavior" (1993:8).

CHAPTER 5

On learning to move oneself

A constructive phenomenology

A method, after all, is nothing which is, or which can be, brought in from the outside…. [A] *determinate* method … is a norm which arises from the fundamental regional specificity and the universal structures of the province in question …   Edmund Husserl (1983:173)

[I]t is not only the worldly facts of birth and death through which transcendental questions about a genesis are to be "constructed," but also the world phenomena of *early childhood development,* insofar as precisely this early period lies beyond the reach of our memory; these are all questions that are raised in psychology under the titles "the origin of the idea of space, of the idea of time," etc., and of course at the essentially inadequate level of the natural attitude. The *transcendental* response to all these questions cannot proceed in intuitive fashion, i.e. it cannot bring the archaic building processes actually to a present or recollective self-givenness, it can only "construct" them…. [Constructive phenomenology] begins in quite *different* problem regions … and in every case does so in a style of "construction" that is in each case *particular,* that is only understandable in view of each problem situation. It thus shows an intrinsic multiplicity of methods …
                                                                Eugen Fink (1995:63)

1. Initial remarks

There is no doubt but that a constructive phenomenology is called for with respect to infancy and childhood, precisely as Eugen Fink indicates. This chapter constitutes just such a methodology in the process of defining itself. The constructive phenomenology appeals to and attempts to consolidate in a harmonious and mutually enlightening way scientific and phenomenological findings — in Husserl's terms, to consolidate the regional specificities and universal structures of infancy and childhood. By the very nature of the topic, the task is a trans-disciplinary one. But how specifically do we initiate this constructive phenomenology? How do we go about recapturing and understanding the complex of experiences we had in learning to move ourselves? Clearly, it is not a matter of recapturing and understanding a past that was never present.[1]

The past in question was definitively present — in the flesh, in the full and vibrant aliveness that we all experienced in yawning and stretching, kicking and grimacing. The methodology, as it unfolds and if it is successful, will bring the foundational ground of that aliveness to life and in the process confirm the value of a trans-disciplinary task. It will demonstrate concretely how phenomenological analyses have the possibility of grounding both scientific empirical studies and everyday observations, in other words, the possibility of exposing unquestioned traditional wisdom lying at the heart of the natural attitude and deepening understandings through phenomenological analyses.

2.   A general introduction to the terrain

Cultural values, ethnic practices, religious beliefs, sexual anatomy and preferences, social class, political affiliations, and all other sources of distinctions and differences among humans aside, we humans have something in common, something beside language, burial practices, tool-making proficiencies, and so on. What we have in common is our natality. We all start out the same way: as infants. Infants are competent, nonlinguistic animate forms. They imitate tongue and mouth movements of adults as early as 42 minutes after birth (Meltzoff & Moore 1983); they distinguish the smell of their mother from the smell of other people (MacFarlane in Stern 1985: 39); they distinguish what is round from what is knobby (Meltzoff & Borton 1979); they move rhythmically as when they nurse in bursts and pauses (Kaye 1982; see also Hendriks-Jansen 1996, Chapter 15); their eyes follow the gaze of their mother (Scaife & Bruner 1975); and more. But the competency of infants is even more impressive than this. Infants learn to move themselves. We are in fact here today — reading this book, climbing these steps, playing this trumpet, formulating this problem, doing this chemistry experiment, excising this tumor — in virtue of having learned to move ourselves. We learned to move ourselves by building on our native kinetic/kinesthetic competencies. We learned without words. We learned without any kind of formal instruction from others. We were our own teachers. We taught ourselves — spontaneously — and at our own pace. We were apprentices of our own bodies. We learned directly from our own bodies what it is to be the animate forms we are. We learned by listening, by being and staying attuned kinesthetically, in an on-going process of feeling the dynamics of our own movement: we felt the effort and shape of our movement; we felt its temporal flow. In our apprenticeship, we learned complex details about our kinetic aliveness — about bending, stretching, turning, lifting, opening, closing, and much more. We learned significant and complex details about the qualitative nature of self-movement: about suddenness, slowness, heaviness, laxness, forcefulness, and again, much more. We learned how these already significant and complex details of our kinetic aliveness gained in significance and became even more complex in the context of our own development, how a newly emerging strength or a newly emerging reaching range gave us new possibilities of movement, thus an expanding repertoire of powers, or "I cans," Husserl's term for those foundational possibilities that are the epistemological cornerstone of our sense-makings (Husserl 1989, 1980, 1970a). We learned our possibilities by moving and having moved — by catching ourselves in the kinetic act, so to speak. (For detailed analyses and discussions of these possibilities and their conceptual import in the context of our own human evolutionary history, see Sheets-Johnstone 1990).

Over an extended period of time, all humans go through the same process of corporeal apprenticeship and learning. In effect, all humans share a common background as novitiates in the art and science of self-movement. They share a common fundamental kinetic repertoire as a result of this process for they are all the same kind of animate form. They all turn, stretch, walk, crouch, jump, hit, punch, recoil, lunge, shake, tremble, and leap in basically the same way. Indeed, our common ground is wordless, as our common natality and infancy and our common movement repertoire so well show. If we pursued a study of that common wordless ground, we might find a relationship between our wordless kinetic beginnings and our later wordless celebrations of movement, as at the Olympic Games, a relationship we could readily spell out in terms of the sheer experience of aliveness, the sheer nonverbal kinetic experience of ourselves and others as animate forms. We need no such study, however, to convince ourselves that fundamental human commonalities lie by way of movement. We need only examine our own experience of movement, observe others about us, and reflect upon what we customarily assume as given and just as customarily relegate to the domain of the merely physical. When we recognize our common infancy and our common repertoire of movement, we discover the common bond that unites us across our individual but species-specific kinetic histories of learning our bodies and learning to move ourselves. In sum, whatever our differences, movement is our mother tongue.

Fundamental facets of our knowledge of the world derive from our basic kinetic corporeal commonalities. As infants, we all explored the world about us. We picked up objects, put them in our mouths, turned them about in our hands, studied them from various perspectives. Through touch and movement, we came to constitute the world epistemologically for ourselves; we came to know a spoon, a ball, an apple, a book, a box, a doll, a chair, a table, and so on, from touching it and moving it directly, and/or from moving ourselves in relation to it. Moving toward objects, approaching them from different directions, stopping in front of them, peering down or up at them, grasping them, mouthing them, we engaged the world on the basis of our tactile-kinesthetic bodies. Clearly, our natural curiosity would be stillborn without movement. Coming to know the world in a quite literal sense means coming to grips with it — exploring it, searching it, discovering it in and through movement. There is no human culture in which movement is not epistemologically central in this way. There is, indeed, no culture in which movement is not our mother tongue. In his phenomenological account of perception, Husserl pinpointed the focal place of movement by the term *the kinestheses*. As detailed in the last chapter, he described how sensing is correlated with movement, that is, how specific perceptions are correlated with specific kinestheses: if I move closer to the table, I see the textured lines on its surface; if I turn my head, I hear the strains of the music more distinctly; if I move toward the tree, I smell the cedar. He described how an orderly, harmonious world is built up on the basis of these if/then relationships, and at the same time how these relationships are based on a repertoire of "I cans." For example, my discovery that if I shut my eyes it gets dark is based upon my ability to shut my eyes; my discovery that if I turn my head the mobile comes into view is based upon my ability to turn my head. Consequential relationships are discovered on the basis of already established powers of movement.[2] But new "I cans" also arise on the basis of already known consequential relationships. For example, based on my knowledge of the relationship "If I close my eyes, it gets dark," I can play "Surprise" or "Owl" with someone, each of us putting our foreheads together, closing our eyes, and on the word "Surprise" or "Owl," opening our eyes. Similarly, on the basis of previously learned consequential relationships having to do with things appearing in view and disappearing from view, I can play peek-a-boo with someone. With more movement possibilities, I learn equally that if I grasp the table leg and then pull on it, I can slide myself across the floor toward it, or if I open my hand and then close it very fast, I can catch the finger put on my palm. In effect, I expand my repertoire of "I cans" on the basis of discovered if/then relationships. We should notice that all of these if/then relationships are enabling or empowering relationships; but they are not on that account simply physical accomplishments. On the contrary, they are conceptually rich experiences. Basic concepts having to do with opening and closing, with closeness and distance, with perspective, with light and dark, with swiftness, with effort, and with myriad other spatio-temporal-energy dimensions and effects of self-movement are inherent in the experience of if/then relationships. There is no bridge to be crossed between thinking and doing. Concepts develop not only in the same sense that abilities and skills develop; they are coincident with the development of those abilities and skills — whether a matter of learning to speak or to read or to stand or to ski. To believe otherwise is to be oblivious of what is there in the experience of self-movement.

Now in describing the fundamental correlation of perception and movement, and the central role of both consequential relationships and of "I cans," Husserl was *not* describing infants. Through a phenomenological methodology and a phenomenological analysis of the experience of perception, he was uncovering originary facets of our knowledge of the world, facets which we can verify any time we wish by turning to our own experience and replicating his phenomenological inquiry. Clearly, however, the originary facets he uncovered, and which we can validate through our own experience, provide insight into infant life. They enlighten us about the key significance of movement in our lives. Indeed, were we immobile — something on the order of the statue that 18th-century philosopher Condillac envisioned, a statue which in the beginning had no senses, but who through Condillac's thought experiment "came to life" one sense at a time beginning with vision and progressing to hearing, smelling, and tasting — we would be incapable of grasping the correlation between sensing and moving that Husserl so well describes. We would be capable only of knowing whatever happened to pass our way, and knowing it only in the sense of having seen, heard, smelled, or tasted it before and of recognizing it as either like or unlike other sights, sounds, smells, or tastes (cf. the notion of exploration — hence movement — as basic to cognition in E.J. Gibson 1988; cf. also studies of searching behavior — "active movement by which an animal finds or attempts to find resources … perhaps the most important kind of behavior that an animal engages in" — William Bell 1991: 1). Most importantly, we would be incapable of learning our bodies. Being statues, we in fact would not really be bodies to begin with and in consequence would be powerless to teach ourselves anything and, in effect, to learn in any robust sense. We would be nothing but singular and isolated sense organs and the world would be nothing but passing stimuli. Only through movement can and does our foundational apprenticeship and learning — our knowledge of ourselves and of the world — take root.

In this general introduction to the centrality of movement to our knowledge of the world, we should also recall from discussions in Chapter Four von Helmholtz's observations concerning spatial relationships as mediated by movement and his insights into the correlation of perception and movement, particularly as he observed that correlation in the activities of young children. We should furthermore call attention to current scientific research on infancy, particularly those studies informed by a dynamic systems approach. This work is innovative and promising precisely because its subjects are real infants existing in — to use dynamic systems terminology — "real time." In other words, these dynamic system theorists take movement seriously; their subjects are not information processors that exhibit certain behaviors or that have input/output devices, but living beings, that is, organisms who interact dynamically with their environment. These dynamic systems theorists are thus not studying behavior in typical third-person style nor are they explaining movement in terms of cortically churned-out motor programs. They are studying what infants actually do in particular contexts in the course of their developing lives. Moreover they do not view infant behaviors as "imperfect versions of adult behavior" (Hendriks-Jansen 1996: 13). A primary value of a dynamic systems approach, particularly in the present general context of movement, is its central concern with *change*. Rather than viewing infant motor development or behavior as either some kind of automatic stage process or insulated turn-on switch from within, dynamic theorists concerned with infant/child development view motor development as a process in which the infant itself is actively engaged, which means a process that is quintessentially structured not in theoretical constructs or neurological programmers but in movement. As infant psychologists Esther Thelen and Linda Smith remark, "Development does not happen because internal maturational processes tell the system how to develop. Rather, development happens through and because of the activity of the system itself," the system meaning the dynamic system which is a composite of the infant, its perceptual and movement capacities of the moment, its immediate surrounds, and its developmental proclivities at the time (Thelen & Smith 1994:305). Moreover from a dynamic systems perspective, cognition is structured in activity, in movement. Knowledge is thus not a pre-existent something that enables an infant to do certain things; it is part of the process of doing them. Knowledge is enfolded in movement. This is the thrust of Thelen and Smith's finer point that, contrary to "the usual developmental stories," integrations of sensory experience in different modalities are not the result of development; they allow development to occur. Similarly, infants discover patterns of coordination in their own movement. In brief, infants are active participants in their own maturational learning, and this on the basis of their own correlated experiences of action and object (Thelen & Smith 1994:187).

Now surely on the basis of their common kinetic apprenticeship and repertoire, all humans in the beginning forge a sense of themselves as animate forms. What kind of sense is this? What is it like to think in movement? What is it like to build up knowledge of the world by moving and touching one's way through it, apprenticing oneself by way of one's body, rather than by way of information, language, or any kind of formal instruction? Consider, for example, how keenly and astutely attuned we are to the slightest movements of others — a flickering of eyes, a pulling in of lips, a waywardness of gaze, a twitching in the neck, a tremoring of hands, a sudden laxity in knees, a momentary grimace, a fleeting constriction in the torso, a sudden intake of breath, a softly beating foot. We are kinetically attuned to each other. No one teaches us how to be attuned. We teach ourselves — nonverbally. Our kinetic inter-attunement has thus nothing to do with mastering a body-language book on the order of popular digests listing typical movements and their typical meanings, nor with having at our disposal culture-specific kinetic dictionaries to which we turn to look up kinetic synonyms and antonyms, much less *derivations*, i.e. kinetic etymologies, which would in fact require a study of primate and even mammalian movement. Our kinetic inter-attunement is grounded in a natural sensitivity to the movement of others, and in a correlative natural sensitivity to kinetic meaning. Dankert Vedeler's work on infant intentionality (1987, 1991), and especially his incorporation of Runeson and Frykholm's "kinematic specification principle" (1981,1983), empirically supports the phenomenologically-based claim of a foundational kinetic bond. How, we may ask, is it possible to deepen our understanding of this bond? And what would it be like to reform our notion of ourselves in such a way as to acknowledge our common birth in movement and our common mother tongue?

3.   Beginning phenomenological considerations

Husserl's basic notions of an "I move" and of an "I do" need further phenomenological elucidation. Although using the terms descriptively in his writings, Husserl did not elucidate the genesis or import of these kinetic structures of experience except to say that "Originally, the 'I move', 'I do', precedes the 'I can do'" (Husserl 1989: 273). Phenomenological philosopher Ludwig Landgrebe (at one time an assistant to Husserl) clarified and extended this seminal initial insight, and in ways that coincide with the lines of current interest: learning to move oneself. His clarification and extension occur in the context of asking about the origin of our capacity for knowledge and of describing how Husserl's phenomenological forms of reflection come to answer the question, at first through a static phenomenology in which reflection upon the object *as meant* leads back to those acts of consciousness by which the object has come to have the meaning it has, i.e. has come to be constituted, and later through a genetic phenomenology in which reflection upon the structures of constituting consciousness itself leads to understandings of transcendental subjectivity — what we might more informally term sense-making consciousness. Landgrebe's point is that the import of Husserl's shift from a static to a genetic phenomenology was never properly specified by Husserl himself. Accordingly, he himself goes on to specify it. He states that "*Static reflection cannot lead to the origin of the acquaintance between ourselves and our constitutive function, which precedes all reflection upon already performed acts*" (Landgrebe 1977: 107; italics in original). What Landgrebe wants to emphasize is that the structures of consciousness that make possible all of our sense-makings are already there and functioning; they are not structures that we can discover through mere "retrospective perception," i.e. through a static phenomenology (107). Given this epistemological impasse, a genetic phenomenology — a phenomenology that aims at elucidating the original structures of constituting consciousness — demands a different kind of reflection. With respect to this different kind of reflection, Landgrebe states that "This peculiar sort of reflexivity, as a prior acquaintance with ourselves, can be understood if we look at the way whereby we are moved in everyday life to interrupt the performance of our acts to reflect on their success or failure" (107). He draws attention to the fact that our "I cans" come to the fore when we suddenly find ourselves unsuccessful in doing what we intended. He writes,

> Then the naive performance is stopped with the consideration which might be formulated in such words as "Why were you unable to do this?" Thus *reflection* is primarily, and always, a *turning back toward what we can do*. But we find out what we can do by exercising our capacity to do what we can do. Husserl was on the verge of discovering this fact when, in the analysis of kinaesthetic ability … he said: "The 'I move' precedes the 'I can." This is true even at an early level of prelinguistic development in the child, while the goal-oriented movement of the parts of its body are practiced and copied. In such activity — with its success

> or failure — the child experiences itself, even at this early stage, as a center and source of spontaneous motion whereby he can bring about, grasp, push away, etc. something in his environment.... The child is already this individual existence, and knows itself as such in terms of experiencing the ability to control his body in the gradually learned ability to govern its motor system. This ability provides the child with its first access to its environment (107–108).

Landgrebe's analysis aims at a foundational clarification of transcendental subjectivity. As the above citation readily suggests, he finds that transcendental subjectivity is, *at its origin*, a kinesthetic consciousness. He affirms that "The ability to move oneself is the deepest-lying transcendental function," that "[t]his *ability to move [oneself] ... is the most elementary form of spontaneity*" (108; italics in original). In effect, the ability to move oneself is foundational to any and all constitutive processes; the *ability* precedes the *possibility* of doing anything, that is, it precedes any "I can." Landgrebe subsequently points out on the basis of this foundational consciousness that the primary form of reflection — the primary form of the relationship of ourselves to our primary "constitutive function" — is a practical one, a reflection upon our abilities: reflection is first and foremost reflection upon ourselves moving, upon ourselves as agents. His two insights are profound. They anchor both consciousness and reflection in self-movement. Landgrebe does not go on to elucidate dimensions of our "deepest-lying transcendental function," but continues, initially at least, to develop his insights along Heideggerian lines (and equally along the lines of Merleau-Ponty), affirming that we are already in the world and functioning with our ability and that reflection cannot break through to a ground prior to that functioning; and affirming further that since a constitutive function that is an ability cannot be intuited but can only be enacted, it itself can never be an object of consciousness apart from its enactment. What Landgrebe is thereby affirming is that reflection is limited; it is powerless to reveal anything prior to the "I move," or "I do," nor can it reveal anything about the abilities — the "I move," or "I do" — themselves. If we follow along the lines of the two insights, however, *and at the same time hew to a phenomenological methodology, in particular to a constructive phenomenology aiming at an elucidation of the phenomenon of learning to move ourselves*, we do not arrive at an epistemological impasse but remain on epistemological track. In turn, we have the possibility of clarifying not only the precedence of an "I move" to an "I can," but the precedence of movement to an "I move."

4. Primal movement and its occlusion by a natural attitude view of movement

We come into the world already moving. We are indeed either movement-born or still-born. When we learn to move ourselves, we do so on the basis of what is already there: an original kinetic liveliness or animation. It is thus not a "functioning Ego" (Landgrebe 1977: 108–109); or a body and a world (a theme throughout the writings of Merleau-Ponty, e.g. Merleau-Ponty 1962: 197–98), or "the existential *fore-structure* of Dasein" (Heidegger 1962: 195), or an "I move" that is already there; it is movement that is already there. To claim ourselves already there in any other way is to view ourselves from an adultist stance that overlooks our beginnings. When we assume that adultist stance, reflection is understandably stymied; we are caught short of being able to dredge up the originating ground of our knowledge, our capacities, our being. In each instance the beginning point of departure for reflection has been pushed forward, accelerated to a vantage point beyond the reach of primal understandings, and to that degree its claims of an impenetrable epistemological boundary are mistaken. We *can* "get back," as the expression goes. But to do so requires a reclamation of nature: our own in its originary form. Of course, this does not mean behaving like an infant again: ceasing to speak, sleeping and eating irregularly, and so on. It means turning ourselves seriously and methodically toward our genesis in nature and discovering the kinetic/ kinesthetic structures of our original humanness. In particular, it means turning attention to our *apprenticeship* and to the grounding of that apprenticeship in animate form, in animation. We can specify what is already kinetically there, not in terms of so many readily performed abilities — e.g. sucking is there, blinking is there, and so on, though such abilities as orchestrations of movement are of considerable constitutive moment in the constructive phenomenological enterprise — but in terms of elucidating the nature of that movement in whose dynamic form we, and indeed, all animate creatures, come into the world. Just as we need not wait for or turn to moments in which we meet or have met with success or failure in exercising our ability in order to understand the original nature of our power to reflect, as Landgrebe wrongly insists we must, so we need not wait for or turn to such moments in order to become aware of the ground on which our abilities emerge. To gain insight into the developing structures of an I that moves, an I that emerges on the ground of movement, we turn to movement itself, to movement that is already there and to the kinesthetic consciousness that is quintessentially and consummately attuned to it. In effect, the task is to elucidate movement as a *natal* phenomenon, and this in a double sense: the phenomenon of being movement-born and the phenomenon of self-movement as it emerges from the phenomenon of being movement-born. As indicated above, the task does not involve us in an itemization and consequent inventory of readily performed natal abilities. But neither does it involve us in an enumeration of behaviors. To pay attention to our genesis in movement is not to classify activities according to function or purpose and thereby demarcate one concerted round of movements from another concerted round of movements — inhaling from exhaling, sucking from swallowing, and so on. When creatures come into the world moving, they are not behaving; they are moving. They are, in a word, *animated.*

But what can be said about this original kinetic liveliness other than that *it is there*?

In Chapter Three, several examples were given of natural, everyday movements that we, as adults, can attend to kinetically: stretching, breathing, sneezing. The essentially *qualitative* character of movement was clearly evident in each case. We can thus appreciate that a phenomenological examination discloses a radically different experience and conception of movement from the experience and conception that hold forth in the natural attitude. In particular, the common notion of movement as a change of position, and the standard dictionary definition of movement as a change of position, find no place within the phenomenology of kinetic experience. Both notion and definition in fact stand in need of correction. At the very least, both need to be identified for what they are: factual views of movement. *As beheld in the natural attitude*, movement is the factual displacement of an object from point A to point B, thus a change of position.[3] Our first task is to confront this view of movement and show how it not only conceals the essential character of movement but impedes a clear conception of movement from the start by centering attention not on *movement* but on *an object in motion*. (For a fully detailed analysis of the difference in the context of dance, see Sheets-Johnstone 1979). In short, to elucidate our original kinetic liveliness, we need to clear a conceptual space in which it can appear. To do this, we shall first examine the natural attitude view of movement in quite general terms and with brief but special reference to how it was confronted by Merleau-Ponty and by psychologist James Gibson. We shall then proceed to extended analyses of both Merleau-Ponty's and Gibson's endeavors to come to terms with movement, attempting to show in each case how a natural attitude view of movement precludes insight into the foundational phenomenon of primal animation.

The natural attitude view of movement as change of position is in great measure fostered by a mathematization of movement, an objectification on behalf of science: a change of position from point A to point B is above all a measurable change. Moreover it is above all a change in location of a particular object which, in the absence of movement, would otherwise be at rest. When Merleau-Ponty is concerned to give an account of movement, he is concerned to foil just this natural attitude view which, with its point by point conception of movement, destroys the unity of movement, and which, with its consistent reference to an object, consistently relativizes movement. His explicit target is not actually the natural attitude view of movement; as throughout *Phenomenology of Perception*, his target is the intellectualist and the empiricist, generalized figures whom he identifies in this instance as "the logician" and "the psychologist," each with his respective rendition of movement (Merleau-Ponty 1962: 267–80). There is no doubt, however, but that the natural attitude is at the base of these renditions as Merleau-Ponty describes them, and that his aim is to overturn a mathematically-informed understanding of movement as a change of position. To this end, he ultimately calls into being a "non-thematized mobile entity" (275), a "[p]re-objective being"(275) which is not objective but whose "changes [of] position" (276, Note 1) are experienced as a "style" (274) by a "prepersonal *I* who provides the basis for the phenomenon of movement" (276, Note 1).[4] We shall examine this seemingly non-natural rendition of movement more closely in a moment. Let us note first that the natural attitude view of movement as change of position is fostered in equally great measure by an instrumental understanding of movement. Psychologist James Gibson's research and writings on perception — in particular, his research and writings on perceptual systems as opposed to traditionally conceived specialized sensory pathways — are geared to this understanding, but in a way that escapes its traditional outlines. Gibson subsumes the phenomenon of movement into the structure of the perceptual systems of sight, hearing, taste, touch, and smell. Thus, in his early major text he speaks of proprioception as visual proprioception, as auditory proprioception, as cutaneous proprioception, and so on, and in his later major text he speaks of, and is concerned in particular with, visual kinesthesis (J.J. Gibson 1966: 37–38, 200–201; J.J. Gibson 1979: e.g. 126, where Gibson states categorically that the pickup of information in "the ambient [optical] array … should in all cases be called *visual kinesthesis*"; italics in original). Ultimately, he transforms the phenomenon of movement into a phenomenon enmeshed in the global phenomenon of "perceptual affordances," the key concept of his later work. His instrumentalization of movement is atypical in that it does not separate out movement *as a means* of perception. In Gibson's account, movement is clearly not merely a physical system actuated toward a perceptual end. On the contrary, movement is conceived as enfolded in perception itself. In his account of "action sensitivity or movement sensitivity," Gibson in fact speaks of "the fallacy" of proprioception; that is, no more than the "exteroceptors" — eyes, ears, nose, mouth, and skin — are proprioceptors "specialized receptors" (J.J. Gibson 1966: 34, 33, 33, 34). It is crucially important to note, however, that, unlike eyes, ears, nose, mouth, and skin, movement does not constitute a perceptual system in Gibson's view. Though no longer a mere physical means, movement nonetheless remains instrumental. It is the way we go about "pick[ing] up information" that is there in the world (J.J. Gibson 1979: 238–263). In the process of picking up information in the world, we of course "pick up information" about our own movement. Proprioceptive information provides the perceiver "awareness of *his own* motion in the world, that is, the awareness of *locomotion*" (1979: 182; italics in original). Though reduced to locomotion in the service of perception, movement is what Gibson might well have termed a "kinetic affordance."

   Although both Merleau-Ponty and Gibson attempt to break out of traditional perspectives on movement, and in this sense attempt to break loose of the natural attitude, in neither case is the attempt successful. The essentially qualitative nature of movement is not given its due because it is nowhere recognized and it is nowhere recognized because the particular methodology in use precludes recognition in each instance.

In effect, it is as if the essential character of movement were nonexistent. Precisely for methodological reasons, it will be helpful to spell out Gibson's and Merleau-Ponty's respective ideas about movement in greater detail. Such an exposition will allow us to appreciate in exacting terms the importance of the phenomenological methodology of bracketing. (It will also of course show how we do not have to wait for the unexpected in order to arrive at insights into either kinesthetic consciousness or into our originary ability to move ourselves, as Landgrebe claims.)

In his first book on perceptual systems, Gibson recognizes "muscular proprio-ception" in the form of muscle receptors that "register effort," but he states that "it is doubtful that there are sensations to correspond." In this same text, he recognizes "articular proprioception" as a "sensitivity to skeletal movement," but appears hesi-tant to accord it any perceptual value, saying only that "[t]here seems to be conscious awareness of the joints," i.e. a feeling of "the angles which the bones make to one another" (1966: 36–37). In short, Gibson's original notion of proprioception is both static and positional; *it is not tied to movement as a dynamically experienced bodily happening.* Running, stretching, swaying, and so on, are just such dynamically experi-enced bodily happenings. So also are reaching, pushing, kicking, and not just myriad other, but *all* other, bodily movements. Though muscular effort and joint angles enter into a kinesthetic awareness of movement in each instance, they enter as features of a globally felt spatio-temporal-energy dynamic. Indeed, muscular effort and joint angles shift in subtle and complex ways in the performance of movement. Hence no move-ment is properly characterized kinesthetically simply in terms of muscular effort and joint angles. Such characterizations are static and positional and belie the dynamic and holistic nature of self-movement. With respect to perceptual systems themselves, there is a further problem. Gibson's notion of perceptual systems coincides with "the five senses." It is thus not surprising that movement has no place as a perceptual system in and of itself, but is recognized only in terms of how it enters into the classic sensory modalities. Though Gibson refigures the latter in innovative and instructive ways as perceptual systems, they remain five in number. In effect, although his central theme is that perception is an *ecological* relationship, that is, a coalition of organism and envi-ronment, and although this ecological relationship re-echoes in theoretical ways von Helmholtz's and Husserl's descriptive accounts of the correlation between movement and perception, Gibson's preferential focus on the five senses — on what we see, hear, smell, taste, and touch — restricts his account of perception. In other words, being riveted on *what* we see, hear, smell, taste, and touch, Gibson's attention is preeminently on the side of the environment and touches only lightly on the side of the organism. In consequence, the phenomenon of movement, self-movement, as a phenomenon in its own right is elided. Indeed, Gibson's environmental focus far outdistances his focus on the organism. The affordant properties of an environment — its support structure and its water sources, for example — are primary, not what correlatively might be termed *the affordant kinetic powers of organisms.* Gibson's uneven attention is a product of his fundamental theory of "information pickup" as well insofar as "[t]he theory of information pickup requires perceptual systems, not senses" (1979:244). Gibson is in fact explicit about his aim. In preface to specifying particulars about his notion of "information pickup," he states quite straightforwardly, "Let us remember once again that it is the perception of the environment that we wish to explain" (1979:239). Accordingly, although he everywhere insists on the equal centrality of living organisms in his ecological approach to perception, declaring, for example, that "Information about the self accompanies information about the environment, and the two are inseparable" (1979:126), or that "The continuous act of perceiving involves the coperceiving of the self" (1979:240), or that "Perception and proprioception are complementary" (1979:157), there is no comparable, substantive elucidation of the complementary, proprioceptively-endowed organism, certainly nothing beyond the observation that "the activities of looking, listening, touching, tasting, or sniffing" are movement activities proper to perceptual systems (1979:244). Given Gibson's uneven account of perception, it is unclear how a "coperceiving of the self" can be anything more than what Sartre would term a prereflective awareness of oneself since one's gaze is always and inexorably world-directed — all the more so when Gibson writes that "Perceiving … is a keeping-in-touch with the world, an experiencing of things rather than a having of experiences" (1979:239). It is worth noting that in his later work, where he introduces the concept of affordances, Gibson at one point seems to accord a slightly more robust nod to "muscle-joint kinesthesis," saying that "visual kinesthesis should be recognized along with muscle-joint kinesthesis." But he nowhere fleshes out the latter. In fact he immediately faults "muscle-joint kinesthesis" because it "does not function during passive locomotion in a vehicle." He concludes that "Visual kinesthesis yields the only reliable information about displacement" (1979:125).

In sum, however insightful and radically novel his notions about the directness of perception and the ongoingness of perception, and however rich and provocative his notion of environmental affordances, his account of movement does less than full justice to the experience of movement, and correlatively, to kinesthesia. What lies at the bottom of his view of movement are residuals of a still natural attitude view. Not only is movement instrumental locomotion in the service of visual perception, auditory perception, and so on; movement is itself a quite subsidiary dimension of the informational structure of all perception. The "muscle-joint" system, Gibson says, provides only "supplementary information" (1979:126). There is no intimation of a qualitative dynamics in this instrumental-informational view. Put in methodological perspective, one can readily and with good reason claim that what is missing is the procedure of bracketing. Without bracketing, Gibson misses the phenomenon of kinesthesia proper, a phenomenon that exists in its own right and that warrants examination in and of itself. By conjoining kinestheses — proprioception — with every other sense modality, Gibson readily misses the qualitative structure of movement. In effect, he does not do justice to the experience of movement — self-movement. His informational thematic is part and parcel of what might be termed the currently trendy natural attitude view of movement: movement is in the service of perceptual "information pickup." While one can readily appreciate Gibson's efforts to show that conceiving vision, hearing, and so on, as so many discrete sensory modalities is wrong-headed, that perception is a matter of integrated systemic functionings, one can readily appreciate even on the basis of naive everyday experiences — of stretching, breathing, and sneezing, for example — that movement is something both more and other than instrumental, and that kinesthesis may afford something both more and other than information. Children, after all, take pleasure in skipping, and adults take pleasure in such games as tennis. In addition, as shown in Chapter Three, kinesthetic consciousness is the foundational source of our concepts of space, time, and force. Moreover we do indeed need to reckon with kinesthesia because we in fact reckon with it in increasingly complex ways from the very beginning. The striking and emphatic comment — striking and emphatic because it is, or should be, so obvious — of developmental psychologists Esther Thelen and Linda Smith is of critical significance in this context. Taking a cue from Gibson's own approach to perception, they state that "*movement must itself be considered a perceptual system*"(1994:193).

One might think that if anyone could show the inextricable bond between organism and environment and elaborate kinesthesia as a perceptual system, it would be Merleau-Ponty. All the more so given his notion of the unity of movement as a certain *style*. But Merleau-Ponty is as far from recognizing the essentially qualitative nature of movement as Gibson, and equally as far from recognizing the quintessential significance of kinesthesia. To show that this is so, we need to consider both his analysis of movement and his notion of motor intentionality.

Merleau-Ponty treats movement in a separate section of his chapter on space in *Phenomenology of Perception*. As elsewhere, his method is to pit the views of the intellectualist against the views of the empiricist, showing how each is wrong and resolving their respective deficiencies through his thematic of the phenomenal body. The problem is that movement does not emerge from the fray as other topics; it is not amenable to the same kind of methodological treatment because neither the empiricist nor the logician can be suitably pinned down in such a way as to allow Merleau-Ponty to emerge victorious. The psychologist's account is especially recalcitrant to his critical strategy. At one point, wrestling with Gestalt psychologists who speak of "dynamic phenomena" apart from objects in motion, Merleau-Ponty declares that "Perception of movement can be perception *of movement* and recognition of it as such, only if it is apprehension of it with its significance as movement, and with all the instants which constitute it, and in particular with the identity of the object in motion" (1962:271; cf. Sheets-Johnstone 1979). Clearly, Merleau-Ponty wants movement to be both all of a piece and identical with the object in motion; he wants to unify movement as against a pointillist view and at the same time to de-relativize it with respect to an object conceived separate from its movement. In short, he wants a non-objective account of movement. But that is not in fact the way he describes it. His statement about what constitutes "perception *of movement*" has contingent clauses which, in the first instance, characterize movement as basically fragmented even if unified, and in the second instance, dissolve the phenomenon of movement into an object in motion. Moreover in elaborating on just what the perception of movement must be, he later declares that "'Dynamic phenomena' take their unity from me who live (*sic*) through them, and who effect (*sic*) their synthesis," a remark that might in a temporal sense sound peculiarly Husserlian. But Merleau-Ponty leaves the notion of 'dynamic phenomena' completely unelucidated phenomenologically and in fact presses for a featureless, i.e. non-dynamical, rendering of movement (1962: 272). Indeed, he designates the phrase "dynamic phenomenon" a metaphor, and does not enlighten us as to its origin. It is not too much to say that in the thirteen odd pages in which he wrestles with movement, Merleau-Ponty valiantly struggles in particular to reconcile movement with objects in motion. There is an aura of uneasiness about the relationship. It is evident, for example, when, in discussing "dynamic phenomena," Merleau-Ponty attempts to identify movement with the object in motion by affirming that it is the perceiver who unifies movement: "it seems to us that a force itself ensures its unity, but this is because we always suppose that someone is there to identify it in the development of its effects" (272).

In sum, the problem of instants and the problem of the relationship of movement to objects in motion are played out in terms of unity and identity, but the critical discussion of intellectualist and empiricist views eventuates in no clear solution. On the contrary, one has the sense that Merleau-Ponty's linguistic recourse to "a mobile entity" is a way out of a tortured reasoning process that has gone and is going nowhere. On the one hand, Merleau-Ponty finally agrees with the logician when the latter "demands some constitution of the 'dynamic phenomenon' itself," but faults him for "present[ing] the identity of the object in motion as an express identity" (1962: 272); on the other hand, he finally agrees with the psychologist when the latter "is led in spite of himself to put a moving body into movement," but faults him for being unclear about the relation between movement and moving body (272). It is at this very end juncture of the discussion that a most unusual series of remarks occurs in which the intellectualist and empiricist positions present themselves as less straightforwardly malleable as in his other investigations of space and spatial phenomena, and in which the underlying aim of Merleau-Ponty's investigations of movement and his seeming impatience in realizing it come to the fore. In uncharacteristically exasperated fashion, Merleau-Ponty remarks, "In the discussion which we have just followed, and which serves to illustrate the everlasting debate between psychology and logic, what, in the last resort, does Wertheimer [the psychologist] mean?" When he goes on in his own words to say precisely what Wertheimer means — "He means that the perception of movement is not secondary to the perception of the moving object, ... and that in short the identity of the object in motion flows directly from 'experience'" — Merleau-Ponty appends a footnote at the end of the sentence, which reads: "It is true that Wertheimer does not say in so many words that the perception of motion embraces this immediate identity. He says so only implicitly" (272). It is odd, of course, to give a final summation of precisely what someone is saying and at the same time note that the person is saying this "only implicitly." But this interpretation clears the air, so to speak. Merleau-Ponty moves immediately from this point to embrace the notion of "a mobile entity" that "is not identical *beneath* the phases of movement, [but] is identical *in* them" (273). Presumably, this move allows a reconciliation of the idea that unity is a function both of the object in motion and of the perceiver: "Motion is nothing without a body in motion which describes and provides it with unity" (272); at the same time, "dynamic phenomena take their unity from me who live (*sic*) through them, and who effect (*sic*) their synthesis" (272).

Though Merleau-Ponty strives to overcome it, the natural attitude view of movement in fact dominates: there is nothing to movement apart from an object in motion. In consequence, movement is nowhere recognized as a qualitative happening but as an event that must in some way be harmonized with moving objects and with points in space and points in time. There is no appreciation of movement *tout court* because, in spite of all efforts against the natural attitude view, movement remains tied to the notion of change of position, the displacement of an object *through* space and *in* time. Even though later affirming that "movement does not necessarily presuppose a moving object, that is, an object defined in terms of a collection of determinate properties" (and adding the following peculiar adequation: "it is sufficient that [movement] should include 'something that moves', or at the most 'something coloured' or 'luminous' without any actual colour or light") (274), Merleau-Ponty never actually considers and reflects upon the phenomenon of movement itself except momentarily and in the most fleeting way in the midst of his searchings. Interestingly enough, in this instance, the object in motion is himself — the one instance, we might note, in which he considers the phenomenon of self-movement. "And yet I walk," he states, "I have the experience of movement in spite of the demands and dilemmas of clear thought, which means, in defiance of all reason, that I perceive movements without any identical moving object, without any external landmark and without any relativity" (269). An awareness of the qualitative structures of movement is latent in just such natural everyday experiences, but only when those experiences are examined outside the natural attitude toward movement, which, as is evident, precludes such an awareness. Moreover even when Merleau-Ponty declares that "If we want to take the phenomenon of movement seriously, we shall need to conceive a world which is not made up only of things, but which has in it also pure transitions," he does not pursue the nature of "pure transitions" but connects them immediately and simply to the style of an object's "passing": "The something in transit which we have recognized as necessary to the constitution of a change is to be defined only in terms of the particular manner of its 'passing'" (275). Thus a bird in flight across his garden is "merely a greyish power of flight" (275). When he finally ties movement by way of a mobile entity to his thematic of the phenomenal body, it is notable that he uses the notion of time to do so. But he does not flesh out any connection between time and movement; he merely avows their dual inherence in the "thickness" of "[t]he lived present" (275). Movement thus turns out to be by declaration rather than by demonstration what it was intended to be from the beginning: something tied to the phenomenal body. Thus Merleau-Ponty writes that "The relation between the moving object and its background passes through our body" (278); "If we can ever speak of movement without an object in motion, it is pre-eminently in the case of our own body. The movement of my eye towards the thing upon which it is about to focus is not the displacement of an object in relation to another object, but progress towards reality" (279); and so on. But a path leading outside the natural attitude view of movement cannot be carved with words. Neither, of course, can a path to the qualitative character of movement. Put in methodological perspective, one can, as with Gibson, readily and with good reason claim that what is missing is the procedure of bracketing. Without bracketing, Merleau-Ponty misses the phenomenon of movement itself. Indeed, from a methodological perspective one can readily and with good reason claim that a phenomenologist investigating movement is remiss if he/she does not consult his/her own experience of movement. It is through such consultation that Merleau-Ponty would have been led to discover precisely those qualitative structures of movement that inform a notion of style, as in the style marking the "passing" of a bird. Moreover he would have been led to discover the cardinal structures of kinesthetic consciousness. In this respect, it is not sufficient to speak of a "motor intentionality" as Merleau-Ponty does. In order for there to be a bona fide motor intentionality in the sense Merleau-Ponty describes, there must be a resonant tactile-kinesthetic body. In effect, to recognize the quintessential significance of kinesthesia, it is necessary to turn to the actual experience of self-movement and to give a phenomenological account of that experience.

More specific justification of this claim is required, for Merleau-Ponty's notion of a motor intentionality would seem already to include an awareness of the quintessential significance of kinesthesia. But in fact Merleau-Ponty devalues kinesthesia in his exposition of a motor intentionality. He states forthrightly, for example, that the body, "[a]s a mass of tactile, labyrinthine and kinaesthetic data," gives us no special spatial orientation whatsoever. Verticality is simply one "spatial level" among all other possible ones. Kinesthesia is thus not privileged in any way: as a sensory "function" or "content," it gives us no definitive ups, downs, tilts, horizontals, or whatever. In a word, it offers us nothing in the way of kinetic meanings: "Our bodily experience of movement," Merleau-Ponty says, "is not a particular case of knowledge" (140). Its only office is to "[provide] us with a way of access to the world and the object," and in this sense is no more than a purely practical kind of knowing (140). Though Merleau-Ponty states that this "praktognosia" "has to be recognized as original and perhaps as primary" (140), and though he goes on to quote neuropsychologist A.A. Grünbaum to the effect that "Already motility, in its pure state, possesses the basic power of giving a meaning," and that "Motility is the primary sphere in which initially the meaning of all significances is engendered in the domain of represented space" (142), he neither stops to reflect upon the conjunction of meaning and our bodily experience of movement nor to account for the foundational significance of the latter. In effect, kinesthetic consciousness is, save for practical purposes, a still-born consciousness, and moreover one that, while acknowledged "as original and perhaps as primary," is nowhere seriously thought of as ever having been vitally present. Clearly, the ready-made mesh of body and world that is always already there, as Merleau-Ponty describes it, and that marks an impassable barrier to knowledge of how things come to have the meaning and value they do, makes movement merely a bridge between body and world, merely "a way of access" by which we reach "the world and the object."

This practical instrumentalization of movement obviously overlooks the apprenticeship we all serve in becoming the bodies we are. When Merleau-Ponty writes that "My body is wherever there is something to be done" (250), he is describing a consummately *adult* body that has passed through its apprenticeship, and, having passed, no longer finds it necessary to look back upon its beginnings or wonder how it all came about, that is, for example, how its fluidity of movement was earned, how its dexterity was attained, how its agility was achieved, or, in a broader and deeper sense, how we first came to discover both ourselves and the world through movement. The past is opaque because it is made opaque, and not because there is no method by which to recover those beginnings in which we learned to move ourselves. In this respect, it is of interest to note that when he introduces his notion of a motor intentionality, Merleau-Ponty does so by linking it with an "I can," i.e. ostensibly with Husserl's notion of an *organ*-ic body, a living body of affections and actions in which, as Husserl says, "I hold sway quite immediately, kinesthetically" (Husserl 1970a: 107). But in fact Merleau-Ponty's "I can" has a decisively different point of reference and meaning. It is already anchored to a world of objects, and its meaning is specified in terms of that ready-made mesh of body and world. Thus, when he writes that "Consciousness is being towards the thing through the intermediary of the body," or more elaborately, that "A movement is learned when the body has understood it, that is, when it has incorporated it into its 'world', and to move one's body is to aim at things through it; it is to allow oneself to respond to their call, which is made upon it independently of any representation" (1962: 138–39), he is affirming a basic bodily unity with the world, a unity achieved not by way of a constituting consciousness, that is, not by way of a building up of knowledge through experience, but by an already intact and functioning "motor intentionality" — a body that "projects" itself into the world.[5] What is lost in the translation of the "I can," so to speak, is the "I move" and the "I do," and the kinestheses that are both their foundation and their unity.[6] In other words, when Merleau-Ponty appropriates the "I can" and translates it into a motor intentionality, he does so without reference either to Husserl's fundamental "kinestheses" or to kinesthesia. In consequence, a motor intentionality "inhabits" our bodies (1962: 139–40), but its dimensions are neither kinetically nor kinesthetically fleshed out. We are given no clue, for example, not only as to the process whereby a body learns a movement and comes to incorporate it into its 'world'; we are given no clue as to how a body *learns to move itself* to begin with. For there to be a motor intentionality, the tactile-kinesthetic body must in fact be constituted. Indeed, we all progressively learn our tactile-kinesthetic bodies on the basis of movement that is simply there, that is, on the basis of that original kinetic liveliness or primal animation with which we come into the world. Moreover we forge our kinetic union with the world on the ground of our progressive kinetic-kinesthetic apprenticeship. It is through having lived and lived vitally in dynamic experiences of movement, through a rich and complex kinesthetic-kinetic past, that we in fact understand Merleau-Ponty's adult notion of a motor intentionality. We grasp what he is pointing to because we have all learned our bodies and because we have all forged a kinetic bond with the world. We can thus agree with Merleau-Ponty that we dwell in our bodies and toward a world. Our bodies are where our kinetic aliveness is that carries us through the day. But that we are at all, and that we are at all disposed in the way we are, is rooted foundationally in our being movement-born; our being-in-the-world is rooted in an originary kinetic liveliness that is there still, residually, at the core of our adult being. Without the procedure of bracketing, the phenomenon of primal animation, of our apprenticeship in learning to move ourselves, and of our kinetic bond with the world, all remain captive of the natural attitude. In consequence, the originary and dynamic structure of movement never comes to light. It is ironic that the quintessential union of body and world that pulses its way poetically through Merleau-Ponty's philosophy is in the end unanimated because animation has been methodologically blocked from view.

Investigations of movement in the natural attitude are prey to beliefs and attitudes that, at bottom, perpetuate misunderstandings of movement, that tie it to objects in motion, to pointillist notions, to a change of position, to information, to instrumentalist conceptions, and so on. What the phenomenological procedure of bracketing allows is precisely a suspension of these encumbered and encumbering understandings of movement. The shift in attitude from the natural to the phenomenological is particularly crucial to an understanding of movement as a *natal* phenomenon. A newborn is not changing position or gathering information: it is animated. It may be making a fist, thus changing the position of its fingers; it may be kicking, thus changing the position of its leg; or it may be crying, stretching, sucking, or doing any number of other things and thereby be said to be changing the position of this or that body part, and certainly to be aware of doing so, but "changing position" or "gathering information" does not properly describe the basic phenomenon of animation. Moreover although each of the above movement examples relies on what we easily and quickly label as a behavior, each is in fact a kinetic episode that we, as adults, partition off from the global phenomenon of animation; each is a kinetic happening occurring along the continuum of a primal kinetic liveliness. Gibson underscores the ongoingness of perception; so should we underscore the ongoingness of a primal kinetic liveliness and a foundational kinesthetic perceptual consciousness. The foundation of perception in fact lies in just such a liveliness. Primal animation is the bedrock of learning to move oneself, and learning to move oneself is the foundation of perceiving the world. To appreciate these relationships requires not *just* phenomenological analyses; it requires the light of empirical studies, and thus what may rightly be called a constructive phenomenology of infancy. In this constructive endeavor, we draw upon our own adult experiences of newborn infants, upon our experiences of self-movement — including what Landgrebe describes as "[our] most elementary form of spontaneity" — and upon scientific studies that illuminate the significance of self-movement in infancy. In so doing, we proceed phenomenologically, that is, by bracketing. It will be helpful to begin with to clarify what this procedure means methodologically with respect to scientific studies of infancy. In particular, we need to show how scientific findings may be used as a point of departure for phenomenological studies, and how, in utilizing such findings, we are in fact following close upon the first methodology Merleau-Ponty used in his study of perception. While we might well proceed on the basis of the precedent Merleau-Ponty set in using scientific findings, a more rigorous explanation is called for, not only to show the adequacy of such a procedure but to make the methodology explicitly available to others. In what follows, it will be helpful at times to advert to "existential analysis" (1962: 136), as Merleau-Ponty specifically termed his method of using case studies of the abnormal in his pursuit of the phenomenology of perception.

5.   Methodological clarifications for a constructive phenomenology

In hewing to a phenomenological approach, we use our adult observations of newborns, (including, if we have them, observations of newborn nonhumans as well as humans), our experiences of self-movement, and scientific findings as a "transcendental clue"; that is, we use each of these sources as our point of departure for doing phenomenological work. In the course of detailing the method of phenomenology, Husserl speaks of an intentional object as a transcendental clue (1973: 50–53). By an intentional object, he does not mean only items such as coffee cups or houses, for example, but a friend we meet on the street, or the experience of joy, or a work of art, or a disagreeable person, and so on. Whatever presents itself to us straightforwardly in experience as meaningful can serve as the point of departure for a phenomenological analysis. What needs clarification in the present context is the use of scientific findings as a transcendental clue. While Merleau-Ponty never speaks of a transcendental clue in conjunction with his use of clinical and experimental scientific material, the scientific literature he consults could indeed be utilized as a *transcendental* clue rather than as a springboard to "existential analysis." Husserl explicitly remarks in fact upon the possibility of utilizing scientific knowledge — in particular, "medical knowledge" — in the pursuit of phenomenology. In the process of considering how we come "to *understand someone's development*" (italics in original), he writes that we must take the person's relationships and their particular temperament into account, and also any vicissitudes that might affect their development such as falling and becoming crippled. He says that "We are not interested here in a real-causal analysis of these consequences. But medical knowledge can be of service toward an integration, in the correct way, of the psychic effects that are relevant for subjective development and consequently toward giving an account of them in the attempt to clarify subjective motivations and subjective development. *Here the physical is serving as an indication of what is to be integrated*" (1989:288; italics added). Certainly Husserl's specification of the use of scientific knowledge in the service of phenomenology may be construed straightaway as the methodological point of departure for Merleau-Ponty's seminal use of pathological material in forging his phenomenology of perception. Through such material, Merleau-Ponty attempts to illuminate normal "subjective motivations and subjective development"; that is, through an existential analysis of the behavior of a neurologically disabled person, he attempts to show by default the nature of our relationship to the world. The utilization of scientific findings in the context of a constructive phenomenology of animation situates us on a quite different terrain. The quest is to understand the normal directly rather than to deduce it from the abnormal. In large measure the quest is precisely "*to understand someone's development*," to understand how primal movement underlies the phenomenon of learning to move oneself, and in reverse terms, how learning to move oneself emerges on the basis of movement that is already there. In this endeavor, the physical will indeed serve as an indication of what is to be integrated. Scientific descriptions of observed infant behavior, of observed infant affects, and so on, together with scientific descriptive accounts of infant experience, will serve as transcendental clues as to what kinetically transpires in infancy such that an "I move" emerges. The descriptions will thus help us to flesh out a constructive phenomenology of animation.

There is a feature of this enterprise that some may well find troublesome and that should be singled out in the context of methodological clarifications, namely, the claim that "the background," as it is consistently referred to in contemporary discourse, not only is not a forever obscure and impenetrable reservoir of capacities or "know-how," but is for all normal humans ultimately and always a basically kinetic background. Though we cannot remember doing so, we all lived through our infancy. Primal animation *is* the background; learning to move ourselves *is etched* on this background. Learning to move ourselves includes not just learning to reach, learning to walk, and learning to pull a toy, for example, but learning to articulate with our tongue and mouths, and with our fingers with respect to their dexterous possibilities. Philosopher John Searle defines background — which he in fact capitalizes and uses "as a technical term" — as "the capacities, abilities, and general know-how that enable our mental states to function." He states categorically that "Background capacities ... are not themselves intentional" (Searle 1992: 175). In other words, we have never been explicitly aware of Background capacities as meanings or values discovered in the everyday world. But how do we know that Background capacities were *never* intentional? In particular, how do we know that the Background is not tied to primal animation and to learning to move oneself? In his concluding remarks where he specifies the Background's "laws of operation," Searle gives as the second law that *Intentionality occurs in a coordinated flow of action and perception, and the Background is the condition of possibility of the forms taken by the flow*" (195; italics in original). This law adumbrates the very notion of primal animation and our first priority of learning to move ourselves. Primal animation and our progressive mastery of self-movement are the condition of possibility of the forms taken by the flow of action and perception in everyday adult life. It is indeed of interest that Searle's "laws of operation" consistently specify the Background as a reservoir of *abilities*, abilities that, to use his examples, range from knowing what to do with one's legs and arms in downhill skiing to knowing that one must match singular nouns with singular verbs in speaking. We may readily ask whether these Background abilities are irrecoverable or whether they are not in essence kinetic abilities, abilities that resonate in distinctive tactile-kinesthetic ways any time we care to notice them. As Searle himself says with reference to matching noun with verb, "I do not have the intention to match singular nouns with singular verbs or plural nouns with plural verbs — I just talk" (195). A child learning to speak might very well say the same, but with this difference: for the child, to say "I just talk" is to say that "my articulatory gestures proceed in just this fashion," or in simpler terms, "I just move my lips and tongue like this." Matching noun with verb follows from just such movement. Consider more pointedly the specific example of an infant learning to reach. Thelen and Smith write that

> First is the question of the infant's *intrinsic dynamics*. In the dynamic systems view, infants discover reaching from an ongoing background of other nonreaching postures and movements. In other words, *before* reaching begins, the system has a landscape with preferred attractor valleys that may be more or less deep, and that reflect both the infant's history and his or her potential for acquiring new

forms. This landscape constitutes the infant's *intrinsic dynamics*. Describing the intrinsic dynamics at each point in developmental time requires studying the trajectories of behavior in real time and how they stay the same and how they change (Thelen & Smith 1994: 250).

When we recognize not only primal animation, but a resonant tactile-kinesthetic body, there is no doubt but that an infant experiences itself in its nonreaching movements and experiences itself in its discovery of reaching proper. The background is experientially present; and it is kinetic through and through.

Like Landgrebe and Heidegger, Searle says that "A good way to observe the Background is in cases of breakdown" (1992: 184), and he goes on to give a concrete instance of someone's actually taking a certain state of affairs for granted, i.e. that "the earth does not move." As Searle relates it, the person (a visiting philosophy professor at Berkeley), following an earthquake, claimed "he had not, prior to that moment, had a belief or a conviction or a hypothesis that the earth does not move" (185). In other words, the person caught himself in the act of having a belief of which he said he was never previously aware in all his life. When we think of such a claim, it is difficult to countenance. Are we so transparent to ourselves as adults that we know with conclusive certainty that we have never entertained a particular thought at any time *in our entire lives*? It is difficult enough to believe that a person who knows enough to speak about "the earth" never learned anything of earthquakes in grade school, much less nothing of the rotation of the earth or its revolution about the sun; in other words, that the person never learned that the earth moves and in a variety of ways. Given the utter self-transparency upon which the claim is based, one would be led to think that the whole of one's past is recoverable, in particular, one's originary kinetic liveliness and the myriad experiences comprising one's kinetic apprenticeship. From this perspective, the belief that we know of the Background only when something goes wrong is an interesting but biased way of appreciating the Background. The belief effectively hides from us our own natality. A clear and unprejudiced way of appreciating the Background is through the phenomenological procedure of bracketing and the development of a constructive phenomenology. Indeed, how can one say anything about the background — what it is, was, or might have been — without first doing a constructive phenomenology? Instead of assuming we can judge conclusively about the whole of our lives as to what we have entertained and what we have not entertained, and instead of taking an authoritative adultist stance, we suspend judgment and turn to our beginnings to see what is there. The task in this sense is akin to answering the question, "What is it like to be a newborn infant?" Sufficient similarity, the criterion proposed by philosopher Thomas Nagel (1979) for knowing "what it is like to be an X" (a criterion analyzed and elaborated in detail in Sheets-Johnstone 1990, Chapter 14), is anchored, and anchored fundamentally, in the tactile-kinesthetic body and kinesthetic consciousness.

Similar remarks may be made of Hubert Dreyfus's and Stuart Dreyfus's notion of "the background" and of their pointed critique of Husserl and his putative ideas about "the background." Though Dreyfus and Dreyfus categorically affirm otherwise, it is not altogether clear that Husserl's "background" was the principle they claim it to be. They state that

> Husserl claimed that the world, the background of significance, ... was a very complex system of facts correlated with a complex system of beliefs which, since they have truth conditions, he called validities. One could, in principle, he held, suspend one's dwelling in the world [i.e. perform the phenomenological epoché] and achieve a detached description of the human belief system. One could thus complete the task that had been implicit in philosophy since Socrates: one could make explicit the beliefs and principles *underlying all intelligent behavior*
> (Dreyfus & Dreyfus 1990: 322; italics added).

In his book, *Ideas II*, which he began in 1912 and last edited in 1928 (see "Translators' Introduction" in Husserl 1989: xi–xiii), Husserl states,

> [C]oncerning the constitution in consciousness of the object prior to the turning of the attention and the taking of a specific position regarding it, we are referred back to the constitution in consciousness of previous objects, to previous acts of attention, and perhaps to previous position-takings [i.e. actual judgments, decisions, and so on]; we are referred back to the data of sensation, to the references back and forth which depend on them, etc. Ultimately we arrive at the 'obscure', 'hidden', representations and representational complexes. Insofar as attention plays a role for this constitution of transcendent unities and multiplicities, we have there implicitly an Ego that is accomplishing some kind of comportment. The ultimate, however, is a *background that is prior to all comportment* and is instead presupposed by all comportment (1989: 291; italics in original).

Husserl goes on to say with respect to this "*background that is prior to all comportment* that "In a certain sense there is, in the obscure depths, a root soil" (292). He does not suggest that the "obscure" or "hidden" is recoverable. He in fact speaks of the "root soil" as our "natural side", "the underlying basis of subjectivity" (292). Given its ties to the natural, it is far more reasonable to connect the background with his notion of "primal sensibility" than to interpret it as "the beliefs and principles underlying all intelligent behavior" that he claimed could be made explicit; that is, it is far more reasonable to connect the background with Husserl's notion of a sensibility that "*does not arise out of immanent grounds*, [but] ... is simply there, it emerges" (346). The background in this sense obviously connects closely with primal animation, but with an important difference: the latter does not emerge; it is "simply there." What *does* emerge is our kinetic apprenticeship, our developing capacity to move ourselves. Moreover the background in this sense is the original ground where perception, action, and cognition are intertwined in the form of incipient and developing intentionalities present in primal animation and in learning to move oneself. What is of moment from this perspective is in fact not whether Husserl actually did or did not believe that "the beliefs and principles underlying all intelligent behavior" — what amounts to "the [entire] human belief system" — can be recovered through phenomenological analysis.[7] What is of moment is the contemporary catch-all called "the background" that is identified with an unrecoverable subterranean ground that is visible only when something goes wrong. In fact, that background is readily open to investigation once we cease ignoring the ground of our common natality and formulate a phenomenological methodology proper to the task of illuminating it. What is of further moment is the direction in which we, as adults, proceed in this task. In the constructive phenomenological endeavor, we start not as we would in normal phenomenological fashion with a present-day adult world, working our way back in genetic fashion, methodically exposing how we come to perceive the world as we do, how we come to believe as we do, how we come to the cultural meanings we do, and so on. We start from the other end, from the world of our natality, and attempt to follow it in its forward movement, concentrating our efforts on understanding how that world comes to be built up. We work in a manner opposite to what Husserl describes as genetic phenomenology, but genetic phenomenology is nonetheless part of the constructive phenomenological endeavor. The question of whether the background is recoverable only accidentally, or whether, being all equally movement-born and having all had to learn to move ourselves, we have within our reach the foundational background for self-understandings, arises precisely in the context of this reverse phenomenology. It arises equally in face of a fundamentally human kinesthetic consciousness by which we all arrive at full-blown intentionalities and conceptual awarenesses of time, space, and force, or in other words, *of the qualitative spatio-temporal flow of life and of our own aliveness.* Surely if we are at a loss to understand our infancy, then we are at a loss to understand the very wellspring of our humanness. Though we adults are self-proclaimed experts, perhaps we are less knowledgeable than we think. Perhaps a skewed conception of infancy and of the phenomenon of self-movement has skewed our conception and rendition of ourselves.

6.   A constructive phenomenology of animation

For any creature that must learn to move itself, that comes into the world unprepared to move immediately on its own in a thoroughly independent fashion in the way that, say, a colt or a lizard or a duckling can immediately or shortly after birth or hatching navigate on its own, there is simply movement, movement that happens to it and is in this sense already there. When this movement is reduced to anatomical specification, it is described in strictly mechanical terms. For a human infant, it is described in terms of knee extension, elbow flexion, head rotation, and so on, together with a listing of correlative muscle engagements. Sacrificing anatomical precision to the colloquial, the movement might be described as toes wiggling, arms flailing, shoulders quivering, mouth twitching, and so on. Whether precise or colloquial, however, anatomical specification cannot possibly do justice to primal animation, not only because a complete anatomical record of all newborn movement would be overwhelmingly tedious if not impossible to compile even with present-day video technologies, but because primal animation would be nowhere evident in such a record. One cannot dissect primal animation anatomically and kinesiologically — or causally — any more than one can itemize it in terms of abilities or categorize it in terms of behaviors. It is equivalent to none of these determinations. Primal animation is the foundational liveliness coincident with being movement-born. By its very nature it entails a tactile-kinesthetic body, a felt body, and thus entails a kinesthetic consciousness. Incipient intentionalities play out along the lines of this body precisely through movement that is already there, through primal animation. They take form on the basis of a foundational kinetic liveliness. It is through these incipient intentionalities of primal animation that creatures who must learn to move themselves, learn to move themselves. By the very nature of their task, they make sense of their own bodies first and foremost. Primal sensibility is thus first and foremost a primal kinesthetic sensibility arising on the ground of primal animation. In the beginning is movement. Landgrebe's "deepest-lying transcendental function," Merleau-Ponty's "phenomenal body," Heidegger's "fore-structures of Dasein," Husserl's "I move" — all have their genesis in primal animation, a kinetic field of incipient intentionalities. *Sheer movement* is thus of moment. *Sheer movement* is the ground on which intentionalities initially develop. They develop coincident with motivations which, equally, emerge on the basis of *sheer movement*. Primal animation is a field of kinetic play from which our initial interests, tendencies, habits, and dispositions arise; our initial turnings toward the world emerge from the background of sheer movement. Whatever the initial motivations and incipient intentionalities might be, they develop by way of a tactile-kinesthetic body. That body is itself the object of motivations and intentionalities — in the form of head turnings, stretchings, and so on. In such ways, the tactile-kinesthetic body is itself constituted: we put ourselves together; we learn our bodies. We do so through movement. From the very beginning, we sense ourselves moving, we feel ourselves kinetically. We are a kinetic-tactile-kinesthetic being; we are a moving-in-the-world being, a *Da-bewegung*. On the basis of movement, we develop an inchoate sense of ourselves as *animate forms*. Clearly, in the beginning, there is movement in the process of forming an "I" that moves, movement in the process of solidifying agency, motivations, intentionalities, regularities, all by way of a tactile-kinesthetic body and kinesthetic consciousness. Our kinetic apprenticeship thus defines an epistemological project, a project grounded in the fact that we do not come ready made kinetically into the world but must learn to move ourselves. Through our kinesthetic consciousness we constitute ourselves as epistemological subjects. We put ourselves together and in the process launch ourselves kinetically into the world. Our tactile-kinesthetic bodies are an epistemological gateway, our opening way of making sense of ourselves and of the world through movement.

Psychological and psychiatric findings readily conjoin with the above broadly sketched constructive phenomenology. They furthermore provide insights on the basis of which further analyses may be made. Two major sources are particularly noteworthy: the clinical and experimental research findings of infant psychiatrist and developmental psychologist Daniel Stern together with the experimental research of infant psychologist Andrew Meltzoff, and the experimental and theoretical research findings of developmental psychologists such as Esther Thelen, Alan Fogel, Linda Smith, and George Butterworth, who approach the study of infancy from a dynamic systems perspective. We will consider each source in turn.

On the basis of his clinical work and developmental research, Stern (1985) describes the period of infancy between birth and two months as a period in which an emergent sense of self "comes into being."[8] He emphasizes the processual nature of this emergent sense of self, a process in which invariants that are the bedrock of integration are recognized and experience in turn becomes organized. He is equally emphatic about an infant's experiencing itself from the start. In answer to the question, "can infants also experience non-organization?" he answers a definitive "No!" Elaborating on the point with respect to the classical notion of infants' experiencing themselves as totally undifferentiated, fused with their mothers and all else in their environment, he remarks that "The traditional notions of clinical theorists have taken the observer's knowledge of infants — that is, relative undifferentiation compared with the differentiated view of older children — reified it, and given it back, or attributed it, to infants as their own dominant subjective sense of things" (1985:46). Traditional wisdom has in this way overlooked the discreteness of infant experiences, that is, the distinctive vividness and clarity of these experiences, and their initial unrelatedness and progressive integration. Specifying the basis of an infant's emergent sense of self in this differentiated and experiential way, Stern states that "In order for the infant to have any formed sense of self, there must ultimately be some organization that is sensed as a reference point. *The first such organization concerns the body*: its coherence, its actions, its inner feeling states, and the memory of all these" (46; italics added). Stern goes on to discuss each of these dimensions under the headings of self-coherence, self-agency, self-affectivity, and self-history, showing in each case how "islands of consistency" (45; phrase borrowed from Escalona 1953) are built up, that is, how an infant comes to identify and to integrate invariants in its experiences of itself. Each dimension is a fundamental facet of "the core self" (46–123). Though implicit, proprioception figures consistently and centrally in Stern's account of each dimension. In one sense, his bodily "reference point" seems so obvious it hardly warrants discussion. With respect to putting things together — organizing experience — what could be more basic than one's tactile-kinesthetic body, most particularly, more basic than making sense of one's body and learning to move oneself? Stern's description of the "coming-to-be" of this bodily organization — what he identifies as the *processes* at the foundation of an infant's putting things together as distinct from their *products* (46–47), but what, as he describes them, might be more finely designated as the fundamental perceptual proclivities and sensitivities of infants — is in fact edifying. In a different way, the description of each process validates the primacy of movement and the tactile-kinesthetic body. In a word, "amodal perception," "physiognomic perception," and "vitality affects" are "processes" that not only allow an infant to relate one experience to another but that resonate in kinetic ways in "subjective experience" (47–61).

Infants readily perceive relationships across sensory modalities. Stern's initial citation in his discussion of amodal perception acknowledges the work of psychologists Andrew Meltzoff and Richard Borton, whose now classic experiment on blindfolded three-week old infants who were given either round- or knobby-nippled pacifiers and who, after the blindfold was removed, recognized visually the particular type of pacifier they had had in their mouths, is well known. Stern speaks of the amodal perceptual capacities of infants as an ability to transfer across sensory modalities. He states with respect to this "innate general capacity" that "We do not know how they accomplish this task" (1985:51). With respect to the infants in Meltzoff and Borton's experiment in particular, he says simply that "They immediately 'knew' that the one they now saw was the one they had just felt" (48). Now one might respond, especially from an adultist perspective, and especially if one mistakes Stern's use of scare quotes around the potent term *knew*,[9] that an infant's amodal perception is unconscious, that the brain of an infant is wired in such a way that amodal perception is programmed, that "deep structures" are responsible, and so on — in short, that the infant does not really know; it just 'knows'. Since there is no reasoning process connected with the ability, one cannot account for the infant's 'knowledge' in any other way than by relegating it to the unconscious, or to a software program, or to "deep structures." In contrast to these explanations, a Piagetian constructionist would describe the infant as putting two schemas together — the haptic and the visual — step by step. Both kinds of explanation, however, fail to take the body into account. If the body is indeed the preeminent reference point, then its primary mode of being, that is, its foundational tactile-kinesthetic liveliness, may with good reason be regarded the touchstone for amodal perception. If what is visually perceived is referred to this centrally and consistently experienced body, then experiments showing infants capable of amodal perception may readily draw on an infant's experiences of its own body, experiences that in fact go back to its *prenatal life*, to explain how an infant can match not only what it sees with what it has previously felt tactilely and kinesthetically, but can match what it sees with what it hears. When infants properly match a moving mouth that they see with a sound that they hear and in fact notice when the latter does not match the former, and when they sanction what they see over what they hear (Kuhl & Meltzoff 1982), then their predilection for *articulatory gestures* is readily apparent. In short, the "innate general capacity" of which Stern speaks is traceable to a resonant tactile-kinesthetic body, and, by extension, to an essentially kinetic bond with the world. This is essentially what Meltzoff and colleagues ultimately affirm in their ongoing experimental investigations (see, for example, Meltzoff 1993; Meltzoff & Moore 1994, 1995a, 1995b). The foundational tactile-kinesthetic attunement of infants is the reference point *sine qua non* for organizing not only their experiences of themselves but their experiences of the world. Their responsivity to articulatory gestures is testimonial to this bond. We will return to this thematic presently. For the moment, it suffices to recall that in the general introduction to this chapter it was noted how attuned we are as adults to the movements of others. Our intercorporeal attunement clearly has its roots in a common body of knowledge spawned in the course of a common infancy. When Stern writes with respect to an infant's ability to find cross-modal matches that "A typology of such events at the experiential level rather than at a conceptual [i.e. abstract] level is greatly needed," we might turn precisely to a constructive phenomenology for an account of how an inchoate sense of the kinetic form of things informs our lives from the beginning.

In his brief account of physiognomic perception, Stern draws on the writings of Heinz Werner, who theorized that physiognomic perception arises as a result of the varying emotional expressions of the human face. Physiognomic perception is thus, according to Werner, geared toward affective qualities such as happy, fearsome, and sad, rather than qualities such as shape, size, and intensity. A sound, for example, may be heard as angry rather than loud, just as a line may be seen as bouncy rather than u-shaped. Affective qualities are similarly amodal in that they are not bound to any particular modality of perception. Though Stern does not mention the accordance, it is of interest to note that affective qualities are invariably tied to movement. A facial expression is not a static facial posturing of one kind or another but a dynamic configuration of a part of one's body; it is arrived at through movement and it is carried forward expressively in movement. Moreover although often construed as contained in the face, any facial expression perfuses the whole body. Sadness, for example, is not merely a drooping look. Sadness is felt in the carriage of one's body, in its sensed weight, in the flow of its gestures, and so on. Facial expressions are an affective condensation of a whole-body dynamic.

What Stern calls vitality affects are the *purely* dynamic aspects of a phenomenon: a *burst* of light, of laughter, or of energy, for example; an *attenuating* sound, pain, or image; a *fleeting* figure, aroma, or touch. Vitality affects substantively inform the experiences of adults as well as infants. As pointed out in Chapter Three, Stern creates this category of experience because "many qualities of feeling that occur do not fit into our existing lexicon or taxonomy of affects." He affirms straightaway that "These qualities of experience are most certainly sensible to infants and of great daily, even momentary, importance"; he states that they are "elicited by changes in motivational states, appetites, and tensions" (Stern 1985:54). Obviously, there is a profound correspondence between vitality affects and the tactile-kinesthetic body. Any time one moves, a vitality affect is present; a certain qualitative dynamic is evident. In describing these affects in infant life and speaking of their experiential character, Stern writes that each vitality affect has a certain "activation tone" or intensity and a certain "hedonic tone" or pleasurableness or displeasurableness about it. He speaks of the former tone as an "activation contour"; that is, in light of its intensity, the phenomenon has a certain dynamic form. That dynamic form can, as indicated, appear across a range of experiences, as in a *burst* of light, of laughter, or of energy. Vitality affects are thus not necessarily tied to what he terms categorical affects, i.e. to distinct affective themes such as sad, fearsome, joyful, and so on. As Stern points out, "a 'rush' of anger or of joy, a perceived flooding of light, an accelerating sequence of thoughts, an unmeasurable wave of feeling evoked by music, and a shot of narcotics can all feel like 'rushes'" (55).

In sum, the ongoing "processes" by which an infant relates one experience to another and that, Stern says, resonate in "subjective experience," defining the structure within which a sense of self "comes into being," are processes definitively tied to tactile-kinesthetic life. While Stern describes these processes in terms of events ongoing in the world of the infant rather than events ongoing in the infant itself, the processes clearly take their bearings from primal animation and the tactile-kinesthetic body. We can appreciate this essentially kinetic relationship of body and world by delving more deeply in a phenomenological sense and more broadly in an empirical one.

The centrality of movement in infant life — if mentioned at all — is typically as quickly passed over as it is acknowledged. When psychiatrist René Spitz poses the question of "how we manage to distinguish the living from the inanimate," and goes on to discuss "how this distinction is made by the infant" (Spitz 1983:148), he begins his account with "a brief review of our knowledge regarding the preliminary stages of visual differentiation between animate and inanimate during the first year of life," stating that "two visual stimuli … reliably provoke the infant's attention and his response to the living." The first such stimulus, he says, is "the percept of the human face and eyes"; the second such stimulus, he says, "is the perception of movement of any kind" (149). While he goes on to speak of *dialogue* — "action and response" dialogue, not verbal dialogue (152) — as the pivotal factor in an infant's distinguishing the animate from the inanimate, he says no more of "the perception of movement of any kind." The fundamental allure of movement is taken simply as a given. It is the unexamined basis for what is patently the more interesting psychiatric phenomenon of dialogue. This attitude toward movement *is one of a number of natural attitudes toward movement.* In this instance, the attitude specifies movement simply as the opposite of stillness. Movement is, in other words, not a phenomenon that warrants examination in its own right.

It is not something that in fact has or could have a *past*, that is, a history in the sense of having had much earlier a character different from the present one, indeed, of having had a certain *originary* character in infancy quite different from "the reverse of stillness." On the contrary, the natural attitude toward movement specifies meanings and values that have the stature of factual truths, factual truths that are incontrovertible, that need no examination but are apparent from the beginning. In actual truth, natural attitude meanings and values fail to accord with the meanings and values of movement in the life of an infant. Regarded in the natural attitude, *movement is bereft of its qualitative structures and resonance*. In effect, its *cardinal features* are categorically absent.

Now if we suspend this natural attitude toward movement and ask why infants are drawn to movement, looking for an answer not in terms of adaptation or survival value, and not in terms of social interactions or cultural groomings, but look to infants themselves, then we are readily led to their originary kinetic liveliness and to the resonance of their own tactile-kinesthetic bodies. If their preeminent reference point for making sense of the world is this very body, then movement will be their match point. In other words, the meanings and values they find in the world will coincide with the preeminently kinetic meanings and values they experience first and foremost corporeally. Movement is indeed their mother tongue. The world may be unfamiliar, but there is a familiar point of origin, that is, a familiar way by which one goes about making sense of it in the beginning.[10]

It is significant that empirical psychological research and not just clinical psychiatric work such as that of Stern accords with this phenomenological account. Psychologist T.G.R. Bower carried out multiple experiments to determine how an infant puts the world of objects together, in particular, how "an infant begin[s] to associate qualities such as solidity with objects that he sees" (1971: 30). The experiments focused on both the featural differences of objects — their size, shape, and color — and on their movement differences — that is, whether they were moving, whether they stopped, whether they disappeared, whether they reappeared. In his discussion of his experimental research, Bower states that "These results show that younger infants [6 weeks to 22 weeks] are not affected by feature differences. For them movement is predominant. They respond to a change in motion but not to a change in size, shape or color" (37). His subsequent comment is of considerable moment in the present context. He remarks that the infants "ignore features to such an extent that I would suggest they respond *not to moving objects but to movements*" (37; italics added). Bower's brief remark clearly dovetails with Spitz's brief acknowledgment of the preeminence of movement. Both the remark and the acknowledgment affirm the priority of movement in infant life: what a young infant sees is seen kinetically, not objectively. The movement that it sees resonates dynamically with its own tactile-kinesthetic body. Kinetic events in the world *match* its own primal animation and burgeoning kinesthetic consciousness. Indeed, its responsivity to movement over objects *makes sense*: it makes sense given a preeminently tactile-kinesthetic body, and it makes sense literally in the way of coming to know the world. In short, an infant's primary path to knowledge is through movement. Like Spitz, Bower does not recognize this fundamental bond with the world because he too does not go on to examine the phenomenon of movement, even though he recognizes that phenomenon as fundamental. Spitz and Bower are not of course alone in their neglect. Piaget, for example, makes a striking remark concerning movement in very early infancy, and just as similarly ignores his own observation. He writes of a two-day old infant that opening and closing the mouth is an increasingly frequent behavior in the absence of any object, but says that he will not go on to consider the behavior further: "During the second day also Laurent again begins to make sucking-like movements between meals while thus repeating the impulsive movements of the first day: His lips open and close as if to receive a real nippleful, but without having any object. This behavior subsequently became more frequent and we shall not take it up again" (Piaget 1952: 25–26). While certainly of moment in itself in exemplifying the standard disregard of movement, Piaget's decision to move on, so to speak, is actually of less moment than his near recognition of *sheer movement*. Attentiveness to sheer movement, an attentiveness that, given the strength and unquestioned status of the natural attitude, virtually demands a suspension of judgment and an institution of the phenomenological *epoché* in order to come to the fore, discloses not a frequent infant *behavior* but the phenomenon of primal animation, the originary kinetic liveliness that is the essence of our natality and the foundation of our original attunement to the world and preference for movement over objects. Our fundamental bond with the world is clearly not a *je ne sais quoi* in need of radical reflection nor is it a non- or near in-articulable opacity impossible to elucidate. It is there before us in the phenomenon of infant life when we bracket our adultist perspective and humble ourselves to acknowledge our true beginnings, which lie not by way of language but by way of movement. What Stern writes of the emergent organizational abilities of infants is apposite in this context. Speaking of their abilities to recognize invariants in both their experien-ces of themselves and their experiences of the world, he states that "The elements that make up these emergent organizations are simply different subjective units from those of adults who, most of the time, believe that they subjectively experience units such as thoughts, perceptions, actions, and so on, because they must translate experience into these terms in order to encode it verbally" (Stern 1985: 67). Clearly, experience is not language, and experience that is there before language must be honored for what it is: the foundation of our knowledge. Not only this, but that foundation is and remains unsurpassed: "The global subjective world of emerging organization," Stern writes, "is and remains the fundamental domain of human subjectivity" (67). Stern accords infant experience a primary and *enduring* status not from a theoretical need, but because his clinical and experimental findings lead him to do so. Perhaps precisely because he is an *infant* psychologist and psychiatrist, he is less wedded to those natural attitude views that preclude a valuing of experience, most particularly, nonlinguistic experience. If we join his insights into the "global subjective world of emerging organization" with all its amodal fluencies and vitality affects to the insightful if passing remarks of Spitz and Bower concerning the foundational significance of movement in infant life, then there are sound empirical grounds for claiming that our fundamental and enduring bond with the world is a kinetic one.

The intricately layered and epistemologically probing investigations of psychologist Andrew Meltzoff offer a further perspective upon this fundamental and enduring kinetic bond. Meltzoff's sophisticated and diverse investigations center on the imitational abilities of infants, beginning with their ability to imitate the tongue protrusions, mouth-openings, and lip protrusions of an adult, and this as early as forty-two minutes after birth. Meltzoff describes the imitation in terms of matching the visual with the proprioceptive, and ascribes the ability to a "supramodal representational system" that, "metaphorically" translated, means that the visual and the motor systems "'speak the same language' right from birth" (Meltzoff 1990: 157; see also Meltzoff & Gallagher 1996: 216, in which an argument is advanced on behalf of an "[innate] system of motor functions" that involves "a set of tacit performances, preconscious, subpersonal processes that play a dramatic role in governing posture and movement," which system and set of tacit performances is designated "the body schema"). He also adverts to "an embryonic 'body scheme,'" that "is present as a 'psychological primitive' right from the earliest phases of infancy" and says that "[t]his nascent notion of self is a foundation from which self development proceeds, not an endpoint that is reached after months or years of interactions with the social environment" (Meltzoff 1990: 160). Now if we carry forward the kinetic thematic as elaborated on the basis of the previous scientific findings, we would explain the extraordinary ability of infants to imitate adult mouth gestures as a kinetic-kinesthetic *dynamic* matching. The 'psychological primitive' that is there from the start is not a "body scheme," whether an abstract image, or a neurological network that becomes established, or a representational schema, or any other kind of hypothetical entity. The 'psychological primitive' is primal animation and the tactile-kinesthetic body that resonates with the spatio-temporal energies of primal animation. "The nascent notion of self" is similarly grounded in primal animation and the tactile-kinesthetic body. Similarly too, what Meltzoff describes as a capacity to copy "pure body movement," that is, not movement with objects — e.g. copying an adult's movement of toys — but movement on the order of facial expressions, has its origin in a dynamically attuned body and an originary kinetic liveliness. The same is true for infants' copying the movement of adults with objects. All such imitation has an essentially kinetic origin. Moreover what Meltzoff distinguishes as structural equivalencies as opposed to merely temporal ones with respect to an infant's recognizing which of two adults is imitating *it*, i.e. *the infant's own movements*, has its origin in the same foundational phenomena. Structural equivalencies are *dynamic* equivalencies; what the infant sees is a replication of the dynamics of its own felt movement. Indeed, Meltzoff states at the beginning of the above-cited article that what he and his colleagues wish to know is whether an infant "can learn something about his or her own body and its possible actions simply by observing the behavior of another" (1990: 146–47). The learning possibilities in question are possibilities not of a "body scheme" or of a "supramodal representational system" but of a tactile-kinesthetic body dynamically attuned to the world. It is not too much to say that, endowed from the beginning with a kinetic reference point — a 'psychological primitive' on the order of primal animation and a resonant tactile-kinesthetic body — *thinking in movement* is an infant's original mode of thinking (see Sheets-Johnstone 1981 and Chapter 12, this text). The 'psychological primitive' that is there from the start is thus not to be construed as an *unperfected*, *undeveloped*, or *crude* stratum that later takes proper adult form. The 'primitive' is *foundational* in both an epistemological and metaphysical sense.

From this perspective, imitation is a dimension of learning to move oneself — precisely as Meltzoff himself suggests when he speaks of the possibility of an infant learning something about his or her body and its possible actions by observing the behavior of another. The extraordinary kinetic responsivity of infants to adult mouth gestures from forty-two minutes onward is, in particular, testimony to a robust and ready capacity to learn to move oneself. The fundamental bond linking infants to the world is indeed dramatically exemplified by their kinetic imitative powers. To approach an explanation of their imitative capacities by attempting to harmonize dissimilar sensory modalities — "the visual" and "the proprioceptive" — is to overlook what is for an infant a unity of experience in virtue of movement, that is, the kinetically unifying bond by which an infant is linked epistemologically to the world. We should note that this link cannot be explained by way of Gibson's "visual proprioception" any more than it can be explained by way of a "supramodal representational system" or a "body-scheme." Primal animation, a resonant tactile-kinesthetic body, and a preeminent attention to movement are the keys to understanding the prodigious power of infants to imitate adult gestures and movements.

Given these broader and deeper insights into the centrality of movement, we can clearly appreciate how self-movement is the epistemological gateway to a world of objects. Such things as hammers and spoons are not just there, ready-to-hand for an infant. We are not born with tools or other items of use in our hands. We come to grasp objects, *grasp them both literally and epistemologically*, through movement. It is topical in this context to point out that philosopher Ralph Ellis, while attempting to show that "imagination is the basic building block of all consciousness," actually adverts to a classic empirical study showing the necessity of self-movement to a knowledge of objects, a study in which kittens are transported in a movement-restricting gondola so that, although they can see a passing scene, they cannot move themselves in relation to it. As Ellis writes, "When deprived of the opportunity to manipulate and interact with the objects they were looking at, kittens ended up being functionally blind" (Ellis 1995: 2–3; see also the classic study by Held & Hein 1963; and Held 1965). When he earlier cites Piaget in support of his claim regarding the imagination, saying that "[e]ven the perceptual consciousness of an infant, according to Piaget, involves imagining what could be *done* with the object *if* the infant *were* to reach out, grasp it, throw it, beat on it, etc." (italics in original), and emphasizing the point that "identifying an object involves imagining how it could be manipulated," he takes for granted the very movement that he later acknowledges by way of the experiment with kittens, the very movement that makes *doing things with objects* possible, namely self-movement. Such movement is not ready-made but achieved: we learn to move ourselves. In sum, when we put together Stern's insights into vitality affects, Meltzoff and colleagues' insights into the proprioceptive and kinetic dynamics of imitation, and Spitz's and Bower's insight into a foundational sensitivity to movement, we see that animate meanings are embedded in experience from the start. They are embedded because they are integral to animate life.

Infant researchers who approach their investigations from a dynamic systems perspective come similarly close to appreciating the foundational role of self-movement in cognition. From a dynamic perspective, the action of an infant is a central and significant dimension of its progressive development. An infant is not simply "growing up," proceeding from behavioral stage one to behavioral stage two, and so on; it is actively involved in its own maturation. In presenting an overview of findings from various sources, Butterworth — whose own theoretical and experimental research has provided original and provocative insights into infancy — notes, for example, that infants determine shape from moving stimuli, that they have "coherent experiences of persons and matter in motion," that they are attuned to "dynamic transitions" and to "spatiotemporal information" (1993: 177–78, 179, 180). On the basis of the evidence he presents, one would be hard pressed not to think that an infant not only moves but responsively understands movement; that is, one would be inclined to say not only that the infant, on the basis of its own primal animation and resonant tactile-kinesthetic body, is movement-born, but that the world speaks to it first and foremost kinetically, dynamically, and that the infant responds in kind. This basic kinetic accord between infant and world is in fact palpably evident in dynamic research findings such as that showing infants adapting the speed of their reach to the speed of a moving object. Dynamic systems researchers speak of this ability in terms of dynamic eye-hand coordinations, that is, in terms of the fact that dynamic transitions are involved in sensory stimulation and that "sensory stimulation carries meaningful information" (Butterworth 1993: 180); they speak of it further in terms of the fact that "event perception is not modality-specific" (Butterworth 1993: 181). In other words, while being action-oriented in the sense of looking at infants in dynamic relation with their environment, and while insisting on the unity of sensory stimulation, they nonetheless pass over *the source* of the dynamic relation and *the source* of the unity. This is in good part because, as with Gibson, they miss kinesthesia; being tethered to a natural attitude view of movement, they miss the phenomenon of self-movement itself. In turn, they miss the preeminence of the tactile-kinesthetic body, an omission one might actually think odd since, from a neurological point of view, the first developing *perceptual system*, apparent soon after conception and dramatically apparent in the varied self-movement abilities of fetuses, is the somatosensory cortex. Previous quotations from the work of Thelen and Smith show an obvious beginning thrust toward the recognition of both primal animation and kinesthesia. When Thelen and Smith write of an *"infant's intrinsic dynamics,"* they are on the edge of realizing primal animation; when they write of the necessity of viewing movement itself as a perceptual system, they are on the edge of realizing the tactile-kinesthetic body. Before discussing their innovative work in greater detail, it will be helpful to consider a Gibsonian conceptual holdover that works against the concrete realization of the primacy of movement.

While clearly profiting from Gibson's direct realism point of view with respect to perception, dynamic systems theorists at the same time and as an outgrowth of Gibsonian theory emphasize *information* over meaning. Gibson states categorically that "The theory that meaning is attached to experience or imposed on it has been abandoned"; and that the only "sort of theory.. [that] will explain perception [is] [n]othing less than one based on the pickup of information" (J.J. Gibson 1979: 238). Information pickup is precisely what environmental affordances provide; information is out there in the world and perceptual systems are designed to pick it up. Thus, it is not surprising that dynamic system theory affirms that "sensory stimulation carries meaningful information in the dynamic transitions involved, whether the energy is radiantly transmitted through vision or mechanically transmitted through oral, tactual, or auditory systems" (Butterworth 1993: 180), and that "the interrelationships between the senses as sources of information about the real world" function as perceptual systems "without the benefit of *foreknowledge,*" that is, "without the need to postulate concepts held in advance of experience" (or, for that matter, without the need to postulate action plans or motor programs of any kind as the source of particular behaviors — a denial of cognitivist assumptions about a cerebral motor executive) (Butterworth 1993: 184). The informational tethering, a facet of the natural attitude toward perception, conceals the centrality of movement, making it simply an instrument of other perceptual systems that generate information. It is not that claims of dynamic systems theorists regarding sensory stimulation and the interrelationship among the senses are invalidated by their tethering to information. It is that they are improperly anchored. Moreover they need deepening and their relationship to phenomenological insights needs to be shown. For example, Butterworth's claim against traditional motor theorists who postulate motor programs, i.e. "prior representation of [an] action," is that there is no "prior representation of the action" but that "[t]he structure of an act is entailed by its own organization in relation to the ecology" (Butterworth 1993: 181). His claim may be grounded phenomenologically: the structure of an infant's act entails — and entails essentially and in an originary sense — primal animation and a tactile-kinesthetic body. It thereby entails acknowledgment of both experience *and* meaning. Teuber's words cited in the epigraph at the beginning of Chapter 2 are of particular significance in this context. Teuber said that "[W]e always start at the sensory end and try to come out at the motor side. I very much agree with the late von Holst when he suggests that we start at the other end and work our why (*sic*) back toward sensation…. It requires some different way of looking." Dynamic systems theorists have in large measure started at the other end because movement is the natural starting place of dynamic theorizing. Starting at the other end explains why their work has brought about a veritable shift in attention, from the hypothetical and static to the actual and dynamic, and provided innumerable insights in the process. But the different way of looking can be extended still further by breaking ties to the natural attitude. When we begin our investigations by suspending judgment, by instituting the phenomenological *epoché*, the familiar becomes strange. In effect, we examine the experience of movement anew, as if experiencing it or meeting it for the first time. In this way, we discover what is there in the phenomenon itself, the phenomenon of self-movement and the phenomenon of movement in the world. Moreover when we go on to freely vary the phenomenon, we discover kinetic invariants. Through this phenomenological methodology, we come to ground the fresh and innovative findings of dynamically-oriented developmental psychologists in the deeper truths of animate life.

The work of Thelen and Smith, and Thelen and Fogel, bears out the above estimation and methodological claim. A particularly significant motif in their writings is *emergence*, that is, the coming-to-be of something new or novel out of what is already present. The notion obviously accords with the notion of an "I move" arising on the ground of primal animation, or, recalling the descriptive account in Chapter Two of kinetic spontaneity, of how kinetic spontaneity arises from primal animation. More finely still, it accords with the earlier descriptive account of how movement forms the I that moves before the I that moves forms movement. An analysis of the motif will exemplify its richness in dynamic systems theory and at the same time its grounding through a phenomenological methodology.

Of "spontaneous infant kicking," Thelen and Smith write that "Kicking is primarily *a manifestation of seemingly nonspecific behavioral arousal*" (1994: 78; italics added); in other words, it is a manifestation of sheer aliveness. They describe the positions in which infants kick — "when lying on their backs and when held upright, and later when prone or even when sitting in a chair" — the situations in which they kick — "infants kick when happy and excited, but also when fussy or uncomfortable" — and the purposes for which they kick — "infants appear to 'convert' kicking movements into instrumental behaviors, e.g. to shake a toy or mobile attached to the crib, or to communicate interest or impatience during a meal" (78). They remark that "In the first few months of life, infant kicking appears to be an especially well-coordinated movement, indeed quite distinct from the much less rhythmic and more seemingly random thrashing of the arms" (78). In preface to their analysis of the "coordinative structure" of crying, Thelen and Fogel remark more broadly upon "the ontogeny of communication" to the effect that "[t]raditional theories of language development … are inadequate because they do not take into account the appearance of communicative expressions in the first weeks and months of life, *long before the infant has control over these expressions*" (Thelen & Fogel 1989:46; italics added). In their analysis proper, they point out that over the first months of an infant's life, crying is preceded or followed by "frown expressions" which, on closer inspection, were observed to be "always accompanied by nonexpressive action patterns." They itemize these related nonexpressive action patterns as follows: "head turning, eye closing and squinting, rubbing the face, eyes, and head with the hands (or into a blanket if prone or into the mother's clothing when cradled), and changes in respiration patterns such as deep breaths, sighs, and gasps" (49). Though not specified in such terms, the account of infant kicking and infant crying both validate primal animation. What is there first and foremost is movement — "nonspecific behavioral arousal," uncontrolled expressions, and "nonexpressive action patterns." In the account of kicking, as is evident, there is even reference to non-directed arm movement, i.e. a "random thrashing of the arms."

In short, infants move. Movement is the ground floor of life. Dynamic systems theorists implicitly recognize this ground not only in their descriptive renditions of kicking, crying, and other infant behaviors, but in the very concept of *emergence*. What emerges is *dynamically assembled*. It is precisely in this sense that *meaning* must be taken into account for it is the keystone of the assemblage. We can see this most clearly by considering the way in which dynamic systems theorists themselves explain emergence. To begin with, what emerges is neither the result of an executive order from on high nor is it a ready-made plan that springs forth. In more exacting terms, it is neither the work of the "central pattern generator" of neurophysiologists nor the result of the "motor program" of experimental psychologists (Thelen & Smith 1994:74). Of the former, Thelen and Smith pointedly comment that "Real data from real frogs, chicks, cats, and humans render the construct of the CPG illusory. What is the pure essence of locomotion when its performance, form, and stability are completely at the whim of the age of the animal, its motivation, and the experimental or observational context?" (74). Of the latter, they write that "If the motor program contains the instructions for the entire sequence of behaviors ahead of time, how can novel and adapted forms be generated?" (74–75). With respect to both, they counter that "the central nervous system is not a computer controlling an electronic output device" (75). They affirm that dynamic analyses of movement take three primary dimensions of behavior into account: the task, the available "organic components" such as an infant's present abilities or leg strength, and the "environmental supports," which include not only immediately surrounding objects and substrate in each particular case, but the presence of parents, caretakers, or other children, for example (73). What emerges, emerges dynamically in "real-time" on the basis of all these factors — it emerges on the basis of a real-life here and now. Experience is in this sense not something that can be denied to the infant; deference cannot be shown to behavior as if that were the only thing to be studied because that is the only thing that is "going on." By the same token, meaning is not something that can be denied to the infant; deference cannot be given to information pickup as if that were the central item of moment. On the contrary, as Thelen and Smith themselves make clear, such factors as *motivation* must be taken into account (312–19). Indeed, they recognize motivation as one of the "hard problems" along with affect, "embodied cognition," and so on (319–327). Information pickup does not generate motivation. Motivation is experienced. It comes from the felt body and is tied to meaning. Similarly, information pickup does not generate affect. Affect is experienced. It comes from the felt body and is tied to meaning. Further still, information pickup does not generate "embodied cognition." The latter, by definition, is corporeal; it is thus not an abstract knowledge but a corporeally resonant knowledge that is tied to meaning. Meaning, as Gibson rightly says, is not "*attached* to experience or *imposed* on it" (italics added). It is embedded in experience — first and foremost by way of the tactile-kinesthetic body.

A final aspect of emergence and dynamic assemblage warrants attention. A crucial and significant phenomenon pinpointed and elaborately modelled by dynamic theorists in terms of topological landscapes with features such as attractors and basins, a phenomenon to which the constructive phenomenology of infancy must in fact apply itself, is the phenomenon of change. Indeed, the constructive phenomenology must take the dynamic modelling of change as a transcendental clue. In following the lines of infant development, dynamic system theorists chart an ongoing sequence of nonlinear transitions from one stable state to another — from one "attractor" to another — in which clusters of dynamic subsystems exist with their own varying landscapes and thus with their own transitional patterns. In effect, change is not a monolithic shift but a complexly fashioned one. A prime example of the intricacy of this shift concerns the stepping movements of infants, movements that, around two months of age, seem to disappear, and then, a month or two before walking begins, reappear. Their disappearance has consistently puzzled infant researchers, and has been traditionally explained as "the inhibition of a primitive reflex by maturing cortical inhibitory centers" (Thelen & Fogel 1989: 41). Various studies by Thelen and colleagues have shown quite otherwise. They demonstrate that the stepping movements do not in fact disappear at all and further, that they are not the result of "a dedicated reflex network" (Thelen & Smith 1994: 89). Rather, they constitute a dynamic event, an event that has its beginnings in utero and that is molded of multiple and subtle components (89). The most prominent components explaining the phenomenon have to do with weight gain and with muscle mass. Infants gain weight rapidly in the beginning months of life, and that weight gain is reflected in a far greater increase in fat tissue than in muscle tissue. These changes affect body proportions and account for the disappearance of the stepping movements; infants simply become muscularly incapable of performing them. When they are submerged in warm water to waist level, the stepping movements readily appear (88–91).

Taking dynamic analyses of just such complex movement systems as a clue, a constructive phenomenology of learning to move oneself would transliterate modellings of landscape changes and anchor them in phenomenological realities. Stern's account of "the global subjective world of emerging organization," and his account of the development of self-agency, self-coherence, self-affectivity, and self-history in the formation of a core self, are both integrally relevant to the task. Each account offers insights into facets of infant experience that are anchored in tactile-kinesthetic life, a life in which, in the course of learning to move oneself, patterns of invariants as well as variants are discovered. Moreover each facet describes a shifting landscape that, in phenomenological terms, is *co-articulated* with all the others; that is, each facet is integrally bound to all others, affecting and being affected by them because all are part of the animated form that is the infant itself. Self-agency is not something that exists apart from self-history, for example, and self-history, for example, is not something that exists apart from vitality affects. Specifying co-articulations means specifying how, against the background of primal animation, changing kinetic possibilities engender changes in tactile-kinesthetic experience, and changing tactile-kinesthetic experiences engender changing kinetic possibilities, and how all such changes engender a range of kinetic structures in the process of redefining and/or refining themselves. Dynamically-modelled landscapes in this way lead to experientially-elaborated ones. The intricately shifting patterns that define change are elucidated with respect to real-life experiences of movement. A constructive phenomenology of infancy would articulate a constructive phenomenology of change in just this sense. To borrow a phrase from Stern, it would articulate the "activation contours" of change that are embedded in learning to move oneself. In this way, a constructive phenomenology of learning to move oneself would readily open out into a phenomenology proper: the phenomenology of change. Dynamic systems analyses of infant development from this perspective offer a prismatic vision of a long-neglected area in Western philosophy. The phenomenon of change is virtually nowhere to be found in phenomenological studies, any more than is a veritable phenomenology of movement. A concern with *dynamics* is far indeed from the *solid* or *object-ive* preoccupations that have long typified Western culture, preoccupations that translate into a concern with being over becoming. The preoccupations dominate not only Western metaphysics but Western epistemological understandings. They coincide with what Thelen and Smith describe as "end-state" fixations in development. For those so fixated, "Development is a movement more or less steadily toward a goal," a goal that is sometimes the end-state that is adult being, particularly as exemplified in the form of language (1994:43). Thelen and Smith point out furthermore that "The end-state is the mechanism in nativist-rationalist approaches [to cognition]," which include information processing theory and connectionist accounts of development. In such approaches, "The end-state (in more or less complete form) is written into the organism and propels it to where it must go." As Thelen and Smith astutely remark, "By putting the end-state in the mechanism [of development], we presuppose what it is we are trying to explain" (43). Clearly a concern with change as a complex dynamic goes against the Western grain. One is tempted to say that, with rare exceptions, it has not received sustained and notable attention since Aristotle's subtle and elaborate writings on change: change as growth, locomotion, and alteration; growth being a quantitative change, locomotion a dimension of soul, and alteration a qualitative change.

In sum, a constructive phenomenology of learning to move oneself has implications for phenomenology as well as implications for dynamic systems theory. It is not of course surprising that a dynamic systems approach to the study of infancy should coincide in remarkable ways with a constructive phenomenology of learning to move oneself. Both recognize movement as a dynamic phenomenon. Moreover for both, the dynamic notion of *emergence* is critical. As noted above, *emergence* for dynamic theorists is a *real* phenomenon, taking place in *real* time, with *real* creatures, in *real* environments. Learning to move oneself is just such a *real* emergent phenomenon. What emerges dynamically in learning to move oneself is an I that moves and an expanding repertoire of "I cans." What emerges equally are spatio-temporal meanings that are dynamically assembled, consistently and integrally, along with movement. Moreover diverse findings showing that infants live in a unified perceptual world, one that is not artificially or linguistically divided up into seeing, hearing, touching, and so on, coincide with the phenomenological insight that we are fundamentally bonded to the world through movement, and further, that we come to know the world through movement, intuitively (see Note 9), precisely in the way we intuitively knew as infants on the basis of our tactile-kinesthetic experiences, and knew without the aid of scare quotes, of qualitative happenings and vitality affects. Such knowing is a manner — or perhaps better, a *style* — of cognition that may be difficult for some adults to acknowledge since it is nonlinguistic and nonpropositional and, just as significantly, has no solid object on which it fastens. It is not, however, on these accounts deniable. On the contrary, we all start out the same way: as infants. And we all learn to move ourselves: without words, at our own pace, directly from our own bodies, on the basis of primal animation. In its various guises, the natural attitude view of movement effectively conceals this past from us; it can accommodate neither primal animation nor a tactile-kinesthetic body nor intuitive kinetic knowing. The tenets to which it is wedded preclude their very existence, much less their acknowledgment. The natural attitude view is in fact encumbered with multiple strictures precluding a recognition of the primacy of movement. Yet however much it precludes, it cannot actually nullify the fact that we were all movement-born, that we all came into the world animated, and that short of this animation, we could hardly have learned to move ourselves. To reflect phenomenologically upon this sheer kinetic spontaneity with which we come into the world, in fact, to reflect upon the sheer kinetic spontaneity with which a vast and incredible diversity of animate forms comes into the world, is to attempt to articulate the very ground of aliveness. Primal animation and tactile-kinesthetic experience are at the core of our infancy and remain the unsurpassed core of our adult being. Indeed, the wonder of being lies in aliveness and the wonder of aliveness originates in movement. Human being, and the being of all who must learn to move themselves, is foundationally and essentially kinetic.[11]

Notes

1.   The theme of a past that was never present is taken up by existentialists (following Merleau-Ponty) as a counter to any foundationalist enterprise, that is, to any endeavor that seeks to work back to the origin of our epistemological understandings.

2.   As this chapter will go on to show, the term "consequential relationship," which comes from the writings of Daniel N. Stern (1985: 71, 76–82), accords conceptually and descriptively with what Edmund Husserl designates "if/then relationships." The accord is of considerable interest not simply because Husserl's writings pre-date Stern's by more than 50 years, but because, as shown in Chapter Four, what is gleaned and elucidated through phenomenological analyses is complemented by what is gleaned through scientific research; and equally, because the yields of both phenomenological and scientific methodologies should in the end be just so complementary since the results in each case derive from empirically structured procedures. Husserl's analyses provide deep and highly detailed epistemological insights into experiential invariants and sensory-kinesthetic correlations, insights that may, of course, be phenomenologically verified by anyone interested in apprenticing him/herself to phenomenological methodology. (Note: For a detailed discussion of how Stern's descriptive accounts of infants accord with facets of bodily life described by Husserl, see Sheets-Johnstone 1996c.)

3.   Perhaps it should be added, *as beheld in the natural attitude in the West*. People's conception of movement is not on anthropologists' inventories, thus the conception is not a studied phenomenon on par with studies of people's conceptions of kin, deities, animals, history, and so on. How people in nomadic or hunter-gatherer societies, for example, behold and conceive of movement is unknown.

4. As we shall see, it is difficult not to find Merleau-Ponty's account of movement tortured because he is at such pains to make his account accord with his theme of a "prepersonal" I and a "prepersonal" world.

5. See Merleau-Ponty 1962: for example, "[C]onsciousness projects itself into a physical world and has a body, as it projects itself into a cultural world and has its habits" (137); "In the action of the hand which is raised towards an object is contained a reference to the object, not as an object represented, but as that highly specific thing toward which we project ourselves" (138).

6. Husserl 1970a: 106: "All kinestheses, each being an "I move," "I do," [etc.] are bound together in a comprehensive unity — in which kinesthetic holding-still is [also] a mode of the "I do.""

7. Dreyfus's and Dreyfus's claim is actually a puzzling if not intemperate one considering Husserl's idea of phenomenology as "an infinite task."

8. Stern actually writes of the infant's "experience of organization-coming-into-being." One could readily claim on the basis of fetal movement — lips opening and closing, forehead wrinkling, head turning, arms waving, and legs kicking — that an emergent self is already "coming-into-being" in the womb as early as eleven weeks.

9. Stern's use of scare quotes is a signal not of a deficient knowing, or knowing "so-called," but of a knowing that is *intuitive*, a knowing that is there immediately with no intermediary epistemological stages, and a knowing that does not break down into the categories into which adults distill knowledge. As Stern points out, "[I]nfants do not see the world in ... terms of our academic subdisciplines.... Infant experience is more unified and global.... [Infants] take sensations, perceptions, actions, cognitions, internal states of motivation, and states of consciousness and experience them directly in terms of intensities, shapes, temporal patterns, vitality affects, categorical affects, and hedonic tones. These are the basic elements of early subjective experience. Cognitions, actions, and perceptions, as such, do not exist" (1985: 67).

10. As should be apparent from usage in this chapter, sense-making describes both an intentional process, thus meaning-grasping (or as Husserl would say, the process of "besouling" as carried out by transcendental subjectivity), and the fundamental epistemic matrix of this process, that is, the kinetic means by which one actively grasps meaning — in virtue of one's mother tongue.

11. Drawing upon material from Chapter Two, Part I, one could go on to show that all animate beings — not just those animate forms that must learn to move themselves — are foundationally kinetic.

CHAPTER 6

Merleau-Ponty

A man in search of a method

[The philosopher] embarks on the task … in his own fashion…. The fashion of a philosopher. Everyone knows how his dance begins…. His first faint step is a question…. [He is] a mind afflicted with a mania for interrogation…. He brings in his whys and hows, the customary instruments of elucidation, which are the apparatus of his own art …   Paul Valéry (1964a: 202, 204)

1. Initial clarification

This chapter is an inquiry in the literal sense of that term. It is a genuine questioning, the immediate purpose of which is to try to understand in a precise methodological sense how Merleau-Ponty forges his philosophy. When we ask how a philosopher arrives at his or her philosophy, specifically when, as with Merleau-Ponty, the philosophy concerns the nature of our humanness and is not a speculative philosophy, we should on careful reflection and analysis be able to give an answer. Yet Merleau-Ponty presents a challenge in just this respect. How he does what he does is not at all transparent. This chapter is thus in a broad sense a meditation on methodology. Its aim is to demonstrate the crucial significance of a transparent methodology in the practice of a philosophy of humanness. Through such a methodology, others may methodologically verify or challenge presented findings; just as importantly, others may carry a given task forward. The line of questioning which we will pursue is self-generated; that is, answers will be provided only in the form of further suggested questions. The close, critical, and persistently searching questions are not a rhetorical exercise. They are an attempt to unravel Merleau-Ponty's philosophy from a methodological perspective, and indeed, to unravel it methodologically. Hence the intent is not to exasperate the reader by an incessant questioning but to engage the reader in the intricacies of an inquiry into the methodological underpinnings of a philosopher's philosophy, a task which necessarily engages her or him in the intricacies of the philosophy itself.

2.   Introduction

How does Merleau-Ponty do what he does? How does he build up a case for his the-sis, from the time he writes *The Structure of Behavior* and affirms behavioral aprioris to the time he writes *The Visible and the Invisible* and affirms the chiasmic nature of flesh? On what does he base his claims? How does he substantiate them? Does he appeal to experience? Does he appeal to facts? Does he appeal to the soundness of his particular interpretations of the facts? Does he appeal to arguments — or does he give arguments? Does he appeal to all of these modes of substantiation? Indiscriminately? Intentionally? On what — in general and in particular — does he expect his readers to weigh his claims and judge their merits?

When we ask what Merleau-Ponty does rather than how Merleau-Ponty does what he does, are we not ultimately asking the same *how* question? For example, does Merleau-Ponty not both jettison phenomenology and profit from the epistemological insights derived from phenomenology? If so, how can he jettison a method from which he has gleaned the very fundaments of his philosophy? Is his jettisoning of the method a consequence of his appropriating Husserl's phenomenology for ontological purposes? In other words, in retooling Husserlian phenomenology for something other than its original epistemological ends, is it at the same time vital (to the forging of his own philosophy) that Merleau-Ponty take Husserl's philosophical labors toward those ends firmly in hand even as he marches them off to completely different ends?

But in fact should we not also ask why Husserl's epistemology breaks open into ontology, or rather, ontologies — into Heidegger's *Being and Time*, Sartre's *Being and Nothingness*, Merleau-Ponty's *Phenomenology of Perception*? What is there in Husserl's phenomenology that spawns "existentialist 'dissidents'" (1962: xiv), as Merleau-Ponty calls them? Is this question merely a question of the history of Western philosophy, perhaps even merely a question of a particular socio-political Western history? Or is it a veritable and profound philosophical question? Does the spawning derive from the method of phenomenology itself? That is, does the phenomenological method itself *as it is practiced*, and practiced particularly with respect to the primary procedure of bracketing or suspending the natural attitude, have the power to stop one existentially short — thus epistemologically dead in one's tracks, so to speak? If so, is ontology — or are ontologies — the necessary consequence of the stopping short? Even were this so, is the ontological derailment of necessity permanent? Is it impossible to get back on epistemological track?

Three historical asides:

1.   Husserl's discovery of phenomenology was a progressive discovery and one that, by its very nature, was not divorced from experience. It was a discovery that

unravelled in a double sense: Husserl progressively discovered both a method and what the method led to: on-going and ever more complex epistemological progeny. In broad terms, he moved from a static to a genetic phenomenology and from a phenomenological Ego to transcendental subjectivity. In the process, he consistently found more than he anticipated; more aptly put, his wonder outran his grasp. Phenomenology — both itself and its progeny — disclosed more and more puzzles, more and more areas needing investigation, more and more questions for study — in short, more and more. Phenomenology thus became both a work-in-progress and an infinite task; it was envisioned as both a provisional labor and an on-going communal undertaking like science. Having begun comparatively simply with external perception, Husserl had, after all, ended with transcendental subjectivity, which presented itself as an epistemologically boundless terrain of study, certainly with respect to any one person's lifetime.

2. With the exception of Sartre in his early work, neither Heidegger, Sartre, nor Merleau-Ponty were wedded to a Husserlian phenomenology, neither to its foundational epistemological labors nor to its communal task. They were not the communally-oriented initial explorers — "First Philosophers" — that Husserl was. For them, Husserl's progressive epistemological investigations and discoveries in phenomenology — most especially with their built-in suspension of the natural attitude — were more immediately an *ontological* discovery. Indeed, and as suggested above, a suspension of the natural attitude *experienced in itself* appears to have disclosed for them something that had not been apparent before; it disclosed an ontological rather than an epistemological subject. Their immersion in Husserlian phenomenology — even were their immersion only in its theory and not in its actual practice — thus gave rise to preeminent concerns with being, not with meaning. Whether only theoretically studied rather than practically carried out, a suspension of the natural attitude — bracketed experience — was the methodological stopping point for these "existentialist dissidents," each of them forging his own ontological perspective upon it. One thus finds Merleau-Ponty at the time of his candidacy to the chair of philosophy at the *Collège de France* (1952), for example, avowedly pursuing an elucidation of "*transcendental Man*," and not an elucidation of Husserl's "transcendental Ego" (1964a: 10), i.e. transcendental subjectivity.

3. Merleau-Ponty's decisive turn toward ontology rather than epistemology, however, clearly occurred earlier. *Pathology* in the beginning was for Merleau-Ponty a substitute for the phenomenological reduction, i.e. the pathway of choice leading outside the natural attitude. It effectuated the bracketing necessary to "doing phenomenology." In effect, Merleau-Ponty made the familiar strange not through a suspension of the natural attitude but through a study of strange humans. Such

humans provided him his first access to "transcendental Man." Other substitute forms of the phenomenological method came later in the course of his philosophy. But phenomenology — Husserlian phenomenology — in truth stopped before any of the substitutions were in place.

Or in truth did it?

Some scholars might want to claim that Merleau-Ponty instantiated new phenomenological methods, precisely ones such as pathology, and in this sense *extended* Husserlian phenomenology.

Did he?

To substantiate the claim, a detailed interrogation of seminal works of Merleau-Ponty is in order, beginning with a consideration of pathology.

3. Pathology

Can empirical facts (about pathology) lead to existential truths (about the normal)? Do certain pathological behaviors actually tell us something about normal behaviors? More finely, do brain lesions linked to certain behavioral deficits actually tell us something about what a lack of those brain lesions means with respect to normal behavior? For example, if lesions in the subthalamic nucleus are correlated with a certain abnormal behavior — hemiballism (involuntary throwing movements) — do normal operations in that same area, i.e. a lack of lesions in that area, function to *restrain* hemiballism? If, neurologically speaking, normal behavior is simply a restraining of abnormal behavior such as involuntary throwing movements, is normal behavior, existentially speaking, not simply a restraining of the same abnormal behavior, thus of a wayward "motor intentionality" (1962: 137–39)? Is it possible to deduce the normal from the abnormal in this way (or in any other way?) with a sense of assurance? If it were, would we by now not have definitive answers as to what makes us (and other animals) tick, both normally and abnormally? Are there more reliable ways of determining existential truths about the nature of human nature? In other words, are there more direct approaches to existential behavioral normality?

If empirical facts about pathology *can* lead to existential truths about normalcy, how does one go about ascertaining those facts in the first place or perhaps go about validating them as facts? Should empirical facts of pathology as they are reported in the literature, for example, be followed up by in-person observations? Should anyone wishing to use the empirical facts gathered by scientists about human pathologies — use them as the basis for achieving existential understandings of human nature — be obliged to ascertain and validate those empirical facts first-hand? Thus, should Merleau-Ponty himself have visited Schneider, for example — as philosopher Ernst Cassirer did prior to utilizing pathological material in formulating his philosophy of consciousness (1957, Vol. 3: Chapter 6)? Should Merleau-Ponty, in addition, have visited the clinic where Schneider was treated, observed other patients, and spoken in person with neurologists Gelb and Goldstein, the doctors who ministered to Schneider and to other patients — precisely as Cassirer did (Chapter 6)? Especially since Cassirer made clinical observations and inquiries in person prior to utilizing pathological material in his philosophy of consciousness — the very same pathological material that Merleau-Ponty used in his phenomenology of perception — on what grounds do we validate, or even favor or commend, Merleau-Ponty's philosophical analysis over Cassirer's? While we may find Merleau-Ponty's criticism of intellectualist explanations of human pathologies of merit, what makes his own explanatory account meritable, and in fact not just meritable, but the rightfully fitting and proper account? How do we go about validating his existential analysis? Do we appeal to our own experience? But how, unless we are pathological, or indeed, if we *are* pathological, can we possibly validate Merleau-Ponty's ontological findings and explanations? Discounting personal pathology, do we rely on his argumentative counters to intellectualist and empiricist interpretations of facts about pathology? But are arguments over interpretations of facts about pathology what *existential analysis* (1962: 136) is all about? If not, then should we simply examine the facts Merleau-Ponty sets forth about pathology and carefully weigh his interpretations of those facts? But are even straightforward interpretations of facts about pathology what *existential analysis* is all about? If the answer to both questions is positive — if Merleau-Ponty's arguments and interpretations are both of singular existential moment — does the answer explain why Merleau-Ponty so strenuously favors facts over essences? In other words, does his defense of *existential analysis* over "the traditional alternatives of empiricism and rationalism" (136), not ultimately rest on facts, and does he in consequence not have to defend facts over against any other foundation? But does he also not have to be sure of his facts in the first place — be sure that they are in fact *facts*?

On the other hand, and especially in view of his writings which readily indicate that he read Cassirer's third volume of *The Philosophy of Symbolic Forms* (*The Phenomenology of Knowledge*, published in 1929) and perhaps even got the idea of using pathological material from his reading of Cassirer, does Merleau-Ponty's account not accord in certain fundamental ways with Cassirer's? Indeed, even though what Cassirer sought from his personal, first-hand investigations into pathology was, in his own words, a "common denominator" that brings together "not so much common factors in *being* as common factors in meaning" (1957, Vol. 3: 275), are the accounts of the two philosophers, insofar as they derive from the same material, not intimately related? In fact, are Cassirer's words, especially with their emphasis, not actually prescient of Merleau-Ponty's use of pathology? Is Merleau-Ponty's quest not precisely the reverse of Cassirer's stated one, that is, a search for "common factors in *being*"? All the same, does Merleau-Ponty's ontology-by-way-of-pathology not skirt clearly along the edges of an epistemology, i.e. along the edges of meaning? And does Cassirer's epistemology-by-way-of-pathology not skirt clearly along the edges of an ontology, i.e. along the edges of being? For example, does the following summary description that Cassirer gives of his quest for a common denominator of consciousness, specifically in its insistence on consciousness as a *global* and *operative* process rather than as a repository of localized, structural events, not dovetail with Merleau-Ponty's quest for a common denominator of being?

> … a view in terms of substance must everywhere be replaced by a view in terms of function; it is not the loss of a faculty that we have here, but the transformation of a highly complex psychic and intellectual process. According as the change affects this or that characteristic phase of the total process, very different pathological pictures arise, none of which need resemble the next in its concrete traits and symptoms but all of which are nevertheless linked together insofar as the change or deviation in all of them points in the same direction. We have sought to establish this general direction while laboring with the detail of particular cases as presented in the descriptions of the most thorough and precise observers; we have sought, in a manner of speaking, to reduce the aphasic, agnostic, and apractic disorders to a common denominator (275; italics added).

When Merleau-Ponty writes that "the life of consciousness — cognitive life, the life of desire or perceptual life — is subtended by an 'intentional arc' … which brings about the unity of the senses, of intelligence, of sensibility and motility," and that "it is this [intentional arc] which 'goes limp' in illness" (1962: 136), is he not gathering together all forms of pathology under one common ontological denominator as Cassirer gathers them together under one common epistemological denominator? From this perspective, and in spite of Merleau-Ponty's vigorous repudiation of "representation" (see, for example, the long footnote in 1962: 138–39), does Cassirer's common denominator — in broad terms, "ideation" — not resonate at all with Merleau-Ponty's common denominator — the "intentional arc"? If one judges that it does not, that their respective accounts of pathology have nothing in common, is one not thereby denying something integral to the history of philosophy? And is one not also close to suggesting that a mind/body split infests not only Cassirer's account in that it is "all mind," but Merleau-Ponty's as well in that it is "all body"?

While it may well appear outlandish to charge Merleau-Ponty with a dichotomization of mind and body, how does one otherwise reckon with certain inconsistencies — with his perplexing use of "having a body" in instances where the phrase is notably inappropriate, for example? Is it conceptually consistent with a professed non-mind/body dualism for Merleau-Ponty to speak of *having* a body in the following contexts?

> [F]ar from my body's being for me no more than a fragment of space, there would be no space at all for me if I had no body (1962: 102);

[C]onsciousness projects itself into a physical world and has a body, as it projects itself into a cultural world and has its habits (1962:137).

Who, we may ask, is this *I* who has a body? What, we may ask, is this consciousness that *has* a body? If the body is "the *vehicle* of being in the world" (1962:139, continuation of Note 2; italics added), and if "being in the world" is consciousness (139, Note 2), then how is dualism avoided? In spite of his eloquently strong anti-Cartesian (and anti-Sartrean) stance, is there not a lingering (or chronic?) dualism (or dualisms?) in Merleau-Ponty's philosophy? Must Merleau-Ponty not come to terms with the difference between *being a body* and *having a body*? Or would he insist that the difference is in fact an ambiguous difference — in the terms of his last writings, that the difference is chiasmic — and that the two expressions are thereby interchangeable?

If a connection between Cassirer's epistemological and Merleau-Ponty's ontological common denominator strains one's credulity, is it an equal strain to affirm common ground between them in the overarching theme of life being there prior to knowledge of it as such, that is, of there being a "prepersonal" life, as Merleau-Ponty, appropriating and ontologizing Husserl's terminology, calls it, or, as he first terms the idea ([1942] 1963), of there being "constants of conduct" or "apriorises"? Does the following short passage from Cassirer not read in spirit as if it came from the pen of Merleau-Ponty?

> Long before it passes into these [cultural] forms, life is purposively formed in itself; it is oriented toward determinate goals. But the knowledge of these goals always implies a breach with this immediacy and immanence of life
>
> (1957, Vol. 3: 275).

Would Merleau-Ponty not agree that there is a breach? Would he not say that knowledge must catch up with existence, that "autonomous functions" — or "determinate goals" — already inform life, and that our epistemological attempts to "catch [existence] at its source"[1] do not coincide with "the ordinary run of living"?[2] Would he also not agree in the deeper and broader sense that, as he puts it, "the internal or logical possibility, solid and incontestable as they may be under the gaze of the mind, have finally their force and their eloquence only because all my thoughts and the thoughts of the others are caught up in the fabric of one sole Being" (1968:110)?

And what of the following words of neurologist John Hughlings Jackson (1915:168) — words that Cassirer quotes?

> In the voluntary operation [i.e. in a voluntary act], … there is a preconception; the operation is nascently done before it is actually done, there is a 'dream' of an operation as formerly doing before the operation. [Note: Cassirer does not quote the further words by which Jackson makes explicit his figurative use of the term

"dream": "We say [dream] figuratively, because we do not mean a visual dream, but having … sensations," i.e. "having incipient motor activity contemporaneous with the intention to move" (169). Clearly, Jackson does not conceive the 'dream' to be a prior neurological "representation"; he conceives it to be part of a global motor intentionality.]

Does Jackson's 'dream' not resound with the notion of an intentional arc as Merleau-Ponty describes it, even as "the preconception" of an operation "nascently done" resounds for Cassirer with the notion of representation? In the most fundamental sense, how do preconception, 'dream', representation, intentional arc differ? Are they all not trying to capture the same truth about animate life? Are they all not affirming, or trying to articulate, whether epistemologically or ontologically, a fundamental truth about the nature of animate life and the relationship of knowledge to that life?

In sum, can there really be no connection whatsoever between the pathological interpretations of Cassirer and those of Merleau-Ponty such that in doing epistemology, one does something with no ontological significance, and conversely, in doing ontology, one does something with no epistemological significance? But then what does one make of Merleau-Ponty's consistent use of Husserl's epistemological findings? Are Husserl's foundational insights, particularly those into the bodily nature of perception and into passive synthesis, not indeed the *sine qua non* of Merleau-Ponty's ontology?

4. Facts

Perhaps the first questions to ask in attempting to understand how the factual is to enter into the philosophical is, what is a fact? and how does one go about sanctioning something as a fact? Is a fact equivalent to observations and descriptions of behavior, the behavior, of course, being the behavior of someone other than oneself? But can such a fact not be merely a putative fact? Can the so-called fact, for example, be in fact deviant if not pathological in that it does not accord with the way things are but is rather a projection of the person making the observations and writing the description? If a fact is really something other than a self-proclaimed, believed-as-gospel truth, or in a larger sense, something really other than a social agreement to stop thinking, then should we not expect it to be substantiated in some way — verified by others as uncontentious, for instance, or as having unquestioned staying power? Otherwise, would not any and all recorded scientific observations be considered *facts*? If this were so, would it not mean that only because someone is a scientist — say, a psychiatrist, psychologist, or neurologist — are his or her observations accorded factual status? But is this not precisely the situation when Merleau-Ponty writes about infant and child behavior in "The Child's Relation With Others" (1964d)? Is his reliance on Lacan, Wallon, and others, for *facts* justified? Or do his analyses and conclusions betray a certain gullibility and innocence with respect to facts, and even to science?

For example, is the descriptive and conceptual jump Merleau-Ponty makes in characterizing infants as confused, undifferentiated, and even pathological, and in characterizing adults as confused (ambiguity-stricken), undifferentiated (in fundamentally significant ways),[3] but normal (*non-infantile?*), reasonable, or is it peculiar? What is the ontological relationship between these two generational sets of individuals, individuals who, Merleau-Ponty indirectly indicates in the above-mentioned essay, occupy two distinct worlds? And how does the change from infancy to adulthood come about? Or should we not hold Merleau-Ponty accountable for this ontogenetical-psychological history? And should we not either ask in light of Merleau-Ponty's earlier descriptive and obviously adult ontology in *Phenomenology of Perception* ([1945] 1962) why human existence starts out *this* way, i.e. why it does not start out "open to the world" (1962:xvii) to begin with? After all, if human existence is *by nature* "open to the world," as Merleau-Ponty urges us to think, how is it that it is *by nature*, at birth and for the first three years (more or less), such a confused, solipsistic package, as Merleau-Ponty tells us in his later essay? How does human existence ever come *by nature* to be otherwise than what it is in the beginning? In particular, does a "syncretic sociability" (1964d:125–52) — our original undifferentiated sense of self and other that Merleau-Ponty affirms as fact following Guillaume, Wallon, and probably Piaget as well — that at six months of age gives way to mirrors — the appearance of an "imaginary *me* ... tear[s] me away from my immediate inwardness," i.e. tears us as infants away from our original "confused reality," as Merleau-Ponty paraphrases "Dr. Lacan's" facts (1964d:136) — does this undifferentiated-to-differentiated, specular-driven passage really fill the maturational bill as Merleau-Ponty claims it does? If so, from where does the *prepersonal* come that Merleau-Ponty consistently invokes, the prepersonal that he invariably describes in ways that unmistakably attach it to *adult* existence alone? Or perhaps we should ask how, if there is an *infant* prepersonal, does that infant prepersonal, being radically different, rise to the existential occasion of an adult prepersonal? On the other hand, if "motor intentionality" basically defines the prepersonal — if "the task to be performed [consistently, and in all normal persons] elicits the necessary movements" — is it not perhaps there from the very beginning? Does an infant not root at its mother's breast, for example? Does it not suck and swallow? Are these behaviors not what Merleau-Ponty calls "autonomous functions"? Are they not, in other words, fundamental aspects of prepersonal life? If this is so, then is Merleau-Ponty not wrong in insisting that an infant is confused, that it fails to differentiate itself from others, that it borders on the pathological? Is he too readily accepting of certain so-called "facts" of infancy? Is it not clear that an infant is, on the contrary, extraordinarily adept and competent (see, for example, Stern 1985, 1990; Butterworth 1983; Meltzoff & Moore 1983)? On yet another hand, and however philosophically inconsistent, does Merleau-Ponty not indeed affirm that everything is there from the start, that both the task to be performed and its elicited movements are already there at hand from the beginning? What else could he mean when he says that "The problem of the world, and, to begin with, that of one's own body, consists in the fact that *it is all there*" (1962: 198; italics in original)? But are round beads that fit into round holes and square beads that fit into square holes there from the start with no apprenticeship? In other words, is there no learning, no random probings or determined explorations, no hesitancies, no dogged persistence, and so on? More basically still, do infants — all infants, our own very young selves included — not have to learn their bodies? Did we all not have to learn to move ourselves? Did we all not in fact discover ourselves in and by moving to begin with, and in so doing learn who and what we are?

Would Merleau-Ponty answer that both learning and apprenticeship are "anonymous functions," or "inborn complex[es]" as he also calls them (1962: 84)? But how, then, can he take as "major fact" that "*the development of consciousness of one's own body* is the acquisition of a representation or a visual image of the body itself, in particular by means of the mirror" (1964d: 125–26; italics added)? What can the learning of our bodies, as a *developmental tactile-kinesthe-tic corporeal phenomenon*, indeed, as a constellation of ongoing tactile-kinesthetic corporeal *experiences*, possibly have to do with a consciousness of our bodies in terms of *mirrors*? Moreover what is a *representation* doing in the midst of what Merleau-Ponty presumably conceives to be an existential analysis of "The Child's Relation with Others"? Or is it an existential analysis? Can an existential account of the development of consciousness of one's own body have anything to do with visual representations short of being, by the strictures of Merleau-Ponty's own canon, an intellectualist account? If Merleau-Ponty affirms that the learning of our own bodies *is* an anonymous function, then precisely because it is a question of consciousness — *corporeal consciousness* — would he not also have to affirm that "the acquisition" of a consciousness of one's own body is likewise an "anonymous function," and this even though it is not only *acquired*, but acquired artifactually, "in particular by means of the mirror"? But what could this mean? How can mirrors enter into so basic an acquisition? Do people in cultures without mirrors lack a consciousness of their bodies? If a consciousness of one's own body is the centerpin of one's learning and apprenticeship, and if learning and apprenticeship have nothing to do with mirrors, then how can "the development of consciousness of one's own body" have anything to do with mirrors? Do not consciousness, learning, and apprenticeship rise or fall together, that is, are not all of them together either anonymous functions or anonymous functions not at all? Moreover would apprenticeship, learning, and consciousness of one's own body–in the sense that one can direct one's attention to it any time one wishes–not in fact be more fittingly and properly described as *autonomous* rather than anonymous functions? Is there not something missing from Merleau-Ponty's account, namely, *a resonant tactile-kinesthetic body*, and, in effect, *a tactile-kinesthetic consciousness*? In turn, would not both one's apprenticeship and one's learning of one's own body be coincident, tactilely and kinesthetically, with "the development of consciousness of one's own body"? And would not such learnings and apprenticeship thereby enunciate precisely, by Merleau-Ponty's very own standard, a *functional* intentionality, that is, in broad terms, an elicitation of movements proper to the task at hand: fitting round beads into round holes, for example, or exploring movements of one's hands and mouth?

In sum, are there not fundamental questions to be asked about how, in a methodological sense, Merleau-Ponty comes to know that everything is there from the start, and fundamental questions too about just what that "everything" includes? Perhaps the most basic questions we might ask in this context are the following: Does immediate experience actually bear out the idea that our apprenticeship and the learning of our own bodies are *anonymous* functions? Or are our apprenticeship and learnings not basic facts of infancy and childhood that are notably noticeable to anyone observing infants and children, and can this apprenticeship and these learnings possibly be founded on anything other than a tactile-kinesthetic body, a body attuned to touch and movement? If immediate experience bears out the latter idea — as Merleau-Ponty himself faintly indicates when, in elaborating on his thesis of an "anonymous and general existence," he observes of himself that, "While I am overcome by some grief and wholly given over to my distress, my eyes already stray in front of me, and are drawn, despite everything, to some shining object, and thereupon resume their autonomous existence" (1962:84), — might it not be possible through reflection, through Husserlian phenomenological inquiry, to uncover something further of these "anonymous functions"? Might one not only make pertinent *self-observations* in the manner of Merleau-Ponty in his grief — thus make *factual* reports of one's own behavior and use such factual reports to support one's case — but might one not also actually practice phenomenology with respect to one's own *experiences*? Why would it not be possible to have *both* a Husserlian phenomenology in the sense of getting back to *epistemological* origins (how we come to make sense of the world with respect to space, time, nature, movement, animals, persons, beads, holes, buildings, books, chairs, and so on) and a Merleau-Pontyian *ontology* (a descriptive metaphysics?) of human existence, which, though phenomenologically-derived, i.e. though rooted in Husserlian epistemological insights, is more immediately concerned with existential facts? Are the two kinds of endeavors mutually exclusive? Should they not in the end, by their very rootedness in a single human nature, complement and validate one another? Why does Merleau-Ponty have a seeming blindspot with respect to this possibility? Why is he in fact so adamant in his criticism of Husserl (and in his disdain of essences as well, when he is himself bent on producing essences — but of this, more later)? Why does he keep biting the hand that has fed him, so to speak, doing continuous battle with Husserl till the end of his life? *What is at stake for him?*

5.   A fundamental liability of a fact-based ontological methodology

Should Merleau-Ponty's writings on infants and children be discounted on the grounds that, in addition to not being a psychologist, Merleau-Ponty was naive and did not realize that received facts (like received wisdom) can be erroneous? But what would such a discounting overlook with respect to his attitude toward facts in the first place? Indeed, since his writings on infants and children were at a midpoint in his career, do they not tell us something important not only about his attitude toward facts but about their methodological place in his philosophy? Might one answer that what is at issue is not a question of "facts" on which Merleau-Ponty relied, but of his ontology, and that in view of this more basic issue, there is a need to consult more seminal works of his in order to investigate in proper fashion his notion of facts and psychology, or more generally, his notion of facts and phenomenology? But might one not counter this response by showing that a similar if not the same problem plagues Merleau-Ponty's seminal works?

For example, is not the very title of the chapter, "The Spatiality of One's Body and Motility," in Merleau-Ponty's *Phenomenology of Perception* misleading in terms of what it contains? Should the chapter not more truthfully be titled "The Spatial-ity of Pathological Bodies and Motility"? In other words, why does Merleau-Ponty not in fact describe "the spatiality of *one's* body and motility" (not to say *his* experi-ence of the spatiality of *his* body and *his* motility)? Because to do so would commit him methodologically to a Husserlian phenomenology? But does Merleau-Ponty not want us precisely to validate *by our own experience* what he is saying in this chap-ter — and elsewhere — and thereby take his analyses as phenomenology? Surely he does not want us to take what he says simply as a theoretical ontology, does he? But as queried earlier, can we possibly validate by our own experience what Merleau-Ponty deduces from pathological case studies? Would Merleau-Ponty answer that phenomenological descriptions of experience do not and cannot dis-close such things as "a basic motor intentionality"? Would he say that when we are at home in our bodies, i.e. not beset by pathologies, such things as our basic motor intentionality are not in evidence? But in everyday life, do we not, for example, grasp the cup, catch the ball, drive the car? — do we — or can we not — draw figure eights in the air, pretend to be a cat, and so on, all "in one fell swoop of the intentional arc" (Kaelin, pers. comm.)? In short, though Merleau-Ponty would answer (again) that it is a matter of a *prepersonal* existence, of anonymous functions, of inborn complexes, of a generalized body — that in the most basic sense, "we don't know how we do it, we just do it!" — can we not explore and reflect upon our own experiences of such everyday movement happenings, and find out for ourselves if such explorations of, and reflections upon, our own movement experiences bear him out? Was not

Husserl's elucidation of "kinestheses", for example, based on just such explorations of, and reflections upon, himself in movement?

If immediate experience did bear out Merleau-Ponty's basic thesis, why would it not be possible all the same through *phenomenological* reflection to uncover something of such "functions" as our "basic motor intentionality"? Again, why is it not possible to have *both* a Husserlian phenomenology in the sense of getting back to *epistemological* origins, and a fully acknowledged *phenomenologically-derived ontology*, that is, an ontology that gratefully recognizes its epistemological rootings in a Husserlian phenomenological methodology? After all, what *are* the ontological truths of human existence? Are there any, pure and simple? If there are, how does one go about ascertaining them? *What methodology is employed*? Does Merleau-Ponty believe (naively take?) scientific findings to be facts, facts that can be straightaway pressed in the service of an ontology? Does he believe that any practice of science produces facts? — and that it does so consistently? always? Is this abiding faith vital to his own ontological "findings"? That is, do *facts* guarantee him a solid and unimpeachable basis on which to ground his ontology of human existence and at the same time distance him from the epistemologically-driven phenomenological methodology he disdains? Furthermore, does this belief (or naive credulity?) allow him to describe existence from afar rather than close-up (*behaviorally rather than experientially*) since scientific findings — facts — are anchored in studies of third-person behavior, not first-person experience? (And does visibility not similarly anchor itself in a preeminently third-person rather than first-person investigation?) Does this same belief (or naive credulity?) afford him a certain credibility to begin with since behavioral reports are taken to be objective, hence more reliable, than experiential accounts, i.e. more reliable than *introspection*, which, incidentally, Merleau-Ponty (1962: 136) aligns with rationalism (intellectualist accounts)? How do we — readers of Merleau-Ponty — treat the *facts* that Merleau-Ponty presents and the *interpretations* that he offers of those facts? How are we to judge them? Do we ourselves need to assess his fact sources by reading Stratton, Gelb and Goldstein, Wallon, Lacan, and others in the original, and, like Cassirer, do we need to visit such places as neurological and psychiatric hospitals and institutes, and psychological clinics and laboratories as well? Do we need to converse with doctors and patients in person, and with infant psychologists and psychiatrists? Further, do we need consistently *to up-date* "the facts"? Is it not true that scientific "facts" change, not only with respect to appraisals of infant life — the conception of an infant as incompetent has been shown over the last thirty years to be a thoroughly erroneous conception, for example, — but with respect to scientific analyses and appraisals generally, all the way from such homely things as the nutrient values of broccoli (*The Register Guard* 1989) to such complex things as the cerebral pathology of schizophrenia (*Science News* 1994: 284)?

What if Merleau-Ponty had in fact analyzed "one's own body and motility" rather than giving us his interpretation of pathological bodies and their motility? Would he have still been able to privilege movement but trivialize the tactile-kinesthetic body? Would he necessarily not have to have taken the latter into serious and detailed account? Could he still have written (1962: 249), in the context of "catching space at its source," that "As a mass of tactile, labyrinthine and kinaesthetic data, the body has no more definite orientation than the other contents of experience, and it too receives this orientation from the general level of experience"? Could he still have declared (1962: 246), in his re-interpretation of Stratton's inverted vision experiments, that head and feet count for nought with respect to orientation? Or would he have realized in the context of reflecting upon these experiments that there is an intact and vibrant body between head and feet; that in inverted vision, a rush of pressure should be felt in the head — and it is not! — and feet should feel no pressure spreading out uniformly against a solid surface — and they do!? Would he have realized that, inverted or not, the body has a definite orientation on the basis of "tactile, labyrinthine and kinesthetic data" (or "contents," as he consistently re-terms "sensations")? Would he have realized that the body has a "preferred vertical" for the same reason, i.e. would he have acknowledged *the felt weight* of his own body and the everyday postural preference it has for the vertical on the basis of its being the animate form that it is?

Does the idea that the "contents of head and feet" (246) count for nought make sense to begin with — especially for Merleau-Ponty? Why would a philosopher of the body, especially one who brings to center stage a motor intentionality, neglect kinesthesia? Why would he not be concerned to explore his own bodily experiences of movement? Was Merleau-Ponty influenced by Piaget in this respect? The question of influence aside, can a similar charge be lodged against Merleau-Ponty that is lodged against Piaget, namely, that more is going on than meets the eye? That is, if movement is at the source of a developing human intelligence, as Piagetian theory affirms, but if, as the same theory affirms, as critics have pointed out, "there is no information *in the structure of sensory stimulation itself*" (Butterworth 1983: 3; italics in original), then does this not mean that, *self-movement is central but kinesthesia counts for nought*? Does the same criticism not apply equally to Merleau-Ponty's "basic motor intentionality"? Is there not a basic conceptual accord in Merleau-Ponty's and Piaget's privileging of self-movement but dismissal of kinesthesia?

Do other chapters in *Phenomenology of Perception* confirm a privileging of movement and trivializing of kinesthesia? When we consult the chapter titled "Space," for example, and the section on the movement of objects, do we not readily find the confirmation? Why, with respect to such movement, does Merleau-Ponty not summon experiences of his own moving body? Particularly since he wants to anchor human existence in the body and to spell out our existential relation to the world in bodily terms, why does he not straightaway consult living human bodies in motion (again, not to say his own living body in motion)? Why, rather than doing so, does he stay strictly with what his eyes see, with his sense of vision alone, putting all the burden of an understanding of movement on sight (1962: especially 278–79, but implicitly in all earlier analyses and discussions as well) — except at one place (269) where, immediately after declaring, "in thinking clearly about movement, I do not understand how it can ever begin for me, and be given to me as a phenomenon," he breaks off and starts a new paragraph with the words, "And yet I walk, I have the experience of movement in spite of the demands and dilemmas of clear thought…"? Why, at this point, does he not follow through? Why does he not elaborate on his "experience of movement," in particular, *on the foundational pan-cultural human experience of walking*? Why does he not reflect on his own "motility"? What prevents him from entertaining the possibility that one's sense of one's own movement epistemologically grounds one's sense of moving objects? Why would a (the?) preeminent philosopher of the body neglect exploring this possibility? Would the act of introspecting self-movement — not to mention doing a phenomenology of self-movement — bring him too close to his body? That is, would the recognition and analysis of kinesthesia, insofar as it is not ambiguous in the least but definitive from beginning to end, constitute a threat to "autonomous functions"? However caught up he might be in rejecting both empiricist and intellectualist renditions of movement, is it not strange that he finally solves the problem he sees in movement by recourse to a hypothetical construct, a "mobile entity" (1962: 273; see also 275, 276 note), which he says is "necessary to the constitution of a change" (275) and which he describes at one point (275) appositionally as "[p]reobjective being"? Is it not strange that he exemplifies this mobile entity, this (form of?) pre-objective being, by a bird in flight, describing its movement in just the terms one would use phenomenologically to describe one's own moving self, i.e. the bird itself, not an observer, "constitutes the unity of its movement" (275)? Why would Merleau-Ponty fail to recognize that our visual sense of the movement of other beings is rooted in just those unified experiences we have of our own movement? Do we ourselves not indeed "constitute the unity of our own movement"? Finally, is it not altogether strange that in a footnote in which he elaborates on the problem of movement, Merleau-Ponty writes both that "The consciousness of my gesture, if it is truly a state of undivided consciousness, is no longer consciousness of movement at all, but an incommunicable quality which can tell us nothing about movement" (275; cf. Sheets-Johnstone 1980 and this text, Chapter 2, Part 2 and Chapter 3), and that "This relative and prepersonal *I* who provides the basis for the phenomenon of movement, and in general the phenomenon of the real, clearly demands some elucidation" (276)? Do these statements not make singularly clear that Merleau-Ponty has in fact bypassed an understanding of the phenomenon of movement, and, at its core, self-movement? Do they not conclusively show that he has bypassed the very kind of examination of movement by which he would have been led to discover that a consciousness of movement *is* qualitative, qualitative because it is of the very nature of movement to be qualitative, and not in an "incommunicable [way] which can tell us nothing about movement," but in ways that speak volubly of a certain *kinetic style*? — a style that is, for example, rushed, sudden, slow, constricted, erratic, weak, heavy, or smooth, a style that has a certain spatio-temporal energy dynamic? Do the statements not show in fact that Merleau-Ponty has failed to elucidate both movement and self-movement, with the result that, rather than having given an account of movement, he has left it needlessly encumbered, not to say shrouded in mystery? At the end of his analysis, are we not in consequence once again at the doorstep (or mercy?) of "anonymous functions"? But in truth is this not where Merleau-Ponty wanted to be in the first place? That is, has he not wanted all along — wittingly or not — to explain our experience of movement in terms of "*inborn complexes*"?

6.   Methodological muddles and opacities

Does Merleau-Ponty confound experience and fact — as when he writes of Husserl (1964c: 90), for example, that "[he] maintained that a mere imaginative variation of the facts would enable us to conceive of every possible experience we might have"? Does Husserl consider the method of free variation to be a variation of *facts* or a variation of *experience*? Is a further confounding apparent in that Merleau-Ponty also equates *facts* with scientific findings — as when he writes (1964b: 24), for example, that "Psychological induction is never more than the methodological means of bringing to light a certain typical behavior, and if induction includes intuition, conversely intuition does not occur in empty space [but] exercises itself on the facts, on the material, on the phenomena brought to light by scientific research"? Is not the double use of the term *fact* — now aligned with experience, now aligned with results of scientific inquiry — peculiarly muddled if not downright contradictory? What precisely is the relationship of an experientially-tethered fact — "I have tied my shoelace" or "I am in the process of tying my shoelace" — to a fact that the practice of science produces — "the earth rotates on its axis"? Are facts procured alike from one's own experience as from science? If this were so, then why would the finding of a fact in the latter case necessitate a particular methodology and in the former case necessitate no particular methodology at all? Or does the derivation of facts from one's own experience require no particular methodology at all?

If one affirmed that, at the very least, the derivation of facts from one's own experience requires introspection — a quintessential and attentive examination of experience that takes place consequent to, or interspersed with, the experience itself — would Merleau-Ponty not emphatically disagree? Does he not want to separate facts — no

matter what he might construe as their source — from any possible suggestion of introspection since the latter, he avers (1964c: 64), "lead[s] to all the difficulties from which
psychology attempted to escape when it decided to become a science"? Does he not
wish precisely to do away with "internal observation" (64)[4] as a methodology in order
to preserve the recognized scientific nature of facts, and, by the same stroke, sanction
a methodology that will found an eidetic psychology, a psychology that he can equate
with phenomenology? But what then happens to experience as a source of facts — notably, the facts of experience to which he refers in a double and even triple sense? In particular, if his claim is true that "The insight into essences rests simply on the fact that in
our experience we can distinguish *the fact that* we are living through something from
what it is we are living through in this fact" (1964c: 54; italics in original), then does
Merleau-Ponty not further complicate the muddle? Where, in fact and in particular, is
his second fact to be found *in experience*? What kind of experience and methodology
brings this second fact — "*the fact that* we are living through something" — to the fore?
Given such a seemingly foundational fact, is it not important that the experience(s)
providing it and the methodology elucidating it be precisely delineated, all the more so
since this existentially-resonant fact anchors Merleau-Ponty's eidetic psychology?

Does Merleau-Ponty not in fact wish in place of introspection to denominate
and claim *radical reflection* — what he also specifies as "phenomenological reflection" and "eidetic reflection" — as his methodology (1964c: 65, 61, and elsewhere)?
Do facts — both experientially-derived facts and scientifically-derived ones — not
provide the very foundation of this reflective methodology? And does Merleau-Ponty
not want specifically to conjoin this fact-based reflective methodology with Husserlian
essences, even as, unlike Husserl, he bases his methodology not on experience per se
but on factual knowledge, and even as he turns his methodology away from epistemology and toward ontology? In short, is radical reflection for Merleau-Ponty not a
radical reflection upon facts — scientific and experiential facts (whatever the latter
might be for him in the context of his methodology) — and, in the case of scientific
facts at the very least, a radical re-interpretation of facts? To this end, does Merleau-
Ponty not explicitly distinguish cognitively between fact and reflection when he states
(1964c: 64), "[R]eflection is not at all the noting of a fact. It is, rather, an attempt to
understand"? If so, then does not his seminal claim (1964c: 65) that radical reflection
"[is] founded on the fact that I am no stranger to myself" need elucidation? Is not the
source of this pivotal fact of moment — in the same way that the source of the second
of his three facts noted above is of moment? Should we not want to be enlightened
about the experiential (scientific?) foundation of this familiar relationship that we have
to ourselves? At the same time, are we not in fact again confronted with the question of
where "*the fact that* we are living through something" comes from? That is, is not "*the
fact that* we are living through something" intimately related to the fact that we are no
strangers to ourselves? More finely put, is it not through or in virtue of the former fact

that we affirm the latter fact? But what kind of experience generates this *Ur* fact? And how does one come to have that experience?

Is there furthermore not a corresponding opacity in that "the fact that I am no stranger to myself" is a fact that is not transparent but on the contrary in need of painstaking clarification? In particular, should we not ask whether "the fact" is really a fact? That is, is the finding — "I am no stranger to myself" — a fact or is it the result of a "radical reflection"? Is the declaration a culmination or a point of departure? Indeed, what precisely does it mean to say that "I am no stranger to myself"? What kind of knowledge is being proclaimed? Is it indeed *factual* knowledge of myself? Or is it rather eidetic (essential) knowledge of myself? Is the question of origin not again clearly of moment? In precise methodological terms, how is it that I discover that I am not a stranger to myself? What is the *source* of this knowledge? — experience? science? psychological induction, a suspension of the natural attitude? introspection? radical reflection? Would a resolution of the question of origin not allow us to determine whether the *fact* is really a fact?

Might we find clues toward a resolution of the question in the remarks Merleau-Ponty makes in exemplifying what an "eidetic reflection [would] ask" (1964c:61)? Might we indeed find clues in specific and general clarifying remarks he makes about knowledge accruing from eidetic reflection? Does he not specifically affirm, for example, that eidetic reflection upon emotion would result in an understanding of "what emotion *means*" (61; italics added)? Does he not more generally affirm that factual investigations are "in need of psychological clarification" (63) to the end that "*[the] one essential meaning*" of the "lived facts" be found and the facts in turn understood (62; italics added)? Does "the fact that I am no stranger to myself" need just such psychological clarification, or does the factual investigation that has disclosed "the fact that I am no stranger to myself" need elucidation? In light of his remarks concerning knowledge accruing from eidetic reflection, is an answer to the question of origin — fact or essential realization? — not indeed pressing? If we parenthetically paraphrase the questions Merleau-Ponty himself poses on behalf of an eidetic reflection on emotion, is the import of the question of origin not heightened even further? "After all," Merleau-Ponty asks (61), "what is it to be moved [what is it to be a stranger to myself]; what is the meaning of emotion [what is the meaning of strangeness]? Can one conceive of a consciousness which is incapable of emotion [Can one conceive of a self which is incapable of a familiarity with itself — i.e. which is a stranger to itself], and if not, why not"? From the perspective of these paraphrased questions, is the so-called "fact that I am no stranger to myself" clearly not a fact at all but an "*essential meaning*"? If so, do we not need to work *backward*? — that is, backward from Merleau-Ponty's radical or eidetic reflection (or psychological induction?) to its source, finding out on what it is based, how it comes experientially (or scientifically?) to be? Alternatively, if Merleau-Ponty has in fact given us a fact, can we — and should we — not justly expect of him an eidetic reflection — a "psychological clarification" — that elucidates it? Is it not of quintessential significance to uncover the "one essential meaning" of this foundational fact? Would Merleau-Ponty answer that his entire philosophy provides that elucidation? — or in other words, that his entire philosophy is "an attempt to understand" how it is that "I am no stranger to myself"?

But does it — or is it? Does his philosophy lead us to an elucidation or understanding of what the fact of being no stranger to myself means? Or, on the contrary, do we already intuitively understand what being no stranger to myself means, even though we have yet to uncover the source of our understanding, to ground our understanding — whether in fact or in experience? Either way, must we not answer to the question of origin and thereby clarify the *Ur* fact Merleau-Ponty so resolutely and positively affirms? Does Merleau-Ponty himself not insist, after all, that an eidetic psychology — an eidetic phenomenology (1964c: 58–59) — is "a clarifying effort"(63)? Does he not maintain (62–63) that such a psychology or phenomenology elucidates the facts that an empirical psychology (and presumably experience?) provides? But would not this very procedure — subjecting facts to radical (or phenomenological or eidetic) reflection in order to discover "the ultimate meaning of these facts" (59) — in this instance be the exact reverse of what Merleau-Ponty intends when he affirms that eidetic reflection is "*founded* on the fact that I am no stranger to myself" (italics added)? Is he not saying that this fact needs no radical reflection? Is he not claiming an unquestionable methodological base line, so to speak, with his *founding* fact? Is this founding fact, in other words, not already or in truth or at the same time an "essential meaning"? Indeed, is Merleau-Ponty not proclaiming an existential foundational truth, particularly with his reference to Heidegger in the very context of specifying the *founding fact*, that is, when he declares (1964c: 65) that "Heidegger would say that I am not hidden from myself"? If Merleau-Ponty were indeed claiming the founding fact as a point of departure for his philosophy, and not as a culmination or essential meaning, then how, since his philosophy is methodologically *based* on this fact, can his philosophy possibly *clarify* this fact? On the other hand, why would this fact, being a *bona fide* fact, be exempt from radical reflection? Why would it not be subject to radical reflection like any other fact, in spite of the fact that it founds his method? Or are we simply to accept his founding methodological fact as given — no questions asked, including the question of whether the fact of being no stranger to myself is actually a fact? Should we not rather press the issue of methodology, and in particular raise the question of whether Merleau-Ponty's dismissal of introspection (not to mention a phenomenological methodology) is merely verbal, a dismissal in word but not in deed?

Surely if it is a fact that I am no stranger to myself, must there not be some perdurable and continuous aspect of myself that provides ever-ready access to this fact, something on the order of an ever-possible, ever-renewable source of validation of the fact, its substantive core, so to speak, of which I have, or can have, experience? If this is so, then how can radical reflection be divorced from introspection, from "internal observation"? Is it sufficient merely to declare, "I am not a stranger to myself" and buttress that declaration with an allusion to how Heidegger would phrase the matter? Do I not *know* myself to be not a stranger to myself? Does "the internal relation of myself to myself" (64), as Merleau-Ponty positively puts the matter in the context of his repudiation of an introspective methodology, and the factual *knowledge* "that I am no stranger to myself," not emanate from my experience of myself? And does it not thereby emanate from evidence gleaned precisely from introspective awarenesses of my experience of myself, and this in spite of Merleau-Ponty's insistence (64) that "internal perception" — introspection — plays no part in radical reflection because such a perception would be the mere "noting of a fact"? But does Merleau-Ponty not specifically require "the noting of a fact"? That is, does he not need to note something specific and integral to our experience of ourselves, something that is iterable any time we care to notice, something that is utterly foundational to our experience of ourselves, something that allows us to claim with conclusive certainty that we are no strangers to ourselves? And where would this integral, iterable, utterly foundational, conclusively certain something come from if not from our tactile-kinesthetic bodies, which are there any time we care to notice? Where in particular would a quintessential familiarity with oneself come from if not from one's tactile-kinesthetic body? Is not this introspectively validatable fact the basis of "*the fact that* we are living through something," and in turn, "the fact that I am no stranger to myself," thus the foundation of my sense of myself as *familiar*? Any time I care to attend, am I not there, tactilely and kinesthetically "living through something"? From this tactile-kinesthetic vantage point, is not the affirmation — "I am not a stranger to myself" — the ready if succinct answer to the three paraphrased questions posed above? That is, in declaring that "I am not a stranger to myself," do I not already know what it is, or would be, to be a stranger to myself? Do I not already know *the bodily felt meaning* of familiarity — and strangeness — because I am fundamentally aware of myself as "living through something"? And do I not already have a bodily felt sense of a self "incapable of an unfamiliarity with itself," i.e. incapable of strangeness? In short, if I *know* that I am not a stranger to myself, if I have arrived at that realization, then have I not *already "radically" reflected* upon "the internal relation of myself to myself" in the course of living through all manner of things? Have I not from birth onward — in all my progressive apprenticeships and learnings and in my developing consciousness — been firmly and foundationally anchored in my tactile-kinesthetic body? And are the facts of all these progressive tactile-kinesthetic experiences not firmly and foundationally etched in my body? Moreover, are the factual observations — experience-based judgments — I have made and still make in the course of these tactile-kinesthetic experiences — the factual observation that I am now, for the moment, balanced securely on my two legs, the factual observation that I am not succeeding in pushing the square knob into the round hole, the factual observation that I must stretch to grasp the apple — are these factual observations the result of a "passive attitude of a subject who watches himself live," as Merleau-Ponty defines "factual knowledge" (64; see also 63)? Or are they precisely the result of "the active effort of a subject who grasps the meaning of his experience" (64), the result of what Merleau-Ponty specifically wants to align not with an introspectively active subject but with the "clarifying efforts" of eidetic psychology and "phenomenological analysis" (63)? In a word, are the foundational facts of one's aliveness — one's "living through something" — not the result of both an active attentiveness and a reflective sensitivity to one's dynamically engaged tactile-kinesthetic body in the challenges, throes, and appetencies of living? Do I in fact not notice myself in ways that attest incontrovertibly to introspection, that is, to an awareness of what I am in just these moments experiencing and/or what I have experienced, thus, how what I am doing and/or have done is efficacious and successful or whether I need to shift my weight, adjust my movement, correct my efforts, desist with the endeavor, pursue a different strategy, and so on?

Yet precisely in this context, must we not heed Merleau-Ponty's own admonition and ask whether, if "internal perception" — introspection — "is capable of error as well as truth" (65) then how can the progressive "radical reflection" that has brought to light my existential familiarity with myself ever be firmly grounded? In particular, how can it be grounded, as indicated above, in the tactile-kinesthetic body? How do I know that I am not in error when I take introspective bearings from my experiences of touch and self-movement? In walking, for example, may I not feel the toes of my left foot to be about six inches from the heel of my right foot, when in fact the distance between toes and heel is seven inches or even eight? But is there any doubt that I feel the toes of my one foot and the heel of my other, and the two at a distance from each other? And is there any doubt that I feel a certain tension in my neck when I turn my head, or a certain amplitude when I stretch, or a certain compression when I crouch, or a certain speed when I run? Is the concern about introspective error a legitimate concern in the present context, i.e. with respect to "*the fact that* we are living through something" and to "the fact that I am no stranger to myself"? Or is it rather, following Merleau-Ponty, a necessary bow to science? What, we may ask again, could possibly ground Merleau-Ponty's foundational existential "fact of being no stranger to myself" other than the tactile-kinesthetic body? In turn, what methodology is there for knowing this body other than a direct experiential methodology? Does the question of introspective error together with the doubts it raises about "internal observation" not result in a neglect of this body? Does it not require our leaving this foundational body behind and unattended? Is this neglect not reflected in Merleau-Ponty's hasty, and in truth, unexamined trivialization and dismissal of "tactile, labyrinthine and kinesthetic data," as we saw earlier in the context of discussing his re-interpretation of Stratton's experiments and his failure to consider sensed bodily weight, pressure, and the like? In a similar but broader sense, is it not reflected in his choice of an interpretive analysis of pathological motility over an experiential analysis of "the spatiality of *one's own* body and motility"? Is his repudiation of introspection in the end not a repudiation of tactile-kinesthetic experience, and in consequence, a repudiation of the very body he needs to ground his philosophy? Is not tactile-kinesthetic introspection — attentive reflections upon our tactile-kinesthetic lives — the pivotal and critical ontological and epistemological source of our being no strangers to ourselves?

In sum, if experience is a source of fact — indeed, our premier source of fact — and thereby the touchstone of an eidetic ontological phenomenology, then can the very bedrock of our experience of ourselves and of the world — movement and touch — be ignored or shunted aside in favor of pathological bodies and other third-person behavioral investigations in psychology? And can Merleau-Ponty in good faith discard internal observation as an error-prone, unscientific methodology, especially since, as his own experientially-based factual observation of his own wandering eyes in the midst of grief indicates, it is a fecund source of knowledge and one that he himself validates as such?

7.   Methodology in Merleau-Ponty's earlier and later work

Would the above line of questioning be tempered by taking into account Merleau-Ponty's later work, especially material from his posthumously published book *The Visible and the Invisible*? After all, does Merleau-Ponty not in these pages explicitly address the question of methodology, treating such issues at length in three successive chapters of a section titled "The Visible and Nature: Philosophical Interrogation"? Should we not examine this book and other later material as well in order to demonstrate a shift in methodological ground? For example, can we fail to notice that in this later work Merleau-Ponty eschews scientific facts and pathological bodies? On the other hand, even given this shift in approach, can we justifiably claim that Merleau-Ponty is now drawing directly on experience as his methodological point of departure and as the very source of his philosophy as well? In particular, might we claim that in certifying a new methodology under the name "Interrogation," Merleau-Ponty finally gives us what he promised but did not give us in *Phenomenology of Perception* when he declared that "Our relationship to the world, as it is untiringly enunciated within us, is not a thing which can be any further clarified by analysis; philosophy can only place it once more before our eyes and present it for our ratification"? When he thus defined his methodology, did he not clearly promise something quite specific in the way of evidence? Did his interpretations of scientific facts and analyses of pathological bodies fulfill this promise? *Can* such interpretations and analyses in fact be put before our eyes and, in effect, be presented to us for ratification? Can we possibly ratify *behavior*? Can we possibly *ratify* Merleau-Ponty's *Phenomenology of Perception*? On the contrary, is it not in *The Visible and the Invisible* that we finally have something we *can* ratify, and this because it is finally a question of appealing to our own experience? If so, is it possible to affirm that in his later work, Merleau-Ponty finally distinguishes *fact* — and *behavior* — from *experience*, and indeed, leaves the former concerns behind?

For example, does Merleau-Ponty not straightaway present us with experience when he declares at the opening of *The Visible and the Invisible* (1968: 3) that "We see the things themselves, the world is what we see"? Is this dual declaration not an affirmation of human experience to which we can give our assent — or dissent? But if we give our assent, do we not meet with a problem? Does ratification mean that we are confirming a visual experience or affirming the declaration of an experiential *fact*, i.e. "We see the things themselves, the world is what we see"? If the latter is so, then does Merleau-Ponty leave us with an unresolved conflict of interest, so to speak, between experience and fact, or are we indeed on new methodological ground insofar as facts can derive from experience and are no longer tethered in any exclusive way to science in general or to the scientific study of behavior in particular? If the latter judgment is the correct one, then what more evidence do we need to show a methodological shift? Indeed, is the double-sided experiential fact — "we see the things themselves" and "the world is what we see," a fact that seemingly bonds subject ("we") and object ("world") indissolubly — not the methodological (and ontological) anchor point of Merleau-Ponty's elucidation of the visible and the invisible? Yet if the double-sided experiential affirmation is indeed equivalent to an experiential fact, then why does Merleau-Ponty immediately speak of the affirmation in terms of a "perceptual faith" that philosophy finds difficult to articulate and that science "presupposes" and "does not elucidate" (14)? How can we possibly believe we are acknowledging an experiential fact if the putative fact is not acknowledged as such, neither philosophically nor scientifically, but is designated a matter of faith? How can we possibly *ratify* what is taken on faith? What can it possibly mean to ratify in this context? If we answer by suggesting that perhaps Merleau-Ponty's earlier work is not pertinent in exacting lexical terms to his later work — hence that ratification is an inappropriate philosophical measure of his later works — are we not still bound to ask how we are to proceed, that is, how we are in a methodological sense to assay, judge, and evaluate, his later philosophical claims? Does ratification not indeed enter the picture in that Merleau-Ponty asks us to give our assent and approval to what he writes? And on what could this assent or approval rest other than our own experience? But then how can we reconcile "confirming experientially" with "taking on faith"? How can our assent be based on experience if ratification amounts to "perceptual faith"? Indeed, are we not still being asked to corroborate what Merleau-Ponty places before our eyes, whether what he places is *Phenomenology of Perception* or *The Visible and the Invisible*? If, at the very most, ratification in the original context Merleau-Ponty uses the term means *to confer* factual status on our experience of our relationship to the world as he describes it, and this on the basis of weighing his work against our own experience, then at the very least, does ratification — again, in the original context Merleau-Ponty uses the term — not mean *to confirm* experience, that is, does it not mean that in reading what Merleau-Ponty places before our eyes, we are being asked to agree with him, to consolidate our beliefs with his, and this inarguably on the basis of our own experience of our relationship to the world?

In short, whether a matter of conferring factual status on experience or of confirming experience, are we not bound in each case to appeal to our own experience? Do we not, precisely on experiential grounds, and not on grounds of e.g. philosophical argument or psychological induction, align ourselves or not with Merleau-Ponty's philosophy? But still, how does this experientially-based agreement or disagreement come about? In a word, how precisely do we go about ratifying? What is the *method* by which we arrive at ratification or non-ratification? Are we not bound to introspect in order to ratify? Must we not reflect attentively on our own experiences of our relationship to the world in order to judge if they coincide with what Merleau-Ponty places before our eyes? In what else could ratification possibly consist if not in an examination of our experiences — of ourselves and of the world? In effect, how can we possibly avoid introspecting what is actually there in our everyday experiences if we are to assent or dissent to what Merleau-Ponty places before our eyes?

Yet by its very nature, does the notion of "perceptual faith" not free us from such a method and such a focal prominencing of experience? That is, is the very highlighting of, and emphasis upon, *faith* a way of avoiding an appeal to common, everyday forms of introspection such as when we introspect our experience of pain in order to tell the doctor about its quality — whether it throbs, is dull, is cutting, is shooting, is sporadic, is intense, and so on — or when we introspect a train of thought in order to examine its associative links or verify its continuity?[5] In broader terms, is the very notion of perceptual faith a way of avoiding epistemology, in particular a way of avoiding appeal to a Husserlian phenomenological methodology with its decisive and unflagging appeal to experience? In this sense, does the very notion of perceptual faith — perhaps especially insofar as *faith* is considered epistemologically vacuous in contrast to *belief* — not provide the conceptual framework for a bifurcation in philosophical paths, a clearly staked fork in the road such that an ontological terrain is definitively and explicitly marked out and distinguished from any form of epistemology? Is perceptual faith not an incisive way of distancing oneself from, if not repudiating, a Husserlian phenomenology from the very start?

If we accede to the notion of perceptual faith (in lieu of experience or experiential fact) as the methodological anchor point of Merleau-Ponty's later philosophy — indeed, as he himself indicates when he says that "philosophy interrogates the perceptual faith … [p]hilosophy is the perceptual faith questioning itself about itself" (1968:103) — are just such philosophical implications and repercussions not indeed plainly evident, not only with respect to the troublesome methodological questions concerning ratification and introspection as discussed above, or with respect to the separation of ontology from epistemology, i.e. Merleau-Ponty's separation of his philosophy from Husserl's phenomenology, but with respect to the methodological nature and purpose of reflection in Merleau-Ponty's philosophy as well? In particular, if "naïve evidence of the world" (1968: 4) — perceptual faith — pushes epistemological concerns conclusively to the side at the same time that it firmly anchors Merleau-Ponty's entire ontology, the *ontological* import of perceptual faith being the fundament of his philosophy, then to what end is reflection of moment, especially insofar as "[o]ur relationship to the world … can[not] be any further clarified by analysis"? What can possibly be the purpose of "*hyper-reflection*," as Merleau-Ponty comes later to designate his method of reflection and to distinguish it from what he calls "[a] philosophy of reflection," the latter being a matter of "methodic doubt" or "a reduction of the openness upon the world to 'spiritual acts'" (1968: 39)? If "naive evidence of the world" is the anchor point for "hyper-reflection," and "hyper-reflection" is reflection that "[does] not cut the organic bonds between the perception and the thing perceived with a hypothesis of inexistence" (1968: 38), then what exactly will "hyper-reflection" furnish if not the formula Merleau-Ponty has already given us in *Phenomenology of Perception*? Will hyper-reflection do anything more than place before our eyes our relationship to the world? In their focal aim (as distinct from the data or evidence to which they appeal), are Merleau-Ponty's earlier and later works not methodologically indistinguishable? Moreover if the relationship between perceptual faith and hyper-reflection is one in which reflection "must suspend [perceptual] faith in the world … so as to *see it*," so as to "read … in the world itself the secret of our perceptual bond with it," then are we not catapulted back to those *aprioris* first met with in *The Structure of Behavior*, aprioris that Merleau-Ponty will now imbue with ontological meaning on the basis of his "seeings" and "readings"? In other words, are we not again in the realm of constants of conduct and preferred behaviors, only now "seeing" and "reading" them as grounded in a basic ontological openness to the world? Is "hyper-reflection," then, not a form of *existential description* — what Merleau-Ponty originally called (his denial of further clarification by analysis notwithstanding) "existential analysis" — and in this sense not actually a form of *reflection* at all? In short, what exactly is the nature of reflection in Merleau-Ponty's later philosophy? Is he actually *reflecting upon something* or is he attempting *to reflect something*, that is, *to reflect something directly as in mirroring*? Is he not trying to capture our openness to the world, thus not trying to *reflect* that openness, i.e. to describe it? What, we may otherwise ask, is he *reflecting upon*?

Is a deeper exposition and understanding of Merleau-Ponty's theory and practice of reflection, especially as they are later articulated, to be found in language? For example, does Merleau-Ponty not tell us (in *The Visible and the Invisible*) that the philosopher must speak the mute world? At the same time, does he not insist that "The philosopher speaks, but this is a weakness in him…. he should keep silent, coincide in silence, and rejoin in Being a philosophy that is there ready-made" (1968: 125)? But does he also not explicitly insist that in rejoining Being in this way and discovering "a philosophy that is there ready-made," the philosopher "must use words not according to their pre-established signification, but *in order to state* [the] prelogical bond" (1968: 38; italics in original)? And does he not go on to affirm that the language of the philosopher "would be a language of which he [the philosopher] would not be the organizer, words he would not assemble, that would combine through him by virtue of a natural intertwining of their meaning, through the occult trading of the metaphor — where what counts is no longer the manifest meaning of each word and of each image, but the lateral relations, the kinships that are implicated in their transfers and their exchanges" (1968: 125)? By affirming, calling upon, or conjuring such a language, does Merleau-Ponty indeed not support his claim that "language is not a mask over Being, but — if one knows how to grasp it with all its roots and all its foliation — the most valuable witness to Being, that it does not interrupt an immediation that would be perfect without it, that the vision itself, the thought itself, are, as has been said, 'structured as a language'" (1968: 126)?[6] Does he not, in summing up his ontology of language, so to speak, aver that "Philosophy itself is language" (1968: 126)? Does he not, therefore, and throughout these passages, aver the philosopher to be something of a medium — a channel for the world's speech? And does it make sense to call this channeling *reflection*? Is it not rather, as indicated above, an act of *reflecting*? Indeed, is not "hyper-reflection" a misnomer in that it suggests an extreme effort at thought when, in fact, it is a matter not of *thinking* at all — of pondering, contemplating, musing, deliberating, lucubrating, examining, weighing, and so on — but a matter of transcribing what is already there by way of what one might call not so much a "prelogical bond" as a linguistic attunement with the world?

But again, how do we ratify this linguistically-attuned philosophy? Moreover how can language avoid what the phenomenological reduction cannot avoid? That is, how can "hyper-reflection" — or language — not be vulnerable to the very lack of completeness Merleau-Ponty consistently finds and criticizes in phenomenological reflection since language too is an *ex post facto* phenomenon, i.e. it too breaks into experience, and thus it too necessarily transfigures what is there? How does language avoid the gap, so to speak? Simply on the basis of Merleau-Ponty's assertion that language *is* the gap, as when he avers that "[t]he thematization of language" (1968: 178) discloses the passage from philosophy to "wild" or "vertical" being to be incomplete, but this incompleteness is "[not] an imperfection … not an obstacle to the reduction, *it is the reduction itself*, the rediscovery of vertical being" (178; italics added)? In other words, are we simply to accept Merleau-Ponty's assertion that language "is not a mask," but that, if one knows how to garden correctly — "grasp [language] with all its roots and all its foliation" — then what one speaks will coincide linguistically with the truth of the world? Is ratification, then, no more than a matter of faith in the wisdom of Merleau-Ponty? Are we simply to believe, as he teaches (1968: 125), that "One has to believe ... that there is or could be a language of coincidence, a manner of making the things themselves speak"?

In the end, are we simply to take Merleau-Ponty's *word*? But again, must even his word not resonate with our own experience? If so, what experience? What experience gives us that ontological moment of truth, that ontological dimension of "wild" or "vertical" being, as Merleau-Ponty terms it? Must we go to an art museum to have such an experience, as "Eye and Mind," Merleau-Ponty's last published essay, suggests? But why are our *organic* bonds with the world not described in terms of *everyday* experiences? Are *organic* bonds, contrary to connotation — indeed, contrary to actual denotation — apparent only in rarified, extra-ordinary experiences, ones not readily come by in the everyday world? If this is so, then how can we believe the organic bonds (or our linguistic attunement to the world) to be *fundamental*? Why does Merleau-Ponty not show us by analysis how, in some quite mundane commerce with the world, an "openness to the world" is latent if not directly manifest? Why must we go out of our way to grasp "the organic bonds between perception and the thing perceived"? Surely however hidden they might be under the burdens and stresses of everyday life, however *invisible* they might be, is it not incumbent upon Merleau-Ponty to elucidate how they are there all the same, in the most mundane of experiences, at the very source of all that we commonly do in the world and think of the world?

Might one not answer that Merleau-Ponty does just that when he speaks of "this red under my eyes" as "a momentary crystallization of colored being or of visibility" (1968: 131, 132), as "a *flesh* of things" with which we are "in a relation of pre-established harmony" (133)? Is the experience of red, after all, not an everyday experience? Could one not answer both "yes" and "no — "yes" because clearly, some things we see, whether a dress or a car, for example, are red, and "no" because clearly, as Merleau-Ponty himself points out, red is not the whole of our vision but "is bound up with a certain wooly, metallic, or porous ... configuration or texture," and because clearly, if red is not the whole of our vision, we may rightfully wonder how we come to separate it out *tout court* — how we might even do so spontaneously — and how we come to experience *it*, and not *it* as some superficial *thing* but as *flesh*? Does Merleau-Ponty actually elucidate this complex experience for us? Does he come close to elucidating it when he gives an extended example of touched and touching, i.e. one hand touching the other as the latter hand touches an object? Does he himself not in fact suggest that this tactile experience — both in particular and in general — is the original of which visual experience is "a remarkable variant" (1968: 133)? Does he not insist that "we must habituate ourselves to think that every visible is cut out in the tangible"? But how exactly is "this red under my eyes," this red that is not the whole of my vision, "cut out in the tangible"? And why, if it is a matter of an "organic bond" would there be any reason to "habituate ourselves" into thinking anything? Why *must* we do anything if it is a matter of an "organic bond"? What place do "*musts*" have in an *organic ontology*?

Is there not in fact a basic and absolutely pivotal methodological problem in that the paradigm tactile experience Merleau-Ponty presents is an utterly foreign experience? How commonly does one hand touch the other as the other is touching an object in the world? Does the reversibility of touched and touching that Merleau-Ponty wishes to demonstrate by his paradigmatic example — "my right hand touches my left hand while it is palpating the things" (1968:133–34) — involve the reader in a novel experiment, or in bodily memories, memories that resonate as readily and powerfully as memories of wandering eyes in the midst of grief? More than this, does the experience itself work in the way that Merleau-Ponty says it works? Does it actually demonstrate to us, immediately and forcefully, a "pre-established harmony"? Do we even frequently touch one hand with another, not to mention frequently touch one with another as the latter is engaged in touching some other object in the world, except when we are wringing, clapping, or clasping our hands together? Do we consistently, in some everyday way, come regularly in touch with ourselves in this way? Certainly, we scratch ourselves, rub our eyes, put our hand to our mouth or forehead, rest our chin on our fist, clean a wound, knead a muscle, lick our fingers, brush our tongue across our lips, cross our legs, and so forth, but how exactly do such experiences show what Merleau-Ponty wants them to show? Are they not, ironically enough, *ambiguous*, in the sense that where chin ends and fist begins, or right leg ends and left begins, are obscure? How can we reverse what is obscure, let alone bring a third item into the reversal? Has philosopher Marjorie Grene, an otherwise strong and articulate proponent of Merleau-Ponty's philosophical ontology, not in fact justly assayed the touched/touching act of reversibility that Merleau-Ponty describes? Are her fundamental sympathies with Merleau-Ponty not apparent to begin with when she declares that it is in the in-between "of hands, of things, of persons, of history, of time, of space" that "we catch a glimpse of Being," and that "the practice of ontology begins" as Merleau-Ponty affirms with just these occasions, even as she goes on immediately to say that "It is here … I must confess, that I find myself, so far, at an impasse"? Are these fundamental sympathies not palpable when she writes that "Every time I read him I have, once more, the sense that his approach to philosophical problems is entirely, overwhelmingly right"? And are they not equally palpable when she writes (Grene 1976:619), "As with no other thinker, I say, yes, so it is — but what about that hand trick? Alas, I cannot make it work"?

Is the problem, finally, that we are without any anchor points in the body itself? A pre-established harmony, an organic bond, a reversibility of touched/touching, an openness to the world, wild Being — all such seemingly corporeally-rooted concepts notwithstanding, is the basic and critical problem not finally the problem of a missing body? What body is it, after all, that Merleau-Ponty pinpoints when he says that "at the origin of every reflection [is] a massive presence to self" (1968:49 [asterisked note]) or when he writes of "the massive sentiment I have of the sack in which I am enclosed" (1968:134)? What is this "massive presence" and "massive sentiment"? Is either the presence or the sentiment contingent on our "having to believe" in a "language of coincidence"? Can either be said to be a matter of perceptual faith? Is it indeed perceptual faith, experiential fact, or simply experience that Merleau-Ponty invokes when he says that "at the origin of every reflection [is] a massive presence to self" or when he writes of "the massive sentiment I have of the sack in which I am enclosed"? Does "a massive presence" or "[a] massive sentiment" require a faith equal to our perceptual faith in the world? Can such "massive" evidence of ourselves possibly be naive as in a matter of faith? Or does "a massive presence to self" not testify amply to itself? And does a massive sentiment of "the sack in which I am enclosed" not do the same? If so, is there any doubt but that such testimony rests on kinesthesia and tactility? If Merleau-Ponty — and we — affirm as much, then does the fundamental proclamation that "We see the things themselves, the world is what we see" tell us the whole story, or perhaps even tell us the story from the beginning as it should be told? At the very least, does it glide over something equally fundamental? Does it omit reference to the felt body? Are we not actually at pains to find this body in the writings of Merleau-Ponty? However much "every visible is cut out in the tangible," is the tangible — and the kinesthetic — given its fundamental due? If it were — if *they* were — would we not know in telling terms where a "massive presence of self" and a "massive sentiment [of self]" come from? Would we not know in detailed *descriptive* terms how the felt body — the tactile-kinesthetic body — is the experiential locus of a "massive presence" and a "massive sentiment"?

Is there furthermore not a historical dimension to take into account with reference to both the tactile-kinesthetic and the visual? Is it not true to say — ontologically as well as epistemologically — that just as we *grow* into the bodies we are, we *grow* into our seeing the things themselves, and that even when we have so grown, we consistently continue to go beyond the things themselves, as we have consistently gone all along beyond the things themselves toward a meaning such that "seeing the things themselves" is not the whole epistemological *or* ontological story? If the aim is not to discredit "the naive evidence of the world" — "the naive evidence" being "the things themselves" as per Merleau-Ponty's definition (i.e. "We see the things themselves, the world is what we see") — but is rather to understand that evidence in terms of a *developing* openness to the world — how we come and have come "[to] see the things themselves" — then is not an ontogenetic viewpoint imperative? In other words, is what Eugen Fink calls a "constructive phenomenology" (Fink 1995:xlvii, 54–66) not imperative, and is a consistently epistemological methodology not imperative also? Is any other account of "the things themselves" not adultist and in this sense deceptively presumptuous? Is it not omitting crucial historical dimensions, telling us far less than the whole story? Is "a philosophy that is there ready-made" taking for granted a world that is *not* there ready-made — not in the sense of there not being an external world that is open and public to everyone, but in the sense of a growing ontological and epistemological structuring of that open, public world, a structuring having nothing to do with language, but with movement and touch? Are we not obliged to acknowledge and examine our *mute* post-natal introductions to being a body and learning to move ourselves, precisely in terms of a *developing* openness to the world, a *developing* capacity "[to] see the things themselves," indeed, of a *developing* "basic motor intentionality"? Is not our tactile-kinesthetic body in this sense fundamental?

8.   The unresolved tension between nature and ontology

Are Merleau-Ponty's concerns with nature topical to the point at issue, in particular, his later concerns with "The Concept of Nature" (1963: Chapters 8, 9; see also Chapter 12)? What indeed is the flesh of the world in Merleau-Ponty's ontology if it is not something *natural*? If flesh is a density of being, if it "is not matter, is not mind, is not substance," but is "a *general thing* ... that brings a style of being wherever there is a fragment of being" (1968: 139), and if it is furthermore "an 'element' of Being" (139), as Merleau-Ponty affirms, in the older sense that water, air, earth, and fire were elements, then should its very character not be coincident with nature? Is it not a *natural* element? In turn, would our *organic* bond with the world not be definitively fleshed out in terms of a *natural* bond? (Would this natural bond not in fact be the foundation of distinctive "cultural bonds"?)

In searching through the facts of nature that science offers (1963, Chapters 9, 12), does Merleau-Ponty not specifically elucidate the intimate relation of nature to ontology? Does he not examine scientific ontogenetical and embryological studies? Does he not take ethological perspectives into account? But in reviewing these studies and perspectives does he not also tether himself to the contemporary passing scene? Is his elucidation of the intimate relation of nature to ontology thus at the mercy of whatever scientific facts happen to be available — and fashionable — at the time of his writing? Can the resulting ontology possibly do justice to the foundational notion he insistently emphasizes, namely, that "*Nature ... 'is there from the first day'*" (1963: 133; italics added)?[7] Can such an ontology possibly capture the essential character of this Nature — the way(s) in which it is manifest "*from the first day*," most especially if its character is essentially dynamic rather than static? Is it possible to reconcile an ontology that favors the immediate — or vertical — over the historical — or horizontal — with a nature that has breadth in a dynamic, changing sense? May we in fact not rightfully wonder whether it is because Merleau-Ponty's aim is to capture the immediate ontological moment — "[i]t is a question of finding … the flesh of the world [in the present] … not in the past" (1968: 267) that he misses any *bona fide* ontogenetic — and evolutionary — dimensions, dimensions that his emphasis upon Nature's "[*being*] *there from the first day*" otherwise strongly suggests? Are the results of this aim as he carries it out not only adultist in the sense noted above, but are they not ahistorical as well in the sense of foregoing a *natural history*? To judge from both the narrowness of his attention to "neo-Darwinism" and the questionableness of his sweeping identification of "Darwinians" with "ultra-mechanism" (1963: 165), may we in fact not wonder whether Merleau-Ponty actually read Darwin? If he had read Darwin — *The Origin of Species, The Descent of Man and Selection in Relation to Sex, The Expression of the Emotions in Man and Animals* — would he not have ended by considering him of central interest in just the sense he considers twentieth-century biologists von Uexküll, Lorenz, and Portmann of central interest? Indeed, are the latter biologists anything but staunch "Darwinians" — and at the same time something quite other than "ultra-mechanists"? Could Merleau-Ponty fail to find in Darwin's writings empirical facts which not only firmly anchor the researches of these scientists, but which support aspects of his own ontology? For example, would he not have found the interconnectedness of life that Darwin details, to be a "scientific fact" of as much moment for his understanding of nature as Portmann's "form values" or Lorenz's "displays" (1963: 163–64)? Would he not have found in Darwin's non-hierarchical perspective upon nature firm scientific support for his claim that "one cannot conceive of the relations between species or between the species and man in terms of a hierarchy" (165)? In brief, would Darwin's empirical facts, together with his highly detailed and richly informative descriptions of animate life, not have resonated in basic ways with Merleau-Ponty's quest to found a "new ontology"?[8] In the most pointed terms, by having gone back to its source, would Merleau-Ponty not have recognized evolutionary theory in its original living contours and avoided reducing it to "selection-mutation" (as he calls it, 1963: 194)? And would he not thereby have discovered the kind of descriptive biological backdrop necessary to the "*general thing* … that brings a style of being wherever there is a fragment of being," namely, *flesh* (1968: 139)? Would he not, in short, have found *descriptive accounts of nature* — descriptive accounts of "coherent structure[s] of … being" (1963: 161) — and thereby been able to elucidate the very *nature of being* he was seeking to articulate?

In sum, rather than attempting "to arrive at [a] new ontology by following the recent development of the [scientific] notion of nature" (1963: 159), should Merleau-Ponty have gone back not only to what preceded "the recent development of the [scientific] notion of nature" but to what constituted the basis of "the recent development of the [scientific] notion of nature," and to what in truth constituted and constitutes the connecting thread of *all* biological studies since Darwin, thus back to what was, and is, at the heart of the scientific concept of nature, namely, evolutionary theory as first spelled out by Darwin in the form of a natural history, of an on-going progression of organic bonds, of an interconnectedness of life and world?

Is Merleau-Ponty's scientific naivety once again apparent, both factually, in his credulous taking as fact whatever science offers in its contemporary practice, and theoretically, in his short-sighted understanding of evolutionary biology and his consequent neglect of what is basically a historical and descriptive understanding of nature? Does this naivety block the possibility of his achieving a credible philosophy of nature and in consequence an ontology in concert with nature, an ontology in which our "pre-established harmony" with the world is transparent? Can an ontology that is in point of fact descriptively free of nature — *living nature* — be anything other than an unnatural ontology? If in Merleau-Ponty's writings there is virtually a single and passing reference to "the waves, and the forests" (1968:155)[9], if there are otherwise no trees, no canyons, no air, wind, rain, stones, crags, leaves, fruits, blossoms, grasses, squashes, seedlings, birds, worms, lizards, sheep, ants, butterflies, and so on, then can the world to which he says we are organically bonded possibly be the world we normally call "the world of nature," the *natural* world? And can the organic bond itself that purportedly ties us — and ties us foundationally — to the world possibly be a *natural* bond, much less a foundational one? Are Merleau-Ponty's world and bond not rather abstractly derived in that neither is described in terms of *natural* experience? Should an articulation of natural experience not in fact flow easily from a language that is "not a mask over Being" but a language that is grasped "with all its roots and all its foliation"? By the same token, if our organic bond with the world is indeed a natural one, should it not be articulated in terms of what is readily there for us naturally and by our very nature? Can the "psychoanalysis of Nature," which Merleau-Ponty wants to set forth and which he identifies with "Existential eternity," with "the flesh, the mother," and with an "*Urtümlich*" and an "*Ursprünglich*" that, he says — most tellingly — "is not of long ago" (1968:267), possibly ground a *bona fide* philosophy of nature, let alone secure us a viable ontology that is at one with the natural world around us? Can an organic bond or a pre-established harmony possibly be shown if, notwithstanding the affirmation "*Nature is there from the first day*," being (and/or Being) is ontologically bodied forth *deus ex machina*, as it were, in ideational psychoanalytic wrappings? If we agree with Merleau-Ponty that "[nature] is *that which makes there be*" (1963:161; italics in original) and that "the pre-existence of natural being, always already there, ... is the proper concern of the philosophy of nature" (1963:147), should we not expect "natural beingness" to be *experientially* specified, particularly when Merleau-Ponty unreservedly and categorically states (1963:152), "Whatever one's conception of philosophy, its business is to elucidate experience"?

Is the unresolved and uneasy status of science in Merleau-Ponty's philosophy — and the consistently confounding tension between fact and experience — once again apparent in the very context of his specification of the "business" of philosophy? If the relation of science to his philosophy (and the relation of fact to experience) were a settled and clarified one, why would Merleau-Ponty, in the process of his inquiry into "The Concept of Nature," declare at the beginning of his investigation of "Contemporary Science and the Signs of a New Conception of Nature" that "There is no need to justify the resort to science," and then go on immediately to state that "[the business of philosophy] is to elucidate experience, and science is a sector of our experience," thus, in effect, proceed to justify "the resort to science" (1963: 152)? In what sense is science "a sector of our *experience*," "a sector" in ways that, seemingly, nature in the flesh — trees, canyons, bees, and butterflies — is not? Does Merleau-Ponty resort to science because it is "a sector of our *experience*," or does he resort to science because certain sectors of science are concerned with the study of the living world of nature, and the relationship of that living world of nature — *precisely as it is rendered by science* — to ontology must be clarified? Does he resort to science because he wants to allow science a voice within his philosophy — because, unlike Husserl, he wants to reconcile, even theoretically join, science and philosophy — or does he resort to science because he wants to avoid resorting directly to *experience*, that is, to everyday, mundane, personal experience in a descriptive, phenomenological sense? What exactly motivates his methodology? And what exactly *is* his methodology with respect to a "resort to science"? What kind of "signs" (see Merleau-Ponty 1964f: 39–83; McCleary 1964: xix–xx) can "contemporary science" provide that might point him in the direction of a solution to the "relation between the problem of nature and the general problem of ontology" (1963: 156)? Can such "signs" properly point him toward certain ontological understandings without pointing him at the same time toward certain evolutionary and developmental ones? More precisely, can Merleau-Ponty claim that "From the interrogation of science philosophy stands to gain an encounter with certain articulations of being which otherwise it would find difficult to uncover" (1963: 152), and at the same time ignore the natural history that informs those "articulations of being"? Indeed, can "certain articulations of being" found in science be gainfully understood short of reference to the natural history in which they are embedded, a history that is, after all, a history not simply of natural beings but natural beings that are *existentially intertwined*? Is it not in default of this history that Merleau-Ponty finds it difficult to negotiate a credible and coherent passage from nature to ontology, science to philosophy, fact to experience, let alone reconcile any one of the pairs?

Is the difficulty not transparent in his declaration (1963: 161) that "Nature" is no more than "that which establishes privileged states, the 'dominant traits' (in the genetic sense of the word)"? Is this scientifically-based rendition of Nature not ultimately coincident with the very "selection-mutation" notion of evolution that he disdains? Is the difficulty not all the more transparent in his subsequent declaration that "nature is an ontological derivation, a pure 'passage', which is neither the only nor the best one possible, which stands at the horizon of our thought as a *fact* which there can be no question of deducing" (161: italics added)? Is nature an ontologically-derived fact — or is it a pre-established ontological harmony? Which end is up, so to speak? Is the difficulty moreover not singularly transparent in Merleau-Ponty's further declaration that "This *facticity* of nature is revealed to us in the universe of perception" (161; italics added)? If nature is simply "facticity," no more than an ontologically-derived fact that, perplexingly enough, seems to exist in a vacuum since a "universe of perception" notwithstanding, no direct experiential strings are attached, how can it give rise to *organic* bonds linking perceiver to perceived? That is, if nature is "*that which makes there be*, simply, and at a single stroke such a coherent structure of a being" (161), then should we not meet with the very forms that instantiate "such a coherent structure of a being"? Where *are* those everyday forms — beetles, ferns, flora, crows, and so on — not to mention humans — that articulate the organic bonds and are themselves "certain articulations of being"? Does Merleau-Ponty's resort to science awaken us to "certain articulations of being" that philosophy would otherwise "find difficult to uncover" — as his allusions to the work of von Uexküll, Lorenz, Portmann, and others clearly indicate — but at the same time relieve us from reflecting upon our own immediate experience of nature? At the very least, in addition to being given scientific facts about locusts and bees, for example (164–65), do we not need facts grounded in the living realities of life itself? In this sense, does a consideration of nature in the form of organic life and in the form of *flesh* not demand a return to experience — simple, mundane experiences such as those Sartre describes when he writes that "My shirt rubs against my skin, and I feel it," or when he writes that "What is ordinarily for me an object most remote becomes the immediately sensible; the warmth of air, the breath of the wind, the rays of sunshine, … all are present to me in a certain way … revealing my flesh by means of their flesh" (1956: 392)?

   Do such simple, mundane experiences not speak to us directly? What prevents Merleau-Ponty from letting nature speak to him in just such a manner? What prevents him from letting nature speak to him to begin with of his own nature, as in that instance when he let his wandering eyes speak to him in the midst of grief? Why does he not in fact let nature speak to him directly in the very ways that, in his later philosophy, he strives to let paintings, touching hands, the mute world, indeed, *language itself*, speak to him directly? Would such a philosophical methodology have led him, inevitably and consistently, to experience, thus from the very beginning to descriptive accounts of the spatiality of his own body and motility, to introspecting, to doing phenomenology in the sense that Sartre was doing phenomenology even as he was doing ontology in describing what he called "a *flesh* of objects" (1956: 392; italics in original)? Would such a philosophical methodology categorically prevent a resort to science, or would it be open to scientific findings? Is there any reason why, in its global purview upon and articulation of Being, a descriptive ontology that is "hyper-reflexive" in a truly experiential sense would be unable to draw upon and gain from a descriptive science, indeed, draw upon and gain in just the way Merleau-Ponty specifies in his interrogation of science on behalf of nature?

Is the unresolved tension between nature and ontology in Merleau-Ponty's philosophy thus the result both of a misunderstanding of the science of nature and of a personal distancing that prevents nature speaking to him directly? Is the unresolved tension thus in part paradigmatic of an unresolved tension in Merleau-Ponty himself, that is, an unresolved tension between a philosophic and poetic voice? When Merleau-Ponty lets "the things themselves" speak to him directly, as when, through what is surely his own experience of philosophy, he says that "Philosophy does not raise questions and does not provide answers that would little by little fill in the blanks" (1968: 105), or when, through what is surely his own experience of science, he says that "Science manipulates things and gives up living in them" (1964e: 159), or when, through what is surely his own experience of painting, he says that "The eye is an instrument that moves itself, a means which invents its own ends; it is *that which* has been moved by some impact of the world" (1964e: 165), or when, through what is surely his own experience of speech, he says that "to understand a phrase is nothing else than to fully welcome it in its sonorous being" (1968: 155), is he not speaking in a voice quite other than the one in which he speaks when he speaks as a philosopher through the data of science or through the traditions of philosophy? Is he not letting poetic speech have a voice in his philosophy? Is it not ultimately *a poetics of language* that he wants to instantiate as his ontological methodology in lieu of a straightforward phenomenology of experience? Does this poetics of language not in fact become more and more apparent in his later work where *passion* is evident, precisely as when he speaks of language, of words that the philosopher "would not assemble, that would combine through him by virtue of a natural intertwining of their meaning, through the occult trading of the metaphor — where what counts is no longer the manifest meaning of each word and of each image, but the lateral relations, the kinships that are implicated in their transfers and their exchanges" (1968: 125)? Is it not *passion* that infuses his language, as it often infuses that of a poet, when, for example, he speaks of the irreducibility of the chiasm as "an inaugural *there is*" (1968: 239), or when he does not speak but conceives himself acting as a channel such that "words ... combine through him by virtue of a natural intertwining of their meaning" and language succeeds in arresting — in capturing — a living moment? Does the character of his philosophy become charged with an urgent and involved energy that emanates from the words themselves? At this point in his philosophy, are not only "the thought" and "the vision" "structured like language," as Merleau-Ponty tells us, but does Merleau-Ponty himself, in Lacanian fashion (see Lacan 1978), become "spoken by language"? Is he not precisely its channel, its medium?

By its very nature, does a poetics of language protect Merleau-Ponty in the sense of providing him a way of being with direct experience — *being with it through language*?

Does it in truth distance him from immediate and consistent experiences of his body, since it is language that is speaking through him *of* the body, indeed, of *the* body? Does it in this sense distance him from global tactile-kinesthetic/affective reverberations, that is, distance him not from his eyes — which he cannot see, thus from the invisible — or from his hands — which he can see, thus from the visible — but from his felt living body that touches and moves as a whole as much when he *reads* as when he *runs*, and that feels hesitation or joy or disgust or confusion precisely as a *massive sentiment*, a massive sentiment that is most definitely not of "a *sack*," much less "a sack" in which an "I" is enclosed"? Is Merleau-Ponty's language — however eloquently impassioned, however richly poetic — not always one step removed from bodily experience, in that, while evoking the body, *it* does not experience it? In this sense, however impassioned and poetic, does Merleau-Ponty's language not go in front of his body in a way similar to the way in which Sartre describes the Look as going in front of the eyes: the Other's eyes remain "at a precise distance … whereas the look is upon me without distance" (1956: 258)? Does the living body in the context of Merleau-Ponty's poetic language likewise remain "at a precise distance … whereas the words are upon me without distance"? Does poetic language in this way relieve Merleau-Ponty from direct contact with experience just as his use of science relieves him of direct contact? Does he himself not say in essence that we ourselves are language when he declares that "Language is a life, is our life and the life of the things" (1968: 125), or when he explains that "because [the philosopher] has experienced within himself the need to speak, the birth of speech as bubbling up at the bottom of his mute experience, the philosopher knows better than anyone that what is lived is lived-spoken" (126), or when he claims that the ideality of meaning in language is an "ideality that is not alien to the flesh" (152) and goes on to affirm that such ideality involves "abandoning the flesh of the body for that of language" (153)? Is it not indeed language that is in the most originary sense, in Merleau-Ponty's own words (1968: 126–27), "open upon the things, called forth by the voices of silence, and continues an effort of articulation which is the Being of every being"? However renown and extolled as philosopher of the body, does Merleau-Ponty's speech not indeed go before his body?

9. Tentative conclusions

Can at least one general and one particular conclusion be reached on the basis of the foregoing inquiry? First, is it correct to conclude that an ontological poetics of language does not threaten epistemology and need not exclude epistemology, that the practice of bracketing — the basic practice of phenomenology that in general terms makes the familiar strange — can open onto an ontological as well as epistemological path, that these two paths need not be opposed and the one privileged over the other, that Merleau-Ponty is preeminently an ontologist rather than a philosopher of the body and that his philosophy is an ontological phenomenology only in the sense that its point of departure is phenomenological, i.e. it takes off from Husserlian insights and attempts to found on that already cultivated ground an existentialist philosophy, a philosophy of the living present which is "always the same" and "ever new" (1968: 267), thus a philosophy that makes foundational claims even as it tries to qualify those claims by "decentering them" (1963: 165)? Second, is it correct to conclude that Merleau-Ponty does not interrogate experience, even though he interrogates perceptual faith and perceptual faith is anchored in experience, that in turn we cannot ratify his philosophy, however much we may find ourselves in accord with it, and that in turn we cannot continue his method because no method in fact exists, even though we may attempt to emulate his hermeneutical re-interpretation of scientific data and/ or attempt to do philosophy "hyper-reflexively," by "rejoin[ing] in Being a philosophy that is there ready-made" (1968: 125)?

10. Optional epilogue

There are remarkable instances in which Merleau-Ponty's ontology resonates with themes in Paul Valéry's writings.[10] In these instances, one might even conceive Merleau-Ponty's philosophy as an ontological elaboration of Valéry's prose. Valéry's "The Problem of the Three Bodies" (in 1964c) is a striking, even classical, essay in this regard. In this essay within an essay, Valéry descriptively identifies and discusses "The Three Bodies" that commonly exist for all of us, the first being "*My Body*," before which "[n]othing moves ... unless this *My Body* traces a corresponding modification that follows or imitates the movement perceived" (1964c: 36–37); the second being the body "which others see, ... an approximation of which confronts us in the mirror or in portraits" (37); and the third being the scientific one, the one that "has unity only in our thought, since we know it only for having dissected and dismembered it" (38). He then suggests that "each of us has a *Fourth Body*." In proceeding to delineate this body, Valéry makes a number of provocative remarks. He says, for example, that "the mind's knowledge is a product of what this *Fourth Body is not*," and follows this definitive statement with the open-ended comment, "Necessarily and irrevocably *everything that is* masks for us *something that might be*... " (39). He confesses that reflection on "the notion of 'body' in general, and on my *Three Bodies*" raises "famous problems ... in the half-darkness of my thoughts," famous problems which, he says, "I ordinarily banish ... from the most sensitive and urgent point of my attention" (39–40). He enumerates some of these "famous problems" and relates them to his *Fourth Body* as follows:

> I seldom speculate on the origin of life and the species; I seldom ask myself
> whether death is a simple change of climate, costume, and habits, whether or not

the mind is a by-product of the organism; whether our acts can ever be what we call free ... and so on. It was against this background of timeworn difficulties that my absurd and luminous idea emerged: "I give the name of Fourth Body," I said to myself, "to the unknowable object, knowledge of which would solve all these problems at one stroke, for it is what they imply" (40).

He defends a reaction against his own creation, saying that.

> as a protest arose within me, the Voice of the Absurd added: "Think carefully: where do you expect to find answers to these philosophical questions [italics added]? Your images, your abstractions, derive only from the properties and experiences of your Three Bodies. But the first offers you nothing but moments; the second a few visions; and the third, at the cost of ruthless dissections and complicated preparations, a mass of figures more indecipherable than Etruscan texts. Your mind, with its language [italics added], pulverizes, mixes, and rearranges all this and from it, by the abuse, if you will, of its habitual questionnaire, evolves its notorious problems [italics added]; but it can give them a shadow of meaning only by tacitly presupposing a certain Nonexistence — of which my Fourth Body is a kind of incarnation" (40).

Does Merleau-Ponty's "body" as it is reflected throughout his philosophy — all the way from a basic motor intentionality to organic bonds, to wild Being, to flesh — not resonate in ways consistent with Valéry's *Fourth Body*? His preeminencing of language aside, does Merleau-Ponty not theoretically consider "the body" the ultimate source? Does he not consider it implied by all we are and do? Further, does it not explain everything in the way that Valéry's *Fourth Body* explains everything? At the same time, does it too not enjoy "a certain Nonexistence" — a certain Invisibility?

Consider a further resonance in a theme Merleau-Ponty himself brings to our attention in a lecture given in 1951. He quotes Valéry as follows:

> No one could think freely if his eyes could not take leave of different eyes which followed them. As soon as glances meet, we are no longer wholly two, and it is hard to remain alone. This exchange (the term is exact) realizes in a very short time a transposition or metathesis — a chiasma of two 'destinies' ...
> (Merleau-Ponty 1964g: 231; italics added).

While Valéry goes on to insist on difference in spite of conjunction — and in almost Sartrean terms, e.g. "You capture my image, my appearance; I capture yours.... What I lack is this me that you see. And what you lack is the you I see. And no matter how far we advance in our mutual understanding, as much as we reflect, so much will we be different... " (in Merleau-Ponty 1964g: 232) — Merleau-Ponty fastens on the *chiasma* itself — on the conjunction, the *exchange*, on what he comes to conceive as a fundamental intertwining of seer and seen. He thus develops the seminal notion of "a chiasma of two 'destinies'" in reverse of Valéry. All the same, the *experienced* chiasma that Valéry describes is the grounding moment that clearly seems to have spoken to Merleau-Ponty directly. The moment resonates with a quite definite sense of recognition, of a felt truth sedimented in bodily being and manifest in our intercorporeal world. Surely it is this moment grounded in visual experience that Merleau-Ponty attempts to recreate tactilely in his paradigm of touching and touched. When hand and hand, or hand and thing meet, there is an *exchange* analogous to glances meeting. Hand and hand, or hand and thing are similarly, "no longer wholly two."

A final instance may be given by drawing again on "The Problem of the Three Bodies." In this instance as in the second, Merleau-Ponty does not develop Valéry's theme theoretically along the lines in which it is originally presented. In particular, he does not carry Valéry's original prose forward ontologically, mining and elaborating it as we might see him doing with respect to Valéry's *Fourth Body*. The theme in this instance is again of experiential moment. In the context of writing of the first of "The Three Bodies" — "*My Body*" — Valéry comments that "the thing itself is formless" (1964c: 36). Though not specifying it in tactile-kinesthetic terms, there is no doubt but that "*My Body*" refers basically to the *felt* touching and moving body. "*My Body*," in other words, is not a *visual* form. This is why Valéry not only says that it is "formless," but more specifically states that "I have no idea of the spatial relations between 'My Forehead' and 'My Foot', between My Knee' and 'My Back'" (36). The odd spatiality of "*My Body*," he says, "gives rise to strange discoveries." In particular, he says that "My right hand is generally unaware of my left. To take one hand in the other is to take hold of an object that is *not-I*." Again, Valéry focuses on essential difference; Merleau-Ponty focuses on reversibility and laterality: the touched can be the touching and the touching the touched. Who, we might ask, is uttering the more fundamental ontological truth? Is Merleau-Ponty's essentially intertwined chiasma the foundational mode of our being-in-the-world, or is Valéry's chiasma of essentially distinct 'destinies' our foundational mode? How would we go about determining which is the fundamental ontological truth? What is the methodology we would use? Is the methodology "a manner of making the things themselves speak," as Merleau-Ponty affirms? But is Valéry also not linguistically attuned to the world? Is language for him too not a "language of coincidence"?

In the context of wondering about the fundamental ontological nature — and meaning — of chiasmic experience, Merleau-Ponty's study of Husserl's *Ideas II* merits brief attention. Merleau-Ponty studied *Ideas II* in manuscript form in 1939 and/or in 1947, the times at which he visited the Husserl Archives at Louvain. In *Ideas II*, Husserl describes the experience of touching and touched hands, of objects touching the body, of the body touching objects, and so on, and at some length. He does so in the process of clarifying localized feelings of touch and movement, that is, of clarifying "*sensings*" by the body of the body itself and of things in the world (Husserl 1989: 152–54 and elsewhere; complex sensings are discussed in other texts as well, e.g. Husserl 1980: 107–111.) Husserl's prose, while exacting and rigorous in its phenomenological truth to experience, is commonly considered heavy, labored, and demanding. It is of considerable interest in this regard to cite the comment of the two English translators of *Ideas II*, one of whom was present when Merleau-Ponty visited the Archives and read the manuscript. He writes: "Merleau-Ponty was a very reserved man, but one of us can remember clearly a conversation with him in which he, with sudden animation, spoke so rapturously of the second *Ideas* and described his study of it as *"une expérience presque voluptueuse"* (Husserl 1989: xvi). The description of Merleau-Ponty and his response are perhaps as perplexing as they are revealing, perplexing because Husserl's scholarly preciseness hardly seems to have rendered experience voluptuous to any of his other readers, revealing because Merleau-Ponty appears to have *experienced* bodily being through Husserl's prose. In other words, Husserl's phenomenology of the body appears to have spoken to Merleau-Ponty directly. At the very least, then, the translator's comment suggests that the paradigmatic experience — or novel experiment, or bodily memory, or "hand trick" — that undergirds Merleau-Ponty's later philosophy, that indeed constitutes what one might consider the foundation of his ontology proper, has an interesting, even fascinating personal history. Much more than this, of course, it indicates that the paradigmatic experience has a history that bridges epistemology and ontology.

Notes

1. I am paraphrasing Merleau-Ponty's remark on space (1962:243: "I catch space at its source ..."; see also 244).

2. Here again, I am applying Merleau-Ponty's remark about space to existence: "We cannot catch it [space/existence] in the ordinary run of living ..." (1962:244).

3. "The indistinction between me and the other does not inevitably reappear [in adult life] except in certain situations that for the adult are limiting situations but are quite important in his life." Merleau-Ponty focuses on love as an example, stating that "To love is inevitably to enter into an undivided situation with another" (1964d:154).

4. Merleau-Ponty also refers to introspection as "internal perception" (1962:64).

5. For a discussion of people's common reliance on introspection, see Sheets-Johnstone 1990:318–21.

6. By "as has been said," Merleau-Ponty means psychiatrist Jacques Lacan, whom he names (without explicit reference to a text) in a footnote.

7. Merleau-Ponty notes here that he is borrowing from Lucien Herr's comment upon Hegel. He uses a slightly different phrase (or translators have translated him differently),

and again puts the phrase in quotation marks in *The Visible and the Invisible*: "Nature is at the first day" (267).

8.   One may well wonder whether such an ontology would not have sizable onto-ecological significance today.

9.   It is in the context of writing of "the very voice of the things" that Merleau-Ponty speaks of "the waves, and the forests."

10.   Paul Valéry was born in 1871 and died in 1945; Merleau-Ponty lived from 1908 to 1961. Valéry and Merleau-Ponty both held appointments at the *Collège de France*, though not during the same years. That Merleau-Ponty highly esteemed Valéry is evident in his relatively frequent citations of him in his writings. Among notable examples other than those given in the present text, see his seminal use of a phrase from Valéry's *Le Cimetière Marin* — *Mes repentirs, mes doutes, mes contraintes/Sont le défaut de ton grand diamant* — at the beginning of Part Two, Chapter I of *Phenomenology of Perception*. "The flawed diamond" is in fact a strategic part of the title of a provocative book on Merleau-Ponty by Peter J. Hadreas: *In Place of the Flawed Diamond: An Investigation of Merleau-Ponty's Philosophy* (New York: Peter Lang, 1986).

CHAPTER 7

Does philosophy begin (and end) in wonder? or what is the nature of a philosophic act?

A methodological postscript*

We dismiss wonder commonly with childhood. Much later we may return. Then the whole world becomes wonderful. But, greatest wonder, our wonder soon lapses. A rainbow every morning who would pause to look at? The wonderful which comes often is soon taken for granted. That is practical enough. It allows us to get on with life. But it may stultify if it cannot on occasion be thrown off.

Sir Charles Sherrington (1953: 100)

Spirality is less conspicuous in animals than in plants... Nevertheless, there are numerous instances of spirality in animal bodies....The problem that is of interest here is why these structures [e.g. fibrils, wood cells, leaf attachments] should be arranged in a spiral *at all.*

Edmund W. Sinnott (1963: 156, 163; italics in original)

[I]n his study of shells ... [the mathematician] first noted that he could describe their general form.... Next, he saw that quite sudden — one might say unforeseen — changes occurred in the forms he was contemplating: the curves and surfaces that made it possible to represent their construction suddenly broke off or degenerated: whereas the cone, the helix, the spiral can well go on 'indefinitely', the shell suddenly wearies of following them. *But why not one turn more?*

Paul Valéry (1964b: 11; italics in original)

Why are there essents [i.e. existent things] rather than nothing?

Martin Heidegger (1961: 1)

1.   Introduction and initial gleanings

Philosopher Janice Moulton's memorable and provocative article, "A Paradigm of Philosophy: The Adversarial Method" (1983), raised critical questions about the ways in which argument and counter-argument fundamentally structure much of present-day (American) philosophy. However much the article spoke out against the limitations and biases of a one-dimensional methodology, called attention to ways in which an aggressive stance is not likely to foster wholesome outcomes, pointed out the error of mistaking the Socratic method to be an adversarial method, and singled out other liabilities as well, the article did not become a ready springboard for further and intense methodological inquiry. For whatever reasons, and in spite of its inclusion in anthologies, the article remains background food for philosophical thought. I want to acknowledge it at the very beginning of this chapter and bring it into more than an anthologized light because although it was not the point of departure for the inquiry constituting this chapter, the inquiry is integrally related to the critical questioning that Moulton articulated.

In this chapter I wonder about wonder and its centrality to a philosophic act. In particular, I wonder if American (and perhaps other) philosophers' concept of philosophy and method of doing philosophy have not progressively changed so that by now, at the tag end of a swellingly scientific and humanistically fractious one hundred years, we have a practice that simply mirrors the times. I subsidiarily wonder whether there is not an abundance of evidence to warrant my wonderings about wonder — for example, the absence of wonder in the ritualized yearly pageant of professional meetings and in the scrivenly discourses constituting the permanent legacy of American (and perhaps other) 20th-century philosophy to future generations.

In classical terms, a philosophic act *always* begins (perhaps even ends) in wonder. Aristotle said, "[I]t is owing to their wonder that men both now begin and at first began to philosophize" (*Metaphysics* 982b: 12). Plato said that "[The] sense of wonder is the mark of the philosopher" (*Theaetetus* 155). Does philosophy still begin in wonder or does it merely begin in lip service to wonder, especially in introductory philosophy courses and texts? Let me put this question on hold and consider first the fact that we read Plato and Aristotle. Why would we assiduously read these ancient Greek philosophers — or any ancient, middle age, or modern philosophers — if, precisely as an act generated in wonder, a philosophic act were not a timeless act? Why would we find what any of these philosophers said to be of moment unless what they thought of the world and of human life mattered to us, and not trivially as a bit of lore to add to our knowledge, but as offering us provocative and perspicuous insights into the nature of the world and human life? As we read any of these philosophers, we do not merely learn what they thought in the rote sense of memorizing the claims they made and the reasons for them. In learning what they thought, we wonder how it was that they came to the ideas and conclusions they did. We wonder about their wonder   what was the reason for thinking water the principal element? or air? or love and strife? Most importantly, we ourselves are moved to wonder. We take up the questions they asked, the issues they raised, the problems they encountered. In short, we ourselves become caught up in philosophy.

But still, why should we be caught up in the questionings and explorations that constitute philosophy? Why indeed — unless, quite apart from being the mark of a philosopher, wonder is a pan-human universal, and being a pan-human universal, is what makes a philosophic act a timeless act? Clearly, if we can join one another across the ages and across cultures in that enterprise called philosophy, it is because of the timeless nature of wonder in face of ourselves and of the world.

The timelessness of wonder has far-reaching significance. It explains why an individual philosophic act is potentially part of a communal task, and in turn, why a communally-practiced philosophy is possible. What a communally-practiced philosophy might be is readily adumbrated in the common sense of *labor*. Questions are not points of departure for exercises in reasoning nor are they the occasion for forensic displays. They are rather of distinctive moment in and of themselves, so much so that we feel their weight, as it were, and in turn labor to address them. Communally addressing them, we seek together to shed light. We inch our way forward. We build rather than do battle together, and in building, profit from each other's insights and errors. Being united in and by wonder, we are attuned totally to the question at issue. We are none of us at stake. The idea that in light of the timelessness of wonder, philosophy might be a communal task, invites us to think and re-think what a philosophic act is and what it might be.

The timelessness of wonder explains furthermore why philosophy is an infinite task. We pick up threads of thought and create new ones. We weave a tapestry that meshes with the past and with our own age. But wonder endures. The end of philosophy is nowhere in sight, or if sighted, signals only the end of personal wonder, which is to say, mistakes the individual tapestry one has woven to be the final one anyone can or will ever weave. On the contrary, our weavings are both alterable and interminable. We never finish wondering. We never come to the end of our questionings and explorations because we never come to the end of our ignorance. This conception of philosophy — as an infinite task — clearly calls into question the implicit pretension of much of present-day Western science to put an end to wonder, claiming as it does in one way or another that it is just a matter of time (and money) until science explains everything there is to know, in effect, that humans will be ultimately all-knowing. Philosopher Patricia Churchland and neuroscientist Terrence Sejnowski, for example, claim as much when they affirm in their book *The Computational Brain* that "it is highly improbable that emergent properties are properties that cannot be explained by low-level properties, or that [emergent properties] are in some sense irreducible, causally *sui generis*, or as philosophers are wont to say 'nomologically autonomous', meaning, roughly, 'not part of the rest of science'," and in light of this affirmation declare that "*the betting man keeps going*" (Churchland & Sejnowski 1992: 2–3; italics added). Equally, Stuart Kauffman in *The Origins of Order* states that "In our proper reductionist mode, we properly seek developmental mechanics, the unrolling machinery of genetic interactions and morphogenetic mechanisms which generate any specific ontogeny. Simultaneously, we suspect that the morphologies we see are expressions of a modest number of fundamental mechanisms each yielding a well-defined family of forms" (1993:641). The reductionist-materialist programs of such philosophers and scientists may certainly engender "a quiet passion," as Kauffman terms his own feelings vis à vis the "intellectual [reductionist] task" (1993:645). Indeed, the feelings of any lay person as well as those of any researcher may conceivably engender wonder as *mechanisms* are uncovered. But *that* wonder is not the point. The point is perhaps most explicitly and piteously exemplified by juxtaposing the notion that "endless forms most beautiful and most wonderful have been, and are being, evolved" (Darwin 1968:460) and the notion that, we humans, being "at home in the universe" and being unavoidably "playful" and "skillful," certain technico-scientific inevitabilities follow — the consequences upon "endless forms most beautiful and most wonderful" be damned:

> We stand on the verge of creating a vaster diversity of molecular forms in one place and time than ever before, we may assume, in the history of the earth, perhaps in the history of the universe. A vast wealth of new useful molecules. An unknown peril of fearful new molecules. Will we do this? Yes, of course we will. We always pursue the technologically feasible. We are, after all, both *Homo ludens* and *Homo habilis*. But can we, *Homo sapiens*, calculate the consequences? No. Never could, never will. Like the grains in the self-organized sandpile, we are carried willy-nilly by our own inventions. We stand in danger of being swept away by the small and large torrents of change we ourselves unleash (Kauffman 1995:148).

Moreover a distinction should be made. Mechanisms do not explain origins; they explain how something works. Furthermore, final causes are not efficient ones and cannot be collapsed into the latter. Sherrington captures this truth well when he writes that "We speak of nerves *for* doing this and that... Nerves seem *for* their purpose, con-structed in view of what *will* be 'wanted' of them. Before ever they function they grow where they *will* be wanted, they make the 'right' connections... Living structure is a mass of Aristotle's final causes" (1953:106–107). Sherrington in fact gives a little publi-cized example, in part quoting Sir Joseph Barcroft: "In the foetus a short channel joins the root of the lung-artery with that of the main artery of the body. Immediately fol-lowing birth the lung enters activity, and this side-tracking of its blood-supply would be disadvantageous. A little before the foetus is actually born this channel is shut by a special small muscle. This muscle 'as far as is known never used in the foetus', 'springs into action at birth' and shuts the channel. 'Having performed its function it degener-ates' and disappears, the channel having in due course become obliterated under dis-use.... It is an instance of a final cause" (1953:106). We might in light of this example question the very idea of gaining total knowledge, i.e. explaining everything in the universe, origins and final causes included — and protest "scoffingly" (see Haugeland 1985:2): Total knowledge? The very idea!

Of course, not everyone is convinced that given sufficient time and money, science will explain everything there is to know. The photograph of a Japanese macaque (*Macaca fuscata*, Plate 1) scurrying bipedally across the savannah might epitomize a skeptic's reasons for remaining unconvinced, and the bipedal macaque might itself be taken as actively protesting such *chutzpah*. In either case it is clear that although present-day Western science undeniably undercuts wonder, it cannot annihilate it short of annihilating humans, and in the process, cutting short their wonder of what a bipedal Japanese macaque, for example, might be up to.

Plate 1. *Macaca fuscata* (from *A Handbook of Living Primates*, by J.R. Napier and P.H. Napier)

I would like to give a remarkable example of the timelessness of wonder by considering two descriptions.

In a 1939 essay, Eugen Fink wrote that "Wonder dislodges man from the prejudice of everyday, publicly pregiven, traditional and worn out familiarity ... drives him from the already authorized and expressly explicated interpretation of the sense of the world and into the creative poverty of not yet knowing...." The displacing structure of wonder, Fink says, "forces man out of that fundamental way of life, one of laziness and metaphysical indolence, in which he has ceased to question. It leads him close to dread, fear, [and] horror ... as well to that great self-movement of man which Nietzsche entitled "the great longing" (1981:24).

Fink's philosophic and experience-based account of wonder as a mixture of fear and longing coincides in striking ways with that of Leonardo da Vinci, who, standing before a great cavern described his experience as follows:

> Urged on by my eagerness to see the many varied and strange forms shaped by artful nature, I wandered for some time among the shady rocks and finally came to the entrance of a great cavern. At first I stood before it dumbfounded, knowing nothing of such a thing; then I bent over with my left hand braced against my knee and my right shading my squinting, deep-searching eyes; again and again I bent over, peering here and there to discern something inside; but the all-embracing darkness revealed nothing.
>
> Standing there, I was suddenly stuck by two things, fear and longing: fear of the dark ominous cavern; longing to see if inside there was something wonderful
> (1959: 19).

Plate 2. *Papio ursinus* (from *A Handbook of Living Primates*, by J.R. Napier and P.H. Napier)

Four hundred years separate Fink and da Vinci. Their experiential descriptions nonetheless converge. Wonder is wonder, a spontaneous feeling variably weighted with fear and longing. Though the feeling may be cultivated, it is certainly not a mere social construction. It has, in fact, an indisputable evolutionary history in that the desire to explore and the fear of exploring are feelings neither unique to humans nor to primates generally. The affective infrastructure of wonder and its evolutionary character are in fact intimately related. In this respect, it will be helpful to clarify aspects of both in more detail.

To begin with, the strikingly convergent descriptive terms by which both Fink and da Vinci characterize wonder should be qualified. Neither fear nor longing are monolithic facets of the feeling of wonder. In particular, the fear aspect of wonder might be precisely specified in one situation as apprehension, in another as hesitation, in another as trepidation, in another as bewilderment, in another as timorousness, and so on; similarly, the longing aspect might be precisely described in one instance as curiosity, in another as eagerness, in another as yearning, in another as fascination, in another as attraction, and so on.

In short, fear and longing come in various affective shades. In turn, their dynamic form — the tactile-kinetic proclivities they embody — is variable. Moreover, whatever their initial shading, they can wax and wane and thus color the global feeling of wonder and its particular tactile-kinesthetic character. The variable and complex experiential infrastructure of wonder can be appreciated all the more finely by considering the context of Fink's and Da Vinci's respective descriptions. Fink speaks of wonder in a philosophical epistemological context; da Vinci speaks of wonder in an empirical epistemological context. That their descriptions should converge, given the different contexts of utterance, is strikingly powerful testimony to the universal character of wonder. At the same time, however, it is evident that a particular shade of fear and of longing is present. Fink speaks of "the displacing structure of wonder," that "drives [man] from the already authorized and expressly explicated interpretation of the sense of the world," in other words, of wonder as unsettling in rousing one from complacency and toward the unfamiliar; da Vinci speaks of wonder in terms of feelings of ominousness and of desire, feelings that are seemingly ambivalent and equipotential in drawing him at the same time toward and away from a particular feature of the world: a cavern. In reading each description, we readily sense a particular character of wonder; that is, we readily grasp the felt sense of wonder Fink describes as different from the felt sense of wonder da Vinci describes. In effect, any particular shading of fear and any particular shading of longing are contingent on the particular situation in which the global feeling of wonder arises; and one's proclivities in face of that global feeling — *ceteris paribus* — are contingent upon that same situation.

With respect to an evolutionary genealogy, one may first of all and with good reason claim that the feeling of wonder is at the very least a primate phenomenon, and this on the basis of its closeness to the feeling of curiosity, and of the clear expression of curiosity not only in many of our primate kinfolk but in mammals generally. The facing photograph of a young chacma baboon (*Papio ursinus*, Plate 2) offers ample testimony to the phenomenon of primate curiosity. It testifies amply to a feeling of wonder as well. William James's observations on curiosity are instructive in this respect. Viewing curiosity as an instinct, James writes that

> Already pretty low down among vertebrates we find that any object may excite attention, provided it be only *novel*, and that attention may be followed by approach and exploration by nostril, lips, or touch. Curiosity and fear form a couple of antagonistic emotions liable to be awakened by the same outward thing, and manifestly both useful to their possessor. The spectacle of their alternation is often amusing enough, as in the timid approaches and scared wheelings which sheep or cattle will make in the presence of some new object they are investigating. I have seen alligators in the water act in precisely the same way towards a man seated on the beach in front of them — gradually drawing near as long as he kept still, frantically careering back as soon as he made a movement. Inasmuch as new objects *may* always be advantageous, it is better than an animal should not *absolutely* fear them. But, inasmuch as they may also possibly be harmful, it is better that he should not be quite indifferent to them either, but on the whole remaining on the *qui vive*, ascertain as much about them, and what they may be likely to bring forth, as he can, before settling down to rest in their presence. Some such susceptibility for being excited and irritated by the mere novelty, as such, of any movable feature of the environment must form the instinctive basis of all human curiosity (1950: Vol. 2, 429).

What is notable from the start is that, from the viewpoint of the feelings themselves, James recognizes the same fundamental affective structures in curiosity that Fink and da Vinci do in wonder. Moreover he implicitly suggests a fundamental continuity in the evolution of wonder from curiosity even though he finds "the instinctive" aspect of curiosity no longer functional in the practice of either science or philosophy. In particular, he writes that "With what is called scientific curiosity, and with metaphysical wonder, the practical instinctive root has probably nothing to do." Although its "practical instinctive root" in curiosity may be difficult to find, scientific and philosophic wonder is not on that account unrelated to curiosity. *Qua* feelings, curiosity and wonder are clearly related. Not only is there an admixture of fear and longing in curiosity as in wonder, but the feeling of wonder *qua* feeling has, like curiosity, an evolutionary genealogy. From this evolutionary perspective, the young chacma baboon is not simply exploring something novel, and being curious in the manner James describes. Its rapt facial expression, its delicate two-hand hold of the object of its attention, and its global bodily inclination toward that object are evidence of a feeling of wonder about the novelty it has discovered and is yet in the process of discovering. Certainly wonder is as physiognomically etched in its bodily attitude as it is physiognomically etched in the bodily attitude of a human infant in face of something "wonderful" it has discovered and is in the process of exploring. Perhaps it is not too much to say that there is even a measure of awe in the young chacma's bodily bearing toward the object.

James's evolutionary views concerning curiosity were undoubtedly influenced by Darwin, who himself wrote in his usual lucid and empirically-tethered manner about curiosity even if not at length about wonder. In the context of describing the mental powers of nonhuman animals, and turning specifically "to the more intellectual emotions and faculties," he observed that

> Animals manifestly enjoy excitement and suffer from ennui, as may be seen with dogs, and, according to Regger, with monkeys. All animals feel Wonder, and many exhibit Curiosity. They sometimes suffer from this latter quality, as when the hunter plays antics and thus attracts them; I have witnessed this with deer, and so it is with the wary chamois [a small antelope], and with some kinds of wild-ducks. Brehm gives a curious account of the instinctive dread which his monkeys exhibited towards snakes; but their curiosity was so great that they could not desist from occasionally satiating their horror in a most human fashion, by lifting up the lid of the box in which the snakes were kept. I was so much surprised at his account, that I took a stuffed and coiled-up snake into the monkey-house at the Zoological Gardens, and the excitement thus caused was one of the most curious spectacles which I ever beheld. Three species of Cercopithecus [guenon monkeys] were the most alarmed; they dashed about their cages and uttered sharp signal-cries of danger, which were understood by the other monkeys. A few young monkeys and one old Anubis baboon alone took no notice of the snake. I then placed the stuffed specimen on the ground in one of the larger compartments. After a time all the monkeys collected round it in a large circle, and staring intently, presented a most ludicrous appearance. They became extremely nervous; so that when a wooden ball, with which they were familiar as a plaything, was accidently moved in the straw, under which it was partly hidden, they all instantly started away. These monkeys behaved very differently when a dead fish, a mouse, and some other new objects were placed in their cages; for though at first frightened, they soon approached, handled and examined them. I then placed a live snake in a paper bag, with the mouth loosely closed, in one of the larger compartments. One of the monkeys immediately approached, cautiously opened the bag a little, peeped in, and instantly dashed away. Then I witnessed what Brehm has described, for monkey after monkey, with head raised high and turned on one side, could not resist taking momentary peeps into the upright bag, at the dreadful object lying quiet at the bottom. It would almost appear as if monkeys had some notion of zoological affinities, for those kept by Brehm exhibited a strange, though mistaken, instinctive dread of innocent lizards and frogs. An orang, also, has been known to be much alarmed at the first sight of a turtle (1981:42–43).

There could hardly be descriptions of nonhuman animal curiosity that tie in more aptly with the affective structures described in the experientially-based accounts of wonder given by Fink and da Vinci.

A further evolutionary perspective on the genealogy of wonder is possible, a perspective some might consider more objective because it is based on artifactual evidence. When we consider our nonhuman kinfolk who, as far back as 60,000 years ago, first buried their dead, we have clear evidence of a concept of death (see Sheets-Johnstone 1990). The ancient gravesites are a testimony to the concept of death, both in terms of a thought-out belief as to what the inanimation of a once-animate form signifies and a thought-out response to that signification. Appreciated in this conceptual perspective, these ancient burial practices were the terminus of a philosophic act, one likely generated and propelled by the feeling of wonder — a fear of the unknown and a longing to make sense of it. This same feeling of wonder in varying ways informs both Western practices and attitudes toward death, and non-Western practices and belief systems that, for example, explain death as a pilgrimage or as a taking of one's place among a panoply of ancestors. The labor of digging gravesites and of specifically positioning bodies within them is a ritual that has not changed over 60,000 years. It is a philosophically-generated ritual informed by the feeling of wonder.

Clearly, the feeling of wonder knows no privileged bounds but spans evolutionary lineages and millennia as it spans generations and cultures. It is a fundamental aspect of our humanness. However much we proclaim our differences from each other in these radically headstrong and fractious postmodern times — creaturely differences as well as intra-human differences — there are ties that bind us, as much to a common evolutionary heritage and to a common world as to a common humanity.

2.   A distinction

Let me at this point differentiate between shallow wonder and deep wonder in order to delineate further dimensions of the timelessness of a philosophic act and to specify a fundamental temporal feature of wonder itself. In everyday life one wonders what to wear, if it will rain, how to fix the faucet, and so on. But there is, or can be, deep wonder in everyday life as well. Wonder in the shallow sense can in fact lead to wonder in the deep sense. When we give in to the feeling of wonder in the deep sense of opening to philosophy, the feeling does not then disappear, as if when we begin our inquiry or meditation proper, we leave wonder behind. On the contrary, wonder fuels the explorations it initiates; it fuels a philosophic act through and through. Acceding to feelings of deep wonder, we are consistently and concurrently driven "into the creative poverty of not yet knowing," and into "the great longing," which is to say, into a bona fide philosophic act. Indeed, only in holding on to wonder, thus to our creative poverty and to our great longing "to see if inside there is something wonderful," do we arrive at a philosophic act. In effect, only what is pursued as well as generated in wonder eventuates in the on-going task that is philosophy. When we let ourselves begin wondering about death or about violence, for example, we give in to our longings to understand something about human life, something we do not understand, something that begs us to pay attention to it, something with which we feel we have to come to terms, even as that something fills us in one way or another with dread or horror, thus even as we feel impelled to turn away. We do not, after all, know where our explorations will take us or what we will discover. This is as true of our wonderings about friendship and love, perception and memory, minds and bodies, as about death and dying. We stand before them too as before a great cavern. Thus, inquiries into what we take to be positive aspects of our lives are not equivalent to philosophic romps. They too partake of that deep wonder that tolerates the anxiety of ignorance as it sustains the eagerness of exploration.

Given the above distinction, one might find it understandable why bona fide philosophic acts are neither central nor common to our culture. Whether because of tossing aside initial wonder or of operating perpetually in the shallows, people easily bypass the extended motivation necessary to clarifying and to investigating, to meditating and to questioning. This essentially wonderless kind of human life may be self-chained to received wisdom, especially received wisdom's most recent scientifically-certified twentieth-century deliveries. The latter are in truth difficult to refuse. Their authority is compelling, extraordinarily compelling. That it is so helps to explain not only why philosophic acts are not central or common in our culture but why they seem to be dying out in areas of philosophy itself. The unspoken credo of 20th-century Western science being to annihilate wonder, it is no wonder that where acts of 20th-century Western philosophers are tightly tethered to science, indeed, where philosophers pursue philosophy in the guise of science or science in the guise of philosophy, ignorance is hardly professed, much less professed a value or an irremediable feature of human existence. Just as lay people can be easily captivated by mountains of authoritative information offered by various sectors of Western science — concerning their genes, their health, their food, their brains, their fitness, their children's behaviors, their own adult behaviors, and so on, seemingly ad infinitum — so also can philosophers; they too can be taken by the models and dictums of science to the point that they give up wondering in the fundamental sense exemplified and discussed above and in turn give up the possibility of engaging in a philosophic act. In such circumstances, vows of creative poverty can hardly be taken. On the contrary, allegiance is solemnly pledged both to the models Western science designates the true models of humans and world, and to the promissory notes Western science writes on its own epistemological and metaphysical behalf. The result is that the complex *experiential* realities of our everyday lives and of the everyday world are jettisoned in favor of experimental findings and laboratory statistics, computer imagings and modellings of brains, a bean-bag genetics of traits and behaviors, and so on. The result is that life, as it is actually lived, recedes into an experiential oblivion.

Now not only is the authority of scientifically-certified received wisdom extraordinarily compelling, but its findings are downright seductive. It is so easy to let someone else examine our lives for us and tell us "how we work" — how our brain functions, for example — or why we behave as we do — how a certain gene is responsible for our criminal behavior, for instance. Buying into these kinds of hard-science "how we work" scenarios, philosophers can be easily seduced into setting up shop with "how we work" scenarios of their own, producing thought experiments that presuppose facts nowhere in evidence, thus with no vital relationship to our actual experiences of ourselves or of the world. Their explorations are fueled less (if at all) by wonder than by wizardry. The hazards of following along the seductive lines of received wisdom (including recent humanistically-certified deliveries), are compounded by the fact that at a cultural level, the *eidos* of our century has been to lock ourselves in, to *fix* ourselves — in a way somewhat akin to the way people in former generations fixed themselves with their concept of predestination. Instead of fixing ourselves with religious gluon, we fix ourselves with what we conceive to be the real stuff: matter or language — *à chacun son gout*. Thus we have — or have had — conclusively predictive accounts of ourselves according to the tenets of behaviorism; ultimate explanations of ourselves in terms of genes or computer-brains; scrively- or conversationally-discursive renditions of ourselves as postmodern non-subjects; and so on. The disposition to fix ourselves with either material or linguistic gluon might be seen as a comforting move — by golly! we know who and what we are in this high-speed, quick-change, high-tech world! — but surely the move is either historically and existentially myopic, and/or it is ethically irresponsible, and/or it is epistemologically stifling. It is historically and existentially myopic if it ignores the evolutionary world and ourselves as creatures within it; it is ethically irresponsible if it conceives us to be behaviorally-perfunctory puppets dangling helplessly from genetic, cortical, or linguistic strings; and it is epistemologically stifling if it distances us from our living bodies, thus from the felt wonder that is part of our living heritage. In each case, the move disposes us to opt for fixity over wonder. We close our senses to the great caverns before us, and to the great cavern that we ourselves are. Moreover, fixing ourselves with the gluon of choice, we hardly conceive of an infinite task, much less of the possibility of taking part in it. We solidify ourselves with theories and dogmas rather than risk ourselves in "the creative poverty of not yet knowing," affirming that we are not only on the right track, but the only track, that, in effect, we have no longings for anything other than more gluon. In sum, present-day received wisdom — of whichever vintage — encourages us to turn away from wonder, from the task of philosophy.

Now of course there is wonder at the intricate workings of a brain, for example, whether those workings are disseminated as information in the popular media or as data in professional journals and at professional meetings. In other words, the information or data that twentieth-century Western science disseminates can be clearly fascinating, even awesome in the sense of stupefying us — as, for example, when we read that the brain houses billions of neurons or that "a single cubic inch of gray matter contains some 100 million cell bodies, with each connected to as many as 60,000 others" (Curtis 1975: 711). Wonder *at* a phenomenon, however — or wonder *at* a possibility, such as the possibility that we might one day introspect our brain states and speak to each other of what we experience in the way of neural firings, (see P.M. Churchland 1985) — is different from wonder in the deep sense of wonder described above. Wonder *at* something is not so much shallow as short-lived, a form of marveling in which we feel a genuine sense of amazement or astonishment in face of something we read or something we see, hear, touch, smell, or taste. Our marveling may even dissolve into a settled fact or piece of information, perhaps particularly when received theory or dogma lead the way and the initial quest has been not so much to comprehend as to fill in informational deficits in a particular epistemological jigsaw. In any case, our wonder *at* something may keep us transfixed for a short while, but we ourselves are not moved to wonder; that is, we ourselves are not impelled to explore, to investigate, to ponder. In essence, we have let someone else do the work for us and continue to let someone else do the work for us. We simply receive the results.

The feeling of wonder is in contrast time-laden. When we ourselves wonder, we give ourselves over to the feeling and sense its particular and possibly varying affective tone. In giving ourselves over in this way, we are moreover aware of the feeling that impels us to inquire, to hesitate, to probe, to vacillate, to ponder, to reflect. In a word, we live with the feeling long enough to feel its character and its demands. Genuine wonder is in this sense time-consuming and for this very reason contrary to late twentieth-century Western life. Indeed, the speed of twentieth-century Western life is not conducive to wonder. It constrains rather than liberates the feeling because only what is fast is cultivated. Coupled with the cultivation of information — gathering it and processing it — the cultivation of speed makes wonder a dispensable luxury. There is so little time, Even with everything running apace and not a minute wasted, there is so little time that one can hardly afford such an indulgence. In effect, only wonder *at* something is possible, for it commits one only momentarily. But when we do in fact wonder *at* something, we tap briefly and only at the surface of wonder. At heart, we remain wonderfully stunted because we deprive ourselves of the full feeling of wonder.

3. Freedom and risks

When we turn away from wonder, we turn away from the possibility of discovering fundamental aspects of our freedom. This is because bona fide philosophical inquiries lead us not only to what might be called professional understandings, insights into certain philosophical questions; they lead us to self-understandings — provided we are listening and realize that "Know thyself" includes wondering about thyself psychologically. Short of this wondering, we remain distant from the very inquiries we undertake. We live out a particular psycho-cultural and/or psycho-familial upbringing, unaware of how we come to have the interests and convictions we do, unaware of the source of our motivations and values, and in consequence, unaware of who we are. We practice philosophy from a distance — a safe distance. Of course, knowing thyself psychologically may be disturbing, so much so that it is what leads us to begin practicing philosophy from a distance. We become unwilling to take any personal risk because in doing so, we open ourselves to unforeseen twists and turns, to outcomes we do not remotely suspect, to feelings we did not know were there, to ideas that are unsettling to our ways of thinking and to our comfortable way of life. We choose in consequence to practice philosophy in the abstract. But where a philosophic act is only an intellectual game — or a mental fitness exercise or a necessary part of one's job — if the act is, in other words, an impersonal act, it cannot possibly be emancipatory. Where there is no felt risk, there is no personal involvement, and where there is no personal involvement, there is no freedom. A philosophic act is an emancipatory act precisely to the degree we learn something from it, which is to say, precisely to the degree that we liberate ourselves from ignorance — not only about the world, but about ourselves, as individuals and as humans, or, more specifically, as individuals and members of a particular species — as a particular *form of life*. A philosophic act potentially leads us to insights into ourselves because, to begin with, the specific questions that intrigue us — free will, solipsism, logic, mind, science, peace studies, aesthetic form, rights, language — have special meaning for us. We thus have the possibility of seeing more clearly into our own motivations and values. In this sense, we might say that in a bona fide philosophic act, the professional is personal. To win our freedom we must practice philosophy close-up.

It is apposite at this point to broach the question of wonder vis à vis actual twentieth-century American philosophic practice: does philosophy begin in wonder or does it merely begin in lip service to wonder? Let us begin answering the question by underscoring the fact that wonder is not an *act*; it is a feeling, a spontaneous affective bodily happening that is *felt*. The act itself — the philosophic act — is a thinking through, a meticulous examination of, a problem, an issue, a question, and a languaging of the results, a formal exposition — in writing or in speaking — of one's findings. But it is an act generated and fueled by wonder. The feeling is part and parcel of the active process of doing philosophy. Indeed, in any philosophic act, thinking, feeling, and doing are conjoined. The generative feeling comes on its own in response to something that we do not understand but that intrigues or awes us. We are involved in a felt bodily sense. Fink's and da Vinci's descriptions of wonder distinctly indicate as much. Can one experience "a great longing" without being a

body? Is "a great longing" experienced somewhere in mental space or is it central-
ized in the chest and diffused as a certain tension throughout the body? Can one fear
a dark cavern if one does not actually experience it as foreboding or threatening —
as "ominous" — in a bodily felt sense? (Cf. James 1950: vol. 2, 451.) Given received
philosophic and cultural wisdom which tells us that feelings are the opposite of
reason — irrational rather than rational — and given the privileged place of wonder
in Platonic and Aristotelian philosophy, one might notice an inconsistency at the
very core of Western philosophy. The point of interest here is not that early Greek
philosophers somehow missed the inconsistency; it is that the inconsistency does
not constitute a problem in present-day American philosophy. It does not constitute a problem because by ridding themselves of wonder, American philosophers rid
themselves of the inconsistency. However much introductory texts and courses in
philosophy extol the birth of philosophy in wonder, feelings are straightaway abandoned as one begins analyzing arguments and understanding philosophy as a form
of argumentation. Wonder is clear-cut from philosophic acts much as old-growth
is clear-cut from hillsides in present-day economic developments: vestiges may be
apparent here and there, but the terrain is virtually stripped. Several pressing and
inter-connected questions arise in consequence. If contemporary American philosophy is fundamentally different from earlier philosophy, how can a philosophic act be
a timeless act? On the other hand, how is it possible that questions posed twenty-five
hundred years ago are still meaningful for us today? More pointedly, if philosophy
properly begins in wonder, how can we begin by arguing for or against a certain
claim and call it philosophy? Is such an act really a philosophic act or should we
rightfully call it something else? If we answer that philosophy properly begins with
argumentation (or that philosophy proper begins with argumentation), then are we
not cutting ourselves off from the very roots of our profession? Moreover are we not
replacing them with something very like lawyer roots in that we argue for or against
something in a thoroughly impersonal manner? Like lawyers, we merely speak "on
behalf"; we argue ideas arbitrarily and for the sake of someone or something else
rather than pursue them for the sake of liberating ourselves from ignorance. Furthermore, where philosophic discourse is argumentatively conceived and structured
in terms of battle, then it is in the nature of a philosophic act to be a competitive
event rather than part of a communal venture; and the point of the act is in turn not
to delve and to understand, but to win rather than lose. George Lakoff and Mark
Johnson illustrate in their book on metaphor the militaristic descriptive language of
arguments, and incidentally and quite briefly raise the question of how an argumentative discourse structured in terms of dance might be different from an argumentative discourse structured in terms of battle (1980: 4–5). Clearly, there is neither fear
nor longing in the latter kind of philosophic discourse except the fear of losing and
the longing to come out on top.

Before pursuing this line of thought further, I should note that the above remarks concerning argumentation in no way constitute an innuendo against critical thinking. They are rather intended to call attention to the fact that there is an initial and on-going need in philosophy for wonder-thinking. Where philosophy is generated and pursued in wonder, critical thinking in fact follows naturally; that is, in following our own wonderings or the wonderings of others, we develop our abilities to reason, our capacities to perceive connections, consequences, inconsistencies, flaws, and so on. We develop our ability to tighten and strengthen our reasoning in the course of pursuing philosophy itself. In so doing, we emancipate ourselves in a further way: in addition to liberating ourselves from ignorance, we progressively free ourselves from ways or habits of thinking that are sciolistic and that lack clarity. We hone our critical skills *as philosophers*.

I would like to crystallize the foregoing wonderings about wonder by drawing out a neglected significance of the bodily engagement of a philosophic act from the feeling of wonder onward.

Though Aristotle suggests differently — when he says that philosophy is for those who are at leisure and that philosophy has no purpose other than itself (*Metaphysics* 982b: 23–28) — a philosophic act can involve taking a stand. Ancient Greek history in fact gives us an eloquent paradigm of a philosophic act that culminates in taking a stand. When Socrates drinks the hemlock, he takes the concluding step of a philosophic act. After painstaking examination of his situation, he chooses death over fleeing the country. Drinking the hemlock is paradigmatic of how a philosophic act need not be exclusively a formally written or spoken act but may be a matter of thinking through one's convictions and values and acting upon them. The act of acting upon them is coterminous with the philosophic act of thinking them through. The notion that philosophy concerns itself only with thinking rather than with thinking and doing is simply not coincident with one of the earliest and most renown events in Western philosophy. Accordingly, a philosophic act is much broader than we might be prone to think. It is not necessarily reducible to language pure and simple; it is not necessarily simply a matter of texts or conversations. It may also be a matter of praxis, praxis enlightened and motivated by insights into one's values, feelings, and beliefs. Indeed, we understand Socrates's drinking the hemlock in the fullest sense only insofar as we understand the stand Socrates was taking. To take a stand is to refuse to separate the professional and the personal. It is at the same time to refuse to separate reason and passion. In this context, it is appropriate to wonder whether one has to be a philosopher — an academically-ordained philosopher at that — to engage in a philosophic act that culminates in taking a stand. In this regard, we might ask whether Pablo Picasso's act of painting *Guernica* was not a philosophic as well as aesthetic act and whether Kurt Joos's act of choreographing *The Green Table* was not similarly a philosophic as well as aesthetic act. We understand these works of art in the fullest sense, after all, only insofar as we understand the stand they are taking — in the same sense that we understand Socrates's drinking the hemlock in the fullest sense only in understanding the stand he was taking.

Let me by way of summation specify how my wonderings would lead me to describe what it is to explore a terrain philosophically.

The ground we want to examine is under-foot: we can *feel* the ground. But if we walk across it with our shoes on, we feel it less and know it less than if we walk it with our bare feet. Walking it in our bare feet, we feel the stones, the hardness, the mud, the unevenness directly. The metaphor may be homely, but the difference between exploring a terrain in shoes and socks, and even shirt and tie, and exploring it with our bare feet is undeniable. In the latter instance, we let the terrain speak to us *directly, personally*. We do not just leave our footprints, but our feet themselves are marked by our contact with the terrain. In effect, the ground we are exploring *touches* us; nothing *professional* separates us from it. When a philosophic act engages us in this way, that is, as a personal act, then our labor on behalf of wisdom is not only a timeless act, an emancipatory act, a personal act. It is ultimately an act of passion. That the *love* of wisdom should result in a *passionate* act is not only reasonable but proper, proper in the sense of *natural*. Where there is no passion, there can in fact hardly be wisdom, for the ardent desire to know has been excised. Moreover when the ardent desire to know is excised in the name of reason, not only what issues forth is unnatural, but the very reasoning creatures themselves are unnatural. They are divorced from the very bodily experiences that would naturally generate and fuel their labor. In practicing philosophy from a distance, they miss both the creative poverty of not yet knowing and the creative labor that comes as its response. In sum, they miss participating in that timeless, passionate labor of love on behalf of wisdom that constitutes a philosophic act.

Note

* The original, longer version of this chapter was given as the invited Keynote Address at the First Annual May 4th Kent State Graduate Student Philosophy Conference titled "What Is A Philosophic Act?" in April 1994.

SECTION III

Applications

CHAPTER 8

On the significance of animate form*

When I look at a living thing, what I see and what first occupies my attention is this mass, all of a piece, which moves, bends, runs, jumps, flies, or swims; which howls, speaks, sings, performs its many acts, takes on many appearances, assumes a multiplicity of selves, wreaks its havoc, does its work, in an environment which accepts it and from which it is inseparable. This thing, with its discontinuous activity, its spontaneous movements springing suddenly from a state of immobility to which they always return is curiously contrived: we note that the visible organs of propulsion, legs, feet, wings, occupy a considerable part of the creature's total bulk; and we discover later on that the rest of its volume is made up of organs of internal work, some of whose outward effects we have witnessed.

Paul Valéry (1964c: 31)

'The patient I will show you today has almost to be carried into the rooms (sic), as he walks in a straddling fashion on the outside of his feet.... [He] sits with his eyes shut, and pays no attention to his surroundings. He does not look up even when he is spoken to, but he answers beginning in a low voice, and gradually screaming louder and louder.... At the end, he scolds in quite inarticulate sounds.'

Now it seems clear that this patient's behavior can be seen in at least two ways, analogous to the ways of seeing vase or face. One may see his behavior as 'signs' of a 'disease'; one may see his behavior as expressive of his existence. The existential-phenomenological construction is an inference about the way [he] is feeling and acting.

R. D. Laing (1963: 29–31; Laing's quote is from a case study by E. Kraepelin)

1. Introduction

Cultural anthropologist George Peter Murdock, in his well-known article "The Common Denominator of Cultures," stated that "what cultures are found to have in common is a uniform system of categories, not a fund of identical elements" (1969: 324). In *The Roots of Thinking* (Sheets-Johnstone 1990), I pointed out that if Murdock's claim is true, then there is a common *conceptual* foundation to all human thought. In other words, in the most fundamental sense human thinking is everywhere standardized on the same model; such diverse concepts as death, size, tool, cleanliness, and drawing are undergirded by a common referent.

Murdock furthermore stated that even with their theoretical differences, competent authorities agree that cultural universals exist. According to Murdock, the basis of these acknowledged universals "cannot be sought in history, or geography, or race, or any other factor limited in time or space, since the universal pattern links all known cultures, simple and complex, ancient and modern. It can only be sought, therefore, in the fundamental biological and psychological nature of man and in the universal conditions of human existence" (1969: 324). Again, in *The Roots of Thinking*, I enlarged upon Murdock's claim. I pointed out that "once a standardized model is acknowledged on the basis of the cultural facts of the matter, and once Murdock's close and accurate reasoning is similarly acknowledged concerning *where* the common denominator of cultures must rest, it is a small step to hypothesize the hominid body as model. What, after all, could be a more universal condition of human existence than animate form? On the one hand, what is more biologically fundamental than the body? On the other hand, what in the most fundamental sense is more psychologically resonant than tactile-kinesthetic experience?" (1990: 293–94).

The initial purpose of this chapter is twofold: (1) to elaborate upon the central claim engendered in the above questions through a re-framing of the questions themselves, in particular, showing that they surface in a philosophical context, transformed, but leading to the same affirmations from their new point of departure; and (2) to articulate the multi-faceted challenge those affirmations pose on behalf of recognizing and comprehending the significance of animate form. The ensuing purpose of the essay is to broaden the perspective upon animate form through critical analyses of twentieth-century Western descriptive terms that purportedly capture the significance of living bodies but that in fact, unlike the term *animate form*, fail to do justice to what is actually there, sensuously present in our experience, mire our metaphysics, and in the end blind us not simply to the recognition of cultural universals but to the possibility of their study and analysis.

2.   Framing the questions anew

We all know that there is a difference between a creature and a stone — between what is animate and what is inanimate — but we seldom ponder the difference or ask ourselves to specify concretely the complex dimensions of animate being. We tend simply to think of the animate as something living, and perhaps also, as something living that moves. Philosopher Hubert Dreyfus and anthropologist Paul Rabinow implicitly call attention to this tendency at one point in their joint book on philosopher Michel Foucault (1983). In analyzing Foucault's power-driven, power-ridden body and in trying unsuccessfully to find out just how "malleable" Foucault envisions this body, they conclude that although Foucault was aware of Merleau-Ponty's "phenomenology of the body," he probably found the "structural invariants [of that body] too general to be useful in understanding the historical specificity of body-molding techniques" (1983: 111–12). In this context, they make the interesting comment that "Reading Merleau-Ponty one would never know that the body has a front and a back and can only cope with what is in front of it, that bodies can move forward more easily than backwards, that there is normally a right/left asymmetry, and so on" (112). They note, moreover, that although "body invariants can be described with much greater specificity than Merleau-Ponty achieved," a basic question still remains; namely, "What is the historical importance of such invariant structures?" (112).

Dreyfus and Rabinow's observational comment and question are provocative. They suggest not only that we are not paying close enough attention to the body and that to do so might lead us to significant historical and pan-cultural insights. Implicit in what they write too is the idea that what we have been ignoring is something under our very noses. How have we missed that the body has a front and a back and can only cope with what is in front of it, or that bodies can move forward more easily than backwards? How have we failed to study the historical and pan-cultural importance of these "invariant structures"? Clearly, it is time for us to consider living bodies and their dispositional powers. Clearly too, it is time for us to become familiar with the evolutionary heritage of living bodies and in so doing discern the importance of their invariant structures. Clearly, it is time to consider animate form.

Let me begin with three different kinds of descriptions of animate form. (The descriptions all focus on power. They derive from research investigations for *The Roots of Power: Animate Form and Gendered Bodies* [Sheets-Johnstone 1994]. Descriptions of animate form do not necessarily focus on power, or, if they do, they do not necessarily focus on the particular kind of power exemplified here. That the following descriptions are topically convergent, however, tightens attention to their singular purpose: to exemplify animate form).

1. "There is no mistaking a dominant male macaque. These are superbly muscled monkeys. Their hair is sleek and carefully groomed, their walk calm, assured and majestic. They move in apparent disregard of the lesser monkeys who scatter at their approach. For to obstruct the path of a dominant male or even to venture, when unwelcome, too near to him is an act of defiance, and macaques learn young that such a challenge will draw a heavy punishment" (Eimerl & DeVore 1965: 109).
2. "He was an inch, perhaps two, under 6 foot, powerfully built and he advanced straight at you with a slight stoop of the shoulders, head forward, and a fixed from-under stare which made you think of a charging bull" (Conrad 1958: 1).
3. "To begin with, the soldier was someone who could be recognized from afar; he bore certain signs: the natural signs of his strength and his courage, the marks, too, of his pride; his body was the blazon of his strength and valour; and although it is true that he had to learn the profession of arms little by little … movements

like marching and attitudes like the bearing of the head belonged for the most part to a bodily rhetoric of honour; … 'The signs for recognizing those most suited to this profession are a lively, alert manner, an erect head, a taut stomach, broad shoulders, long arms, strong fingers, a small belly, thick thighs, slender legs and dry feet'.… Recruits become accustomed to 'holding their heads high and erect; to standing upright, without bending the back, to … throwing out the chest and throwing back the shoulders.… [T]hey will be taught never to fix their eyes on the ground, but to look straight at those they pass … [and] to march with a bold step, with knee and ham taut, on the points of the feet, which should face outwards'" (Foucault 1979: 135–36).

The first description is taken from a primatological study, the second from *Lord Jim* by Joseph Conrad (actually the novel's first lines), the third, from Foucault's *Discipline and Punish*. In a general sense, the different descriptions might be termed "scientific" (evolutionary) "literary" (aesthetic), and "cultural" (socio-historical).

It would be surprising if anyone were puzzled by the described bodily comportments, acts, or requirements, or failed to perceive commonalities among them in spite of the different literatures from which they derive. But precisely on these grounds, we should wonder with respect to each of the three descriptive passages, why just these bodily comportments, acts, and manners of moving and not others?; that is, why do these bodily comportments, acts, and manners of moving have the precise meaning and power they do? The passage from Foucault serves nicely to draw out the significance of the question. This is because, while both his own descriptions and the descriptions from the military manual he cites are highly detailed with respect to the bodily conformations, carriages, and acts proper to a soldier, the semantics of those conformations, carriages, and acts are taken wholly for granted. Foucault nowhere spells out why it is that the body is the site of power relations or how it is that the body is accessible to disciplinary technologies. In brief, he does not ask, Why just these bodily builds, comportments, and manners of moving? Because he is remiss, however, we should not be. We should indeed ask the question, or rather questions: Why erect heads? Why forward-looking eyes? Why broad shoulders? Why thick thighs? Why laterally-turned feet? Why bold steps? Why not sunken chests, downcast eyes, drooping mouths, medially-turned feet, and stout bellies? What is unsoldierly about such a body?

3.   The animate is not arbitrary — or the semantic specificity of living bodies

Our concept of power, like other *fundamental* human concepts, derives from animate form. Fundamental human concepts in fact derive from our primate evolutionary heritage, as do the correlatively fundamental behaviors that instantiate them, behaviors such as staring and standing erect for the purpose of intimidating or threatening others. The following description concretizes the claim in exacting terms:

> Suppose that a dominant male [baboon] is annoyed by a squabble. Its first reaction will be to stare at the offenders. The stare is long and steady, with the animal's whole attention concentrated behind it. If the stare is not enough to quell the trouble, it pulls back the skin on the top of its scalp, drawing back its ears and opening its eyes wide.... If the facial threat is still not enough to impose order, the male stands erect, with its body tensed and the fur on its mane stiffened. [The] baboon may bark, take a few steps forward, slap the ground threateningly and take a few more steps. Finally, if it still feels defied, it will give chase   (Eimerl & DeVore 1965: 109).

*The animate is thus not arbitrarily animate; on the contrary, there is a built-in seman-
tic specificity in the movement of living bodies.* The previous descriptions give clear evidence of this fact as well. It is remarkable, then, to read that "[I]n man there is no natural sign," and that "It would be legitimate to speak of 'natural signs' only if *the anatomical organization of our body* produced a correspondence between specific gestures and given 'states of mind'" (Merleau-Ponty 1962: 188–89; italics added). These statements are perplexing, all the more so coming from the pen of Merleau-Ponty. The idea aside that we experience something definitively apart from our bodies called "states of mind," surely it is evident that the anatomical organization of our body, and in fact the anatomical organization of all animate forms, produces just such a correspondence. Surely it is evident that if bodily comportments and corporeal and intercorporeal behaviors were arbitrary with respect to "states of mind," — "states of mind" meaning ostensibly moods, feelings, affective tone, and the like — we would find no primate (in some cases even mammalian) and cross-cultural commonalities in acts such as staring, advancing straight at someone, or comporting oneself in a soldierly manner. Surely it is evident that if bodily comportments and corporeal and intercorporeal behaviors were arbitrary with respect to "states of mind," there would be no common ground for inventing a social communication system, or for a social life much less a cultural tradition to take root to begin with. Surely it is evident that the same or quintessentially similar anatomies and the same or quintessentially similar physiologies cannot possibly give rise to totally different tactile-kinesthetic and affective experiences. Darwin long ago observed that "Terror acts in the same manner on [nonhuman animals] as in us, causing the muscles to tremble, the heart to palpitate, the sphincters to be relaxed, and the hair to stand on end" ([1871] 1981: 39). Certainly in terms of human societies (and in terms of some nonhuman primate societies as well: see, for example, McGrew 1992; Tomasello 1990), there are cultural differences in bodily bearings and expressions with respect to "states of mind," but this does not

make the "states of mind" arbitrary with respect to the body nor does it make the body a merely superficial phenomenon on which "states of mind" are arbitrarily inscribed, culture by culture. "States of mind" are indeed rooted in "the anatomical organization of our body." They are grounded in animate form, in our being the bodies we are. How else explain the soldierly body that Foucault describes? How else explain why a soldierly body does not have a sunken chest and stout belly? Moreover how else explain why in hearing or reading descriptions of bodily comportments and corporeal and intercorporeal behaviors, whether those offered by primatologists, novelists, or Foucault, we need no interpreter, but know immediately — in our bones — what it is to stare and be stared at, what it is to be tall or large, what it is to walk in an assured, majestic manner or with a bold step, what it is to charge like a bull. We know what it is because intuitively we know what it is to be an animate form — perhaps even more keenly given precisely those fundamental primate behavioral commonalities such as staring and standing erect, a *primate* animate form. Indeed, that we in no way doubt that primatologists, and that even lay people like ourselves, correctly understand and describe nonhuman primate behavior attests to an intuitive awareness of what it is to be a primate animate form.

(Two parenthetical comments warrant insertion at this point. The first is that, just because cultures differ linguistically is no reason to assume that they differ kinetically. On the contrary *all* humans move forward more easily than backward; *all* raise their eyebrows in surprise; *all* eat by putting food into their mouths; *all* reach for things they want and back away — or run away — from those they fear. Everything is *not* culturally relative or culturally constructed. The second comment, put in the form of a question, makes the same point but from a different perspective. How could dramatists and choreographers possibly create movements, gestures, and intercorporeal spatial relationships that we as an audience intuitively understand as having a particular qualitative character or feeling dynamic if there were no natural concordance between our own everyday movements, gestures, and intercorporeal spatial relationships and particular feelings, in other words, if there were no natural concordance between our tactile-kinesthetic and affective bodies? In finer terms, and with respect to the emergence of modern dance, was not the discovery of its early pioneers precisely the fact that everyday human feelings have a certain felt dynamic and that any particular dynamic, creatively elaborated in movement, can be immediately understood as mirroring the life of a certain feeling? Perhaps the most concise way of summing up these parenthetical comments is to say that we are all of us first and foremost *bodies*, even though we are all of us indoctrinated into thinking we are first and foremost minds (or linguistic founts), that minds have no essential relationships with bodies, and that bodies can in consequence be culturally inscribed in whatever way any particular group of minds in the form of a particular culture or society deems proper).

Now were we to begin actually fathoming what it is to be the bodies we are and how they are the foundation of "invariant structures," we would first of all attempt to make animate form explicit. We would pay attention to it and acknowledge the diversity of our experiences, personally in the form of our own bodies, conspecifically in our observations and interactions with other humans, and inter-specifically in our observations and interactions with other species. Given this empirical grounding, we could then attempt to comprehend it, study and analyze it to the end that our human form of life and the animate world of which we are a part are corporeally and intercorporeally illuminated.

From this perspective, it is of the very nature of the task to pinpoint creaturely similarities and differences, that is, to understand ourselves in the context of evolutionary continuities and discontinuities, and in the process to give historical scope to those fundamental corporeal and intercorporeal ways of being that anchor our culturally-universal humanness. This historical dimension of the task is extraordinarily similar to the historical dimension Edmund Husserl spells out with respect to a phenomenological understanding of cultural traditions: "These [cultural] forms," he says, "have arisen as such not merely casually"; they have arisen "through human activity ... even though we generally know nothing ... of the particular provenance" that brought any one of them about. "In this lack of knowledge," he says, "[is] an implicit knowledge, which can ... be made explicit, a knowledge of unassailable self-evidence. It begins with superficial commonplaces such as that everything traditional has arisen out of human activity, that accordingly past ... civilizations existed, and among them their first inventors, who shaped the new out of materials at hand ... " (1981b: 256). In short, what Husserl describes in terms of cultural traditions is in every way pertinent to those fundamental behaviors and experiences that mark us as human. They too have arisen as such not merely casually; they too have a history; that history too can be made explicit.

By opening the door to an evolutionary history, the study of animate form leads to the discovery and delineation of invariant structures that are in truth corporeal archetypes. These archetypes range all the way from "form values" — Adolph Portmann's term for morphological patternings, attributes, and conformations by which one animal recognizes another as being, for example, sexually disposed, male or female, young or mature, the alpha member of the group, and so on (1967) — to what may correlatively be termed "animate values" — postural, gestural, or otherwise kinetic patterns which articulate particular kinds of social relationships such as invitations, threats, reassurances, comfortings, and assaults, or which are affectively expressive of feelings such as fright, sadness, surprise, disgust, and so on. A number of these archetypal kinetic patterns were first described by Darwin in *The Expression of the Emotions in Man and Animals*. Moreover many archetypal bodily expressions have since been cross-culturally documented by ethologists and psychologists (for example, by Ekman 1989, 1992; Eibl-Eibesfeldt 1979). Archetypal animate values, however, pose a complex challenge for unlike form values, in the strict sense of morphology, they are (or can be) differentially modified by cultures. Because the complexity of the challenge is rooted precisely in the fact that the natural and the cultural are densely intertwined, the challenge of distinguishing what is cultural from what is evolutionarily given is substantial. To take up the challenge, however, and to meet it successfully is ultimately to map our pan-culturally invariant corporeal heritage, thereby coming to know the idiosyncratic ways in which cultures have specifically reworked that heritage — by exaggerating, suppressing, neglecting, or distorting aspects of it. In effect, to meet the challenge is to comprehend how evolutionarily given corporeal archetypes give rise to culture-spawned ones.[1]

To trace the roots of culture-spawned corporeal archetypes to their origins in evolutionary history is necessarily to call into question the highly influential philosophical legacies of both Foucault and Merleau-Ponty. In particular, it is to question both Merleau-Ponty's relativism and his allegiance to human uniqueness on the one hand, and to press Foucaultian post-structuralists for answers to fundamental questions about the body on the other. Foucault's claim that "Nothing in man — not even his body — is sufficiently stable to serve as the basis for self-recognition or for understanding other men" (1977: 153; also in Dreyfus & Rabinow 1983: 110) and Merleau-Ponty's claim that "Man is a historical idea and not a natural species" (1962: 170) are both clearly claims that deny a human evolutionary genealogy, or at most, recognize it as humanly meaningless. In default of this genealogy, however, we humans are categorically placed outside nature. In effect, nothing binds us in a common humanity. Cultural universals, if they exist, are mere flukes; there is no common ground in which they are rooted. From this critical perspective, to meet the challenge of animate values is to acknowledge and to re-instate "man's place in nature," not of course by simply assenting to the inclusion of that place as a stage within an evolutionary chronology, but rather, by recognizing that an understanding of that place is crucial to human self- and world-understandings, including the understanding of cultural universals.

A concrete if brief example of the cultural reworking of a corporeal archetype will illustrate specifically how fundamental cultural practices and beliefs derive from what is evolutionarily given, or in other terms, how animate form is indeed a semantic template, the standard upon which fundamental human concepts and comportments alike are generated. The following sketch of how the evil eye derives from staring will show how *a heightened form of power relations* derives from *the natural power of optics* that is part of our primate evolutionary heritage.

4. A sketch of the evil eye as a derived archetypal form

According to ophthalmologist Albert Potts, the evil eye is part of the World's eye; the World's eye, he says, is the way in which "all the world exclusive of scientists looks upon the eye" (1982: 79). The evil eye dates far back into antiquity — about 4500 years. It can be traced back to pre-Semitic Sumerian cuneiform texts. It can also be traced back to the Book of Proverbs in which one reads: "Eat thou not the bread of him that hath an evil eye" (Proverb 23.6). Not only is the belief old, but the idea that one can injure and even gravely harm others merely by looking at them is not peculiar to a single culture or even several cultures. It is found extensively in Indo-European and Semitic cultures. It has furthermore been studied by scholars from highly disparate fields: anthropology, religion, classics, ophthalmology, psychiatry, sociology, folklore (and now, to a limited extent, philosophy). What are the mechanics of this power? Where does it come from? No one has offered an explanation of the pre-eminent power of the eye to inflict actual harm. On the one hand, there is only the vaguest suggestion by an anthropologist, quoting a passing reference in the *Encyclopaedia of Islam*, that in spite of its being a psychological rather than sociological phenomenon, the evil eye might be connected with "the naturally injurious power of a strange and staring look" (Spooner 1976: 79). On the other hand, there is a strongly compelling beginning account that initially claims that visual behavior exists along a continuum from seeing to what we might call "evil-eyeing," the act of staring being midway on the continuum. The account, however, turns into a discussion of the "accusatory logic" by which a person attributes an accident or harmful incident to the gaze of another (Siebers 1983: 29ff.).[2] Yet that the eye has *power* is in the first place experientially evident. The eye has power to see, to apprehend, to take in an entire scene, to seize upon the finest details.[3] Moreover the eye has power *to move*. Our discovery of its power to move is part of that repertoire of "I cans" that each of us discovers and consolidates in our infancy and that grounds our sense of ourselves as autonomous agents. In other words, our eyes are at our command, albeit in a thoroughly distinctive way from torsos and heads, arms and legs. Eyes furthermore have communicative powers. A poignant and eloquent testimonial to these powers is implicit in the remark of a young autistic person, who, though lacking normal social understandings, was acutely observant: "People talk to each other with their eyes," he said; "What is it that they are saying?" (see Frith 1993: 113). With specific respect to the communicative power of eyes to control others, numerous descriptions of nonhuman primate visual behavior show clearly that by staring, one animal can convey to another that it wants the other to desist in some activity. This power of optics in human societies is no less evident, as witness not only empirical studies and reviews such as those of sociologists (e.g. Henley 1977; Lloyd & Archer 1985) and psychologists (e.g. Webbink 1986) that document staring as dominant behavior and lowering, averting, or blinking the eyes as submissive behavior, but those lucid and varied descriptions that philosopher Jean-Paul Sartre (1956) gives of the Look and that testify to the painful extremities to which being in the eyes of another can lead. Clearly, staring is a means of controlling not simply what another does but how another feels. It has an affective as well as behavioral component. At the very least it is a way of making another person feel uncomfortable. Accordingly, if one wanted to augment one's power over another person, one might do it by intensifying what one's eyes can already do. It is not a great epistemological leap at all from the knowledge that one can cause another person to feel uncomfortable by staring at them to the belief that one could, or might, inflict actual harm on them by intensifying the stare. On an experiential scale, actual harm is an intensification of acute discomfort. The perplexing question is precisely how one intensifies the power of the eye. If we are to show how an evolutionary corporeal archetype can be culturally reworked, in this instance, how it can be exaggerated, we must consider how the transition from acute discomfort to actual harm — from staring to evil-eyeing — could possibly be effected, or how, in other words, one could be led to conceive of the eye as having power at a distance, namely, the power actually to injure others without touching them.

Obviously, common experience leads us rightfully to believe that to harm someone, there must be contact. What is interesting is how a closing of the visual distance between persons draws on the very power of eyes that present-day, erudite Westerners readily acknowledge and esteem so highly: the power of eyes to shed light on the world, their power to see into the nature of things, the penetrative perspicuity of the visual sense. We praise just this power in our upright selves when we praise that "we are born to see, bound to behold" (see Straus 1970). The evil eye is a negative metaphysical reworking of this positive fundamental epistemological power of eyes to see into the nature of things; that is, the closing of the visual distance is at once a matter of corrupting the positive epistemological power of eyes to enlighten us about the world, and a matter of endowing a mere look with an intercorporeal power beyond the stare, namely, with an intercorporeal power to do evil, neither act — the corrupting or the endowing — being necessarily carried out in a conscious way at all. (I might incidentally note that the question of whether the evil eye was in fact a conscious power or not was discussed as early as the 14th century by an Arab historian. See Dundes 1981:259–60.) To begin with, one already intuitively knows the intercorporeal power of eyes to intimidate and to threaten by staring. The evil eye is an intensification of this archetypal power, even a maximization to the fullest since an evil eye can cause death. The intensification is effected by a metaphysical borrowing as it were. Not that the evil that the eye performs travels on light from the eye. Rather, evil replaces light as an *emanation*. Like light, evil is something that can *emanate* from the eye. Indeed, there is a metaphysical similarity in that, like light, evil that is cast by the eye is non-material. Its non-materiality, however, does not cancel out its reality as an *emanation*. On the contrary, it speaks all the more eloquently of the numinous power of the eye to cast something from itself, to give off effluvia of one sort or another. In describing this discharging power, Sir Francis Bacon actually spoke of the eye as *ejaculating* evil. In fact, across a diversity of cultures, the evil eye is symbolically related to the phallus.[4] This symbolic relationship, and other intra-corporeal symbolic relationships as well, are well-documented in the literature on the evil eye.[5]

So long as erudite intellectualists scoff at folk notions such as the evil eye and dismiss such everyday, pan-cultural and primatological intercorporeal behaviors as staring, just so long will they fail to distinguish culture-spawned corporeal archetypes from those that are evolutionarily given, and in effect fail to understand how fundamental cultural practices and beliefs derive from our evolutionary heritage. At a finer level, just so long will they fail to begin fathoming the bodies they are — and the bodies they are not — and thereby fail to understand how in both a phylogenetic and ontogenetic sense, thinking is fundamentally modelled on the body. Just so long too will concepts and behaviors be reduced to mere social constructions and unexamined genuflections be made to received authorities who, though never having justly examined living bodies, pronounce upon them at times as if witnesses to gospel truths. Animate form is out there in the world for anyone to see; it is neither reducible to social constructionist thought nor nullified by relativistic theses. It is what humans and nonhumans are in the deepest possible sense. It is the generative source not only of our fundamental practices and beliefs, but of our individual and species-specific "I cans," those possibilities of being and doing that Husserl called upon us to recognize and which we have yet to comprehend. As the above sketch shows, serious inquiry into the beliefs and practices of living bodies leads to deepened understandings of archetypal animate values and to deepened understandings of the complex ways in which the very form of living bodies is dynamically elaborated. It leads us to uncover corporeal archetypes and to trace the ways in which cultures and individuals work and rework them, ultimately in life-enhancing and life-destroying ways, which is to say, ultimately into complex socio-political tapestries. In a word, serious inquiry leads to a semantics of animate form.

5. The fundamental challenge of animate form and its lexical-conceptual consequence as exemplified in two critical analyses

Animate values present an even more basic challenge, one that has sizable implications for typical Western conceptual allegiances and separatist academic practices, and this because the very idea of animate values unsettles the complacent tradition of those allegiances and practices. In the most basic and at the same time broadest sense, the challenge of animate values demands a corporeal turn, in particular, a turn toward the animate. Given the earlier re-framing of the questions and given too the semantic specificity of living bodies, the import of such a turn should be evident: it is the move by which we initially make animate form explicit, that is, bring it forward into experience. It is on the basis of this initial move that we have the possibility of discovering cultural universals and their grounding in our common evolutionary history. Only by a concerted turn toward the animate do we have the possibility of elucidating the essentially corporeal terrain on which the relationship of culture to nature — and mind to body — is forged. Clearly, as with the linguistic turn earlier this century, in turning toward the animate, we turn toward something we have long taken for granted, and in so doing give living bodies — animate forms — their living due.

That a steadfast and continuing focus on the body and a correlative progressive elucidation of animate form should lead to a critical examination of the commonly-used terms by which the living body is typically identified, referred to, and/or incorporated into present-day Western philosophy, should not be surprising. When what is latent in experience is brought to light, it can disturb conventional terminologies — not to say conventional thought — and this precisely because what is brought to light is not subsumed or subsumable within the conceptual domains of those terminologies. On the contrary, what is brought to light calls those domains into question at the same time that it itself demands proper languaging, that is, a descriptive vocabulary commensurate with experience. A critical examination of conventional terminologies will show that in contrast to animate form, these terminologies do not properly describe what is actually there, sensuously present in our experience. The examination will indeed demonstrate not just the experiential inaptness of the terms but the ways in which the terms create a muddled metaphysics. The examination will in this sense show how language can — and does — deceive us, whether through our own laxity and tendency toward linguistic habituation or through the beguilements of language itself. Most importantly, the examination will show that the deception results in a disregard if not denial of pan-cultural invariants because it effectively hides from experience "the fundamental biological and psychological nature of man and ... the universal conditions of human existence" — or in short, animate form.

Two terms in particular testify to the linguistic deception: "lived body" and "embodiment" (the latter in all its linguistic variations). I begin with embodiment, or more precisely, I begin by lodging a complaint — against embodiment.

The term "embodiment" (and variations thereof) is often used to affirm the fact that we are bodies and that they count for something. We read, for example, that "My embodying organism is ... constituted as my *orientational locus in the world*" (Zaner 1981: 38); we read that there are "feminine structures of erotic embodiment" (Dallery 1989: 54); we read that "feminist embodiment resists fixation and is insatiably curious about the webs of differential positioning" (Haraway 1988: 590); we read that "the universalism of the generalized other is already schematized ... by the 'intercorporeality' of our embodiment" (Levin 1988. 334); we read of a recent interdisciplinary summer Institute titled "Embodiment: The Intersection of Nature and Culture," and find that those attending studied "the phenomenon of embodiment," and that the "Institute ... encourage[d] a multidisciplinary discussion of embodied mind" (Dreyfus & Hoy 1994). Serious examination of such affirmations and proclamations on behalf of "embodiment" shows that the term is little more than a lexical band-aid covering a three-hundred year old Western wound. In using the term, we are actually perpetuating a divide that has not healed and will never heal so long as the terms of the division remain part of our thinking. They remain part of our thinking because we have not yet fathomed what it is to be the bodies we are. The term "embodiment" testifies to just this fact. It is not an experientially apposite term; indeed, it seems in the present-day Western world to be a consumer-oriented one. Like our fast cereals and TV dinners, our organism is packaged, our minds are packaged, our gender is packaged, our selves are packaged — all thanks to the packaging magic of "embodiment." Verily, we are not making the abstract concrete, as a quality — courage, for example — is made concrete by *its* embodiment; we are making the concrete abstract, thereby hoping to make two things one, and, in particular, or so it seems, to make the thing we prize the most at home *in* this thing we call the body. The problem is that there is no recognition of animate form in this lexical exercise. There is only a vain attempt to *include* a living body in the proceedings by nodding affirmatively in its direction and duly wagging our tongues, as if by incantation we can not only properly acknowledge ourselves as living bodies but fathom their meaningfulness by using them as a cover for what we privilege and want to protect. In reality, however, we are simply covering over and per-petuating a schizoid metaphysics. In reality, we do not look around and see embodied beings or experience ourselves as embodied, unless, of course, we perceive others and experience ourselves precisely *as packaged*.

It might be noted that the term "disembodied" at least has justifiable clinical usage — as in psychiatrist R.D. Laing's work, for example — and perhaps cosmologi-cal or religious significance as well — the phenomenon of death inspires metaphysical answers in the form of spirits as well as metaphysical questions in the form of being. The term "embodied," on the other hand, while it might claim cosmological justifica-tion — some might conceive themselves as embodied in their life here on earth and disembodied thereafter — can certainly not claim clinical justification. Does a clini-cian ever describe someone as "embodied," for example, when she/he finds the person to be psychologically healthy? Even cosmologically, embodiment gives rise to meta-physical problems. This is not only because the dichotomizing Cartesian trappings of "embodiment" cannot be avoided. It is also because only when we are dead does "embodiment" purportedly provide the proper description of what it is — or was — to be alive. This manner of proceeding is akin to taking pathology as the fundamental path to truth about human life. It recalls the words of brain neuroanatomists Walle Nauta and Michael Feirtag who, in repudiating the idea that lesions provide the means of identifying normal localized brain functions, point out that, while destruction of the subthalamic nucleus "leads to the motor dysfunction known as hemiballism in which the patient uncontrollably makes motions that resemble the throwing of a ball," the normal function of the intact subthalamic nucleus is not therefore the suppression of motions resembling the throwing of a ball. "[T]he condition," they go on to affirm, "represents only the action of a central nervous system unbalanced by the absence of a subthalamic nucleus" (Nauta & Feirtag 1979: 88).

Clearly, we must not confuse either normal or pathological disintegration (especially experimental pathological disintegration) with phenomenological analysis; that is, we must not take the description of what is there when something dies or falls apart as the basis for a description of the intact experiential structure itself. This is to fall into errors akin to the error of Merleau-Ponty when he tries "to catch space at its source" (1962: 243ff.); he finds "space at its source" in George Stratton's experimental studies of inverted vision. To unmuddle our thinking, we must go back to everyday human experience. Thus, with respect to embodiment, we must ask ourselves not only *what* it is that is embodied and challenge ourselves to describe it, but ask ourselves *how* it is embodied and challenge ourselves to describe in experiential terms just how the *what* we believe to be embodied — a mind, a soul, a spirit, a self, our organism, or whatever — is embodied by the body.

Alternatively, we need to ask ourselves what it is we actually *do* perceive, not just visually in the form of other bodies, but kinesthetically and tactilely in the form of our own body. Animate form, after all, describes not just what is out there in the world for all to see; it describes what we ourselves are. In one of the simplest of senses, this truth translates into the seeming experiential banality that in moving, we change our felt shape and in changing our felt shape, we move. What could be more obvious than *our own animate form*? But what at the same time could be more overlooked? — perhaps especially by sophisticated "embodied" adults who have long since forgotten the corporeal epiphanies of their childhood and who are dumb to recite those most basic learnings of their infancy to which they are all beholden. Embodiment fails to do justice to animate form; it fails to recognize the primacy of movement and its dynamic tactile-kinesthetic-kinetic correlates. When we have recourse to "embodiment," we avoid coming to terms with bodies, with what is actually there, sensuously present in our experience, precisely as with the experience of moving and changing shape — or with the experience of a front and a back and of moving more easily forward than backward.

We should note that use of the term "animate form" is not an attempt to side-step the classical mind/body split or to redress the wrongs of a descriptively disfiguring dualism in the manner of the term "embodiment." It is rather an attempt to describe precisely what we experience, to pinpoint the way in which we actually perceive and understand ourselves and one another, in fact, the way in which we perceive and understand *all* living creatures, human and nonhuman, and this in order that we might gain insight into the ties that bind all humans in a common humanity and a common humanity in a common creaturehood. It is of considerable interest in this regard to recall that animate form is what Husserl consistently if implicitly recognizes in speaking of "animate organisms" and "psychophysical organisms." In other words, in attempting to elucidate the essential nature of animal nature, he consistently emphasizes its *animation* (see especially Husserl 1989). He consistently describes humans and nonhumans as "animated," and even describes works of art as "animated," a description that ties in significantly with the familiar notion of art as *organic* form. Correspondingly, in fact, "form" in the phrase "animate form" has aesthetic overtones. Animate *forms* have an aesthetic dimension in the sense that their physiognomic presence — their qualitative character — rather than, for example, their utility or their mere recognition, is what is of immediate moment in experience. Indeed, mere recognition presupposes physiognomic awarenesses without which there could be no recognition of any kind; similarly, concern merely with a (human or nonhuman) creature's utility demands prior cognizance of its particular bearing and attitude, its particular orientation and comportment, short of which utilization to any end would be impossible since one could hardly get a handle — figuratively or literally — on the creature to begin with. Though we might rarely make this physiognomic dimension explicit, it is there in our experience. When we read about a creature who stares at a social offender, for instance, and finding staring insufficient, "pulls back the skin on the top of its scalp, drawing back its ears, and opening its eyes wide," we intuitively understand the escalated proceedings; when an individual larger than we are advances directly at us, we intuitively understand the possibility of assault; when we see a human or nonhuman creature lower itself before another, we intuitively know it to be deferring in some way to the other. We intuitively understand in each case because animate forms are indeed animate — they present ever-changing physiognomies — and physiognomic perception is fundamental to our way of relating to the dynamic world of animate forms. Physiognomic perception is furthermore fundamental to the way in which we relate to the changing countenances of the world itself: its brightness, coldness, darkness, warmth, texture, sounds, and so on. (See Stern 1985, 1990 on physiognomic perception; see also Meltzoff, e.g. 1981, which implicitly shows imitation to be physiognomic).

It is apposite to point out in this context that words uttered in conversation can often if not typically block our awareness of animate form, and this because they block physiognomic perception. The words we utter tend to go in front of us, as it were, and correlatively, we hang our attention on the words that are there in front of the person speaking to us.[6] When, by a shift of attention, we disregard the sounds (in a manner akin to flicking off the TV sound control or plugging our ears), animate form immediately surfaces. Similarly, if something unfamiliar or unexpected intrudes upon the flow of words we or others are uttering — a twitch in the cheek, for example, a fluttering of the eyes or a trembling of hands — animate form precisely calls attention to itself, momentarily muffling the words. In such situations immediate awareness is deflected away from the linguistic and toward the physiognomic features of experience.

When we open ourselves directly and deliberately to animate form by way of a corporeal turn, we find the term "lived body" as experientially wanting as the term "embodiment." This is not to deny the enormous contribution the term "lived body" made to redressing on the one hand, a belittling, even opprobrious, view of the body traceable all the way back to Plato as well as to Descartes, and on the other hand, a scientific view of the body as a strictly material entity. The intent here is only to question the term's experiential precision and descriptive aptness and in so doing suggest reasons for considering a change in terminology. In a very general sense, the reasons may be reduced to five observations:

1. The phrase "the lived body" identifies one body, but only in contrast to another body, i.e. the "lived" as opposed to the merely "physical," "objective," or "seen" body;
2. The phrase "the lived body" thus sets up and perpetuates a dichotomy, and it is only on the basis of this dichotomy that the phrase is meaningful;
3. The phrase "the lived body," though attempting to pinpoint an experiencing body, has no historical, social, or ecological reference; it thereby appears solipsistically-oriented, i.e. each of us has his/her own "lived body," but there is no basis for making any connections among them, whether historical, social, or ecological;
4. The phrase "the lived body" appears to identify a passive body, i.e. something lives the lived body;
5. The phrase "the lived body" thus again sets up and perpetuates a dichotomy.

(Before proceeding, a parenthetical comment is warranted with respect to the fourth observation. The comment is best introduced by way of the question, what is it that lives the lived body? Sartre [1956], for example, tells us that consciousness lives the body as the contingency of its being. But we might note that the question, what is it that lives the lived body?, is like the question, what is it that the body embodies? Accordingly, we might surmise that, after all, in each case it is just a matter of a grammatical snare. In view of the previous discussions, however, we have reason to question that judgment. Indeed, in each case we can see that there is not a grammatical snare but a conceptual flaw; the terminologies do not accurately describe what is there, sensuously present in our experience, neither our experience of ourselves nor our experience of others, whether other humans or other species. Sartre's body that is lived by consciousness, for example, is a Cartesian specimen that is belied by Sartre's own perspicuously faithful descriptions of bodily life. One can be a dualist — a Cartesian in the sense of recognizing meaning [or more generally, consciousness or mind] as a non-material aspect of experience — and not demote the body in the process. On the contrary, one can show how the body is in the most fundamental sense at the very origin of meaning, at the very origin of meaning because it is in the most fundamental sense at the origin of thinking [see Sheets-Johnstone 1990]).

The five observations testify to a body that in one way and another does not properly coincide with a living body as it is actually experienced. Sartre's (1956) identification of a lived body in contrast to a physical body and Merleau-Ponty's (1962) identification of a lived body in contrast to an objective body testify not to what is sensuously present in experience, but to something each philosopher is trying to set off in a conceptually distinctive manner. Because precision matters in descriptive accounts of experience, however, terminology matters. "Lived body" jibes with experience only insofar as it obliquely specifies an individual body; you have yours and I have mine, but that is all. From this perspective, the problem in the first as in the last analysis is that our individual bodies exist in a formless, static vacuum. Granted no one can experience my bodily experiences, still, my body to begin with is not an anomaly. My creaturely form is not unique. *My altogether human form is indeed a cultural universal.* Second, when the body I alone experience is descriptively, thus conceptually, set over and against another kind of body, a phenomenological understanding of bodies — thus a *pan-cultural* understanding of bodies — is fundamentally and ironically compromised since that other kind of body — that so-called physical thing — is an intimate dimension of myself, in fact, one apart from which I would not be the body I am and in turn not have the experiences I have. Third, when the body I alone experience is passively defined — it is "lived" — my bodily experience and my experience of other bodies (nonhuman as well as human) tend toward thinghood. My body and the bodies of others are conceived sites of happenings rather than dynamically moving forms. Living bodies — human and nonhuman — are indeed normally experienced not as sites of happenings but as forms of agency, that is, as animate forms. Insofar as what is experientially true of creatures generally and of humans in particular (and in effect, what is a pan-hominid attribute) is neglected, a phenomenological understanding of bodies is again compromised. Finally, a formless, static vacuum is apparent in the fact that a "lived body" must be granted an environment, including not only a surround of other like and unlike "lived bodies," and a surround that has a particular historical context with respect to the unfolding of its own life and the lives of others as well, but an actual ground upon which it, like other "lived bodies," walks, takes its bearings, and moves about. In short, a "lived body" does not in and of itself imply a spatio-temporal world; it does not in and of itself imply a historical, social, or ecological situation, nor, in consequence, does it in any way imply those ties that bind us in a common humanity, in a larger common creaturehood, and to a common global earth. On the contrary, we have explicitly to *situate* a lived body, to *position* it, and even then, we are dumb to find in it any conceptual threads which might imply a surrounding creaturely world.

This balky, carping, perhaps to some, even mammoth, claim demands justification in further detail.

We watch a spider crawling or spinning its web; we watch a gull digging in the sand; we watch lionesses hunting; we watch ants crawling in a file; we watch someone walking toward us. In each case, we apprehend animate form. We apprehend a certain kind of livability in the world: a living creature that has a certain way of relating to what is immediately present, a certain way of moving and being still, a certain way of perceiving the world that is made evident by its actions and stillnesses. In brief, we apprehend a living creature whose kinetic articulations and silences give way to particular spatial orientations, bodily contours, energies, centers of interest, and so on.

"Lived body" does not capture this *living* dimension of other creatures. It does not even capture this living dimension of oneself. An adjective attached to what is basically conceptualized as a *thing* does not a living form make. The division between a physical body and a lived body, while certainly appropriate within the context of some of Sartre's descriptive accounts both of the Other and of bad faith (e.g. his famous waiter; 1956:59), and while capturing too the ethos of Western medicine and Western sexist practices, does not fundamentally describe the bodies we are. Living forms are first and foremost existentially fit (Sheets-Johnstone 1986a). Physical and lived bodies are quintessentially coherent. They define precisely a certain livability in the world. They describe creatures who make their distinctive ways in the world by being the bodies they are. In other words, "hands and a big brain would not have made a fish human; they would only have made a fish impossible" (Howells 1959:341).

Clearly, the phrase "the lived body," while attempting to reclaim living aspects of the body from relentless reductions by Western science and while resurrecting the body from centuries-old Western cultural devaluations, elevates the body to a place of prominence at the cost of misrepresenting it. A closer look at the concept of existential fit and its relevance to a critique of the lived body will in turn more closely pinpoint the source of the terminological inaptness.[7]

While in existential studies, the physical and lived bodies are consistently described as oppositional, no creature in the world is a physical specimen upon which a certain mode of living is grafted, and neither is it a certain mode of living upon which a certain enabling physicality is grafted. From what point of view, then, is the opposition discovered and conceptualized? It is not the definitive conclusion of a phenomenology of the body, an insight discovered through a thoroughgoing, foundational description of human bodily life. It is discovered in the analysis of certain bodily experiences tempered by two already drawn dichotomies: that of the self and the social (or the private and the public), as in Sartre's "my body for me and my body for others," and especially that of the existential and the scientific, as in the writings of Merleau-Ponty and other existential philosophers. In brief, it is a description and conception of the body that is rooted in certain views and/or practices common to the Western world. From this perspective it is a preeminently *cultural* conception of bodily being; that is, it is through and through a culturally relative conception. To balance the corporeal scale in the direction of cultural universals, one needs to dig below the surface of the cultural and consider the phenomenon of bodily being from a more basic perspective, a perspective in which the fundamental life theme of existential fit is everywhere apparent. A fish, for example, is a creature which lives the life of a fish. That a fish is a creature which lives the life of a fish is rooted not in causally or teleologically reductive accounts of behavior but in the quintessential coherency of "physical" and "lived" bodies — in existential fit. What is existentially fit is existentially viable. An intact readiness exists to take up the living of a life. A particular subject is not merely alive in the world but livable. Moreover not only a particular subject is livable but a particular *kind* of subject is livable. While individual livability has its origin in existential fit, so *kinds* of livability have their origin in its differential expression. Hence what is necessary is an understanding of sensory-kinetic domains. In other words, any particular domain of "I cans" (Husserl 1989, 1970, 1980) is the differential expression of existential fit.

In *The Structure of Behavior* (1967 [1942]), Merleau-Ponty speaks of a species as elaborating stimuli in a manner "which is proper to it" (129); he speaks of stimuli intervening "according to what they signify and what they are worth for the typical activity of the species considered" (130); he speaks of situation and reaction participating "in a structure in which the mode of activity proper to the organism is expressed" (130); he speaks of "the conditions of life … [being] defined by the proper essence of the species" (174). What is this *propriety*, this appositeness without which forms of life in both an existential and evolutionary sense would not be possible? What is this *propriety* which is acknowledged but passed over in silence? This a priori manner of elaborating a stimulus, this mode of activity proper to the organism, this stimulus intervening according to what it signifies and what it is worth for the typical activities of the species considered — all these proprieties are in truth testimonials to existential fit, to the differential expression of animate form. The character of being proper to a certain species, the character of species themselves in terms of proper essences, both are an affirmation of a quintessential coherency of "physical" and "lived" bodies. The "physical" and the "lived" are not two distinct developmental forms meeting and happening in the same creature. What exists and evolves are not parts but wholes, not fragments of life, but life itself. What is "lived," then, in an existential-evolutionary sense is more properly described as different sensory-kinetic worlds: these fins, these eyes, this fur, these wings, these ears, these arms, these legs, and so on, are a certain opening onto the world; they bespeak certain sensory-kinetic powers and sensitivities, a certain kind of livability in the world, a certain domain of "I cans," a certain *propriety* of being — in a word, *a certain animate form.*

Unlike "lived body," *animate form* situates us directly in the context of a natural history, a natural history from which we have not escaped through some kind of sleight-of-culture but of which we are irrevocably a part. "Lived body," by isolating us from our natural history, by purportedly describing what it is to be human but not acknowledging our experienced social, historical, and ecological kinships, opens the door to social constructivist thought at the same time that it blinds us to its deficiencies. Living bodies are in consequence easily conceived to be through and through mere surfaces for cultural inscriptions, hardly the stuff of which universals are made. If we ask of what such bodies are constructed, we could only be told that they are constructed of sheer physiology and sheer mechanisms, which is to say sheer body-denigrating Cartesianism and Western scientific reductionism. To insist that bodies are just such pure social constructions, sex too being a social construction on the basis of genetic genitalic anomalies, is in truth to insist that something like pentadactylism is a social construct. If biologically anomalous bodies — what were formerly called "sports," creatures falling short of normal or typical animate form by way of biological anomalies of some kind or another — are taken as evidence of the falsity of biological classifications, then of course nothing is left but to regard *all* corporeal characters by which biological classifications are normally made as socially determined. In effect, there are no "sports" because there is no corporeal standard for any creature, perhaps in the end, no standard for creaturehood itself. In the words of a character in a William Saroyan play (1960), "There is no foundation all the way down the line."[8]

Clearly, this line of reasoning is erroneous. With respect to pentadactylism, for example, a sport might have three fingers or a missing thumb, but whatever the pentadactyl anomaly, the creature does not thereby invalidate the classification "pentadactyl" — any more than it invalidates its classification "vertebrate," "primate," "chimpanzee" or "human." Moreover though evolutionary gradualism and even punctualism obviously engender the idea of ongoing multitudinous variations leading to new species and are thus anchored in the idea of incessant change rather than in the idea of eternal forms, neither gradualism nor punctualism denies species as a readily experienced and readily identifiable group of creatures. In effect, neither mutability nor anomalies invalidate biological classifications. The foundation of cultural universals in animate form can in turn not be denied.

In sum, we need to take seriously the fact that a human body has a front and a back, that it moves more easily forward than backward, that it has five fingers on each hand, that it closes its eyes to sleep, that it spontaneously smiles when just a few weeks old, that it spontaneously stands and moves on its own, that it babbles, cries, sings, and speaks, that it gestures, crouches, cringes, leaps, and dances. The term "animate form" adumbrates these corporeal matters of fact and possibilities. The task in mapping cultural universals is to be true to these facts and possibilities — these truths of human experience — and in so doing arrive at understandings of the origin of our culturally diverse conceptual and comportmental histories. Insofar as animate forms are central to our experience, they constitute the central strand of our understandings, which is to say that animate forms are intending and knowing subjects. They are creatures caught up in making their way in an ever-changing world. They are creatures whose bodily logos endows them with a capacity for survival, but a capacity that is always at the mercy of *circonstances*, as Lamarck modestly termed what we now know to be the fragility of ecological balances and relationships. To the degree we lose touch with that central strand of our understandings, we lose sight of ourselves and others — other humans *and* other species — as Darwinian bodies, bodies that are products of a natural history, integrated wholes, whose mental powers and emotional expressions evolved no less than their physiologies and anatomies.[9] Correlatively, we lose sight of the possibility of understanding how our Darwinian bodies are as much the foundation of a common humanity as they are the foundation of multiple and diverse cultural practices and beliefs. In a broader and equally significant sense, we correlatively lose touch with history, that larger, natural history not only of which we are irrevocably a part, but a history the recognition of which is integral to the very future of this planet.

Notes

* This chapter appeared originally in *Analecta Husserliana* Vol. LV (Sheets-Johnstone 1997). Shorter versions were presented as guest lectures at the University of Oregon and Duquesne University in 1994 and at the University of Arhus (Denmark) in 1996.

1. For a detailed theoretical account of the relationship between the natural (or evolutionarily given) and the cultural as well as detailed analyses of corporeal archetypes and their cultural reworkings with respect to power, see Sheets-Johnstone 1994a. (Note: The example of the evil eye, which follows in this text, first appeared in Sheets-Johnstone 1994b.).

2. Siebers's book is, in fact, an attempt to understand the evil eye from the viewpoint of the *doer*, not the recipient, of the evil eye. As Siebers points out in the preface, "Although many studies of the evil eye exist, not one of them includes the perspective of the accused fascinator" (1983:xii).

3. In this context we might recall the poet Giacomo da Lentino's wonder with respect to an adored woman: "How can it be that so large a woman has been able to penetrate my eyes, which are so small, and then enter my heart and my brain?" See Couliano 1987:22.

4. Freud remarked on the relationship saying that there is a "substitutive relation between the eye and the male member which is seen to exist in dreams and phantasies" (Freud 1959:383–84). Obviously the Oedipal complex as first formulated by Freud is a testimonial to the relationship.

5. It is notable — and ironic — that Lacan speaks of the evil eye as "that which has the effect of arresting movement, and, literally, of killing life" (Lacan 1978:118), or in other words that in describing the "anti-life, anti-movement function" of the evil eye (118), Lacan equates *movement* — not the unconscious, not language, not the Other — with *life*. However fundamental the equation, and however natural and spontaneous its recognition, the equation and its components are hardly constituents — seminal or otherwise — of Lacan's psychoanalytic (see Sheets-Johnstone 1994 for a psychoanalytic analysis of Lacan's psychoanalytic).

6. There is a similarity between words going in front of physiognomies and *The Look*, as Sartre describes it, going in front of the eyes. "The Other's look," Sartre writes, "hides his eyes; he seems to go *in front of them*. This illusion stems from the fact that eyes as objects of my

perception remain at a precise distance which unfolds from me to them … whereas the look is upon me without distance" (Sartre 1956:258). The same can be said of words in everyday conversation.

7.   The exposition of existential fit is taken from Sheets-Johnstone 1986a.

8.   Saroyan's *The Time of Your Life*. The words are uttered several times over in the course of the play by an otherwise near-mute character. Philosophically speaking, the phrase could, of course, be uttered with equal conviction by a foundationalist to a relativist or by a relativist to a foundationalist.

9.   As I pointed out in Sheets-Johnstone 1992b and 1996a, Darwin's thesis concerning the evolution of mental powers and emotions has never been disproved; it has only been ignored. See Darwin 1981 [1871] and 1965 [1872]; see also Sheets-Johnstone 1990 for more on Darwinian bodies.

CHAPTER 9

Human speech perception and an evolutionary semantics*

> I listen to two people speaking in a language which is unknown to me. Do I therefore hear them talk?
>
> Henri Bergson (1991:109)

> Linguistic conventions and standard forms do not leap full grown from the egg.
>
> Jerome Bruner (1983:69)

> Let us … consider again *spiritual living beings,* those beings animated in a special sense, i.e. human beings (but of course all animals are included)…. [T]he apprehension of that person there, who dances, laughs when amused, and chatters, or who discusses something with me in science, etc., is not the apprehension of a spirit fastened to a Body…. [I]n his movements, in his action, in his speaking and writing, etc., [the person] is not a mere connection or linking up of one thing, called a soul, with another thing, the Body. The Body is, as Body, filled with the soul through and through. Each movement of the Body is full of soul, the coming and going, the standing and sitting, the walking and dancing, etc. Likewise, so is every human performance, every human production.
>
> Edmund Husserl (1989:251–52)

1. The motor theory of speech perception

If asked what we perceive when we perceive speech, we would likely say that we perceive the sounds made by the speaker, not the articulatory gestures the speaker makes in producing the sound. As psychologists Alvin M. Liberman and Ignatius Mattingly note (1985:3), "Surely it is these [acoustic] signals, not the gestures, which stimulate the listener's ear." Yet in more than forty years of speech research, and in collating his findings with a broad spectrum of related research, Liberman and his various associates have vindicated the motor theory of speech perception. They have shown in a quite conclusive way that, as he and Mattingly say (1985:25), "the object of perception is motoric." This means that understanding what another person is saying is contingent upon one's somehow sensing the articulatory gestures producing the sounds the person utters: "To perceive an utterance … is to perceive a specific pattern of intended gestures" (3). Liberman and Mattingly use the word 'intended' "because … the gestures are not directly manifested in the acoustic signal or in the observable articulatory movements" (3). Speech perception is thus not a matter of lip-reading, for example, any more than it is a matter of word-reading: "the perceived event is neither [visual nor auditory]; it is, rather, a gesture" (17).

The major reason that the gestures are not directly manifested, either acoustically or visually, is that they are co-articulated, any particular sound — an *a* sound, for example — being gesturally influenced by sounds that immediately precede and follow it — a *k* sound, for example, or a *b* sound. Because gestures are co-articulated, the relationship between sound and gesture is not simple — a particular gesture being coincident with a particular sound — and speech is not a succession of one discrete phoneme after the next. As Liberman and Mattingly point out (1985:3), if a simple relationship obtained between sound and gesture, "it would matter little whether the listener was said to perceive the one or the other." On the other hand, if speech were nothing but the production of single phonemes, speakers "could speak only as fast as they could spell" (13). What Liberman and colleagues have found over the many years of their research is that gestures producing phonemes are co-articulated in complex ways such that speech perception cannot be explained by general auditory principles.

It is of particular interest to note that originally, Liberman and those working with him emphasized covert mimicry as the source of a listener's understanding of another's speech. In other words, speech perception was linked to speech production by way of covert or internal imitation. Although not explained as such, covert imitation would have to have been conceived as being thoroughly spontaneous and thoroughly informative of the sensory feel of the gestures since, as Liberman then maintained, "perceiving the gesture was a matter of picking up the sensory consequences of covert mimicry" (Liberman & Mattingly 1985:23). Correction of this behaviorist model of speech perception involved new research findings, a disavowal of traditional behaviorist interpretations, subsequent adoption of a different explanatory paradigm, and utilization of related research data showing, for example, that people who lack control of their articulatory organs since birth are still capable of perceiving speech, and that infants, who of course do not speak, can nevertheless categorize phonetic differences just as speaking adults do.

Not surprisingly, Liberman and colleagues' new explanatory paradigm is a cognitivist-computational one: speech signals are "computed by an analogue of the production process — an internal, innately specified vocal-tract synthesizer … that incorporates complete information about the anatomical and physiological characteristics of the vocal tract and also about the articulatory and acoustic consequences of linguistically significant gestures" (Liberman & Mattingly 1985:26). In short, a "language module" in the brain decodes the speaker's speech and in fact distinguishes linguistically significant gestures from non-linguistically significant ones.

It is of further theoretical interest to note that in this new explanatory paradigm, Liberman recognizes the necessity of invariant gestures. As he and Mattingly point out (1985: 3), there must be "invariant gestures of some description … for they are required, not merely for our particular theory of speech perception, but for *any* adequate theory of speech production." On the motor theory account, speech production and speech perception "share the same set of invariants" (3), namely, gestural constants coincide with the anatomical and physiological characteristics of the vocal tract. These invariants are of course part of the fund of information incorporated by the "internal, innately specified vocal-tract synthesizer." Although showing that gestural invariants are topologically distinct, that "instances of a particular gesture always have certain topological properties not shared by any other gesture," Liberman and colleagues emphatically argue that the characteristic invariant properties "must be seen … not as peripheral movements [that is, *not as the actual gestures the speaker makes*], but as *the more remote structures that control the movements*" (Liberman & Mattingly 1985: 22, 23; italics added). In other words, invariant properties are attached not to the gestures themselves but to neurological happenings in a brain. Indeed, Liberman and Mattingly state that "These [brain] structures correspond to the speaker's intentions" (23).

The motor theory of speech perception thus comes full-circle: gestural invariants are not real-life gestural events but structural components of a "vocal-tract synthesizer" in the brain that specifies anatomical and physiological properties of speech and distinguishes linguistically significant gestures from non-linguistically significant gestures. Speech perception is a matter of the synthesizer's matching its structural components to a speaker's intentions. Thus, on the one hand, while you may think that *you* are perceiving the speech of another — that *you* are understanding what the other is saying — it is really your vocal-tract synthesizer that is taking it all in. On the other hand, since it is your vocal-tract synthesizer that is producing your own speech, there appears to be nothing particularly *motoric* at all about it, any more than there is anything particularly motoric at all about your perceiving the speech of another. Your articulatory gestures are for you as for the other nothing more than on-going synthesizing events in your respective brains. Articulatory gestures that are purportedly the very source of speech production and speech perception are thus reduced to a hard-working but thoroughly hypothetical entity — a synthesizer — which, given its formidable experiences, knowledge, and tasks, appears more and more to resemble a homunculus in a brain.

2. Expanding upon the critique

Three major research findings anchor Liberman's motor theory of perception: (1) speech perception is a gestural event; (2) it does not hinge on imitation; (3) it is founded on invariants. When these three major findings are corporeally interpreted, rather than interpreted in cognitivist-computational terms, the motor theory of speech perception turns out to be a clear acknowledgment of tactile-kinesthetic invariants and analogical apperception. This is first of all because a corporeal interpretation of the data acknowledges from the very beginning what the cognitivist-computational explanation both presupposes and fails to acknowledge. The cognitivist-computational explanation presupposes a subject who is in fact capable of making articulatory gestures, that is, *it presupposes a sound-maker*. Indeed, there seems little sense to speak of linguistically significant gestures or of gestural invariants if there is nothing in the way of an actual creature, one capable of making sounds and of articulating in a systematic way. By the same token, the cognitivist-computational explanation presupposes *a sentient subject*, a subject aware of his/her own body, thus aware in a tactile-kinesthetic sense of the gestures he/she makes. To insist on the necessity of gestural invariants "for *any* adequate theory of speech production," but then to say that these invariants have nothing to do with "peripheral movements," that is, nothing to do with the actual gestures the speaker makes, is to deny to the individual producing speech any kind of sensory experience. Surely the gestural invariants that are necessary "for *any* adequate theory of speech production" constitute precisely those sensed bodily constants which make possible the very learning of a language, not to say which made possible the very *invention* of language in the first place. Liberman and Mattingly appear on the edge of acknowledging as much, save for the inclusion of a critical qualifier. They write that "Until and unless the child (tacitly) appreciates the gestural source of the sounds, he can hardly be expected to perceive, or ever learn to perceive, a phonetic structure" (1985:25). While "tacitly" could mean simply "outside of the child's focal awareness," something of which the child is only subliminally aware, given "an internal, innately-specified vocal-tract synthesizer," such a meaning is unlikely. In other words, the word "tacitly" appears linked to what is being orchestrated by a language module in the child's brain. In effect, it allots to a brain what properly belongs to a living body. In so doing, it precludes forthright acknowledgment of sensed bodily constants because it precludes the recognition of a sentient body to begin with. In sum, to say that a child "(tacitly) appreciates the gestural source of the sounds" is to ignore the child's own experiences of itself as a sound-maker, experiences beginning early in its infancy. It is, in more radical terms, to cut the child off from its own bodily experiences, the tactile-kinesthetic experiences of its own developing articulatory gestures. Insofar as the synthesizing link that Liberman and colleagues postulate between speech perception and speech production becomes located in a thoroughly hypothetical cortical structure that takes the place of a concrete, empirically present, sentiently experienced living body, one might say that their theory preempts the ultimate invariant required of any credible theory of speech perception, namely, a flesh and bone speaker, a living articulator of sounds.

It is important to point out that the fact that some persons have been since birth at a loss to *control* their articulators in no way precludes their having tactile-kinesthetic articulatory experiences. That they cannot speak in a *systematic* way is not evidence against sentience — or learning. The situation is akin to infants' babbling and cooing. Although infants cannot imitate adult speech, in their vocalizing gestures they are nevertheless aware of themselves as sound-makers. Moreover if they learn to control their articulators, they necessarily come to an awareness of certain if/then relationships, a kind of relationship that psychiatrist Daniel Stern, physicist-physiologist Hermann von Helmholtz, and philosopher Edmund Husserl all emphasize as basic to understandings of the world. In particular, infants discover quite specific tactile-kinesthetic/aural relationships in moving their tongue, lips, and velum in various ways — i.e. such and such movements/touchings, such and such sounds, or, in Husserlian terms, if this (tactile-kinesthetic event), then this (aural event). It is also worth noting in this context that deaf children do not lack anything in the way of a speech apparatus. What they lack is precisely the capacity to appreciate themselves as sound-makers and in turn the capacity to bisociate articulatory gestures with heard sounds, or phonetic elements (see Sheets-Johnstone 1990: 158–63).

Now it is, of course, true that appreciation of the relationship between articulatory gestures and sounds is ordinarily far from one's awareness once one has learned basic speech. Adults — and children of five years at least — are seldom aware of what they are doing inside their mouths or with their lips when they are speaking, unless, for example, they are rehabilitating themselves in the aftermath of a stroke or learning a new word. In this sense, it is true that appreciation of the gestural source of sounds is tacit in everyday speech, "tacit" precisely in the sense of being outside of focal awareness. We should note, however, that rather than epistemologically blanketing the appreciation of the gestural source of sounds by the word *tacit* — the equivalent of saying "we don't know how we do it, but we do it!" — we could attempt to elucidate how we come to synthesize articulatory gestures and phonetic elements, that is, how we both actively and passively relate tactile-kinesthetic and aural modalities in our early experiences of babbling, in our later inchoate experiences of speaking, and in our still later experiences of speaking as full-fledged adults. Passive synthesizing is not to be confused with a mysterious happening in a repository we designate "the unconscious"; nor, of course, is it to be confused with mysterious happenings in a mechanism we designate an "internal, innately-specified vocal-tract synthesizer." Passive synthesis — a term that comes from Husserl — is rather a constitutive part of any process of sense-making, whether a matter of speech perception, traffic perception, chocolate perception, velvet perception, or symphony perception; it is part of an epistemological process.

In a very general sense, passive synthesis is always there in experience because whatever the experience, we never get the thing — speech, traffic, chocolate, velvet, or symphony — all at once and always the same. Our knowledge of the world is experientially constructed; it is furthermore built up dynamically in conjunction with accrued meanings from past experience. When philosopher Ronald de Sousa, in reviewing Liberman's research, comments that "Our phonetic perception is crucially conditioned by our own capacity to produce speech, though the process involves neither inference, nor argument from analogy, nor imaginative effort" (1987: 155), he is underscoring a particular aspect of this very point, namely, that our adult capacity to link perception and production does not typically involve an active intellectual doing of some kind— inferring, arguing from analogy, or imagining, for example — a kind of doing that we typically associate with thinking or reasoning. Liberman and Mattingly themselves stress that no such effortful activity is involved when they say that the shared invariants of speech production and speech perception are "not a *learned* association, a result of the fact that what people hear when they listen to speech is what they do when they speak" (1985: 3; italics added). Clearly, the designation *tacit*, unlike passive synthesis, does not do justice to this pointed lack of effortful activity; in the context of Liberman's theory, it connotes merely something underground, not something processual and constructive, certainly not something that is consistently part of our epistemological grasp of the world, something which can in fact be elucidated — one might even say, if the term were not already in use, "de-constructed" — through phenomenological analyses. Moreover neither does it do justice to the actual activity inherent in sense-making, that is, to the actual involvement of a subject in discovering him/herself as both a sound-maker and a maker of sound meanings. An acknowledgment of passive synthesis, unlike a blanketing *tacit* appreciation, in fact entails no wholesale denial of activity since not only is passive synthesis itself a kind of activity, a *synthesizing* activity, but it is not the whole story; it is an aspect of a global epistemological process that is intentionally active. Indeed, "until and unless" infants and young children are aware of themselves first as sound-makers — in babbling and cooing, in gurgling, in tapping and smacking their lips together, and so on — and then, as *articulators* of sound — in saying "mama" and "dada," for example — "[they] can hardly be expected to perceive, or ever learn to perceive, a phonetic structure." In other words, *contra* Liberman, short of tactile-kinesthetic awarenesses developing in normal experiential fashion in the course of infancy and early childhood, not only is the production of speech impossible, gestural invariants and language itself are impossible.

With respect to this very point, a further insight into speech perception is evident. If it is true that the object of perception is motoric, then an explanation of speech perception on the basis of something other than "an innately specified vocal-tract synthesizer" is clearly available. This further alternative explanation is based on a faculty already there, namely, analogical apperception. On the basis of our experiences of our own body, we consistently apperceive the tactile-kinesthetic and affective feelings of others — as when they lift something heavy, for example, or when they smile, or when they slip and fall, or when they go out and slam the door. In each case, we make co-present — we *app*erceive — something that is not actually there sensuously present before us — in a way similar to the way in which we make co-present the inside of a book when we in fact see only a red or blue or green surface and take it to be an outside that covers a sheaf of pages with writing on them: we apperceive the heaviness of the suitcase someone is lifting, the joy in someone's smile, the unexpectedness and pain of someone's fall, the anger in someone's exit. However elaborated by culture our modes of expression might be — however much we are the product of particular cultural groomings — our experiences of our own bodies are the consistent basis of our apperceiving the tactile-kinesthetic and affective feelings of others. Accordingly, if the motor theory of speech perception is correct, it can be further explained on the basis of analogical apperception. In speech perception, we make co-present — we *apper*ceive — the articulatory gestures of others along with their sounds. Thus, in speaking with someone, we do not perceive their articulatory gestures directly, but apperceive them; that is, we make co-present with the aural event the tactile-kinetic corollaries of the event, and this on the basis of our own tactile-kinesthetic experiences as articulators of sound. What is 'intended', as Liberman puts it, can thus be readily explained on the basis of both actual sentience — first hand experience of one's own articulatory gestures — and analogical apperception — making co-present with the actual sound event the articulatory gestures of another.

Now one of the puzzles of any semantical system is how elements of the system are differentiated from elements outside the system. In Liberman's motor theory of speech perception, the internal, innately specified vocal-tract synthesizer distinguishes between speech and non-speech. This is quite a feat — even for a brain. It suggests that the synthesizer, being innately specified, has already within its grasp a notion of the sound of airplanes, tractors, windstorms, the crackling sound that a fire produces, the sound of one's own chewing, and so on. It suggests that the synthesizer is cognitively akin to philosopher Jerry Fodor's Mentalese (1975) — a single language of thought in which every possible word is already represented in the brain. In contrast to this extraordinary, not to say preposterous scenario, the claim of analogical apperception is modest, and, being modest, is far more plausible. But it is also far more plausible because it is rooted in an experiencing subject, a live individual. Consider, for example, that analogical apperception can readily explain how it is that speech sounds are distinguished from non-speech sounds, not only the non-speech sounds of wind, rain, cars, phones, and even music, but also the non-speech sounds of a foreign language. Though the latter sounds might be classed as speech because emitted by humans, the sounds of a foreign language are non-speech sounds for anyone incapable of making sense of them. Where there is no tactile-kinesthetic foundation for analogizing in the sense of a basic articulatory familiarity with the language, there is no apperception. This is why we in fact readily distinguish between *our own tongue* and that of another. We find the other's tongue foreign, i.e. non-sensical, because we have no articulatory experience with it. We cannot in consequence apperceive the gestures of the foreign speaker. In turn, we cannot discern phonetic structure. Only at the point where we can begin to sense the articulations of the native speaker do we begin to have a grasp of the "foreign" tongue, an understanding — precisely in a tactile-kinesthetic sense — of where one word ends and another begins. Imitating the sounds of a native speaker, we enact the articulatory gestures the native speaker enacts in producing the sound; understanding the sounds of the native speaker, we apperceive the gestures by which the native speaker articulates the sounds. When Liberman writes that "acoustic patterns are identified as speech by reference to deep properties of a linguistic sort: if a sound can be 'interpreted' by the specialized phonetic module [the brain's vocal-tract synthesizer] as the result of linguistically significant gestures, then it is speech; otherwise, not," he fails to acknowledge just such human perceptive and apperceptive capacities. Ultimately, he fails to acknowledge both the tactile-kinesthetic/aural explorations through which we realize our possibility of becoming sound-makers to begin with, and the powers of analogical apperception that have developed from infancy onward and that undergird all of our social communication. What he puts in a brain is corporeally and intercorporeally 'out of the mouths of babes' in its very inception. When it comes to foundational psychical faculties — or to parsimony — a hypothesized entity in a brain is no match for a sentient living body.

There is actually a deep irony in overlooking a subject in the form of an empirically present, sentiently resonant body and to favor a brain instead, since to overlook sentience is in fact to overlook the brain. Considerable cortical space is given over to tactility and to movement (Penfield & Rasmussen 1950). By comparison, an "internal, innately specified vocal-tract synthesizer" — a so-called "brain module" — has little or no empirical reality. It is a hypothetical explanatory structure that does more for theory than for fact. Tactility and movement, in contrast, are localized body part by body part along the topmost frontal profile of the brain hemispheres. Indeed, it is of particular significance that "the great somatic sensory systems of the body," as well-known neurosurgeon Wilder Penfield terms them (1975:16), have been finely mapped, and that of all areas of the body, the lips and tongue (along with the face and feet) are the areas most prominently represented, the pharynx (toes, hands, and genitals) being not too far behind. To take no account of an experiencing subject in the form of a felt tactile-kinesthetic body, especially if speech perception has its roots in speech production, is to disregard cortically-significant corporeal matters of fact.

The result of discounting the felt tactile-kinesthetic body has perils beyond irony. An "internal, innately specified vocal-tract synthesizer" is also a blow to parsimony. Such ontological creations as "vocal-tract synthesizers" — like cognitive maps and feature analyzers — populate a bland, grey cerebral landscape with explanatory artifacts, creating something like a cerebral mall.[1] Not only does a sentient body offer a more parsimonious explanation of speech production and speech perception, but recognition of a sentient body also accords in general terms with psychologist Lloyd Morgan's long-acknowledged canon, which stipulates that a higher psychical faculty should not be invoked to explain a behavior if the behavior can be interpreted by a lower psychical faculty. Abstract ontological entities on the order of vocal-tract synthesizers are clearly more sophisticated and higher-ranking faculties than mundane corporeal matters of fact on the order of tactile-kinesthetic experience, tactile-kinesthetic invariants, and analogical apperception based upon those invariants. But tactile-kinesthetic invariants and analogical apperception based on those invariants clearly afford the most basic and most direct explanation of how we manage to produce speech ourselves and how we make sense of the speech of others. At the most fundamental level, the computational explanation leaves out *experience.* Yet why would one want to overlook or even deny the fact that when we learned our native tongue, we literally learned our native tongue: we babbled and cooed, we made sounds, we discovered ourselves as sound-makers and in the process learned what we could do with our tongues. Why would one want to say instead that when we were very young, i.e. before we ourselves could speak, a language module in our brain came to life and began computing the articulatory characteristics of people who were speaking to us? Why, especially with recent international research on infants showing their capabilities to discern one phoneme from another and to recognize in a preferential way the language they have heard since birth over another language (Mehler et al.: undated; Eimas 1975), why would one not rather say that through their own lingual explorations and experiments, and through their own aural abilities to discern and to distinguish linguistic features that they consistently hear, infants not only learn the phonemes, prosodic elements, and intonations of their parents' language, they come to know what they can do with their tongues. Their initial discovery of themselves as sound-makers leads to their discovery of themselves as articulators. They develop a repertoire of I can's with respect to the articulatory gestures of their culture's language.

Now interestingly enough, tactile-kinesthetic experience and invariants together with analogical apperception offer the most direct explanation of nonhuman animal communication as well. In particular, they accord with empirical evidence concerning the presence of comsigns in groups of social animals, the practice of tactical deception in primates, and the phenomenon of inter-animate communication generally. A consideration of evidence demonstrating these aspects of inter-animate life — primate life in particular — will in fact suggest fundamental evolutionary continuities. It will show how tactile-kinesthetic bodies are central to social communication and to a social semantics, and how an evolutionary understanding of any communication system and semantics is rooted in an understanding of intercorporeal sense-making. By examining such evidence, we can probe the import of tactile-kinesthetic experience and invariants, and analogical apperception in further interesting ways.

3.   Comsigns and tactical deception

Primatologist Stuart Altmann (1967) coined the term comsigns to refer to those behaviors of a group or species that are common to virtually all members in the group or species. In effect, comsigns are characterized by an interchangeability with respect to "sender" and "receiver" in any communicative process. A honeybee, for example, can be either sender or recipient of information concerning the whereabouts of a sugar source. Similarly, a vervet monkey can be either sender or recipient of information concerning the presence of a leopard. Though Altmann does not elaborate upon the concept of a comsign in bodily terms, it is obvious that comsigns could only arise on the basis of a common tactile-kinesthetic body, which is to say on the basis of *a common body of experience*. Short of an *experiencing body that is tactilely and kinesthetically common to all*, no language — verbal or nonverbal — could be standardized: there would be no honeybee dances, no alarm calls, no human speech. In each case, no grounds would exist for inventing, discovering, or establishing communicative acts. Tactile-kinesthetic bodies, felt bodies, are the *sine qua non* of communication since signals, dances, calls, speech, gestures — all need to be standardized along common experiential lines. In short, for any language whatsoever to be standardized, the language — be it wolf howlings, sheep bleatings, goose honkings, honeybee dances, bird songs, vervet calls, or human speech — must be producible by all, and to be producible by all, a common tactile-kinesthetic body is required.

Observations of tactical deception in primates supports and strengthens the notion of comsigns. To begin with, certain everyday behaviors are both producible by, and meaningful to, all members of particular groups of primates, be they baboons, gorillas, macaques, or chimpanzees, for example, and it is because they are meaningful to all members of the group — *uniformly* meaningful to them — that the behaviors can be used by one individual in the group to deceive other individuals in the group. One primatologist writes of an old female mangabey (an Old World monkey species), for example, who, "would often use distracting tactics to get a [piece of] food when the male was sitting over it. She would pace around him, keeping her eye on the food and in coming closer would 'accidentally' walk over a piece of [the] food which would, of course, remain in her hand as she strolled off" (Whiten & Byrne 1988: 237). Walking and pacing are natural acts common to these (and other) primates. Walking close to another who is sitting is similarly a natural act common to all. The acts can be used deceptively precisely for this reason: they are natural acts common to all. A more elaborate instance of tactical deception concerns the behavior of a gorilla who was observed walking with others in a relatively straight line along a narrow trail. The gorilla spied a choice vine that was partly hidden. She sat down by the side of the trail and began to groom herself. When the others were all out of sight, she stopped grooming herself, rapidly climbed into the tree, broke off the clump of vine, descended with it, and hastily ate it "before running to catch up with the group" (Whiten & Byrne 1988: 237). As with walking and walking close, sitting down and grooming oneself are natural acts common to many primates. They can be used deceptively precisely for this reason.

An interesting remark made by philosopher Ludwig Wittgenstein is topical here. Wittgenstein wrote that "The origin and primitive form of the language game is a reaction; it is first from this that the more complicated forms can grow. I would say that language is a refinement. 'In the beginning was the act'" (1980: 31).[2] Now undoubtedly, we can assume that by "language," Wittgenstein means *human* language, but if we take his remark in an evolutionary sense, that is, if we take it more broadly in terms of an *evolutionary semantics*, it becomes clear how and why bodies are of critical moment to all "language games." All acts are tactile-kinesthetic phenomena; that is, acts are generated by living bodies, living bodies that are sensitive to their own movement and to the movement of others. We may thus with good reason strongly urge that, in lieu of "act," movement is the more appropriate term: "In the beginning was movement," not a mere happening or doing, but a bodily-resonating event, and as such meaningful, meaningful not only to the moving creature itself but apperceptively meaningful to creatures perceiving the movement. How else explain how interanimate meanings evolved? How else explain how creatures came to agree on the meaning of certain behaviors? How, for example, did certain postures come to be indicative of threat? How did others come to be indicative of invitation? How did others come to indicate reassurance? How did others come to indicate friendliness? How did creatures come to agree on what this signal, this gesture, this movement, this posture, this orientation *means*? Surely they did not have a conference. Surely they did not discuss the matter and take a vote. Moreover how else explain the origin of *comsigns*? How else explain how communal signals evolved, signals that by definition — *com-signs, signs that are common to everyone* — are bodily-mediated meanings, meanings that are dynamically realized, which is to say meanings that are literally embodied in movement?

The foregoing discussion of comsigns and tactical deception shows that intercorporeal sense-making is not only an apperceptive phenomenon, but an evolutionary fact of life. There is no doubt then but that speech, like all forms of inter-animate social communication, *evolved*. There is no doubt either but that initial articulatory gestures were founded on tactile-kinesthetic invariants and that these invariants were invariantly meaningful from the start. Studies in the symbolic structure of primordial language in fact make the relationship between articulatory gesture and meaning abundantly clear. They furthermore call into question the received assumption that the primary function of language is and always has been to name things. Recent research in anthropological linguistics confutes this assumption (LeCron Foster 1990, 1992, 1994a: 387–389, 1996; see also LeCron Foster 1978 & Sheets-Johnstone 1990, Chapter 6). Extensive studies of root forms show both that the referents of primordial language were motional-relational complexes, not objects, and that the symbolic structure of primordial language was anchored in iconic sounds rather than in arbitrary ones. A common articulatory movement aptly illustrates this relationship. To make the sound "m," we press our lips together. All reconstructed root forms of the sound "m" refer to bilateral relationships that are spatio-kinetically analogous to the act of bringing the lips together — "the fingers or hands in taking or grasping," for instance, or "two opposed surfaces in tapering, pressing together, holding together, crushing, or resting against." In primordial language, the sound "m" thus named a particular motional-relational complex. It might have referred to resting against nest materials as in sleeping or against the earth as in standing, for example; or to pressing together as in copulating; or to crushing as in chewing food or to pounding one thing with another; and so on. In effect, what the linguistic reconstruction of the symbolic structure of primordial language shows is that articulatory gestures were of primary semantic significance, which is to say that the felt, moving body, the tactile-kinesthetic body, was the focal point of symbolization.

It is of interest in this context to point out several observations made by neurologist Oliver Sacks (1993) in his clinical treatment of a person he calls Virgil, a person who, after forty-five years of blindness, has his vision restored. Sacks notes the difficulty Virgil has in synthesizing what he sees after he has regained sight. Virgil sees specific features of a cat, for example — perhaps its paws, its ears, or its legs — but he can neither readily nor easily see the cat. His knowledge of the world to this point has been tactile-kinesthetic, a sequentially built-up knowledge as distinguished from a visual, instantaneous knowledge. As Sacks points out, we precisely *learn* to see in this instantaneous visual way. We build up our knowledge of objects in the world by moving about them, by changing our vantage point so that we see them in different profiles; we tactilely explore things; we study them in moments of concentrated stillness and are alert to their movement. In short, our knowledge of the visual world is progressively achieved; only after a long tuition is it instantaneous. And indeed, Sacks writes that Virgil enjoys seeing shapes and movement over trying to see objects as such, that shapes and movement intrigue and fascinate him. Something quite similar can be said of infants. The investigations of clinical psychiatrist and developmental psychologist Daniel Stern discussed in Chapter Five give ample testimony to this fact. Given what intrigues and fascinates Virgil and what intrigues and fascinates infants as well, we might surmise that vitality affects and physiognomic perception underlie our way of perceiving the world. They constitute the basic qualitative aspects of things. It is not surprising, then, that the reconstructed root forms of primordial language should refer to motional-relational complexes rather than to objects as such.

From this evolutionary vantage point upon speech and its tactile-kinesthetic foundations, we readily come to a specific kind of appreciation of the beginnings of language, an appreciation first of its *invention* and second, of what its invention necessarily entailed in the way of *bodily invariants*. Speculative accounts of the origin of language easily ignore these basic appreciations. Dennett's scenario offers a brief case in point. "The first of our ancestors to speak," he writes (1991:200), "almost certainly had a much more laborious time getting the hang of it, but we are the descendants of the virtuosos among them." In this near-creationist scenario, *words* appear ready-mades rippling from the mouths of "our ancestors," the latter merely having had to practice moving their mouths to "get the hang of [them]." But for "[t]he first of our ancestors," speaking was precisely not an already established process, as speaking — and writing — is for a twentieth-century child (or was for a fifteenth-century, or even fifth-century B.C. child), or, it might be added, as skiing or surgery or watch-repairing is for a twentieth-century adult ignorant of and/or unaccustomed to these practices. One "gets the hang of it" only in situations where one's own practice makes perfect the doing of some already set behavior. In short, when human language is taken as a pre-established entity to "get the hang of," it is actually being taken for granted. We do not only not consider *how* our human form of language began; we do not properly consider *that* it began. We somehow ignore the fact that at some time in our remote evolutionary history, language in the form of speech was created from scratch: there was no ready-made form, whether churned out cortically or *deus ex machina*, whereby hominids one day began conversing verbally with each other. When we seriously consider this fact, we come to consider seriously both the primacy and complexity of the articulatory gestures of speech. As suggested in the previous section, we approximate to an appreciation of this primacy and complexity when we experience the unfamiliarity of a foreign language. Not only are our tongues not fluent, moving with ease, but our ears cannot distinguish where one word ends and another begins. We are at a loss for words because we are at a loss to comprehend in a tactile-kinesthetic sense the articulatory gestures of the language being spoken. We approximate similarly to an appreciation of the primacy and complexity when we consider how infants come to speak. Indeed, if speech perception depends upon speech production, then surely we must in part take a clue from infants in order to understand what was necessarily entailed in the invention of language. An awareness of oneself as a sound-maker was first of all crucial to the invention of a verbal language. An awareness of what one could do with one's tongue and lips and supralaryngeal tract was equally crucial. So too was an ability to control one's tongue, lips, and supralaryngeal tract in specific repeatable ways. In sum, the more one thinks seriously of what was necessary to the invention of language in the form of speech, the more one is also led to take a clue from Condillac, a philosopher who explicitly began his eighteenth century account of the origin of language not with a certain view of how it arose — to wit, it arose ready-made, a gift from divine providence — but with a living scenario by means of which he literally fleshed out a recreation of its origin. Though not spelled out in detail, his reconstruction shows how the new sound language was patterned on already existing natural sounds; it describes how certain lingual sensitivities and capacities were vital to the invention of the new sound language; it describes the central role of the tongue and the necessity of its flexibility; and so on ([1756] 1971). In short, by his thoughtful reconstruction, Condillac implicitly emphasizes both the primacy and the complexity of the articulatory gestures of speech at the dawn of language.

A final consideration merits attention in the context of this evolutionary perspective on speech, a consideration that ultimately both reinforces the notion of movement as a match point (see Chapter Five) and suggests a basic affinity between feeling and thinking. To lead up to this affinity and to put it in its proper light, we might best note in advance how unreasonable some might think it to say that we can explain the phenomenon of human speech perception by acknowledging the listener's body of articulatory experience, that is, by acknowledging how the latter serves as a semantic template for understanding others, since we know by our own experience that in our typical everyday speaking life, attention to our own articulatory gestures, let alone to those of the person who speaks to us, is buried in what French philosopher Paul Ricoeur once designated *the said* (1991: 146). What bears emphasizing in this regard, however, is that originally, we made sense in bodily ways, and indeed, made sense not only *with*, but *of* our bodies. In particular, both prior to and in the course of our learning a language we were necessarily attentive to what we were doing inside our mouths, to the tactile-kinetic play of our lingual gestures and how they felt. When we learned our mother tongue, we spontaneously learned the specific tactile-kinesthetic invariants peculiar to it. As noted earlier, Liberman has spoken of these invariant gestures as 'intended', the perceiver of speech distinguishing the gestures through his/her physiologically and anatomically knowledgeable vocal-tract synthesizer. The foregoing reinterpretation of his research has shown, however, that gestures coincident with *the said* are not buried in the brain but are apperceptively given with the said. 'Intended gestures' are analogically apperceived. Accordingly, we recognize and respond to linguistically significant gestures not because a brain module picks them out, that is, not because a cortical entity discerns linguistic sound from non-linguistic sound, but because we are sentiently attuned to the bodies of others as linguistic sound-makers through our own experiences of ourselves as sound-makers. In short, we have already made articulatory sense of our own bodies and that articulatory sense of our own bodies serves us as a semantic template. Speech perception — not merely the hearing of sound from human lips, but the recognition and understanding of such sound as speech — thus involves an analogical transfer of sense from our own tactile-kinesthetic body to the tactile-kinesthetic body of another. The linkage is guaranteed by our foundational attunement to movement and to the invariants of our mother tongue. There is no "covert mimicry" involved with respect to these invariants, but there is what might be termed an empathic dimension insofar as a felt moving body is at either end of the transfer.

In analogically apperceiving the felt moving body of the other in the act of listening to its sounds, *and in thus apperceptively transforming mere sound into sound-making*, we might indeed say that our intercorporeal sense-making is an inchoate form of empathy: it draws on our own experience of ourselves as sound-makers and has its origins in tactile-kinesthetic invariants. But we might equally say that in apperceptively transforming mere sound into sound-making, our intercorporeal sense-making is an extraordinarily sophisticated form of empathy. In other words, the tactile-kinesthetic transfer of sense that makes human speech possible is not simply the same kind of transfer of sense that makes empathy possible; the former transfer has its roots in the latter transfer. Put in the perspective of an evolutionary history, the conjunction of empathy and language in fact becomes remarkably suggestive. That empathy was a necessary intercorporeal precursor of human language accords first of all with present-day estimations of the high social value of cooperation in the evolution of hominids. Empathy is consistently mentioned in studies on this topic (see e.g. Caporael et al. 1991). For example, cooperative group-hunting and group-living activities associated with tool-making indicate that the social capacity to empathize was of critical significance to the evolution of hominids. One well-known paleoanthropologist even writes specifically of caring for others in the context of evidence from australopithecine times of broken bones having healed (Wolpoff 1980: 150). While human language is conservatively estimated to have originated 300,000 to 400,000 years ago, rudimentary tool-making, by artifactual evidence, is dated as far back as two to two-and-a-half million years (Wolpoff 1980). If the evolutionary scaling of empathy to cooperative social ventures is correct, then the capacity to make felt sense of the travails and contentments of another preceded the invention of human language by some one-and-one-half to two million years and laid the intercorporeal foundations for the very possibility of social communication in the form of human speech.

Interestingly enough, an evolutionary relationship between empathy and speech perception is strongly suggested by ontogenetic studies of imitation and empathy as well as by phylogenetic evidence and theory. That day-old human infants cry when they hear their peers cry,[3] and that at five months they select an image of a face mouthing the vowel they hear over an image of a face mouthing a different vowel (Kuhl & Meltzoff 1982, 1984), indicates both an ontogenetic developmental relationship and an impressively close conjunction in transfer of sense between entrainment — readily described as a form of inter-animate imitation — and empathy, and between empathy and speech perception.

When both empathy and human speech are viewed as the forms of intercorporeal sense-making that in truth they are, the capacity for "feeling at a distance," for sensing the felt body of another, can clearly be seen to have extraordinary evolutionary import. This fact should serve as a caveat for considering empathy and language to be binary opposites of each other, emotions — or "the passions" — being opposed to thinking — or rationality — or, in the finer axiological terms of a binary oppositionality, empathy being esteemed on the one hand an interesting but frou-frou aspect of human life, and language, on the other hand being esteemed the absolute and *suigeneris* crown. Forms of life have their origins deep in evolutionary history. In no instance are they simply the result of particular cultural groomings. To view forms of life in evolutionary perspective is indeed to discover their common roots. With respect to human speech perception, this means discovering something about the way in which we make sense both directly, in speaking, and indirectly, in apperceiving the speech of others. Movement is indeed our match point. That this lingual tactile-kinesthetic sense-making is closely related to empathy strongly suggests that where meaning is corporeally enacted, then intercorporeal sense-making only makes sense.

4.   Challenging counter evidence

In order to draw out a further fundamental dimension of intercorporeal sense-making, we will shift gears in radical fashion and consider evidence of human speech perception that is explained neither by "an internal, innately specified vocal-tract synthesizer" *nor* by tactile-kinesthetic invariant articulatory gestures. Such evidence will obviously present a formidable challenge to the previous critical analysis.

Kanzi is a bonobo chimpanzee (*Pan paniscus*) who comprehends spoken English at the level of a two-and-a-half-year-old human child.[4] He learned English spontaneously when, for the first two-and-a-half years of his life, he observed experimenters attempting to teach English to his mother, who, it turned out, was unable to comprehend the symbols used to teach the language. These symbols were arbitrarily designed graphic forms assembled on a wired keyboard. Each symbol represented a word: chase, for example, or apple, or refrigerator, or television. When a symbol on the board was pressed, an English word would be heard. Kanzi picked up a command of spoken English by means of the symbolic keyboard.[5]

Now clearly, Kanzi does not have "an internal, innately specified vocal-tract synthesizer … that incorporates complete information about the anatomical and physiological characteristic of the vocal tract" since not only does he not have a human brain; he does not have a human body, i.e. a human anatomy and physiology. The question of how he learned to comprehend normal English sentences on the order of "Get your ball" or even "Put the lemon in the water" and quite outlandish sentences on the order of "Can you throw a potato at the turtle?" must thus look to quite other explanations — and understandings — of his abilities. An experientially-based tactile-kinesthetic explanation is also deficient in explaining how Kanzi comes to have a two-and-a-half-year-old's comprehension of English. Kanzi does not have a human tongue, lips, or supralaryngeal tract; hence Kanzi cannot make articulatory gestures peculiar to human speech. Of equal importance is the fact that Kanzi never babbled and cooed, and so never proprioceptively explored and felt a range of buccal gestures and appreciated their correlation with certain sounds — though obviously, he correlated *other* kinds of articulatory gestures and sounds. A video tape of Kanzi and his immediate family and human care-givers gives substantive hints of the basis of his learning. Although these indications do not result in an explanation of how he was able to put together in a semantically resonant manner visual symbols on a keyboard and sounds uttered by human speakers, and of how he was ultimately able to comprehend a human speaker directly, without the intermediary of a keyboard, they unequivocally show us something fundamental about animate life, something familiar but not ordinarily made explicit about the nature of living creatures. In particular, they show us how an individual raised in circumstances quite unnatural to its species-typical ways of life may, *through its own native proclivities*, makes sense of the world in which it finds itself.

On many occasions the video tape shows Kanzi with a particular facial gesture that is typical of the facial gesture humans make in listening attentively to another human's speech. In these instances, Kanzi's eyes, like the eyes of a listening human, are alert and poised; they are not flitting about, but are held in readiness, as if on the edge of seizing something. This kind of focused eye gesture is starkly contrasted with the evasive and erratic eye movements of a person who is frustrated to understand, a person who knows there is something to be understood but cannot understand it. The person may indeed become quite noticeably agitated, as agitated as a child who, seeing others comprehending how something works and being unable himself or herself to comprehend how it does, becomes fitful and eccentric, precisely, as a matter of fact, in the way in which Tamuli, Kanzi's sibling, who had no language training and who was brought up as a control subject, becomes fitful and eccentric when asked to respond to spoken questions or requests by pressing the appropriate symbol on the keyboard. Tamuli's movement is noticeably wild: she seizes the cord attached to the keyboard, for example, begins chewing on it, then jerks it out of her mouth, twists her body this way and that, and in general moves in a thoroughly unfocused, highly perturbed and convulsive manner. One is readily inclined to say that she understands that something is going on with the keyboard for she sees it instrumentally connected with the behavior of others — thus she sees that the board *means something* — and further, that she understands that something is expected of her by others with respect to doing something with the board — something in the way of *meaning-grasping* — but that she cannot make sense of the questions, of the requests, of the board — of the situation. *Meaning* escapes her. The semantic void is readily apparent in her frantic, fitful, and unfocused movement. The difference between her nervous, anxiously darting eyes and Kanzi's alert and ready ones is emblematic of the totally different bodily dynamics of each bonobo: Kanzi's whole body is held in rapt attention; Tamuli's whole body is in a frenzy.

Before putting these qualitatively distinct bodily dynamics in the perspective of an evolutionary semantics and drawing out their fundamental animate significance, a single observation warrants attention. Kanzi, like all living creatures, is not a piecemeal arrangement of parts but a living whole, a creature that is from the start and in all of its doings, all of a piece. As suggested from the above descriptions, explaining his comprehension of spoken English from a whole-body perspective entails an appreciation of his bodily dynamics — the character of his animation as he is engaged in the world. What is of particular interest in this regard is that neither Kanzi's vocabulary nor his comprehension of English include a definitive sense of himself as a physical body, a physical body with head, arms, legs, fingers, elbows, and so on. His vocabulary and comprehension revolve for the most part about objects — a stuffed animal, a vacuum cleaner, a blanket, a rubber band, and foods of many different kinds[6] — about doing something active such as chasing or tickling — and about going to a particular place out of doors. His care-takers/trainers, in fact, remark in their notes — quite in passing — that while Kanzi is "asked about body parts … he does not know them well, even though these are words that have been on his keyboard for some time" (*Bonobo People* "Data Base": 7). In comparison with his extensive linguistic knowledge of objects — most especially what we human observers would take to be important objects like *food* — Kanzi's lack of linguistic knowledge of his own body parts is significant. It is significant in that it says something important and specific about his sense of his own body and, by extension, his sense of the bodies of others. This sense may be glossed in terms of the having or not having of a physical body *as such*. As analyzed and discussed at length elsewhere (Sheets-Johnstone 1990, Chapter 8), physical bodies *as such* are springboards to analysis and manipulation. To have a physical body *as such* is to be capable of analyzing one's body as a composite of such and such body parts together with a knowledge of their practical and kinetic possibilities — manipulation, rotation, and so on. Nonhuman animals do not have physical bodies *as such*. Their physical bodies are inseparable from their living bodies. Their living bodies are *felt*. As felt, they are perceived as dynamically engaged in the world in some way or other — fighting, snarling, exploring, eating, pulling, resting, pursuing — or dynamically self-engaged — scratching, grooming, shaking, or turning, for instance, or crouching, reaching, or stretching. By this very token, the living bodies of animate creatures are co-terminous with the animals themselves. Physical bodies *as such* have no separable place in their world as do the physical bodies of humans. In effect, the bodies of other creatures appear to them not as *physical things* but as other creatures, *dynamic* other forms that are physiognomically portentous in some way or other: threatening, inviting, playful, fearful, and so on. In a word, the physical body of the other is equally all of a piece with its living body.

Now if we take this whole-body dynamic seriously and if, in turn, we take *attentiveness* seriously as a certain physiognomically distinct bodily bearing, the challenge of the counter evidence leads us to a broad and deep understanding of Kanzi's ability, broad and deep precisely in the direction of an evolutionary semantics.[7] Indeed, if we recall the notion that in the beginning is not the word but *movement*, and if we take into account not only the above descriptions of the total bodily dynamic of Kanzi and Tamuli, but the earlier expositions and examples of comsigns and of tactical deception, we are led to an acknowledgment of a fundamental semantic propensity of animate life. What I would like to do is to sketch out this fundamental propensity, in part to draw out its import to an understanding of language — language not in the narrow sense of referring only and exclusively to human language, but language taken in the broader sense of an evolutionary semantics — and in part to specify in finer detail a pan-animate feature of life.

5. On the evolution of an evolutionary semantics

In studies of animal life, considerable attention is given to communication — to signalling behaviors. Yet while consistent reference is made to a displayer and to a displayed-to animal, reference to the process whereby meaning originates and is solidified between the two creatures is rare and marginal. One well-known primatologist, for example, remarks only briefly and in passing on the importance of the displayed-to animal. She writes that "Once an intention movement has acquired meaning, or predictive value, *and this is a matter of the evolution of the receiver rather than the animal making the movements*, it may presumably come under selection pressure as a signal" (Rowell 1972: 94; italics added). She goes on then to discuss how efficiency and safety are necessary to a signal being selected — that is, acquired. Although she does not say so explicitly, it is nonetheless clear from her remark that it is the displayed-to animal that solidifies meaning. Insofar as the displayed-to animal validates the movement of the other as meaningful, we might say that it acquiesces to meaning. It is just its assent to meaning — whether a matter of another's posture, gesture, facial expression, display, extended movement sequence, orientation, or any other bodily kinetic event — that is of interest from the viewpoint of an evolutionary semantics. In effect, it is just its assent to meaning that needs examination. In particular, the basic question that demands answer is, how does a displayed-to animal come to validate a movement or gesture of another as meaningful? How does a displayed-to animal come to acquiesce to meaning and thus officially instantiate a particular moment of a language or semantics?

Let me approach this question by way of a distinction. As noted in the previous chapter, we all know that there is a difference between a stone and a living being — a difference between the animate and the inanimate — but we seldom ponder the difference or ask ourselves to specify the complex dimensions of animate being. We tend simply to think of the animate as something living, and perhaps also, as something living that moves. What I would like to suggest here in the way of a deeper understanding of the animate is that living beings are primed for meaning; they come ready-made with a readiness to understand, with a readiness, that is, toward meaning. A stone is not out there in the world ready for meaning. And it is not because a stone lacks culture that it is not out there in the world ready for meaning. It is because a stone is not animated. It shows no responsivity toward meaning. It is not quickened toward meaning. As we saw in Part I of Chapter Two, responsivity is in fact a feature regularly itemized by biologists in their definitions of life: "the capacity to respond is a fundamental and almost universal characteristic of life" (Curtis 1975: 28). Moreover as we also saw, just such a feature is present even in bacteria:

> Processing in a bacterium may be thought of as a sort of molecular polling: … the positive "votes" cast by receptors in response, say to increasing concentrations of sugar are matched against the negative votes produced by increasing concentrations of noxious compounds. On the basis of this continuous voting process, the bacterium "knows" whether the environment, on the whole, is getting better or worse. The results of this analysis appear to be communicated by electrical signals to the response centers. The final stage, the response, consists of a brief change in the direction of rotation of the several stiff, helical flagella that propel the bacterium. The result is that the bacterium founders briefly and then strikes out in a new direction, once again sampling to see whether the environment is improving or deteriorating." (Keeton & Gould 1986: 452)

A bacterium too is primed for meaning. It goes toward and away from things; it approaches them or avoids them on the basis of whether they are of value or toxic. A bacterium finds meanings in its world and moves accordingly. A stone is precisely not primed for meaning in this way. Living creatures — organisms — are in fact intentionally active. Described mechanistically as self-enclosed, self-replicating systems, they are described simply as material objects. Their very livingness is passed over and with it their very natural propensity toward meaning. Living creatures validate another's gesture or posture as meaningful because they are by nature meaning-seekers. They have a built-in readiness toward meaning. It is notable that Daniel Dennett takes just such a readiness for meaning for granted and thereby validates just such a semantic propensity. In laying out what he calls his heterophenomenological method and differentiating that method from what he calls "'pure' phenomenology" — a phenomenology that actually has no resemblance to continental phenomenology but is simply a pejorative synonym for an already pejorative term, namely, introspection — he says that we "effortlessly — in fact involuntarily — 'make sense'" (1991: 75). It is notable too that when he makes this statement, he is speaking specifically of human speech. He says that "We effortlessly — in fact involuntarily — 'make sense' of [a] sound stream in the process of turning it into words" (75). He encloses the words *make sense* within single quotes, presumably to alert us to the fact that, as per his hard-driving materialist stance, it is not really *we* who are making sense; our brains are making sense. All the same, there is no mistaking his validation, especially when a page later (76), after affirming that, "the uttered noises are to be interpreted as things the subjects *wanted to say*, of *propositions* they meant to *assert*, for instance, for various *reasons*," he goes on to say that "In fact, we were already relying on some such assumptions in the previous step of purifying the text," that is, in the previous step of his heterophenomenological method where pure sounds are turned into words by stenographers. In short, what Dennett assumes throughout his heterophenomenology is a readiness to meaning, an active predisposition to make sense of the world, a receptivity to meaning that, as an abundance of empirical evidence shows, is there from the start, from the moment of our natality and the natality of all animate life.

Recent dynamic system accounts of bootstrapping — or scaffolding — in infant/child development make a similar assumption. A readiness to meaning underlies the processes described. For example, when Paul van Geert, a psychologist/dynamic systems theorist writes of how a child's cognitive development is bootstrapped by others or by the child itself with respect to its own immediate growth level, he exemplifies the process by language learning, pointing out how, "with increasing confidence [in language learning] … children become more attentive to their own errors, are able to use increasingly complex information concerning those rules, pay more attention to those sentences that reflect the linguistic features they are currently acquiring, and so forth." Similarly, he points out how, in a mutually supportive relationship, such as that between a parent and a child, growth in the one modifies growth in the other "either by increasing the [cognitive] carrying capacity, or the [cognitive] growth rate, or both" (1993: 313). In each case, he is describing a cognitive situation that takes a readiness for meaning for granted. There could hardly be an increased attentiveness, for example, or an increased cognitive carrying capacity short of this grounding. For one individual to affect the cognitive growth of another, or for an individual's own cognitive growth level to affect its own carrying capacity, there must first be a semantically-oriented subject; there must first be a meaning-seeker.

We see just this semantically-oriented subject concretely and many times over in the video of Kanzi: Kanzi's bodily dynamic capsulates a readiness to meaning; just as clearly, Tamuli's capsulates a frustrated readiness. Living creatures are indeed disposed toward meaning. Animation and meaning go hand in hand. Psychologist Jerome Bruner's thoughtful explorations of a child's "entry into meaning" (1990, Chapter 3) are apposite here. In developing an account of how "quite young human beings 'enter into meaning', how they learn to make sense, particularly narrative sense, of the world around them" (68), Bruner speaks explicitly of "prelinguistic 'readinesses for meaning'"(72). In so doing, he is led to sketch out a "biology of meaning," underscoring the innateness of the "readinesses" and the capacity for language (69). Although his preeminent concern is with the development of language, i.e. a child's affinity for *narrative* meaning,[8] and although he affirms that "The newborn, we say, cannot grasp 'meanings'" (68), his very postulation of an inborn readiness or disposition to meaning is significant and actually belies the lack of meaning that he says we attribute to newborns. His postulation is equally significant in the context of his emphasis on the importance of action. Linguistic meaning, he says, focuses attention on *"human action and its outcomes"* (78; italics in original): narratives are tied to "plot structures" (45) and are linked exclusively, he says, to a social world. Accordingly, insofar as "prelinguistic 'readinesses to meaning'" make ready the mastery of language, they must be similarly focused. In other words, implicit in Bruner's conception of an "entry into meaning" is the idea that "prelinguistic 'readinesses to meaning'" are tied to movement, to animation, to "I can's," to a capacity to act in the world. Moreover although his concern is not with readinesses that fall outside a preeminently narrated and narratable social world — readinesses that would, for example, embrace an infant's sense-makings with its toys, with the play of shadows on the wall of its room, with the movement of the mobile above its head, with the making of a fist with its own hand and fingers, and so on, or, that would embrace a bonobo's sense-makings of a keyboard with non-iconic symbols on it, symbols which, when pressed, result in certain sounds being heard — Bruner gives indications of recognizing just such broader 'readinesses to meaning' when he writes, for example, of the fact that a nine-month-old infant will follow the trajectory of an adult's gaze, and if it finds nothing there, "[will turn] back to check not only the adult's direction of point but the line of visual regard as well" (75). The indications are more pointedly apparent still when he speaks of performing "habituation experiments" with infants, experiments that attest to the ready attention of infants to novelty: "Infants reliably perk up in the presence of the unusual," he states; "they look more fixedly, stop sucking, show cardiac deceleration, and so on." Furthermore, he says, "[t]hey not only perk up in the presence of, but also gesture toward, vocalize, and finally talk about what is unusual" (78). In a word, Bruner's "prelinguistic 'readinesses to meaning'" readily embrace a broader world than the immediate social world of other human beings. His own well-known experimental observations of infants as well as those of others clearly show that narrative meaning is only one form of meaning. More broadly, they show that "prelinguistic 'readinesses to meaning'" are not necessarily tied exclusively to a social world, to language, to narratives, or to a "protolinguistic 'theory of mind'" (Bruner 1990:75) at all. They are tied rather to the world generally, and this because a readiness to meaning is a fundamental dimension of life. Living creatures — organisms — are *primed for meaning*. Not only can we recall the bodily dynamics of Kanzi and Tamuli, we can recall the vitality affects and the physiognomic and amodal perceptions that infant psychiatrist Daniel Stern identifies and that were discussed in Chapter Five. Moreover disregarding Bruner's characterization of "prelinguistic readiness" as "a form of mental representation" — "a highly malleable yet innate representation that is triggered by the acts and expressions of others and by certain basic social contexts in which human beings interact" (1990: 73) — and characterizing it rather as a whole-body dispositional readiness toward meaning, a sheer semantic bodily propensity, we readily see it as clearly etched in the lives of nonhuman animals as of human ones. A disposition toward meaning is a pan-animate disposition. How otherwise explain the presence of comsigns or the possibility of tactical deception? How otherwise explain the provenience and evolution of inter-animate meanings, inter-animate meanings that are not only intra-species meanings but inter-species meanings as well? A readiness toward meaning is a biological matrix. Like corporeal representation (Sheets-Johnstone 1990), it is a matrix evident in the evolution of animate forms. It is thus neither limited to our own hominid lineage nor is it the result of our being social animals, creatures who live in groups. By the same token, and with respect to our ontogenetic past, it is not limited to *praxis* (cf. Bruner 1990: 73, 74). An ontogenetic readiness toward meaning is not confined to an infant's or young child's mastery of practical understandings of social interactions — in a broad sense, of "the perils to Agentivity in a tough [social] world and how one copes in that world by deed and by word" (Bruner 1990: 84). A readiness toward meaning is phylogenetically and ontogenetically geared to the global but particular world in which creatures — ourselves included — find themselves, and find themselves from the very beginning of their lives. It is the backbone of their burgeoning knowledge of themselves and of their developing commerce with the world-at-large, as when they explore a terrain, recognize a food source, play with others, study an object, care for a young one, court a possible mate, defend a territory, become perturbed at the sight of something alien, choose to flee rather than fight, greet a friend or conspecific, discern a rival, build a nest — or learn the intricacies of a keyboard and its correlated sounds. A readiness to meaning is everywhere apparent because living creatures are semantically-oriented subjects. What Bruner terms "a biology of meaning" informs the lives of all living creatures not in virtue of language, but in virtue of the fact that from the beginning, we are all of us primed for meaning. The same biological matrix is at the core of all our lives.

Husserl once remarked that primal sensibility "is simply there" — it emerges with life itself (1989: 346). The same may be said of primal movement; it too is simply there. Unless we are stillborn, primal animation informs our lives from the beginning. The same is true of a readiness toward meaning: it too is simply there — it too emerges with life itself. Meaning is in fact what primal sensibility and primal movement are all about. Husserl's perspicuous analysis of "receptivity" — a foundational perceptual disposition toward the world — is significant in this context. Receptivity is not at all a passive disposition but an active one (Husserl 1973b: 71–194). Husserl described it as a natural "*turning toward*" the world (1973: 76–79; italics added), a natural, active, spontaneous inclination toward sensing, and a natural, active, and spontaneous interest in that which is sensed. This foundational perceptual disposition toward the world is a foundational aspect of all creaturely life; it is co-extensive with a natural turning toward meaning, and of a natural power to grasp meaning, as in grasping the meaning of a displaying animal, or in grasping the import of a rustling sound that we hear behind us, or in grasping the words we read on a page. Living creatures, ourselves included, are thus responsive in a sense beyond the sense in which biology texts speak of responsivity. We are all of us *semantically* responsive, just as we are *semantically* receptive. We are all of us inherently meaning-seekers and meaning-finders (for references to related bio-semiotic research, see Note 7). Meaning-seeking readily explains why it is the receiver, the displayed-to animal, that solidifies meaning and indeed, why it assents to meaning in the first place. It straight-away recognizes the world and other creatures in its world as having semantic value. For all of us, to be intentionally active is to move spontaneously toward meaning and in virtue of meaning. We take it for granted, as it were, that, whatever the situation, we will find other creatures meaningful and the world in general meaningful; and indeed, both are consistently full of meaning for us. They are as consistently meaningful for nonhuman creatures as for human ones. Acknowledgment of this disposition toward meaning constitutes the beginning step in understanding Kanzi's spontaneous move toward a keyboard and his mastery of its correlated visual and aural symbols. It constitutes as well the beginning step in understanding Tamuli's wild and erratic movement in the presence of the keyboard. If one were to forge a bio-ontology on the basis of life being a movement toward meaning, a literal turning toward the world, the ontology would be well described as being-toward-meaning. Clearly, this ontology would not favor or single out humans in the least. On the contrary, and as indicated, being-toward-meaning describes all animate forms, not just the animate form that is human.

A final word may be added. No species can forge a language for which its body is unprepared. As pointed out and discussed in the previous chapter, there are two biologically-based semantics. In addition to built-in morphological semantics, or form values, to use Adolph Portmann's term (1967) — the distinct coloration of male and female birds of many species, for example, or the distinct black coloration of a newborn infant olive baboon (*Papio anubis*) in contrast to the brown-gray-olive coloration of an adult — there are animate values that define a species-specific semantics structured in each case on the basis of species-specific possibilities of movement — distinctive but also variously overlapping kinetic possibilities peculiar to animate forms (see Chapter One, this text). Species-specific semantics are integral to dynamic forms of life. There could hardly be comsigns if living forms were immobile. There could hardly be a propensity toward meaning at all since meaning demands animation. Responsivity, as in the flight of a bee or butterfly to certain color-patterned flowers, is a testimonial to this foundational semantic-kinetic relationship. An evolutionary semantics would surely move us closer to its understanding; it would surely move us closer to an appreciation of the way in which the primacy of movement and the primacy of meaning in the natural world are essentially intertwined. By the same token, it would surely move us closer to an understanding of how our own meaningful lives, perhaps especially, our own linguistically meaningful lives, are fundamentally related to the meaningful lives of other creatures. It would, in other words, attune us to the fact that sense-making is a fundamental way of life rooted in a diversity of animate forms and tactile-kinesthetic bodies, and in a foundational readiness toward meaning.

Notes

* A shorter version of this chapter was presented at Trondheim University (Norway) in December 1996 and at a Philosophy Forum at Albright College in March 1997.

1. This objection to exclusively modular explanations of human speech perception compliments and supports John Searle's objection to cognitive-computational explanations of behavior on the grounds that they proliferate homunculi (Searle 1990a, 1984). Note too that "feature analyzers" are common in speech research and have a long history. See, for example, Cutting & Eimas 1975; Masland 1972.

2. I first learned of Wittgenstein's remark through linguist Patrick Coppock, whom I thank for the reference. Though not explicitly credited by Wittgenstein (though perhaps suggestively credited by being enclosed in scare quotes), the remark actually comes from Goethe's *Faust* (Part I, line 1237: "*Im Anfang war die Tat*"), when Faust challenges the idea that "In the beginning was the Word." Interestingly enough, Husserl too uses the aphorism. He uses it in specifying his new beginning, i.e. what it means methodologically to turn toward the life-world in the phenomenological attitude. He writes that "As is the case with all undertakings which are new in principle, for which not even an analogy can serve as guide, this beginning takes place with a certain unavoidable naivete. In the beginning is the deed" (Husserl 1970:156).

3. The original study showing that infants two-and three-days old cry in response to hearing other infants cry was done by Simner 1971. A subsequent study by Sagi and Hoffman (1976) showed that one-day old infants cry in response to hearing other infants cry.

4. Kanzi was raised at the Language Research Center at Georgia State University. A video was made by Japanese researchers visiting the Language Research Center and is available from the Center. Savage-Rumbaugh and Lewin co-authored *Kanzi* (1994).

5. The earlier reference to bisociation is topical with respect to an explanation of Kanzi's linguistic ability, for here, as with deaf children, an understanding of the sensory-kinetic foundations of the normal development of speech are of moment. To explain Kanzi's ability in bisociative terms would entail first an analysis of the way in which visual symbol (keyboard icon) and aural element (sounded word) come to be semantically linked with an object or doing or place in the world. Important in this analysis is an understanding of the active role of Kanzi himself: he makes things happen as a result of pressing a key, that is, he causes certain sounds to be heard. Kanzi's ability to comprehend spoken English, that is, by itself, in the absence of a visual icon on a keyboard, is an ability to recognize sound alone — *the sheer*

physiognomy of sound — as meaningful. The situation might be akin to the mastery of reading, in which instance a sheer visual physiognomy presents itself as meaningful.

6.   In this regard it is of moment to note that in the experimental circumstances in which Kanzi lives, operant conditioning limits his abilities; that is, Kanzi is consistently given *food* rewards. Increments in learning are not rewarded with, what one might call advanced challenges. One might well wonder what would happen if he were given other kinds of rewards — crayons, a flashlight, a microscope, a recording of Mother Goose nursery rhymes, a recording of Benjamin Britten's "A Young Person's Guide to the Orchestra," a recording of Mozart's "Eine kleine Nachtmusik," and so on. Moreover what would happen if he were not rewarded at all? After all, he learned in the beginning spontaneously and presumably out of a sheer natural curiosity.

7.   I first presented the idea of an evolutionary semantics in terms of *corporeal representation*, both the fact (morphological) and the practice (based on species-specific tactile-kinesthetic invariants) of such representation (Sheets-Johnstone 1990). For a full analysis and discussion of corporeal representation as a biological matrix, see the above, Chapter 5. A readiness for meaning is a further biological matrix. The interesting and detailed semiotic work of Claus Emmeche (1991, 1994), Jesper Hoffmeyer (1996), and Hoffmeyer and Emmeche (1991) on behalf of semiotic understandings of creaturely life has a quite different point of departure — Charles Sanders Peirce's theory of signs — but converges in important ways with the evolutionary semantics proposed here.

8.   What is significant about narrative meaning in the present context is its focus on actions and their outcomes, exactly as Bruner emphasizes. Narrative meaning is dynamically oriented; at the very least, it consistently enfolds a sense of agency. More than this, it appears to enfold those dimensions of self that Stern identifies as aspects of a core self: a sense of agency, a sense of coherence, a sense of affectivity, a sense of history.

CHAPTER 10

Why a mind is not a brain
and a brain is not a body*

> To say ... that a man is made up of certain chemical elements is a satisfactory
> description only for those who intend to use him as a fertilizer.
>
> Herbert Muller (1943: 107)

1. Introduction

If we take evolution seriously, we are compelled to realize that an exclusive focus on
brains — in the name of understanding in a cognitive sense who and what we are — is
misguided. It is as misguided as the singular focus of those paleoanthropologists who
not that long ago insisted that "big brains came first."[1] When finally the artifactual evidence was allowed to speak for itself, paleoanthropologists found that big brains did
not come first. Movement came first. Labor came first. These historical truths should
by themselves temper present-day proclivities to see everything in terms of brains.
Moreover if paleoanthropologists can right their record-keeping and generate a credible picture of our evolutionary past on the basis of empirical evidence, then we should
be able to right our theoretical bias and generate a credible picture of mind and body
on the basis of empirical evidence. Our major concern in this chapter will be to right
our theoretical bias. In particular, we will consider our origins — ontogenetic as well as
phylogenetic — in the light of three notable conceptual hazards we readily encounter
in present-day cognitivist studies: an undue elevation of language, a radical materialism, and a Meccanized neurology. Critical examination of these hazards will allow an
empirically credible picture of mind and body to come into view.

2. Minds and language

In the beginning was — and is — not the word.[2] In the beginning was — and is —
movement. In fact, in the beginning is always *animate form*. We see this ontogenetically as well as phylogenetically. Newborn creatures *move*; stillborns are precisely
stillborn. Life, including human life, is in the most fundamental sense not a matter of
brains or language; it is most basically a matter of tactile-kinetic powers, including, but

not limited to, those tactile-kinetic powers that at some time in our remote hominid past led to the very invention of a verbal language and that make present-day human speech possible. When Daniel Dennett asks "What is it like to be a human infant?" and answers "My killjoy answer would be that it isn't like very much," he justifies himself by saying, "How do I know? I don't 'know', of course, but my even more killjoy answer is that in my view of consciousness, it arises when there is work for it to do, and the preeminent work of consciousness is dependent on sophisticated language-using activities" (1983:384). Dennett's view is not only unexamined and unsubstantiated, but flies in the face of available empirical evidence, namely, the extraordinarily varied and impressive data gathered in the last twenty-five years and more on human infants.[3]

If we begin our understandings of consciousness — or mind — with Dennett's emaciated notion of infants, we begin in fact with a *deus ex machina* world. We are, in effect, academic creationists who believe in immaculate linguistic conception. We espouse the view that language arose *de novo* — a decidedly counter-evolutionary notion — or we fail altogether to think about the question of how a verbal language could possibly have arisen. In this latter respect we lag far behind the thoughtful reflections of Condillac whose inquiries into the origin of human knowledge, as indicated in Chapter Nine, led him to an in-depth reflective recreation of the origin of language "according to the ordinary course of nature" — in pointed contrast to a view of language as a gift from divine providence ([1756] 1971:171). We are moreover linguistic dogmatists who, with our adultist priorities, confer no status at all on those who do not measure up to our lingual standards, thus not only decreeing there are developmental Rubicons to be crossed to achieve our unique adult status but denigrating in the process what we ourselves once were but are incapable of remembering what it was like being.

Now in the first place, and as suggested above, a well-recognized evolutionary axiom states that there is nothing *de novo* in nature, in other words, that in the natural world, there is nothing that has absolutely no antecedents; everything has a history. Clearly, we must begin with that history, *our* history, if we are to understand who and what we are, in particular, if we are to understand mind or consciousness. To do this, we obviously must become acquainted with our past and understand and accept ourselves as we were, both ontogenetically and phylogenetically: we must comprehend the heritages that have shaped us as individuals and that bind us in a common humanity. In effect, we must give up masquerading as something we would like to be or something we fancy ourselves as being, and accede in the end to the truths of our human condition. In the memorable if sportive words of Swami Beyondananda: "we must drive our karma and curb our dogma" (Bhaerman 1991).

In the second place, it might seem that our very inability to remember ourselves as infants — the word 'infant' deriving from Latin, "not to speak" — is sufficient reason for denigrating infancy. After all, were something *really* going on in that period of our lives, we would know it and remember it. Not only this but we would be able to *speak* of it, and with first-person authority. In this justificatory tone, we might easily invoke the immaturity of a human infant's neurological system as empirical testimony to its cognitive deficiencies. But as suggested above, a denigrating and even blank slate rendition of infancy is readily refuted by evidence that has been gathered on human infants in the last twenty-five years and more and that attests to a prodigious cognitive capacity — for imitation (Meltzoff 1981; Meltzoff & Moore 1977), for self/other discriminative abilities and intermodal fluencies (Stern 1990), for basic arithmetic skills (B. Bower 1992: 132), and for much, much more (e.g. Butterworth 1983, 1991; Butterworth & Hopkins 1988).[4]

Further and broader problems attend a language-tethered consciousness that have nothing to do with infancy per se. Because of its exclusive emphasis on language-using activities, a language-tethered consciousness comes perilously close to denying what might be called generic experience, and this because language-using activities obviously depend on there being something to talk about. They depend precisely upon *experience* in the ordinary, everyday sense of perceiving things, being affected by them, exploring them, moving away from them, playing with them, intently studying them, and so on. Surely if there is no substantive experiencing consciousness, then there can hardly be anything to talk (read or write) about to begin with since there is no awareness that such and such is happening, and to oneself rather than to someone else; no awareness that such and such is present, and at the center rather than at the periphery of action; and so on. If, as Dennett says, consciousness arises only when it has work to do and the preeminent work of consciousness *depends* on sophisticated language-using activities, then he is putting something close to a garrulous horse before an empty cart. Moreover his formulation is reminiscent of Descartes's "*cogito, ergo sum*" and subject to the same kind of jest, *viz.*, whenever I am not speaking (reading or writing), I am devoid of consciousness. Finally, if it were true that the preeminent work of consciousness *depends* on sophisticated language-using activities, then, as indicated above, we could only wonder how on earth language itself could have gotten started. A sizable consciousness is necessary to the invention of language, beginning with a consciousness of oneself as a sound-maker and ending with a full-blown and acutely perceptive consciousness of the articulatory gestures of speech (Sheets-Johnstone 1990). Indeed, as a phenomenon in its own right, the very invention of language defines a situation in which — to paraphrase Dennett — "there is work for consciousness to do," not a *deus ex machina* consciousness capable of immaculate linguistic conceptions, but an already discerning and creative consciousness knowledgeably attuned to itself and to the ways of the world.

3. The radical doctrine of eliminative materialism

There is another place at which one might be tempted to anchor one's assessments of minds that constitutes an equally notable hazard. One might claim that metaphysically speaking, there is nothing that is non-material, and not just from the beginning of time, so to speak, but to any end one could possibly imagine. Mind — or consciousness — is a figment of our folk imagination, and our folk imagination is itself a figment of that figment. Accordingly, with this claim one is easily in the lap of eliminative materialism (P.M. Churchland 1981; P.S. Churchland 1986, 1992). By way of spelling out the tenets of this doctrine critically and in further detail, I would like to note something about it that is basically puzzling. I would in fact like to confess, however blatantly autobiographical, that the reason I had — and still occasionally have — difficulty with the doctrine of eliminative materialism is that the phrase "eliminative materialism" is a verbal necker cube. What we are supposed to understand by the phrase is that the mind, that is, what is putatively non-material, is in the process of being eliminated by our expanding understandings of neurophysiology, in particular, the neurophysiology of the brain. When our neurophysiological knowledge of the brain reaches its promised fulfillment, nothing but a pure physicalism will remain. In the end, we will thus see how misled we have been to think in terms of minds or consciousness, for there are no such things as minds, no such things as mental events, processes, or entities. We boil down to neural firings and our ultimate ability will be to speak in terms of these neural firings. We will become fluent in the neurological language of our brains. In effect, the material brain will have eliminated the non-material mind and in the process cleared up all of our nagging metaphysical and epistemological problems.

The phrase "eliminative materialism" may, however, be equally understood as a materialism in which matter is self- rather than other-eliminating, that is, as a process in which matter *decreases* rather than increases — like an animal devouring its own tail, or more concretely, perhaps like an opossum that, caught in a trap, eats off its own shackled appendage. According to this opposite but equally cogent sense of "eliminative materialism," the phrase specifies a matter that progressively shrinks, to the point that only what is absolutely essential remains. The long and short of the essential in this construal of the doctrine of eliminative materialism is the brain. In effect, a material brain ultimately eliminates a dispensable material body. The same corporeal elimination is of course at the heart of the rightly-construed sense of eliminative materialism as well. This is because in both readings, the brain is firmly planted centerstage in an ever-expanding pool of neurophysiological light. It is only a question of what the light directly obliterates. In the first reading, the light directly obliterates the mind; in the second reading, the light directly obliterates the living body. More finely expressed, the difference between the two readings lies in the fact that in the second reading, the elimination of the living body is not simply the by-product of an all-consuming attention to the brain. The living body is eliminated directly on the grounds of its strictly marginal importance. It is accordingly eliminated from the scene, not just pushed back into the wings where it might hover expectantly or remain "on call" as needed, but out the door and onto the street, an outcast that, like those socio-political outsiders called "the homeless," has no intrinsic value.

In spite of the possibility of alternative readings, it might be said that it matters not at all in what sense one understands eliminative materialism; the basic reality — a brain that is the be-all and end-all of a fundamental and absolute physicalism — is the same, exactly what one would expect from a necker cube, verbal or otherwise. The alternative readings, however, are substantively instructive, metaphysically and epistemologically, and this because, whether specifying a swelling or shrinking matter, the doctrine of eliminative materialism progressively subtracts corporeal matters of fact, and with them, insights into the cognitive heart of our ontogenetic and phylogenetic humanness. From this perspective, it might indeed be said that eliminative materialism is not simply or *inter alia* an egregiously pretentious program; it is a grave mistake. However glorious and rising our neurophysiological knowledge of the brain, what is being ignored and finally made to disappear under its banner is animate form, and with animate form, all those conative and cognitive possibilities and constraints of being that fundamentally inform our lives and are the very stuff of our being. In short, it might indeed be said that our present-day love affair with brain neurophysiology is leading us astray. It blinds us to the fact that in the most fundamental sense, we are living bodies and that where goeth living bodies, so also goeth minds, not in the sense of a twosome, but a onesome. Our own evolutionary history conclusively demonstrates to us the sobriety and truth of this claim. What began in movement and in labor — what began in the body with bipedality and with tool-using/tool-making — is indissolubly linked to thinking and to conceptual expansions. Consistent bipedality brought with it new sexual signalling behaviors; tool-using/tool-making brought with it new ways of living in the world. Radically new possibilities and constraints attached to and developed from these new bodily practices (Sheets-Johnstone 1990). Our own evolutionary history thus teaches us that to catapult the brain to prominence and in the process to eliminate the living body is to eliminate the source of those fundamental conceptual changes that are the hallmarks of hominid evolution. The living body and its tactile-kinesthetic correlates are the basis of our ontogenetic conceptual and comportmental histories as well as of our phylogenetic ones. We learn to reach, and in the process measure shapes and distances; we learn to stand alone, and in the process gauge new spatial relationships, bodily alignments, balance, and weight. We think first of all in movement. Thinking is in fact foundationally modelled on the body, on animate form. To affirm otherwise is to fall into the error perhaps best exemplified by the primatologist (Harding 1975: 255) who wrote that "Nonhuman primates have brains capable of cooperative hunting," as if when summoned by hunger, it is primate brains that go out to do battle on the savannah. Clearly, brains do not think any more than brains perceive or judge. Such possibilities are the province of living bodies, of animate forms.

4.   Dressing up: The broader eliminative-materialist picture

The wearing of a lab coat signifies science or at least has the aura of a scientific undertaking. In this respect it signifies distance, for in science, a distance is placed between
oneself and the objects one manipulates. For this very reason, a lab coat can easily
make people forgetful of living bodies. Indeed, lab-coated personnel commonly trade
in tissues and organs, in bodily fluids, in chemically preserved specimens, in fragmented wholes, and have little or no traffic either with the dynamics or with the fleshly
warm feel of living bodies. The inert mass that lies before them on the laboratory table
is an object of study, and to be such, must be and in fact has already been object-ified.
A physician's white coat can easily make people forgetful of humanness for similar
reasons. As Dan Blumhagen, himself a medical doctor, points out in "The Doctor's
White Coat," the garb of the physician derives from the laboratory; the coat is powerfully symbolic of scientific authority and knowledge; as such, it strengthens the image
of the physician as "active scientist" and the patient as "passive material" (1979: 115).
Blumhagen's point is reminiscent of Maurice Merleau-Ponty's just observation that
"science manipulates things and gives up living in them" (1964e: 159).

Now suppose a group of philosophers unexpectedly were to find an eliminative
materialist philosopher lecturing in a lab coat. There is no inert mass lying on a laboratory table and there is not even a laboratory table to begin with. The gathering is not in a
laboratory but in a large lecture hall and the philosopher is not concerned with bodies at
all but is lecturing on the brain, using a pointer to indicate this and that place on various
diagrams of the brain that are cast on a large screen by an overhead projector. The more
perplexed might conclude that eliminative materialism is linked in a fundamental way
to the wearing of lab coats even though in the present instance there is nothing dissectable, thus no potentially messy material at hand. In other words, the practical answer
to the question of why people wear lab coats — to keep from getting splattered with
the stuffings of once-animate forms — is incongruous here. The group of philosophers
might thus be led to ponder the deeper significances of a lab coat indicated above. The
course of their reflections might be briefly sketched in the following way:

At a purely pragmatic level, a philosopher lecturing on brains is in no need of
protective garb. The philosopher is not dealing with pulpy tissues, slippery organs, and
such but with physico-chemical events, with neural firings and the like which, incidentally, are actually nowhere in sight. The lab coat hence indeed appears to be purely
symbolic — like "The Doctor's White Coat." More than this, the symbolic effectiveness to which it aspires is aptly described in a passage from Blumhagen — appropriate
paraphrasings being supplied: philosopher for physician, audience for patient.

> The relationship between a philosopher and his audience is serious and
> purposeful, not social, casual or random.... For a long time it has been

customary for individuals in society to dress rather formally when conducting serious business, and less formally when they are at leisure. The philosopher's dress should convey ... a sense of seriousness of purpose that helps to provide reassurance and confidence.... Casual ... dress is likely to convey ... casual or inattentive professional handling of [the] problem (Blumhagen 1979:111–12).

Read symbolically in this way, the lab coat transforms the philosopher into an authoritative scientist-physician who understands the mind/body problem thoroughly and knows how to minister to it. Correlatively, the audience that has a mind/body problem and that gathers to hear its problem addressed immediately sees that its concerns are being accorded the highest recognition; a master of the subject is about to treat the problem and heal it. Further reflection, however, shows that the symbolic effectiveness of the lab coat cannot cover over certain doxic and conceptual infelicities of the actual situation. In particular, close attention to the tendered treatment shows the master philosopher to be a devout believer in a kind of promised land, that is, in an as yet unrealized consummate brain neurophysiology. On the basis of this belief, the philosopher reduces the mind/body problem to one big nervous fixture that is straightaway and without question regarded both in detachment, and as basically detachable, from living bodies. Close attention, in short, reveals a philosopher attempting to do away with the mind/body problem by scientizing it, laundering it so that it comes out clean, without all those bothersome epistemological spots and metaphysical stains. With this revelation, it becomes clear that to protest the treatment, mere de-frocking will not do. That is, simply asking for the removal of the lab coat will in no way preclude a continuing exclusive focus on the brain and thereby save the mind/body problem from reductive extinction. This is because the aspired-to symbolic authority of the lab coat is actually just dressing. The coat is in fact no more than an extreme instance of routine practice among materialist-oriented philosophers, namely, to take on the guise of the scientist and, in effect, to practice philosophy scientifically.

These reflections lead to the conclusion that "The Philosopher's White Coat" is symbolic of a core problem that might be termed "the cover-up" problem, but that can be more fruitfully analyzed as a compound philosophical problem that is the source of sizable and unwitting confusions. As indicated earlier, a centerstage brain in an ever-expanding pool of neurophysiological light brings with it a thoughtless, one might even say absent-minded, but straightforward and progressive forgetting of living bodies.[5] It brings with it as well a thoughtless — again, one might even say absent-minded — substitution of body by brain. Forgetfulness and substitution together create a kind of clandestiny of the living body that renders it homeless and in effect eliminates it from concern. The ensuing irony is unmistakable. While cognitivists in general and eliminative materialists in particular are ostensibly, in the very terms of their discourse, solving the mind/body problem, there is in fact no body in sight. They are in fact most frequently attempting to solve the quite different "mind/brain" problem — of which more later. The philosopher's white coat is thus less a matter of where one's allegiances lie or of devout belief than a matter of probity. If collapsing living creatures into brains compromises living bodies — precisely as the earlier image of hungry, battling brains on the savannah succinctly illustrates — then a centerstage brain in an ever-expanding pool of obliterating light is philosophically out of joint with life. Living creatures are neither brains in disguise — cerebral events either on the march or waiting to happen, as it were — nor are they a ruse science must unmask for what they are: containers of cerebral neurophysiological happenings, pure and simple, containers that are in essence the neurological equivalent of the lumbering vehicle that carries genes about.

The desire to transform twentieth-century philosophy into a twentieth-century science readily explains why eliminative materialists — and cognitivists generally — go to the brain as to the oracle at Delphi for answers to their mind/body problems. The brain makes the problems dissectable in essence if not in fact. Indeed, for an eliminativist as for many a cognitivist, privileging the brain and appealing to it for solution already count as a dissection of the mind/body problem. On their view, the dual acts strip the problem to its core and expose it for what it is: at the near limits, something only a brain can solve; at the extreme, a misconception to begin with. It is not surprising, then, that philosophers conduct thought experiments featuring brains in vats to raise and solve issues about "the mind/world relationship" (Putnam 1981:6),[6] for example, or "to lead us to the beginnings of a theory — an empirical scientifically respectable theory — of human consciousness" (Dennett 1991:4). Brains in vats, kept alive by proper "nutrients," are attached to "a super-scientific computer which causes the person whose brain it is to have the illusion that everything is perfectly normal" (Putnam 1981:6) or they are the playthings of "evil scientists" who can manipulate them neurologically to have certain experiences (Dennett 1991:3–4). Whatever the specific scenario, where just such privilegings and appeals are made, one big nervous fixture is taken to be the definitive emblem of humankind. All true believers must ultimately come there as to neurological Mecca, make their respectful genuflections, and do their intellectual work.

5. Pause-for-thought problems with neurological mecca

That the belief in a neurological Mecca is itself, on the cognitivist's account, merely a neurophysiological happening inside the brain, and as such enjoys no privileged position with respect to other beliefs, should give pause for thought. After all, if beliefs, desires, wishes, convictions, feelings, and so on, are but neurophysiological brain events, what reason is there to claim the priority of one belief (desire, wish, conviction, feeling) over another?[7] The question is not only important; it is critical to the very doctrine of a thoroughgoing materialism.[8] How can one set of mere neural firings possibly be valued over another? Can the brain neurophysiology that is identical to the doctrine of materialism be shown to have, say, "greater survival value" than the brain neurophysiology that is identical to the doctrine of vitalism? Can the brain neurophysiology that specifies a belief in the primacy of a computational brain possibly be privileged in anything but an arbitrary manner over the brain neurophysiology that specifies a belief in the primacy of living bodies? Can the strength of a belief possibly be deemed a measure of its value — as with an undeviating belief in a consummate brain neurophysiology, for example? But surely the strength of any particular belief counts for nought, not only because the strength of any particular belief is only a matter of neurophysiology, either "more" neurophysiology or "less" neurophysiology, but because the neurophysiological strength of a belief in materialism, for example, might be equal to the neurophysiological strength of a belief that bananas are good to eat. Clearly, if there are no minds and no living bodies to be taken into account, if minds and living bodies are separately and together totally explained by brain neurophysiology, then the reasonability of eliminative materialism or any other type of cognitivism which whittles away at body and mind so that in the end only neural states remain is undermined. Such doctrines call materialism itself into serious question by their very extremism. Indeed, their funneling of minds and bodies into human brain neurophysiology is the equivalent of shooting themselves in the foot, however that foot might be believed to be only a materially represented one in a brain.

The self-undoing of a Meccanized materialism aside, concrete knowledge of the lives of so-called "lower" creatures such as those that entomologists study should also give pause for thought. Darwin wrote, for example, that "the brain of an ant is one of the most marvellous atoms of matter in the world, perhaps more marvellous than the brain of man" ([1871] 1981: 145). Why did he say this? Because he realized that "there may be extraordinary mental activity with an extremely small absolute mass of nervous matter" (145). He made these remarks on ants in the context of reflecting upon the human brain and its evolutionary development, noting that "the wonderfully diversified instincts, mental powers, and affections of ants are generally known, yet their cerebral ganglia are not so large as the quarter of a small pin's head" (145). The specific interrelated points he was making were (1) that "[as] mental faculties were gradually developed, the brain would almost certainly have become larger," but (2) that "intellect can[not] be accurately gauged by the cubic contents of … skulls" (145). Darwin's observations should prompt one to wonder on what grounds human — not to mention ant — intellect can be wholly explained in terms of "nervous matter" at all. They raise robust, even galvanic, doubts as to whether, via material shrinkings or swellings, consciousness or mind can be thoroughly "neuralized" and thereby thoroughly explained by a materialist account. We might recall that sociobiological entomologists E.O. Wilson and Bert Holldobler wrote a 732 page book on ants (1990) — on brainless, purportedly ungifted, mechanical creatures endowed with only a single gan-glionic cell. In an earlier article, they described the remarkable alarm and recruitment systems of African weaver ants, systems that attest to the veracity of Darwin's obser-vations concerning both the "mental powers" and "affections of ants" (Holldobler & Wilson 1978). Indeed, lest it be thought that Darwin was waxing sentimentally about either the "mental powers" or the "affections of ants," we should note that Holldobler and Wilson describe the "hostility and aversion" of African weaver ants, and their "cooperative ability" as seen in their recruitment of others to a food source, which of course means food-sharing (1978: 19, 21). Their descriptions might be dismissed as maudlin anthropomorphisms, but only if the exact behaviors referred to could be described in other terms exactly equal in meaning to the original. To render just such alternate descriptions would suggest that Holldobler, Wilson, and other entomolo-gists had acceded — or could accede — to philosopher Thomas Nagel's dreamed-of "objective phenomenology" (1979: 179). They would know exactly what it is like to have the subjective experiences of an ant; in effect, they would know what it is like to be an ant (see Section 6 below on the question, "What is it like?"). On the other hand, we should note that sociobiologists' typical dismissal of their descriptive language as simply a *façon de parler* is hardly credible.[9] *Façons de parler* are clearly *façons de penser* (see Sheets-Johnstone 1992b: Note 33; 1996a: Note 37).

In the most fundamental sense, Darwin's entomological observations prompt one to take evolution seriously. What evolves is not simply physical matter; mental powers and affections likewise evolve. Indeed, multiple dimensions of being inform animate life, each dimension being integrally part and parcel of the evolution of spe-cies. Darwin offered specific evidence of these dimensions in the two books he wrote subsequent to *The Origin of Species*: *The Descent of Man and Selection in Relation to Sex* ([1871] 1981: Volume I, Part I) and *The Expression of the Emotions in Man and Animals* ([1872] 1965). Materialists who worship at neurological Mecca tend to over-look this larger Darwinian picture. They gravitate toward behind-the-scenes expla-nations as it were and forego explanations grounded in natural history. In the process of doing so, they bypass the wonders and complexities of animate form, precisely those wonders and complexities described by Darwin in his studies of creatures mak-ing their diverse ways in the world. Those wonders and complexities are not *passé*. On the contrary, they are regularly described by field biologists such as Wilson and Holldobler. They are even remarked upon from time to time in essays in the popular media. In a review of Wilson's book on biological diversity, for example, *Time* maga-zine writer R.Z. Sheppard observed that "An explanation of how species evolve may require more attention than *Homo televideous* is willing to muster. Hang in. Accounts of the author's field experiences convey an excitement of discovery that many read-ers last felt as children examining insects in a patch of grass" (Nov. 16, 1992: 101). Sheppard leaves no doubt but that, in the beginning at least, animate forms are a source of wonder. They are definitive of the wonder of life itself and of its history. It is not surprising, then, that they attract not a passing attention but a rapt and fascinated interest, literally enlivened by a sense of the animate. Wonder in face of animate forms puts us back in touch with natural history, a history that can otherwise founder, like wonder itself, as a result of the vapid energies and torpid interests of *Homo televideous*. The irony is that *Homo televideous* is, at least partially, a product of the "at home" syndrome of American science, its mundanization of life and cosmos. Where twentieth-century American scientists take up the generally chummy and casual end-of-the-century American *Zeitgeist*, they fuel the invidiously lazy habits of *Homo televideous*. *Time* essayist Barbara Ehrenreich captures the *Zeitgeist* well in her commentary on NASA's telecast reports of Sojourner's rock explorations on Mars. As she succinctly describes it, "we are making things seem tame and familiar before we even know what they are." Apropos of NASA's "cuddly" naming of rocks, for example, and of its "Coochy-coochy-coo" descriptions of Sojourner's interactions with them, she legitimately decries our cultural penchant for cuteness over wonder. In "the cutest little universe you've ever seen," she writes, "there is nothing out there — either in the mythic past or the distant reaches of space — that can't be labeled, depicted and potentially marketed by the late 20th-century American entertainment culture" (August 25, 1997:82). Clearly, *Homo televideous* and the "at home" syndrome are locked together in the same fatuously emaciated and intellectually-debilitated view of life, one bereft of wonder and of a resonantly deep appreciation of animate life and its evolutionary history.

We should note that words which attempt a makeover of evolution are an equal threat to the larger Darwinian picture, words of those with a talent for fantasy and a disregard of our own natural history. Two well-known instances will suffice to make the point. The makeover that philosopher Jacques Derrida forthrightly proposes is a new "history of man" in the name of "grammatology as a positive science" (1976:85). The makeover is perhaps most aptly described as a science-fiction *tour de foppery*, for the new text-making creature that Derrida brings to life is not even a figment of its former animate self. It is without hands and teeth, and perhaps most remarkable of all, it is no longer even upright. It is a piece of "toothless humanity that would exist in a prone position using what limbs it had left to push buttons with" (button-pushing being vital to its text-making).[10] Derrida writes one body out of existence and another into existence with the neat stroke of a pen, clearly a knock-out performance. Psychiatrist Jacques Lacan's makeover is in substance no different. Animate form is again compromised, in this instance not through replacement but through redefinition. Lacan's psychoanalytic body is a body that is quite simply full of holes: a *corps troué* creates space for the phallus, Lacan's omnipotent, overarching, and privileged signifier (Lacan 1978; for a critical analysis, see Sheets-Johnstone 1994a, Chapters 7 through 10). It is notable that the two cavalier makeovers of animate form are actually on par with present-day Western conceptions of the body as a bin of disposable, exchange-able, augmentable, rearrangeable, or otherwise endlessly re-do-able parts. Such a body falls within the tradition of that well-remembered and well-studied French philoso-pher who so deftly originated the mind/body problem. After concluding "*I am, I exist*" ([1641] 1984, vol. 2, 17), but before asking "what shall I now say that I am?" and going on to conclude that he is a thinking substance (18), Descartes asks himself, "What then did I formerly think I was?" (17). He answers that "the first thought to come to mind was that I had a face, hands, arms and the whole mechanical structure of limbs which can be seen in a corpse, and which I called the body" (17). In effect, what adds up to "the body" is (1) a possession, (2) a purely visual entity, (3) a mechanical system of parts, and (4) a corpse-like appearance.

Informational-computational and reductionist renditions of mind typically fall too within this recognizably Cartesian tradition of failing to give the living body its due and to this extent coincide conceptually with postmodern thought. In these cogni-tivist renditions, however, the body is not only stripped of its livingness; it is no longer something for which one is obliged to give a direct account of some kind or other, as with grammatology, psychoanalysis — or Descartes. Privileging the brain takes care of the matter; the neurophysiology of the brain explains everything, including the liv-ing body. Particularly difficult conceptual confusions are created, however, when such explanations are put to the test, specifically in scenarios in which brains in vats are stimulated by (evil) scientists or (super-scientific) computers. This is essentially not only because scientists or computers are putatively the generative source of a vatted brain's perceptions, movements, words, and thoughts — in other words, vatted brains merely carry out orders on the order of "thou shalt see (grasp, say, or wonder) such and such" — but because a vatted brain, however nutrient rich the solution in which it is immersed, is not a viable synecdoche. Indeed, thought experiments featuring brains in vats give one considerable pause for thought and warrant extended examination.

Dennett's most recent brain-in-a-vat scenario dramatically illustrates the extraor-dinary conceptual difficulties. Moreover because his descriptive narrative is so gen-erous, his scenario exemplifies basic problems with brain-privileging that might otherwise go unnoticed and thereby shows how actually ill-fitted a hypothetical brain in a vat is to shed light on the mind/body problem in the first place. In fact, as we exam-ine Dennett's scenario, we shall see that the more details that are supplied about the workings and experiences of a vatted brain, the hotter and deeper the water gets vis à vis the credibility of the aim of the thought experiment: to shed light on the mind/body problem via an "empirical scientifically respectable theory of human consciousness."

Putting the reader in the position of being a brain in a vat, Dennett writes that the scientists

> arrange to wake you up [from your comatose state] by piping stereo music …
> into your auditory nerves. They also arrange for the signals that would normally

come from your vestibular system or inner ear to indicate that you are lying on your back, but otherwise paralyzed, numb, blind…. They might then go on to stimulate the tracts that used to innervate your epidermis, providing it with the input that would normally have been produced by a gentle, even warmth over the ventral (belly) surface of your body, and (getting fancier) they might stimulate the dorsal (back) epidermal nerves in a way that simulated the tingly texture of grains of sand pressing into your back. 'Great!' you say to yourself: 'Here I am, lying on my back on the beach, paralyzed and blind, listening to rather nice music, but probably in danger of sunburn. How did I get here, and how can I call for help?' (Dennett 1991: 4; italics added).

Extended examination of the difficult question, "Where do the words come from that you, a vatted brain, say to yourself?" will aptly illustrate why a brain cannot stand in place of a living body — or mind — and why in turn vatted-brain thought experiments cannot shed light on the mind/body problem.

One might think to begin with that, obviously, insofar as a brain in a vat is beholden to its hardware, the words the brain utters to itself could only come from scientists or computer. In other words, no matter how well fed, without connections that determine what it feels and what it believes, a vatted brain is nothing but pulpy tissue. To judge from Dennett's narrative scenario, however, the words appear to be the *spontaneous* self-utterances of the brain in the vat, i.e. of you, a "person." The innocent, self-reflective words that pour out of you, however, pose a problem. Either they are being put into your mouth by the scientists/computer or the scientists/computer are reading your brain, so to speak. If the words are being put into your mouth, then it must be explained how it is possible for the scientists/computer to know your experience of your condition to the extent that they know unequivocally what you are actually thinking verbally to yourself. In finer critical terms, it must be explained how it is possible for the scientists/computer to *arrange* that you speak words *to yourself* and for those words to be *self*-reflections, *veridical* self-reflections. Short of compromising the thought experiment, it is impossible for you to be fooled here too, that is, fooled in addition to thinking yourself first of all a "person." In other words, at this "meta-experiential," i.e. reflective, level, it is imperative that your verbal thoughts and feelings about yourself be your own self-reflective evaluations of your situation and not simply the musings of others. Alternatively, if scientists/computer are reading self-generated thoughts and feelings out of your brain, then the very logic of the thought experiment collapses since you, a vatted brain, are designed to be no more than a neurological/computational device and have nothing more in the way of experiences than what you are provided. Certainly you have neither an actual body to be sunburned nor an actual mind to worry that you are. Indeed, the very purpose of the thought experiment is to show that it is possible *to control* a brain by neurologically feeding it certain pre-determined experiences. It is in essence to find out — *in Dennett's own words* — how "to *force* the brain in the vat to have a particular set of … intentions" (italics in original), thereby to control its cerebrations and at the same time to sustain its illusion that it is a normal human (1991:10). The purpose is clearly not to find out what a brain in a vat, given certain experiences, might be thinking to itself — although conceivably, it might be argued that it is precisely *those* kinds of intentions, e.g. "I'm possibly in danger of sunburn," "How did I get here?," that the scientists/computer want to elicit — in a thoroughly controlled way, of course.

The alternative answers to the question of where the words come from pose further and more complex questions that warrant examination. Indeed, when we look closely at each alternative answer, we find a complex of internal problems, unsettling implications, and/or unjustified assumptions. What we will do is consider each answer from this closer perspective and bring central facets of the complex to light.

If the inner speech of the vatted brain were actually that of a normal, intact human, we would say that its self-reflective self-utterances were triggered naturally and spontaneously by both its perceived and affectively-felt bodily situation. In Dennett's scenario, however, the verbalized self-reflections, while seemingly triggered naturally and spontaneously by the vatted brain's perceived and affectively-felt bodily situation, are precisely *not* part of the situational "arrangement" — i.e. the music, the supine position, the grains of sand. They are, neurologically speaking, an unaccounted-for reflective *answer* to the arrangement. Indeed, they indicate that the vatted brain is not thoroughly controlled, but has experiences in excess of its forced feedings. Accordingly, if we suppose, counter to the very logic of the thought experiment, that you, a vatted brain, are capable of the spontaneous self-reflections Dennett describes, we would have to ask how scientists/computer could be privy to those self-reflections. To be privy to them would mean that scientists/computer could not only translate experience into neural firings but that, in a reverse fashion, they could translate whatever neural firings they picked up from a vatted brain into experience, *including neural firings putatively identical with verbal thoughts*, i.e. "ideational" neural firings. It would thus mean not merely that they could work the neural language both ways, translating perceptions and movements into discrete constellations of neural firings, and discrete constellations of neural firings into perceptions and movements. It would mean that they had cracked the code of all codes. Supposing they had done so, they would be able not only to *give* experiences to a vatted brain via precise neural stimulations as in Dennett's scenario, but they would be able to read its self-generated neural firings as *specific self-reflective experiences*. They would be able, in effect, to read the brain's mind — notwithstanding the fact that a brain does not have a mind. Hence, in a way closely akin to philosopher Jerry Fodor's "language of thought" by which every possible sentence is conceived to be already present in a human brain's neurological circuitry (Fodor 1975), every conceivable self-reflective experience would be neurologically accessible, for either generation or reading, by scientists/computer. In a word, if the self-reflections are indeed the spontaneous ones of the vatted brain, then there is no doubt but that the ultimate alchemy has been achieved.

In this context it should be noted that although in Dennett's narrative the vat-ted brain's spontaneous verbalized self-reflections seem part of a singular experience, there is in fact a shift from a third-person to a first-person account of the situation. The shift, from one perspective, highlights precisely the basic critical question at issue, and, from the opposite perspective, makes it appear precisely that scientists/computer can work the language both ways, thus ostensibly cancelling out the critical question. But the shift nevertheless raises the deeper question of whether spontaneous first-person, self-reflective self-utterances can be made by anything short of a living body, or at the least, short of being "arranged" in accordance with *some* living body's experience. This is because *a felt bodily sense of a situation* is absolutely essential to spontaneous self-reflective self-utterances upon the situation. In a word, *somebody* must know what it is like. In effect, there is no way in which a tactile-kinesthetic *corps engagé* can possibly be left out of the picture.

By examining the notion of spontaneity more closely, we can elucidate in greater detail the necessity of a body, in particular, a tactile-kinesthetic body, to the vatted-brain's first-person account and at the same time delve more deeply into the complexities entailed in alternative answers to the basic question "Where do the words come from?" We should note to begin with that the vatted brain's first-person self-reflective inner commentary on its bodily situation appears spontaneous and unrehearsed in just the way that the speech of one person to another person in everyday life appears spontaneous and unrehearsed. The vatted brain's inner commentary, however, is not just *apparently* spontaneous; it is *necessarily* spontaneous — in the very way that one's own inner speech is not simply apparently spontaneous but necessarily so. Whatever the thoughts that pop into one's head, they are not other than what they are. In just this way, the vatted brain does not choose its verbal thoughts; they simply appear. Accordingly, if we assume, as we are supposed to, that the vatted brain is akin to a normal, intact human, then the words it utters to itself upon its bodily condition cannot be anything but what they are, i.e. these particular words and none others, verbal reflections of its very own upon its immediate situation. When we understand the thought experiment to the letter with its third-to-first person shift in this way, we find the vatted brain's first-person self-reflective inner commentary on its situation to be indeed spontaneous. In consequence we find that its inner speech is *not* something that is force-fed to it by scientists/computer. On the contrary, the very spontaneity of its inner speech validates its viability and the alchemical wizardry of scientists/computer.

The origin of the vatted brain's spontaneity is nonetheless difficult to explain. Even if we suppose, as the thought experiment would seem to urge us to suppose, that each word the vatted brain utters to itself is neurologically identifiable, the words as a descriptive-judicative whole are not to be found anywhere in its neurological circuitry prior to their being self-uttered. Yet the vatted brain's spontaneity requires finding them somewhere; a mere vatted brain could not otherwise spontaneously utter them to itself. The neurological wherewithal of its spontaneity would be lacking. Yet even if the words as a descriptive-judicative whole were neurologically embedded prior to their being self-uttered — in broader terms, even if every possible spontaneous self-reflective verbal thought were correlated with a particular and known sequence of words in the form of a particular and known sequence of neural states — still, the particular sequence of neural states composing the particular spontaneous inner speech of the vatted brain would have to be definitively prompted or elicited; some specific state of affairs would have to propel that particular sequence of neural states and none other into existence. Presumably, the specific state of affairs that prompts the vatted brain's spontaneous self-reflections is its particular bodily situation, i.e. its felt bodily sense of being stranded on a beach, paralyzed, and blind. Yet surely there are other options; that is, surely the same bodily situation could conceivably call up other self-reflections. There is no reason to suppose, for example, that the vatted brain's felt bodily sense of being stranded on a beach, paralyzed, and blind might not conceivably provoke self-reflections on death or on glasses of water, rather than on the danger of sunburn and calls for help. Spontaneity would otherwise be a ruse; it would reduce to a finite series of fixed self-utterances, particular self-utterances being elicited for each and every conceivable situation in which a vatted brain might find itself, self-utterances that, incidentally, to keep their appearance of spontaneity, would have to undergo periodic changes commensurate with the vatted brain's age, state of alert-ness, facility with language, and so on. Moreover we might note too that the vatted brain's immediate bodily situation cannot actually by itself motivate into existence the particular sequence of neural states that it does, unless its spontaneity is an ersatz spontaneity. Its immediate bodily situation is a necessary but not sufficient condition. To entertain thoughts of sunburn and of danger, the vatted brain must have had past bodily experiences in which just such possibilities or eventualities were lived through, or it would have to have heard comparable warnings from others and understood them in a bodily felt sense. It would have to have learned, for example, not only that there might be danger in lying exposed to the sun, but that in a situation of danger, one might call for help. In short, not only is a living body essential to the credibility of the vatted brain's spontaneity — as to the credibility of the thought experiment itself — but a particular living body is essential. In this sense, plucking a brain out of the blue will not do. The credibility of a vatted brain's putatively spontaneous verbal self-reflections depends upon the life history of the person whose brain is plucked.

Clearly, the origin of a vatted brain's spontaneous self-reflections is an unresolved and perplexing question. Suppose, however, that we discount the necessity of a con-cern with a vatted brain's past experiences and learning and put momentarily to one side the essentiality of a living body. Suppose too, of course, that we discount the problem of finding neurological equivalents and consider the problem of reading a vatted brain's spontaneous self-utterances resolved. Suppose, in other words, that we take the vatted brain's verbal self-reflections as a kind of self-questioning and self-evaluation that *is* of the moment, precisely as Dennett's scenario indicates. We might still wonder whether its spontaneity is not more properly the achievement of scientists/computer. After all, if the thought experiment runs its true course, then the task of the scientists/computer is to constrain the vatted brain to finding just the situational verbal meanings it does — i.e. danger of sunburn, finding help — that is, to entertain just these thoughts and none others, and thus indeed "to *force* the brain in the vat to have a particular set of … intentions." Now for scientists/computer to control a vatted brain's "spontaneous" self-reflections in this way involves a great deal. To begin with, that scientists/computer can put spontaneous self-reflective verbal thoughts and verbalized affective feelings into a vatted brain's neurological circuitry, not just *any* thoughts and feelings but situationally *sensical* self-reflective verbal thoughts and feelings, means essentially that *they themselves know what it is like to be a body, specifically a body lying on the beach in such a condition*. It means that, short of being vatted brains themselves that are controlled by more advanced (evil) scientists or by a more gifted super-scientific computer, they have either themselves to be living bodies or to be capable of finely and accurately simulating living bodies, specifically, living bodies experiencing the particular kind of beach experience they have given the brain in the vat. They would otherwise not know what kinds of self-reflective words would make sense to put into the vatted brain's figurative mouth, words that would jibe with its felt bodily situation. Giving considerable conceptual latitude and being imaginatively generous in the extreme, one might say that one could imagine scientists/computer "arranging" for a brain in a vat to sense something, to move something, or to speak aloud. Short of being a living body, however, or of being capable of finely and accurately simulating a living body, one cannot imagine how scientists/computer could "arrange" for a brain in a vat to speak to itself in a spontaneous self-reflective way about the particular situation in which it finds itself and for those particular words to describe accurately the way it feels and what it believes about its situation. But "forc[ing] the brain in the vat to have a particular set of … intentions" involves even more than this. The vatted brain's inner speech is not simply a testimonial to such and such sensory experiences, i.e. a testimonial to its being in such and such a (perceptual) neurophysiological state; it is testimonial to something far more complex — precisely as intimated by the spontaneity problem. It is a testimonial to *introspection,* in this instance, to a spontaneous introspective report to itself on its present experienced feelings and beliefs. It is worth noting in this respect that scientific behavioral experiments on nonhuman (and human) animals are similarly a testimonial to introspection. Such experiments are *designed* in terms of certain introspective findings and of a certain range of possible intentions in light of those introspective findings. They are designed, in other words, in terms of certain feelings, thoughts, and proclivities one finds — or might find — *within oneself* were one in the same in or similar situation in which one is placing the nonhuman or human subject. The *verbal* "combinatorial explosion problem" with respect to the vatted brain's inner speech arises precisely in this introspective context and is solved within it as well. The "combinatorial explosion problem" (Dennett 1991:5), Dennett's phrase for what motor physiologists term the degrees of freedom problem — and phenomenologists might designate the kinesthetic motivation problem — refers to the enormous range of possible variability in any given movement. (The problem is considered and discussed in detail below.) A vatted brain's inner speech being in principle like its voluntary movement, it similarly presents a "combinatorial explosion problem" to be solved. As emphasized above, the vatted brain could have thought otherwise about its situation, whether a matter of having different interpretations of the situation and uttering a variety of different words — for example, "Alas! This feels like Waikiki all over again!" — or whether a matter of having the same verbal thought about getting help but in a different form — e.g. "I wonder if anyone is lying next to me." Scientists/computer solve the verbal combinatorial explosion problem in the only way they can: on the basis of introspection, that is, on the basis of reviewing their own possible thoughts and feelings were they in such a situation, and opting for a particular inner speech. In effect, and in spite of Dennett's giving no indication of their doing so, scientists/computer, in addition to "arranging" the vatted brain to hear music, to be aware of itself as lying on a beach, and so on, "arrange" it to feel in immanent danger, to wonder about its situation, and to voice its feelings of danger and wonderment in inner speech. They put particular, well-chosen words into the vatted brain's figurative mouth. In effect, being in fact the achievement of scientists/computer, the vatted brain's seemingly spontaneous self-reflections are from this perspective an illusion; the vatted brain is, after all, being fooled here too. It is indeed a dupe. Its putative spontaneous and unrehearsed self-reflections are in actuality the neurologically transferred self-reflections of scientists/computer; more precisely, they are the introspectively achieved self-reflections of a living body (or something capable of finely and accurately simulating a living body), one that knows from its own personal experience what it is like — or what it might be like — to be in the beach situation of the vatted brain.

Now if scientists/computer have not in fact arranged for the vatted brain to voice feelings of danger and wonderment in inner speech, then given the scenario, one can only acknowledge that the vatted brain is experiencing something more than what has been arranged for it. It indeed has a mind of its own, one that is capable of spontaneous and unrehearsed self-reflections. Correlatively, scientists/computer have merely tuned in, neurologically speaking, to its inner speech. But this scenario-in-excess is plainly troublesome, not only because it presupposes the ultimate alchemy to be a *fait accompli* — scientists/computer picking up every possible neurological twitch and translating it instantaneously and impeccably into thought — but because everyday capabilities that go unannounced as such — e.g. "how can I call for help?" — and that have entered Dennett's scenario raise the seemingly intractable question of agency. The question of agency in fact makes the very point that Dennett goes on to raise following his scenario all the more telling. He notes that, following their success with the music, the grains of sand, and so on, scientists could proceed to tackle "the much more difficult problem of convincing you [a brain in a vat] that you are … *an agent capable of engaging in some form of activity in the world*" (1991:5; italics added). The extreme difficulty of the problem is actually twofold, not onefold as Dennett describes it. To begin with, the problem turns on the fact that what is tactilely and especially kinesthetically felt in the course of any act depends upon just how one performs the act, and just how one performs the act depends upon how one is motivated to perform it, how one feels at the time of its execution, the position in which one currently is, and so on. In short, an agent capable of engaging in some activity in the world performs the activity in a certain way. Dennett speaks of this difficulty in computational/engineering terms, i.e. in terms of "combinatorial explosion," but the difficulty is more precisely articulated in experiential terms, i.e. in terms of kinesthetic motivation, or in kinematic terms, i.e. in terms of degrees of freedom. The latter phrase derives from the highly esteemed Russian physiologist Nicolas Bernstein (Bernstein 1984). It pinpoints the fact that any particular movement has a range of possible executions. When I lift my leg flexed at the knee, for example, I can lift it from my hip joint, knee joint, or ankle and big toe joints; I can lift it against — or as if with — resistance, I can lift it effortlessly, and in any number of ways between these two extremes; I can furthermore lift it minimally or in an exaggerated fashion, abruptly or in a sustained manner, with a slight or maximal lateral or medial rotation, with a rounded or straight spine, in conjunction with an untold number of other possible concomitant bodily postures; and so on. The possibilities are virtually limitless. The point is that a particular constellation of kinesthetic motivations or degrees of freedom attends the actual movement and that how I actually lift my leg will determine what I feel proprioceptively. Now if the purpose of the thought experiment is not to read the vatted brain's mind but to force-feed it its desires, beliefs, and so on, or in other words, to make the vatted brain intend certain experiences and to give it the experiences it intends, then accordingly, if I am the brain in the vat, my kinesthetic motivations must be controlled by scientists/computer, but in such a way that my sense of agency is uncompromised. This means that the kinetic combinatorial explosion problem must be solved and, in effect, that I can be duly duped into thinking that I am an "agent capable of engaging in some form of activity in the world." Yet even supposing magnanimously — even madly — the degrees of freedom problem solved and thus affirming what is in truth an agency *manqué* to be experienceable by me as a proper sense of agency, a second difficult problem remains.

Granted that all neurological correlates of every possible human movement with all its possible variations are not only identified and controllable, but immediately available as orchestrated wholes, how can scientists/computer possibly know in sufficient time precisely how a vatted brain not only wants to move but will actually move? If "wanting to move" — say, wanting to get a book off the shelf — is nothing more than moving — getting the book off the shelf — then where does the immediately available kinetically orchestrated whole that institutes the particular "wanting to move" come from? Notwithstanding the fact that motor programs have fallen from grace in good measure due to the probing research of dynamic systems analysts and that in consequence the very idea of immediately available kinetically orchestrated wholes is unfounded, a vatted brain's sense of agency would seem to depend upon them. If a vatted brain's wanting to move is coincident with its moving, then to preserve its sense of agency, scientists/computer would have to recognize its movement intention in the form of a motor program and duly stimulate the proper efferent impulses coincident with it. From this perspective, however, there is a fundamental critical problem that reduces to the fact that, given a vatted brain, "efferent stimulation" or "efferent impulses" light up nothing corporeal at the other end. In other words, while there are sensory cortical areas that light up with sensory experiences upon proper stimulation of the proper afferent nerve stumps, whatever might be meant by "efferent stimulation" or "efferent impulses" — stimulation of, or impulses from, the motor, supplementary motor, or premotor cortex, or the cerebellum, the basal ganglia, stumps leading to the pyramidal tracts, and so on — the stimulation or impulses go nowhere; no actual movement results. The problem that the movement blank presents is putatively addressed by providing the vatted brain with immediate tactile-kinesthetic feedback that reflects the missing movement, *putatively* because such tactile-kinesthetic provisioning leaves totally unresolved the question of *just what the efferent system is actually providing in such a situation*. Indeed, given a vatted brain, what could possibly be meant by "an efferent system" — other than fantasized if not theoretically defunct "motor programs"? Until "an efferent system" or "efferent stimulation" are specified, one can hardly take for granted that scientists/computer know what to feed back to a vatted brain in the way of sensory experiences since exactly what the vatted brain is efferently spewing forth on its own, i.e. what its own movement intentionalities are, or alternatively, what efferent effluences scientists/computer are causing it to spew forth, is not elucidated in the least. Not only this but the idea that a complete and intact efferent system exists in a vatted brain is a thoroughly untenable idea to begin with. A vatted brain has no spinal cord, for example, and a spinal cord is mandatory not only for reflexive movement but for voluntary movement as well (Kelly & Dodd 1991; Rowland 1991; Gordon 1991). Moreover if some motor responses to sensory feedback are mediated by the spinal cord alone — they occur too quickly to be mediated by the brain (Rosenbaum 1991: 137) — then a vatted brain's putative motor programs are at the mercy of efferent deficits that preclude the possibility of mediated movement responses. These spinal deficits are not compensated by the mere having of higher centers; the role of the spinal cord in movement cannot be taken over by other parts of the central nervous system. How then, given no spinal cord, do scientists/computer stimulate a vatted brain such that it experiences itself doing what it wants to do, or what scientists/computer want it to do? However unwavering and thorough the attention to afferent sensory feedback, the question of a vatted brain's fundamental efferent deficiencies is unresolved. The conclusion might well be that just as a spinal animal has cortical deficits, so a cortical animal has spinal ones.

Certainly if an efferent system was no more than a set of pre-established movement possibilities — a set of full-fledged motor programs devised by scientists/computer — then the vatted brain's movement choices would be limited to whatever particular kinetic repertoire scientists/computer might give it. In turn, the vatted brain might experience itself as an agent even though in reality it would be merely an agent *manqué* in a second sense. In this case, however, it is quite possible that the vatted brain would realize it is being duped. It could, after all, conceivably wish to do something for which it was not programmed; in effect, it could "want to move" — take it into its head to play ice hockey, for example — but find that nothing happens. Moreover a further complication is conceivable, one that dramatically highlights the intimate relationship between spontaneity and agency. Whatever a vatted brain's initial (forced) intention — to reach for a glass of water, for instance — there is nothing that would prevent it from changing its mind in the course of its moving — it might opt at the last minute to reach for a glass of iced tea instead — yet it finds its last-minute option inexplicably cancelled: it finds itself with the glass of water in its hand. Can scientists/computer possibly cope with, much less predict, the intentional vagaries of a vatted brain? Can they possibly control its spontaneity without undermining their very attempt to convince it that it is "an agent capable of engaging in some form of activity in the world"?

Alternatively, if "wanting to move" is construed not as coincident with the movement but as pure kinetic intention — nothing more than the pure desire to move — then an efferent system is superfluous. All that is needed is recourse to the code of all codes; that is, scientists/computer have merely to be tuned in neurologically to the vatted brain's desire: "to get a book off the shelf." But a fundamental critical problem with ""efferent stimulation" or "the efferent system" arises all the same in this context. To begin with, afferent stimulation is not efferent stimulation and cannot take the place of the latter. Providing afferent stimulation coincident with getting a book off the shelf is equivalent to providing documentation, not initiation, of movement. *Afferent stimulation by itself does not provide a sense of agency*; it lets the vatted brain know the degree to which its limbs are flexed or extended, for example, whether it is moving slowly or quickly, and so on, and in this sense allows the vatted brain the possibility of altering its direction, for example, or its range of movement. The central and sizable import of "the efferent system" and its relation to a sense of agency are exemplified by default in philosopher Hilary Putnam's vatted brain scenario. Assuming that he is a vatted brain speaking aloud to other vatted brains (Putnam assumes what he calls "a *collective* hal-lucination"), Putnam says that "Of course, it is not the case that my words actually reach your ears ... nor do I have a real mouth and tongue. Rather, when I produce my words, what happens is that the efferent impulses travel from my brain to the com-puter, which ... causes me to 'hear' my own voice uttering those words and 'feel' my tongue moving, etc." (1981:6–7). What Putnam is saying is that motor impulses from his brain, via transcription by super-scientific computer, cause certain quite particular, wholly coordinated "uttering" movements, and thus in turn certain correlative tactile-kinesthetic and auditory sensations. Efferent impulses thus directly cause the vatted brain to feel and hear its missing body. On what grounds, however, do these "causally potent" efferent impulses arise?[11] What Putnam is necessarily assuming in this fantasy scenario is that within his vatted brain is a motor program to produce words, that that motor program is intentionally booted up, so to speak, and that it in turn causes appro-priate efferent impulses, i.e. impulses that cause words to be uttered and thus his voice to be heard and his articulatory gestures to be felt. Putnam thus obviously makes an even further assumption. A sense of agency clearly informs his vatted brain's produc-tion of words; his assumed motor program is intentionally motivated. Indeed, if there is a motor program to produce words, there is a motor programmer, an "I" — precisely as Putnam indicates when he writes, "when I produce my words" — that is the source of a desire to speak, and moreover speak not just *any* words, but most specifically *these* words and no others.

Now as suggested above, a sense of agency comes only in part from sensory feed-back. It comes to begin with from a sense of actively initiating movement oneself.[12] In default of this sense of actively initiating movement himself, Putnam *qua* vatted brain would feel himself a pawn, in a manner similar to the way in which unanaesthetized patients undergoing brain stimulations feel themselves pawns in the hands of the neu-rosurgeons probing their brains. In a section titled "What the Patient Thinks," in his book *The Mystery of the Mind*, well-known neuroanatomist Wilder Penfield sums up patient response to brain stimulation as follows:

> When I have caused a conscious patient to move his hand by applying an electrode *to the motor cortex* of one hemisphere, I have often asked him about it. Invariably his response was: "I didn't do that. You did." When I caused him to vocalize, he said: "I didn't make that sound. You pulled it out of me" (1978:76; italics added).

A correlative indication of a lack of agency is found in the section titled "What the Electrode Can Do":

> The electrode can present to the patient various crude sensations. It can cause him to turn head and eyes, or to move the limbs, or to vocalize and swallow. It may recall vivid re-experience of the past, or present to him an illusion that present experience is familiar, or that the things he sees are growing large and

coming near. *But he remains aloof* [italics added]. He passes judgment on it all. He says "things *seem* familiar," not "I have been through this before." He says, "things are growing larger," but he does not move for fear of being run over. If the electrode moves his right hand, he does not say, "I wanted to move it." He may, however, reach over with the left hand and oppose his action (1978: 76–77).

Granted that electrical stimulation of the motor cortex resulting in crude movement is not the same as direct stimulation of efferent nerves in a vatted brain resulting in purportedly fine-tuned, wholly orchestrated movement, the analogy between Putnam *qua* vatted brain and anaesthetized patient with respect to a lack of a sense of actively initiating movement oneself nevertheless holds. No matter that efferent impulses are generated in each case, and in each case are causing movement. Moreover, as emphasized, in neither case does afferent stimulation suffice for a sense of agency. An unanaesthetized person has sensory feedback just as a vatted brain in a thought experiment has sensory feedback. Sensory feedback is not at issue. What is at issue is a causally potent efferent system that can make movement happen but that does not generate a sense of agency along with the movement. Clearly, the problem of agency is an outstanding problem. The person whose brain is being stimulated and who experiences certain bodily happenings, experiences no sense of agency. A stimulated brain is an observer brain that notes at a distance what is present; it is itself uninvolved in the experience. Its perceptions are precisely not enmeshed with movement, and its movement is precisely not felt as a self-initiated act. Dennett himself affirms that the problem of "convincing you [a vatted brain] that you are … an agent capable of engaging in some form of activity in the world" is "a much more difficult problem" than the problem of afferent stimulation. While sensory arrangements such as the hearing of music and the awareness of being in a supine position do not really tax the scientists' "technical virtuosity" according to Dennett (1991: 4), "your paralysis" very definitely does. When the scientists "tackle the more difficult problem of convincing you that you are not a mere beach potato," they start "with little steps," he says (5). Nonetheless, the moment "they decide to lift part of the 'paralysis' of your phantom body and let you wiggle your right index finger in the sand," they meet immediately with the "combinatorial explosion" problem (5). Dennett skirts the problem, offering a glib and murky solution that is no solution at all. He skirts it precisely because he cannot answer it. If we heed the readily available empirical evidence from Penfield, we readily see why: however one might stimulate a person's brain such that movement happens, the movement is not experienced by the person as actively initiated, that is, as spontaneous self-movement. In analogous fashion, whatever the efferently orchestrated movement activity in which a vatted brain engages, the vatted brain will not itself have the sense of actively initiating the movement: something other than itself will be felt to be making it happen. We may thus genuinely wonder whether it is not wayward, even a conceit, to think "the much more difficult problem" materially solvable. Penfield strongly suggests that it is materially insoluble when he writes — immediately after the foregoing description of what an electrode can do — "There is no place in the cerebral cortex where electrical stimulation will cause a patient to believe or to decide," and when he goes on to affirm in the next section (titled "Activation by Epileptic Discharge") "There is *no* area of gray matter, as far as my experience goes, in which local epileptic discharge brings to pass what could be called "mind-action." ... I am forced to conclude that there is no valid evidence that either epileptic discharge or electrical stimulation can activate the mind" (1978: 77–78). We might note that other kinds of findings confirm his view. For example, "readiness potential" recordings from the scalp are present prior to voluntary movement (Pickenhain 1984: 515; Asanuma 1989: 77–81); "preparation of a voluntary movement extends far down into the spinal cord and even engages muscles that do not have a share in it" (Granit 1977: 167). Coupled with the fact that an internationally recognized theory of action (based on Bernstein's research) centers on the "permanent anticipatory activity of the organism," i.e. activity that aims at "modelling the future" (Requin, Semjen, Bonnet 1984: 482), these findings unequivocally suggest that there is a good deal more to movement than efferent stimulation of, or efferent impulses from, an impeccably-tuned brain, vatted or not.

In sum, can a vatted brain really tell us something about who and what we are? Only in a doubly negative sense. On the one hand, what it is like to be a mind is not what it is like either to be a brain *tout court* or to be a brain in a vat; on the other hand, neither a brain *tout court* nor a brain in a vat is equal to a living body.

6.   From problems with neurological mecca to the question "what is it like?"

Unlike materialists who reduce animate form to neurophysiological circuitry and thereby life to a network of neural connections, philosopher Thomas Nagel gives implicit if unwitting recognition to animate form in his justly noted inquiry "What Is It Like To Be a Bat?". He does so in the process of attempting to specify what he calls subjective experience. Beginning his inquiry with the remark that "Consciousness is what makes the mind-body problem really intractable," he goes on to declare that "Without consciousness the mind-body problem would be much less interesting. With consciousness it seems hopeless" (1979: 165–66). A bit further on he states that "fundamentally an organism has conscious mental states if and only if there is something that it is like to *be* that organism — something it is like *for* the organism. We may call this the subjective character of experience" (166).

To be noted closely is the distinction that Nagel wants to establish by his added conditional, and indeed to insist upon, namely, that the problem is not to specify what it is like for *me* to be a bat, but what it is like for *a bat* to be a bat. He underscores the necessity of the distinction in a further way in a footnote (170, Note 6) where he states that "the analogical form of the English expression 'what it is *like*' is misleading. It does not mean 'what (in our experience) it *resembles*', but rather 'how it is for the subject himself'." It is instructive to point out that Dennett, in answering his own question about what it is like to be a human infant, appears not to have distinguished between the two "likenesses," for his answer is not an answer a human infant would give; it is an answer a human adult — perhaps particularly a certain kind of *male* human adult — would give. In other words, for Dennett, it would not be "like very much" to be a human infant because human infant consciousness does not correspond to what consciousness is like for Dennett, a human (male) adult.

To get at a conception of what it is like to be a bat — or conceivably, an infant — Nagel suggests devising an objective phenomenology. Such a phenomenology, he says, would not depend upon either empathy or the imagination to close "the gap between subjective and objective" (1979: 178). Without examining in depth why he would want to discount empathy and the imagination, and in a seemingly negative and belittling way at that, we should at least recognize that empathy and the imagination are forms of sense-making, and as such, can hardly be considered epistemologically worthless. In addition to phenomenological analyses that show analogical apperception in everyday social life to be contingent on empathy (see Husserl 1973a: Fifth Meditation), empirical studies by both developmental psychologists and infant psychiatrists, thus data from both experimental and clinical sources (see, for example, Meltzoff 1995; Stern 1985, 1990), show that empathy and the imagination are fundamental ways in which we gain our epistemic hold on the world. There is thus little reason to discount them from consideration in attempting to spell out "what it is like to be an X" — as if an objective phenomenology were no more than an austerely pristine scientific exercise. Insofar as an objective phenomenology is a descriptive account that sets forth what it is like to be an X for those individuals who are incapable of having the experiences of an X, something must bridge the gap between the two. A formidable clue as to what the something is, thus what is essential to Nagel's proposed and dreamed-of "objective phenomenology," is provided by Roger Sperry's notion of the brain as an organ of and for movement (1952; see also Cotterill 1995 & Kelso 1995).[13] If movement does indeed bridge the gap, then it may justifiably be said that for individuals lacking the experience of an X to grasp what X's experience is like, it is necessary that they grasp what it is like to be a body they are not. It may thus be justifiably said that an objective phenomenology depends for its realization on both empathy and imagination.

Sperry first of all stresses many times over that perception is not a simple impression — a "passive registration in brain tissue of a pattern of sensory excitation" or a "mere passage of sensory patterns into passive brain protoplasm" (1952: 306, 302). His strong emphasis on a non-reductive conception of a living capacity recalls the stronger words of Herbert Muller who, in underscoring that "the fundamental fact in biology ... is the organism," wrote, "To say ... that a man is made up of certain chemical elements is a satisfactory description only for those who intend to use him as a fertilizer" (1943: 107). (One could, of course, update Muller's 1943 observation: to say that a man is made up of certain computational and programmable elements or certain cortico-neuronal modules is a satisfactory description only for those who intend to use him as a computer or a brain.) Following a description and discussion of his many experiments, Sperry spells out his view of perception in unequivocal terms:

> If there be any objectively demonstrable fact about perception that indicates the nature of the neural process involved, it is the following: In so far as an organism perceives a given object, it is prepared to respond with reference to it.... The preparation-to-respond in perception is a demonstrable fact. All that need be questioned is whether it may not be a consequence of, rather than a part of, the cerebral process which actually constitutes the perception itself. In this regard we may emphasize again that the structure of the brain, as well as what is known of its physiology, discourages any effort to separate the motor from the sensory and associative processes. To the best of our knowledge there is only a gradual merging and transformation of the one into the other, with nothing to suggest where perception might end and motor processes begin (1952: 301).

A few paragraphs later, after considering further evidence, he reiterates the same basic fact: "Perception is basically an implicit preparation to respond" (302). It should be noted that this view of perception is far from idiosyncratic. Zoologist Jacob von Uexküll, for example, whose analyses of *Umwelts* is well-known upholds a similar view. Speaking of the functional way in which animals (humans included) distinctively perceive their distinctive worlds, he writes of the priority of the *functional* or *effector* tone of objects — the *sitting* tone of chairs, the *eating* tone of food, the *climbing* tone of ladders, and so on. Whatever the perceived object, its specific meaning is created and established through action (1957: 46–50).

Now in order to profit fully from this beginning clue as to the central significance of movement to understandings of what it is like to be a mind and a body, it will be helpful to clear the ground of hindering assumptions and confusions.

The earlier summation notwithstanding, the words "brain" and "body" are often used interchangeably by avowed physicalists, dualists, and what might be called ontological free-lancers. Nagel himself, for example, begins by speaking of the mind body problem only to go on to speak of "reductionist euphoria" and to say that "[i]t is most unlikely" that any reductionist account "will shed light on the relation of mind to brain" (1979: 166) — as if the mind-body problem is a macro-edition of the mind-brain problem. The seeming interchangeability of body and brain is in fact cause for question: is the brain really equivalent to the body, the *living* body? The rationale for those disposed to answer "yes" would seem to be that the living body is actually nothing more than a mechanical rig for getting about in the world. Ergo, to speak of the brain as the body is to recognize the fact that the body is merely the servant of an in-charge physico-chemical executive system. In this consummately materialist way of thinking, whatever the actual experiences of a living body in the way of movement, gestures, skillful activity, explorations, curiosity, laughing, crying, making love, gazing at the Grand Canyon, and so on, they are merely folksy ways of construing certain physical facts. But while the brain on this thoroughgoing physicalist view replaces the living body, a living body can in fact hardly be reduced to a brain, and not only because the materiality of a living body is hardly identical to the materiality of a brain — a brain has no muscle tissue, fat deposits, or fibrous proteins, for example — nor because a living body cannot be explained evolutionarily in terms of a brain in a rationally credible way — the explanation would require, *inter alia*, a brain-tethered teleology of the evolution of bodies, the latter evolving wholly on the basis of what particular evolving brains would materially require, for example, *legs* in order to hunt cooperatively or *ears* to aid in the location of sound — nor because a living body lacks the privileged axiological stature of a brain. It can hardly be reduced because there is something incommensurable about the idea of being able to reduce *both* mind and body to a brain. Classically and by the materialist's very conception, a body has no substantive connection to mind — specifically in the indispensable and intimate ways that a brain does such that indeed, brains are said to explain mind(s) completely. Hence, to reduce both body and mind to the same material entity is equivalent to compressing two incommensurable entities into the same substance.

On the other hand, if we examine the reduction of body to brain carefully, we see that however much the latter is accorded total supervisory powers over the former, its grasp falls short of its purported powers. A brain, for example, cannot speak for a living body. When neurologically-recognized language areas of the brain are stimulated, nary a word is uttered. Indeed, stimulation of Wernicke's area, for example, produces aphasia (Penfield & Rasmussen 1955: 89–91; Penfield 1966: 220–21); a privileged but empty autonomy reigns. In spite of such facts, however, it might actually seem that, thanks to a thoroughgoing materialism, the brain is bringing the body closer to the mind. In other words, a rapprochement of body and mind occurs by dint of the fact that the brain is chummy with both. On closer metaphysical inspection, however, it becomes clear that the brain is simply gaining ground right and left. Mind and body are not coming together at all; they are merely being swallowed up by a metaphysically omnivorous brain. In view of this fact, one might rightly claim that what with displacing bodies on one side and minds on the other, the brain is being overfed. Its diet is stretching it in two directions at once such that its metaphysical elasticity may eventually snap. Indeed, to put brains in the place of bodies and minds confounds Nagel's original question because it does away not only with the subjective experience of a bat but with the bat itself. In place of the bat is a computational device in the form of "nervous matter," granted a particular kind of nervous matter, but nervous matter all the same. Such confounding brings to mind philosopher Albert Johnstone's important observation that the mind-brain problem and the mind-body problem are two quite separate metaphysical-epistemological problems, each requiring its own special attention (Johnstone 1992). The former problem is rooted in epistemological-metaphysical puzzles related to the Representational Theory of Perception; the latter problem is rooted in epistemological-metaphysical puzzles related to first-person experience. The transmutaton of a bat into nervous matter readily suggests an amplification of Johnstone's observation, namely, that the triumvirate — mind, body, brain — gives rise to a third problem, the brain-body problem, of which brains in vats are paradigmatic. The problem is actually a twentieth-century invention that threatens to plague Western thought and culture in the same ongoing and crippling way that the mind-body problem has plagued Western thought and culture for the past three hundred and fifty years. It is based on a misconception of the brain and a misconception of bodies. The significance of Sperry's hypothesis that the brain is an organ of and for movement dawns fully in just this context. An appreciation of its implications is helped along dramatically by a consideration of Dennett's inadvertent insight that "consciousness arises when there is work for it to do." In particular, stripped of their proper bodily connections, *brains, including brains in vats, have no work to do.* It is precisely their distance from living bodies that makes them travesties of life and their close equation with minds — "equation" in the sense that they explain minds materially and thus do away with them metaphysically — that makes them heuristically effete. As sole performers in philosophical thought experiments or as sole performers in scientific empirical ones, brains are as devoid of animate powers as any postmodern grammatological agent or gaping psychoanalytic body. If we ask in this context, "What is it like to be a mind?" or, "What is it like to be a brain?" we would have to answer that "It is not like very much" for the very cogent reason Dennett supplies us: "[C]onsciousness ... arises when there is work for it to do."

Let us take Dennett's insight literally. To say that consciousness arises when there is work for it to do means that there is a *corps engagé*, and for there to be a *corps engagé* means that there is movement, labor, gesture, comportmental patterns, expressive behaviors — in short, a living body, an animate form. Especially for a creature that must learn to move itself, there is work for it to do. Especially for a creature that must learn to hunt in order to feed itself, there is work for it to do. Especially for a creature that must learn to defend itself, there is work for it to do. Especially for a creature that must cope with environmental exigencies, there is work for it to do. Especially for a creature that improves its situation, maximizes its resources, or invents new ways of living, there is work that it does and work for it to do. What Dennett's insight suggests coincides in broad terms with Sperry's hypothesis: the brain is an organ of and for movement. His hypothesis is validated by the evolutionary progression paleoanthropologists discovered when they found that movement and labor came first, i.e. that three million years ago there were hominids who were consistently bipedal and that two and a half million years ago there were hominids who were tool-makers. With respect to Sperry's hypothesis, it is in fact of moment to note that neither bipedality nor tool-making is unique to hominids. Japanese macaques and gorillas, for example, walk bipedally; chimpanzees fashion certain kinds of sticks for termite fishing (Teleki 1974), for example, and elephants fashion fly-swatters from various available materials (Hart & Hart 1993). The kinetic capacities and accomplishments of species other than the one we recognize as human thus warrant recognition.[14] Indeed, the message from this evolutionary vantage point might be best put by paraphrasing Churchland: "We humans — like all creatures — are creatures of movement. And we should learn to live with that fact." Certainly creatures have brains, or nervous matter equivalent to brains. It is not brains, however, that invent tools or that at times carry themselves bipedally to display their penis, for example, or to maximize their size. It is living bodies, bodies for whom "perception is basically an implicit preparation to respond." It follows, then, that if there are such things as minds and bodies, they can only be found in their true colors in the midst of life, which is to say in a corps engagé, a body in which perception and movement are, as in Sperry's view, inextricably bound.

Earlier critical facts about agency point to the importance of taking seriously the fact that sensory and motor systems are intertwined, and not passively, but in an active sense. Sperry's conceptualization of their relationship is indeed noteworthy for it illustrates the centrality of agency to an understanding of perception. By way of contrast, we might ask whether (evil) scientists or (super-scientific) computers could possibly capture the subtleties of "an implicit preparation to respond." More pointedly, we might ask whether cognitivist accounts with their central focus on information-processing — on "input" and "output" — and their characterization of the brain as a computational device do not distract us from the primacy of movement and the centrality of agency. Indeed, we can hardly refrain from reading them as promoting a view directly antithetical to that of Sperry: passive pieces of protoplasm are exactly what information-processing machines, brains *tout court*, and vatted brains are all about. Finally, we might ask by way of contrast whether cognitivist accounts do not mislead us in their one-dimensional model of mind, not only as if perception was nothing more than a matter of incoming information, but as if the evolution of animate form was simply a matter of different information-processing machines. Like movement and agency, mind in the Darwinian sense of a range of mental powers is a dynamic dimension of living creatures. Indeed, curiosity, imitation, attention, imagination, reason, memory — mental powers that Darwin enumerates and discusses — are powers peculiar to animate forms, powers that, unlike the powers of any information-processing machine, are through and through keyed to unfabricated real-life experiences of living creatures in the throes and pleasures of their day-to-day lives.

In sum, it seems reasonable for us to take note of, and heed the conclusions of those earlier researchers who had less stringent theoretical agendas and who did without computational models both in their studies of brain neuroanatomy and neurophysiology and in their direct clinical stimulations of the brains of conscious subjects. How, in fact, can we possibly discount their findings and conclusions? How can we possibly eschew the results of actual experimentation and clinical studies in favor of artifactual entities and fantasy scenarios? Rather than pedastalling the brain — most notably our own human one — should we not rather turn to "the life of organisms," to "manifestations of persistent wholes" (Haldane 1931: 26, 13), to animate form, to living creatures in the midst of life in order to understand what it is like to be a mind and a body?

7.   Zeroing in on why a mind is not a brain and a brain is not a body

At their most fundamental level, subjective experiences are tactile-kinesthetic experiences. They are experiences of one's own body and body movement; they are experiences of animate form. These experiences are the bedrock of thinking. Our evolutionary history documents this claim (see Sheets-Johnstone 1990). The claim is moreover documented methodologically by Darwin's condensed observation that "experience shows the problem of the mind cannot be solved by attacking the citadel itself. — the mind is function of body. — we must bring some *stable* foundation to argue from" ([1836–1844] 1987: 564). An interesting critical sidenote is instructive here. While Darwin's thought is that "we must *bring* [italics added] some *stable* foundation to argue from," sociobiological anthropologist Donald Symons, in quoting Darwin, changes "bring" to "find" (1979: 43). The change signals a decided shift in attitude and conceptual approach. To *find* "some stable foundation to argue from" indicates that we should we look around, seeking for something to give us an anchor point from which to argue the claim that "the mind is function of body." To *find* is thus highly suggestive of the position of cognitivists who would argue that the brain is the stable foundation, the brain being conceived as the body to which the mind may be reduced. To *bring* "some stable foundation" indicates something quite different. To begin with, what is to be argued is not that the mind *is* a function of body: that function is already the fact of life Darwin matter-of-factly states it to be. Darwin's statement is indeed not a speculation; it is an observation. In effect, what we must *bring* are solid evidential grounds showing the validity of the observation. In other words, what we must do is gather together empirical facts substantiating that "the mind is function of body."

Lest it be thought that too much is being made of Darwin's statement — why should we intellectually honor his observation that "the mind is function of body"? — we should note that the statement is not an armchair pronouncement any more than it is a speculation. It is a methodological observation based on years of experience as a naturalist and world-wide observer of nature. In other words, the observation that "the mind is function of body" is as much rooted in the data Darwin collected in his studies of animals as is the observation that more creatures are born than can possibly survive. Accordingly, a careful reading of his observation turns us in a very different direction from brains — whether *tout court* or vatted. Indeed, if we take Darwin's observation seriously, then we see it is utterly misguided to reduce mind or body to brain in order to understand "the problem of the mind." We need rather to examine living ways in which "the mind is function of body." When we do so, we view ourselves within a natural history and put animate form first. Sperry's thesis together with both his earlier research findings and the research findings of others puts us onto just such an evolutionary path at the same time that it directs us toward a correlative re-thinking of the brain.

Quite early in his career, Sperry remarked that

> An objective psychologist, hoping to get at the physiological side of behavior, is apt to plunge immediately into neurology trying to correlate brain activity with modes of experience. The result in many cases only accentuates the gap between the total experience as studied by the psychologist and neural activity as analyzed by the neurologist. But the experience of the organism is integrated, organized, and has its meaning in terms of coordinated movement (1939: 295).

A number of years later, he pointed out that to approach mental activity in terms of motor activity is not to affirm that what is experienced as subjective "resides within any motor reaction or within the motor system" (1952: 309); subjectivity is not, in other words, *located* in any motor area of the brain. If pushed to say just where in cerebral terms subjective experience lies, Sperry said that "we could only suggest vaguely those brain centers midway functionally between the sensory input and motor output, where the coordinated action of the entire motor system may be governed as an integrated whole." Sperry's view, in short, is that *the function of consciousness is coordinated movement.* The view clearly coincides with Darwin's idea that "the mind is function of body." Moreover it clearly coincides both with an appreciation of the foundational significance of tactile-kinesthetic experience and evolutionary understandings of animate form. It coincides as well with the principle of responsivity as a "fundamental and almost universal characteristic of life" (Curtis 1975: 28). It is notable too that Penfield's conclusion, framed in terms of consciousness, is similar to Sperry's: "Consciousness," he said, "is not something to be localized in space ... [It is] a function of the integrated action of the brain," final integration likely taking place "in those neuronal circuits which are most intimately associated with *the initiation of voluntary activity and with the sensory summation prerequisite to it*" (1966:219; italics added).

Sperry's and Penfield's intimate linking of subjective experience or consciousness with self-movement — "mental activity with motor activity" — is a validation of the foundational significance of the tactile-kinesthetic body. Together with a conception of the brain as an organ fundamentally in the service of movement, it is a view of the fundamental nature of organic life, a view that is implicitly if not explicitly supported by a variety of research findings. In his general introduction to the physiology of movement (1991), for example, David Rosenbaum discusses a range of seminal experimental findings: that active (rather than passive) movement facilitates perceptual identification of an object and memory of the previous position of a part of the body (1991:23); that the perceptual-motor system with respect to distinguishing self-motion from environmental motion is astonishingly sophisticated at a quite elementary evolutionary level (24–25); that the phenomenon of coarticulation (the term refers to speech production, specifically, to the fact that phonemes are not discretely formed entities, or as Rosenbaum puts it, "the simultaneous motions of effectors … help achieve a temporally extended task") demands an account of psychological as well as physiological constraints (15); and that the polishing performance of piano-polishing robots is enhanced when they are equipped with tactile sensors (47). Such examples unequivocally reinforce both the notion of the primacy of movement and the fundamental significance of tactile-kinesthetic experience. The two themes in fact meet in Rosenbaum's recognition of the import — and problem — of intentionality. Rosenbaum states that "Movements are made in response to perceptual input and intentional states," but "where," he asks, "do intentional states come from?" (1991:71). He is not naive enough to think either that the question is a simple one or that motor physiologists have the answer. Nonetheless, he suggests the importance of "the physiological substrates of voluntary performance" (71). As he points out, *the mere intention to move precipitates activity throughout the brain before movement even occurs.* For example, there is diffuse activity "over virtually the entire cerebral cortex" one-and-one-half seconds before the electromyographic recording of finger movement (71). Moreover he also points out that "virtually all areas of the brain, when stimulated strongly enough, give rise to some form of overt behavior." He makes a similar point when he notes that in the production of movement, many areas of the brain are active. "A motor act," he says, "is the product of the orchestrated activity of many brain centers" (70–71). Clearly, experimental data relevant to the study of human motor control support Sperry's view both that the brain is an organ of and for movement and that self-movement and intentionality are intimately related.

In a recent book based on symposia of the Neurosciences Institute — a book on perceptual categorization and learning titled *Signal and Sense: Local and Global Order in Perceptual Maps* — ten of twenty-four chapters are devoted to movement (motion, action, or behavior). Among these is one in which anatomist Roger Lemon discusses the possibilities of mapping the output functions of the motor cortex. Lemon highlights the fact that unlike neurons in sensory areas of the cortex, motor cortex neurons "do not respond very well to sensory stimuli in anesthetized preparations," that in fact "the full wealth of the somatosensory input to area 4 [the motor area] can be appreciated only in a conscious animal" (1990: 343). Such a finding, of course, calls into question the very premisses of computational models of brain (the brain, brains) since not only efferent outputs from, but afferent inputs to, the motor cortex defy fine-grained neuronal analysis and hence reduction to neurological algorithmic formulae. To analyze the movement of a conscious animal — and not artificial movement induced in a laboratory but spontaneous, everyday in-the-world movement — in the neurologically fine terms demanded would, after all, mean to specify, in addition to afferent inputs, the movement effect of each and every possible neural motor impulse as it would play out in concert with each and every other possible neural motor impulse. Consider too that "the difficulty in studying the role of the motor cortex in motor learning is that the motor cortex is also concerned with the execution of learned motor skills" (Asanuma 1989: 120). In other words, there is a procedural problem in that "the routine method for studying the function of a given structure in the central nervous system is to remove that structure and observe the resulting deficit." But as neuroanatomist Hiroshi Asanuma points out, "removal of the motor cortex abolishes not only the ability to learn the skill, if it exists, but also the learned motor skills themselves" (1989: 120). Anatomist Paul Johnson similarly points out "inherent [methodological] difficulties in the study of the motor system," noting, for example, "the necessity of allowing and yet controlling animal behavior" (1992: 242). Procedural problems aside, there is a problem in the fact that since all neural impulses are the same, the task of determining what each and every impulse purportedly specifies in the way of a single movement's complex of spatio-temporal dynamic qualities — the movement's force, its direction, its range, its duration, and so on — appears doomed from the start. Indeed, that there is "multiple representation of movements, muscles, and individual motoneurons within the primary motor cortex ... resulting [in] convergence of output on target structures from different, often discontinuous, regions of the cortex" (Johnson 1992: 315); that in fact "[m]any different investigators have reported that a particular movement can be elicited from different and often discontinuous regions within a particular area ... of the cortex" (Johnson 1992: 331); that there are "overlapping outputs to different motoneurons/muscles, [s]ome of this overlap [being] due to single neurons influencing multiple muscles (its 'muscle field'), including reciprocal effects on antagonist muscles (Johnson 1992: 331; see also 338–343); that "the principal effect of electrical stimulation is to *disrupt* voluntary movement" (Johnson 1992: 317); that there is no 'private line' linking a given corticospinal neuron with a single muscle" (Johnson 1992:321); that "trains of stimuli are essential to produce overt movements" (Johnson 1992:323) — in other words, whatever the movement, it is a question of mapping a temporally complex rather than discrete neuronal sequence; and so on — all these findings strongly suggest that the task of sorting out and mapping the motor functions of the brain of a conscious animal is not simply a complicated affair but an impossibility. In a quite general way one might think of this impossibility as a function of co-articulation, the latter in a far broader sense than simply the co-articulation of phonemes in speech production. Indeed, *all* bodily movement is at *all* times co-articulated, and differentially so according to the moving individual's bodily and environmental circumstances. In other words, bodily movement is always of the whole organism to begin with, and added to this fundamental whole-body kinetics are kinetic variables such as immediate posture, tonicity, energy, spatial orientation, strength, movement experience, age, and, of course, the variable of the specific situation itself — its obstacles, its formality or casualness, its dangers, and so on. Even if the movement is "the same," just such fundamental variables enter differentially into the production and final form of the movement. In light of the difficulties presented at the neurological level by multiple representation, overlapping, and so on, Lemon's suggestion is to concentrate on goal-directed movements that have different "motor 'strategies,'" each 'strategy' calling into action different "cell clusters" (Lemon 1990:315–16). He arrives at this suggestion after reviewing experimental work and returning to his original question concerning the functional output of the motor cortex: what does the output "represent"? (345). It bears emphasizing that what Lemon is looking for is neither an identity relationship between mind and brain nor an identity relationship between brain and body; he is looking for "correlates" between "performance," i.e. actual movement, and the motor cortex, i.e. the brain (348).

It bears emphasizing too in this context of reviewing investigations of the motor cortex that electrical stimulation of a brain does not produce "natural processes of movement" (Lemon 1990:316);[15] a definitive distinction exists between volitional movement and experimental stimulation of a brain. Lemon states not only that "This point has been made repeatedly" (1990:317), but that, as noted above, "the principal effect of electrical stimulation is to *disrupt* voluntary movement." He states further that, with respect to electrical stimulation, there is not a one to one relationship between cortical stimulation and movement or muscle response (1990:323), that movement not only depends upon "trains of stimuli" but that the movement itself depends "on the level of cortical excitability and on ongoing cortical processes, including voluntary 'focusing' on a particular muscle or movement" (323). In this respect, the "striking difference" that he notes between motor and sensory cortices is of fundamental significance. "A given motor cortex neuron," he writes, "can change its relationship with its neighbor in a behaviorally contingent manner, firing simultaneously during one movement and in reciprocal fashion during another. The flexibility of this relationship between individual components of a cortical cluster is no doubt a property of the especially extensive neuropil of the motor cortex: It suggests that individual neurons are able to move in and out of functionally different groups" (1990: 347).[16] Given the fundamentally *unstable* relationships of motor cortex neurons, the general and at the same time profound lesson appears unequivocal: *neurological motor happenings are as unpredictable as human movement itself.*

A further aspect of the striking difference between motor and sensory cortices lies in the startling fact that the motor cortex may be altogether silent even as the creature in question is moving. In his general discussion of the physiological foundations of movement, Rosenbaum makes this very point. He cites a study, for example, in which the motor cortex was absolutely silent even in the midst of highly agitated activity on the part of the subject. In short, there is little ground for believing in the identity of brain and body when a consistent match between movement and corticomotoneuronal activity is not to be found. Moreover although one could interpret the finding as an interruption of natural functioning, the fact that electrical stimulation of a brain is not sufficient to induce meaningful, coordinated movement is compelling evidence as to why a mind is not a brain and a brain is not a body. It is compelling first of all because Penfield and Rasmussen's brain stimulation studies show that apart from such basal acts as swallowing, there are no orchestrated motor programs that are run off upon stimulation of the motor cortex. It is compelling furthermore because Penfield and Rasmussen specifically and strongly emphasize that what is elicited by brain stimulation is on the sensory side "crude" (1955: 232)[17] and on the motor side elementary if not similarly "crude" (140–41): what is elicited is far removed from "skilled performance" (232). Even more pointed is their summary observation that "The movements produced by cortical stimulation are never skilled, acquired movements but instead consist of either flexion or extension of one or more joints, movements which are not more complicated than those the newborn infant is able to perform" 47). Clearly, coordinated movement is the privileged domain of a living creature — a *corps engagé*, a subject capable of subjective experience, including, we may note, a subject such as a fly. Following experimental distortion of its visual field, a fly — the subject of an experiment by noted physiologist Erich von Holst — was observed to have anticipated changes in its visual field in conjunction with its movement and to find those anticipated changes unfulfilled: "When the fly attempted to move on its own, it took a step one way or the other and then stood stock still, frozen!" (Rosenbaum 1991: 24). There was, as von Holst stated, "a central catastrophe!" (von Holst 1973: 142).

When the neurological and living facts of the matter are seriously considered, that is, when coordinated movement, co-articulation, highly flexible connections among corticomotor neurons, multiple representations, overlapping, and events such as inexplicable silences are taken into account together with the degrees of freedom problem discussed earlier, they indicate that a vast range of kinetic possibilities exist and that these possibilities are tied to a level of experience — an intentional, subjective strata — beyond that elicited by either afferent or efferent modes of electrical stimulation. They indicate precisely a subjective element within the organization and performance of movement. In effect, what studies of the motor regions of the brain teach us is that in actuality there is an indefinitely great number of possible coordinations and performances and that, its crudity aside, any particular movement elicited by electrical stimulation is arbitrary insofar as it is unconnected both to the normally complex and integrated totality of ongoing movement of an individual animal — humans included — and to any actual and particular kinetic context of utterance. One may with good reason conclude that it is because a *stable* mapping of the motor cortex is indeed impossible — given its flexibility, its silences, its multiple representations, its overlapping responses, and so on — that Lemon proposes a "truly functional" understanding of the motor cortex on the basis of "goal-directed behavior" (1990: 350). D. Denny-Brown, in his well-known book *The Cerebral Control of Movement* published some twenty-four years before Lemon's article, made the similar but broader observation that "The cerebral cortex is responsible for goal-directed behavior" (1966: 199). Such behavior can be defined, of course, only in terms of a living subject. Charles S. Sherrington, the founder of modern neurophysiology, aptly captured this fact when he wrote that "The dog not only walks but it walks to greet its master" (1953: 190). In light of the purposiveness of its movement, Sherrington noted, the character of the motor act changes from a "generality of purpose" to a "narrowed and specific purpose fitting a specific occasion." Commenting on this change of purpose, he added, "The change is just as if the motor act had suddenly become correlated with the finite mind of the moment. It is just as if the body and its finite mind had become one!" (1953: 190).[18]

When we take intentionality in the broader epistemological sense of *meaning* rather than in the narrower pragmatic sense of *purpose* or *goal-directed behavior*, we see the quintessential "oneness" in proportionally broader perspective. We see, in other words, that movement and meaning are in the most fundamental sense intertwined, phylogenetically and ontogenetically. They go hand in hand in the lives of living creatures. They are primal aspects of animate form. Moreover neither can be reduced to brain neurology. The tactile-kinesthetic body is indeed not simply a body of the neurological moment. It is a body that has both a natural and individual kinetic history. It is a body rich in movement memories, expectations, and values, a body that has in consequence developed certain kinetic dispositions, habits, and ways of responding. Like the fly, for example, that moved and in moving anticipated certain visual fields in conjunction with its movement, tactile-kinesthetic bodies have expectant meanings consistent with the moving bodies they are. Animate forms move to begin with in ways consistent with the bodies they are. They move too in ways semantically consistent with the bodies they become in light of their experiences of moving, which is to say both that tactile-kinesthetic bodies are changing bodies and that meanings discovered in the course of moving are carried forward. Movement and intentionality are indeed plaited into the very being of animate forms. Making sense is in the most basic sense a kinetic activity.

Close reflection on the above research findings in conjunction with vatted brain thought experiments testifies in further ways to the truth of this basic fact of life. It does so by bringing to light a sizable fly in the nutrient-rich waters of vatted brains. The fly's outlines were evident earlier when the question arose of just what a vatted brain's efferent system might be. What passes as an efferent system in a vatted brain are instant readings of desired experiences and instantaneous stimulations of the sensory, i.e. afferent, correlates of the desired experiences. In short, in the thought experiments, intentionality, *contra* Rosenbaum's indications, is mapped; motor cortex, *contra* Lemon's indications, is mapped, albeit by tactical deception — i.e. by way of afferent feedback. The sizable fly is thereby able to work its sizable magic but in the process thoroughly undermines the credibility of the thought experiment. It brings to pass the best of all possible worlds — not only for any vatted brain, but for creators and manipulators of vatted brains as well. A vatted brain leads an utterly fantastic life far removed from what we know to be everyday reality. For example, it could dance a tarantella though it never did a single plié in its life; it could kick field-goals though it never so much as touched a football and was ignorant of the game; it could perform heart surgery though it never spent a day in medical school — such is its giftedness in light of the technical virtuosity of its controllers, who can instantaneously orchestrate neurologically whatever movement it intends. Of course the instant kinetic satisfactions involve even further neurological sleights of hand. The sizable fly makes reflex actions, the role of muscle spindles, and the like, superfluous; the neurophysiological situation is such that "the integrative action of the nervous system" and "a final common path" are unnecessary (Sherrington 1947). So long as what is desired is read correctly and what is fed back afferently is always on target — so long as scientists/computer do not miss a trick either in reading desire or in providing afferent sensory correlates — there is no problem in simulating *movement that is not actually there*. The net result, however, is that a vatted brain is a preeminently sensory system — a desire-processing device — whose motor yearnings, whatever they might be, are instantly fulfilled, thanks to the alchemical wizardry of its manipulators. But like information-processing systems, it operates essentially in only one direction. In the context of cautioning that "movements can never be discussed as if they took place in a vacuum," motor physiologist Ragnar Granit emphasizes the purposiveness of movement, the end result that we "demand" and that we measure against kinesthetic and (commonly) ocular feedback (1977: 160). A vatted brain does not function at all in this normal way. It is not bothered with the need for corrections or adjustments. It moves perfectly at every moment, though literally never lifting a finger. Indeed, when scientists/computer *let* it wiggle its finger as per Dennett's scenario (1991: 5), it is immaterial whether the *letting* is an act deferent to the desire of an active agent or the forced movement of passive nervous matter. In either case, what the vatted brain experiences is instant wish-fulfillment. What vatted brains would thus tell us about "the mind/world relationship" or about "the beginnings of a theory — an empirical scientifically respectable theory — of human consciousness" is worlds away from what we actually experience in our intact, kinetically active everyday lives.

A final perspective upon the seemingly insoluble problem of mapping the motor cortex warrants mention. It might best be introduced by the straightforward assertion of brain neurologist Apostolos Georgopoulos following his summary of research on the motor cortex that spells out how its conception has changed over the past twenty-five years, including the changed notion of it as simply "a muscle controller" to a view that encompasses the notion of "the process of movement generation." Georgopoulos asserts that "The main take-home message from the studies summarized above is that motor cortex is complex!" (1992: 180). Some years earlier, brain neurologists Walle Nauta and Michael Feirtag reflected skeptically on the very quest to map the motor system, and this precisely on the grounds that the motor system is thoroughly enmeshed as a singular organized whole with perception, a view deriving not only from their own research but from Sperry's original research and conclusions. They pointed out that with the 1870 discovery that electrical stimulation of the neocortex produced muscle twitches on the side of the body opposite to the point of stimulation, a quest began to map the "motor system" (1979: 105). They noted that "The quest continues to this day, and one may fairly ask whether it can ever be completed" (105). In support of their skepticism, they presented an example:

> Consider area 19, a band of neocortex distinct in cell architecture from neighboring zones and situated not far from the visual cortex. When area 19 is stimulated electrically in an experimental animal, the eyes of the animal turn in unison to the contralateral side, that is, the gaze moves to an alignment directed away from the side of the brain receiving the electric current. It is therefore tempting to call area 19 a "motor" area. To do so, however, would be arbitrary, because from another point of view area 19 is sensory; it is known to reprocess information that has passed through the visual cortex (105–106).

Given Nauta and Feirtag's conclusion — "The lesson is that no line can be drawn between a sensory side and a motor side in the organization of the brain" (106) — mapping the motor cortex again appears to be a task defied by the very nature of the case. But there is a further lesson we can draw, one supported as well by the above-discussed research findings generally, namely, that an understanding of movement is tied to understandings of the dynamics of actual creaturely life, hence to expectations, volition, purpose — in broad terms, to understandings of animate form and intentionality. Lemon's more modest proposal to seek neurological motor "correlates" of "goal-directed behavior" in fact strongly suggests that what has been learned from brain research, i.e. from neurological studies of the motor cortex, is both that brains are attuned to the dynamic nature of creaturely life and that the dynamic nature of creaturely life makes a reductive neurology impossible. Accordingly, a mind is not a brain and a brain is not a body. In turn, a shift in conceptual understanding of the nature of life is in order: a shift from a reductionist concern with brains *tout court* to a concern with living bodies. Such a shift brings with it the realization that volitional movement is performatively defined by living subjects and that goals are intentionally defined by the same living subjects. The problem of mapping the motor cortex — whether with a view to neurologically specifying motor programs or to neurologically specifying a complete lexicon of discrete neuron-muscle connections — is thus a pseudo problem. More finely put, the kinetic possibilities built into motor systems defy formulaic representational mappings in the same way that the spontaneity built into the movement of living creatures defies standardization. In effect, the idea of predicting and controlling the movement of living creatures in a corticomotoneuronal sense through proper stimulation of their brains is a pipe dream. Indeed, a brain in a vat should have a pipe in its mouth.

8.   How by exchanging brain technology for history we give ourselves the one-two punch

Looking back on reductive cognitivists' claims in the light of the above matters of cerebral fact, one can only conclude that neurological Meccaland is a mirage. Reductive metaphysical claims in consequence take on proportionately broader and more alarming implications. When by way of these claims we exchange brain technology for natural history, we give ourselves the "one-two punch." The one-two punch is "the destruction of natural processes on the one hand and their replacement by technocratic constructions on the other" (Reynolds 1991: xi). By thus giving up our place in nature, we fail to understand what it is to be the animate forms we are. We mismeasure, miscalculate, and misconceive ourselves. Indeed, in giving ourselves the one-two punch, we knock ourselves out.

Like any other organ of the body, the brain is part of an integrated dynamic system geared to the actual everyday dynamics of life itself. To view it as an informational or computational device is to miss the animateness of animate form and thereby to abandon a fundamentally evolutionary perspective. An informational-computational view of the brain is indeed a culturally relative view spawned by and congenial to twentieth-century Westerners infatuated with technological ingenuities. To see living forms as computerlike "Darwin machines" (Calvin 1987) is both an affront to Darwin's foundational sense of a natural history and a radical extension of Cartesianism; as if our bodies were not enough, we now insist that our minds are machines. This auto-mechanization of ourselves is clearly mechanomorphic. As such, it should be subject to a rule of thumb akin to Morgan's canon (1930). Morgan's canon decrees that whatever can be explained in terms of lower functions should not be explained in terms of higher ones, not because of parsimony, as is often thought, but because lower faculties evolved before higher ones and are therefore more commonly distributed. Translated in terms of mechanomorphism, Morgan's canon would decree that whatever can be explained in terms of animate form should not be explained in terms of mechanical form not only because animate forms, having evolved before human-spawned mechanical ones, are therefore more commonly distributed, but also because *only* such forms, being animate, can explain what it is to be a mind and what it is to be a body.

Notes

* This chapter is a substantially expanded version of an invited essay that appeared in a *Festschrift* for Ashley Montagu: *Race and Other Misadventures: Essays in Honor of Ashley Montagu in His Ninetieth Year* (Sheets-Johnstone 1996e).

1.   So taken were these paleoanthropologists with the comparative largeness of the human brain vis à vis other creatures — Neandertals excluded if not brushed aside and conveniently explained away — it took them a long time to realize their error. Sherwood Washburn, for example, in a 1960 article outlining how the emergence of tools gave rise to *Homo sapiens*, discusses the difference in brain size between what he calls "man-apes" and "man." He then cautions that "size alone is a very crude indicator, and … brains of equal size may vary greatly in function." He immediately continues this cautionary note with the statement, "My belief is that although the brain of *Homo sapiens* is no larger than that of Neanderthal man, the indirect evidence strongly suggests that the first *Homo sapiens* was a much more intelligent creature" (1960:71). To say that "the brain of *Homo sapiens* is no larger than that of Neanderthal man" is misleading: the brain size of Neandertals is *definitively* larger than that of *Homo sapiens* (see, for example, Relethford 1990:355–59). The larger brain size is difficult precisely because we want to say that larger brains equate with smarter creatures. Obviously, this creates a problem. If bigger is better, then *Homo sapiens* comes out on the short end of the stick. Furthermore, the indirect evidence that Washburn alludes to but does not specify can only refer to non-anatomical data. He most probably has cave paintings in mind. But the problem is that there are also burial sites that pre-date cave painting and these burial sites house the remains of Neandertals. Neandertals thus had a concept of death — a rather sophisticated notion indicating an intelligence certainly on par with creatures whose artistry we revere.

For a brief but pointed discussion of "brain primacy," see Gould 1980:108–25, especially 116–17; see too Brace & Montagu 1965, especially 122–71.

2.   While "rudimentary vocal communication" is believed (by some) to go back two million years, the oldest date suggested for a verbal language, i.e. for speech, is 300,000 years ago, coincident with the appearance of early *Homo sapiens*. See Bruce Bower 1989.

3.   In point of fact, the wrong-headedness of the view even flies in the face of what might be seen as readily available philosophical evidence. An advertisement in an issue of *Jobs for Philosophers* addressed the need for a postdoctoral fellow in the History, Philosophy, or Sociology of Science and Technology. Its specifications included the following desiderata: "The candidate's AOS [area of specialization] should be relevant to the teaching of a joint graduate research seminar on the role of models in science and technology. Familiarity with the use of non-linguistic forms of representation such as diagrams, graphs, equations, simulations, and scale models would be desirable." Given Dennett's criterion for consciousness, one might well wonder whether the duly appointed philosopher, being fluent in nonlinguistic forms of thought, would not have grave deficits in consciousness.

4.   Even were we to put aside the impressive and irrefutable evidence of infant capacities, capacities that we do not remember, honest reflection shows that forgetfulness is not necessarily a measure of stupidity but a very real dimension of our humanness. We recall not only little if anything at all of how we originally or progressively put things together or made sense of them as infants, we recall little if anything at all of how we made sense of Beethoven's Ninth Symphony, Kant's *Critique of Pure Reason*, bicycles, or dinner knives. In short, we remember far less than we think, both in the sense of priding ourselves as lucid and exacting retainers of knowledge and in the sense that what we remember commonly reverberates with as much or more affective intensity as cognitive intensity.

5.   … though it would seem, of course, and in multiple and varied important senses, never quite a forgetting of one's own body and possibly never either a forgetting of the bodies of one's immediate family or circle of friends.

6.   It should be noted that Putnam's concern is to show that vatted brains, however functionally equivalent to our brains, cannot think linguistically to themselves or say to others that they are vatted brains. His concern is, in other words, not with the neurological credibility of the thought experiment — its conceptual viability — but rather with the credibility of vatted brains' linguistic so-called "references" to objects in the external world — e.g. "there is nothing by virtue of which their thought 'tree' represents actual trees" (1981: 13). His criticism of vatted brain thought experiments thus bypasses the more fundamental critical issues raised in this chapter.

7.   Of course, one could answer that although no neurophysiological brain event can be true or false, still, the assumption that a brain represents reality by such things as cognitive maps best explains the spatial abilities of creatures, including ourselves. On these grounds, which verge on survival criteria, one belief, in spite of its being a mere neurological event like any other belief, might be said to be more likely to be true than another. To such an answer, however, one could retort that the assumption proliferates cognitive entities no one has ever seen and can never hope to see. Such entities thus end up having the same status as minds: in whatever way they might be conceived related to, or correlated with, material happenings, they are immaterial.

8.   A paraphrasing along materialist lines of Albert Johnstone's epistemological findings (on behalf of refuting skeptical theses about the world) makes the point emphatically:

> The belief in eliminative materialism, functionalism, or any other cognitivist theory that collapses mind/body problems into brain neurophysiology is but one of an indefinitely great number of similar possible beliefs. Of these countless beliefs there is no apparent reason to prefer any one to any of the others.... In these circumstances, a claim that alleges the truth of one rather than that of another is quite unjustified and even irrational. Indeed, one might say that it attains a higher level of irrationality. It is not merely gratuitous, which is to say, unsupported or without reason. Nor is it simply arbitrarily chosen, since no better supported than its rivals. It is what might be termed *limitlessly arbitrary*.... No rational thinker ... can seriously assert such a claim, or refuse to see it as but one of an indefinitely great number of equally conceivable states of affairs (Johnstone 1991:319–20).

9.   See, for example, Trivers's "Parental Investment and Sexual Selection" (1972). Under the heading "Desertion and Cuckoldry," Trivers speaks in general behavioral terms that purportedly describe all animate reproductive life and takes external as well as internal fertilization into account. He writes that "To discuss the problems that confront paired individuals ostensibly cooperating in a joint parental effort, I choose the language of strategy and decision, as if each individual contemplated in strategic terms the decisions it ought to make at each instant in order to maximize its reproductive success. This language is chosen purely for convenience to explore the adaptations one might expect natural selection to favor" (146). The first question is, Is there another language? The second question is, If there is another language, are equivalents to the terms "desertion" and "cuckoldry" to be found in it? If they are not to be found in it, then the conceptual underpinnings of Trivers's general parental theory evaporate and a second, third, and conceivably limitless number of other theories can emerge alongside the first — each with its own descriptively convenient vocabulary.

However much sociobiologists might protest that their descriptive language is only a *façon de parler*, it is nonetheless the only language they have. Given the *socio* dimension of their biology, they must give precisely an account of social relations. In other words, whatever the genetic programming of any particular social relation, it is still an event in the lives of the creatures concerned. Sociobiologists recognize this fact when they say that creatures find "sweet" the activities in which they engage. Clearly, there is an experiential dimension to social behavior. Recognition of this fact demands a language geared to describing experienced feelings toward others. Any charges of anthropomorphism must be viewed in this context. They must also of course be viewed in the context of the limits of human knowledge and of the way in which humans seem naturally to parlay knowledge of themselves into a knowledge of other creatures — including other humans.

10.   Derrida is actually appropriating noted paleoanthropologist André Leroi-Gourhan's work in an egregiously distorted way. His button-pushing specimen is patterned on Leroi-Gourhan's science fiction specimen, which Leroi-Gourhan describes as having "a large cranium, a minuscule face, and a scanty body," in other words, a *corps* not *engagé* but "*étriqué*." See Leroi-Gourhan 1964, Vol. 1:182–183. For a full critical discussion of Derrida's evolutionary makeover and his appropriation of Leroi-Gourhan, see Sheets-Johnstone 1994, Chapter 4:"Corporeal Archetypes and Postmodern Theory."

11. Mind has "causal potency," Roger Sperry says, not in any mystical sense, but in the empirically-derived sense that any coherent system acts holistically in ways that control and determine the behavior of its parts (Sperry 1990:384–85). One might say that it is vatted brains in thought experiments that have causal potency in a mystical sense.

12. We might note how a recognition of agency falls through the crack when movement theory disputes are waged in either/or terms of efferent/afferent systems, avowed centrists — efferent theorists of motor programs — differing diametrically from avowed peripheralists — afferent theorists of sensory feedback. Some years ago when the argument between centrists and peripheralists was in its prime, J.A. Adams wrote that "I must point out that a very limited idea of a motor program is necessary for any theory of movement because a movement must be started and feedback does not occur until a fraction of a second later" (quoted in Requin et al. 1984:479). Clearly, any adequate account of agency demands a recognition of both intentionality and kinesthesia. Exclusively neurological concerns with movement can easily deflect awareness away from this fact either because the realities of self-movement go unnoticed or because they are swamped by theory.

13. Cotterill's concern with movement is from the viewpoint of a biophysicist who, in attempting to explain "the unity of conscious experience" in neurological terms finds much of merit in "'the old motor theory of thought'" (1995:290, 293). His emphasis upon the tactile-kinesthetic body, though not identified as such, is notable, as when he points out that "[an] organism's response might, viewed externally, appear to be an *out*put, but to the organism itself it is an *in*put" (294–95). Of moment too is his brief suggestion that qualia are inherent in our experience of movement, even if he does not specify in what such qualia consist.

　　Kelso similarly recognizes the centrality of movement: "It is important to keep in mind ... that the brain did not evolve merely to register representations of the world; rather, it evolved for adaptive action and behavior. Musculoskeletal structures coevolved with appropriate brain structures so that the entire unit functions together in an adaptive fashion" (Kelso 1995:268). He goes on to say that "Edelman arrived at a similar conclusion," i.e. "For him, like me, it is the entire system of muscles, joints, and proprioceptive and kinesthetic functions plus appropriate parts of the brain that evolves and functions together in a unitary way" (268).

14. The accomplishments of those early hominids who made tools, of those later hominids who, by strong indirect evidence, had rudimentary counting skills (Montagu 1976), and of those still later hominids who buried their dead, are the accomplishments of hominid species other than the one we recognize as our own human one. The only ancient artifacts connected exclusively with our distinctly *human* lineage — with *Homo sapiens sapiens* — are paleolithic cave drawings.

15. Lemon is actually quoting a phrase from John Hughlings Jackson. See John Hughlings Jackson 1931.

16. With respect to "striking differences," to be noted too, for example, is the fact that while small areas of the sensory cortex receive input "predominantly from one receptor or a few receptors of the same modality located nearby," small areas of the motor cortex receive "converging input from different receptors" (Asanuma 1989:35).

17.   Stimulation of the visual cortex, for example, actually produces nothing but "dancing lights," "black and white things," "[a] radiating gray spot which became pink and blue," "[an] undulating black wheel," "colors," "flickering light," and so on — *there are no objects*, nothing "which might suggest the things [one] has seen in past experience and learned to know" (Penfield & Rasmussen 1955:208).

18.   The whole passage reads, "The dog not only walks but it walks to greet its master. In a word the component from the roof-brain [that "increases the finesse, skill, adaptability and specificity of the motor act" beyond a reflex manoeuvre] alters the character of the motor act from one of generality of purpose to one of narrowed and specific purpose fitting a specific occasion. The change is just as if the motor act had suddenly become correlated with the finite mind of the moment. It is just as if the body and its finite mind had become one!" (bracketed insert from p. 189). Sherrington describes the roof-brain as "*par excellence* that organ where motor act and finite mind get into touch with one another" (1953:189). Though running counter to the very idea that the mind is not a brain, we might note that well-known neuroanatomist Ragnar Granit (1977) pointedly underscores Sherrington's view in the very title of his book *The Purposive Brain*.

CHAPTER 11

What is it like to be a brain?

The touchstone of the evolution of mammals from primitive reptiles has been the development of an increased level of activity … The skull has been affected primarily by the great enlargement of the brain needed in an active animal …. In the evolution through reptiles to mammals, numerous changes occur in the nervous system which are related in large measure to the increased activity and flexibility of response of mammals. A major change in the brain is the evolution of a neopallium, or neocortex, in the cerebral hemispheres to which sensory impulses are projected and where many motor impulses originate …. Another important change is the great enlargement of the cerebellum. This is correlated with the increased complexity of muscular movement …

Warren F. Walker (1975: 75, 214)

The feeling of an unbridgeable gulf between consciousness and brain-process … This idea of a difference in kind is accompanied by slight giddiness … When does this feeling occur in the present case? It is when I, for example, turn my attention in a particular way on to my own consciousness, and, astonished, say to myself: THIS is supposed to be produced by a process in the brain! — as it were clutching my forehead.

Ludwig Wittgenstein (1963: 124)

1. Introduction

This chapter attempts to pinpoint in exacting terms an answer to the question, what it is like to be a brain. In the beginning, and at several subsequent points, it paraphrases in outright ways passages from Thomas Nagel's justly famous and durable article, "What Is It Like To Be a Bat?" (1979). It does so with a view to highlighting how, when the same question is asked of a brain as of a bat, a conceptually affinitive state of affairs becomes evident. While the respective questions differ in the basic kind of problem they generate, they nevertheless give rise to philosophically analogous puzzles and philosophically analogous battle lines, which is why many of Nagel's locutions may be so readily paraphrased and many of his sequences of ideas so readily duplicated — as in the opening paragraph that follows:

The brain is what has been making the mind/body problem really intractable of late. That is why current discussions of the problem get it obviously wrong. Without *the brain*, the mind/body problem would be a different problem, i.e. it would be a veritable mind/body problem, whereas with *the brain*, it is hopeless. It is hopeless not only because the mind/brain problem is conflated with the mind/body problem. It is hopeless because the most important and characteristic feature of the brain is poorly understood; in fact, it is not even acknowledged. On the contrary, it is taken for granted and in consequence consistently ignored. Careful examination shows that no currently available concept of the brain takes it into account. The present inquiry into brains in general and *the brain* in particular will lead us to the heart of the matter. Indeed, it will allow us to see how a hard-driving materialism is empirically opaque and deviant, as much in its neglect of what is most important and characteristic of a brain as in its neglect of living bodies, that is, bodies which exist not only in real-time — to borrow a phrase from dynamic systems theorists — but in real-space and which move with real-energies.

2. Beginning findings

Brains are widespread. They are present in different sizes and shapes at many levels of animate life. Although we are aware of ganglia and such in invertebrate organisms, some persons are prepared to deny evolutionary continuities, that is, to deny that there are structural or formal analogies in different types of head-end neural matter, and, along the same lines, to deny that there are analogies in "mental powers" — e.g. attention, memory, reasoning, and other capacities that Darwin specified as "mental powers" (1981). Yet no matter how the material form may vary, the fact that organisms have material formations in their head-ends *at all* — whether brains or infinitesimally small ganglia — means basically that there is something that it is like to be a brain — or ganglia — something that it is like *for the brain (or ganglia) itself.*

Now it cannot be claimed that that something is experiential in nature since the brain is an organ, not an organism. Hence, any experiential ascriptions to brains must be in error since they wrongly impute to brains something that properly belongs to organisms. A prime way in which *the brain* renders the mind/body problem intractable, even incurable, consists precisely in the fact that present-day investigations, discussions, and analyses of *the brain* abound in just such experiential ascriptions. Rather than explaining how living organisms — humans included — assess something dangerous in their environment or interact with conspecifics, accounts of organic life degenerate into accounts of brain life. For example, we read that "The [barn] owl's brain perceives depth using the same computations it uses to determine the location of sounds. To locate a sound, the brain assesses the difference in the time the sound takes to reach each ear" (Pennisi 1993: 133);[1] another states (as noted in Chapter Ten) that "Nonhuman animals have brains capable of cooperative hunting" (Harding 1975: 255). Insofar as a brain is not an organism, on what grounds can one say that a brain locates sounds?; on what grounds can one say that brains hunt together cooperatively? If a brain can locate a sound, then a brain can *hear*; if brains can hunt together, then they can *move together in concert* on the savannah. To think that brains can, and do, do such things is to think that there is such a thing as a day in the life of a brain.

Now clearly, such an idea is misguided: a brain does not have a life. The first challenge is thus to specify what it is like to be a brain without making experiential ascriptions. What is wanted is an absolutely objective description of what it is like to be a brain — a heterophenomenological account, as Dennett might call it, such an account being one that follows a "*neutral* path leading from objective physical science and its insistence on the third-person point of view, to a method of phenomenological description that can (in principle) do justice to [what is] most private and ineffable ..." (Dennett 1991:72; italics in original).

Perhaps the first point to notice in answer to the challenge is that it is dark; that is, to be a brain is to be unilluminated. An equally significant way of putting the point is to say that any objective description of what is it like to be a brain must acknowledge the fact that brains are *inside*. Brains never show themselves directly except by way of surgery or accidents, or by way of dissections; they show themselves indirectly only through experimentation. Accordingly, they never show themselves except (1) when they are either medically or traumatically exposed, (2) when they are set out on laboratory tables, or (3) when they are in other than ordinary everyday conditions. To draw attention in this phenomenological manner to the way in which, and the conditions under which, a brain shows itself is to underscore the fact that, whatever the exceptional conditions in which they show themselves, and however normally hidden away and inaccessible, brains are considered to be *normally active*, and to be so continuously until the moment the organism in which the brain inheres, dies.

What is the evidence for claiming they are? What warrant do we have for thinking that there is something called *brain activity*? And what exactly is the nature of this activity?

Current research and textbook accounts of brains document their activity in the course of an individual's eating, being aggressive, speaking, sensing, sleeping, behaving sexually, learning, and across many other domains of animate existence. Studies show, for example, that the brain has "nutrient-sensitive detectors," or more specifically, that other organs (eyes, nose, mouth, stomach, duodenum, and liver) signal the brain that food has been eaten and is "on the way to absorption" (Carlson 1991:415); they show that "the gut talks to the brain over ... [vagus nerve] fibers" (Raloff 1996:343);[2] they show that the brain has different "mechanisms" for each of three aggressive behaviors — offense, defense, and predation — and that the ventral tegmental area of the midbrain is "involved in" offensive behavior and not in either defensive or predatory behavior, lesions made in the tegmental area disrupting only the animal's attack behavior (Carlson 1992:306); they show that different naming tasks "[boost] blood flow in

different parts of the temporal lobe" (B. Bower 1996:234);[3] they show that "[a]wait-
ing an impending touch or shock to the fingers produce[s] substantial drops in blood
flow in the parts of the somatosensory cortex that deal with facial sensation, while
the region concerned with finger sensation [holds] steady" (B. Bower 1995:38).[4] The
above studies postulate brain activity on the basis of experimental lesions, of specific
cranial nerve connections, of hypothetical mechanisms such as "detectors," and of
imaging techniques that monitor blood flow. Other data postulate brain activity on
the basis of other practices: electrical activity mapping, for example, direct stimulation via electrodes, and the use of radioactive compounds rather than blood flow as
a standard of measurement. (For complete descriptions of the various techniques, see
Carlson 1991, Chapter 5; for a brief discussion of different methods, see Roediger et al.
1987:55–56.) Whatever their procedures, all research findings support the claim that
brains are normally active: they are the site of neurological, electrical, and metabolic
happenings. Many of these findings show further that, as indicated above, brain activity is correlated in quite specific ways with behavior, memory, attention, and myriad
other facets of everyday animate existence (Carlson 1992; Roediger et al. 1987). What
the findings do not show, however, in spite of showing correlations, is that neurological, electrical, and metabolic brain activity is anything other than neurological, electrical, and metabolic. Thus, according to the facts of the matter — the facts of the matter
in the literal sense of being empirically-gathered facts about matter — to be a brain is
to be on the inside, in the dark, and engaged in neurological, electrical, and metabolic
activities.

In an anatomical sense, of course, to be a brain is more than this. Anatomically,
to be a brain is to be a chunk of superficially convoluted tissue that is internally par-
titioned in various ways and that is laced through and through with neural ganglia,
fibers, and tracts. Although laced through and through with neural matter, the chunk
of tissue is insensitive. When electrodes are inserted into brain tissue, there is no discomfort to the creature whose tissue it is. The insensitive chunk of tissue comes in two
colors: white and gray — gray on the outside, white on the inside. While such anatomical facts as these add to our knowledge of what it is like to be a brain, they do not
broaden or deepen our knowledge in the sense that we need to broaden and deepen it.
If we are to "do justice to [what is] most private and ineffable," then something further
in the way of understanding brain activity is obviously required. In particular, what we
need to know, or at least what we need to begin to fathom, and in non-ascriptive terms,
is what exactly is going on *inside*?

We may note in this context a certain irony in the fact that, although the architecture and organization of the brain is known in great detail, what the brain actually
does in terms of its architecture and organization is not necessarily known at all.
Research findings notwithstanding, *the actual activity of the brain* — what generates it and in what it consists — is obscure. Indeed, none of the above facts of the

matter sheds light on the question of its actual activity. Crucial information is thus missing from the above preliminary "heterophenomenological" account. What is missing is not merely functional information — how each specific part of the brain works, for example. We can appreciate this fact by considering remarks philosopher Patricia Churchland makes in the process of giving an account of the cerebellum. At the beginning of her account she states that "With only some exaggeration it can be said that almost everything one would want to know about the micro-organization of the cerebellum is known." Shortly after, at the start of her next paragraph, she writes that "Exactly *what* the cerebellum contributes to nervous system function is not well understood" (Churchland 1986: 412, 413; italics in original). The *functional* ignorance of which Churchland speaks is altogether different from what we might hesitantly but boldly call a *material ignorance*. In other words, it is not a question of what a cerebellum contributes but what a cerebellum is doing, i.e. what is going on inside? In still other terms, the most fundamental facet of what it is like to be a brain has to do neither with its structure nor with its function. It has to do with the fact that to be a brain is *to be active*; *it is to be something other than simply an inert piece of matter*. Indeed, research findings show that a brain is continuously and differentially "busy." Hence it is not surprising that most if not all research on the brain is concerned with an investigation of some form of brain activity. If we discount experiential ascriptions — "detecting," "talking," and so on — what we have left is precisely activity.

 We may properly designate this fundamental facet *the kinetic character of brain matter*. This character is not captured by any of the familiar renditions of brain matter — in particular, not even by functional ones, for though functional ones tell us how various parts of the brain are "involved in" various living functions, or just "*what*" various parts of the brain contribute to nervous system function, they do not tell us anything about how a brain is *active*. To account for this fundamental feature of brain matter, what is needed is an *expansionist* program, that is, a program that explains how it is that brain matter is active and not just matter, pure and simple. Such a program would account for something that is not presently accounted for in materialist accounts of brains in general and *the brain* in particular, something that is, on the contrary, unacknowledged from the start but at the same time assumed and taken for granted. If materialism is to be a defensible doctrine, then materialist accounts of brains, rather than being reductionistically oriented, must be expanded to incorporate the basic kinetic character of brain matter. Indeed, any materialist account that fails to deal explicitly with its kinetic character is less than empirical, or in Dennett's terms, less than heterophenomenological. Hewing to "the method of heterophenomenology" means "never abandoning the methodological scruples of science" (Dennett 1991: 72). Clearly, if something crucial about brain matter is being ignored, then scruples *are* being abandoned.

The problem is that incorporation seems impossible given present-day matter-pure-and-simple materialist doctrine. Contemporary accounts of brain matter are accounts either of something static in the form of spatially discrete pieces of architecture — sulci, amygdala, lobes, and optic chiasma — and/or of something substantial — blood, glucose, sodium, potassium, for example, substances that are physically present, or absent, and in certain quantities, at some place or other at some particular time. In a word, current materialist accounts are inhospitable to movement. They are inhospitable to the idea that movement is a built-in feature of brain matter, let alone a fundamental feature. This is why the kinetic character of brain matter does not fall within the explanatory framework of current materialist theory and why brain activity remains an enigma. In other terms, this is why functional accounts can be given of "activity," these accounts being basically statements about what a part of the brain does and/or what it is good for, and why kinetic accounts of brain activity are lacking. A hard-driving — not to say, eliminative — materialism cannot explain matter in motion but can only take it for granted, slipping it into explanations in trivializing ways, but otherwise ignoring it completely, as when Paul Churchland writes that "a nervous system is *just an active* matrix of cells, and a cell is *just an active* matrix of molecules" (P. M. Churchland 1984:21; italics added). Indeed, *a hard-driving materialism neglects aspects of life on both sides of its reductionist equations.* It neglects not just "the subjective"; it neglects the kinetic. Matter pure and simple — even "more complex and powerful matter" (P. M. Churchland 1984:21) — stretches in neither of these directions.

We can pursue the point at issue and further clarify its importance by specifying deficiencies in common materialist conceptions of brain matter. We can do this most effectively by taking a simple but fundamental example of what it is like to be a brain; namely, to be consistently run through with neural firings.

3.   Neural firing: A phenomenological inquiry

Scientists and lay people familiar with science would undoubtedly answer positively if asked if they believed that neurons fire. Their positive answer clearly affirms brain activity; neurons fire in the brain as they fire elsewhere in the body. But what precisely does it mean to say that neurons fire? In what does neuron firing consist? Literature on the subject is quite specific: "When an action potential shoots down an axon, the neuron is said to have *fired*" (Bernstein et al. 1994:97). If we ask what an action potential is, we find again that literature on the subject is quite specific: "[an] abrupt change in the potential of an axon is called an *action potential*" (Bernstein et al. 1994:97). If we want the phenomenon defined in still more specific terms, or if we want a more elaborate description, it too is readily available. The abrupt change in potential is the result of "a force called an *electrochemical potential*" (Bernstein et al. 1994:96). The force "drives positively charged molecules (sodium) toward the inside of the cell ... [though] many are kept outside by the [cell] membrane" (Bernstein et al. 1994:96). Gates along the axon open and close allowing these otherwise "excluded" (sodium) molecules to "rush into the axon, stimulating the next gate to open, and so on down the axon" (Bernstein et al. 1994:97). What opens the gates is "stimulation of the [nerve] cell [which] causes depolarization near a particular gate" (Bernstein et al. 1994:97). The progressive opening of gates "and the change in electrochemical potential spreads like a wild rumor all the way down the axon" (Bernstein et al. 1994:97).

To judge from this detailed account, there is a good deal of activity going on in an axon when a neuron fires. When we consider the fact that a human brain has approximately 100 billion nerve cells (Bernstein et al. 1994:107), and that the speed of an action potential may be as fast as 260 miles per hour (Bernstein et al. 1994:97), we can hardly trivialize brain activity or take it for granted, especially since, in spite of believing that neurons fire, and in spite of being able to say in what the firing consists, i.e. in "an action potential shoot[ing] down an axon," we cannot grasp what the activity is actually like. Temporally, spatially, and energetically, the brain is abuzz with activity in a way totally different from the way in which we are abuzz with activity. The "wild rumor" dynamics of neuron firing are not our dynamics. Though clearly a form of motion, neural firing is not similar to any motion that we make or could make, and there is no reason to suppose that it is like anything we can experience or imagine ourselves experiencing. Indeed, *shooting down* is fundamentally an *alien* form of motion for us. We have no experience of ourselves as a force shooting down anything, much less at 260 miles per hour, and much less doing something like opening gates along the way. Imaginative possibilities are foreclosed for the same reason that actual experience is foreclosed: they necessitate our being a body other than the body we are. In more precise terms, they necessitate our imagining ourselves kinesthetically experiencing an utterly foreign motion. To think ourselves capable of such imaginings is to conflate visual and kinesthetic modalities, i.e. a visual image of some kind or other with an imagined kinesthetically-experienced event. What we discover in a visual image is not *what it is like* to be a neuron firing, but only what the verbal description, "action potential shoot[ing] down an axon," prompts us to discover — most likely an imaginary non-specifiable fast-moving something whizzing by us at eye level. Even if we try imagining ourselves gradually metamorphosing bodily into a neuron, we still find nothing in our constitution that enables us to imagine what it would be like to move in the way an action potential moves in "shoot[ing] down an axon." Clearly, it is the kinesthetic event that we need to experience or imagine in order to say what it is like to be a neuron firing, for it is only that experienced or imagined event that will tell us what brain activity is like — in the same way that only such kinesthetic experiencings or imaginings will tell us what it is like to be a bat.

Now if we cannot grasp what it is actually like, then how is it possible to describe what it is like, not only in terms of "a wild rumor," but metaphorically[5] from the very beginning: an action potential *shoots down an axon*. In particular, while allusion might be made to "shooting pains," for example, there is no direct analogy we can make to kinesthetic bodily experiences. How, then, did the idea of *a force shooting down a material object* ever arise? What were the original grounds for describing a neuron firing, or even speaking of the *firing* of a neuron to begin with? How did neurophysiologists arrive at this description? The basic question is clearly not a question of direct observation since no one can actually see an action potential shooting down an axon, i.e. see an electrochemical potential herding sodium molecules toward the inside of a cell and sodium molecules opening gates along an axon. The basic question is rather a conceptual one. In the broadest of terms, and especially in light of a radically austere twentieth-century Western conception of matter, how does brain matter come to be conceived as dynamically energized and changing rather than as inert? Is all matter really matter-pure-and-simple? Or is there something about brain matter that is crucially different from the matter of a table or a telescope or a car, or from the matter of a stone, a clod of earth, or a body of water? Would scientists and lay people alike not say that the former kind of matter is precisely neither interchangeable with, nor equivalent to, the latter kind? Clearly, the very conception of matter is in question, and not only this, but as intimated above, the very terms of the description pose a fundamental conceptual puzzle. If action potentials are not directly witnessed but only inferred, one may rightly ask on what basis they are inferred. How does the dynamic event that constitutes a neuron firing comes to be conceived? *Where does the concept of an action potential come from*?

Since action potentials are kinetic in nature and are themselves claimed to be the result of a moving force, one can begin to answer the above questions only by taking movement into account. Putting the questions in kinetic perspective, a beginning answer might be formulated in the following general terms: whatever any particular movement might be, if we can describe it kinetically, then in some sense we know what it is like, and this in spite of our having no such movement experiences ourselves and of our not being able to imagine ourselves moving in such ways. If this general rule were not true, descriptions of movement on the order of action potentials shooting down an axon and electrochemical forces driving positively charged molecules would not gain currency. They would not be sanctioned as bona fide descriptions of what is going on. If we ask what basis there is for sanctioning the descriptions, we have only ourselves to look to — and correlatively, only to look to ourselves. The fact that we move supplies all the answer we need: we know experientially what it is to move, even though we do not know either experientially or imaginatively what it is to move *in those ways*. However alien the motion of *shooting down* an axon — however incapable we are of particular kinesthetic experiences and imaginings — our conception of an action potential, as of our consequent explanations of brain activity, derives from our own moving bodies. In other words, the very idea of an action potential, including the basic idea of an electrochemical *force*, traces back to dynamic experiences we have of ourselves in movement, and of ourselves as making things happen through movement. The relevant kinetic concepts and the descriptive language have their origin in our own bodies. In effect, in a crucial epistemological sense, the starting point for conceiving and describing an action potential — an unobserved but inferred moving force — is on the side of the observer, not the observed.

The idea that our concept of force derives from our own bodily experiences of moving is not a new idea. Eighteenth-century British empiricists — John Locke, George Berkeley, and David Hume — in different ways underscore their common conviction that neither innate ideas nor reason supplies the grounds for the concept of force; the concept comes from experience. Ironically, however, their arguments on behalf of experience rarely take experiences of actual living bodies into account. The experiences they consult or describe, when they consult or describe experience, concern for the most part the movement of things in the world, not the movement of their own bodies. For this reason, their arguments do not so much present concrete evidentially-grounded claims as abstract reasoned-out ones. To make a genuinely empirical case for an origin in experience, evidence must be brought forth showing that the concept of force is anchored in self-movement, that is, in a sentiently moving body, the tactile-kinesthetic body. No such body makes an appearance in any of the arguments the empiricists present. When Locke, for example, does cite living bodies (rather than bodies such as billiard balls), he remarks that "barely by willing it, barely by a thought of the mind, we can move the parts of our bodies which were before at rest." He goes on immediately to give this power to the mind and says no more of the moving body itself. In modern terms, he, like Hume and Berkeley, fixate on the efferent side of movement and are oblivious of the reafferent or kinesthetic side. They take up the idea of will, volition, and the like, and totally ignore the tactile-kinesthetic body.

In his history of the muscle sense and of innervation feelings, historian of science Eckart Scheerer points out the central (and largely overlooked) role of nineteenth-century philosopher Johann Jakob Engel who, as Scheerer notes, may be properly regarded "the father of the muscle sense" (Scheerer 1987: 176). Engel sharply admonished Locke and Hume for neglecting the muscle sense in favor of reflection. He reproached Hume, saying that "He ought to use his muscles, but instead he uses his eyes; he ought to grasp and struggle, and instead he is content to watch" (176). Scheerer emphasizes Engle's critical point that "feelings of innervation" — will, volition, and the like — are not *ideas*, as Locke and Hume affirm, but incipient bodily tensions. He furthermore calls attention to Engel's insight — that "muscles are organs by which we acquire ideas about external objects" — and quotes his criticism of Locke and Hume: if the latter two philosophers had paid attention to their own muscles, "they would, while going through the number of external senses, have fixed their attention on this muscle sense.. and would have found in it the original source of our concept of force" (177). Scheerer himself points out that "a purely contemplative attitude" (176) cannot possibly lead to an understanding of force. The attitude is unanchored in any felt bodily presence. The point is well taken: if the concept in question is a kinetic one, one must reflect not in a vacuum as it were but in the context of experiences of one's own body. The very idea of force — whether an action potential shooting down an axon and opening gates as it travels, or an army driving a wedge, or a train pulling out of a station — is conceptually contingent upon kinesthetic experience, experiences of a sentient moving body, a body aware of itself in the process of moving. Such a body is not indifferent to movement and to rest, in the style of Galileo and Descartes. On the contrary, such a body is quintessentially attuned to the rest and movement of its own body, and in consequence, quintessentially attuned to the richness and subtleties of its own dynamics in the process of moving.

The point is significant from a further perspective. A Galilean-Cartesian construal of motion shifts attention away from the kinds of fundamental concerns Aristotle had about movement toward not only mathematical concerns but inertial ones. Rather than taking movement as something to be understood and explained in its own right, a Galilean-Cartesian construal makes it simply a possible condition of matter. The latter orientation in essence frees matter of any inherent kinetic other than an inertial one based on its resistance to change. Accordingly, matter is charged only with — in Newton's later terms — "the force of inactivity." In effect, the latter orientation purifies matter and ultimately homogenizes it. Coincident with this homogenous view of matter and arbitrary view of motion is the idea that movement is simply a change of position. Descartes formulates this definition exactly: Motion, he says, is "the transfer of one piece of matter, or one body, from the vicinity of the other bodies which are in immediate contact with it, and which are regarded as being at rest, to the vicinity of other bodies" (Descartes [1644] 1985, 233). The definition puts movement in its place, so to speak; it effectively nullifies any sense of its dynamic, reducing it to mere transport. At the same time, it makes matter the focal point of attention; what matters is the stuff — the "piece of matter" or particular body — that happens to be transferred or not transferred. That stuff simply persists in doing whatever it is doing — moving or resting — until such time as its resistance is overcome, and, if it is moving, it ceases to move, or if resting, it ceases to rest. This inertial notion of matter and motion actually puts to rest any sense of a living world. *It reduces the kinetic to the positional and the happenstance.* When matter in motion is arrested in this way, so also is life; when movement is viewed as no more than an arbitrary condition of matter, so also is life. When the world in all its particulars is viewed basically as a collection of purely material objects, life is indeed metamorphosed into a series of stills.

Quite obviously, brain activity does not accord with this series of stills — any more than does a living world of living creatures. When movement is brought to a standstill, *all* animate powers are stilled. Indeed, the living world is no longer *animate*. Something essential is missing, something which is the very source point of our concept of action potentials and of electrochemical forces. An action potential shooting down an axon has nothing to do with the transfer of a piece of matter from one place to another. It has nothing to do with the perseveration of a present state. The very idea of an action potential rests not on a concept of matter, especially inertial matter, but *a concept of movement*, a concept of dynamic energy. That concept derives from the concept we have of ourselves as moving bodies. That same concept informs our concept of our bodily insides — not only our various unobserved and unobservable organic systems, but also our various unobserved and unobservable organs, including our brains. Everything inside is conceived to be in the process of doing something; everything inside is conceived to be *alive with activity*. We readily affirm that *there are forces inside of us and things inside of us that move*, that our insides are not *inert*, that, on the contrary, only when we are dead are they inert. The entire description of a neuron firing coincides with this dynamic conception we have of our bodily selves. It is anchored in a kinetic terminology, a terminology that belies a conception of matter as mere stuff that is arbitrarily at rest and arbitrarily active. It in fact takes for granted at the same time that it specifies, a concept of *living* matter, that is, matter in motion.

Now if, on the basis of our own kinetic lives, we know in some sense what it is like for a neuron to fire, then however unacknowledged and unarticulated the relationship between our own experiences of movement and our concept of a neuron firing, and however imperfect our knowledge of the latter given its remoteness from actual experience, we have at least a schematic kinetic conception of what it is like for a neuron to fire — what it is like to move and in moving make things happen. This schematic *non-linguistic* kinetic conception is solidified linguistically by the words chosen to describe metaphorically what happens when a neuron is active, i.e. when a neuron fires. Neither the nonlinguistic conception nor its linguistic formulation, however, are coincident with what neuron firing is like *for the neuron*. This is not because it is not like anything for a neuron insofar as a neuron has no sensory system that gives it a sense of its own movement in the way that kinesthesia gives us a sense of our own movement. It is not a deficiency on the part of the neuron; it is a deficiency on our side, a deficiency over and above our inability to imagine what it is like to be a neuron firing because we are the bodies we are and not some other kind of body, that is, because our bodily structure does not permit us to generate directly concepts of the requisite type. This further deficiency is basically a theoretical deficiency, not a corporeal one. What additionally prevents our knowing what it is like *for the neuron* is a matter of our not being able to fathom within the confines of twentieth-century Western science how it is that matter comes to be animated. However much we may know of sodium molecules, depolarization, cell membranes, and so on, we know nothing of how an energy dynamics comes to suffuse matter, and how matter comes to be in motion. We are not close to conceiving where potentials or forces come from. In short, we believe in kinetic facts beyond the reach of our understanding, facts whose exact nature we are not close to conceiving.

4. Distinguishing information and ability

Before substantiating the above claim in further ways, showing how a hard-driving materialism actually exacerbates our ignorance by denying it, and how this state of affairs encourages us to believe beyond our conceptual reach, it will be helpful to examine and clarify a distinction. The distinction might easily be related to Ryle's original distinction between "knowing that" and "knowing how," but the guise in which we will consider it is more cogent to present concerns. When David Lewis writes that "knowing what it's like is not the possession of information at all ... [but is rather] the possession of abilities" (1991: 234), he seems to be in quasi-agreement with the first of the two above conclusions: knowing what it is like to be a neuron firing — or to be a brain — is contingent on certain abilities we possess. These abilities, however, are not the abilities Lewis specifies — "abilities to recognize, abilities to imagine, abilities to predict one's behavior by means of imaginative experiments" (1991: 234). As we have seen, imagination plays no foundational role art in our basically kinetic conception of what it is like for a neuron to fire, and as for recognition, we lack the direct experience to begin with of "an action potential shoot[ing] down an axon." At the most basic level, the relevant abilities are the ability to move in certain ways and in virtue of moving in those ways, the ability to make certain other things happen. We experience just such abilities in everyday life, as when we push a door hard so that it slams shut, or when we hammer a nail into wood, or when we rock a baby to sleep, or when we bump into someone and that someone falls down, or when we startle someone by walking into a room unexpectedly, and so on. Clearly, we have the ability to move, and in moving, make other things happen — in a way akin to the way in which an action potential "shoot[ing] down an axon" makes other things happen (see Sheets-Johnstone 1979: 41–42). All the same, we cannot know what it is like for a neuron to be firing because as pointed out above, we do not have anything like *that* particular ability — i.e. the ability to shoot ourselves forward at exorbitant speed at the same time changing the very nature of the path we are traversing. What we do have, in virtue of our movement abilities, is the conceptual foundation for understanding movement, and it is this conceptual foundation that allows us not only to understand the idea of "an action potential shoot[ing] down an axon"; the conceptual foundation also allows us to formulate the process in the first place. It allows us, in other words, to conceive of an action potential, of a self-propagating force, of molecular attraction, and of shooting and firing to begin with. What allows us to claim that we know what we are talking about when we talk about a neuron firing are kinetic concepts rooted in our own movement experiences and abilities. These foundational concepts allow us both to grasp and to formulate the idea of a neuron firing. We can thus conclude that we know what it is like for a neuron to fire not from the perspective of a neuron, but from the perspective of our own kinetic abilities and experiences. It is important to emphasize that this conclusion is grounded in facts concerning our own animate existence, facts ascertainable not on the basis of a heterophenomenological study of (or heterophenomenological questionnaire given to) other humans, but on the basis of awarenesses we ourselves have and judgments we ourselves make in the context of our own experiences of movement, awarenesses and judgments of which we can give a solid phenomenological description.

The limited, quasi-concurrence about the role of abilities in "knowing what it is like" notwithstanding, Lewis's distinction is not relevant to the question of what it is like to be a neuron firing, let alone to conceptual foundations. His point in distinguishing between information and ability arises in a quite other context and has a quite specific aim, which turns on the fact that materialist and functionalist explanations of brains are threatened by the very idea of "knowing what it is like." The idea opens the door to qualia — to pains (Lewis's main concern), to colors, and to all such qualitative aspects of everyday life. Lewis's aim is to save materialist and functionalist doctrines from the admission of qualia. His materialist-functionalist strategy is, quite obviously, to explain qualia in terms of matter and function, thus ultimately reducing so-called "qualia" to *states* of *the brain*. The fact that movement experiences are inherently *qualitative* as well as dynamic — and hence pose perhaps the greatest challenge to a qualia-free ontology, in addition to constituting precisely the kind of experience that Lewis must dismiss if he is to save materialism-functionalism from ontological infestations — will not concern us at this point. The immediate concern is theoretical, not phenomenological: saving materialist and functionalist doctrine is possible only at the expense of movement. To appreciate what results from this theoretical oversight, let us consider Lewis's "smart data bank."

Lewis tells us that "a smart data bank ... can be told things, it can store the information it is given, it can reason with it, it can answer questions on the basis of its stored information" (1991:234). If his conjectured "smart data bank" is an alias for *the brain*, as surely he intends it to be, then what "shoots down an axon" is not an action potential but *information*. In other words, *the brain* is not the site of kinetic happenings; it is the site of information-processing. Accordingly, information is without question, i.e. *ipso facto*, understood as being embedded in brain matter. The question of *how* it is embedded is answered by reference to "coding." That is, materialists-functionalists claim that through experimental evidence, one can determine — either now or in the future — how in each case information is embedded in certain structures according to the coding used by those structures. For example, rods and cones are photoreceptors that are differentially responsive to light, i.e. they are coded to light of different wave lengths (Carlson 1992:160–61). Whether a code is actually known or not, an informational conception of brain matter allows one to speak of stimuli such as light waves and sound waves, of receptors such as eyes and ears, of feature analyzers or brain modules such as vocal tract synthesizers (see Liberman & Mattingly 1985; see also Chapter Nine, this text), and of detectors such as temperature monitors; that is, it allows speaking of *things*, things on the body and in the brain that carry, send, or receive information. How such things as light or sound waves — or in the case of taste, such macro-items as salt, chocolate, or lemons — are transformed into information is a matter of structural coding — of "taste-sensitive neurons," for example (Carlson 1992:204).

The above elaboration should suffice to show that an informational "smart data bank" account of brain matter is clearly tractable in a way that a kinetic account of matter is not. In particular, matter is *manageable* in informational terms, even instantly so. It does not balk when we put information into it, such as when we speak of messages being exchanged by brain and gut, or when we speak of name recognition in terms of increased blood flow in a certain region of the temporal lobe, or when we speak of certain tongue papillae being receptive to sourness. What matters, both with respect to what comes in in the way of matter — a light wave, for example — and what is cerebrally dealt with in the way of matter — a neuron firing, for example — is *information*. *The brain* is congenial to this materialist-functionalist conception and is exactingly conceived in pure-and-simple matter terms. What the conception leaves unexplained, of course, is how information *enmatters itself* — in a way similar to the way in which the conception of a neuron firing leaves unexplained how matter moves itself.

Now information has a palpable concreteness, a remarkable stability, quantifiability, and even spatio-temporal specificity about it that movement lacks. It is not surprising, then, that matter — the prevalent twentieth-century Western conception of matter — is not docile in the same way when it comes to movement. Indeed, even with such "forces" and "things" as — and "concepts" of — "an *electrochemical potential* [that] drives positively charged molecules toward the inside of [a nerve] cell," we do not begin to understand how matter comes to be animated. We do not begin to understand how it is that some matter attracts and repulses other matter. We are that much further baffled by how matter that happens to be inside and at a distance from other matter comes to be kinetically set off by that other matter. When we stop to question how materialist and functionalist doctrines can implicitly affirm that matter simply moves itself, or at the very least implicitly deny any importance to an explanation of motion by ignoring the very question, we realize the explanatory bankruptcy of the doctrines. In materialist-functionalist accounts, electrochemical potentials, action potentials, and other such "forces" or "things" are taken as givens, givens apparently arriving out of the blue or idling about at the ready until driven to animating matter from time to time. In any event, such "forces" or "things" are neither explained nor considered as needing explanation. In point of fact, the question of movement never arises in informational accounts of matter. On the contrary, movement is taken for granted in the rush of information. What Lewis and other hard-driving materialists overlook is the fact not only that information is not equivalent to explanation but that no amount of information can generate an explanation. "[A] smart data bank," however much "it can store ... information," however much "it can reason with [its information]," however much it can tell us about how something works, cannot explain how brain activity itself comes to be. In effect, it cannot explain itself. Its own workings — its own activity — remain a mystery.

An explanation of brain activity clearly requires something quite other than data. It in fact requires opting out of blindered materialist notions of brains in general and "smart data bank" notions of *the brain* in particular. It requires recognizing that an informational account of brain activity omits something crucial, something that Aristotle long ago recognized when he asked, "how will there be movement, if there is no actual cause?" (*Metaphysics* 1071b: 29–30). Electrochemical potentials, action potentials, chemical attraction, and the like, though conjuring dynamic "forces," "things," or events, are powerless to supply an "actual cause." Though invoked to explain certain happenings, they are explanatory constructs that themselves remain unexplained; they conjure energy out of the blue. As enfolded without question in processes of information-processing, they are summarily caught up in a pure and simple materialism that aims to remain pure and simple. Contrary to Aristotle's concerns about the necessity of explaining how matter comes to be animated — how "[m]atter will surely not move itself" (*Metaphysics* 1071b: 30) — materialists implicitly affirm quite simply that "matter surely *does* move itself." Clearly, so long as one hews to a reductive materialist account of brain activity, one cannot begin to conceive how matter — mere matter — can be animated, how it itself can be the source of dynamic happenings. From this perspective, it becomes obvious that the central problem with "knowing what it is like to be a brain" is not that *we* lack an ability — the ability to know what it is like *for the neuron* to be a neuron firing, i.e. to be animated. The central problem is that *a pure and simple materialism* lacks an ability, the ability to explain how it is that matter — *mere* matter — can be in motion, active, animated.

The central problem is in fact not that far from home. Even if conceiving themselves as "creatures of matter" — "more complex and powerful" matter than that of their "fellow creatures," but matter all the same (P. M. Churchland 1984: 21) — reductive materialists know from their own abilities and experiences that *they move themselves*. If they know from their own experience that they initiate movement, that movement does not simply happen to them, then they must necessarily take seriously the question of how matter comes to be animated, how there is such a thing as a neuron firing. The brain, after all, with all its neurons, is abuzz with activity, in a "wild rumor" way quite dissimilar from the way in which materialists themselves are abuzz with activity in their everyday lives, but in a way that is equally kinetic. Can reductive materialists answer to what *drives* all this activity? Indeed, can they explain how matter appears to animate itself — to change itself from potentiality to dynamic actuality, as Aristotle would likely say? Or are they at a loss to explain the motion — the animation — of matter? Is their lack of explanation not related to the fact that *the brain's* motor programs, so long cherished as explanatory devices, are currently being challenged and conceptually displaced by explanations of movement that are dynamically attuned to the animation of living forms themselves — as research in the area of infant and child development shows? (For a detailed exposition, see Thelen & Smith 1994; for a more general exposition of dynamic systems theory and of the self-organizing processes underlying dynamic systems, see Kelso 1995).

In sum, detailed physico-chemical descriptions of what happens when a neuron fires explain nothing in the way of the kinetic character of matter for the descriptions stop short of explaining *how it is that a neuron fires*. They fail to explain the fundamental phenomenon putatively being witnessed, i.e. movement. Does matter move itself? If not, what generates its *activity*? If *action potentials* animate matter, where do *action potentials* come from? And what exactly does it mean to say that they are *self-propagating*? Is animism necessary to a complete account of matter, living matter?

5. Animism

Animism is regarded a pernicious practice by traditional Western science. It may be defined as the practice of calling into existence an animating force of some kind, a force whereby otherwise inanimate objects are endowed with capacities such as responsivity if not actual motion and thus endowed with life. But animism is also often regarded a way of bringing what is unknown, mysterious, unpredictable, or outside one's control within the realm of what is known and controllable, a way of reining in, perhaps even taming, what otherwise lies beyond the reach of one's understanding. In this sense, it makes what is unknown like oneself, thus, in effect, knowable. In just this way, personifying the brain demystifies it: the brain "infers," the brain "anticipates."[6] We are chummy with the brain; we can say what it is thinking and/or doing in the same way that we often say in the ordinary course of our lives what other people are thinking and/or doing. While one might claim that this way of speaking of the brain is merely a *façon de parler*, others might with reason counterclaim that *façons de parler* are *façons de penser* (see Sheets-Johnstone 1992b: Note 33; Sheets-Johnstone 1996a: Note 37).

Moreover one must admit that, whatever matters of fact are known about brains today, they give no indication whatsoever that a brain is able to do such things as infer or anticipate, let alone locate sounds or hunt cooperatively. On the contrary, matters of fact on the order of both those itemized at the beginning of this chapter and those having to do with neuron firing show clearly that to be a brain is to do brain types of things, not person or creaturely kinds of things. A valid heterophenomenology (Dennett 1991) can hardly deny this fact about brains. The actual situation is thus quite odd in that we read consistently of *the brain* in *animistic* terms. We find current articles on such topics as "[h]ow the brain knows when eating must stop" (Raloff 1996: 343). In such instances, brains appear to be invested with animate powers. They are spoken of in terms of their singular feats: a brain "shapes up thoughts in milliseconds rather than millennia, and uses innocuous remembered environments rather than the noxious real-life ones" (Calvin 1987: 33).[7] In this golden age of science, how can *animism* flourish? And how can scientists themselves practice what they preach against?

Perhaps the simplest and most direct answer is that animism does not flourish at all. The idea of matter as an inert chunk of stuff is outmoded. Twentieth-century quantum physics has shown that the fundamental stuff of matter is continuously in motion, albeit in a motion we do not witness first-hand. By showing it to be continuously in motion, quantum physics has demonstrated that the inanimate is fundamentally animated, animated not in the traditional animistic sense, but animated precisely in the sense of moving *causa sui*: the world of matter is astir with motion. This simplest and most direct answer, however provocative in itself, nonetheless fails to defuse the charge of animism. This is because brain activity is implicitly if not explicitly conceived as something over and above quantum motion. The conception is readily apparent in contemporary informational models of the brain. Where brains are conceived as information-processing machines, brain activity is precisely something not on-going in a quantum-mechanics sense, but something present differentially and/or only potentially: brain activity changes character, for example, as brain waves change character; brain activity hangs there at the ready, so to speak, and springs forth — like an action potential — only under specified conditions at specified places and times; and so on. By implication, motion comes in packages, just like the information it carries; that is, bundles of specified information come in bundles of movement at specified locations at specified times. Insofar as movement is simply a function of information-processing, the very notion of matter in motion virtually disappears under the weight of information. Motion is no more than the means whereby the latter is processed. It is thus not *movement* but information that characterizes brain activity, and it is precisely the informational character of brain activity that allows *the brain* to be spoken of animistically.

A second answer, again rather simple, might be that brain scientists, brain-science philosophers, and cognitivists generally, are doing no more than giving *the brain* functional inputs and outputs; that is, they are giving sensory-cognitive functions to *the brain* on the basis of its demonstrated neural, metabolic, and electrical activity. In so doing, they are simply rounding out the functional input-output picture. Put more finely, insofar as brain activity means that something is going on, then if, for example, eating is going on, *the brain knows* eating is going on; if hunting is going on, *the brain knows* hunting is going on; and so forth. The all-inclusive functional picture means merely that, given its activity — or more particularly, given the fact that now this area is active, now that area is active, or alternatively, given the computational idea of parallel distributed processing — the brain is sensorially or motorically engaged in some way or other; it is taking things in and anticipating, for example, or it is locating a sound and thereby executing a response. With its mechanistic compressions, this rather easy answer slurs over distinctions and cannot possibly hope to avoid the charge of animism. The charge is warranted in that *life* is being predicated of mere matter; mere matter is conceived as having something akin to creaturely *soul*, something that has motivations, interests in the world, and so forth. The unqualified boldness of the answer also claims our attention. The boldness is of special interest not only because, as pointed out in the beginning, experiential ascriptions have no place in an answer to the question of what it is like to be a brain. It is of special interest because an astonishing irony exists in the fact that, unlike the cautious and limited use of experiential ascriptions in studies of nonhuman animals, there is no cautiousness here at all. On the contrary, there is a forthright, self-possessed confidence in ascribing sensory-cognitive experiences to *the brain*, a confidence that is plainly evident. In contrast to the frequent use of quotation marks around terms reservedly or uneasily used to ascribe sensory-cognitive capacities to nonhuman animals, no quotation marks enclose sensory-cognitive ascriptions to *the brain*. We never read, for example, that "the brain 'assesses'" or that "the brain 'recognizes'," but we quite commonly read, for example, that "the wolf 'assesses'" or "the parrot 'recognizes'." The complete lack of hesitance in according sensory-cognitive powers to brain matter — most notably the brain matter of humans — and the comparatively extravagant hesitance in according sensory-cognitive powers to living creatures other than humans reveals a predilectional animistic practice as pervasively striking as it is nowhere justified. Indeed, nothing more than received wisdom, *tel que*, dictates that "mental powers" be accorded in generous fashion to brain matter and in miserly fashion to any form of life that is not human.

A third answer, seemingly simplistic but actually more complicated, might charge that the idea that brain scientists, philosophers, and even lay people are engaging in animism is outlandish, that all committed materialists need do to set the record straight is adjust their focus — and terminology — so that rather than speaking in terms of an all-pervasive elementary physicalism, they speak in terms of an all-pervasive elementary *physicalism animated*. But physicalism animated is not only quite a trick to explain — where does motion come from? for example, why is the surface membrane of some neuronal fibers "excitable"? (Bernstein et al. 1994: 96) — or why is there motion rather than stillness? for example, why are there brain waves? — it is a trick requiring a reconceptualization of materialist doctrine. It requires admitting a kinetic character into the domain of brain matter such that brain matter is not simply matter pure and simple any longer, but matter having the potential, *in and of itself*, to move and/or to generate motion, and in moving or generating motion, to make things happen. Moreover at the most basic level, the reconceptualization harbors a contradiction. It requires acknowledging the fact that matter — understood in a broad sense — both moves itself and does not move itself. It moves itself insofar as it fires, propagates, and flows, for example; it does not move itself insofar as it is, for example, a stone. Hence, there must be different kinds of matter: matter that is nonliving and matter that is living, any matter constituting living forms being different in some crucial kinetic — thus *animated* — way(s) from matter that has no connection with living forms. Yet there are singular instances in which nonliving matter, in spite of its being unlike living forms, *does* move itself. Perhaps the most prominent instances are earthquakes, volcanoes, and tides. A simple and ready kinetic distinction between nonliving and living matter is thus not that simple and ready to come by. Perhaps this is why Paul Churchland tries to show that "no metaphysical gap" exists between living and nonliving systems. But perhaps this is also why he speaks so easily of a nervous system as "just an active matrix of cells," and of an active matrix of cells as "just an active matrix of molecules" without bothering in the least to explain how *active* matrices come to be or why they are crucial aspects of the particular kind of matter that constitutes nervous systems.

Although the reconceptualization might appear at first to harbor a further and more pressing contradiction for hard-driving materialists, it would not necessarily do so at all. This is because while committed materialists would hardly deny that brain matter moves itself insofar as it generates propagations and firings, for example, such materialists would deny that it is animated in the traditional animistic sense. In other words, committed materialists would remain reductionists, and in remaining reductionists, would only seemingly be caught in a contradiction. It is not immediate-evidence-in-hand that buttresses their reductionist stance, of course, but only a promissory note: however poorly understood it might be at present, the manner in which *the brain* converts neuronal, metabolic, and/or electrical activity into thoughts and other mental phenomena (and presumably into hops, skips, jumps, and other physical phenomena), will eventually come to light. Clinging firmly to this belief — or is it faith? — committed materialists avoid any contradiction. They can readily admit that at a micro-level, matter does indeed move itself: action potentials, electrochemical potentials, and the like, are indeed self-generated by matter. But admitting as much does not mean that reductionism will not succeed. While motion may complicate the material picture, they might say, it does not jeopardize it. On the contrary, measurements of blood flow, for example, indicate sites of brain activity, and sites of brain activity indicate sites of cognition of one sort or another (or, presumably, hops, skips, jumps, and other physical phenomena of one sort or another). Clearly, for committed materialists, an animated brain is not an animistic one. Physicalism animated thus presents no contradiction. In fact, hard-driving materialists might claim that it presents an opportunity. Not only does physicalism animated not fundamentally alter materialist doctrine, these materialists might claim, it does not threaten it in the first place by introducing animism. This is because the charge of animism, if correctly understood, is aptly, even splendidly, vindicated by reductionist materialist doctrine. Brain activity is not just *correlated* with believing, judging, recognizing, and the like; it is *identical* with such cognitive functions. Hence, to speak of brains inferring, locating sounds, and the like, is thoroughly justified. Brain activity is the very stuff of a person's thinking, believing, judging, recognizing, and so on. A person's brain is animism personified, the ultimate in living matter, the exemplar incarnate of physicalism animated.

Reasoning in such ways and keeping the faith, as it were, committed materialists might hope to defuse physicalism animated in its menacing animistic guise. So long as brain activity is identical to cognitive and other forms of mental activity (and presumably identical to hops, skips, jumps, and other forms of physical activity as well), materialism is safe. To shoot down an axon is to think (or presumably, to skip). A committed materialist's thinking might be said to be reminiscent of Freud's in this respect, but with all tenses collapsed into the present. For Freud, the rule was that "where the id was, there the ego shall be." For a materialist, where the neurons fire and where the blood flows, there the thoughts are (or equally, where the neurons fire and where the blood flows, there the hops, skips, and jumps are). All the same, physicalism animated in its *other*, unsettling and challenging, animistic guise remains: How explain the motion of matter? Indeed, how explain the animation of living creatures? As noted earlier, such *things* as motor programs — instances of what might be termed "reified neurology"[8] — have been and are being critically rejected as explanations of creaturely motion. The above parenthetical inclusions concerning *movement* are hence topical rather than marginal. They specify not merely other, trivial, less consequential concerns, but constitute a genuine challenge for materialists. However consistently ignored in favor of narrowly specified acts of perception and cognition, movement too must fit into the materialist's explanation of "mind," which means that movement too must be explained by something other than a convenient compendium of motor programs or behavioral rules housed in a brain; it too must find a credible explanation.

Now the charge of "mysterianism" on the one (theoretical) hand, and the charge of miscarriages of heterophenomenological justice through phenomenological magic on the other (methodological) hand, are charges that can be levelled at materialists themselves, precisely as specified in the questions above. The possibility of levelling these charges may ultimately be traced to the fact that the charge of animism in one form or another holds good whether materialist claims succeed or not. If committed materialists make good on their promissory note, they are animists of the first order, animists not in the traditional sense, but animists in the sense of affirming the essentially animate nature of brain matter. If they fail to make good on their promissory note, they are still animists, animists in the traditional sense of imputing an aliveness to something that is not in and of itself alive at all even though in this instance it is part and parcel of something that *is* alive, namely a living individual. In the first instance brain matter is quite simply matter in motion; in the second instance brain matter is also quite simply matter in motion, but matter in motion requiring explanation. In either instance, however, matter surely does not move itself; hence in either instance, a committed materialist is a committed animist.

With respect to the general charge of animism and to its possible answers, an internal theoretical problem has been passed over which warrants critical attention. If we seriously ponder the issue of animism, we readily see that accepting a committed materialist's experiential ascriptions to *the brain* — whatever the context might be in which those ascriptions are formulated — commits us ultimately to beliefs beyond the reach of any available facts. In turn, we readily see that, with their promissory note intact, materialists can continue to evade charges of animism only if we accept their experiential ascriptions; they can continue to speak of *the brain* as perceiving, inferring, and so on, but only if we accept their functional-informational and/or identitist accounts of brains. In short, they can continue to exacerbate our ignorance by encouraging us to believe as fact something for which there is no evidence only if we too pledge allegiance to *the brain*. If we seriously ponder the issue of animism further, however, we see that the very charges that materialists bring against non-reductionists (against the idea of there being "an irreducible subjective") can be brought in reverse fashion against the materialists themselves. Materialists have charged non-reductionists with being "mysterians" and with being "phenomenologists." Yet what is more mysterious, after all, than the animation of matter? And what is a less *neutral* stance than the studied neglect of motion by heterophenomenologists? The charges — the original materialist ones against the non-materialists, and the reverse non-materialist ones against the materialists — are enlightening to consider and warrant comment.

6. Reversing materialist charges

Owen Flanagan's original charge against those he terms "the mysterians" (notably Thomas Nagel and Colin McGinn) is that "[they] think that consciousness will *never* be understood" (Flanagan 1991: 313). The reason they think it will never be understood, or think it at the very least presently "intractable," is that our very nature prevents our understanding how what is physical links up with what is psychical, or that we have at present not the slightest clue as to how they are related (Flanagan 1991:313). Flanagan argues strongly against these "mysterian" views; unlike the mysterians, he does not believe that we are permanently stuck with what he and most other philosophers term "the mind/body problem." It is important to point out in passing that the consistent conflation by philosophers of the mind/brain problem with the mind/body problem is a fundamental problem in itself, one in dire need of quite separate attention. In the immediate context, the conflation is of secondary moment, but it does not remain so, as will be evident. Flanagan's charge against the mysterians is a theoretical one; his concern is to show that there can indeed be a naturalistic account of consciousness. To sustain his claim and his theoretical charge, he appeals to empirical data, especially data from neuropsychology and cognitivist science. In doing so, his aim is to show, *contra the mysterians*, that "a coherent sketch can be given" of consciousness," and if this coherent sketch can be given, then we are on our way to a naturalistic explanation of mind. Thus, he states that "After all, what is actual is possible"; in other words, because the sketch is rooted in "the actual" — it is based on empirical data — the complete picture of consciousness is possible (1991:314). In fact, however, there is a considerable not to say Brobdingnagian gap between the actual and the possible and it is filled by nothing more than the committed materialist's promissory notes. The manner in which *the brain* converts its activities into thoughts and other mental phenomena is a missing explanatory link, a mystery *par excellence*. *This* mystery is nowhere acknowledged by committed materialists. Empirical data and promissory notes are offered in its place. Yet the mystery remains no matter how much empirical data is gathered and reported, no matter how much hypothetical material is added, and no matter how many promissory notes are written, even written by distinguished persons. Thus, whatever Flanagan tells us about the brain and the number of neurons it has, for example, or about the presence of "functionally distributed processors vertically and horizontally communicating back and forth" (1991:316), we are no further ahead in solving the fundamental mystery of conversion; we are not any closer to cracking the ontological code. Not only this, but with respect to certain descriptive passages within his empirical review of brain activity, a central nagging question resurfaces: how is it that matter moves itself? what explains brain *activity*? When Flanagan says, in the context of describing how "a depolarization pulse … runs down an axon" (1991:315), i.e. how a neuron fires, that "[n]euronal cells are almost always jittering," and that a depolarization pulse "is simply a very powerful jitter, a jolt," he does not pause in his recitation to wonder how matter is in motion (316); he does not pause to reflect upon the basic self-moving or movement-generating nature of brain matter. Yet what, after all, explains the fact that "neuronal cells are almost always jittering"? Is almost continuous jittering not a mysterious phenomenon, something about which we should inquire? Is solving this mystery not basic to an understanding of conscious-ness in the precise reductionist sense in which hard-driving materialists want us to understand consciousness? For example, if "neuronal cells are almost always jitter-ing," how can materialists speak of brain *states*? At the very least, are they not bound to explain something *kinetically primal* about brain states? At the very most, are they not bound to recognize that *states* are theoretical abstractions? In a broad sense, one might say there is a rush to epistemology before the ontological work is done, that is, a rush toward establishing an epistemological construct of *the brain*, making the brain savvy, as it were, before brains are actually understood, and not only in themselves as particular pieces of matter, but as material parts of intact living organisms. One might in fact point out that it is erroneous to prominence the brain epistemologically as a wholly separate organ, let alone as a machine, most especially a Darwin machine (Calvin 1987; see also Note 7, this chapter), since, *contra* the notions of those who perform brain-in-a-vat thought experiments or who confound intact living organisms with a constellation of discrete material events, not only do brains have connections to other parts of the body, and in ways which make it impossible to say precisely where a brain ends and other bodily parts begin, but brains are dependent upon those very connections for their everyday functioning. In sum, until basic understandings and missing explanatory links are furnished, it seems not only foolhardy but anthropo-morphic in the extreme to believe that jittering pieces of anatomy are equivalent to forms of consciousness. The belief is akin to a belief in the occult. In this respect com-mitted materialists can be labelled "mysterians." However impressive their empirical data, however innovative their hypothetical offerings and modellings, and however seductive their promissory notes, they are covering over bona fide immaterialities — meanings, concepts, memories, recognitions — with a neurophysiological wishlist. They are twentieth-century alchemists bent on transmuting mind into matter.

Daniel Dennett's original charge against "phenomenologists" is in essence a dis-crediting of those who think the question of consciousness can be answered in any way other than through a scientific methodology, namely, a methodology he terms "het-erophenomenology." This methodology bypasses the limitations and false impressions of introspection, and indeed, as Dennett puts it, "dissipate(s) the 'magic' in the phe-nomenological garden" (1991:65). In a word, *hetero*phenomenology, unlike its garden variety relative, is an objective "phenomenology," one based on the "*[interpret[ation] of] verbal behavior*" (78; italics added). Only such a "phenomenology," one rooted in third-person narratives or story-telling accounts of experience, can "do justice to the most private and ineffable subjective experiences" (72) i.e. to consciousness. We should note that Dennett's objective phenomenology is notably different from the one called for originally by Thomas Nagel (1979). The aim of Nagel's objective phe-nomenology is to permit access to the consciousness of creatures other than humans; with its pivotal reliance on language, Dennett's objective phenomenology is obviously rooted in human narrative discourse. It is no surprise, then, that a Dennettian brain is essentially an organ of and for language. While Dennett goes to great length to spell out how rigorously objective his heterophenomenology is, how *neutrality* governs its procedures through and through, his fundamental reliance on language as *the* source of data is hardly neutral. Indeed, while straightforwardly acknowledging his all too human approach — i.e. "if consciousness is anywhere, it is in [humans]" (1991:73) — he stacks the cards from the start by yoking consciousness to language. Dennett's heterophenomenologist — a scientific experimenter — begins by asking subjects to give verbal reports of their experience. By transforming raw sound reports — "*raw data*" (1991:74) — into more developed data, i.e. by giving the reports to three different stenographers for transcription (three different stenographers in order to assure objectivity [75]), and then *by interpreting* the generated stenographic texts as "a record of *speech acts*," a heterophenomenologist is able to explain a subject's verbal reports as "intentional," that is, as statements about certain beliefs, desires, or "other mental states that exhibit *intentionality* or 'aboutness'" (1991:76). In the course of this compound procedure, however, a quite unexplained and remarkable shift takes place. The heterophenomenologist desists in thinking about and characterizing a subject as a mere "noise-emitter" (1991:76); the heterophenomenologist begins thinking about and characterizing a subject as "an agent" — in Dennett's own continuing words, as "indeed a rational agent" (1991:76). Why does the notion of intentionality catapult Dennett into a conception of the subject as an agent? Because only if the subject is an agent and not a mere "noise-emitter" does it have mental states. The significance of this "intentional stance" theorem is critically assayed below. The point of moment now is less conceptual than methodological. Taking a critical stance toward Dennett's shifting characterization of the subject and generalizing the critique, we would say that committed materialists are covering over immaterialities not only with a doxastic wishlist but with pull-the-wool-over-your-eyes data; as heterophenomenologists, they are producing magic in their own gardens. Let us look at the issue more closely from a methodological point of view.

If heterophenomenology is compared line for line, as it were, with "'pure' phenomenology" (Dennett 1991:69), then the neutrality stance of the experimenter is a stand-in for a phenomenologist's procedure of bracketing. However, the suspension of the natural attitude, as it is described in phenomenology, is being carried out not by the person whose experience it is; it is being carried out by the person who is carrying out an experiment on the person who has had the experience. In effect, "neutrality modification" — to use a descriptive phrase from Husserl — is on the side of the scientific observer. Moreover while the so-called neutrality modification of the heterophenomenologist may seem as if it is an objective manoeuvre, it is not. The heterophenomenologist can readily be charged with bypassing rigorous examinations of experience in favor of verbal reports about experience, verbal reports that, for example, take language — its relativity, its preciseness, and so on — for granted, just as they take the "noise-emitters" use of language — his or her verbal acuity, preciseness, and so on — for granted. The heterophenomenologist's magic is to think that by running putative "raw" sounds through certain procedures — scientifically processing them in intricate mechanical and symbolic ways — one arrives at subjective experience, i.e. one becomes privy to a subject's private and ineffable world, and without in any way relying on introspection. In this latter respect, a further methodological point warrants comment. Precisely because Dennett has equated phenomenology with introspection but bypassed the actual method of phenomenology that transforms everyday introspection through a suspension of the natural attitude, he fails to see that, in the same way that scientific training is needed to make scientific observations, to design scientific experiments, to interpret scientific data, and so on, so phenomenological training is needed to practice phenomenology. In short, the phenomenological method as practiced is not equivalent to everyday introspection. As a method, it too requires training.

The above general critique aside, there are two further reverse charges concerning neutrality that may be brought against heterophenomenologists. The first of these may be introduced by asking why it is Dennett identifies subjects in the dual way he does. To put the question in slightly different perspective, why is it necessary to transform "noise-emitters" into "agent[s], indeed ... rational agent[s]"? What necessitates this conceptual move *within Dennett's heterophenomenological methodology*? If the subject of the experiment in the beginning is regarded only as a data source, as Dennett himself specifies, that is, only as a source of sound or only as a source of electroencephalographic or videotape recordings, then on what grounds is he or she (supposing such a distinction even allowable) transformed into something that, at the end of the methodological procedure, has mental states and acts coincident with those states? On the magical face of things, heterophenomenologists appear to wield sizable power; in the process of their investigations, they instantiate subjects as what we might call "real persons" — at least those subjects who run the heterophenomenologists' methodological gauntlet and qualify as such. They are furthermore the sole arbiters of meaning: in the course of performing their magic, and by the very nature of their methodology, they determine just how "uttered noises are to be interpreted" (1991:76), thus what the subject "*wanted to say*," for example, or "*propositions* [the subject] meant to *assert*" (1991:76). Duly interpreted wantings and assertions are in turn dubbed the wantings and assertions of duly authenticated rational agents, i.e. veritable speakers. Indeed, mere noise-emitters have nothing to say; only through the offices of a heterophenomenologist do they become rational agents. Presumably, were a heterophenomenologist not able to interpret a text he/she was given, indeed, were stenographers to begin with unable to transcribe the "raw data" they were given, then whatever the original noise emitted by a subject, it would not be the noise of one who has desires, beliefs, and so on. Only by dint of heterophenomenolgists' interpretative authentications do speakers emerge who have mental states and who produce rational utterances about them.

The intentional stance of the heterophenomenologist is clearly and without question authoritative. And it is just as clearly and without question anything but neutral in that a heterophenomenologist can withhold agency from anything that, for example, merely hoots or babbles and does not give verbal reports. In this respect, gibbon apes and infants are clearly short-changed. In a further respect, of course, the brains of such individuals are also short-changed since, like infants and gibbon apes themselves who are not unchanging things, brains also develop and mature. On the basis of the evidence Dennett presents on behalf of his methodology, a neutral observer would rightly judge that in a heterophenomenologist's eyes, infants and gibbon apes have not a hope of a fair hearing with respect to possible "private and ineffable" experiences because they cannot give a verbal report and have it transcribed and interpreted; they remain mere noise-emitters. In this context, we might recall Dennett's answer to the question, *what is it like to be an infant*? He writes, "My killjoy answer would be that it isn't like very much. How do I know? I don't 'know,' of course, but my even more killjoy answer is that on my view of consciousness, it arises when there is work for it to do, and the preeminent work of consciousness is dependent on sophisticated language-using activities" (1983: 384). Can this be the voice of a neutral, objective heterophenomenologist? Is heterophenomenology a valid phenomenology or is it a by-guess-and-by-golly phenomenology?

The second charge is related to the first. It has to do with a less than empirical view of the functional purpose of brains. Clearly, Dennett's heterophenomenologist, insofar as s/he is wedded to language, is wedded to a particular conception of the brain: brain activity is essentially the activity of a language machine — though we might note that in less heterophenomenological moments, Dennett describes brain activity as essentially the activity of an information-processing machine (1991: 433). In either case, however, the preferred view of brain activity not only fails to take account of infants and gibbon apes but of animate life generally. What it overlooks is not a matter of behavior; what it overlooks are veritable agents, creatures who move themselves. Behaviors can be run by hypothetical "motor programs" in the brain, and can thus be written off as merely mechanical manoeuvers. Movement presents a challenge because the movement of animate forms is not always and everywhere predictable. If it were, there could hardly be innovations in behavior (see Sheets-Johnstone 1992b, 1996a, 1996b). It is equally because creaturely life is not reducible to a lifetime tape but shifts and changes in response to environmental shifts and changes. Indeed, the world itself as an environing surround is not reducible to a tape. Motion, change, flux — such terms define both creaturely *Umwelts* and creaturely life. Roger Sperry's characterization of brains in terms of movement is consistent with these kinetic facts of life and more generally, with an evolutionary perspective on the animate world.

Dennett's heterophenomenologist, in contrast, considers *the brain* neither an organ of and for movement, nor a neural system serving movement in the evolutionary sense of integrating information "to provide a basis for effective, life-preserving movement" (Gray 1991: 185). *The brain* is an organ of and for language. It is an organ for processing linguistic information and speaking our mind. It is a brain only a comparatively sedentary human could love.

In sum, materialist charges can be reversed. In the process, they can teach a metaphysical lesson, namely, that to enshrine matter reductively as the ultimate stuff of the world is to shackle oneself to a metaphysics at odds with the nature of the world. To suppress movement is to suppress the fundamentally dynamic principle of motion that informs the world, the world not only in the grand sense of the natural world with its oceans, winds, erosions, meteors, rotations, glaciations, and more, but in the modest sense of the natural worlds of animate forms and in the smaller sense of the natural worlds internal to those animate forms. The kinetic character of brain matter in particular is as unexplicated and unelucidated by reductivist materialist doctrine as the subjective character of experience. In asking what is it like to be a brain, however, in contrast to asking what is it like to be a bat, we meet materialists on their own ground. That is, rather than charging materialists to account for something we think their account of the world omits, we charge them with accounting for something their account of the world necessarily includes, yet something which their account consistently ignores or trivializes. Indeed, we inquire about something their doctrine takes for granted and fails properly to acknowledge much less explain. That something is essential to an understanding of brains. Brains are organs, living organs, inside living creatures. As such, they are actively engaged in being brains; they are not actively engaged in worlds beyond their own internal one. The challenge that confronts hard-driving materialists concerns precisely the kinetic character of brain matter. That challenge is precisely a metaphysical one: to explain how it is that brain matter is dynamically energized, how it is that forces rush through it, propagating currents, making this and that happen. In a larger sense, of course, the metaphysical challenge is to explain the kinetic character of life. How does movement come to inform the lives of animate forms? Clearly there is something essentially motile about living matter. What is the nature of this essential motility? What is the metaphysics that will elucidate this nature? A studied material ignorance cannot fill the metaphysical breach.

Notes

1.   Pennisi is reporting on the work of Hermann Wagner of the Max Planck Institute for Biological Cybernetics in Tübingen, Germany.

2.   Raloff is quoting Gerard P. Smith of the Cornell Medical Center in White Plains, New York.

3.   Bower is reporting on studies carried out at the University of Iowa College of Medicine.

4.   Bower is reporting on studies of Wayne C. Drevets and colleagues at Washington University School of Medicine in St. Louis.

5.   Oxford English Dictionary, meaning #3 of *shoot* (p. 728): "a motion or movement (of a thing) *as though* shooting or being shot in a particular direction" (italics added).

6.   "If you see the back of a person's head, the brain infers that there is a face on the front of it" (Crick & Koch, 1992:153); "Overall, our brain is the most powerful anticipation machine ever built" (Flanagan, 1991:319; Flanagan is actually elaborating on a remark by Daniel Dennett that he has just quoted, namely, that "all brains are, in essence, *anticipation-machines*" [319]).

7.   For an example of how philosophers appropriate in so seemingly ready and uncritical fashion Calvin's oxymoronic notion of a Darwin machine — oxymoronic insofar as it is inconceivable that Darwin would have animistically attributed to brains what he so perspicuously described in terms of living creatures, much less that he would have ended by reducing living creatures themselves to machines — see Flanagan 1992:40–46, a section titled "The Evolution of Darwin Machines."

8.   One might judge reified neurology to be no different in character from reified genetics, as in the genomic reification of diseases or the genomic reification of traits such as perfect pitch. Reification is reminiscent of preformationism, a doctrine which held that the complete organism was inside the germ cell. It seems that just as we have today the genomic equivalent with respect to such things as diseases and traits inside genes, so we have the neurological equivalent with respect to fully formed motoric behaviors inside nerve cells.

CHAPTER 12

Thinking in movement*

And what is *thinking?* — Well, don't you ever think? Can't you observe yourself
and see what is going on? It should be quite simple. You do not have to wait for it
as for an astronomical event and then perhaps make your observation in a hurry.
Ludwig Wittgenstein (1963:106)

As I was led to keep in my study during many months worms in pots filled
with earth, I became interested in them, and wished to learn how far they acted
consciously, and how much mental power they displayed.... [A]s chance does
not determine the manner in which [they drag] objects [leaves or paper] ... into
[their] burrows, and as the existence of specialized instincts for each particular
case cannot be admitted, the first and most natural supposition is that worms try
all methods until they at last succeed; but many appearances [i.e., observations]
are opposed to such a supposition. One alternative alone is left, namely, that
worms, although standing low in the scale of organization, possess some degree
of intelligence. This will strike every one as very improbable; but it may be
doubted whether we know enough about the nervous system of the lower animals
to justify our natural distrust of such a conclusion. With respect to the small size
of the cerebral ganglia, we should remember what a mass of inherited knowledge,
with some power of adapting means to an end, is crowded into the minute brain
of a worker ant. Charles Darwin (1976 [1881]:19–20,58)

1. The twofold purpose

What I hope to do in this chapter is elucidate both the experience and foundations
of thinking in movement. The foundations include both the evolution of animate
life of which we humans are a part and our own human develomental background.
I begin with a descriptive account of what I take to be a paradigmatic experience
of thinking in movement, the experience of moving in an improvisational dance.
Thinking in movement is at the core of this experience, indeed, a *sine qua non* of
the realization of its aesthetic form. In taking this experience as paradigmatic, I
hope only to show how its dynamically-tethered thematic typifies such thinking, *not*
that all experiences of thinking in movement accord with it. Forms of thinking in
movement can differ considerably. Thinking in movement in infancy, for example,

can have practical, self-instructional, or explorative ends in contrast to the aesthetic ones of improvisational dance. So also with animate life generally. It is possible thus to distinguish structures in one kind of experience of thinking in movement from those present in another. What a descriptive account of the experience of thinking in movement in improvisational dance will provide is a bare bones example of such thinking, a laying out of the qualitative nature of its essentially dynamically-tethered thematic, or in other words, an example in which the qualia or cardinal structures of movement and of thinking in movement are magnified.

2.   Dance improvisation: A paradigm of thinking in movement

A dance improvisation is unique in the sense that no score is being fulfilled, no performance is being reproduced. The dancers who are improvising understand this uniqueness in the very manner in which they approach the dance. They have agreed to follow the rules, as it were, of a dance improvisation, rules that might very generally be summed up as: dance the dance as it comes into being at this particular moment at this particular place. More detailed and possibly restrictive rules might structure a dance improvisation, rules that specify, for example, a certain kind of improvisation or certain sequences of movement: "contact improvisation only," for instance, or "fast group movement to alternate with slow, large individual move-ment." Such rules notwithstanding, the aim of the dancers is not to render some-thing planned or choreographed in advance. Whatever the framing rules might be that act as a constraint upon movement, the aim of the dancers is to form move-ment spontaneously. It is to dance *this evening's dance*, whatever it might turn out to be. In view of the uniqueness of *this evening's dance* — as of all *this evening's dances* — the common aesthetical question of ontological identity does not arise. In other words, being the only one of its kind, *this evening's dance* is not measured against or viewed with respect to other performances nor is it measured against or viewed with respect to a score. Ontological status is thus not an issue. Unlike a set piece of choreography — Marius Petipa's and Lev Ivanov's *Swan Lake*, Mark Morris's *Jeal-ousy*, Twyla Tharp's *Red, White, and Blues*, Alvin Ailey's *Revelations*, for example — *this evening's dance* is a singular performance. It is either in the process of being created — in the very process of being born — or it is not at all. If pressed for an artistic comparison, one might say — though only in a quite broad and general sense — that a dance improvisation is akin to a jazz jam session wherein a group of musicians literally make music together. They bring something into being, some-thing which never before was, something which will never be again, thus something that has no past or future performances but exists only in the here and now of its creation.

In view of its unique appearance, it is not surprising that a dance improvisation is commonly described as an unrehearsed and spontaneous form of dance. What is not commonly recognized, however, is that that description hinges on the more fundamental characteristic suggested above, namely, that in a dance improvisation, the process of creating is not the means of realizing *a* dance; it is *the* dance itself. A dance improvisation is the incarnation of creativity as process. Its future is thus open. Where it will go at any moment, what will happen next, no one knows; until the precise moment at which it ends, its integrity as an artwork is uncharted. It is in virtue of its perpetually open future, its being in the process of being created, that a dance improvisation is unrehearsed and spontaneous. Because no set artistic product exists in advance or in arrear, the dancers have nothing in particular to practice or perfect in advance, nothing in particular to remember in order to keep. Their improvisation is process through and through, a form which lives and breathes in the moving flow of its creation, a flow experienced as an ongoing present, an unbroken now that is something akin to what Gertrude Stein called a "prolonged present" (1926: 16–17), to what William James (borrowing from E.R. Clay) called "a specious present" (1950, vol. 1: 609), and to what Henri Bergson called "a live present" (1991: 137), that is, an ongoing flow of movement from an ever-changing kinetic world of possibilities.

How is such a dance possible? How can dancers create a dance on the spot? To unravel the nature of an ongoing present and discover its generative core requires a description of the creative process from the perspective of a dancer engaged in the process. In the course of giving this description, we will find that what is essential is a non-separation of thinking and doing, and that the very ground of this non-separation is the capacity, indeed, the very experience of the dancer, to be thinking in movement. To say that the dancer is thinking in movement does not mean that the dancer is thinking *by means of* movement or that her/his thoughts are *being transcribed into* movement. To think is first of all to be caught up in a dynamic flow; thinking is itself, by its very nature, kinetic. It moves forward, backward, digressively, quickly, slowly, narrowly, suddenly, hesitantly, blindly, confusedly, penetratingly. What is distinctive about thinking in movement is not that the flow of thought is kinetic, but that the thought itself is. It is motional through and through; at once spatial, temporal, dynamic. The description that follows will attempt to capture this motional character.

I should emphasize in advance that the account is basically descriptive, not theoretical. As such, it is not an *argument* for a certain conception of dance improvisation. The purpose of the analysis is not to claim or document a theory about dance improvisation but to describe as accurately as possible, indeed, to capture, the essential character of a dance improvisation as it is experienced by a dancer to the end that the kind of thinking that lies at the core of its spontaneous creation is clearly elaborated. The account may in this sense certainly be elaborated further; it may be amended; and so on. It is offered as a phenomenological account. Precisely because its aim is to render the experience of the dancer justly, it leaves an objective kinetic language behind, the latter language tying us to facts about the experience rather than leading us to a conception of its living quality or character. In other words, what is of interest is not that I flexed my knee, for example, or that I circumducted my arm, or that I saw another dancer out of the corner of my eye, but the experienced kinetic reality of these events. What is wanted, as may be readily apparent, is a first-person descriptive account, an account of the experience of thinking in movement as it is lived first-hand. If in the course of the description phrases or terms appear precious or fanciful verbal excesses, their successive elaboration should clarify their meaning such that anyone interested in grasping the process of creating an improvisational dance is led to the heart of that experience and to an understanding of its inherent structure: thinking in movement.

To say that in improvising, I am in the process of creating the dance out of the possibilities that are mine at any moment of the dance is to say that I am exploring the world in movement; that is, at the same time that I am moving, I am taking into account the world as it exists for me here and now in this ongoing, ever-expanding present. As one might wonder about the world in words, I am wondering the world directly, in movement. I am actively exploring its possibilities and what I perceive in the course of that exploration is enfolded in the very process of my moving — a density or fluidity of other dancers about me, for example, or a sharpness and angularity in their movement. The density or fluidity, like the sharpness and angularity, are not first registered as a perception (still less as stimuli, and certainly not as sense-data), a perception to which I then respond in some manner by doing something. Qualities and presences are enfolded into my own ongoing kinetic presence and quality. They are absorbed by my movement, as when I become part of the swirl of dancers sweeping by me or am propelled outward, away from their tumultuous energies, or when I quicken to the sharpness of their movement and accentuate its angularity or break out of its jaggedness by a sudden turn and stillness. In just such ways, the global dynamic world I am perceiving, including the ongoing kinesthetically felt world of my own movement, is inseparable from the kinetic world in which I am moving. Sensing and moving do not come together from two separate regions of experience, fortuitously joining together by virtue of their happening in, or being part of, the same body. Perceptions are plaited into my here-now flow of movement just as my here-now flow of movement is plaited into my perceptions. Movement and perception are seamlessly interwoven; there is no "mind-doing" that is separate from a "body-doing." My movement is thus not the result of a mental process that exists prior to, and is distinguishable from, a physical process in which it eventuates, nor does my movement involve no thinking at all. To separate myself into a mind and a body would be to perform a radical surgery upon myself such that a vibrant kinetic reality is reduced to faint and impotent pulp, or excised altogether. In effect, the separation would deny what I experience myself to be: a mindful body, a body that is thinking in movement and that has the possibility of creating a dance on the spot.

The dynamic world that I and other dancers are together exploring is inseparable from the dynamic world we are together creating. Thus, with respect to possibilities, it is not as if I am contemplating — or must contemplate — a range of options in order to choose from among them a ripest course of action, given now this, now that present situation. My possibilities at any moment in the ongoing present are not explicit and neither is my choosing. Again, the idea that thinking is separate from its expression — a thought in one's head, so to speak, existing always prior to its corporeal expression — is a denial of thinking in movement. Certainly a movement might occur to me prior to its actual performance. For example, in the course of improvising, I may have a particular kinetic image or a particular kinetic inclination. At the same time that I am moving, I may have an image of a leg extension, for instance, or a fleeting image of a particular movement quality — perhaps a strong and abrupt upward movement of my arm. Similarly, at the same time that I am moving, I may have an inclination to run toward another dancer or toward a particular place on the stage. Such thoughts, while emerging within the experience of an ongoing present, do not interrupt the flow of movement which is the dance. I do not stop moving; I am not impeded in any way, brought to a standstill by the passing image or inclination and made to choose explicitly what I shall do. On the contrary, I might indeed extend my leg or thrust my arm upward or run toward another dancer or toward a particular place on the stage. The image or inclination is a kinetic form within a form, a motional thought that momentarily intrudes itself into, or superimposes itself upon, the ongoing process of thinking in movement. Insofar as thoughts *of* movement are thoughts within the global form — thinking in movement — they can be distinguished from the latter. Thoughts *of* movement are experienced as discrete events: I have an image of a certain leg extension, an image of a certain strong and abrupt movement of my arm, and so on. Within the context of improvisational dance, such thoughts arise autonomously; they are spin-offs of thinking in movement rather than the result of an ongoing process of thinking in images while moving or the result of any deliberative thinking, e.g. "what if I ..." or "shall I ..." or "if I were to ...," and so on. In the same way that my sensings and movings are not sequential happenings but integrally entwined facets of a dance that is a dynamic form in-the-making, so I am not mentally exploring a range of possibilities first, and then later taking some action in consequence of them.

Thoughts *of* movement are not the only way in which discrete movements might find their way into the ongoing present of the dance I am creating. I might, for example, think my way into movement that, by certain cultural standards, is distinctly referential in one way or another. I might shrug my shoulders, for instance, or wave to a dancer leaving the stage, or push another dancer off balance, or fall into the arms of a nearby dancer. But this is only to say that, within the context of improvisational dance, thinking in movement is not limited to thinking in what one might call *dance* movement. Hence, the incorporation of movement and gestures from everyday life that have certain culturally recognized meanings is always possible. It should be added, however, that such gestures or movements do not necessarily make the dance symbolic nor make the particular movement symptomatic. To use the above examples in turn, the dance in which such a movement happens is not thereby a dance about resignation, a dance about partings, a dance about aggression, or a dance about love. While each of the movements might be read off as standing for something, for the dancer creating the dance, it is the dynamic patterning of movement, its subtleties and explosions, its range and rhythm, its power and intricacy that are foundational, not its referential value as such. Thus, in *this evening's dance*, a particular movement is not "about" something any more than a smile is about pleasure.

Any process of thinking in movement is tied to an evolving, changing situation. Hence, if one would speak at all of a systematic reasonableness of meaning, it would not be in terms of an externally imposed scheme of some kind but in terms of *a kinetic bodily logos*, a body that, in thinking in movement, grasps the global qualitative dynamics in which it is enmeshed. To be thinking in movement means that a mindful body is creating a particular dynamic as that very dynamic is kinetically unfolding. A kinetic intelligence is forging its way in the world, shaping and being shaped by the developing dynamic patterns in which it is living. Thus again we see that possibilities at any moment do not stand out as so many recourses of action; possibilities are adumbrated in the immediacy of the evolving situation itself, a situation that moment by moment opens up a certain world and certain kinetic ways of being in that world. In improvisational dance, possibilities arise and dissolve for me in a fluid complex of relationships, qualities, and patternings without becoming thematic for me. We see again too, then, that choices are not explicitly made. Rather, a certain way of moving calls forth a certain kinetic world and a certain kinetic world calls forth a certain way of moving. It is as much a matter of the fluid complex moving me as it is a matter of my moving it, and at the core of that phenomenal kinetic world is a moving intelligence, a kinetic bodily logos.

There is a further way in which the actual moment by moment creation of the dance may be described as my thinking in movement. The movement that I actually create at any moment is not a *thing* that I do, an action that I take, a behavior in which I engage, but a passing moment within a dynamic process, a process that I cannot divide into beginnings and endings. There is a dissolution of my passing movements into my perpetually moving present and a dilation of my perpetually moving present into my continuing movements. The sequential, waving gesture I am now making with my arm, for example, is spilling over into a turning movement I am now making with my head, and the turning movement I am now making with my head is spilling over into a bending of my torso and a sideward leaping in a direction opposite to that of my turning head. I have indeed made each of these movements — I have moved my way into them in the course of improvising — yet they are not detachable moments. They have no separate or separable existence for me. They are like the passing stages of a forward-rolling spiral that at the same time coils back on itself in the process of rolling forward. Even were the sequential, waving gesture I am now making with my arm to dissolve into stillness or end abruptly, I could not say when the gesture ended and when the stillness began, or that the stillness was not an ongoing creation of the dance. My thinking in movement is not an assemblage of discrete gestures happening one after the next, but an enfolding of all movement into a perpetually moving present. Thinking in movement is an experience in which the qualitative dynamics of movement combine to form an ongoing kinetic happening. A singular kinetic density evolves that is nothing other than this moment in which my arm is sequentially waving, this moment in which my head is turning, this moment in which my torso is bending, and so on. My experience of an ongoing present exists only in virtue of these immediate moments, that is, in the actual here–now creating of this gesture or movement. But this gesture or movement is itself an opening out of the dance, a process of moving. It has a spatio-temporal thickness or dynamic density about it. The turning movement I am now making with my head capsulates the dance, as it were, gathering up in its momentum all that has gone before and all that might lie ahead. Each actual movement of the dance has such a dynamic density, a density that stretches out the present moment, transfiguring it from a mere momentary bodily happening into a qualitative kinetic fullness or plentitude that radiates outward and into the ongoing qualitative process of motion that is the dance. My perpetually moving present is in this sense indistinguishable from the actual movement I am here and now creating. Thinking in movement, I am aware of a qualitative dilation and dissolution of movement, even a mutability of here–now movements and the moving present that is the dance.

There is one further aspect to be touched on in this descriptive account of improvisational dance. We have seen that, in contrast to a quite particular reification of thinking and/or to a conception of thinking as an exclusively mental event, thinking in movement is a way of being in the world, of wondering or exploring the world directly, taking it up moment by moment and living it in movement, kinetically. Thinking in movement is thus clearly not the work of a symbol-making body, a body that mediates its way about the world by means of language, for example; it is the work of an existentially resonant body. An existentially resonant body creates a particular dynamic world without intermediary. In improvisational dance, the world it creates is neither a part of the everyday given world nor a temporary fictitious world, but a protean world created moment by moment. Experienced as an elongated or ongoing present, it is a world in which there are no befores or hereafters, no sooner-or-laters, no definitively expected endings or places of arrival. For just such reasons, the dance being created is not a dance that the dancer might acknowledge as being "about" something, unless that something were movement itself. To appreciate and to understand such a phenomenon is akin to appreciating and understanding what Gertrude Stein meant when she said, "a rose is a rose is a rose." Clearly a rose is not about something. Neither is it a jumble of petals. The same may be said of a dance improvisation. The kinetic intelligence that creates the dance informs the dance itself. No more than the dancing body must movement stand for or refer to something beyond itself in order for the phenomenon to be dance. To have meaning is not necessarily to refer and neither is it necessarily to have a verbal label. Movement — animation — can be in and of itself meaningful.

To appreciate — and indeed, to fathom — such nonlinguistic strata of experience, we turn toward that which is animate; we find in our highly symbol-laden human world patches where thinking in movement comes to light. In so doing, we discover that fundamental creative patterning of thought that is founded upon a kinetic bodily logos; we discover mindful bodies, thinking bodies, bodies that, in improvisational dance, break forth continuously into movement and into this dance, bodies that moment by moment fulfill a kinetic destiny and so create kinetic meanings. When we reflect upon our experience of moving in just such ways, examining the experience from a phenomenological perspective and discovering the phenomenon of thinking in movement, we are in turn propelled to rethink our notion of thinking — and in the process, to realize that insights gleaned from a descriptive account of improvisational dance have consequences for epistemology and evolutionary accounts of animate life as well as for aesthetics.

Before proceeding to a consideration of these broader topics, it will be helpful to consider two assumptions about thinking, assumptions that, the preceding descriptive account notwithstanding, might otherwise impede a clear and unprejudiced grasp of what it is to think in movement. The first assumption has to do with thinking itself and has several layers. To begin with, it is commonly assumed that thinking is tied to language and that it takes place only via language. It is furthermore commonly assumed that thinking and language are tied in an exclusive way to rationality. The basis for these assumptions seems itself to be an assumption: that thinking, language, and rationality form a holy, albeit human, triumvirate, a congealed sacred hallmark of preeminently *human* existence. To link thinking, language, and rationality in this manner, however, is to claim a necessary and inherent interdependence before examining the evidence from experience itself and prematurely to declare impossible something that may not be impossible at all, and perhaps, on the contrary, quite common, i.e. thinking in movement. Moreover to deny peremptorily the possibility of thinking in movement on the basis of the foregoing assumption(s) may readily involve a further assumption, namely, that thinking takes place only by means of something, in particular, a symbolic system of some sort — e.g. mathematical, linguistic, logical — a system having the capacity to mediate or carry thought referentially. As the previous descriptive account has demonstrated, however, to affirm the possibility of thinking in movement is to regard movement neither as a vehicle for thinking nor as a symbolic system through which reference is made to something else. Indeed, steadfast and serious reflection on the phenomenon of improvisational dance shows that movement is neither a medium through which a dancer's thoughts emerge nor a kinetic system of counters for mediating his or her thoughts; movement constitutes the thoughts themselves. One might in this context paraphrase Maurice Merleau-Ponty's remarks upon language and say that, in order to understand what it means to think in movement, "*movement* must somehow cease to be a way of designating things or thoughts, and become the presence of that thought in the phenomenal world, and moreover, not its clothing but its token or its body" (Merleau-Ponty 1962:182). Similarly, one might paraphrase neurologist Kurt Goldstein's remarks upon language and say that, "As soon as man uses *movement* to establish a living relation with his fellows, movement is no longer an instrument, *no longer a means; it is a manifestation, a revelation of intimate being and of the psychic link which unites us to the world and our fellow men*" (quoted in Merleau-Ponty 1962:196).

Whether a matter of binding thinking exclusively to language and rationality or a matter of tying it exclusively to a symbolic system of one kind or another, the first assumption is essentially based on a reification of thinking. It is thus based essentially on a substantive rather than processual metaphysical conception and understanding of thinking. It is important to emphasize that neither the reification nor the substantive conception of thinking are unfounded; they are only narrow. In other words, what the previous descriptive account of improvisational dance challenges is not *a* linkage between thinking and language or between thinking and rationality, nor *a* linkage between thinking and symbolic systems of thought, but the view that there are no other forms of thinking, that thinking is wholly dependent on, and to that extent limited to, symbolic structures of thought, hence that it is transactable only in terms of a hard currency like language, and furthermore that it proceeds in a strictly linear fashion, its progression being marked by a systematic reasonableness that develops on the basis of exact and particular connections between what are in essence bead-like thoughts arranged in propositional sequences and/or on the basis of specific syntactic rules demanded by the symbolic counters or currency utilized. What the descriptive account of improvisational dance suggests is that to reify thinking in this exclusively linguistic, or more broadly, symbolic, manner is to perpetuate a metaphysics that is at odds with experience, and in fact, not simply at odds with a particular kind of aesthetic experience, but with a fundamental form of experience. What it correlatively suggests is that such reification is axiologically unwarranted in that it exalts humankind at the expense of denying dimensions of human experience, i.e. dimensions of thinking which, though nonsymbolic may nonetheless be designated rational and which, from both a developmental and evolutionary perspective, may in fact be evidenced across a broad spectrum of animate life.

The assumption rooted in a reification of thinking and a substantive metaphysics may be accompanied by a parallel assumption rooted in a Cartesian separation of mind and body. To assume that thinking is something only a mind does, and doing or moving are something only a body does is, in effect, to deny the possibility of thinking in movement. If thinking is furthermore assumed to be always separate from its expression — a thought in one's head always existing prior to its corporeal expression — then thinking must necessarily be transcribed — or, given a strictly linguistic conception of thinking, *transliterated* — into movement. When the mind formulates a thought, for example, the tongue and lips move to express it; when the mind thinks of going to the store, the body complies by walking or driving it there. The notion that thoughts must be corporeally transliterated, that they exist separately from and prior to their expression, has been justly criticized by philosophers such as Wittgenstein and Merleau-Ponty. "When I think in language," Wittgenstein points out, "there aren't 'meanings' going through my mind in addition to the verbal expressions" (1963: 107). Merleau-Ponty similarly points out that "speech is not the 'sign' of thought, if by this we understand a phenomenon which heralds another as smoke betrays fire…. Nor can we concede … that it [speech] is the envelope and clothing of thought" (1962: 181–82). Although in these examples it is a question of *language* and not of movement, the same critical insights into the phenomenon of *thinking* apply. What the descriptive account of improvisational dance challenges is not the possibility that thinking, or a single thought such as an image, never occurs prior to its overt expression in some form, that is, prior to a movement or an action of some kind. When one thinks in general terms about what one will say prior to expressing the thought verbally to others, verbal thinking clearly occurs prior to its active expression. What the descriptive account challenges is the notion that thinking always and necessarily takes place in this way, thus that the mind is always one thoughtful step ahead of the body, always there beforehand to mobilize it into action.

There is an aspect of this assumption that we would do well to clarify in some detail. Though typically so regarded, movement is hardly given its due when presumptively conceived merely as the medium of a body's everyday transactions with the world. Movement is, on the contrary, first and foremost the natural mode of being a body — a ready and perpetual kinetic susceptibility and effusion, as it were, of animate life. Serious reflection on this fact readily leads one to the realization that animate forms readily inhabit movement in the literal sense of living in it and that thinking in movement is foundational to being a body, as much an epistemological dimension of bodily life as a biological built-in that makes sense. One aspect of this naturally kinetic manner of being — this spontaneous thinking in, and opening up into movement — is implicit in Merleau-Ponty's remark that Cezanne's description of himself as "thinking in painting"

is a description of a process in which "vision becomes gesture" (1964e: 178). His remark
is clearly not intended to mean that movement follows perception, i.e. doing follows
seeing, but that perception is interlaced with movement, and to the point, we might
add, where it is impossible to separate out where perception begins and movement ends
or where movement begins and perception ends. The one informs the other — inextricably, and all the more inextricably when it is a question not of *vision* becoming gesture,
but of *movement* becoming movement. Consider, for example, the two basic ways in
which thinking in movement may enter into the creation of a dance. One can readily
distinguish between thinking in movement in and of itself and a kind of thinking in
movement that is analogous to Cezanne's "thinking in painting." The distinction is in
fact integral to an understanding of the difference between improvisational dance —
what we might characterize as the creation of dance as artistic process — and non-
improvisational dance — the creation of dance as artistic product. In creating the latter
kind of dance, a choreographer obviously thinks in movement as she creates the dance,
precisely in a way similar to the way in which Cezanne "thinks in painting." In broad
terms, what Cezanne does with hand and brush, the choreographer does with other
bodies. Moreover, like the painter, she also stands back from time to time and views
the work in progress with an eye to judging its form — to changing the timing of a
particular movement sequence perhaps, or of attenuating a particular gesture, or of
cutting a whole passage because its dynamics are discordant. Thinking in movement is
thus a compound process for a choreographer. One might characterize the difference
between an improvisationally choreographed dance and a non-improvisationally choreographed one in terms of how the process of thinking in movement stands in relation to the actual making of the dance, i.e. in terms of whether the process of thinking
in movement is at times "transcendental" to the dance or at all times "immanent" in
the making of the dance, or in other words, whether thinking in movement is at times
"thought about action" or consistently and throughout "thought in action" (Harrison
1978: 34).[1] The difference may furthermore be characterized as an outside/inside difference. Obviously, in improvisational dance, there is no critical or creative outside eye.
Thinking in movement is all from the inside. The choreographed form evolves spontaneously from the ongoing process of thinking in movement. Non-improvisational
dances are choreographed from the outside; hence, thinking in movement may at any
time in the choreographic process be a critical thinking in movement at the same time
that it is a creative thinking in movement. In formally judging a dance, or in changing
its dynamics in any way, a choreographer is casting a critical thinking eye at the kinetic
form she is in the process of creating. Viewing the dance with a moving eye that is
consummately absorbed in the movement of moving bodies, she is caught up in a flow
of kinetic thought, perceptually experiencing the dance as an unfolding kinetic drama,
a dynamic form-in-the-making (Sheets-Johnstone 1966 [1979, 1980]). Thinking in
movement in this choreographic way, she is not only turning "vision into gesture,"

but also gesture into vision; in the act of choreographing, she is transforming dance into movement — her "vision into gesture" — and movement into dance — "gesture into vision." In effect, while a further dimension of thinking in movement opens up in choreographing a dance from the outside, perception and movement are not thereby separable moments of the process of thinking in movement. Whether choreographed from the inside or outside — in one non-stop choreographic swoop or in sections over a period of time — the basic process of thinking in movement is the same. By having turned attention exclusively to improvisational dance, we have been able to flesh out this basic process undistracted by critical concerns, and to show how this mode of thinking, by its very nature, is the work of a mindful body.

3. Thinking in movement: Our human developmental background

In Chapter Five, in the context of showing how experimental psychological research on human infants coincides with the phenomenological notions of primal animation and of a kinetic attunement to the world, or how, in other words, movement is foundational — "primitive" — in both an epistemological and metaphysical sense, it was stated that an infant's first mode of thinking is in movement. This insight into our original mode of thinking can be further elucidated and in fact substantively documented in ways that draw on developmental as well as experimental research on infants. Studies of language development that are concerned not merely with words, but with experience before language, are particularly instructive and relevant to this elucidation and documentation. Well-known infant-child psychologist Lois Bloom's first book, for example, a monograph titled *One Word at a Time*, was concerned in part to show that first single-word utterances are in fact "conceptual rather than linguistic" (Bloom 1993: ix). The single-word utterance "bye-bye," for instance, is pegged to someone's leaving the room; it is not a locutionary statement as such, or, as Bloom describes it, a "syntactic" one. Single words are initially paired with *happenings* of some kind or other — thus "down," as in getting down from a chair; objects are paired with certain *perceived dynamics* — thus "tick-tock," as in noticing a clock. In her recent book *The Transition from Infancy to Language*, Bloom fleshes out this conceptual terrain in the process of reviewing the literature on infant development and in her related discussions of topics such as movement and change, general object knowledge, and object concepts. She does so not in great detail but to a sufficient degree to afford a general sense of what is there before language. In other words, she approaches a child's progressive mastery of language by beginning with the life of the child as an infant, in particular, with those "developing cognitive abilities in infancy that bring the infant to the threshold of language at the end of the first year" (1993: 35). It is of critical importance to emphasize that in so doing, Bloom does *not* address the relationship between movement and thinking, or use the terms nonlinguistic and linguistic, or in fact concern herself in any central sense with *thinking*; the central terms of her discourse are cognition and affect. It is of equally critical importance to emphasize that her account of the transition from infancy to language is nevertheless replete with references to movement that incontrovertibly support the notion that infants think in movement. The value of her account in the present context consists precisely in these dual facts. In what follows, the underlying thematic of *thinking in movement* will be brought to the surface.

One of Bloom's first references to movement unequivocally attests to its primacy in the life of an infant and to its cogency in the development of language. Bloom states that "The foundation for the semantic structure of language ... is in the theories of objects, movement, and location that begin to be formed in the first year of life" (1993: 37). The ensuing discussion — in fact, the section that immediately follows — is devoted to "Movement and Change" (37). Though not stated outright in the discussion, it is clear that an infant's burgeoning idea of objects is tied not to a simple visual experience of them — to *looking* at them — but to noticing whether they change, how their appearance is different in different circumstances, whether they change in conjunction with what the infant itself does with them, including how it moves in relation to them, thus also including how, though it does not locomote itself, how the act of being carried about by others affects its relation to objects, and so on. We might note that such a "theory of objects" coincides basically with what both von Helmholtz and Husserl affirm about the constitution of objects. As shown in Chapter Four, both von Helmholtz and Husserl describe how we learn about objects originally by moving in relation to them and by noticing their changing appearances in concert with our movements. Moreover this same kinetically-tethered "theory of objects" has further resonances. When Bloom, in the section on "Movement and Change," speaks of feeding bottles and blankets having "a dynamic quality" according to where the infant is in relation to them, how the infant moves or is moved by others relative to them, how they, as objects, move or do not move, and so on (38), her words recall in an abbreviated way Stern's much more highly elaborated account of vitality affects (discussed in Chapter Five). "A blanket," she says, for example, "appears when the baby is put down to rest, and then it disappears when the baby is taken up for feeding and playing.... [M]oreover, its movements are integrated with the baby's own twisting, turning, trying to rise up, and so forth" (38). It is furthermore significant that Bloom first mentions in just this dynamic context the fact that "when [children] begin to say words, their earliest words express something about objects that move" (38). As Bloom points out, this empirical finding about the centrality of movement to earliest words has in fact been made by many researchers (272, Note 10). Bloom herself goes on to make a most provocative comment. She states that "Both conceptual categories and eventual linguistic categories build on an infant's nascent theories about objects, motion, space, and causality, and these theories originate in the early experiences that come about with movement and change in location."

Now by "conceptual categories" Bloom obviously means categories prior to language since she goes on to mention "eventual linguistic categories." In effect, though not named as such, Bloom implicitly acknowledges that infants have nonlinguistic concepts, concepts in advance of language, indeed that they have *theories* in advance of language since it is theories about "movement and change" originating in early experiences of movement and change that ultimately spawn "linguistic categories." Of further moment is that although psychologists disagree on how an infant arrives at a "theory of objects," and disagree as well as to the nature of that theory, they are in accord that "movement and invariance in the face of change" (39) are central to an infant's theory of objects. In other words, movement is the foundation of our epistemological construction of the world; even while some objects are static — like walls or pieces of furniture — there is movement in relation to them. What is crucial, then, is making sense of what is invariant amidst change. Indeed, as Bloom emphatically points out in reviewing a study by T.G.R. Bower — the study referred to and discussed in Chapter Five — which showed that infants were less disturbed or did not even notice that an object changed, but became quite "disturbed when the path in which it moved changed" — "*Movement* [is] the critical factor: either the movement of the object or the path of movement or the infant's head movement while following the object" (40). Clearly, *thinking in movement* is our primary way of making sense of the world. We see this truth enunciated again in the conclusion drawn from experimental research, namely, that "infants as young as 2 to 4 months of age can track a moving object and anticipate its reappearance" (40). Infants as young as 2 to 4 months of age are *thinking in movement*: to *anticipate* is first of all to think ahead, as in expecting something to happen; to expect the reappearance of an object that has been moving along a certain path and disappears at a certain point on that path is *to think ahead dynamically*, i.e., *to think in movement*. Moreover if an infant's perception of objects and "theory of objects" matures in conjunction with movement — its developing perception of objects being tied both to the movement of objects and to its own movement — then again, an infant is *thinking in movement* (see Ruff 1980).

As Bloom implicitly shows, "physical knowledge" matures in conjunction with an infant's developing "theory of objects" (43–46). By physical knowledge Bloom means such properties as solidity, object permanence, and even such things as gravitational effects. Infant researchers have long remarked on the fact that infants are attracted to novelty; they habituate to what is regular or expected and pay particular attention to what is unusual. The latter phenomenon — "preferential looking," as Bloom at one point describes it (43) — is regularly used as an empirical measure of an infant's perceptions, expectations, interests, and so on. Drawing in particular on a series of research studies of child psychologists Elizabeth Spelke and Renée Baillargeon that utilize this standard technique, Bloom describes how infants even as young as two-and-a-half months have a sense of object continuity and solidity, and how those at six months have a beginning appreciation of gravity and inertia (43–44). In summing up these studies, she writes that "In all these experiments, infants demonstrated these abilities with respect to objects that *move*" (44; italics in original). Again, empirical research validates the claim that infants are *thinking in movement*. Indeed, the research itself all but articulates the truth. Precisely by *thinking in movement*, infants are gaining knowledge of "objects, motion, space, and causality" — and, we could add, of time. In progressively attaining to physical knowledge about the world in ways that are integrally tethered to movement, they are gaining knowledge about invariant and variant spatio-temporal and dynamic features of the world. We should perhaps emphasize once more that it is not Bloom's intention to present a case for movement or for thinking in movement. On the contrary, as initially suggested, the case is made by itself. We see this yet again when, after underscoring the importance of "objects that *move*," Bloom writes — a few lines later — that "A theory of objects clearly begins very early in infancy, and experiments have shown its beginnings in perceptions of objects that move in relation to a physical field" (45).

When Bloom goes on to consider what she terms "relational" concepts, the basic developmental phenomenon of thinking in movement is implicitly elaborated in further ways. Relational concepts develop outside of language. They develop on the basis of observation. Bloom defines them by saying that "Children learn about relationships between objects by observing the effects of movement and actions done by themselves and other persons" (50). It is instructive to note that Bloom's "relational concepts" are akin to what Stern describes as "consequential relationships" and to what Husserl describes as "if/then" relationships. All three are descriptive of the same basic phenomenon. An infant notices, for example, that slapping bath water causes a splash; closing one's mouth impedes the insertion of food into it; pulling on a blanket brings it closer; pushing against a bottle or a ball causes it to roll on the floor; being picked up has a certain feel to it and changes the way things in the surrounding world appear; and so on. Bloom's "relational" concepts — and their kin — are *not* language-dependent. Moreover they are not simply stepping stones integral to language development, thus essentially "pre-verbal" or "pre-linguistic" phenomena. On the contrary, they are the fundamental backbone of an infant's — and an adult's — knowledge of its surrounding world. They are the bedrock of our notion of objects, motion, space, causality — and time — just as Bloom points out. They derive from experiences in which and by which infants attain concepts of different objects and gain "physical knowledge" generally. Though just such concepts and knowledge are undeniably basic to an infant's ultimately having something to talk about, at least some of these concepts and some of this knowledge may never even wend their way into language. In other words, they are not *necessarily* articulated or even articulable. What a blown-up balloon does, for example, when it is suddenly untied is hardly expressed by the word "deflates" or the words "splutters about." The actual dynamic kinetic event is not reducible to a word or even to a series of words. We all have knowledge of just such physical events just as we all have nonlinguistic concepts of their dynamics. We have this knowledge and these concepts because we have all been nurtured by an original capacity to think in movement, a capacity that does not diminish with age but merely becomes submerged or hidden by the capacity and practice of thinking in words.

Psychologist Jerome Bruner's focal emphasis upon narrative as the primary form of discourse and upon the central place of action in that discourse affirms this very insight. He writes that when young children "come to grasp the basic idea of reference necessary for any language use … their principal linguistic interest centers on *human action and its outcomes*" (1990: 78). His point is that narrative structure is, in the beginning, concerned with movement, in particular, with "agentivity" (77). "Agent-and-action, action-and-object, agent-and-object, action-and-location, and possessor-and-possession," he says, "make up the major part of the semantic relations that appear in the first stage of speech" (78). A particularly interesting experiment implicitly demonstrates the ready concern of infants with movement in Bruner's sense of "agentivity." In this experiment, luminous points are placed at eleven anatomical joints strategic to human walking — i.e., ankles, knees, elbows, and so on. When set in motion, the luminous points create the illusion of a person walking (or running or carrying or throwing or involved in other acts). Not only do adults readily see a person walking (or engaged in other acts: see, for example, Runeson & Frykholm 1981, 1983), but three-month-old infants do also. When the eleven luminous points are randomly organized and set in motion in computer simulations, or when the moving point-figure is turned upside down and set in motion, a coherently moving shape is no longer perceived (Bertenthal & Pinto 1993; Bertenthal, Proffitt, Cutting 1984).[2] Though some infant researchers have tied the experimental findings to the notion of infants having a "body schema" — a body schema "that permits not only the control of their own bodies but also the recognition of their fellow humans" (Mehler & Dupoux 1994: 108) — no such hypothetical explanatory entity is actually necessary. Even as a fetus in utero, an infant has a sense of gravity, i.e. of the vertical; even as a fetus in utero, an infant has a sense of its joints, i.e. through kinesthesia. Though as an infant, it has never itself walked, it has seen others walking; and again, even as a fetus in utero, it has a tactile-kinesthetic sense of its own body as an articulable, essentially dynamic form. "Agentivity" specifies a dynamic concept of action coincident with this articulable, essentially dynamic form. "Agentivity" is thus intimately related to *primal animation*. Primal animation indeed is the epistemological ground on which *thinking in movement* develops, hence the ground on which the concept of "agentivity" develops, agentivity in conjunction with both one's own actions and the actions of others, as is evident in a three-month-old infant's recognition of a coherent moving form that in fact exists only sketchily as a luminous point-figure.

Aspects of this original mode of thinking warrant consideration with respect to their differences from linguistic thinking and with respect to the fact that in many cases, as the earlier balloon example suggests, what is thought in movement is opaque to language. With respect to differences between thinking in movement and thinking in words, attention might first be called to a coincidence highlighted in an earlier publication (Sheets-Johnstone 1996c). Both Husserl and Stern remark upon a certain lack of fit between language and experience, as evidenced by the disruptive character of language with respect to actual experience (Husserl), or by the elision of experience by language (Stern). Husserl writes that

> It is easy to see that even in (ordinary) human life, and first of all in every individual life from childhood up to maturity, the originally intuitive life which creates its originally self-evident structures through activities on the basis of sense-experience very quickly and in increasing measure falls victim to the *seduction of language*. Greater and greater segments of this life lapse into a kind of talking and reading that is dominated purely by association; and often enough, in respect to the validities arrived at in this way, it is disappointed by subsequent experience (1970b: 362; italics in original).

Stern observes that there is a "slippage between experience and words," noting that experiences of self having to do with a sense of coherence and continuity, for example, "fall into a category something like your heartbeat or regular breathing" (1985: 181). He goes on to say that "[P]eriodically some transient sense of this experience is revealed, for some inexplicable reason or via psychopathology, with the breathtaking effect of sudden realization that your existential and verbal selves can be light years apart, *that the self is unavoidably divided by language*" (181; italics added). In one sense, of course, Stern's observation straightaway validates Lacanian psychoanalytic theory: language *is* Other, but it is not necessarily the Other that Lacan proposes. In fact, in a quite different sense, Stern's notion of a self-divided-by-language is wholly contrary to Lacan's psychoanalytic and this because at its core, the self is, and has been, a distinctly different self in just the way Stern has previously described, both clinically and experimentally. The core self is an *existential* self, a preeminently bodily presence that carries with it a sense of coherence, agency, affectivity, and continuity. In the descriptive terms Husserl uses many times over, the core self is fundamentally *animate* and *animated*. Thus both the "originally intuitive life" that Husserl describes and the core or existential self that Stern describes are anchored in a dynamics of aliveness that is not simply a state of being that is there before language, but an aliveness that language, when it does emerge, can and often does fail to capture. Indeed, such a linguistic feat, we might say, is not the mission of language; one word after another, while potentially itself a highly dynamic happening, is not equipped to render — at least in an everyday, non-poetic way — the qualitatively dynamic metaphysics of aliveness — of breathing, for example, or of the synaesthetic experience of waves crashing relentlessly upon a shore. What moves and changes is always in excess of the word — or words — that tries to name it. Thinking in movement is different not in degree but in kind from thinking in words. Words are not sharper tools, more precise instruments by which to think about dynamics, by which to hone our sense of space, time, energy, causality, or "agentivity". When the definitive shift into language takes place, that is, when thinking in words comes to dominate thinking in movement, a foundationally rich and subtle mode of thinking is displaced and typically subdued, commonly to the point that it is no longer even recognized as a mode of thinking. Experience itself may be fundamentally transformed if the shift is so compelling and overpowering, and so ultimately transforming of the person, that any other form of thinking is categorically denied.

Earlier in his career, Stern wrote of certain infant behaviors as being "resistant" to language. He termed these nonverbal behaviors "intention movements" (1981:47), following along the lines of ethological studies and attempting to show how the behaviors were biological built-ins in the service of communication. The nonverbal behaviors he singled out were "gaze, head orientation, upper and lower body orientation, spatial positioning, and assumption of posture and distance" (45). He spoke of these nonverbal behaviors in the context of an infant's readiness or unreadiness to interact with others, viewing readiness and unreadiness not as an either/or condition of the infant, but as dynamic behavioral possibilities existing along a continuum. What is of moment is Stern's emphasis on the fact that these nonverbal communicative behaviors are neither transformed nor transformable into language; that is, while some infant nonverbal behaviors such as pointing or reaching for an object might be viewed as "'proto-linguistic' (or linguistic precursors) because they later become linguistically encoded" — as pointing, for example, becomes "gimme" (54–55) — some of their nonverbal behaviors such as averting their gaze or lowering their head "will never undergo an analogous [linguistic] transformation" (55). In discussing the reasons for their resistance to linguistic encoding, Stern points out that a word naming a behavior has none of the effect of the actual behavior itself; language is thus not equal to the communicative power of these nonverbal behaviors. He points out further that the nonverbal behaviors are dimensional rather than categorical in character; they transmit or signal "gradient information" (57–58): postures, gaze, upper and lower body orientation, and so on, have a variable affective tone according to *how* they are enacted; they signal a variable level of arousal, for example, according to *how* they are enacted. Though Stern does not speak of affective variability in such terms, there is no doubt but that the gradient character of the nonverbal behaviors is through and through a question of spatio-temporal dynamics: an infant can slowly or suddenly avert its gaze with respect to another person; it can turn its head away abruptly coincident with its sudden gaze aversion, thus intensifying its unreadiness to interact with someone; it can turn its upper torso minimally toward another person, let its head follow minimally, and then make brief eye contact with a person, thus tentatively showing a readiness to interact; and so on. Endless spatio-temporal intercorporeal dynamics are possible. In contrast to "a verbal message" (58), the "gradient information" is precise in character. It is also transmitted with greater speed than a verbal message. In short, there is a richly subtle and complex nonverbal world that is there from the beginning of all of our lives, a dynamic world that is neither mediated by language nor a stepping stone to language, but that is literally significant in and of itself and remains literally significant in and of itself, a dynamic world articulating intercorporeal intentions that, although clearly affective in origin, are enmeshed in "agentivity," in expectations, in consequential relationships, and thereby in the phenomenon of thinking in movement (cf. Bull 1951).[3]

When Stern in his later writings examines the impact of language, he consistently emphasizes and reiterates the differences between a nonverbal and verbal world. He again points out, for example, how "Language is slow," how "Words cannot handle global experiences well," how language in fact "breaks apart rich, complicated global experiences into relatively impoverished component parts," how language "is clumsy at noting gradations between its categories," how it "may split thought away from emotion," and how some experiences such as "looking into someone's eyes while he or she is looking into yours ... can simply never be captured in words; at best [such experiences] can be evoked by words." He states further that for the young child, language "creates a wide gulf between [a] familiar nonverbal world of experience and [a] new world of words," that the "schism is confusing and at times painful." In fact, "for the first time in [its] young life," a young child, "has to hold onto two different versions of the same event." He says that "Life will now ... be lived more in parallel," that "The simple wholeness of experience has been broken," but that "the verbal and the nonverbal constructions of experience will live together all the same" (1990:114).

Now while the advent of language is radically intrusive on Stern's account and to that degree may appear misconceived if not incomprehensible to many, his account is difficult to discount. To begin with, serious and extended study of a subject may well turn up findings that are radically incompatible with popular beliefs and attitudes. In this respect, Stern's account cannot be peremptorily dismissed because it is informed by years of both clinical experience with infants and developmental research into infancy, a time of life, we might note, with which we are all familiar in varying degrees, but which most of us have never actually studied either close-up or longitudinally. At the very least, what Stern's professional findings call upon us to do is to suspend judgment, to listen carefully to what is being said, to reflect carefully upon it, and then, to the best of our own abilities and situation, test out what is being said in the light of our own observations of infants. The idea that infants are nothing until they speak, that there is no thinking outside language, that there is not even consciousness outside language — all such ideas are readily open to question when we turn in this suspended way "to the things themselves." More than this, insights are gained into language itself. When we go back to infancy and seriously attend both to Stern's account and to what is there in the form of living flesh before us, we can hardly miss the fact that *language is not experience and does not create experience*. We readily discover this fact because we can indeed hardly miss it: infants experience themselves and their surrounding world. They are animate forms in an animate world: they are reaching, kicking, smiling, pulling, turning, babbling, and more — and they consistently notice and respond to things that move. They are *sensibly* caught up in the primacy of something quite other than words. They are caught up in the primacy of movement and in thinking, not in words, but in movement.

When we listen and attend in this way, when we read descriptions of infant behaviors and interactions, when we observe infants, when we reflect back upon our own fundamental knowledge of ourselves and the world, we realize that our most basic human concepts are foundationally corporeal concepts; they derive from our own dynamic bodily lives. When we turn to any basic spatio-temporal or dynamic concept, the concept of distance, for example, and ask how we first *thought about* distance, in what terms we came to conceive of distance, or how we first came to have a concept of suddenness, in what terms we first experienced and thought about it, we realize straightaway that we did so nonverbally. These fundamental spatio-temporal concepts are not in the least language-dependent. They are first and foremost *corporeal concepts* (Sheets-Johnstone 1990). As infants, we forged just such concepts. Although we have a word to designate them, there is nothing basically linguistic about them in the least. Corporeal concepts in each case derive from experience and in no way require language for their formulation. Moreover the idea that language is there implicitly as some kind of ultimate and proper conceptual form, a kind of conceptual destiny toward which we inexorably progress as toward what, in an evolutionary context, Stephen Jay Gould describes as "the summum bonum of bigger brains" (see Chapter One, this text), is a notion at odds with corporeal matters of fact. Infancy is not a *pre*-linguistic or *proto*-linguistic state of mind.[4] It is not a *primitive* state of being, an antediluvian, prehistoric, barbarian time of life. Infancy is infancy, a period in our lives that affords all of us the crucial opportunity to experience the world and ourselves directly, as animate forms, and correlatively, to know the world and ourselves in their most basic terms: dynamically, kinetically. If anything, *language is post-kinetic*. Fundamental spatio-temporal-energic concepts come from experiences of movement, both in the form of self-movement and in the form of the movement of individuals and things in one's surrounding world. Even with such spatial concepts as that of light and dark, we do not need words or even need to witness a sunrise or sunset; blinking suffices. Indeed, our own bodily changes, our own bodily processes, quantitative ones as in growth and development as well as qualitative ones as in feelings of hunger giving way to feelings of satiety — an experience that Stern describes for an infant as a *"hunger storm ... that passes"* (1990: 31–35, 36–43) — are temporal processes. We live in and through the changes. As adults, we tend not to follow the temporal dynamics of change closely. We would thus not likely say, for example, that hunger "sweeps through [our] nervous system like a storm, disrupting whatever was going on before and temporarily disorganizing behavior and experience." Nor would we ordinarily say that our hunger then "establishes its own patterns of action and feelings, its own rhythms" (Stern 1990: 32), making us breathe faster, for example, and more jaggedly. Yet what *is* the experience of hunger for an adult? As infants, hunger affected us in just such ways and when we were fed, sucking produced rhythms that overrode the fast and jagged breathing rhythm. When as adults we begin recognizing the fecundity and breadth of our tactile-kinesthetic bodies and corporeal concepts, we wean ourselves in reverse: we back down the linguistic ladder from which we customarily see and appraise ourselves — and other creatures — a ladder whose ascension has been richly prepared for in earlier ways, but that appears to us now virtually untainted by them. We come back down to earth and recontact that original ground which gave us our first footings and which has never actually disappeared but has only been buried under a pedestalled and myopic view of language. Weaning ourselves away from the thought that all thought is language-dependent, and equally, from language-dependent thought, we wean ourselves away from a basically object- or substance-tethered metaphysics. In turn, we afford ourselves the possibility of grasping the momentous significance of movement and change, and of attaining to a metaphysics quintessentially attuned to the dynamic nature of animate forms and an animate world. A process metaphysics accurately describes the natural world, the living forms that inhabit it, and the natural contours of life itself. Thinking in movement is not only coincident with that metaphysics; it is the methodological point of departure for its formulation. Precisely as Heraclitus indicated: bodies *step* into *running* rivers.

4. Thinking in movement: Our phylogenetic heritage

Killdeer are ground-nesting birds that protect their young in two basic ways depending upon the immediate danger. When approached by predators who will eat their young, they move away from the nest and flutter their wings as if injured; when cattle approach who might trample their young, they remain at the nest, spreading their wings in a conspicuous display, which action ordinarily deflects the cattle away from the nest (Griffin 1984: 36), or they lunge toward a cow's face "thereby startling it and causing it to veer away" (Ristau 1996: 80).

Instances of thinking in movement abound in the literature on nonhuman animal life just as they abound in the literature on human infant life. That the killdeer's behaviors *are* examples of thinking in movement, and not merely blind, robotic behaviors adaptively favored by natural selection, is an issue that will be duly addressed. Of moment now are the distinctive movement dynamics of the killdeer in each situation. As instances of *thinking in movement*, the dynamics are aptly fitted to the circumstance; each movement dynamic is in its own way a reasonable act in the service of kin-protection. Similarly, each movement dynamic has its own integrity as an act of kin-protection. To be effective, movement dynamics must be just so structured. Focusing attention on the movement dynamics of these protective acts highlights the extended and more complex spatio-temporal dynamics of predator-prey interactions,[5] where, as ethologist Donald Griffin points out, "The stakes are extremely high. For the prey it is literally a matter of life and death. For the predator, success or failure in a particular effort is less crucial, but its survival and reproduction depend on succeeding reasonably often" (1984: 73). The prize being on the one hand to stay alive, and on the other, to have a good meal, prey and predator are at near corresponding risks. The drama that evolves between and through them is clearly played out in movement, a kinetic drama through and through. Precisely because it is a spontaneous dynamic interaction not orchestrated in advance, but played out from moment to moment, it is a drama that involves thinking. To claim that there is no thinking involved would in fact be absurd. It would be absurd to claim, for example, that predator's and prey's progression of movement is tied to a set of rules that algorithmically specify both the immediate moment and the global event, as if the animals involved were following a script, their every movement being orchestrated in advance. Moreover it would be equally absurd to claim that the thoughts the animals think exist separately from the movement the animals make, or in other words, that the animals' thoughts are successively transcribed into movement — as if one of two hungry female lions in tandem strategic pursuit of a zebra were first thinking in some way to herself, "Let's see, if I head off the zebra from this direction, perhaps Mary over there will move up on its right flank and ...," the lioness then following through by bodying forth her thoughts in the flesh. All such claims overlook the obvious: predator and prey alike are thinking in movement; their progression of thought — their process of thinking in movement — is tied to the evolving, changing situation itself, the situation they themselves are dynamically creating moment by moment in their very movement. That dynamically evolving situation develops its own logic, i.e. its own reasonableness and integrity, and it develops that logic on the basis of a *kinetic bodily logos*, a natural kinetic intelligence that is there from the beginning in both prey and predator and that evolves on the basis of experience. In stalking, in chasing, in avoiding — in other words, in crouching, creeping, sprinting, racing, suddenly changing directions, putting on speed, and so on — prey and predator alike make their way in a kinetically intelligent manner, a manner that is at once spontaneous and contextually appropriate. Agonistic situations in which pursuit and flight are dominant themes demand just such a kinetic intelligence, an intelligence that is not a fixed and static body of knowledge but a dynamically evolving intelligence that grows and changes on the basis of past experience. The reproductive success of prey and predator alike depends on just such an intelligence.

The old division between instinctive and learned behavior is a spurious one, as most biologists have come to realize, an oppositional way of thinking that does not accord with facts of life. In their classroom text *Biological Science*, William Keeton and James Gould, for example, state that "[I]t is extremely unlikely that any behavior can be classified as strictly innate or strictly learned: even the most rigidly automatic behavior depends on the environmental conditions for which it evolved, while most learning, flexible as it seems, appears to be guided by innate mechanisms." They conclude that "*Instincts* ... can be defined as the heritable, genetically specified neural circuitry that organizes and guides behavior," and that "behavior that is thereby produced can reasonably be said to be at least partially innate" (Keeton & Gould 1986: 554).[6] Instructive cases in point that confirm this conception of behavior are paths and shelters. Animals that make paths for themselves are not automatons blindly following a motor program, any more than are human animals who blaze trails or build roads. As Keeton and Gould's remarks implicitly indicate, creatures — including human ones — build according to what is available and/or at hand, according to what the contour of the land allows, according to what construction and/or destruction is in fact required if a path, trail, or road is to be successfully made, and so on. Moreover what starts out in a happenstance manner may be progressively improved. Griffin points out, for example, that a vole runway "may have started as an incidental result of repeated walking over the same route, but its users soon work on it actively, nibbling away at the lower parts of some plants while leaving in place the blades of grass that lean over the runway." In this way, they make the runway smooth, level, and "almost invisible from above" (Griffin 1984: 96). The building of shelters correspondingly involves thinking in movement and tailoring one's building accordingly. The nest-building of weaverbirds provides an exceptional example; its nest incorporates not only an extraordinary number of possible stitches and fastenings, but ones requiring complex weavings. Ethologist W.H. Thorpe diagrams nine different styles, including a half hitch, an overhand knot, an alternately reversed winding, a series of interlocking loops, and a slip knot (Thorpe 1974: 149). In the context of discussing instincts understood as genetically-determined behaviors, Thorpe emphasizes the fact that experience affects genetically-generated behavior. In other words, instincts are malleable; their particular realization depends upon an individual's past experience, for example, upon whether, in the course of an action, an individual is interrupted in its activities, upon what available resources provide, and so on (Thorpe 1974: 134–171). Griffin makes this very point with respect to nest-building behaviors when he states that however instinctive the behavior might be, "nest-building is anything but a stereotyped and fixed sequence of behavior patterns" (1984: 107–108). In the context of discussing various aspects of nest-building, such as whether a bird repairs a damaged nest or abandons it and builds a new one, he remarks upon the flexibility and sensibleness of their choice, but states too that "This is not to say that birds never do foolish things in the course of nest building." He proceeds then to relate how blackbirds may become confused, starting to build "many nests in some artificial structure that has many similar-looking cavities." Their confusion, he says, appears to be about just where the nest should be located and ends in their not completing any nest. He goes on to say with respect to this behavior that "we tend to infer a total lack of thinking when animals do something foolish and wasteful of effort. But we do not apply the same standard to members of our own species, and we never infer a total absence of thinking when people behave with comparable foolishness" (1984:109). The point is an important one. To say animals think is not to say that they think infallibly, or as Griffin puts it, it is not to say that their thinking "always corresponds perfectly to external reality." Just like humans animals, nonhuman animals make mistakes. "[E]rror," however, as Griffin points out, "is not the same as absence of thought" (109). By a similar token, instinctive behavior is not the same as absence of thought.

Intelligence in action is instinctive. *All* animals — humans included — could hardly survive much less reproduce if intelligence in action were not instinctive. In just this sense, a kinetic bodily logos is at the heart of thinking in movement. It is what makes such thinking spontaneous and contextually appropriate to the situation at hand. It is what ties thinking not to *behavior* but to *movement*, that is, to kinetic meanings, to a *spatio-temporal-energic semantics.* Instinctive behaviors are malleable precisely because they are fundamentally kinetically dynamic patterns and not chunks of behaviorally labeled "doings." To think in movement is not to think in monolithic comportmental wholes: eating, mating, courting, defending, aggressing, threatening, and so on; it is to think in dynamic terms — in terms of speed, postural orientation, range of movement, force, direction, and so on. Behavioral variations exist precisely because *kinetically dynamic possibilities* exist. It is just such kinetically dynamic possibilities that distinguish one creature from another: one creature runs faster than another, is more agile over a rough terrain than another, is more awkward in climbing than another, is less easily aroused or startled than another, is quicker to withdraw than another, and so on. From this essentially kinetic vantage point, the malleability of what are called instinctive behaviors, indeed, their *evolution*, is a matter of movement. Instincts have their genesis in animation — primal animation. When circumstances change, ways of living change, and these changes in the most basic sense are a matter of movement possibilities. A kinetic bodily logos is not some kind of adaptive mechanism; it is a real-life dimension of animate forms. An intelligence of action is a built-in of animate life. Thinking in movement is the natural expression of this elemental biological character of life.

When ethologist Niko Tinbergen relates in some detail a range of animal behavioral studies of colleagues over a twenty-five year period, his descriptions implicitly exemplify again and again a kinetic bodily logos and the phenomenon of thinking in movement. An especially impressive example concerns the seven-year study of a species of sand wasp (*Ammophila*) by G.P. Baerends and J. van Roon (at that time students of Tinbergen). The sand wasps in question live not on open land but in "knee-deep Heather" in a terrain that has "few outstanding landmarks"; what is more, they carry their "heavy prey [caterpillars] home walking over the ground below the Heather shrubs" (Tinbergen 1968: 104–105). In other words, in supplying caterpillars to their young buried in the ground, the female wasps walk the highly uneven ground below the heather; they cannot fly there. But this is not all. Each female wasp has two, three, and sometimes more nests at one time — what Tinbergen describes as a "telescoping of broods" (112). This means, of course, that she must remember the location of more than one nest. Furthermore, after constructing each nest originally and laying an egg on the first caterpillar she places in it, she makes two more calls to each nest over a period of days, provisioning each one according to its needs. An interesting difference between these wasps and what was, at the time, a more highly studied species (*Philanthus*) concerns the former's building habits. Although *Ammophila* already build their nests in a highly overgrown and therefore visually difficult terrain, rather than leaving the sand they excavate in building the nest by the nest itself, thus giving a clue as to its location, they carry it away so that a sandpile does not distinguish the nest from its surrounds. To arrange the physiognomy of the landscape in such a way, that is, to create a certain spatial semantics, is to think in movement. Moreover the building of the nest itself is a complicated process of thinking in movement: the female digs earth, pushes pebbles or bits of wood into the shaft that she makes, "works sand among the pebbles," "rakes sand," and so on (Tinbergen 1968: 106). In the course of provisioning the larvae, for example, she clears sand away that has dropped into the opening as a result of her removing the pebbles to enter the nest, and she uses her head as a hammer against the pebbles so as to close the nest after a visit. What is more, when she first returns to the nest after initially building it and laying her egg atop a caterpillar, she does not bring anything the next time, but simply "calls," as Tinbergen puts it, to evaluate the needs of the larva. Only after doing so does she return with caterpillars — in the amount necessary to sustain the larva. In other words, what she does next — what is literally her next move: to find one, two, or three more caterpillars to bring back to the nest — is each time determined by what she finds on her inspection. As Tinbergen emphasizes many times over, "All the time she remembers where all the nests are and, roughly, in what stage they are" (Tinbergen 1968: 114). Perhaps the purest and most sophisticated example of the wasp's thinking in movement concerns her ability to home in on the nest with the food. The wasp invariably climbs either a bush of heather or a young pine tree, and then, "Arrived at the top after a laborious climb, she turn[s] in various directions, as if having a good look round. Then she [takes] a long jump, which [is] always in the direction of her nest. The weight of the caterpillar decide[s] how long this 'flight' [will] be…. The wasp then [begins] to walk, stumbling and plodding along over the rough ground." Although starting out in the right direction, she might make a wrong turn or even go in loops. She will then again climb a heather bush or young pine, look around again, and again, make another jump — in the correct direction of the nest. Various studies clearly show that the wasp's movement is tethered to landmarks — landmarks such as tufts of grass or a clump of pebbles or pine cones — "the positions of which she has to learn" (Tinbergen 1968: 120).

Thinking in movement is not only the natural expression of a kinetic bodily logos; it is the natural noetic sequel of actual experiences of movement, both self-movement and the movement of others. As indicated earlier, experiences of movement are the generative source of concepts of agentivity, of if/then relationships, of spatio-temporal invariants. They generate expectations; they are replete with kinetic concepts having to do with energy, distance, speed, range of movement, direction — in short, with a complex of dynamic qualities inherent in the experience of movement itself. Consider, for example, the seemingly simple behavior of moving away from something noxious. Zoologist John Paul Scott writes that

> Escape depends on some power of movement. A paramecium quickly withdraws from an injury, and even the sluggish ameba slowly crawls away…. [T]hose forms which can move at all retreat or withdraw in some way. Even clams can disappear quite rapidly into their native mud, as anyone who tries to dig them out soon discovers. Snails, turtles, and other animals with hard shells often escape by simply withdrawing into their armor…. An opossum which is overpowered will go completely limp and apparently lifeless for several minutes, then suddenly bound to its feet and escape if it is no longer held. Similar reactions are seen in turkey buzzards (1963: 70–71).

The tendency to place all such movement — or at least all such movement of "lower animals" — in the category of reflex behavior does less than full justice to the actual situation. An animal, even a so-called "lower animal," can, for example, hesitate before crawling away or withdrawing, just as it can hesitate before re-emerging after withdrawing. Consider the behavior of fan worms. As invertebrate zoologist Martin Wells observes, "Touch them, or pass a shadow across [their] filtering crown, and they vanish [i.e. "duck very quickly"] down their tubes, only emerging, with great caution and very slowly, after a matter of several minutes" (Wells 1968: 80). Now surely if a fan worm moves "with great caution and very slowly," however that caution and slowness might be actually measured objectively and quantified, then it can move with either a bit more or a bit less "great caution," and similarly, it can attenuate even further or accelerate just a bit its very slow movement. In short, it can vary its movement. In fact, it is reasonable to assume that the several minutes that elapse before a fan worm reappears, and its great caution and very slow movement in reappearing, are all variable according to the variability of the circumstances themselves. In some real-life situations, for example, should a touch or shadow appear again in the course of its cautious and very slow reappearing, a fan worm will again "duck very quickly," interrupting its slow and cautious re-emergence. Clearly, a kinetic intelligence is at work in the observed behavior of fan worms. There is nothing wayward at all in this understanding and explanation of animate life, wayward in the sense of putatively ignoring the concept of adaptation and of natural selection and proffering another, we might say, "mindful" understanding and explanation in its place. On the contrary, a kinetic bodily logos — in essence, primal animation, surface recognition sensitivity, proprioception, kinesthesia, and the capacity to think in movement — is of the very quintessence of adaptation and selection. Animate forms that are born to move but that fail to be sensitive to their surrounds, that fail to be sensitive to their own bodies, and that in turn fail to think in movement do not survive. They are deficient in the very business of living. However circumscribed the range of their movement possibilities, however restricted their particular *Umwelt*, their lives depend on being responsive to a particular surrounding world as it is at this particular moment in this particular place. As was emphasized in Chapter Two, the world is not the same one day to the next and neither is a creature's life. Moreover creatures are themselves spontaneous; they move motivated by their own dispositions to move. Even anemones, animals one thinks of as sedentary, are spontaneous, generating activity on their own, and not just in response to stimuli in their surrounding world (Wells 1968: 40). Further still, individual animals can and do change their behaviors as a result of experience. Again, even anemones, animals one thinks of as totally programmed, demonstrate this capacity of animate life (Wells 1968: 42).

The focus on "lower animals" has been intentional. The tendency of many, perhaps all too many, humans is to order animate life hierarchically and to belittle what lies "below" — wherever that dividing mark might be drawn. In contrast, at least some humans readily accredit a kinetic bodily logos to "higher" animals, however indirectly. Abundant examples exist that validate the accreditation. Well-known primatologist Jane Goodall relates two incidents that, even in their brief description, straightaway illustrate and implicitly affirm a kinetic bodily logos in action. One of the related incidents concerns a chimpanzee who saves his much younger brother from severe treatment by an adult male. The younger brother's temper tantrum — the result of being hurled away by a female in estrus — was irking not only to the female but to the alpha male who was courting her. Hearing the tantrum, the older brother "who had been feeding some distance away, came hurrying up to see what was going on. For a moment he stood surveying the scene then, realizing that Pax was in imminent danger of severe punishment, seized his still screaming kid brother by one wrist and dragged him hastily away!" (1990: 199). The other related incident concerns a group of six male chimpanzees and is equally if not more telling since it involves concerted intelligent action. The group of males came upon a female baboon carrying a small infant and feeding in a palm tree. All of the chimpanzees stood gazing up at the baboon, "their hair bristling." One of them slowly climbed a tree close to the one in which the baboon was feeding and to a height where he was level with her. Then two other males climbed two other trees so that one chimpanzee was "now stationed in each of the trees to which their victim could leap. The other three chimpanzees [waited] on the ground." The first chimpanzee suddenly leaped into the baboon's tree. The baboon made a huge leap into a tree in which another chimpanzee was stationed. That chimpanzee seized the baboon and pulled her infant away from her. All six chimpanzees subsequently shared the infant as a meal (1990: 128).

Each incident clearly indicates a kinetic intelligence at work, a spontaneously integrated and reasoned course of action. In neither case were the chimpanzees taught what to do, for example. Neither had they practiced, nor were they practicing, a "behavior." Rather, they were *kinetically attuned* to a particular situation at hand. Kinetic attunement is the work of a kinetic bodily logos, a logos that comes with a creature's being the animate form it is. From this perspective, the designations "higher" and "lower" are clearly inappropriate; each creature is what it is and is not another thing. It is quintessentially suited, and in multiple ways, to the life it lives. Not only is there an existential fit with respect to its physical and living body — what might roughly be described as a fit between its anatomical and animate form (Sheets-Johnstone 1986a) — but an existential fit obtains between the organism and its environing world, a fit that is kinetically expressed. Each species of animate form is kinetically suited to the life it lives by way of an intelligence that is of the very nature of the form itself, an intelligence that is plaited into its very tissues and expressed in the sensible ways in which it lives its life. In sum, a kinetic bodily logos is an instinctive disposition toward intelligent action. It is a disposition that is common to all animate forms of life.

We might note that it is incomprehensible how any so-called purely instinctive behavior could otherwise have gotten started. It would be absurd, for example, to think that the first living form was programmed to some *behavior* or other in advance of its leading any particular kind of life. To be viable, instinctive behaviors have to be effectively tethered to particular environing circumstances, which in fact can only be faced at the moment the animate form first encounters them. More than this, however, it is not *behavior* that first appears. In the beginning is not *behavior* any more than it is — or was — *words*. In the beginning is — and was — movement, sheer movement. What lives moves, and in moving, goes toward and away from things. It is in the process of spontaneously moving about that animate forms discover aspects of the world, and it is on the basis of this process of spontaneous movement and discovery that instincts are formed. Certain movements are instinctively ingrained because organisms *find satisfaction in them.* It is not too much to say that they realize that their movement works, *and that in consequence, they do again what they did* when in a similar situation, *and again do what they did* when in a similar situation, and so on. In short, instincts do not have their origin in *habits.* Instincts have their genesis in movement, in primal animation; they start kinetically. They have their origin in responsivity, in the fact that creatures are *responsive* and in the fact that their responses, however accidentally they might arise, do not take place in a vacuum and are certainly not proprioceptively blind, but make sense or are dangerous, or unproductive, or have any number of other possible consequences for the creatures themselves. What starts out in movement, in exploration or by chance, is kinetically taken up, repeated, even honed and fine-tuned in dynamic, spatio-temporal ways; or it is kinetically abandoned and a different kinetic exploration and strategy are tried. Instincts develop on the basis of movement and ways of moving. They are fundamentally forms of thinking in movement, and it is because they are fundamentally forms of thinking in movement that they are malleable.

If responsivity is a near universal characteristic of life, if perception is a preparation to respond, if the fundamental nature of organisms is not to be neural repositories of information, much less information-processing machines, but to be kinetically alive to, and in, their respective worlds, then it is readily understandable why thinking in movement is a built-in disposition of animate forms. The not uncommon tendency to carve at certain self-serving human joints and thereby make honorific and pejorative distinctions on the order of "this one thinks," "this one does not," generates and reinforces an arrogantly biased metaphysics and epistemology. A broader sense of the animate is not only needed but proper in that that broader sense accommodates facts of life as enumerated in any biology text: mealworms congregate, cats pounce; creatures move toward and away from things in their environment. Animation is a primary fact of life — and thinking itself, as noted earlier, is itself a form of animation: moving forward, backward, quickly, slowly, narrowly, broadly, lightly, ponderously, it itself is kinetic.

5.   Summation

A common kinetic thematic suffuses improvisational dance, human developmental life, and the lives of animate forms. In each case, a non-separation of thinking and doing is evident; so also is a non-separation of sensing and moving. In each case, qualities and presences are absorbed by a mindful body in the process of moving and thinking in movement; a dynamically changing spatio-temporal world emerges. A finer dimension of this common thematic is furthermore evident. Through the dynamics their movements explore and articulate, dancers bring forth a particular — though not necessarily singular — qualitative world. *This evening's dance* may be gay and buoyant, for example, playful in its energies, zany in its interactions, and so on; or it may be intense and brooding, a world in which movements appear portentous and ominous, where relationships appear on edge and threatened; or it may be erratic in its swings from one dynamic contour to another, the whole united by a kinetic logic having its own unspoken integrity. Just so in the living world of animate forms, where playfulness, wariness, fitfulness, and so on, are all kinetic possibilities. Moving organisms indeed create kinetic melodies — to borrow neurologist Alexandr Luria's evocative phrase (1973:179) — by the very fact of their aliveness. These melodies are created because qualia are inherent in movement, inherent in the dynamically moving bodies of animate forms. They are the foundational kinetic units, the cardinal structures of movement and of thinking in movement. A dynamically attuned body that knows the world and makes its way within it kinetically is thoughtfully attuned to the variable qualia of both its own movement and the movement of things in its surrounding world — to forceful, swift, slow, straight, swerving, flaccid, tense, sudden, up, down, and much more.

Caught up in an adult world, we easily lose sight of movement and of our fundamental capacity to think in movement. Any time we care to turn our attention to it, however, there it is.

Notes

* This chapter is a substantively expanded version of an article that first appeared in *The Journal of Aesthetics and Art Criticism* (Sheets-Johnstone 1981).

1.   Harrison spells out the difference I am drawing between improvisational and non-improvisational dance in terms of "a creator who is 'transcendental' to his creation and [a creator who is] ... imminant (*sic*) in the process of his creation's coming to be" (1978:34). I came across his book after having written the original *Journal of Aesthetics and Art Criticism* article, but found his mode of distinguishing between "thought in action" and "thought about action" — the focus of his second chapter — richly topical.

For a full phenomenological account of dance as a dynamic form-in-the-making, see Sheets-Johnstone 1966.

2.   See Runeson 1994 for an informative critique of computer-simulated point-light display experiments as against point-light display experiments of actual humans in action.

3.   Bull's theory is posturally, i.e. neuromuscularly, based. A certain preparatory motor attitude — what might be termed a certain corporeal readiness — is the requisite basis of a certain action or range of possible actions. Feelings "come into the picture" between the preparatory attitude and the action (1951:4). A "motor attitude" is thus "the initiator of feeling as well as action" (1951:5).

4.   An analogy might be made to silent films, the value of which could hardly be captured by the designation "pre-linguistic."

5. It is of interest to call attention to the fact that hunting behavior is not studied in laboratories and could hardly be studied in laboratories. Predator-prey interactions are not amenable to experimental designs. They are spontaneous, real-life interactions that can be captured in nothing less than real-life situations. Recording animal behaviors in these situations — who does what, under what circumstances, and so on — gives a sense of the intensity of the drama, but only indirectly gives a sense of the phenomenon of thinking in movement that necessarily informs it. Consider, for example, the fact that a predator chasing a fast-running prey animal must aim its charge ahead of where the prey animal is and that when the prey animal changes directions, it must adjust its own directional charge accordingly.

6. An egregious and lamentable error should be pointed out in Keeton's and Gould's text. In their introduction, they state that "To early 'mechanistic' philosophers like Aristotle and Descartes, life was wholly explicable in terms of the natural laws of chemistry and physics." A reading of *De Anima* should be required reading for all biologists, along with *The History of Animals*, *Parts of Animals*, *Movement of Animals*, *Progression of Animals*, and *Generation of Animals*, and also some excellent commentary texts, especially what is considered "the bible" with respect to Aristotle's biology: *Philosophical Issues in Aristotle's Biology*, edited by Allan Gotthelf and James G. Lennox.

Twenty-first century reflections on human nature: Foundational concepts and realities

CHAPTER 13

Animation

The fundamental, essential, and properly descriptive concept

1. Introduction

When we strip the lexical band-aid '*embodiment*' off the more than 350 year-old wound inflicted by the Cartesian split of mind and body, we find *animation*, the foundational dimension of the living. Everything living is animated. Flowers turn toward the sun; pill bugs curl into spheres; lambs rise on untried legs, finding their way into patterned coordinations. The phenomenon of *movement* testifies to animation as the foundational dimension of the living. Morphogenetical kinetic capacities testify as well to animation: cells divide in complex processes of mitosis and meiosis; seedlings mature; trees heal the cuttings humans make on them (Sinnott 1963). In short, self-regulated movement and growth testify in a different but equally fundamental way to animation. As Aristotle lucidly and succinctly observed 2500 years ago, an observation duly recognized epigraphically at the beginning of Chapter 2, Part II: "Nature is a principle of motion and change" (Aristotle 200b: 12).

We would do well to begin our investigations of life by acknowledging that principle, and in turn, acknowledge animation as the foundational ground of life itself. Animation encapsulates what is fundamental to life, the vibrant and spirited way living creatures come into the world and the vibrant and spirited way that is gone when they die; it engenders dynamics, the essence of life in all its varied and vital kinetic contours; it articulates in an exacting linguistic sense the living wholeness of animate forms and is thus properly descriptive of life itself. What is fundamental is that we are indeed *animate* forms of life, and as such, are necessarily and from the beginning subjects of a world, an *Umwelt* in von Uexküll's sense. The dynamics essential to our progressive sense-makings of ourselves and of the world are intrinsic to and inherent in our primal animation and in our being the particular animate forms we are. To ignore, neglect, or pass over animation is thus to ignore, neglect, or pass over the fundamental, essential, and properly descriptive phenomenon: the bedrock of our being and feeling alive. In what follows, we will take a critical and constructive path toward an illumination of these threefold dimensions of animation by examining a linguistic formulation in cognitive neuroscience — *enaction* — that, together with practices and habits in various domains of present-day science and philosophy, obfuscates them. We will do this by focusing attention on affectivity and the fundamental phenomenon of animation that is both its biological — that is, its evolutionary — and existential foundation.[1]

2. Basic realities of affectivity

Affectivity is a staple of life. In the most rudimentary sense, it is what motivates creatures to approach or avoid. In this sense, it is one aspect of what is biologically specified as a defining feature of life, namely, 'responsivity' (Curtis 1975), a feature affectively characterizable as interest or aversion, hence as movement toward or away from something in the environment (see also Schneirla 1959). As empirically and phenomenologically shown elsewhere, there is a *dynamic congruency* of affectivity and movement in the everyday lives of animate forms (Sheets-Johnstone 1999, 2006). That this biologically basic dynamic relationship goes largely unrecognized is odd. Humans are, after all, normally in proximity to other humans every day of their lives. They have feelings of comfort or discomfort, security or insecurity, solicitude or annoyance, disappointment or elation, and so on, in relation to them and normally move in ways coincident with the dynamics of their feelings. In the ordinary course of everyday human life, the affective and the kinetic are clearly dynamically congruent; emotion and movement coincide. If they did not normally coincide, there would be no possibility of *feigning* by kinetically *enacting* emotional dynamics. The word *enacting* is precisely correct in this instance, for it is a matter of putting something into a form of a specified kind, in this instance, a kinetic form, which means going through the motions of X, that is, putting a non-felt feeling into a performance, as in, for example, shaking hands with, and smiling at someone whom one actually detests. Grammatically, the word '*enact*', as the etymology of its prefix indicates, means "to bring [something] into a certain condition or state," precisely as in the word's common usage: 'to make into a law'.

However presently favored the term, it falsifies rather than aptly captures — much less entails recognition or understanding of — the fundamental, everyday, *wholly spontaneous and natural* qualitative affective-kinetic dynamics that commonly permeate our lives: neither the qualitative *affective* dynamics that ordinarily motivate and inform smiling and shaking hands, for example, nor the qualitative *kinetic* dynamics normally created in shaking hands and smiling. Though its aims as a corrective within cognitive science are surely laudable and its emphasis on dynamics and utilization of dynamic systems theory are surely laudable as well (Varela, Thompson, Rosch 1991; Thompson 2007), the denotational ties of *enaction* to "the performance or carrying out of an action" (Thompson 2007: 13) make the neologism conceptually amiss on two counts: it bypasses any inherent linkage to affect and it packages movement into a specified deed of some kind, reducing a kinesthetic/kinetic dynamics to no more than a duly labeled 'act' like 'walking', for example, or 'hammering'. It thus falls far short of doing justice to the spatio-temporal-energic qualitative dynamics of affect and movement and falls short equally of realizing their dynamically congruent relationship. The double lapse is readily exemplified in an 'enactive' rendition of emotion that begins by etymologically specifying the latter as "literally mean[ing] an outward movement" (ibid.: 364). In the critical discussion that follows, I single out the writings of philosopher Evan Thompson not only because his book *Mind and Life* gives the most authoritative, highly developed, and thorough presentation of enactive theory and "the enactive approach" but because Thompson originally began writing *Mind and Life* with Francisco Varela before Varela's untimely death. Thompson's work figures centrally for two further reasons: first, although Francisco Varela is customarily regarded the originator of the term 'enaction' and of an enactive approach to cognition, Thompson was one of the co-authors of the book in which the term and approach were originally spelled out (Varela, Thompson, Rosch 1991);[2] second, since Varela's death, Thompson has taken on his mantle, so to speak, having written articles by himself and with others on enaction as well on neurophenomenology (e.g. Hanna & Thompson 2003; the topic "neurophenomenology" was initiated by Varela: see Varela 1996, 1999c).

To begin with, etymologically, emotion does not mean "an outward movement." As the OED specifies, the first meaning of emotion (*e-motion*), now obsolete, had to do not with feelings but with migrations of people from one place to another. A now obsolete second meaning of emotion was aligned with a physical "stirring" or "agitation" in a worldly sense, a meaning that allowed a writer in 1758 to comment on "The waters continuing in the caverns … causing an emotion or earthquake." What the OED sets forth and defines as the figurative (since seventeenth century) meaning of emotion, including (since early nineteenth century) its psychological meaning, has to do generally with feelings: "Any agitation or stirrings of mind, feeling, passion," as in a writer's reference to "the emotions of humanity" (1660), and as in analytical psychological writings in which emotion is defined as "feeling or affection (e.g. of pleasure or pain, desire or aversion, surprise, hope, or fear, etc.) as distinguished from cognitional and volitional states of consciousness." To be noted is the fact that the prefix *e* derives from *a*, the original Old English meaning of which is defined as "implying motion onward or away from a position, hence *away*, *on*, *up*, *out*, and thus with verbs of motion implying *intensity*." To be noted specifically too is the fact that the prefix *e* in the word *emotion* is given simply as deriving from Latin and meaning "out."

The above various etymological usages strongly suggest that, as the word is commonly used and understood today, emotion arises *out of* or *from* motion, motion in the sense of felt dynamic stirrings, felt inner commotions — a bodily "earthquake" as it were, spanning a strikingly varied range of possible dynamics and thereby a strikingly varied range of possible magnitudes or intensities. The commotions, being thoroughly dynamic in nature, are thus quite inadequately described as "the welling up of an impulse within" (Thompson 2007: 363–64). Though Thompson goes on to point out the "close resemblance between the etymological sense of emotion — an impulse moving outward — and the etymological sense of intentionality — an arrow directed at a target, and by extension the mind's aiming outward or beyond itself toward the world," concluding that "[b]oth ideas connote directed movement" (364), he remains tethered to language and stops short of investigating emotions themselves and the dynamic congruency of emotions and movement. It is, in short, not enough to *connote* movement, whether ideationally or linguistically.[313] To begin with, *impulse* does not do justice to the dynamics of emotions, which do not just motivate movement. As indicated above, they *inform* movement every step, turn, gesture, clenching, or quivering of the way. Indeed, the affective quiverings, tensions, lightnesses, shudderings, pressures, constrictions, extensions, heavinesses, and so on, that one feels in a thoroughly corporeal sense in anger, anticipation, compassion, worry, and shame, for example, are ongoing dynamic affective happenings. Hence, whatever the dynamic stirrings and informings, they are qualitatively distinct, which means they have a formally recognizable bodily-felt character. A normal individual does not confuse his or her feelings of sadness with those of embarrassment or pride, for example, those of fascination with those of contempt, those of anxiety or annoyance with those of conviction or hostility. It is important to note explicitly in this context that although there are words for emotions, names that duly label them as those just mentioned, "the things themselves" are not *objects* like tables and chairs, and are indeed not *things* to begin with. On the contrary, 'the things themselves' — emotions — are dynamic, processual happenings. They are not *states* of being but precisely *moving* phenomena that are *movingly* experienced, not only in the sense of a dynamic congruency between affect and movement — real-life feelings of fear being dynamically congruent to real-life kinesthetic feelings of running away, real-life feelings of joy being dynamically congruent to real-life kinesthetic feelings of running toward — but in the sense of *emotions* themselves, which are not static entities, but phenomena that run their course, waxing and waning, exploding, attenuating, constricting, expanding, bubbling, reverberating, all in ways that can be intricately subtle and complex. In a word, *emotions move through the body at the same time that they move us to move.* Again, they do so in distinctive ways: fear moves the body and moves through the body in ways different from trust; delight moves the body and moves through the body in ways different from grief (Sheets-Johnstone 2006b; English translation of same in Sheets-Johnstone 2008, Chapter 7). In each instance, we are not simply "acting" or "behaving." We are caught up in the dynamics of the immediate life we are living, even as that immediate life might be focused or fixated on past or possible future happenings or on riveting aspects of our immediate situation. In sum, we are first and foremost animate beings who, in being animate, are alive to our animateness, which is to say that whatever affects us moves through us, permeating the whole of our being and moving us to move in ways dynamically congruent with the ongoing stirrings and commotions we feel. It might be noted that such understandings of our foundational animation anchor concepts such as *pre-reflective self-awareness* in the dynamic realities of kinesthesia and the affective/tactile-kinesthetic body.

The above clarifications rooted in both etymology and in actual experience show unequivocally that bona fide elucidations of emotion begin with the nature of emotion itself. In this respect, the studies of psychiatrist Nina Bull and of psychologist Joseph de Rivera are eminently instructive, the former shedding light on postural attitudes, the latter on movement attitudes, both of which, one might say, delimit emotions no less exactingly than a dictionary delimits the meaning of words. What Bull analyzes in terms of felt postural dynamics as reported by subjects hypnotized to experience a certain emotion, de Rivera analyzes in terms of the nature of the bodily movement manifest in different emotions, that is, the way in which "we experience ourselves ... as *being moved*" (de Rivera 1977:11). Postural attitudes constrain affective meaning in the sense of channeling it along certain lines, indeed, along the literally felt lines of the particular emotion itself. For example, of the experience of fear, one subject within Bull's experimental research states, "First my jaws tightened, and then my legs and feet ... my toes bunched up until it hurt"; another subject, being locked hypnotically to the feeling of joy and asked to experience depression, states, "I feel light — can't feel depression" (Bull 1951:59 and 85, respectively). De Rivera's analyses, which Hartvig Dahl describes as a "geometry of emotions" (Dahl 1977:4), underscore the distinctive spatial motifs of the moving body in different emotions, most essentially their extensional or contractive nature. (For a full discussion of both Bull's and de Rivera's analyses, see Sheets-Johnstone 1999).

Rather than attending to the emotionally caught up *corps engagé* as in the studies above, Thompson's enactive analysis of emotion is skewed by being set exclusively within the framework of protentions, relying thus heavily on the notion of a movement disposition — "the welling up of an impulse," a "readiness to action" (Thompson 2007:361, 363–364, respectively). While that perspective approximates to the fact that emotions move us to move, it does not, as indicated above, elucidate the fact that emotions are themselves dynamic, moving through us in subtle and complex ways. Thus, to elucidate the nature of emotions through the example of 'averting the eyes' (ibid.: 376–377; see the original 'generic' use of the example in Varela & Depraz 2005) is to skip over the phenomenon itself, that is, the nature of emotions themselves, relying instead on a quasi-Wittgensteinian 'this is what we do' when we are embarrassed, distressed, fearful, or ashamed. Methodologically, it is to start *behaviorally*, presumably with the intent of working backward. Each of the fore-named emotions, however, that is potentially connected with "averting the eyes" courses through the body in a distinctive way. In Aristotelian terms, embarrassment is what it is and is not another "thing"; so also is distress, fear, and shame. Thompson uses the example of 'averting the eyes' in a quasi-Wittgensteinian manner in large measure because, while strongly engaged by phenomenological writings and with a strong desire to make good the promise of a "complementary and mutually informing" 'neurophenomenology' (Thompson 2007: 14), his predilections and sympathies lie far closer to a brain-oriented "primordial dynamism" than to a veritable phenomenological, i.e. *experiential*, "primordial dynamism." (ibid.: 360–381). These predilections and sympathies are straightforwardly apparent in his statement that "Emotion is embodied in the closed dynamics of the sensorimotor loop, orchestrated endogenously by processes up and down the neuraxis, especially the limbic system," and in his follow-up statement that "The enactive approach can thus provide a theoretically significant, superordinate concept of emotion and can ground that concept in large-scale dynamic properties of brain organization" (ibid.: 365). When he furthermore states, "The guiding question for an enactive approach to emotion is well put by [neurobiologist Walter] Freeman: 'How do intentional behaviors, all of which are emotive, whether or not they are conscious, emerge through self-organization of neural activity in even the most primitive brains?'" (ibid.), he leaves no doubt that his "neurophenomenological approach to the structure of experience" (ibid.: 381) falls short of doing justice to the lived-through dynamic realities of emotional experience.

3. Primal animation

What is missing in Thompson's account of "enactive emotion" (ibid.: 362–366) is the basic reality of animation that defines the organism as a whole and that, in defining *the whole organism*, is the conceptual portal to understanding the dynamics of experience from top to bottom and bottom to top, i.e. in the full sense of animate being. Indeed, the "primordial dynamism" that Thompson takes as the defining nature of "emotion and valence" (ibid.: 360–381) rests on animation. Its anchorage in animation is clearly evident in his emphasis on "the feeling of being alive" — on "affective core consciousness or sentience" (ibid.: 354–355). It is of interest to note that his use of the term "primordial dynamism" appears to have been taken — no citation is given — from Czech philosopher Jan Patočka, whose original use of the term is precisely to designate the source of our experienced feelings of aliveness, the ground floor of our existence as it were. Patočka states, "Our primary experience of ourselves is ... an experience of the primordial dynamism that manifests itself in our awareness of our existence as a moving, active being" (Patočka 1998 [1968–1969]: 40). Tethering "primordial dynamism" to our sense of aliveness in experienced movement, Patočka in fact proceeds — though giving no reference to Husserl — to reiterate Husserl's classic linkage between sensing and moving, that is, between perception and the kinestheses (Husserl 1970, 1989). He states (Patočka 1998 [1968–1969]: 40),

This dynamism appears as distinctively linked to that which orients us in our movements, that is, to the phenomena appearing in our sensory fields, and that in such a way that our energy is always focused on something, on what we are doing. I listen and I am stretched out in the direction of the lecturer. When I am writing, the energy of my sensory fields and the posture of my movements focus on what I am doing; that becomes the center.

Oddly enough, in spite of their focal attention on movement, sentience, and on "the feeling of being alive," we find a virtual absence of *kinesthesia* in both Patočka's and Thompson's accounts of primordial dynamism. The virtual absence warrants attention: it signals precisely an *in*attention to the dynamics of experienced feelings and a corresponding *in*attention to the fundamental dynamic congruency of affect and movement that informs our lives. *Primal animation* (see this text, Chapters 3, 5, 12), a descriptive term coined and used prior to the discovery of "primordial dynamism" in the writings of Patočka and Thompson, concretely links our sense of aliveness to movement, *to kinesthesia and to our tactile-kinesthetic bodies*. The descriptive term resonates along the lines of "primordial dynamism" but with the following significant differences: unlike Patočka's "primordial dynamism," which, "as we experience it, characterizes the spatiality of our physical presence" (Patočka 1998 [1968–1969]: 41), primal animation derives most fundamentally from movement and is thus not simply a spatial but a spatio-temporal-energic phenomenon; analogously, unlike Thompson's "primordial dynamism," which is limned exclusively as a temporal phenomenon, notably, a matter of temporal protentions epitomized in emotion as a "readiness to action" (Thompson 2007: 361), primal animation is a spatio-temporal-energic whole, a kinetic liveliness originally in the service of learning our bodies and learning to move ourselves in face of a surrounding world (see this text Chapter 5). That kinetic liveliness is consistently qualified affectively: infants are curious, apprehensive, enchanted, or absorbed, for example. Indeed, while "movement forms the I that moves before the I that moves forms movement" (this text Chapter 3: 119; Chapter 5: 229), infant movement is continuously and unfailingly informed affectively. That original kinetic-affective liveliness in face of a surrounding world endures developmentally and is differentially articulated throughout our lives. Most significantly, in epitomizing our sense of aliveness, primal animation and its ongoing dynamic realities do not remain unspecified in an experientially unanchored "sentience" or "feeling of being alive." On the contrary, they describe the all-inclusive and spontaneously arising affective, tactile/kinesthetic, sense-making, subject/world nature of our being, precisely as encapsulated in the fact that we come into the world moving; we are not stillborn (Chapter 3: 117). That we come into the world moving means we are cognitively attuned in a sense making manner discovering ourselves and our surrounding world in and through our affective/tactile-kinesthetic bodies from the very beginning. Affectivity is indeed quintessentially evidenced in our earliest cries and in our earliest and ongoing feelings of wonder, wonder at the world and at our own bodily being. Correlatively, our affective/tactile-kinesthetic bodies are the bedrock of our developing 'I cans' in face of the world such that we come to know it.

Primal animation brings with it the most primitive form of consciousness, which is consciousness of one's own movement, hence "kinesthetic consciousness." This form of consciousness develops in the womb. Indeed, tactility and kinesthesia are neurologically the primary senses to develop. In a broader sense, this consciousness is a "kinetic consciousness." It includes a developing consciousness of one's movement as a three-dimensional happening "in space" and is intimately tied to a basic responsivity to movement in one's surrounding world, most importantly to a distinction between the animate and the inanimate (Spitz 1983). Primal animation thus clearly accords with Husserl's classic insight into the foundational complementarity of perception and movement. It straightaway validates the fact that, as pointed out at the very beginning of Chapter 3 (113), "[n]ot only is our own perception of the world everywhere and always animated, but our movement is everywhere and always kinesthetically informed."[4] Primal animation is furthermore the conceptual corollary of what Scott Kelso fittingly describes as "intrinsic dynamics," dynamics that define "coordination tendencies," including both subtending older patterns or habits and spontaneously arising patterns that arise in the formation of a new skill (Kelso 1995: 162–164). These tendencies and the patterns themselves are intrinsic in the double sense of defining coordination dynamics at the level of both brain and behavior. They accord with Aristotle's insight that nature is a principle of motion and change and with phenomenological groundings of "sentience" and "the feeling of being alive" in the phenomenon of animation.

The phenomenological groundings are of particular significance for an enactive cognitive science in which the questions of *sentience* and of *feeling alive* loom large (Thompson 2007: 229, 231). Indeed, though "*sentience*, the feeling of being alive and exercising effort in movement" (ibid.: 161) are aligned with consciousness by some philosophers and neuroscientists — Thompson cites Maine de Biran, Antonio Damasio, Jaak Panksepp, and Hans Jonas in particular — Thompson rejects the alignment on the grounds that "this immanent purposiveness does not entail consciousness" (ibid.: 162). Thus, he states that while "one might describe consciousness in the sense of sentience as a kind of primitive self-aware liveliness or *animation of the body*" (ibid.: 161; italics added), the description is not viable.

4.   Enactive resistances and their biological refutations

The reasons Thompson specifies for disavowing the entailment and rejecting the description are of moment to consider, especially since he himself states that the initial reason is "controversial" (ibid.: 162). The reasons run as follows: First, the description does not coincide with autopoietic theory and autopoietic selfhood and hence is not applicable to autopoietic organisms like bacteria: such "minimal cellular" organisms lack "intentional access" to their "sense-making" (ibid.). Second, Thompson states that "it seems unlikely that minimal autopoietic selfhood" would have a "pre-reflective self-awareness" since the latter "would seem to require" a nervous system (ibid.). Finally, Thompson reasons that consciousness must be "situate[d]" with respect to an unconscious, and were consciousness to obtain "down to the cellular level," such a situatedness would be "difficult, perhaps impossible" (ibid.).

Questions may surely be raised with respect to these interrelated reasons. We may ask with respect to living organisms such as bacteria, for example, why a minimal intentionality, i.e. minimal forms of meaning, would not coincide with "minimal cellular selfhood"? In particular, why would bacteria, in changing direction, not be propelled by an if/then intentionality, meaning that, when they change direction, they expect to get away from whatever they are finding noxious, and correlatively, by setting out in a different direction, they are searching for a better environment? In changing direction, bacteria are "going beyond" in a Husserlian phenomenological sense of meaning: their 'turning away from' is both aversive and expectant; their 'starting out anew' is both explorative and anticipant. Their changes in direction are, in short, motivated. In truth, they are motivated in just the sense that Thompson claims "protention is motivated" (ibid.: 361). In effect, why would self-moving forms of life, i.e. non-sessile creatures, *not* have "intentional access" to their "sense-makings"?

A related question naturally arises regarding the thesis that pre-reflective self-awareness requires a nervous system, a thesis bolstered by Thompson's earlier claim set forth in the context of specifying "the enactive approach" in cognitive science, namely, that "[t]he nervous system ... creates meaning" (ibid.: 13). The idea that meaning is *created* by the nervous system is rather odd. Oddness aside, we may surely affirm that intact living subjects, not nervous systems, create meaning, and in this context point out that a bacterium is a living subject. It initiates a change in direction because it finds the current environment unsuitable or "noxious" (Keeton & Gould 1986: 452). It is thus not simply counterintuitive but self-contradictory to say that a bacterium is unaware of itself turning away and making a directional change since the turning and change come about through its own self-movement. The lack of a nervous system does not therefore preclude meaning, neither in the sense of "creating" meaning nor in the sense of meaningful movement. Darwin's classic statement concerning the mental capacities of ants is relevant in this context (Darwin 1981 [1871]: 145):

> "It is certain that there may be extraordinary mental activity with an extremely small absolute mass of nervous matter: thus the wonderfully diversified instincts,

mental powers, and affections of ants are generally known, yet their cerebral ganglia are not so large as the quarter of a small pin's head. Under this latter point of view, the brain of an ant is one of the most marvellous atoms of matter in the world, perhaps more marvellous than the brain of man."

Evolutionary forms of life are clearly living subjects of particular *Umwelts*, and as such create *synergies of meaningful movement*, synergies that assure their survival. (For more on synergies of meaningful movement, see Sheets-Johnstone 2011a).

Finally, there is an all-or-none aspect to Thompson's denying a "cellular" level of consciousness. The all-or-none aspect has to do with evolutionary continuities, the disavowal of which seems to lie in a conflation of 'cellular' in the sense of cells within an organism, including the brain cells of humans, with cellular in the sense of prokaryotic forms of life. The former are not equivalent to the latter. Bacteria, in other words, are not equivalent to muscle cells, for example, or nerve cells. As shown at some length in Chapter 2, Part I, bacteria — "[t]he oldest and most abundant group of organisms in the world" (Curtis 1975: 290) — are sensitive to surface events and to themselves with respect to those events: they can sense both the environment and themselves with respect to the environment. Biologists have in fact empirically demonstrated that the capacity of bacteria to recognize the difference in concentration of a chemical rests on their memory of an immediately past concentration in relation to an immediately present concentration (Curtis & Barnes 1989: 131; Curtis 1975: 297). Such recognition and memory lend further credence to the thesis that, as discussed in Chapter 2, Part I, *surface recognition sensitivity* in the service of movement was the forerunner of proprioception in the form of *external* organs subserving movement — external organs such as the slit sensilla of spiders and the campaniform sensilla of insects — and that proprioception was the forerunner of kinesthesia, i.e. of *internal* organs subserving movement. Of import in this context are not only Sperry's observations that the brain is an organ of and for coordinated movement, but that the primary function of consciousness or subjective experience is *coordinated movement* (see Chapter 10 and Kelso 1995). The significance of self-movement and the consciousness of self-movement through the entire evolutionary spectrum of self-moving forms of life can hardly be ignored. In short, "*animation of the body*" is of singular moment to sentience, feeling alive, and consciousness, however much it conflicts with Thompson's notion of "immanent purposiveness."

5.   Further reflections on animation

The empirical realities of animation are of moment in both an individual and evolutionary sense, and this because the realities naturally engender *life, time, and affectivity as well as movement*. These four dimensions are not just intimately linked but intermeshed, interwoven one with the other such that any one is not present without the others.[5] The *concept* of animation, a concept that derives from the realities of animation, is thus understandably a corrective to theoretical-linguistic band-aids, not just the band-aid of "enactive," as in the awkward notions of "enactive emotion" and "enactive evolution" (Thompson 2007: 362–366 and 215–218, respectively), and the band-aid of "embodiment," but the band-aid of "embedding" in order that a subject, notably a human, is connected to a "world." A dichotomy of subject and world is either blatant or latent in all these band-aids and is in all instances ironic. The irony is justly prominenced when the dichotomy is put in evolutionary perspective. Plants and Fungi, major evolutionary groups in their own right, are unquestioningly tied to their environments: they suffer no subject-world dichotomization at the hands of scientists or philosophers, though it is surely pertinent to note that very few forms in either group move in the sense of self-movement (Curtis 1975: 288). Yet bacteria and Protists, self-moving forms of life, the latter being a major evolutionary group comprising paramecia and amoeba, for example, do not suffer the dichotomization either. Nonhuman animals are also exempt. Humans alone, notably modern, present-day ones, languish, ensnared in a subject/world divide. It is no wonder that cognitive scientists and philosophers strive to alleviate their suffering by eradicating the dichotomy. In truth, the problem is one of their own making, a fabrication of thought, making necessary, in today's cognitive science language, an "embedding" of "the subject" in "the world," or in the language of some existentialist philosophers, a "chiasm" or intertwining of subject and world (Merleau-Ponty 1968). Animation is a corrective to such "embeddings" and "chiasmatic" solutions: it is the *mot juste* that properly describes living creatures as living and thus necessarily, that is, *naturally*, in the full sense of *nature*, links them inseparably to and within a spatio-temporal world distinctive to their ways of living, i.e. to an *Umwelt* (von Uexküll 1928, 1957).[6]

It bears notice too that animation is of distinctive moment with respect to what is commonly termed "background consciousness." Any form of life that moves itself — any *animate form* — knows itself to be moving not because there is a *self* in the verbal locution but because there is a kinetic consciousness of some kind, *a consciousness subserving movement*, hence not out of grammatical necessity, but out of biological necessity. Thus if "homeodynamic regulation of the body" is an indication of "background consciousness" (Thompson 2007: 354), then surely the motility of bacteria qualifies as "background consciousness," and this in spite of the fact that background consciousness is aligned with "dynamic *neural* activity" (ibid.: 355; italics added). "Background consciousness" is indeed a perplexing locution, a linguistic camouflage of something needing explicit elucidation by way of empirical facts of life. Thompson affirms that "background consciousness depends crucially on brainstem structures and processes," an affirmation close to Panksepp's theory of "core emotional affects" (Panksepp 2005), but an affirmation too entailing recognition of the "wide connectivity" of the cerebellum that includes but is not restricted to its functions in posture and volitional movement (Schmahmann 2000:ix). Expanding on his affirmation, Thompson states that background consciousness

> "is inextricably tied to the homeodynamic regulation of the body and includes a primary affective awareness or core consciousness of one's bodily selfhood. Background consciousness in this fundamental sense is none other than sentience, the feeling of being alive, the affective backdrop of every conscious state. Sentience — or primal consciousness or core consciousness — is evidently not organized according to sensory modality, but rather according to the regulatory, emotional, and affective processes that make up the organism's basic feeling of self. For this reason, the search for content NCCs [neural correlates of consciousness] in a particular sensory modality such as vision runs the risk of missing the biologically and phenomenologically … fundamental phenomenon of sentience, whose affective character and ipseity (nonreflective self-awareness) underlie and pervade all sensory experience" (Thompson 2007:354–355).

We are clearly revisiting the looming questions of sentience and feeling alive compounded by the question of a "non-reflective self-awareness," questions capsulated perhaps in the question: Just what *is* the "affective character" and the "non-reflective self awareness" of sentience? Moreover if *sentience* "is evidently not organized according to sensory modality," but "underlie[s] and pervade[s] all sensory experience," is the word not simply a twenty-first century lexical remake of the nineteenth century word "'coenesthesia'? These questions cannot be properly answered in a Nagelian-inflected 'what is it like' language (Nagel 1974; see below for further discussion and examples). They require a phenomenologically grounded *experiential* accounting. In effect, the affective/tactile-kinesthetic body, the *felt* body, can hardly be ignored since it is precisely the experiential foundation of "the fundamental phenomenon of sentience," "the feeling of being alive," and hence definitive of "primal" or "core" consciousness." In turn, and contrary to Thompson, *all* sensory modalities cannot be excluded in an elucidation of sentience, "primal," "core," or "background" consciousness: kinesthesia and proprioception are foundational from the beginning of life onward.

Infant psychiatrist and clinical psychologist Daniel Stern's account of core consciousness and of an emergent self are of prime importance in this regard (Stern 1985, 1990). They open us to our own ontogenetic history and wean us away from an adultist as well as purely theoretical neurology by providing substantive empirical grounds for core consciousness and sentience. As spelled out in detail in Chapter 5, they do so in real-life terms, that is, in terms of the dynamics of the felt affective/ tactile-kinesthetic body. Of further importance in this regard, however, is Thompson's keen and just emphasis on the crucial role of "midbrain and brainstem structures" to "affective core consciousness or sentience." His statement that "virtually the entire neuraxis seems essential for consciousness in the widest sense of the term" (Thompson 2007: 355) coincides with recent re-estimations of the cerebellum, for example. Indeed, recent brain research shows that the cerebral cortex is not up there alone with respect to cognitive functions, but is part of a sizable and integral neurological system that is "embedded" *in toto* in living organisms — *animate* organisms.

6.   Animation and current scientific research on *the brain*

Two aspects of animation are of particular significance with respect to recent brain research, aspects that augur a paradigm shift in current studies of *the brain* and consciousness. The first of these concerns empirical research highlighting the functional value of anatomically lower regions of the brain, lower in the sense not only of being spatially lower than the cortex but of being consistently judged of no relation to the (higher) faculty of cognition. Research studies of Swedish neuroscientist Bjorn Merker show that a "primary consciousness" obtains in young children who either before or after birth have suffered medical problems leaving them without a cortex (Merker 2007). As succinctly stated in a science journal, studies of these children show that a "[b]asic awareness of one's internal and external world depends on the brain stem, the often-overlooked cylinder of tissue situated between the spinal cord and the cortex" (Bower 2007: 170). The second concerns a growing awareness that current experimental research on *the brain* ignores the "intrinsic activity" of the brain, activity in the form of energy consumption existing apart from any immediate environmental stimulation, hence what neuroscientist Marcus Raichle terms the brain's "dark energy" (Raichle 2006). Indeed, brain responses to stimuli measured through functional magnetic resonance imaging (fMRI) utilize a proportionally small energy output, perhaps "as little as 0.5–1.0% of the total energy budget" (ibid.: 1249). The surprisingly unrecognized tie-in of "intrinsic activity" with Kelso's foundational investigations and analyses of "intrinsic dynamics" aside, the favored suggestion put forth is that "the brain's enormous intrinsic functional activity" has to do with "predictions about the future," i.e. that its "enormous" activity is not simply a matter of balancing excitatory and inhibitory neural activity, but of being in the service of the future — what rightly and more precisely might be called *temporal and cognitive wakefulness*. It is notable that Raichle ends his report on the "dark energy" of the brain by quoting William James. He states, "William James presciently suggested in 1890 that 'Enough has now been said to prove the general law of perception, which is this, that *whilst part of what we perceive comes through our senses from the object before us, another part* (and it may be the larger part) *always comes ... out of our own head*'" (ibid.: 1250; James 1950, vol. II: 103). Raichle concludes that "[t]he brain's energy consumption tells us that the brain is never at

rest" and that "[t]he challenge of neuroscience is to understand the functions associated with this energy consumption" (ibid.). In phenomenological terms, the larger
part of the brain's energy consumption would be tied precisely to being temporally
and cognitively awake, which means (among other things) having retentions as well as
protentions in both Husserl's sense of inner time consciousness making possible the
constitution of objects (Husserl 1966) and the experiential sense of recollections and
anticipations making possible a cognitively meaningful global present.

Each recent piece of research confirms the need to look at the foundational phenomenon of animation and to wean ourselves away not only from *the brain* as if it were
the oracle at Delphi, but away from a separation of brain from body as if the morphology of nature categorically and axiologically divided us into an elevated top and an
inelegant bottom, away too, we might note, from a categorical separation of faculties
such that one has virtually to plead the case for a non-separation of cognition and
emotion (Thompson 2007: 371), and finally, away too from a separation of a philosophy of the organism from a philosophy of mind as if one could sever nature, creating
a division between living and sentience and hence between living and sense-making
(ibid.: 236–237; see also Sheets-Johnstone 2008, Chapters V and VIII). Indeed, so long
as one is wedded to the notion that the human mind–body or "body–body problem"
(Hanna & Thompson 2003; Thompson 2007; see also this text Chapter 14) will be
solved when we can scientifically determine that "there is something it is like to be that
body," i.e. that body "whose organizational dynamic processes can become constitutive of a subjective point of view" (Thompson 2007: 237; see also Zahavi 1999, 2000,
2005), one will remain closed to the dynamic realities of animation that, as indicated
earlier, constitute the all-inclusive and spontaneously arising affective, tactile-kinesthetic, sense-making, subject/world nature of human life. It is not *like* something to
feel curious or joyful; it is not *like* something to hop, skip, and jump or run one's hand
over velvet; it is not *like* something to doubt or to agree; it is not *like* something to hear
the wind or see a tree. Each experience is what it is. The challenge is not to determine
scientifically "what it is like to be that body." The challenge is to language experience,
which, to begin with, quintessentially requires phenomenological attention to experience and a concomitant recognition of the fact that language is not experience.

7.   Animate organisms, affectivity, and the challenge of languaging experience

That we are first and foremost *animate* organisms is a truth Husserl consistently recognized. The truth merits highlighting if not accentuating. In his lifelong studies of
sense-making — of constitution, be-souling, meaning-bestowing, sedimentations,
horizons, protentions, retentions, and more — Husserl wrote not about *active* — or
enactive — organisms; he wrote not about *embodied* organisms; he wrote not about

embedded organisms; he wrote throughout about *animate organisms.*[7] Animation is the ground floor of our being alive in all its affective, perceptual, cognitional, and imaginative guises, stages, practices, and surrounding worlds. In other words, animation grounds the full range of those intricate and varying dynamics that constitute and span the multiple dimensions of our livingness. Moreover it bears emphasizing that animate organisms are subjects of a world. Indeed, animate organisms, being subjects, are never without a surrounding world. Husserl makes this point sharply in the context of contrasting the natural and humanistic sciences. In the latter sciences, scientists are oriented

> "toward men and animals not as bodies to be investigated in the attitude oriented toward nature ['nature' as in physics, for example, or chemistry] but as men (or animals) who have their bodies as living bodies, who have their personal surrounding world, oriented around their living bodies as the near-far world and, at the same time, in the manners of appearing of right-left, up-down — all these manners of appearing standing in a successive relation of dependence to subjective manners of 'I move my living body' in a system of kinestheses which can be realized even voluntarily. The thematics of the human being includes what is valid for him as surrounding world, what is valid for him within this surrounding world, both his individual and also the communal surrounding world; the 'how' of the appearance of this surrounding world which can be grasped reflectively, not only for him but also for the community; how the manners of appearance belonging to the communicating individuals correspond to one another; how each individual gives his being-human a position in the space of the surrounding world as the zero-point object of the oriented surrounding world in experiential apperception..." (Husserl 1970: 331–332).

In short, Husserl is at pains to underscore the fact that living bodies — animate organisms — are not entities in a vacuum but are kinetically, affectively, thematically — *experientially* — anchored to and engaged in meaningful ways in a surrounding world, i.e. engaged in *synergies of meaningful movement* that support their survival. The importance of these meaningful ways can be highlighted by citing the inadequacy of treating emotions under the rubric of "coping behavior," and by showing the corollary needs to address the living dynamics of affectivity and to take seriously the challenge of languaging experience.[8]

That meaningful ways of moving are motivated in the sense of finding something noxious, for example, and moving away from it can hardly be denied: life-enhancing capacities are part and parcel of animate life. Synergies of meaningful movement are affectively driven. It is thus puzzling that the dynamics of affective experience remain virtually unattended in the humanistic sciences. If the living dynamics of affectivity are sidelined in the pursuit of a cognitive science of *the brain*, however, they are surely unthinkingly but no less emphatically marginalized when emotion is parsed as it were and treated under the aegis of "coping" behavior

(Varela 1999a, 1999c; Varela & Depraz 2005; Thompson 2007). In such circumstances, *coping* is taken as the basic landscape on which emotion "occurs," ostensibly because, as Varela originally described it, coping defines a break in transparency, that is, a break in our "unreflected absorption" in the world as we go about our everyday business — as we go about "hammering," for instance, as in Heidegger's classic example (Heidegger 1962: 98), the example taken up by Varela. Varela avers that "This standard Heideggerian vignette can be extended to all embodied actions, that is, actions in a fluid context where there is always a mixture of immediate coping and concurrent secondary activities of language and mental life" (Varela 1999c: 299). Whatever might be meant by "embodied actions" — the idea of disembodied ones is difficult to imagine — coping is clearly attributed to all human actions "in a fluid context," which means along with hammering not only reaching, sitting, pushing, throwing, walking, greeting, and so on, all of which take place in a fluid context, but gasping, moaning, even whistling: all are "embodied actions." Varela goes on to affirm that

> "[t]he loss of transparency is never distant from a dispositional affective tone …
> and that different degrees of breakdown in transparency and the multiple
> manners in which it happens opens a panoply of affective tonalities: fear, jealousy,
> anger, anxiety, self-assurance, and so on. Accordingly, the word 'emotion' is used
> here in its specific sense: the *tonality of the affect that accompanies a shift in
> transparency*. Affect, on the other hand, is a broader dispositional orientation
> which will precondition the emotional tone that may appear (ibid.: 299–300;
> italics in original).

The critical point at issue here is not the distinction Varela draws between emotion and affect, but what he claims to be "the specific sense" of the word 'emotion', namely, an affective tonality accompanying "a shift in transparency" — in Heideggerian terms, accompanying a "breakdown" — the shift or breakdown resulting in the need to "cope." An emotion in this sense is devoid of its inherent qualitative dynamics. Elation has its own affectively-felt dynamic contours; so also do disappointment, pride, delight, jealousy, and grief. None is simply a tonal accompaniment in a pragmatics of "embodied actions" in response to vicissitudes of life. "Coping" indeed moves the dynamic realities of emotion to an entirely different plane, distilling them into an ancillary aura hovering over thoughts of what to do about a shift or breakdown, as when "the hammer slips and lands on the finger. … [The] breakdown brings the transparent equipment into view, and a new set of action-assessments begins" (ibid.: 299). When Thompson "explore[s]" the link between emotion and the protentional aspects of temporality, he moves away from a recognition of the inherently distinctive qualitative dynamics of emotion in just this way. Focusing on emotion in terms of "an action tendency or readiness for action" and "skillful coping" (Thompson 2007: 361, 374–375), he follows Varela's dual leads: on the one hand, "Coping is a readiness or dispositional tendency for action in a larger field, an *ontological readiness*, that is, an expectation as to the way the world will show up" (Varela 1999a: 132); on the other hand, "The loss of fluidity in coping is never distant from a dispositional affective tone" (ibid.).

A further equally basic and critical point is that "transparency acquisition" is taken for granted; it is nowhere recognized as the animate engagement with the world that it is, an animate engagement that has a particular affective-kinetic dynamic. In effect, the very attainment of 'transparency' — of *familiarity* — is nowhere accounted for. It obviously rests on animation, on a corporeal-kinetic engagement with the world such that *learning* takes place to begin with, the learning that grounds 'transparency'. The basic question that needs to be asked is: How is it that 'doings' become familiar? The answer is clearly rooted in dynamics, in the qualitative tactile-kinesthetically felt kinetic dynamics of hammering, of brushing one's teeth, of sweeping, of typing, of playing a Bach prelude, and so on. *Familiar dynamics* are woven into our bodies and are played out along the lines of our bodies; they are kinesthetic/kinetic melodies in both a neurological and experiential sense (Luria 1966, 1973). A *melody* to begin with is a *qualitative* phenomenon, qualitative in virtue of its spatio-temporal-energic character. Varela's description of his "exaltation" at a concert is testimony to the fundamentally qualitative character of melody and its qualitatively experienced dynamics (Varela & Depraz 2005: 67–68). When melody is a matter of movement in Luria's sense — when the melody is being played *by oneself*, whether a matter of writing one's name, playing the flute, dancing, brushing one's teeth, ice skating, or running with the ball — creation and constitution of the *kinesthetic/kinetic* melody are phenomenologically concurrent (see this text Chapter 3: 132; see also Sheets-Johnstone 2006a: 371ff). The melody is kinesthetically felt and has an affective character generated by the very movement that produces it at the same time that the very movement that produces it is kinesthetically constituted as an ongoing qualitative affective-kinetic dynamic: it is heavy or light, moderately fast or solemnly slow, has swelling crescendos and fading diminuendos, and so on. It has what Stern identifes as "vitality affects" (Stern 1985). Indeed, its qualitative dynamic might perhaps at times be felt as rushed, attenuated, awkward, abrupt, delicate, jagged, fluent, and so on, all of such felt affective-kinetic qualities entering into the overall dynamic, the affective tonalities of the melody modulating the kinetic patterning throughout and the kinetic patterning modulating the affective tonalities throughout. It is surely clear then that *familiar* dynamics are not *embodied*; like emotion itself, *they are through and through already a bodily phenomenon.*

To be noted too is that 'averting the eyes', an example originally given by Varela and Depraz and taken up by Thompson in the context of a discussion of the neuro-dynamics of "skillful coping" (Varela & Depraz 2005; Thompson 2007), is actually an example at odds with the idea that emotion is "the welling up of an impulse within" since "coping behavior" is not "emotion experience." The experience of an emotion — whatever that emotion might be — is in other words something more and in fact something other than a "*precipitating event* or trigger" (Thompson 2007: 376), and indeed, something more and in fact something other than "an action tendency or readiness for action" (ibid.: 361). When Thompson writes that "[i]n the flow of skillful coping, we switch activities as a result of the attractions and repulsions we experience prereflectively," that "[s]uch emotional fluctuations act as control parameters that induce bifurcations from one present moment of consciousness to another," and that "[i]n this way, emotion plays a major role in the generation of the flow of consciousness, and this role can be phenomenologically discerned in the microtemporality of affect" (ibid.: 374–375), he attempts to situate emotions within a temporal dynamic. But as indicated, his account of emotion passes over emotion itself *as it is experienced*. When he gives as example seeing an angry face directed at him, he identifies a "complex *feeling tone* of startle, surprise, fear, and distress [that] strikes like an electric shock" (ibid.: 376–377). He passes over any description of the complex emotional dynamics themselves, complex dynamics that warrant examination, particularly with respect to how startle, surprise, fear, and distress are substantively different, yet substantively interrelated in the experience, seemingly finding that likening them all to "an electric shock" suffices.[9] Indeed, he goes on immediately instead to describe a "*motor embodiment*": "I turn my eyes and head to look away, and I quickly speed up my pace (*motor embodiment*)" (Thompson 2007: 377). "[M]*otor embodiment*" is a term originally used by Varela and Depraz in the context of their original discussion of 'averting the eyes', a discussion in which they furthermore speak of "embodied movement" in an attempt to specify the relationship between affect and movement (Varela & Depraz 2005: 68, 69, respectively). The latter locution, we should note, is an epistemological tautology of the first order. It highlights the basic challenge of languaging experience.

8.   Concluding thoughts on the importance of recognizing and languaging the qualitative dynamics of life

That the enactive method of beginning behaviorally and putatively working backward is flawed proves itself in the fact that a real-life engagement with emotion itself never surfaces. The term 'motor embodiment', a seemingly 'higher octane' additive to enaction, is an impediment to understandings of emotion and of its grounding in animation. A motorology will never approximate to recognition or understandings of emotion as a qualitatively dynamic phenomenon duly experienced as such, much less recognition or understandings of movement as a qualitatively dynamic phenomenon and duly experienced as such. By the same token, one cannot retain the term 'motor' — as in "sensorimotor subjectivity" (Thompson 2007), "sensorimotor profiles"[10] and the like — and profess to be giving a veridical account of experience, notably, a phenomenologically informed account. Motors have nothing to do with experience or with animate organisms. The qualitative affective-kinetic dynamics of grief that fold the body inward in spatially contorted and rhythmically writhing ways contrast strikingly with the qualitative affective-kinetic dynamics of joy, for example, that spatially expand the body outward and infuse it in a lightness and buoyancy that are spatially and temporally open-ended. A motorology furthermore precludes recognition of experienced corporeal-kinetic intentionalities that correlate with neurological corporeal-kinetic patternings (Sheets-Johnstone 2005). Such intentionalities are appropriately specified not in terms of sensorimotor processes but in terms of sensory-*kinetic* realities (Sheets-Johnstone 1990, 2005). In short, a motorology precludes arrival at a complementary dynamics of experiential and neuronal processes, processes admirably recognized and encapsulated in Scott Kelso's concept of *coordination dynamics* and in his and Engstrom's concept of complementarity Kelso 1995; Kelso & Engstrøm 2006; see also Sheets-Johnstone 2004). While the language of an enactionist's neurodynamics is 'down pat' in a vocabulary that includes dynamic system terms such as non-linear, attractors, bifurcations, parameters, and so on, the language of an affective-kinetic experiential dynamics is, in contrast, nowhere to be found much less even noticed as missing in neurophenomenological and enactive approaches. It is occluded in large measure precisely by a "*motor embodiment*" vocabulary. The latter all too easily and erroneously reduces movement to "the form of facial and posture changes, and differential action tendencies or global intentions for acting on the world" (Varela & Depraz 2005:68; Thompson 2007:376). Similarly, it all too easily and erroneously passes over kinesthesia, subsuming it — apparently — in "*autonomic ... muscle tone manifestations*" (Varela & Depraz 2005:68) or in "*interoceptive embodiment*, in the form of complex autonomic-physiological changes ... to [sic] muscle tone" (Thompson 2007:376). Clearly, kinesthesia and the broader term 'proprioception' cannot be transmogrified into forms of 'action' or 'embodiment', or into a motorology and in any way retain their essential phenomenological qualities, qualities foundational to animate life. Indeed, tactile-kinesthetic invariants ground our basic species-specific human repertoire of movement possibilities and undergird our affective social understandings.[11] A first step toward capturing these essential qualities and invariants is recognition of sensory-*kinetic* bodies, not sensorimotor ones.

In sum, actually lived through experiences of emotion and movement that are dynamic through and through and whose dynamics resonate in bodily-felt spatio-temporal-energic experiences warrant full and assiduous attention and languaging. To bring this language to the fore is correlatively to bring a descriptively refined acuity to "emotion experience" such that the dynamics of affect and movement and their congruency that is present from the beginning of human life (Stern 1985, 1990; Sheets-Johnstone 1999, this text Chapter 5) is manifestly evident. An enactivist approach, in passing over this history, is adultist. It takes familiarity for granted, the familiarity that allows 'transparency' — a term that might well be qualified as the adult luxury of an "unreflected absorption" in the world — to be realized. We are not born with a ready-made transparency either of ourselves or of the world: as shown at length and in depth in Chapter 5, we learn our bodies and learn to move ourselves. In the course of this learning we become familiar with ourselves as animate beings in a surrounding world. We explore ourselves and the world about us and build up habits on the basis of our growing familiarities. We develop a repertoire of 'I cans' (Husserl 1989). 'Transparency' is not only not a ready-made but is grounded through and through in experience, which itself is grounded in both our evolutionary heritage to explore and make sense of the world and in the actual explorations and discoveries we all made as infants. In a word, it is grounded through and through in animation. By failing to consider the basis of our developing familiarity with ourselves and the world, we fail to consider our inborn responsivity and those affective-kinetic coordination dynamics that are rooted in our being the animate organisms we are. Animate organisms — what I describe as animate forms[12] (e.g. Sheets-Johnstone 1994) — do not have to be embedded in the world. Neither do they have to be embodied in their actions, their emotions, their cognitions, and so on, and so forth.[13] The term embodiment and all its derivatives are in truth linguistic embalmers. Instead of conceptually enlivening what they qualify — emotions, actions, subjectivity, experience, metaphor, conversation, perception, and so on — they conceptually embalm it, dressing it up in fashionable garb, i.e. garb that makes it look as if what they qualify is a living phenomenon, part and parcel of something right here and now in the flesh. Such embalmings attempt to resurrect a once animate and animated body that over centuries of inquisition has been academically masticated into bits and pieces — a veritable corps morcelé. In contrast, animate beings come ready-made for living and for being described in their livingness without the need of lexical qualifiers or revivifications. They are already in and of the world because they are animate and animated: they are already living, and being already living, are already making sense of themselves and of the world in which they find themselves and of which they are a part.

Notes

1.   For more on an evolutionary-existential relationship, see Sheets-Johnstone 1986, 2008. For more on the relationship between biology and phenomenology, see Sheets-Johnstone 2007a.

2.   The word *enaction* as defined originally by Varela, Thompson, and Rosch reads: "We propose as a name the term *enactive* to emphasize the growing conviction that cognition is not the representation of a pregiven world by a pregiven mind but is rather the enactment of a world and a mind on the basis of a history of the variety of actions that being in the world performs" (1991:9).

3.   Thompson relies on language as well as on ideas. His reliance on language to connote rather than on experience to demonstrate is evident in his immediate follow-up remarks

on intentionality and its "dynamic striving" for "fulfillment." After citing Husserl's "drive-intentionality" and Patočka's term "'e-motion'" for such intentionality, Thompson states, "This term ['e-motion'] connotes movement." He goes on to explain that the "instigation" of movement is by "'impressional affectivity'" and the dynamic of "'constant attraction and repulsion,'" the latter two quotes being from Patočka's writings (Thompson 2007:364). Clearly, in this instance too, "connoting movement" is vastly different from describing movement in the flesh via phenomenological analysis and in turn discovering and elucidating the dynamic congruency obtaining between emotions and movement. Whether by way of lexical or ideational connotation, emotions and their relationship to movement remain abysmally underexamined in Thompson's account.

4.   Our awareness of our own movement, however, is not everywhere and always at the focal point of our attention. Indeed, infancy apart, kinesthesia is commonly marginalized in everyday human adult awarenesses. All the same, as noted at the conclusion of Chapter 12, "Any time we care to turn our attention to it, however, there it is." The importance of this observation will surface again in Chapter 14.

5.   It is notable that *self-movement* was present at the inauguration of life on this planet. Though a sizable, even temporally unimaginable evolutionary gap exists between Monera and Protists on the one hand and Animals on the other–bacteria originated 3 to 3 1/2 billion years ago, protists 1.2 to 1.4 billion years ago, while the first insects appeared only 400 + million years ago, and the first birds and mammals only 180 + million years ago (Curtis, 1975:307; Keeton & Gould 1986:152)–self-movement abides across the enormous span of time. In fact, along with chromosomes, i.e. the presence of DNA, motility is the only evolutionary character present, though at near nil representation in Fungi and Plants, across all major evolutionary groups (see Curtis 1975:288).

6.   See also Cassirer (1970). Cassirer explains (251) why there are *Umwelts:* "Every organism … has a world of its own because it has an experience of its own."

7.   Though Darwin did not write about animate organisms as such, he certainly wrote similarly of human and nonhuman animals, their mental powers and their emotions (Darwin 1981 [1871], 1965 [1872]), giving attention throughout to evolutionary continuities.

8.   The challenge at times begins with an understanding of experience itself. Surely it is intact living individuals who experience, not brains any more than livers or cochlea. While certainly contributing to understandings of the neural architecture of emotions, neuroscientist Jaak Panksepp, perhaps as a result of the present climate of apotheosizing *the brain*, contributes also to an already astonishing number of experiential attributions to *the brain*. He writes, for example, "In my view, emotional feelings represent only one category of affects that brains experience" (Panksepp 2005:162). Other examples from equally prominent neuroscientists were given in Chapter 2, Part II: 82–83.

9.   For an indication of how these are different emotions in a scientifically determined sense, see, for example, Landis & Hunt 1939 on the startle reflex and Darwin 1965 [1872] on surprise and fear. For a phenomenological exposition of how startle and fear are pathologically related in schizophrenia, see Sheets-Johnstone 2007b, target article with commentaries and response.

10.   Noë 2004. It is odd that Noë takes the concept of *profiles* and the *perspectival* aspect of objects from Husserl without making reference to Husserl. Obviously the words do not belong

exclusively to Husserl's phenomenology, but Noë's use of them — "*sensorimotor profiles*" and "*perspectival properties*" — clearly derives from Husserl's seminal notion of profiles and the perspectival experience of objects. Moreover Noë's ensuing emphasis on "*self-actuated* movement" as the key to everyday perception — "Only through *self*-movement can one *test* and so *learn* relevant patterns of sensorimotor dependence" (2004:13) — is a reiteration of what Husserl recognized and identified experientially as the "*unitary accomplishment* which arises essentially out of the playing together of two *correlatively related functions*" (Husserl 1989:63; italics in original), namely, the coordinate systems of sensing and moving: perception and kinesthesia.

It is odd too that in his book titled *Action in Perception* (2004), Noë mentions kinesthesis a total of three times, an under-acknowledgment that is at variance with his requirement that "A neuroscience of perceptual consciousness must be an enactive neuroscience — that is, a neuroscience of embodied activity, rather than a neuroscience of brain activity" (227). In fact, his enactive, or as he terms it, *sensorimotor* "approach to perception," in which human "possession of sensorimotor skill" figures centrally (33), belies the required 'embodied' rather than "brain" neuroscience. 'Sensorimotor skill' is conceptually and linguistically oxymoronic, a conceptual-linguistic marriage of two incompatible bed-fellows, the one motorological, the other experiential. We do not experience our skills motorically but kinesthetically, that is, we experience them and indeed learn them to begin with in hands-on, first-person experience, any and all references to something 'motor' being patently a reference to non-experienced brain areas.

Finally, although Noë affirms that "perceiving is a kind of skillful bodily activity" (p. 2), that we possess "a battery of sensorimotor skills" (87), that "seeing requires sensorimotor knowledge" (103), that things have "definite sensorimotor profile[s]" (117), and so on, he never brings to light the experiential realities of movement undergirding such activity, skills, knowledge and profiles, nor does he explain just how "*self*-movement" generates *skill* in the first place. On the contrary, he states simply that "You have an implicit practical mastery of ... patterns of change" with respect to your own movement (ibid.). Surely we should ask where our implicit practical mastery comes from and on what it depends. Just as surely we would find, if we examined the matter, that the answer involves familiarity, a familiarity constituted on the basis of having learned one's body and learned to move oneself. Just as surely too we would find that it involves what Husserl emphasizes many times over as the free play of kinestheses, "an essential part of the constitution of spatiality" (Husserl 1989:63) and what child psychologist Jerome Bruner speaks of as "agentivity," that is, an infant's and young child's avid and central interest in agent and action (Bruner 1990). Indeed, Noë's account, being devoid of a developmental history, is adultist: no reference is made, for example, to well-known child psychologists Esther Thelen's and Linda Smith's analyses of the dynamics of movement and kinesthesia (Thelen & Smith 1994); of child psychologist Lois Bloom's discussion of the centrality of consequential relationships in infant development, relationships that, being noticed by infants, are clearly *nonlinguistic* (Bloom 1993); of infant-child psychiatrist Daniel Stern's discussion of self-agency (Stern 1985); and so on. All of these research citations would provide a foundation for his affirmation that "*self*-movement" is the basis of learning and of "skillful bodily activity." The absence of the foundation is particularly striking in view of his concluding affirmation that "[a]n account of consciousness as a natural phenomenon will be a tale, not about the brain, but about our active lives" (231).

In sum, Noë's usage and re-wording of Husserlian phenomenology appear to be ways of cognitivizing Husserl's insights for analytical consumption. Just as enactivists argue against computationalist and representationalist views of knowledge (cognition, perception, and so on) and in the process put experience into a language that fellow scientists and philosophers of various persuasion will understand, so Noë and cohort sensorimotorists argue against a propositionalist view of knowledge (cognition, perception, and so on) and in the process put experience into a language that fellow analytic philosophers of mind will understand.

11.   See Sheets-Johnstone 1990; on the topic of "comsigns," see also Altmann 1967. When this chapter was originally published in *Continental Philosophy Review,* I answered specifically to a reviewer's concern by stating explicitly that, with respect to emotions and affectivity, I was not presenting a phenomenological developmental account as played out in ontogenetical social relations. I specified, "What I am presenting is a phenomenological exposition of the nature of emotion as it is engendered by and in the primal phenomenon of animation. In other words, I am giving a phenomenological description of the ground floor of affectivity and emotions, their "root soil" (Husserl 1989:292), which is animation, precisely as implied if not explicitly evident in Husserl's consistent concern with the animate, i.e. with the *animate* organism. A developmental history of *intersubjectivity* in the form of social affectivity is thus not the theme of this article, a theme that would necessitate not just phenomenological descriptions focused on exacting ontogenetical elucidations of our emotional maturation vis-a-vis parents, caretakers, playmates, and so on, but precisely, as indicated in the text, a phenomenological account of pan-cultural human tactile-kinesthetic invariants to begin with."

12.   "By *animate form* is meant a species-specific body with all its various spatial conformations, and attendant everyday postures, modes of locomotion, movements, and gestures" (Sheets -Johnstone 1990:5; see also Sheets-Johnstone 1994a).

13.   For seemingly open-ended "embodiments," including even "embodied movement," see Gibbs 2006.

CHAPTER 14

Embodied minds or mindful bodies?

A core twenty-first century challenge

1. Introduction

Movement — animate movement — is coming to the fore, though not yet called by its real name. A seemingly ineffable murkiness clings to the realities of movement, making it appear less than immediately knowable. The word *action*, like the word *behavior*, appears in contrast definitive. It wraps something up neatly and efficiently. An action — or act — has boundaries; it is or can be readily recognized and identified; it is objective in the sense of being a demonstrable solid out there in the world, hence something that is or can be straightforwardly investigated. In short, it has precisely the specificity that movement lacks. It is indeed much more difficult, a veritable challenge, to examine movement, except as a quantified or quantifiable entity. With easily available equipment, one can readily measure amount of force, for example, distance traveled, and speed and range of movement; one can readily specify direction, time of initiation, and time of termination of movement. Such quantifications of movement, however, ignore the very core of animate movement. They bypass completely the central and singularly significant character of animate movement, namely, the *qualitative dynamics* that are inherent in the *experience* of movement. (For an in-depth, thoroughgoing descriptive analysis of movement inside and out, see Sheets-Johnstone 2010.) Indeed, *action* and *behavior* ignore kinesthetic experience and the spatio-temporal-energic qualities inherent in that experience. In lending themselves straightaway to objectification and unquestionable specificity, they actually package movement in the same way that embodiment packages the mind, subjectivity, the self, and all those other otherwise vague and seemingly intangible less-than-physical existential realities. One readily sees the efficiency of the practice in many recent books in cognitive science and philosophy (e.g. Thompson 2007; Jeannerod 2006; Noë 2009, Grammont, Legrand, Livet 2010), books in which one reads over and over again of *action*, a term that has more or less taken over the former labeling role of behavior. Yet however linguistically subverted, one has to admit that wherever there is animate movement, an individual of whatever order is not just doing something — "acting" — but is *experiencing* it kinesthetically and/or proprioceptively. Moreover animate forms of life are not *motoric* forms, not mechanical robots of one sort and another that, in moving, experience themselves as motors; they are *kinetic* forms of life that, in moving, experience a kinetic happening, as in moving toward or running away from something. Such kinetic experiences are not like being shoved or poked into movement by someone or something. Moving toward and running away are initiated by the individual itself in relation to its surrounding world — in von Uexküll's term, its *Umwelt*. It bears notice that no one teaches the individual how to move toward or to run away. Its basic faculties and possibilities for movement come with its being the body it is. Kinetic bodily experiences, however, can also be autonomous involuntary movements, as in the continuous rise and fall or in and out of breath. Animate creatures have nothing to do to keep such experiences going, and, as with moving toward and running away, no one taught them to breathe, for example, or even to laugh (on "laughing" rats, see Panksepp & Burgdorf 2003). Accordingly, whatever our bodily movement — whether we voluntarily initiate it or not — we can simply pay attention to it, noticing its dynamics, and noticing too how those dynamics play out according to how we are motivated to move as we are now moving, how emotions and thoughts, whether topical or aberrant, color the dynamics, and so on. Our attention to something as simple as our breath, as in Buddhist meditation, can indeed be kinesthetically illuminating and illuminating too of the dynamic congruency of movement to emotions and the semantic congruency of movement to cognition (for more on such congruencies, see Sheets-Johnstone 1999, 2011a).

In what follows, we will broaden and deepen just such insights into movement from three perspectives: mind, brain, and the conceptually reciprocal concepts of receptivity and responsivity as set forth in phenomenology and evolutionary biology, respectively. Each perspective will elucidate fundamental aspects of movement that have been and continue to be neglected or ignored altogether since the turn of the century in research and writings on consciousness, subjectivity, embodiment, "motor" topics in general — e.g. motor skills, motor learning — and more. Conjointly, the perspectives will meet the core 21st century challenge by showing that the synergies of meaningful movement that abound in everyday life and the kinesthetic memory that sustains them attest not to embodied minds but mindful bodies.

2.   Mind

What do we see when we look at the mind? Constant change…. There is ceaseless movement, filled with plans, ideas, and memories.

Joseph Goldstein & Jack Kornfield 1987:47

[E]very unity of cognition, in particular every real one, has its 'history' … what the *thing* [*Sache*] itself is — that becomes evident … only in its history, which brings the unities and their moments to prominence by setting the constitutive manifolds in motion. In the method of phenomenological kinesis both things are separated at once: the essential direction of intentionality [its history]and its intentional correlates.   Edmund Husserl 1980 [1912]: 117–118

[H]uman behavior — from neurons to mind — is governed by the generic processes of self-organization. Self-organization refers to the spontaneous formation of patterns and pattern change in open, nonequilibrium systems…. [R]egardless of the level of description … the same basic pattern-forming principles are in evidence.   J.A. Scott Kelso 1995: xi–xii

I would say that in my scientific and philosophical work, my main concern has been with understanding the nature of reality in general and of consciousness in particular as a coherent whole, which is never static or complete, but which is in an unending process of movement and unfoldment. Thus, when I look back, I see that even as a child I was fascinated by the puzzle, indeed the mystery, of what is the nature of movement…. [T]hen there is the further question of what is the relationship of thinking to reality. As careful attention shows, thought itself is in an actual process of movement. That is to say, one can feel a sense of flow in the 'stream of consciousness' not dissimilar to the sense of flow in the movement of matter in general.   David Bohm 1995 [1981]: ix

In his well-known and justly revered two-volume work *The Principles of Psychology*, William James wrote a lengthy (66-page) chapter titled "Stream of Thought." Early on in the chapter, he calls attention to the "constant change" of what he broadly characterizes as "thought": "We all recognize as different great classes of our conscious states. Now we are seeing, now hearing; now reasoning, now willing; now recollecting, now expecting; now loving, now hating; and in a hundred other ways we know our minds to be alternately engaged" (James 1950, vol. 1: 230). After further analysis and discussion, he notes, "it is obvious and palpable that our state of mind is never precisely the same" (ibid.: 233). Still later, he concludes that consciousness "does not appear to itself chopped up in bits…. It is nothing jointed; it flows. A 'river' or a 'stream' are the metaphors by which it is most naturally described. *In talking of it hereafter, let us call it the stream of thought, of consciousness, or of subjective life*" (ibid.: 239; italics in original).

In the course of describing the stream of consciousness, James notes at several points how language can throw us off track in our quest for understanding, that is, how "language works against our perception of the truth" (ibid.: 241). His point is that either by naming or by breaking experience into parts, language deters us from seeing the unbroken flow, the essential "unity of consciousness" (ibid.: 240; see also James's asterisked note in acknowledgement of Brentano's notion of the unity). He observes, for example, "The transition between the thought of one object and the thought of another is no more a break in the *thought* than a joint in a bamboo is a break in the wood. It is a part of the *consciousness* as much as the joint is a part of the *bamboo*" (ibid.).

In the course of his penetrating and meticulous descriptive analyses, he calls attention to the temporal nature of consciousness and urges us to take into account its dynamics in the form of "fringes" that adhere to what we might call "thoughts-in-process," that is, fringes of meaning (ibid.: 281) and of relations that are discordant or harmonious (ibid.: 259). The fringes and relations are due, James states, to "the influence of a faint brain-process upon our thought" (ibid.: 258). James characterizes 'brain-process' in terms of "nerve-action" (ibid.: 242) (or "brain-action," e.g. ibid.: 257), a term recalling Darwin's "nerve-force," the third of the principles Darwin set forth that account for the natural gestures and expression of emotions in animals, human and non-human, in face of their surrounding world (Darwin 1965 [1872]). In fact, James himself speaks of principles, namely, "the principles of nerve-action" (James 1950, vol. 1: 242) and limns them first and foremost along the lines of a basic temporality, namely, *flow*: "[N]o state of the brain can be supposed instantly to die away. If a new state comes, the inertia of the old state will still be there and modify the result accordingly.... If recently the brain-tract a was vividly excited, and then b, and now vividly c, the total present consciousness is not produced simply by c's excitement, but also by the dying vibrations of a and b as well." He describes the interrelated dynamic as "three different processes coexisting, and correlated with them a thought which is no one of the three thoughts which they would have produced had each of them occurred alone" (ibid.). A few pages later, he sums up, stating, "As the brain-changes are continuous, so do all these consciousnesses melt into each other like dissolving views. Properly they are but one protracted consciousness, one unbroken stream" (ibid.: 247–48).

Two aspects of James's experientially-anchored, detailed descriptive analyses are of particular moment with respect to the topic of mind. First, his analyses of the stream of consciousness obviously tie in with the epigraphs at the beginning of this section: with Therevada Buddhist insights into impermanence and the nature of mind; with Edmund Husserl's analyses of the decisively temporal way in which we build up knowledge of the world about us; with Pierre de Fermat laureate Scott Kelso's studies of complex systems in terms of their self-organization, their metastable nature, and their coordination dynamics at all levels; with physicist David Bohm's notion of movement as fundamental to understandings of both consciousness and cosmology. Second, while they resonate in strikingly contrasting ways with present-day neurological reductionism, they resonate in strikingly complementary ways with present-day findings about the brain that directly and indirectly highlight its temporal nature, and in doing so call attention to the waywardness of a pointillist, static, part-by-part, often modular conception of the brain that not only fails to accord with the streaming, flowing, historical nature of consciousness but with the dynamically interconnected whole of which the brain is a part and that in actuality constitutes *a whole-body nervous system*. James in fact conceives the brain neither as an autonomous neurological organ distinct from the body as in much of present-day neuroscience, of which more in the section that follows — and certainly not as the subject of experience — nor as a system of parts. He construes the brain dynamically: "*The 'entire brain-process' is not a physical fact at all.* It is the appearance to an onlooking mind of a multitude of physical facts. 'Entire brain' is nothing but our name for the way in which a million of molecules arranged in certain positions may affect our sense" (ibid.: 178). Indeed, it is notable that the entry for the item 'brain process' in James's index reads: "see *neural process.*" We will address this second aspect of James's work in the course of the following section on the brain, but one aspect of it is pertinent in the present context of mind. In particular, one of James's conclusions in his two-volume study of psychology is cogent to a *dynamic* view of the brain as distinguished from a "solid" view derived from mechanical and mathematical perspectives. As will be shown, the dynamic view coincides in a diversity of ways with the epigraphs at the beginning of this section, ways that warrant our attention.

James observes,

> [W]hen you give things mathematical and mechanical names and call them just so many solids in just such positions, describing just such paths with just such velocities, all is changed ["changed" from what James calls the quite different "sentimental, moral, and aesthetic" perspective]. Your sagacity finds its reward in the verification by nature of all the deductions which you may next proceed to make. Your 'things' realize all the *consequences* of the names by which you classed them. The modern mechanico-physical philosophy of which we are all so proud ... begins by saying that the *only* facts are collocations and motions of primordial solids, and the only laws[,] the changes of motion which changes in collocation bring. The ideal which this philosophy strives after is a mathematical world-formula, by which, if all the collocations and motions at a given moment were known, it would be possible to reckon those of any wished-for future moment, by simply considering the necessary geometrical, arithmetical, and logical implications (James 1950, vol. II: 666–67).

He later adds: "Take any ... mathematico-mechanical theory ... They are all translations of sensible experiences into other forms" (ibid.: 669).

While James does not use the term 'dynamic', his observations and assessments clearly attest not to *solids* but to dynamically resonant "sensible experiences" that reverberate throughout the whole body: "Using sweeping terms and ignoring exceptions, *we might say that every possible feeling produces a movement, and that the movement is a movement of the entire organism, and of each and all its parts*" (ibid.: 372; italics in original). His conclusion: "*A process set up anywhere in the centres* [i.e. "nerve-centres," as in the circulatory, respiratory, visceral neural systems including bladder, uterus, and so on] *reverberates everywhere, and in some way or other affects the organism throughout, making its activities either greater or less* (ibid.: 381; italics in original).

The idea that everything is connected to everything else is hardly new. What warrants attention here is a substantive and thoroughgoing affirmation of the principle with respect to animate organisms. A "solid" approach to the body, for example, would have it that throwing, for example, happens in the arm; that kicking happens in the foot and leg. The "solid" stance is clearly nonsensical. Throwing and kicking are dynamic whole-body movements, the actual kinetic sequence of which could hardly unfold 'just in the arm' or 'just in the foot and leg'. Mind and the temporal flow of thought and feeling — the stream of consciousness — and the nervous system, *which includes the brain*, are no different. Thinking, doubting, planning, rejoicing, ruminating, examining, fearing, wanting, craving, grieving, and so on, resonate in dynamically congruent ways throughout the organism, precisely as James describes: everything "*reverberates everywhere.*" Concentrated ongoing attention, which one might think an exception, is no different: it too is dynamically congruent, in this instance with a stilled, alert, and intently focused tactile-kinesthetic/affective body. In effect, mind is not a solid and is not reducible to something solid, i.e. to *the brain*. The brain itself is part of the "reverberating" neurophysiological dynamic living whole.

The four epigraphs support the above elaboration of James's notion of a whole-body kinetic as opposed to a collocation of "solids." The writers, meticulous and perspicuous individual researchers, each from an entirely different perspective and indeed experts in their areas of study, observe, like James, that mind is not an unvarying, static entity; movement is of the very nature of mind.[1] Brains in turn could not be otherwise, except, of course, when considered purely as an anatomical organ like any other organ of the body — heart, liver, pancreas, and so on, organs dissected from the whole, and specified as being made up of such and such parts and residing at such and such a place in the body. The import of recognizing *dynamics*, what James might call the *interlocked and interlocking dynamics of sensible experience*, could hardly be more clearly highlighted.

The point in calling attention to the distinction between solid and dynamic conceptions of mind, and more generally of living beings at all levels of description, is not to pit a mathematico-mechanical school of thought against an experientially-tethered one. The point is rather *conceptual*, and even *metaphysical*, not in the sense of referencing or conjuring something *beyond* the physical, but in the sense of approaching ultimate truths about the reality of mind by way of firmly grounded e*pistemological* understandings of its nature. To be so firmly grounded is to take the unfolding dynamic nature of experience seriously, and correlatively, to take the challenge of languaging experience seriously (on the latter topic, see Sheets-Johnstone 2009: Chapter XV). It is or should be obvious that short of experience, there would be no science and no philosophy. Precisely in epistemological terms, there would be no wonder, no questioning, no doubting, no exploring — no mindful investigations. There would be no experiments, no laboratories, no machines to measure this and that, and so on. Short of experience, there would be not only no knowledge, but no motivation to seek knowledge, no desire to inquire into this or that, no excitement about delving, no inquisitiveness, no curiosity. Experience is the bottom line of knowledge, the epistemological basis of all forms of *gnosis*. It is not abstract, but grounded in affect and movement, and in sensibilities and cognitions deriving therefrom. In a word, it is grounded in the fact of our being — in Husserl's exacting term — *animate organisms*. It is thus grounded in animation. When we are dead, we precisely no longer experience. We are no longer *animate*. Our primary source of animation — our tactile-kinesthetic/ affective body — no longer generates movement and feelings, and correspondingly, an affective-kinetic-cognitive relationship to the world.

It should be noted that *mind* is a rarely used term in phenomenology where, if anything, it has a psycho-ontological rather than epistemological meaning (see Husserl 1980: 22). The comparable or correlative term in phenomenology is *consciousness*, in some instances, *psyche* or *subjectivity*, and in a special sense, *transcendental ego* or *transcendental subjectivity*. A close resemblance in meaning, however, is apparent between the two words (for a detailed account, see Sheets-Johnstone 2011b), and at times a conceptual concordance is evident between the two. Husserl at one point states, for example, that intention is "a mode of consciousness, of 'mindedness' (*Zumuteseins*)" (Husserl 1970d [1900], vol. 2: 565). Moreover it should be noted that like James, Husserl does not use the word "dynamics," yet dynamics are of the very nature of *constitution*, that is, the way in which we make sense of the world about us, the way in which we put things together from our myriad experiential relationships to them. As the epigraph above shows, Husserl describes cognition in terms of its *history*, the manner in which and the modes by which each and every one of our extant cognitions has been built up. Constitution is in other words *a dynamic process*. It attests to a mind in motion, a flowing unity of awarenesses, to a mindful body attuned to its surrounding world. Indeed, we come to know the world not only through moving in relation to our surrounding world, but by the inner temporal workings of consciousness which, through sedimentations, horizons, protentions, and retentions, conjoin present awarenesses with those past, those at the margins of awareness, those on the cusp of the future (Husserl 1966). Thus, on the basis and in the light of our ongoing experiences of ourselves and the world about us, our cognitions are continuously affected by what we remember, what is peripheral as well as what is focal in our attention, and what we anticipate. Dynamics thus aptly describe the nature of our knowledge, knowledge of ourselves and of the world about us. In Jamesian terms, they describe the non-solid nature of mind and animate life.

Dynamics are essentially modes of animation. They are present at all levels of animate being, as Kelso has so admirably shown in his extensive and ongoing studies of *coordination dynamics* (Kelso 1995; Kelso & Engstrøm 2006). These detailed and broadly investigative studies anchor a temporal rather than purely spatial concept of mind; that is, they bring to the fore the fact that there are "neither purely stable nor purely unstable" states (Kelso & Engstrøm 2006, p. 10), that *metastability* aptly describes dual co-existing tendencies at all levels of being, i.e. tendencies to bind together and to maintain independence, whether the elements under investigation are living creatures or neurons in the brain (ibid.: 112). Kelso's "twinkling metastable mind" (Kelso 1995:225; Kelso & Engstrøm 2006:148) is a direct, rigorously documented descendant of Sherrington's well-known "enchanted loom, where millions of flashing shuttles weave a dissolving pattern, always a meaningful pattern though never an abiding one" (Sherrington 1953:184). Not only is the meaningful pattern dynamic, but the harmony of effective movement is, as Sherrington explicitly points out, "not a harmony built out of parts in the sense of [being] merely a product of harmonious parts." On the contrary, and in accord with Aristotle's concept of *form*, the living moving system is itself "the cause of the harmony of its parts" (ibid.: 180).

Kelso significantly expands Sherrington's insight into the self-generated harmony of living systems, and this via his concept of metastability: metastability is a self-organizational phenomenon, a foundational feature of living systems. As the epigraph at the beginning of this section intimates, to say that a system is *self-organizing* is to say that its *coordination dynamics* are the result of spontaneously emerging and dissolving patterns (Kelso 1995; Kelso & Engstrøm 2006). The patterns emerge and dissolve in virtue of the system being an open one, a system in which what we might call the "membrane" between the system — whatever its level — and its outer world is permeable. Two aspects of Kelso's exposition of metastability are of particular moment with respect to James's notion of "solids." The aspects — as will be apparent — are actually interrelated.

First, Kelso explicitly rejects a "solid" notion of the brain, solid in the sense of a neuron by neuron or even module by module explanation of its workings. On the basis of highly disciplined studies of PET scans and fMRI imagings in addition to his own experimental research, he observes, "Neither the brain nor its individual neurons are linear.... When one examines brain images before they are subtracted from each other, one sees activity distributed all over the place. There are no centers for reading and speaking, even though each task may selectively involve *in time* certain areas more than others" (Kelso 1995:273). Moreover in answer to causal explanations, motor programs, and the like, he points out that "Self-organizing systems have no deus ex machina, no ghost in the machine ordering the parts" (ibid.: 9), and later specifies that "the linkage between coherent events at different scales of observation from the cell membrane to the cerebral cortex is *by virtue of shared dynamics*, not because any single level is more or less fundamental than any other" (ibid.: 229). Perhaps most incisive is his implicit criticism of typical causal notions of mind. Recalling Jung's idea that conscious and unconscious are two aspects of the same singular reality, and in keeping with the thesis of complementary dynamic *tendencies* rather than fixed *states* as anchoring living systems, he and co-author David Engstrøm straightforwardly acknowledge, "It is unknown whether the segregation~integration of the brain [i.e. the neuronal tendencies to function independently as well as to coordinate] corresponds to the unconscious~conscious mind." They proceed to point out that, "If true, such a novel correspondence principle would seem a rather more agreeable solution to the mind~body, psycho~physical problem than the usual story of how one-way neural firings are causing mental events" (Kelso & Engstrøm 2006:148. As Kelso and Engstrøm explain, the tilde [~] "does not represent a simple concatenation of words, but rather indicates the inextricable complementary relationship between them," as in individual~collective, for example [xiv–xv]). In short, Kelso and Engstrøm remind us not only that "neurons in the cortex are patently multifunctional" (ibid.: 151) but that "[t]hinking arises as spontaneous, self-organized patterns of brain activity created by interactions among myriad interacting neurons and neural assemblies" and that because a reciprocal causality obtains, thinking "modifies the activity of the very neurons and neural assemblies that create it" (ibid.: 115).

Second, a compelling relationship exists between the self-organizing coordination tendencies that Kelso and Engstrøm describe and a mind perpetually on the move that Buddhists describe. The relationship is compelling specifically with reference to notions of a self. In particular, Kelso and Engstrøm first cautiously suggest that "spontaneous self-organizing coordination tendencies" might be "the source from which the sense of biological agency springs," and in turn, that coordination dynamics hint at the possibility that "awareness of 'self' could emerge from self-organization (a term that by definition paradoxically means the organization of patterns without an organizer, *without a self*)" (ibid.: 11; italics in original). They later reiterate the parenthesized theme of a "no-self" in terms of the entrained ticking of pendulum clocks: "whether through vibration in the wall or displacement of the air, [coupling] enables the clocks to become mutually entrained, that is, *coordinated without any coordinator at all*" (ibid.: 112; italics in original). It is well known that Buddhists view the "self" to be nothing more than a concept. "The truth of our being is simply this process of flowing change" (Goldstein & Kornfield 1987:56); 'the self', or 'I' "is an idea, a name we apply to a constantly flowing pattern of ephemeral mental and physical phenomena" (ibid.: 135). The confluence of thought is striking precisely because the idea of "no-self" is affirmed from such different perspectives. The further confluence in understandings of *mind* is what one might term the foundational paradox of *self*-organization on the one hand and the foundational paradox of direct experience of no-self on the other:

> The only way to effectively maintain the illusion of the self's solidity is to keep churning out thoughts, plans, programs and the rest. If we keep them coming, we can quickly paste it all together and it seems to make something solid. But when the mind begins to quiet down, the whole structure begins to slip, and from the ego's point of view that is scary… [there is] no enduring entity behind the scenes controlling the show. In truth what we are is this changing process; there is nothing substantial or solid (ibid.: 145).

In short, "Insight comes from the realization that observation is going on without an observer" (Goldstein 1983:62).

Clearly, when we acknowledge the living dynamics of life itself, we are a long way from thinking and conceptualizing along the lines of "collocations and motions of primordial solids," including the primordial solid of a self. The topic of the self in relation to mind is relevant from a further perspective. It is finely articulated in Buddhist psychiatrist Mark Epstein's discussion of "self" in his book *Thoughts Without A Thinker*. Epstein first calls attention to how we humans commonly have and cultivate a spatial rather than temporal 'sense of self'. He then points out that "mindfulness means being aware of exactly what is happening in the mind and body *as* it is occurring: what it reveals is how much of a flux we are in at all times" (Epstein 1995: 142). He acutely observes that "[w]ith the mindfulness practices comes a shift from a spatially based experience of self to a temporal one" (ibid.), and further, that as the shift occurs, "it becomes impossible to ignore just how removed we all are from what [psychiatrist Stephen A.] Mitchell has called the 'rushing fluidity' of our everyday experience" (ibid.: 143).

Just why we not only are removed but commonly remain removed is a question worth pondering. Recognizing a temporal self entails recognizing one's life as ultimately terminal. It means recognizing a "punctuated existence" (Sheets-Johnstone 1990: Chapter 8; 2009: Chapter 4). In Heidegger's language, it means recognizing that, ontologically speaking, we are all 'being-toward-death'. The temporal is — or may be — fearful in just such respects. Goldstein and Kornfield implicitly recognize this fact when they point out that "from the ego's point of view," it is "scary" to realize that "there is nothing substantial or solid" (Goldstein & Kornfield 1987: 145). In contrast to a temporal self, a spatial self has nothing to fear: it is solid, firmly shaped and firmly situated. It acts and behaves: it does this and that. Its actions and behaviors are temporal, but not temporal in a deeply and veritably flowing, i.e. *kinetic*, experiential sense. Certainly each act — or behavior — has a beginning and an end, but the way we conceive it and the name we give it package that beginning and end, succinctly specifying but not describing or delineating in any way not only *what* is kinetically unfolding between beginning and end, i.e. *movement*, but *that that 'what' is always unfolding in a dynamically qualitative manner*. A spatial self simply does what it does: runs, gets into a car, puts an arm in a sleeve and a fork in its mouth, reads, talks, kisses, hugs, and so on. Mindfulness discloses something altogether different in the way of a self. Its temporal character comes to the fore and is obviously elusive, fleeting, not to be pinned down: habitual movements come and go; patterns of thought come and go; feelings come and go; ideas come and go — all of these dimensions of life coming and going with their unique qualitative dynamics (see Sheets-Johnstone 2011b). The erstwhile solidity of the spatial dissolves in and into the dynamic flow of the temporal. The flow is experientially epitomized in the natural in and out of breath. Not that breathing lacks spatial localization, but that it is first and foremost a dynamic *temporal* happening. As Epstein points out, a "breath-based experience" is one of "fluidity" (Epstein 1995: 146), but attended to, is no longer one of the "rushing fluidities" of everyday life.

It is hardly surprising then that "awareness of breathing provides a unique opportunity for one to integrate time into the self experience" (ibid.: 145).

To realize and acknowledge that animate forms of life are indeed animate and that their animation articulates a dynamic is to realize and acknowledge that meanings unfold in and through a mindful body, and that mind as elucidated in Buddhist observations and that the temporal dynamics of consciousness as elucidated in Husserl's observations are natural complements of one another. Indeed, impermanence and constitution are epistemologically related. Constitution is not only a temporal phenomenon in itself — as indicated above, it is a matter of putting the world together in the service of sense-making — but a temporal phenomenon that answers epistemologically to what Goldstein and Kornfield finely describe as the "constant change" of mind, that is, to the Buddhist truth of impermanence (Sheets-Johnstone 2011b). The one perspective indeed implicitly validates the other: short of the realities of impermanence, there would be no need for constitution; short of the realities of constitution, there would be ongoing impermanence devoid of sense-making. In each instance, a mutual complementarity obtains (for more on complementarity, see Kelso & Engstrøm 2006). One might say that Nature provides animate beings with the ability to compensate for the fluidity of motion, mind, and time. They are thereby enabled to gain knowledge of themselves and the world about them. Aristotle's observation quoted epigraphically at the beginning of Chapter 2, Part II and again in Chapter 13 is once more strikingly relevant in just this epistemological sense: "Nature is a principle of motion and change.... We must therefore see that we understand what motion is; for if it were unknown, nature too would be unknown" (*Physics* 200b: 12–14). When we understand motion — constant change, internal time consciousness, qualitative kinetic dynamics, metastability, stream of consciousness, and more — we approximate to basic understandings of Nature in terms of both impermanence and constitution. Nature is essentially in constant flux, impermanent, and animate beings are part of Nature. It is pertinent too in this context to reiterate a theme prominent in Chapter 2, Part I, namely, that the world is never the same from one day to the next and that an animal's movement can thus not be absolutely programmed, running on something akin to a lifetime tape. It follows that for those animate beings who must learn their bodies and learn to move themselves to begin with, and this in conjunction with making sense of the world about them, that internal time consciousness is virtually mandatory, an epistemological recognition of the realities of Nature in terms of both constitution and impermanence. Constitution is Nature's way of counterbalancing the incessant flow of everyday, real-time, real-life experience. Internal time consciousness is in other words the backbone of our affective-kinetic-cognitive life. Indeed, it is the backbone of those kinesthetic/kinetic melodies that constitute what neuropsychologist Aleksandr Romanovich Luria recognized as everyday "complex sequential activities": writing one's name, calculating a sum, and so on (Luria 1966, 1973). Such abilities run off by themselves because they were once learned, which is to say that the temporal structure and flow of each melody was at one time inscribed in a mindful body and remains inscribed in a mindful body as a theme with variations according to "circonstances," to borrow once again from Lamarck (see this text pp. 23, 318).

Bohm's concept of motion as the ground floor of mind and cosmos, hence of Nature in the broadest sense, is further testimony to the temporal dynamics and metastability of Nature. Although obviously giving us "solids" in the form of flora and fauna, Nature endows them with motion in the form of what Aristotle perceptively enumerated as growth, change, and locomotion, though not necessarily all three in all forms of life. Bohm is virtually alone among contemporary scientists in recognizing Aristotle's acumen. In the course of clarifying his notion of "flowing movement" that is prior to the reality of "things" (Bohm 1995 [1981]: 12), he discusses Aristotle's notion of causation, calling attention precisely to his notion of *form* and distinguishing the word from "its modern connotation" as signifying something "not very significant … as in 'formal dress' or 'a mere formality'" (ibid.: 12). As he points out, in Aristotle's time, the word *form* signified something quite different: "an inner *forming activity* which is the cause of the growth of things, and of the development and differentiation of their various essential forms" (ibid.). Bohm succinctly limns Aristotle's conception of form as "*an ordered and structured inner movement that is essential to what things are*" (ibid.) He goes on to note that *form* — in just this sense of a causative inner kinetic dynamic — "was considered to be of essentially the same nature for the mind as it was for life and for the cosmos as a whole" (ibid.: 13). His point is to show that mind, being part of Nature, is to be understood as "the flowing movement of awareness" (ibid.). Though not in any way recognizing Husserl's phenomenological analyses of perception and cognitional awarenesses in the form of concepts and the nature of internal time consciousness, Bohm's sequence of thought is through and through Husserlian. With respect to the flow of awareness, he writes, "one is aware of each aspect as assimilated within a single whole, all of whose parts are inwardly related…. [T]hey are to be considered as aspects of the *forming* activity of the mind," an activity that gives rise to a "particular structure of concepts" (ibid.). In short, and in phenomenological terms, we put things together, making sense of ourselves and the world, in the course of our flowing awarenesses. Inner time consciousness is indeed adumbrated in Bohm's notion of an "undivided wholeness in flowing movement" (ibid.: 14). Moreover though he too does not use the word *dynamics*, his point is clearly to emphasize the dynamics of Nature — *movement* — over a mechanics of Nature. In the process, he calls attention to the fact that Aristotle's notion of formative and final cause are far from central in present-day physics. He writes that "law" in present-day physics

> is still generally conceived as a self-determined system of efficient causes, operating in an ultimate set of material constituents of the universe (e.g. elementary particles subject to forces of interaction between them)…. [T]hey tend to be conceived as

separately existent mechanical elements of a fixed nature. The prevailing trend in modern physics is thus much against any sort of view giving primacy to formative activity in undivided wholeness of flowing movement (ibid.).

What he goes on to describe as the ensuing "fragmentary" world has political implications (ibid.), but it also quite clearly has epistemological implications and straightforward epistemological effects in terms of how living beings and physical world realities are conceived and how they are studied and understood. His formulation and exposition of an implicate order is grounded in a total or holistic continuous unfolding that is not reducible to a mechanics. Whether one takes up his more detailed and complex notion of an implicate/explicate order is not of moment in the present context. What is of moment is his emphasis on a non-reductive view of Nature, a view that singles out what we may not inappropriately or impertinently, or even brazenly term *the primacy of movement*: "What we are saying is, then, that movement is basically such a creative inception of new content as projected from the multidimensional ground [of sequential "moments" of time]. In contrast, what is mechanical is a relatively autonomous sub-totality that can be abstracted from that which is basically a creative movement of unfoldment" (ibid.: 212).

3. The Brain

> Everything you hear, feel, see and think is controlled by your brain. It allows you to cope masterfully with your everyday environment and is capable of producing breathtaking athletic feats, sublime works of art, and profound scientific insights. But its most amazing achievement may be that it can understand itself.
> Advertisement of a course — "How Your Brain Works" — offered by
> The Teaching Company (*Science News* 2009: 3)

> It would be nice to know what the neurons are doing, but we don't with this method. And that's life.
> Nikos Logothetis of the Max Planck Institute for Biological Cybernetics.
> (Quoted by Sanders 2009: 18)

> For there is no such thing as face or flesh without soul in it; it is only homonymously that they will be called face or flesh if the life has gone out of them, just as if they had been made of stone or wood.
> Aristotle *Generation of Animals* 734b: 24–26.

> I've been so excited by this whole presentation of this session because everybody is coordinated into one unit, but what has fascinated me is the absence of the body below the neck [laughter].
> Unidentified audience member at "Emotions Inside Out" Conference
> in a panel discussion on "Expression" (Ekman, Campos, Davidson,
> deWaal 2003, p. 273)

Motors are neither conceptually nor linguistically compatible with animation. They are not compatible with *life*. The issue is not trivial. It is precisely conceptual and linguistic, and in turn constitutes a challenge: the challenge of languaging experience. Motoric talk and writing preclude thinking along the lines of life itself, along the lines of experience. Motors are man-made products, indeed, artifacts masquerading as life. As is evident from the previous chapter's criticism of the term "motor" in relation to animate life, a misuse of language is a conceptual obstacle to ferreting out and elucidating the truths of experience (see also Sheets-Johnstone 2006 on "myness"). More will be said presently in this section of motoric talk and writing, but surely a sizable hint of the problem is apparent in the difference between functional approaches and explanations and experiential analyses. Ezequiel di Paolo, who has worked in artificial intelligence and cognitive science, writes, "The movement of meaningful action can be convincingly emulated in an artificial system but this is not the same as the system acting meaningfully. The robot may look scared and retreat when yelled at but this may be only a sophisticated illusion … Being functionally scared is not the same as being scared … The vast majority of current work on robot emotion … [places] almost exclusive reliance on pure functionality" (Di Paolo 2005: 443).

We readily see the elision of real-life emotions in cognitive science not only in artificial systems studies but in present-day concentrated attention on *the brain*. The preeminence of *the brain* has grown enormously in the past decade and outgrown the significance of, and perhaps even general interest in all other internal organs, except as the latter are wracked by disease or painfully afflicted. Motors of course figure centrally in this preeminence, not only as in motor skills, motor learning, and motor control, but precisely in such oxymoronic notions as a "sensorimotor subjectivity" (e.g. Thompson 2005, 2007). Critical reflections on present-day research on *the brain* will highlight pitfalls in the practice and demonstrate basic faults in the enterprise itself.

A statement in an article titled "Destination Brain," whose concern is with pollutants that "may inflame more than the lungs," is a striking case in point. In the context of discussing the wider effect of these pollutants on young children, science writer Janet Raloff states that "through a new battery of medical and cognitive tests, [the investigating scientist] found that something has been ravaging the youngsters' lungs, hearts — and, especially troubling, their minds" (Raloff 2010: 16). Certainly we may ask why ravaged minds — obviously considered homologous to ravaged brains by way of "Destination Brain" — should be "especially troubling," that is, any more troubling than ravaged lungs and hearts since unravaged lungs and hearts are as essential to human life as unravaged minds. In fact, since aliveness would otherwise be compromised, are not unravaged lungs and hearts essential to unravaged human minds to begin with? Moreover the problem is not just that mind and brain are considered as one, but that a body/brain divide is now *au courant* and effectively replaces the classic body/mind divide. We readily see this new divide not only in science but in philosophy, precisely in statements such as "Brain, body, and world — each plays a critical role in making us the kind of beings we are" (Noë 2009: 184). While the idea behind the latter statement is to demote the brain from its preeminence and conceive it instead as one "player" en par among others, the critical point is missed, namely, that the brain is neurophysiologically — *functionally considered* — an integral part of the nervous system and the nervous system is indeed *a singular system*, one spanning the entire body from head to toe and dedicated centrally to the coordinated dynamics of living bodies. As earlier chapters have shown, the research and writings of neurophysiologist Sir Charles Sherrington and psychologist Roger Sperry affirm this fact in multiple and exacting ways as does the work of neuropsychologist Aleksandr Romanovich Luria. When *the brain* is preeminenced as it is in today's neuroscience and certain realms of philosophy, it is severed from its neuromuscular coordinates. The idea that the brain is an organ separate from the body actually defies anatomy and is nothing more than a theoretical legerdemain. The fundamental significance of the *neuromuscular system* to life is in turn no longer recognized and studied as it was recognized and studied in *Man and His Nature* (Sherrington), for example, and in *The Working Brain* (Luria). In effect, the bedrock of all those *synergies of meaningful movement* that abound in the everyday lives of humans — as in the everyday lives of all animate organisms — are nowhere to be found in present-day studies of *the brain*, nor are the initial kinetic forays of human infants and other young animals that lead to the formation of those synergies of meaningful movement. Rather than an elucidation of the formation of those synergies and of their retention into adulthood, we have, as amply documented earlier (see Chapter 2, Part II and Chapter 11), experiential ascriptions to *the brain*, ascriptions accomplished by an anatomical sleight of hand that cleaves in two what is in its living reality clearly all of a piece. Comparable experiential ascriptions are patently not made to lungs in terms of breathing, for example, or to the heart in terms of pounding — or for that matter to the stomach in terms of food processing: we do not read of lungs 'finding the quality of air rich and exhilarating', of the heart 'balking at the pace to which its ventricular contractions are put', or of the stomach 'determining the textural quality of the apple that has come its way'. The proper question, then, is why *experience* should be exclusively ascribed to the body organ we call "the brain" and not to these other bodily organs. The ascriptions indeed decorticate an otherwise intact living individual and rivet attention in turn not on an ensuing decerebrate rigidity of the body as in "the olden days," but on a *literally dis-embodied* mass of cortical folds, neurons, and blood flows together with a recording of their exact location. Indeed, these decortications readily open the gate to "*the brain* pure and simple."

The manner in which third-person and first-person accounts of life are related, that is, the manner in which neurological happenings and experience are related can be conceived causally, in which case the relationship is epiphenomenal, or it can be conceived complementary. Kelso's fine-grained account of a "shared dynamics" (Kelso 1995: 229) obtaining at all levels shows precisely how a complementary relationship obtains (see also Kelso & Engstrøm 2006). The dynamics are not the same at all levels, but are precisely *complementary*. There are thus alternatives to reductionism, just as there are alternatives to modeling (Kelso 1995: 228). It is notable that at least some cognitivists and neuroscientists are aware of the reductionist tendency and the problem it presents. In the concluding chapter of an edited conference book titled *Mind and Motion*, the three editors (two psychologists and a scientist from the Max Planck Institute for Human Cognitive and Brain Sciences) state, "As recognized in other chapters in this volume, perhaps the single largest threat to true and comprehensive understanding of the bidirectional links between cognition and action is the reductionist tendency" (Raab, Johnson, Heekeren 2009: 322). It should be noted that the book's collection of essays was addressed to the question of how "an agent immersed in a situation that require[s] appraisal and action" decides what to do (ibid.: 320). Interestingly enough, in their conclusion, the editors declare that reductionism "was manifest [in essayists' explanations] in many forms, none of which contributed very positively to our ultimate [research] goals" (ibid.: 322). Kelso's extensive and penetrating research studies of coordination dynamics is edifying as to why. Kelso writes,

> "Most neuroscientists are reductionists. They follow the time-honored thesis of classical physics, namely, that macroscopic states can be explained through microscopic analysis. Ultimately, the mind will boil down to molecular biology, which can be reduced to chemistry, which can be reduced to physics … where the ultimate goal for some is to find the 'God particle'.… But studying the elementary components of the system is not enough. At each level of complexity, novel properties appear whose behavior cannot be predicted from knowledge of component processes alone. To reduce a person's behavior to a set of molecular configurations is, as English neurobiologist Steven Rose once said, to mistake the singer for the song" (Kelso 1995: 227–228).

Rose, a seemingly lone voice in today's neurobiology, has in fact written and continues to write emphatically and at length beyond the 1980 article that Kelso cites of why reductionism is a false doctrine and why its adherents are on a failed mission (e.g. Rose 1982a, 1982b; Rees & Rose 2004). He writes not only of the fact that brain neurons and their interconnections are highly individualized, contingent on individual histories, but the fact that the relationship between neuronal histories and their present "state" is unknown: "There may be an indefinite number of histories of neurons from conception to the present time which could be interpreted as meaning the experiencing of a red bus coming towards me — and equally there might be an infinite number of experiences that could be inferred from any particular pattern" (Rose 2005: 217). Rose's point actually recalls Bohm's notion of a multidimensional rather than linear, i.e. mechanical, reality. More damning still to a reductionist credo is Rose's thought

experiment with a cerebroscope, a device, Rose believes, to have been theorized originally by psychologist Donald Mackay. The device is capable of specifying the activities
of all 100 billion neurons in the brain at any time. Rose envisions the possibility of a
powerful cerebroscope capable of recording "a person's neural activity from the first
moment of detectable neural activity in the foetus onwards, and focus it on the brain of
someone trying to decide whether an argument is false or not" (ibid.: 219). He states,

> "Once again we will expect all sorts of brain regions to light up as some
> proposition is examined, semantically, syntactically, compared with related
> propositions extracted from memory, and so forth. The cerebroscope will in due
> course also register the final decision, yes or no, to the truth or falsity of the
> proposition — but would it be able to detect the actual *content* of the argument
> leading to the conclusion? I suggest not; the cerebroscope is at the limits of its
> powers in identifying the brain regions that *enable* the mental process involved
> in the argument. It is at this point, I suggest, that neuroscience may be reaching
> its theoretical limits in its efforts to understand the brain in order to explain
> the mind" (ibid.: 219–220).

In this context, Rose in fact makes the interesting point that description and explanation are two quite different aspects of mind. While some — Rose identifies philosopher Thomas Nagel with whom he disagrees — believe that descriptive accounts are
the province of "higher" mental functions and explanatory accounts are the province of
"lower" ones, Rose points out that "[h]owever comprehensive the cerebroscope's record
of the neural activity taking place when I experience the sensation of being angry or
in love, drafting this sentence or designing an experiment, the account will only be
descriptive. It is the words, read or spoken, which are explanatory." Moreover he adds,
"For sure, explaining the brain is helping us describe and understand our minds, but it
is not going to succeed in eliminating mind-language by relocating it into some limbo
dismissible by the cognitive illuminati as mere 'folk psychology'" (ibid.: 220).

The distinction between description and explanation is of moment and in ways
beyond that based on Rose's cerebroscope. In a limited sense, the distinction exemplifies the distinction between phenomenology and science, that is, a distinction between
knowledge of what Husserl describes as *the things themselves* and knowledge of how
things work or come to be. In a quite broad sense, it exemplifies the distinction between
the essential character of a thing and a causal account of it. But further still, descriptive accounts are the very basis of an explanatory science: the thing itself — whatever
it might be — is first and foremost insofar as experiences and observations of it are the
ground floor of any investigations. Its description thus matters and the terms in which it
is described thus matter and matter foundationally. That mattering and its foundational
significance are determined by the way in which the phenomenon is perceived and correlatively conceived in the first place. The dynamic, qualitative realities of animate movement, for example, can readily degenerate into talk of behavior and action when little

or no thought is given to *animate movement*, the veritable object of actual experience. In short, and in Rose's terms, descriptions are foundationally significant to a veridical "mind-language" (ibid., note p. 139; see also 215–16). The fundamental challenge in any endeavor to understand a particular phenomenon is, as I have elsewhere shown, *to language experience* (Sheets-Johnstone 2009: Chapter XV; see also Sheets-Johnstone 2002, 2005). Outside of literature, little thought is commonly given to the challenge. But the omission is not a sign of its importance. On the contrary, *descriptive foundations* are the bedrock not only of literature and phenomenology, but of life sciences (Sheets-Johnstone 2002). Darwin's writings attest extensively and even eloquently to this fact. Moreover the epigraphs of this section attest in notably different but exacting ways to their significance and to the hazards of reductive explanations. Reductionism indeed turns us away not only from experience but from recognizing the challenge of languaging experience; it deflects attention away from the fact that language itself is not experience and from the ensuing need for, and the fundamental importance of solid descriptive foundations. It is furthermore imperative to recognize that different levels of description are possible. Kelso indeed stresses "how important it is to choose a level of description appropriate to the phenomenon one wants to understand." The example he gives to demonstrate the importance is relevant to the present discussion:

> Since our ultimate goal is to understand mind, brain, and behavior in terms that reflect life itself (stabilities, transitions, crises, etc.), why are we talking about low-level ion channel kinetics at all? On the face of it, ion channels and single neurons are irrelevant to understanding brain and behavioral function. That's why bio-physicists study ion channels and psychologists study mental abilities, right? Of course this is the very myth I want to debunk. Yes, the molecular mechanisms of ion flows in permeable membranes must be clarified in detail. Yes, it's useful to study cognitive functions in their own right. Here, however, the search is for *level-independent principles*.... [W]e don't expect the dynamics to be the same at all levels (Kelso 1995: 235; see also Kelso & Engstrøm 2006: 201–203).

Kelso goes on to point out that "the patterns of switching that [are] seen between openings and closings of ion channels parallel the pattern of percept switching when people look at ambiguous figures. In fact, both can be understood in terms of intermittent processes in a nonlinear dynamical system" (Kelso 1995: 235).

The dynamic parallelism — "the shared dynamics" — that Kelso points out is theoretically similar to what Rose terms a "translational relationship": "[The] pattern of neural activity translates into the seeing of red, and seeing red is simply what we call in mind language the phenomenon that we call in brain language the activity of a particular ensemble of neurons" (Rose 2005: 215). A theoretical similarity is equally apparent with respect to the idea of "conceptual complementarity" and to a denial that we need to build a bridge between first- and third-person methodologies as Francisco Varela specifies (Varela 1996). As shown in an article titled "Preserving Integrity Against Colonization," "conceptual complementarities exist between constitution in a phenomenological sense and coordination in a dynamic sense." In light of this conceptual relationship, I affirmed that

> [a] genuine reconciliation of first- and third-person methodologies asks us to discover just such conceptual complementarities and to trace out in detail their common ground. It does not require bridge-building because conceptual bridges are already there. What it does require is listening and learning from each other, immersing ourselves in studies and concepts outside our own discipline, and expanding our understandings of life by examining and elucidating the animate ties that bind us in a common humanity, in a common creaturehood, and in a common quest for knowledge (Sheets-Johnstone 2004: 259).

In sum, the core challenge to understandings of animate life rests foundationally not on preeminencing *the brain* or on reductionism to *the brain*, but on descriptive foundations that elucidate the complexities and subtleties of animate life and that result in concepts tied to those complexities and subtleties. Meeting the challenge demands attention to ontogeny and to evolutionary forms of life. In precisely this context, we properly ask: is a nascent human infant, an infant chimpanzee, a baby lamb, or a newborn chick an embodied mind or a mindful body? Each newborn individual is a particular animate form of life entering into a particular lifeworld. What each discovers through its observations and explorations and ultimately solidifies are inborn capacities for *synergies of meaningful movement* (see also Sheets-Johnstone 2011a). These synergies attest to the foundational animation and dynamics that motivate, inform, and constitute its experiences. Accordingly, we may in turn ask: are its feelings, recognitions, images, and movements conveniently packaged — are they embodied? and embodied ultimately in a brain? — or do they in fact arise and resonate corporeally in a full-body sense to begin with? Are they, in other words, not the natural experiences of a mindful body, just as the synergies themselves are the naturally culminating capacities of a mindful body? What may be specifically limned as the natural subject-world integrity of animate forms of life may be elucidated on the one hand through constitution in a phenomenological sense, namely, a putting together or a synthesizing of aspects of things experienced in the world — in Husserl's term, "profiles" of things — and on the other hand through spontaneous pattern formations that are the bedrock of those coordination dynamics that inform animate bodies at all levels. What the integrity and indeed inherent coherency affirm is a complementarity of mind and motion. That complementarity is in fact described by Husserl at an even finer level, a level that resonates with James's stream of consciousness:

> [C]onsciousness of the world … is in constant motion; we are conscious of the world always in terms of some object-content or other, in the alteration of the different ways of being conscious (intuitive, nonintuitive, determined,

undetermined, etc.) and also in the alteration of affection and action, in such a way that there is always a total sphere of affection and such that the affecting objects are now thematic, now unthematic; here we also find ourselves, we who always and inevitably belong to the affective sphere, always functioning as subjects of acts but only occasionally being thematically objective as the object of preoccupation with ourselves (Husserl 1970a: 109).

When we add to the above reflections on *the brain* and related themes bona fide studies of ontogeny and of natural history, we find that the joints at which many a present-day life scientist carves are not necessarily the joints of nature or even joints at all. We find this fact validated in natural history, for example, when we read in detail of the quintessential importance of the reticular system in the brain stem that is central to arousal and attention and thus to consciousness, and of the coordinating functions of the cerebellum that enter into cognitive as well as kinetic capacities — capacities such as verbal language. Artificial joints can in fact give rise to conceptual arthritis in the sense of enlarging the significance of a part, arthritically hardening it and distorting the structure of the whole in the process, which is also why, in turn, artificial joints can give rise to linguistic surgeries and therapies on the order of "embodiments" that attempt to sew the whole back together, in effect, to reconstitute the original, wholly natural holistic form, or on the order of reductive motorologies that serve to gloss over or explain away any experiential phenomenon by making it happen "here." With respect to these linguistic stop-gap measures and operations, researchers would do well to heed, and heed from the beginning of their labors the long-ago cautionary words of Socrates, who stated in the context of discussing kinds of knowledge, that "division into species [should be] according to the natural formation, where the joint is, not breaking any part as a bad carver might" (*Phaedrus* 265 E). Moreover, as he elsewhere admonished, "we certainly should divide everything into as few parts as possible" (*Statesman* 287). In finer terms, then, instead of taking up a preeminently *cognitive* science, for example, and trying to reshape it to match the realities of life itself through linguistic implants on the order of *embodied* action (Varela, Thompson & Rosch 1991, e.g. 172–180), *embodied* language (Gibbs 2006), *embodied* cognition (Varela, Thompson & Rosch 1991: 147–184), *embodied* subjectivity (Zahavi 2005: 156–163), *embodied* self-awareness (Zahavi 2002), *embodied* simulation (Gallese 2007),[2] *embodied* self-experience (Zahavi 2005: 197–206), *embodied* mind (Thompson 2007), and even (wonder of wonders!) *embodied* movement (Gibbs 2006: 127, 130, 134; Varela & Depraz 2005: 69), or through linguistic transplants that conceptually disfigure the truths of experience by encasing them in a motorology, as in talk of sensorimotor subjectivity (Hanna & Thompson 2003; Zahavi 2005; Thompson 2007), sensorimotor profiles (Noë 2004), motor intentionality, motor control (Merleau-Ponty 1962), motor schema, motor intention (Gallagher 2005a, 2005b), and the like, we would do well to take seriously the thesis of the previous chapter. We would do well, in other words, to begin with the fundamental fact of animation that integrally and explicitly informs the evolution of animate forms of life and that indeed constitutes the basic evolutionary fact of animate life.

The combined moral to be drawn from detailed observations of infants, natural history, and the words of Socrates is succinctly illustrated by a fundamental and enduring concept in Edmund Husserl's writings. The concept is precisely that elaborated in the previous chapter: Husserl wrote of bodies, but did not write of *embodied* organisms; he wrote of action, but did not write of *active* or *enactive* organisms; he wrote of the world, but did not write of organisms being *embedded* in the world. He wrote simply, directly, and from start to finish of *animate* organisms. *Animation* is indeed the ground floor, the ontological and epistemological bedrock of human self-understandings and indeed of human pan-animate understandings, understandings that include but do not separate out in exclusive and privileged ways either *the brain* or cognition as the point of entry to those understandings. A striking correspondence in methodological priority in fact exists between Socratic and Husserlian investigations in their mutual call to turn to the experienced realities of life itself. In the *Cratylus*, Socrates asks Cratylus whether one can learn things as readily through names as through "the things themselves," and later states, "How *real existence* is to be studied or discovered is, I suspect, beyond you and me. But we may admit so much, that the knowledge of things is not to be derived from names. No; they must be studied and investigated in themselves" (*Cratylus* 439 A; italics added). Husserl's classic dictum, "to the things themselves" is a reiteration of Socrates's earlier dictum. In particular, Husserl states, "to judge rationally or scientifically about things signifies to conform *to the things themselves* or to go from words and opinions back to the things themselves, to consult them in their self-givenness and to set aside all prejudices alien to them" (Husserl 1983: 35). When we heed Socrates's and Husserl's keen insight into the manner in which we would best gain knowledge of ourselves and the world about us, including the lifeworlds of all animate forms of life, we realize that animation naturally conjoins affect, cognition, and movement, that it is the natural whole from which we separate out different features, and that to recognize this natural whole from the start puts us in the position of not having to join artificially or to try to conjoin what we have already in our ignorance separated in advance. Clearly, we would do well to attend to the fundamental realties of life itself that are ontogenetically and phylogenetically grounded in affectively and cognitively informed movement — in animation.

A major part of the effort in this section has been to single out divergent ways of thinking that occlude recognition of these realities, and this as a way of showing from a further point of view and at greater depth (see Chapter 10) the perils of construing *the brain* as the oracle at Delphi, the shrine to which all questions concerning humans are addressed and from which all bona fide explanations of humans emanate. Though not centering on the brain as oracle, philosopher Arthur Danto, in his provocative essay,

"The Body-Body Problem," hones in on these perils in a distinctive way that is both edifying and challenging and that propels us toward further insights. He does so by setting forth the difference between "the body that is me and the body that is merely mine" — "the minded body and the mindless one" (Danto 1999: 197), pointing out that "[an] eliminative strategy … haunts contemporary discussion" and that "according to [this eliminative strategy] the entirety of folk psychology, as it is abusively called, must give way to another kind of theory altogether, one based upon the findings of a future neurophysiology." He states, "With this replacement must come an erasure of the boundaries between the body as lived and the body ["of a future neurophysiology"]…. [T]he body that is me will itself wither as a concept, to be replaced with the body that is mine" (ibid.: 201).

Although he does not explicitly say so, the difference is linguistically expressed as the difference between being a body and having a body: "having a body" objectifies the realities of "being a body." In doing so, it obviously makes the body amenable to a thoroughly scientific account, not so much to a "neurophysiological" account, as Danto specifies, but, as in today's highly exclusive world of neuroscience, to a "neuroscientific" account, an account that quite obviously reduces to *the brain*. It is of considerable interest from the perspective of experience that Danto underscores the fact that with respect to the bodies we are, "we probably know very little the Greeks did not know" (ibid.: 197). He points out in fact that that body

> is close philosophical kin to what the Phenomenologists call the lived body: it is the lived body that enters into the basic human enterprises of working, fighting, and love…. It is the body as we see it represented on Grecian vases, in conduct we understand as we understand the body in most artistic representations of it, however exotic the traditions these come from. We perform, mainly, the sorts of actions and the kinds of thoughts and feelings the Greeks share with us: the body is the emblem of our common humanity (ibid.: 197–198).

Danto's recognition of our emblematic humanity and his cautionary words about an eliminative science that lacks recognition not to say respect for "the lived body" ring with unmistakable clearness. It is odd that they are not cited much less taken up in the context of later writings on "the body-body problem." When philosopher Evan Thompson emphasizes the centrality of kinesthetic experience to perception with due and strong reference to Husserl's phenomenology (Thompson 2007: 231–232) and underscores the need to understand "bodily self-consciousness" (ibid.: 248–252), but then speaks in terms of "sensori*motor* subjectivity" (ibid.: 243–266; italics added), the seeming gain in understandings of what he identifies as "the body-body problem" (with no reference to or citation of Danto) is aborted. Putative phenomenological insight into body-subject and body-object is not sustained nor are Danto's earlier pan-human phenomenological insights into the lived body. Linguistic surgical tetherings take the place of *bona fide* elucidations. Like Merleau-Ponty's "motor intentionality," a "sensorimotor subjectivity" leaves out fine-grained analyses of actual experience, what Thompson expressly seeks in his concern with "bodily self-consciousness." While the word 'motor' in English refers in an extended physiological sense to that which "convey[s] an impulse that results or tends to result in movement, as a nerve" and the word 'motoric' in both a psychological and physiological sense "pertain[s] to, or involve[s] muscular movement" (*Webster's New Universal and Unabridged Dictionary 1996*), neither word ever approaches much less recognizes *the dynamic kinesthetic realities of movement*. In short, while a sensorium is patently part and parcel of subjectivity, a motor is patently inadequate to any account of subjectivity whatsoever. Hence, a subjectivity grounded equally in sentience and movement is not a sensori*motor* subjectivity, but a *sensory-kinetic* subjectivity (for more on the propriety of sensory-*kinetic* over sensori*motor*, see Sheets-Johnstone 1990) whose sensorium is properly paired with the experienced kinesthetic dynamics of life itself — again, precisely as Husserl indicates not only in his consistent concern with *animate organism*, but in his pairing of sensing and movement in perception: "[T]he courses of appearance go hand in hand with the orchestrating movements of the lived-body".... The lived body is ... an entire system of compatibly harmonizing organs of perception" (Husserl 2001: 50). Indeed, as the natural history of consciousness (Chapter 2, Part I) indicates, a stunning spectrum of sensory-kinetic modes of living in the world defines the biological diversity of life (see also Sheets-Johnstone 1986a, 2009: Chapters III and VII).

A final point warrants attention in this context. The term *action* (see, for example, Dreyfus 1991, 2000; Noë 2004; Thompson 2007) is no match and certainly no substitute for movement. Like its motor correlate, it cannot approximate to a recognition and understanding of the qualitative kinesthetic/kinetic dynamics of movement, the substantive ground of our habits (or for that matter, to an understanding of our "skillful coping": see Dreyfus 1991, 2000) and of our learning our bodies and learning to move ourselves in the first place. In fact, *action* is no match or substitute for movement any more than behavior is a match or substitute. Neither action nor behavior open insight into the cardinal structures of kinesthetic consciousness that were set forth in Chapter 3, structures that ground the synergies of meaningful movement that inform our lives and that ground our habits. More generally, cardinal structures of movement emanate in a qualitative dynamic that grounds our recognition of the style of others — their way of walking, laughing, and so on. We in fact commonly recognize the qualitative kinetic dynamics of those in our immediate surrounding world far more readily than we customarily recognize our own. To recognize our own style requires us to turn to our own experience of movement and to witness the truths of our own experience. To turn in this way and to witness these truths in the overarching world of today's neuroscience seems near heretical. As philosopher Mary Midgley wisely reminds us, however, "Our inner experience is as real as stones or electrons" (Midgley 2004: 32). Though using the word "action, she calls attention to the reality of inner experience when she observes, "When we say that someone acts freely, deliberately and responsibly, this does *not* mean that a separate soul does so…. It simply means that *he or she does this action as a whole person*, attending to it and being well aware of what [he or she is] doing…. Of course this agent needs to have a brain — and no doubt some genes … [b]ut it is he or she, the whole person, who uses that brain, just as [he or she uses his/her] legs to walk and [his/her] eyes and hand in writing" (ibid.: 33). Her affirmation of "inner experience" is in the service of affirming that individual humans make individual choices with respect to their action and that their choices are not causally explainable in terms of their brains.

While many neuroscientists proceed in lock-step in their march to reductionism, others are clearly marching counter-step: in a vigorous and challenging nonlinear dynamic, to be exact (Kelso 1995; Kelso & Engstrøm 2006); in substantive recognitions of the personal-historical nature of life (Rose 2005: e.g. 186); and in substantive other ways, as in Raichle's recognition of the brain's "dark energy," that call into definitive question the notion of both an isolated neuron-by-neuron and an isolated module-by-module notion of the brain. As noted in Chapter 13, in concluding his findings on the dark energy of the brain, Raichle quotes James to the effect that "*whilst part of what we perceive comes through our senses from the object before us, another part* (and this may be the larger part) *always comes … out of our own head*" (Raichle 2006: 1250; James 1950, vol. II: 103). Together with fellow neuroscientist Dongyang Zhang, Raichle in fact has found that "'visible' elements of brain activity — neuronal responses to environmentally driven demands — account for less than 5 % of the brain's energy budget, leaving the majority devoted to intrinsic neuronal signaling" (Zhang & Raichle 2010: 1). In a later article, he explains how typical neuroscientists running imaging experiments attempt "to pinpoint the brain regions that give rise to a given perception or behavior." For example, "If researchers wanted to see which brain areas are important during reading words aloud (the 'test' condition) as opposed to viewing the same words silently (the 'control' condition), … they would look for differences in images of those two conditions … and essentially subtract the pixels in the passive-reading images from those in the vocal image." He points out that, "Representing data in this way makes it easy to envision areas of the brain being 'turned on', during a given behavior, as if they were inactive until needed by a particular task" (Raichle 2010: 30). What Raichle's studies have shown is that while a mind may be at rest — "when you are daydreaming quietly in a chair, say, asleep in a bed or anesthetized for surgery — dispersed brain areas are chattering away to one another" (ibid.: 28). Raichle has termed this activity "the brain's default mode network" (ibid.) and describes what is ongoing in the network as "intrinsic activity" (ibid.: 30). The term recalls Kelso's earlier identification and explication of "intrinsic dynamics," an identification and explication that constitutes the backbone of Thelen and Smith's descriptive account of infant reaching, which was cited and discussed in Chapter 5. Intrinsic dynamics describe the coordination tendencies of any self-organizing system. At a neurological level, brains are just such a system; they have their own intrinsic dynamics (in addition to previous references, see, for example, Kelso 2005, 2009; De Luca, Jantzen, Comani, Bertollo, & Kelso 2010). Intrinsic activity and intrinsic dynamics in fact seem complementary perspectives on the brain: the one in terms of a brain — or mind — putatively at rest, the other in terms of a brain — or mind — unequivocally in motion.

Intrinsic dynamics and intrinsic activity should surely give us pause for thought about reductionist thinking. Research findings with respect to each should in fact put the previous and present section in face of one another such that we could, in conclusion, pointedly ask whether a neuron by neuron, or module by module, or any other form of reductionist thought concerning *the brain* can do justice to the ever-changing nature of mind, that is, to the patently obvious experience of constant flow — of thoughts, feelings, movement, images, memories, expectations — and correlatively, to the intrinsic dynamics and intrinsic activity of the brain itself, an organ which, as highlighted previously, is part of a singular whole-body nervous system, a system which itself is part of a whole-body movement system, and that system part of a whole-body person We might in this context paraphrase the epigraph from Aristotle quoted at the beginning of this section: "For there is no such thing as a brain without a full-fledged body, that is, a mindful body; it is only homonymously called brain if the real-life animation has gone out of it, just as if it had been made of stone or wood." Along similar lines, we could say that the "unbridgeable gulf" between "consciousness and brain-process" of which Wittgenstein speaks (see epigraph, Chapter 11) is bridged by the foundational complementarity that informs all mindful bodies. In a pivotally central but also ironic way, "embodied minds," like other current "embodiments," serve reductionist interests and goals, occluding the reality of mindful bodies.

4. Receptivity and responsivity: Reciprocal concepts in phenomenology and evolutionary biology

> Five years ago the concepts of 'mind' and 'consciousness' were virtually excluded from scientific discourse. Now they have come back, and every week we see the publication of new books on the subject. Reading most of this work, we may have a sense of disappointment, even outrage; beneath the enthusiasm about scientific developments, there is a certain thinness, a poverty and unreality compared to what we know of human nature, the complexity and density of the emotions we feel and of the thoughts we have. We read excitedly of the latest chemical, computational, or quantum theory of mind, and then ask, 'Is that all there is to it?'
>
> Oliver Sacks 1995:101

[I]n the words of Louis de Broglie over 60 years ago, *philosophy* — literally, the love of wisdom — and *science* — from the Latin word *scio*, 'know" — have become polarized, segregated disciplines … What a strange world it is, where the love of wisdom and the pursuit of knowledge are separate enterprises!

J. A. Scott Kelso & David A. Engstrøm 2006: 183

There is obviously a difference between looking in the sense of investigating from the inside and looking in the same sense from the outside. The complementarity of the two forms of investigation mirror the basic complementarity of phenomenology and science, a complementarity that has the possibility of enlightening researchers on both sides. The possibility is readily apparent in two basic dimensions of animate life: receptivity and responsivity, the former being a central phenomenological character of animate life, the latter a central biological character. Both dimensions were discussed in various contexts in earlier chapters. The concern here is to examine them precisely in terms of their complementarity. That their complementarity is substantively significant is — or should be — immediately evident: whatever the animal, it could hardly be responsive if it were not receptive to begin with, that is, attentive, alert, and aroused in some way as in interest, excitement, or apprehension, for example. Correlatively, receptivity would count for nought if the animal were incapable of being responsive in some way, as in moving toward, away, or against. The two dimensions are natural to animate organisms, beings whose surrounding world is not just clearly present to them, but just as clearly interests, excites, or disturbs them to move in some way. At root, the dimensions are grounded in, and conceptually descriptive of, an affective/tactile-kinesthetic body, not two different bodies but two different aspects of the singular body that is the animate form itself. The two dimensions furthermore anchor the broader complementarity of existential fit, that is, the integral relationship obtaining between physical and lived bodies (Sheets-Johnstone 1986, 2009: Chapter III), the bodies that constitute the "body-body problem" of which Danto writes. More will be said of the affective/tactile-kinesthetic body and of the integral relationship obtaining between physical and lived bodies in the course of offering a more detailed account of each dimension.

Husserl considers receptivity to be a "phenomenologically necessary concept" that is "in no way" to be thought of as opposed to "activity" on the part of the subject. "On the contrary," Husserl affirms, "receptivity must be regarded as the lowest level of activity. The ego consents to what is coming and takes it in" (Husserl 1973: 79). He describes the experience of this first stage of receptivity as an affection, meaning that something in our surrounding world stands out for us or "'strikes'" us (ibid.: 76.) He states, for example, that "Through its intensity, the datum stands out from a multiplicity of coaffecting data. This occurs, for example, when, in the sensuous sphere, there is a sound, a noise, or a color which is more or less obtrusive" (ibid.). Moreover, he states that "a thought which suddenly emerges can be obtrusive, or a wish, a desire, can get through to us from the background with insistence" (ibid.) He points out that though the latter is nonsensuous and thus is not distinguished in a qualitative way, it is no less impelling along a continuum of weak to strong (ibid.: 76–77). He also points out from the beginning that receptivity is "prepredicative," meaning that the subject of experience is not yet involved in affirming or denying, that is, not yet involved in what he calls "position-takings" with respect to the "striking" or "obtruding" object. The affective pull of an object in the world, or of a thought or image or feeling, means simply that we are open both inside and out to whatever arises or appears, whether from within or without, and duly affected by it.

Because he is explicating perception first and foremost, and in particular the cognitive subtleties and complexities involved in perception, Husserl focuses attention on 'turning toward' as a second stage of receptivity, a turning toward in attention, not in actual movement. When the subject "yields" to the "stimulus," a transformation occurs: "there is a tendency of the intentional object to pass from a position in the *background of the ego* to one *confronting the ego* (ibid.: 77). Accordingly, in Husserl's terms, "the being-attracted, the being-affected" results in the *tendency to give way* (ibid.: 78). As he points out, the tendency runs along a gradient, both respect to its intensity and its temporal character. We thus begin to see initially how responsivity is the complement of receptivity. Turning toward in receptivity is a prelude to cognition; it presages an incipient recognition of something, an insipient recognition that results — or can result — in an actual movement in relation to it.

When put in the broader context of animate life generally, we can readily recognize and appreciate the relevance of receptivity and its concordance with certain descriptions offered by biological researchers. Receptivity is indeed a pan-animate phenomenon, descriptive of nonhuman as well as human life. It is conceptually related to von Uexküll's notion of "functional tone," for example (see this text Chapter 10): there would be no "functional tone" if an animal were not receptive in the first place, which is to say if, *from the beginning, there was not a subject-world relationship*. Most importantly too, receptivity is not only a perceptual disposition toward the world, as discussed in Chapter 9 (343 ff.), but, as Husserl indicates, a disposition toward an individual's own thoughts, feelings, memories, and so on — in short, toward whatever arises from within as well as whatever appears from without. Before we or any animate form of life turn toward, we are first of all struck by something and in this sense are simply the recipients of whatever comes to our awareness. The natural inborn capacity to be affected is thus a core phenomenon of animate life, a "primal sensibility" (Husserl 1989: 346). Husserl's exposition of receptivity is in fact of moment precisely in directing our attention toward *affectivity*, and more specifically still, toward deeper examinations and expositions of affectivity in relation to movement. In other words, receptivity — being affected and turning toward — leads us to an acknowledgment of what was referred to at the beginning of this section as the affective/tactile-kinesthetic body, and in turn to the dynamic congruency of affect and movement, that is, to a rec-ognition of the dynamic concordance of feeling in an emotional sense and feeling in a kinesthetic sense (see Sheets-Johnstone 1999, 2009: Chapter VIII). We can validate this concordance in the briefest way by noting that we can feign an emotion by going through the motions congruent with its dynamics and that we can restrain the expres-sion of an emotion by inhibiting its dynamics. We literally could do neither — and would never even be led to the possibility of doing either — were there not an inherent and naturally integral dynamic bond between the two kinds of feeling.

The above account of receptivity lays the ground for understandings of the seman-tic congruency of movement and meaning: how we move — as well as how we perceive the movement of others — is concordant with intentionality in a phenomenological sense, that is, in the sense of meaning. To elucidate this semantic aspect of receptivity more fully, consider first that receptivity was elucidated by Husserl as what is there — "pre-given" — prior to any theoretical act or cognition (Husserl 1989: 9–10). Its most succinct formulation might be said to be in his observation that "To be awake is to direct one's regard to something" (Husserl 1973: 79). Being awake is thus the ground floor of receptivity and thus undergirds the incipient form of responsivity, notably, the tendency *to turn toward*. In finer terms, the primary *"tendency to give way"* (ibid.: 78), to be affected by that which comes to awareness in pure attraction, is grounded in awakeness, an awakeness that carries with it not just the tendency, but the very pos-sibility of giving oneself over to it. In effect, while *to be awake* is first of all to be open to attractions and to tend toward being actually attracted and affected, *to be awakened* is actually to tend to turn toward the attraction. Hence Husserl's distinction: to be not just awake but awakened "means to submit to an effective affection" (ibid.: 79).

This wholly natural life experience of being awake and being awakened is clearly not some kind of passive capacity of the individual or subject — "the ego" in Husserl's terms. It is an active capacity, one that presages cognition, as Husserl indicates when he characterizes it as "the lowest level of activity" (ibid.) and elsewhere as "the root soil," the basis on which cognitions are constituted (Husserl 1989: 291–292). In "consent[ing] to what is coming and tak[ing] it in," the subject lays the ground for cognitions of its surrounding world. In effect, short of receptivity, there would be no knowledge of the world. There would indeed be nothing rather than something, for there would be no primordial awakeness, no primordial tendency or capacity to be affected, hence no awakened impulse to turn toward any object, i.e. no "effective affection." Knowledge would in effect be literally stillborn. Short of awakeness and being awakened, affectiv-ity and movement would never come to life, and in turn, short of affectivity and move-ment, knowledge would never come to life. We might recall from Chapter 5 not only that "we come into the world moving; we are precisely not stillborn," but that "[e]very-thing cognitive leads back … to movement, to animate nature" (118). Cognitivists who forego such basic truths of the animate nature of humans and all that animate nature engenders overlook natural dispositions and foundational capacities. They obviously do so at the peril of basing a science in findings that fail to explain the foundational realities of life itself: knowledge — cognition — is tied to affect and to movement. On the basis of these realities we come naturally to appreciate that the meaning that informs our movement — and informs our experience of the movement of others — is implicit in its dynamics. Humans and animate forms generally are not simply moving capriciously, unwittingly, or nonsensically through a kinetic form of one sort or another. On the contrary, in moving as they do, they are creating a certain dynamic that moves meaningfully through them. The concordance of meaning and dynamic is as apparent in the sustained fluidity of raising an arm overhead to signal someone as in the sudden and forceful raising of an arm to strike something. The dynamics are not just "telling" or "informative," but substantively structure meaning.

We might note specifically in this context of awakeness and being awakened and their essential relationship to cognition and meaning that a surrounding world naturally impinges on any animal, human or nonhuman. In Husserl's terms, "the tendency which precedes the *cogito*" is an "*obtrusion on the ego*" (Husserl 1973: 78). A surrounding world is, in a full sensory sense, an ongoing source of attraction that affects any animate organism in one way and another. In other words, it is open to its sounds, sights, smells, and its tactile aspects. We can thus appreciate again that neither we nor any other form of animate life needs to be *embedded* in a world: we are all already natural subjects of a natural world. That we are all naturally attracted and affected recalls a fundamental insight of Aristotle set forth earlier in the Aristotelian account of consciousness (Chapter 2, Part II), specifically, that "every body that has soul in it must … be capable of touch." In fact, all animate forms of life are in touch with something solid, liquid, or vaporous; as indicated, they are never out of touch with something. It should come as no surprise then that being awake, attracted, affected, and turning toward point us to a further basic truth of animate existence; namely, that following the tendency to being open to whatever attracts, to being duly affected, and to the successive tendency to turn toward, one can in actual fact turn away. In other words, the tendency to turn toward can propel one not only to turn toward in actual fact and continue on in interest and in veritable cognitive pursuits, but to turn away or against (Sheets-Johnstone 2007b). In short, one's actual movement response in face of a surrounding world is not always one of interest or in the interests of cognition, as in curiosity, puzzlement, and the like, but may be in the interests of protecting oneself from harm or of defending oneself against someone or something that may harm one. Thus the tendency to turn toward what attracts and affects may immediately reverse itself and impel one to run away or to strike out, to crouch or to hide, and so on. Receptivity is thus indeed not a static state of being, but a dynamic dimension of our aliveness; as Husserl emphasizes, receptivity is not *passive* but *active*. However low he places it on the experiential scale of cognition — of "apprehending" the object directly — he recognizes its living reality. It is no wonder then that he observes that every "higher" act has its foundation in affect and action, that "each free act [an act involving reason or cognition] has its comet's tail of nature" (Husserl 1989: 350; for more on Husserl's sometimes vexed relationship of "sensibility" and "reason," see Sheets-Johnstone 2007b).

We might furthermore in this context recall the opening epigraph of Chapter 1, namely, Darwin's judgment as to "the problem of the mind" and the approach proper to the problem: "Experience shows the problem of the mind cannot be solved by attacking the citadel itself. — the mind is function of body. — we must bring some *stable* foundation to argue from." As I have emphasized, and tried to show elsewhere as well, that stable foundation is patently the body, the living body that feels and moves, and in so doing, comes to cognize its surrounding world. More than thirty years ago Husserlian scholar Robert Sokolowski vindicated the claim when he wisely observed, "In phenomenological analysis, the description of apparitions and profiles as noemata must be supplemented by a description of the kinesthesia and sensibility that are their noetic counterparts" (Sokolowski 1974: 96). Kinesthesia and sensibility in other words are not mere physical or material apparatuses but have to do with consciousness. Moreover Sokolowski concluded his justifications for this requirement in part by noting that "[e]ven our capacity to perceive is not as basic as kinesthesia for it depends on the latter for its own possibility" (ibid.: 96–97). Our capacity for self-movement and our experience of self-movement are indeed cornerstones of our sense-makings. No wonder that Husserl wrote of a "root soil" (Husserl 1989: 291–92) that is the natural background of all comportment.

In sum, not just the better part of wisdom, but the whole of wisdom would be to recognize receptivity as an essential fact of life. However much its reality remains for the most part a neglected topic in phenomenology, not simply an overlooked dimension of animate life, but an overlooked foundational dimension, it remains both a natural and essential dimension of living forms that move themselves and that are moved to move themselves.

In a way similar to the way in which receptivity is a neglected topic in phenomenology, so responsivity is a neglected topic in science. In light of its centrality to animate life, it too is not prominenced in the foundational way it warrants. Responsivity is implicit in talk of "behavior," of "action" or "acts," and of "reaction to stimuli," but when swallowed up in such talk, its own evolutionary reality fails to come to light. Consider, for example, the following recent account on the *Natural History* website of ants helping a comrade who was trapped (Konkel 2009):

> Helpful acts, such as grooming or foster parenting, are common throughout the animal kingdom, but accounts of animals rescuing one another from danger are exceedingly rare, having been reported in the scientific literature only for dolphins, capuchin monkeys, and ants. New research shows that in the ant *Cataglyphis cursor*, the behavior is surprisingly sophisticated. Elise Nowbahari of the University of Paris North, Karen L. Hollis of Mount Holyoke College in South Hadley, Massachusetts, and two colleagues mimicked a natural situation — an ant restrained by collapsing sand and debris. But hidden beneath the sand was

a nylon snare holding the ant firmly in place. The ant's nestmates consistently responded by digging around the victim and tugging at its limbs until they found the trap, then biting at the nylon strand. Potential rescuers did not, however, do the same for unrelated ants or insects of other species. The ants' ability to discern and then tackle the unfamiliar nylon snare demonstrates cognitive and behavioral complexity, unlike such simple actions as digging or limb pulling, which could arguably be elicited by a chemical distress signal. Nowbahari and Hollis distinguish rescue behavior from other cooperative acts in that both participants risk physical harm (rescuing ants could themselves be trapped under falling sand), with no possibility of reward for the rescuer aside from the benefits of kin selection.

The "consistent response" of the ants attests to responsivity's being an underlying natural disposition, a disposition that is — or can be — present early on. Consider, for example, the responsivity of red-eyed embryo frogs that hang in a mass on leaves that dangle over tropical ponds. The embryonic frogs can distinguish perturbances caused by storms from perturbances caused by snakes biting into their mass. The older ones respond or not respond accordingly; that is, they "feel the vibes" and when necessary, they can "cut and run," i.e. older embryos can detach and flee when it is a snake that is moving them about (Milius 2009: 29). In Chapter 2, Part I, attention was called specifically to examples of responsivity in a biology text: "mealworms congregate in dampness; cats pounce on small moving objects … the capacity to respond is a fundamental and almost universal characteristic of life" (Curtis 1975: 28). Moreover Darwin's observations of animate life abound in accounts of responsivity and in fact attest to the capacity to reason in relation to responsivity. "Few persons," he states, "any longer dispute that animals possess some power of reasoning. Animals may constantly be seen to pause, deliberate, and resolve. It is a significant fact, that the more the habits of any particular animal are studied by a naturalist, the more he attributes to reason and the less to unlearnt instincts" (Darwin 1981 [1871]: 48). In fact, after giving a number of different examples of animal reasoning prior to or in the course of responding, he remarks, "The muleteers in S. America say, 'I will not give you the mule whose step is easiest, but *la más racional,* — the one that reasons best'; and Humboldt adds, this popular expression, dictated by long experience, combats the system of animated machines, better perhaps than all the arguments of speculative philosophy." (Darwin 1981 [1871]: 48)

Surely further testimonials are hardly needed. What is needed is an appreciation of how easily this fundamental and almost universal characteristic of life can be verbally transposed into behavioral talk of one kind or another rather than illuminated in terms of its real-life movement dynamics. As with receptivity, short of such illumination, understandings and insights into the realities of life itself are short-circuited. In contrast, when the most basic of phenomenological and biological concepts are put side by side, there is no question of their mutual relevance, which is to say of their fundamental complementarity. Looking and investigating from both inside and outside perspectives, phenomenologically as well as biologically, and biologically as well as phenomenologically, we not only elide the hazards of reductionism but discover that both forms of looking and investigating are mandatory to veridical accounts of life itself. An article titled "Eureka! Brain Makes Mental Leaps" amply testifies to the need for such looking and investigating. The article exemplifies the unquestioned strength and status of common reductive practice at the same time that it unintentionally highlights its basic fallibility. In demonstrating that rats have an "aha" moment when confronted with a new system of reward through an experimental program that tracks their prefrontal cortical activity, the researchers declare, "It is not clear whether the change in brain activity causes the insight, or the other way around" (Ehrenberg 2010: 9).

What *is* definitively clear is that the causal ambiguity stated by the researchers affirms not only the possibility that reductionism may be fallible, but that, in affirming the contrary possibility, i.e. that brain activity causes the insight, reductionism implicitly affirms the possibility that certain prefrontal cortical neurons rather than the rats themselves see blinking lights, press levers, and obtain or not obtain food rewards.

A reductive stance most commonly reduces to a motorological stance in terms of motor control, motor skills, motor learning, motor programs, and so on. Like the lexical band-aid of embodiment, a motorology is no substitute for descriptive accounts of experience, specifically both phenomenologically-based and biologically-based descriptive accounts of animate experience. Such accounts are at the core of conceptual understandings of animate life. The direct observations of Darwin and of Alfred Wallace gave rise to just such accounts as did those of physiologist Hermann von Helmholtz, for example, and as do those of Husserl and of infant psychiatrist Daniel Stern, for example. In short, a motorology does not and cannot account for the dynamic realities of life itself, realities that are foundationally grounded both ontogenetically and phylogenetically in animation, and correlatively, in the kinesthetic and proprioceptive experiences of animate organisms living their everyday lives.

Finally, precisely with respect to the complementarity of receptivity and responsivity and of basic phenomenological and biological research findings, methodological clarifications are in order. A phenomenological methodology, like a scientific methodology, takes verification to be not just of prime importance but a prime necessity. Verification of the validity of an account of experience through phenomenological replication of the experience is essential not only in terms of affirming validity, but in terms of opening new questions in an ongoing spiral of inquiry (see Sheets-Johnstone 2009). From its inception, the project of naturalizing phenomenology (Petitot, Varela, Pachoud, Roy 1999) cuts short the possibility of such replication and spiraling inquiry, that is, it cuts short the possibility of turning attention to the actual practice of phenomenology, directing attention and research instead, as Francisco Varela envisioned it, to a program of "reconciliation" by way of "pragmatically build[ing] the bridges between third- and first-person" (Varela 1999c: 273). As Varela tersely enjoined, "Keep the insights from the founding father [Husserl] and then move on," though he pointedly recognized at the same time that "neurophenomenology might make the grand old man [Husserl] turn in his grave" (ibid.; see Sheets-Johnstone 2004 on this topic). In spite of his urge to train people in the actual practice of phenomenology (see Varela 1996), Varela's methodological imperative has in large measure been followed, which is why, perhaps, in order to incorporate experience into their theoretical program, cognitivists tend straightaway simply to take over fundamental phenomenological findings and shape and use them in ways compatible with their interests (e.g. Varela's neurophenomenology: 1996, 1999a, 1999b, 1999c; see also this text Chapter 11 on Dennett's heterophenomenology). Husserl's exposition of perception as a combined process of sensing and kinesthesia is a particularly pointed example in the present context. As literally noted (note 10) in the previous chapter, philosopher Alva Noë takes over Husserl's methodologically arrived at insights not only without due credit, but without any evidence of having methodologically replicated and verified Husserl's findings, neither directly with respect to "the two-fold articulation" of sensing and kinesthesia that undergirds different "profiles" of objects (Husserl 1970a, 1989: 63; see also, e.g. Husserl 2001: 50–51), nor indirectly with respect to the body as "the zero point of orientation" (Husserl 1989: 61). Cognitive scientists and philosophers also refer to Merleau-Ponty in their efforts to illuminate the inherently bodily nature of experience (e.g. Thompson 2007; De Preester 2003; Bermúdez 2003). As indicated from the beginning of Chapter 6, however, Merleau-Ponty's methodology is in question. As that chapter shows, Merleau-Ponty incorporates findings of science into his understandings of bodily life and uses them as a point of departure for getting at "existential truths" of normal human capacities, experience, and behavior. Thus his ready "usefulness" to cognitivists, but a usefulness that elides methodological precision insofar as it lacks anchorage in the basic practice of phenomenology. It is thus not surprising that his "motor intentionality" (Merleau-Ponty 1962) is not equivalent to Husserl's "kinestheses" or intentionality (Husserl 1989, 1983).[3] In short, the direct move to "naturalize" phenomenology ignores the need to verify by one's own experience, and this by actually learning the method and actually practicing phenomenology, thereby acquainting oneself directly with its findings and proceeding from there to verify, to question, and so on, that is, to practice philosophy "close-up," experientially, as specified in Chapter 7. As its very formulation makes evident, "naturalizing phenomenology" otherwise makes for an unequivocally unequal partnership.

It is worth noting in this context that Husserl's phenomenology, while certainly no substitute for an objective scientific methodology, is a *complementary* methodology in a further sense. It illuminates the very ground of objective science, and this because any objective science necessarily begins with experience. Scientists could indeed not describe any observations or even begin to design an experiment if they did not, to begin with, experience something in particular that interests them, something that "obtrudes" and "strikes" them, something to which they were obviously in the beginning precisely "receptive." They would in turn not be led to apprehend the particular phenomenon as puzzling, worth studying or describing, or be led to design an experiment by which they could attempt to investigate it and explain it, and so forth: they would obviously not in other words be "responsive." Experience is the ground floor of science. It is the basic stuff of life itself, the pith of what it means to be alive. The fundamental nature of that ground floor is describable in terms of both *animation* and *dynamics*. To be alive is from an evolutionary perspective *to be a body, to have a surrounding world, and to be able to move in an efficiently and affectively knowledgeable way in relation to that surrounding world*. Moreover to move is in each instance to articulate a particular qualitative dynamic, a spacetimeforce or spatio-temporal-energic dynamic as shown in Chapter 3, not only as in walking, but in walking hesitantly, quickly, determinedly, restively or restlessly. Not only do aliveness and movement-affective dynamics go hand in hand, but aliveness, movement-affective dynamics, and world are of a biological-existential piece. Indeed, death terminates aliveness, movement-affective dynamics, and world at a stroke. It puts an end to receptivity and responsivity, the most basic dimensions of life, the incontrovertibly dispositional capacities of mindful bodies.

5.   Afterword on kinesthesia

When movement is called by its real name, kinesthesia will necessarily come to the fore. It will do so both because the experience of movement cannot be ignored and because the neurophysiology of movement in terms of muscles, tendons, and joints can no longer be short-circuited by talk of motor programs, motor happenings, action, or behavior. For these very reasons, kinesthetic memory will likewise come to the fore. The real-life kinetic/kinesthetic neurophysiology of nerve, muscle, and bone puts us in touch with dynamics that are there at all levels of animate being and with the hallmark of life that is their source: animation.

As shown in Chapter 5, sense-making begins with learning one's body and learning to move oneself. That primordial kinesthetically rooted sense-making is the backbone of broader sense-makings in the double sense of making sense oneself and making sense of one's surrounding world, a world not merely of objects but of other animate forms of life. The broader sense-makings are indeed descriptive of human sociality: making sense oneself with respect to others and making sense of others. As with the sociality of other animate forms of life, these broader social sense-makings are foundationally an intercorporeality grounded in kinesthetic/kinetic realities, which is to say in tactile-kinesthetic/affective bodies, bodies attuned to their own felt dynamics in feeling their way literally and metaphorically about the world. These bodies are the "root soil" of all comportments, the "comet's tail of nature" undergirding all perceptual-cognitional experience (Husserl 1989: 292–93, 350).

Being grounded in tactile-kinesthetic/affective bodies, our doubly meaningful social sense-makings are clearly not a matter of sensations. Indeed, the kinesthetic/kinetic living dynamics of our intercorporeal lives are not to be confused with sensations, whether from within or without, any more than kinesthesia is to be equated with or defined as "momentary sensation[s] of movement" (Husserl 2001: 52). As pointed out and discussed elsewhere (Sheets-Johnstone 2006a: 368), to use eye movement as a paradigm of movement is to overlook the fact that saccadic movement is not only temporally punctual and spatially pointillist — precisely as indicated by "the momentary sensation of movement" — but that eye movement is a two-dimensional, not a three-dimensional phenomenon. It is thus *not* equivalent to movement of the body proper. As shown elsewhere (ibid.), the inherent qualitative dynamics of movement go unnoticed in talk of sensations, in many instances because kinesthesia is reduced to bodily *position*, the complex dynamic experience of bodily *movement* going unrecognized and remaining unexamined. We might furthermore note that there is no way of elucidating the nature of a person's *style* in a phenomenologically lucid manner by way of sensations. The way in which movement and feelings flow forth in another person is the basis of what we think of as their *style*: the characteristic way in which they laugh, walk, are surprised, greet others, and so on. What is again imperative is an understanding of dynamics, in particular, kinetic and affective dynamics. In fact, as we shall presently see, two forms of kinesthetic experience are possible: self-movement has both an inside and an outside. As will become apparent by way of extending Husserl's original probings into the "interior" and "exterior" of movement (see Sheets-Johnstone 2008: Chapter V), the dual character of movement is the source of its social significance.

To gain insight into such understandings of movement requires not just deeper understandings of kinesthesia but straightforward recognition of kinesthesia and its non-sensational character in the first place. The kinesthetically felt dynamics of movement are akin neither to a shove, an itch, a flash, a prick, a jolt, nor even to a series of shoves, itches, flashes, pricks, or jolts; they are not equivalent to *sensations* or even to an amalgamation of *sensations*.[4] As noted above and pointed out and discussed elsewhere at length (Sheets-Johnstone 2006; see also 2008: Chapter V, 198–199), sensations are spatially pointillist and temporally punctual bodily events. In distinct contrast, movement is an ongoing spatio-temporal-energic dynamic that is first of all felt as such. In our everyday lives, it unfolds in a way similar to the way in which Husserl describes a melody: it too "runs off" (Husserl 1966: 48ff.); it too has a temporal structure, and a spatial and energic one as well. In short, the kinesthetically felt dynamic of our movement is a streaming, not a pointillist/punctual event, and it is precisely its dynamic streaming that rings in familiar ways in common everyday experience. Any familiar dynamic in other words constitutes an ongoing qualitatively inflected kinetic that has its own created spatio-temporal-energic character, the qualitatively inflected dynamic running off like a major theme with variations depending on circumstance. In Luria's apt words, it is a kinesthetic/kinetic melody. When we are already at home with any particular movement pattern or when we practice a particular pattern and through repetition learn it, its qualitatively inflected kinetic dynamic is of the essence of kinesthetic memory. As elucidated and emphasized elsewhere (Sheets-Johnstone 2003, 2009: Chapter X), melody and memory are dynamic images of one another, precisely as Luria indicates when he identifies kinetic melodies as "*integral kinesthetic structures*" (Sheets-Johnstone 2003: 74; Luria 1973: 176, italics in original). Because of the familiarity of the qualitatively inflected streaming, that is, because of the everyday familiarity of the dynamic even with its circumstantial variations, we commonly pay it no attention, our "concernful gaze," as Heidegger might put it, being directed elsewhere. As pointed out at the close of the first edition of this book, however, "any time we care to turn our attention to it ... there it is" (see further below on this topic and note 6).

Especially in light of present-day writings about embodiment and enaction, it is astonishing that an awareness of the qualitative dynamics of one's own body movement goes virtually unmentioned, remaining under-researched and in fact unexamined, or that when actually mentioned, is erroneously defined and in turn egregiously misapprehended, its integral value to life totally ignored.. As exemplified and discussed at length in Chapter 2, Part I, *animate* bodies — members of the Kingdom Animalia — are clearly living forms that make sense of their surrounding world through movement, at the same time sensing the dynamics of their own movement in relation to that world; they do not perceive their surrounding world like statues in face of whatever is in front of them. The sensory modalities that are cornerstones of their awareness — kinesthesia, proprioception, and tactility — are central and indeed pivotal dimensions of what makes their survival possible. In particular, contrary to received wisdom apparent in both philosophical and scientific writings and as noted in passing above, kinesthesia is preeminently not a *positional* sense but a *movement sense*, the experience of which constitutes a specific qualitative dynamic. Neurophysiologist Jonathan Cole and philosopher Shaun Gallagher, in aligning the perception of one's own movement with body image, reduce kinesthetic experience precisely to a positional knowledge of the body when they write: "I can tell you where my legs are even with my eyes closed." They positionalize movement even further when they state, "Proprioceptive awareness is a felt experience of bodily position that helps to constitute the perceptual aspect of the body image" (Gallagher & Cole 1998: 137). As shown in detail in Chapter 2, Part I, proprioception is *an evolutionary fact of animate life having to do preeminently with the experience of movement through bodily deformations.* Moreover as shown in that same chapter and in Chapter 3, *kinesthesia* is a *bona fide* sensory modality in its own right, one rooted in a neurophysiology that gives us an immediate sense of our own movement dynamics. On that indisputable neurophysiological basis, it should cease being swallowed up for ease in handling — whether wittingly or unwittingly — in proprioception (e.g. Gallagher 2003). Clearly, a gross injustice is done to the intricacies and complexities of movement when its distinctive sensory modalities are neglected or regarded simply a matter of positional knowledge. Not only philosophers and neuroscientists, but psychologists perpetuate the injustice. Wayne Weiten, for example, in the newest edition of his psychology textbook states, "The *kinesthetic system* monitors the positions of the various parts of the body. To some extent, you know where your limbs are because you commanded the muscles that put them there. Nonetheless, the kinesthetic system allows you to double-check these locations" (Weiten 2007:160; italics in original). In sum, the neglect of kinesthesia together with the reduction of kinesthesia and proprioception to positional knowledge are, like the equation of the experience of movement with sensations, an egregious instance of received ignorance.

The implicit prominencing of kinesthesia by default in a scientific textbook on movement validates the above critical observations. Physiologists Barbara Gowitzke and Morris Milner, in a chapter titled "The Proprioceptors and Their Associated Reflexes," are pointedly concerned with neural circuitry that permits stereotypical responses in human and nonhuman animals. They write, "Fortunately, neural control of muscles, whether activity is unconscious or deliberate, is mostly involuntary: muscles are smoothly regulated by reflex mechanisms" (Gowitzke & Milner 1988:256). They in turn state, "The voluntary contribution to movement is almost entirely limited to initiation, regulation of speed, force, range, and direction, and termination of the movement" (ibid.). However "limited" Gowitzke and Milner judge the contribution of voluntary movement in relation to involuntary muscular activity, their implicit recognition of the foundational qualitative character of movement and the wholly autonomous variables of initiation and termination can hardly be ignored, any more than can the fundamental significance of kinesthesia. Any voluntary movement sequence is in the first place initiated; its spatial, temporal, and energic qualities can be modulated circumstantially; and the sequence or kinesthetic melody can be terminated at will. Accordingly, kinesthesia is incontrovertibly a built-in of voluntary movement. Unlike vision, hearing, taste, and smell, it cannot be voluntarily closed down: we cannot shut out our kinesthetically-felt bodies as we can shut out vision by closing our eyes, shut out noise by clamping our ears, shut out smells by pinching our nose, shut off tastes by closing our mouths. Our tactile-kinesthetic bodies cannot in fact be dampened in any way except through pathological disaster. In Chapter 2, Part II, following Aristotle's observation that touch was essential to animate being, it was pointed out that we are never out of touch with something. Something similar can be said with respect to movement. Not only is movement essential to animate being, but, as discussed in Chapter 5, we come into the world moving; we are precisely not stillborn. Our primordial animation is with us from the beginning to the end of our lives.

While kinesthetic experience certainly does *not* commonly constitute our focal everyday adult awareness, it is indisputably at the margins or horizons of our awareness in the form of a dynamic — as noted above, most commonly a familiar dynamic which, in light of its familiarity, runs off virtually by itself (see further below on familiar dynamics and note 3 for erroneous understandings of same). It is notable that kinesthesia is precisely the sense modality that was lost by IW—IW being the patient whom Cole and Gallagher describe at length in terms of body image and body schema. Though the modality was lost, IW nonetheless acknowledged that he had a "crude" sense of effort. Cole and Gallagher give no concrete phenomenologically-informed elaboration of this "crude" sense of effort, which, by definition would seem incontrovertibly to be rooted in kinesthesia, i.e., in felt bodily tensions and directional impulsions. As I commented elsewhere, "If cognitive science is to make use of experiential reports, it should insure that reportees are trained if not in phenomenological methodology, then in 'auto-sensory observation' (Jacobson 1967, 1970). IW's report of 'a "crude" sense of effort' (Gallagher & Cole 1998: 137) is tantalizing in this respect. What is this 'crude' sense?" (Sheets-Johnstone 2003: 90; also in Sheets-Johnstone 2009: 275, note 14). Motor programs, motor acts, motor capacities, motor abilities, motor intention, motor schema, motor strategies (Gallagher & Cole 1998; Gallagher 2005b) — motor talk in general — offer no hope for enlightening us about such experience. On the contrary, such talk consistently bypasses any recognition of kinesthetic experience and indeed covers over any need for it.[5] A preeminently postural notion of the body encased in the notions of "proprioceptive information" and "proprioceptive awareness" (Gallagher 2005b: 43–47) does the same: it loses sight of our foundational animation and the qualitative dynamics of movement that inform our everyday lives. We might rightfully observe, in fact, that if we actually had a kinesthetic system that preeminently registered position and not movement, we would certainly know the particular spatial form of our body when it is still, as in a photograph, but we would not know in a substantively kinetic sense how we arrived at that position or how to get out of it.

The qualities of movement set forth in a descriptive analysis in Chapter 3 were not pulled out of the drawer of an ivory-tower desk much less out of a laboratory hat filled with speculatively or even introspectively arrived at possibilities, but were discovered in the course of following Husserl's classical phenomenological method and of engaging in a phenomenological analysis of movement. With respect to bodily-felt qualia generally, it is notable that the essential nature of the body is not *to be in pain* (e.g. Chalmers 1996) or *to see colors* (e.g. Thompson 2007; Noë 2004, O'Regan & Noë 2001a, 2001b, Thompson, Noë, Pessoa 1999), but *to move*. It would thus seem imperative to concern ourselves with animation, to investigate movement, self-movement, and in turn, determine its essential character. All the more so since, as shown and detailed in Chapter 5, movement is our mother tongue. The social dimension of this central ontogenetical truth can be profitably spelled out precisely in these terms: in the beginning, we relate to others in and through movement, through a *kinesthetically-and kinetically-inflected* intercorporeality (see Stern 1995). This social dimension testifies in profound ways to the core significance of movement in our lives, its dynamic qualitative structure and its affective resonance. That verbal language is post-kinetic (Chapters 3 and 12) in fact testifies not only to corporeal concepts — nonlinguistic concepts (see also Sheets-Johnstone 1990) — but to our original and primary form of social communication. Affective modes of receptivity and responsivity to others, affective accordances and disaccordances with others, and so on, are anchored and articulated in bodily movement, including the bodily kinetics of vocalization. Stern's detailed descriptive accounts of "affect attunement" (Stern 1995) are relevant in just this context. Before words intercede, we relate to others in and through movement and in notably affective as well as effective ways. Our social lives are indeed rooted in a dynamic intercorporeality that is kinesthetically and affectively resonant through and through.

Requisite to finer understandings of this dynamic intercorporeality is a mandatory clarification of kinesthetic experience, namely, recognition of two distinct modes of kinesthesia, the first definitively felt, the second definitively perceived (Sheets-Johnstone 2008, 2010, 2011a). In today's world of neuroscience, little recognition is given to either mode, much less to their distinction, and this in good measure because little recognition is given to kinesthetic afference, certainly not to the exacting and penetrating degree to which Luria attended to it and realized its fundamental import (Luria 1966, 1973). Indeed, in twenty-first century brain-tethered neuroscience, it is as if the sensory modality that is kinesthesia, the premiere one to develop neurologically along with tactility, did not exist. Texts devoted to fetal/embryonic development implicitly highlight the criticality of the omission and its import.

That fetuses suck their thumb, for example, is testimonial to the primordial significance of animation and the tactile-kinesthetic body that is its foundation and of the initial sensory neural structures to develop: movement and touch — not vision, smell, hearing, or taste — are primary in a neurologically developmental sense. But there is a fourth corporeal dimension that is experientially relevant to each of these primary modalities, namely, inner and outer, or inside and outside. While we commonly think of up/down, side/side, and front/back as constituting the three-dimensionality of our bodies, there is also an experienced fourth dimension that distinguishes what is experienced within from what is experienced without. In phenomenological circles, drawing on what Merleau-Ponty transformed on the basis of Husserl's quite different original analyses (see this text, Chapter 6, and Husserl 1989: 154–59), present-day philosophers commonly wax on about the reversibility of the touched and touching hand, about their *chiasmatic* relationship, as Merleau-Ponty described it (Merleau-Ponty 1968). But kinesthesia has a veritable double mode of reality all its own that Husserl first described and that is seldom if ever explicitly recognized. A notable exception to common practice are the perspicuous and enlightening probings of philosopher Søren Overgaard that focus on Husserl's initial findings about kinesthetic experience, specifically, the fact that it has both an interior and an exterior (Overgaard 2003; see Sheets-Johnstone 2008, Chapter 5 for a full discussion). In essence, these findings and probings point toward two possible kinds of awarenesses of self-movement. In particular, the confusion of kinesthetically-based *perceptions* of one's bodily movement and kinesthetically-based *feelings* of the dynamics of one's movement ties in with the fact of movement having both an outside and an inside. As shown elsewhere (Sheets-Johnstone 2008), the experience of self-movement can follow along the lines of a felt dynamic or of a perceived three-dimensionality, the latter extending, when objectively expanded, into a four-dimensionality of space-time. Its *felt* dynamic describes a particular spatio-temporal-energic pattern or *dynamic line* (Sheets-Johnstone 1966 [1979/1980]). If the movement is habitual, its dynamic line unfolds like a familiar theme, a theme having variations according to circumstances, as noted above, as in the basic spatio-temporal-energic pattern that defines walking that has specifically varied spatial, temporal, and energic qualities depending upon whether one is rushing or sauntering, invigorated or fatigued, and so on. Sneezing, a classic example of an involuntary dynamic to which the dynamics of laughing, yawning, and sobbing, not to mention breathing might be added, is witness to the fact that common human movements, both voluntary and involuntary, are all kinesthetically felt dynamic themes with variations. Their particular dynamic is or can be keenly felt even as they run off by themselves: any time we care to pay attention to their unfolding dynamic, there it is.

This existential fact of life was already indicated not only in the closing sentence of the original edition of this book, as indicated above, but in Chapter 6 with respect to the tactile-kinesthetic body (see page 256). [6] A ready and familiar example — namely, the everyday practice of brushing one's teeth — makes the point incontrovertibly. Were someone else to brush your teeth, you would immediately recognize the fact that you yourself were not brushing your teeth, not simply because you saw someone standing before you holding your toothbrush and moving it about, but because *you would definitively feel a foreign dynamics running off inside your mouth.* A totally different tactile-kinetic melody would be unfolding. Tactility and kinesthesia are indeed commonly intertwined: our tactile-kinesthetic bodies are the bedrock of the dynamic invariants that shape our everyday lives, and this because we are indeed *animate* organisms and are always in touch with something (e.g. Chapter 2, Part I: 53). In the same way that the particular dynamic flow of a nursery rhyme may be vocalized with nonsense syllables — transliterated into 'dá-de-dá-de-dá-de-dá' as in "Mary Had A Little Lamb" — so the dynamic line of any movement may be vocalized and its dynamics brought audibly to the fore, its manner of flow and its accents duly recognized. To be attentive to the inherent dynamics of movement is to be attentive to the fact that *the felt experience of movement is precisely a matter of a qualitatively-inflected dynamic.*

It is furthermore revealing as a style, one's own as well as that of others, as shown in Chapter 3, Section 7 and mentioned briefly elsewhere (see Subject Index).

The *perceptual* experience of self-movement is rooted in an awareness of one's movement as taking place in a surrounding world, a dynamic kinetic reality that has an objective if fleeting presence. What is perceptually realized first and foremost is the three-dimensionality of one's movement; that is, the spatial volume of one's movement becomes apparent, and with it — at least at times — the possible collision of one's movement with nearby objects or other persons. The fact that one is or can be perceptually aware of one's movement as a kinetic worldly reality is obviously significant with respect to interpersonal relations; one can become aware of the literal or figurative impact of one's own movement dynamics on others. A point of core significance in this respect is the fact that one does not need to "embed" oneself in the world: self-movement, and specifically, our natural capacity to perceive our own movement, already testifies to a surrounding world and to the experience of that surrounding world as an open — or closed — expanse.[7] The capacity to perceive our own movement is part and parcel of learning: learning to jump rope, to serve, spike, and set up a ball in volleyball, to write one's name, to ride a bicycle, to hammer a nail, to make a surgical incision — and to begin with, to turn over, to crawl, and to walk. Such a perceptual capacity is not basically a *motor* skill or a matter of *motor* control: it is basically the experience of *living movement*, of an experiencing *living body*, hence of *kinesthesia*, which in this learning instance constitutes a perceptive attention to the spatial, temporal, and/or energic aspects of our movement as it unfolds in a particular surrounding world. Initial learnings aside, a quick side-stepping movement in our otherwise even-gaited and straightforward path in order to avoid an oncoming object is testimony to such a perceptual capacity as is the effort to increase the reach of our arm overhead in a tennis serve in order to increase its kinetic force. It should perhaps be pointed out specifically that perceiving our own movement as a three-dimensional happening or a constellation of spatial, temporal, and energic aspects is not contingent on vision. We do not, in other words, have to *see* our own movement in order to be aware of it as a kinetic reality in the world (cf. Dennett [Chapter 2, Part I: 48]: "Do something and look to see what moves.").

In sum, self-movement has an inside and an outside, either of which can be the object of our attention and hence constitute our experience. We have merely to shift from our natural attitude with all its built-in presuppositions and unexamined assumptions and begin examining movement itself, not from afar but close-up, experientially rather than behaviorally (see this text: 249, 295). Indeed, we would do well to allow ourselves "the poverty of not yet knowing" and to engage in "the creative labor that comes as its response" (295).

A final concern comes with this shift in attitude, namely a concern with efforts toward "naturalization," an energetic enterprise in present-day cognitive science and philosophy and in present-day neuroscience. With lexical markers already in hand to label phenomena, many such researchers forge ahead in unswerving reductive ways. Their blindered determination to naturalize is in other words a dogged attempt to cerebralize. It is dogged in that it is precisely a persistent, tenacious, even stubborn effort to subvert any talk of movement into some form of "brain talk." Such naturalizations of movement patently distort the real-life experiential realities of movement: its dynamic congruency to affective feelings, its semantic congruency to meaning, and its ontogenetical import as the foundation of spatio-temporal-energic concepts that are the basis of verbal language. The dogged attempt is indeed — to borrow the subtitle of a book by Giorgio Agamben (Agamben 2007) — a "destruction of experience," and this even though, as shown and discussed in the previous section, experience is necessarily the bottom if unacknowledged line of any such research, indeed of any research program. The practice of naturalizing transforms movement and kinesthetic experience into something other than themselves, as when, for example, in module-by-module explanations, "the link between affect and action" is cerebrally located in critical ways to the orbitofrontal cortex. The orbitofrontal cortex can certainly be "active" in laboratory experiments centering on affect and action, but as indicated earlier in the "aha" rat experimenters' comment, there is a question as to whether the activity in the orbitofrontal cortex is cause or effect, and further, the problem of experiential ascriptions to *the brain*. Moreover, in broader terms, there is the more basic question of whether a causal explanation — in Aristotle's terms, an efficient cause — gives us the ultimate truth about a phenomenon.

Naturalizing actions is a sophisticated form of reductionism that actually does an injustice to Nature. Who we are and what we are have a *natural* history, a history in which our human *nature* has its roots. Naturalizing elides that history. In particular, it commonly ignores completely *the evolution of humans*, neither taking into account nor recognizing to begin with our primate heritage, much less our mammalian one. In many ways, naturalization thus appears a self-centered practice, thoroughly narcissistic in its blindered elevation of human preeminence and prestigious uniqueness in the form of a brain. It furthermore appears a covert form of objectification, a transformation of something putatively less than empirical, i.e. something merely experiential, thus "subjective," into something irrefutably empirical: *the brain*, an experimentally testable and duly tested anatomical object. Put in this perspective, the three beginning entries in the dictionary definition of naturalizing should actually be embarrassing to naturalizing academics. The first definition reads: "to confer upon (*an alien*) the rights and privileges of a citizen"; the second, "to introduce (organisms) into a region and cause them to flourish *as if native*"; the third, "to introduce or adopt (*foreign practices*, words, etc.) into a country or into general use" (*Webster's New Universal Unabridged Dictionary, Revised and Updated:* italics added in each instance). In each instance the process of naturalizing involves a positively identified outlander, outsider, or stranger of some kind being brought into "the fold." The fourth definition is obviously more congenial to naturalizers and is undoubtedly preferred: "to bring into conformity with nature." The problem, however, is that *movement and kinesthesia already conform with nature.* They are not alien, non-native foreigners to nature. On the contrary, they emanate from nature. *Each is already a wholly natural phenomenon.* Indeed, it is *action*, not movement, that necessitates the conforming move. The concern with action is so narrowly focused that it occludes not only the very possibility of recognizing kinesthesia but the very possibility of recognizing evolutionary realities that connect kinesthetically and proprioceptively endowed human animals with kinesthetically and proprioceptively endowed nonhuman ones. When philosopher Dorothée Legrand (Legrand 2010: 170), for example, in defining "bodily intention," states that "at the level of action, the body relates to the world in a meaningful, motor and nonintellectual way," she postulates an unnatural body, a body that fails to accord with migrating animals who are kinesthetically and intellectually active and acute navigators and with hunting animals who are kinesthetically and intellectually active and acute judges, for example, not to mention seeing-eye dogs who are kinesthetically and intellectually active and acute guides. As the exemplifications and discussions of our phylogenetic heritage in Chapter 12 show, *thinking in movement* is a basic capacity of animate forms of life (see also Sheets-Johnstone 1986 on hunting and intelligence). Moreover in failing to take evolution into serious account, Legrand's account of "action," like other typical neuroscience and philosophical accounts (e.g. Maasen, Prinz & Roth 2003; Prinz 2003a, Prinz 2003b, Hommel 2003; Noë 2004,) is opaque to studies of stone tool-making and tool-using, for example, not only by great apes — chimpanzees, gorillas, and orangutans — but by capuchin monkeys, crows, and dolphins (Bower 2009). With their academic grids in place, such researchers fail utterly in thinking "action" can take them to understandings of animate life.

It is notable that in the introductory chapter of *Naturalizing Intention In Action,* Franck Grammont poses the question of the meaning of "naturalizing." He states, "Literally, naturalizing an epistemic object is to make it 'natural' in the sense of making it concrete and graspable by empirical sciences" (Grammont 2010: 4). Clearly we may ask: does movement need such "naturalizing"?; does kinesthesia? "To the things themselves," Husserl's famous dictum, has perhaps never been more apt. The natural attitude with all its prejudgments, assumptions, and biases that are already in place and reign *unquestioned* preclude understandings of "*real existence.*" A shift away from the natural attitude opens experience precisely to "the things themselves," and in turn, in light of phenomenological practice, to a realization of the challenge of languaging experience. The things themselves are no longer ready-mades and knowledge of them is no longer a matter of naming. Being true to the truths of experience becomes a linguistic as well as purely epistemic challenge, a quest in itself. The truths of experience are occasionally straightforwardly asserted in reductive tracts, but at the same time remain unplumbed and unelucidated, their fundamental import going unrecognized. A prime, even tantalizing example occurs in the context of neurophysiologist Marc Jeannerod's chapter titled "Consciousness of Self-Produced Actions and Intentions" in his book *Motor Cognition: What Actions Tell the Self*. After recognizing that "kinesthetic cues clearly relate to a self-generated movement: they are 'first-person' cues in the sense that they can only conceivably arise from the self," he goes on to concern himself with "a longstanding controversy" concerning the role of these kinesthetic cues with respect to non-sensory cues "represented by central signals originating from various levels of the action generation system." He asks whether "conscious knowledge about one's actions" come from the former or the latter? He points out that "experimenters have consistently failed to resolve this issue, mainly because of the methodological difficulty of isolating the two sources of information from one another." In particular, he states, "*There are no reliable methods for suppressing kinesthetic information arising during the execution of a movement*" (Jeannerod 2006: 55–56; italics added).

Jeannerod's statement concerning "kinesthetic information" should be not only an eye-opening insight into the foundational reality of kinesthesia, but a formidable prod to examine precisely what *is* there in kinesthetic "information," that is, to examine meticulously and thoroughly through phenomenological analysis precisely what is there *in insuppressible kinesthetic experience*, and not only in terms of invariant qualitative structures, but in terms of thinking, concepts, and congruencies as indicated above. In following through on this examination, one would discover that "naturalizing intention" by means of "indirectly asses[ing] the mental states we experience on the basis of their underlying mechanisms and behavioral expressions such as neuronal activities and actions" (Grammont 2010: 4) leads us in an entirely different direction, a direction having nothing to do with kinesthesia and virtually nothing to do with movement insofar as movement is dismissively defined as "[e]lementary components constituting actions" (ibid.: 13).

Such unpromising omissions of kinesthesia and degradations of movement notwithstanding, "*real existence*" cannot remain interminably suppressed if only because the insuppressible reality of kinesthesia cannot remain interminably ignored. The "elementary components constituting action" will eventually engage researchers. A concern with real existence, after all, can hardly be passed over by scientists or philosophers. Investigating what is elementary and studying what is real coincide both with scientists' quest for knowledge and philosophers' love of wisdom. However swallowed up at present or called by something other than its real name, kinesthesia and movement are on the rise. They are coming slowly to attention and out of the shadows in which they have been kept, both observationally and conceptually. When submerged in talk of action and acts, of embodiment, behavior, enaction, and the like, and when transmogrified into motorological talk, not only are the experiential and demonstrable empirical realities of kinesthesia and movement occluded, but we are in turn impeded from realizing their foundational import and from reaching veritable understandings of our core animation that is there from the beginning of our lives and is precisely gone when we die. Indeed, when we die, it is not that we can no longer act, that we are no longer embodied, that we can no longer behave, that we are no longer capable of motor skills, that we are no longer the beneficiaries of a putative central pattern generator, and so on, but that we cannot *move,* that we cannot feel ourselves *moved to move,* and that we cannot feel the *qualitatively meaningful and affective dynamics of our own movement.* The kinesthetically and affectively structured synergies of meaningful movement that ground our lives as humans and that themselves are grounded in our ontogenetical and phylogenetical histories are gone. When present in the elementary and real-time existence of our aliveness, those synergies of meaningful movement that abound in our everyday lives and the kinesthetic memory that sustains them attest resoundingly to the fact that we are not embodied minds but mindful bodies.

Notes

1.   Though oddly enough omitting reference to Kelso's extensive research and writings on the dynamics of complex systems, i.e. brain and behavior, and of their coordination at all levels of animate being, van Gelder and Port's 1995 book *Mind as Motion* underscores the importance of recognizing dynamics, in particular the dynamics of cognition, and the importance of shifting away from a computational and representational view of mind.

2.   Gallese's guest lecture, given in conjunction with his receiving the 2009 Arnold Pfeffer Prize, is titled "From Mirror Neurons to Embodied Simulation: A New Perspective on Intersubjectivity." However fascinating and of moment the finding of "mirror neurons," Gallese's précis of the lecture succinctly demonstrates an allegiance to a reductive mode of thought, what we might justly term a runaway reductionism that elides the realities of animation and the qualitatively inflected living dynamics that are its hallmark, in essence, eliding what Husserl recognized as the "interior" and "exterior" of movement (see Section IV: Afterword on Kinesthesia) by reducing our "intercorporeity" to "representations" in the brain. Herewith Gallese's précis as given in the announcement of the prize and guest lecture:

> Our seemingly effortless capacity to perceive the bodies inhabiting our social world as goal-oriented individuals like us depends on activity within a shared "we-centric" space. I have proposed that this shared manifold space can be characterized at the functional level as *embodied simulation,* a basic functional mechanism by which our brain/body system models its interactions with the world.
>
> The mirroring mechanism for action and other mirroring mechanisms in our brain represent sub-personal instantiations of embodied simulation. Embodied simulation provides a new empirically based notion of intersubjectivity, viewed first and foremost as intercorporeity. Embodied simulation challenges the notion that

Folk-psychology is the sole account of interpersonal understanding. Underlying our capacity for "mind reading" is intercorporeity as the main source of knowledge we directly gather about others. Parallel to the detached third-person sensory perception of social stimuli, internal non-linguistic "representations" of the body-states associated with actions, emotions, and sensations are evoked in the observer, as if he or she were performing a similar action or experiencing a similar emotion or sensation.

By means of an isomorphic format we can map others' actions onto our own motor representations, as well as others' emotions and sensations onto our own viscero-motor and somatosensory representations. Social cognition is not *only* explicitly reasoning about the contents of someone else's mind. Our brains, and those of other primates, appear to have developed embodied simulation as a basic functional mechanism that gives us a direct insight of other minds, thus enabling our capacity to empathize with others.

3.   See Gallagher 2010 for an attempt to promote — one might almost say eulogize — Merleau-Ponty's *Phenomenology of Perception*, and this in terms of his conjoining science, in particular the study of pathologically disturbed humans, and phenomenology in that book.. Merleau-Ponty's use of pathology obviously offers a platform and even a lexical template in its employment of terms such as body image and body schema for today's scientists and philosophers who, rather than showing cognitive- and neuro-science and phenomenology to be conceptually complementary projects (see Sheets-Johnstone 2004), seek to *fuse* them by various means, and who, in addition, rather than fathoming in a phenomenologically rigorous sense *normal* everyday human experience, want to read off the normal from the pathological. Indeed with respect to the latter and contrary to Gallagher's claim, Merleau-Ponty does not "treat kinesthesia" (Gallagher 2010: 184), i.e. he does not examine phenomenologically the experience of self-movement. If he had done so, could he honestly have written of the body "[a]s a mass of tactile, labyrinthine and kinaesthetic data" (see this text: 287–88 for references), for example, and of the "massive sentiment" of a "massive presence to self" (ibid.: 305), or perhaps most tellingly, could he have failed to follow up his own query about movement, instead declaring, "in thinking clearly about movement, I do not understand how it can ever begin for me, and be given to me as a phenomenon" (ibid.: 289)? Clearly, one can hardly claim that Merleau-Ponty "treats kinesthesia." As shown in the original chapters of this text as well as in the added chapters of this second edition, such fusings and readings actually cut phenomenology short by short-circuiting the very methodological project initiated by Husserl, a project that spawned foundational and integral insights into body and movement that clearly open a vast terrain for further study, but insights too that may be appropriated by others, including Merleau-Ponty, to serve quite other ends. See too Sheets-Johnstone 2010 for phenomenologically grounded analyses and understandings of movement inside and out.

4.   To define kinesthesia on the basis of etymology as *sensation* (e.g. Petit 2010: 201–202) is misleading This derivative meaning actually falls short of the basic nature of kinesthetic experience, which is dynamic and dynamically felt, not perceived. See further in this text for the distinction between the two kinds of kinesthetic experience. See too Sheets-Johnstone 2010.

5. So also does the word "processing" as invoked with respect to information, i.e. 'processing information'. As English literature scholar Simon Beesley (Beesley & Joughin 2001) comments (pers. comm.), "In all but a few instances in cognitivist literature, so it seems to me, the term "processing" could be replaced by "gubbins" with no loss of meaning.

6. In view of this consistently recognized existential fact of life, Gallagher makes an egregious error in stating, "Sheets-Johnstone ... claims that movement constantly generates a qualitative, proprioceptive, and kinesthetic consciousness of our bodies," or in other words, that kinesthetic consciousness is "a constant bodily awareness" in a focal sense. Sheets-Johnstone does nothing of the kind. See Gallagher 2005:60–61. See also Gallagher 2003:53 where Gallagher attributes to Sheets-Johnstone the idea that "One is said to be proprioceptively aware of one's own body, to consciously know where one's limbs are at any particular time as one moves through the world." Again, Sheets-Johnstone says nothing of the kind. Gallagher completely overlooks the dynamic realities of kinesthetic experience, precisely what Sheets-Johnstone is at pains to elucidate. See too Sheets-Johnstone 2006:387, note 5 for further notice of these errors. For more on kinesthesia and proprioception from a psychotherapeutic perspective, see Sheets-Johnstone 2010.

7. In contrast to this existential truth, see, for example, philosopher Andy Clark's "information-theoretic lens" of "embodiment" through which the "cognitive roles of body, action, and environment" are to be understood (Clark 2008:54).

References

Agamben, Giorgio. 2007. *Infancy and History: On the Destruction of Experience,* trans. Liz Heron. London: Verso.

Altmann, Stuart A. 1967. "The Structure of Primate Social Communication." In Stuart A. Altmann (ed), *Social Communication Among Primates.* Chicago: University of Chicago Press, 325–362.

Aristotle *De Anima*

Aristotle *Generation of Animals*

Aristotle *Metaphysics*

Aristotle *On Generation and Corruption*

Aristotle *Physics*

Asanuma, Hiroshi. 1989. *The Motor Cortex.* New York: Raven Press.

Bartenieff, Irmgard & Dori Lewis. 1980. *Body Movement — Coping with the Environment.* New York: Gordon & Breach.

Bartenieff, Irmgard, Martha Davis & Forrestine Paulay. 1970. *Four Adaptations of Effort Theory in Research and Teaching.* New York: Dance Notation Bureau.

Beer, Randall D. 1995. "Computational and Dynamical Languages for Autonomous Agents." In Timothy van Gelder & Robert F. Port (eds), *Mind as Motion: Explorations in the Dynamics of Cognition.* Cambridge, MA: Bradford/MIT Press. 121–147.

Beesley, Simon & Sheena Joughin. 2001. *History of 20th Century Literature.* London: Hamlyn.

Bell, David. 1990. *Husserl.* New York: Routledge.

Bell, William J. 1991. *Searching Behavior: The Behavioral Ecology of Finding Resources.* London: Chapman & Hall.

Benesh, Rudolf & Joan Benesh. 1969. *An Introduction to Benesh Movement Notation: Dance,* rev. ed. New York: Dance Horizons.

Bennett, Jonathan. 1971. *Rationality.* London: Routledge & Kegan Paul.

Bergson, Henri. 1991. *Matter and Memory,* trans. Nancy Margaret Paul & W. Scott Palmer. New York: Zone Books.

Bermúdez, José. 2003. "The Phenomenology of Bodily Perception." *Theoria et Historia Scientiarum,* vol. VII, no. 1: 43–52.

Bernstein, Douglas A., Alison Clarke-Stewart, Edward J. Roy, Thomas K. Srull, Christopher D. Wickens. 1994. *Psychology,* 3rd ed. Boston: Houghton Mifflin Co.

Bernstein, Nicolas. 1984. *Human Motor Actions: Bernstein Reassessed,* ed. H.T.A. Whiting. New York: Elsevier Science Publishing Co.

Bertenthal, Bennett I. & Jeanine Pinto. 1993. "Complementary Processes in the Perception and Production of Human Movements." In Linda B. Smith & Esther Thelen (eds) *A Dynamic Systems Approach to Development: Applications.* Cambridge, MA: Bradford Books/MIT Press, 209–239.

Bertenthal, Bennett I., D.R. Proffitt, & J.E. Cutting. 1984. "Infant Sensitivity to Figural Coherence in Biomechanical Motions." *Journal of Experimental Child Psychology* 37: 214–30.

Bhaerman (Swami Beyondananda). 1991. "Drive Your Karma, Curb Your Dogma: Swami Beyondananda's Guidelines for Enlightenment." Austin, TX: Lite Headed Productions.

Bloom, Lois. 1993. *The Transition from Infancy to Language: Acquiring the Power of Expression.* New York: Cambridge University Press.

Blumhagen, Dan W. 1979. "The Doctor's White Coat." *Annals of Internal Medicine* 91: 111–116.

Bohm, David. 1995 [1981]. *Wholeness and the Implicate Order.* London: Routledge.

Bonobo People. Video tape and "Data Base." Language Research Center: Georgia State University.

Bower, Bruce. 1989. "Talk of Ages." *Science News* 136(2): 24–26.

Bower, Bruce. 1992. "Babies Add Up Basic Arithmetic Skills." *Science News* 142(9): 132.

Bower, Bruce. 1995. Brain Activity Calms Down to Expectations." *Science News* 147(3): 38.

Bower, Bruce. 1996. "Creatures in the Brain." *Science News* 149(13): 234.

Bower, Bruce. 2007. "Consciousness in the Raw." *Science News* 172(11): 170–172.

Bower, Bruce. 2009. "Chimp Chasers Join Artifact Extractors to Probe the Roots of Stone Tools." *Science News*, November 21, 2009: 25–28.

Bower, T.G.R. 1971. "The Object in the World of the Infant." *Scientific American* 225(4): 30–38.

Brace, C.L. & M.F. Ashley Montagu. 1965. *Man's Evolution.* New York: Macmillan Co.

Bruner, Jerome. 1983. *Child's Talk: Learning to Use Language.* New York: W.W. Norton & Co.

Bruner, Jerome. 1990. Acts of Meaning. Cambridge, MA: Harvard University Press.

Brues, Alice. 1959. "The Spearman and the Archer — An Essay on Selection in Body Build." *American Anthropologist* n.s. 61: 457–69.

Bruzina, Ronald. 1995. "There Is More to the Phenomenology of Time Than Meets the Eye." Paper presented at the Center for Advanced Research in Phenomenology, Florida Atlantic University, November 1995.

Bull, Nina. 1951. *The Attitude Theory of Emotion.* New York: Nervous and Mental Disease Monographs (Coolidge Foundation).

Burnyeat, Myles. 1992. "Is an Aristotelian Philosophy of Mind Still Credible?" In Martha C. Nussbaum & Amélie Oksenberg Rorty (eds), *Essays on Aristotle's "De Anima."* Oxford: Clarendon Press, 15–26.

Butterworth, George. 1983. "Structure of the Mind in Human Infancy." In L.P. Lipsitt & C.K. Rovee-Collier (eds), *Advances in Infancy Research*, Vol. 2. Norwood, NJ: Ablex Publishing, 1–29.

Butterworth, George. 1993. "Dynamic Approaches to Infant Perception and Action: Old and New Theories about the Origins of Knowledge." In Linda B. Smith & Esther Thelen (eds), *A Dynamic Systems Approach to Development: Applications.* Cambridge: MIT Press/ Bradford Books, 171–187.

Butterworth, George & B. Hopkins. 1988. "Hand–Mouth Coordination in the Newborn Baby." *British Journal of Developmental Psychology* 6: 303–14.

Calvin, William H. 1987. "The Brain as a Darwin Machine." *Nature* 330: 33–34.

Caporael, Linnda R., Robyn M. Dawes, John M. Orbell, Alphons J.C. van de Kragt. 1989. "Selfishness Examined: Cooperation in the Absence of Egoistic Incentives." *The Behavioral and Brain Sciences* 12: 683–739; Continuing Commentary 1991. *The Behavioral and Brain Sciences* 14: 748–753.

Carlson, Neil R. 1991. *Physiology of Behavior*, 4th ed. Boston: Allyn & Bacon.

Carlson, Neil R. 1992. *Foundations of Physiological Psychology*, 2nd ed. Boston: Allyn & Bacon.

Carpenter, C.R. 1963. "Societies of Monkeys and Apes." In Charles H. Southwick (ed), *Primate Social Behavior.* New York: Van Nostrand Reinhold, 17–51.

Carruthers, Peter. 1989. "Brute Experience." *The Journal of Philosophy* 86(5): 258–69.

Cassirer, Ernst. 1957. *The Philosophy of Symbolic Forms*, Vol. 3: *The Phenomenology of Knowledge*, trans. Ralph Manheim. New Haven: Yale University Press.

Cassirer, Ernst. 1970. *An Essay on Man*. New York: Bantam Books.

Chalmers, David. 1996. *The Conscious Mind*. New York: Oxford University Press.

Churchland, Patricia S. 1986. *Neurophilosophy: Toward a Unified Science of the Mind/Brain*. Cambridge, MA: MIT Press.

Churchland, Patricia S. & Terrence J. Sejnowski. 1992. *The Computational Brain*. Cambridge, MA: Bradford Books/MIT Press.

Churchland, Paul M. 1981. "Eliminative Materialism and the Propositional Attitudes." *The Journal of Philosophy* 78: 67–90.

Churchland, Paul M. 1984. *Matter and Consciousness: A Contemporary Introduction to the Philosophy of Mind*. Cambridge, MA: MIT Press.

Churchland, Paul M. 1985. "Reduction, Qualia, and the Direct Introspection of Brain States." *The Journal of Philosophy* 82 (1): 8–28.

Claesges, Ulrich. 1964. *Edmund Husserls Theorie der Raumkonstitution*. The Hague: Martinus Nijhoff.

Clark, Andy. 2008. "Embodiment and Explanation." In *Handbook of Cognitive Science: An Embodied Approach*, ed. Paco Calvo & Antoni Gomila. Amsterdam: Elsevier, 41–58.

Clark, Eve V. 1973. "Non-linguistic Strategies and the Acquisition of Word Meanings." *Cognition* 2: 161–82.

Clark, Eve V. 1979. "Building a Vocabulary: Words for Objects, Actions and Relations." In Paul Fletcher & Michael Garman (eds) *Language Acquisition*. Cambridge: Cambridge University Press, 149–60.

Condillac, Etienne Bonnot de. 1971 [1756]. *An Essay on the Origin of Human Knowledge*, trans. T. Nugent. Gainesville, FL: Scholars' Facsimiles and Reprints.

Condillac, Etienne Bonnot de. 1982 [1754]. *Treatise on the Sensations*, trans. Franklin Philip. Hillsdale, NJ: Lawrence Erlbaum.

Conrad, Joseph. 1958. *Lord Jim*. New York: Bantam Books.

Cotterill, Rodney M.J. 1995. "On the Unity of Conscious Experience." *Journal of Consciousness Studies* 2(4): 290–312.

Couliano, Ioan P. 1987. *Eros and Magic in the Renaissance*, trans. Margaret Cook. Chicago: University of Chicago Press.

Cowley, Geoffrey & Amy Salzhauer. 1995. "Humankind's First Steps." *Time*, 28 August 1995: 64.

Crick, Francis & Christof Koch. 1992. "The Problem of Consciousness." *Scientific American* 267(3): 153–159.

Crowell, Steven. 1996. Commentary. Husserl Circle meeting

Cunningham, Merce. 1968. *Notes on Choreography*, ed. Frances Starr. New York: Something Else Press.

Curtis, Helena. 1975. *Biology*, 2nd ed. New York: Worth Publishers.

Curtis, Helena & N. Sue Barnes. 1989. *Biology of Cells*, 5th ed. New York: Worth Publishers.

Cutting, James E. & Peter D. Eimas. 1975. "Phonetic Feature Analyzers and the Processing of Speech in Infants." In James F. Kavanagh & James E. Cutting (eds), *The Role of Speech in Language*. Cambridge, MA: MIT Press, 127–148.

Dahl, Hartvig. 1977. "Considerations for a Theory of Emotions." Preface to *A Structural Theory of Emotions* by J. de Rivera, p. 4. New York: International Universities Press.

Dallery, Arleen B. 1989. "The Politics of Writing (The) Body: *Ecriture Feminine*. In Alison M. Jaggar & Susan R. Bordo (eds), *Gender/Body/Knowledge*. New Brunswick, NJ: Rutgers University Press.

Damasio, Antonio R. & Hanna Damasio. 1992. "Brain and Language." *Scientific American* 267(3): 89–95.

Danto, Arthur C. 1999. *The Body/Body Problem: Selected Essays*. Berkeley: University of California Press.

Darwin, Charles, 1965 [1872]. *The Expression of the Emotions in Man and Animals*. Chicago: University of Chicago Press.

Darwin, Charles. 1968 [1859]. *The Origin of Species*, ed. J.W. Burrow. New York: Penguin Books.

Darwin, Charles. 1976 [1881]. *Darwin on Earthworms: The Formation of Vegetable Mould Through the Action of Worms with Observations on Their Habits*. Ontario, CA: Bookworm Publishing Co.

Darwin, Charles. 1981 [1871]. *The Descent of Man and Selection in Relation to Sex*. Princeton: Princeton University Press.

Darwin, Charles. 1987. *Charles Darwin's Notebooks, 1836–1844*, Paul H. Barrett, Peter J. Gautrey, Sandra Herbert, David Kohn, Sydney Smith (eds). Ithaca: Cornell University Press.

da Vinci, Leonardo. 1959. *Philosophical Diary*, trans. Wade Baskin. New York: Wisdom Library.

Dawkins, Richard & J.R. Krebs. 1978. "Animal Signals: Information or Manipulation?" In J.R. Krebs & N.B. Davies, *Behavioral Ecology*. London: Basil Blackwell, 282–309.

De Luca, Cinzia, Kelly J. Jantzen, Silvia Comani, Maurizio Bertollo, J.A. Scott Kelso. 2010. "Striatal Activity During Intentional Switching Depends on Pattern Stability." *The Journal of Neuroscience* (March 3, 2010) 30/9: 3167–3174.

Dennett, Daniel C. 1983. "Intentional Systems in Cognitive Ethology: The 'Panglossian' Paradigm Defended." *The Behavioral and Brain Sciences* 6: 343–390.

Dennett, Daniel C. 1991. *Consciousness Explained*. Boston: Little, Brown & Company.

Dennett, Daniel C. 1995. *Darwin's Dangerous Idea*. New York: Simon & Schuster.

Dennett, Daniel C. 1996. *Kinds of Minds*. New York: Basic Books.

Denny-Brown, Derek. 1966. *The Cerebral Control of Movement*. Thomas: Springfield, IL.

De Preester, Helena. 2003. "Meaning: What's the Matter?" *Theoria et Historia Scientiarum*, vol. VII, no. 1: 195–205.

de Rivera, Joseph. 1977. *A Structural Theory of the Emotions*. New York: International Universities Press.

Derrida, Jacques. 1976. *Of Grammatology*, trans. Gayatri C. Spivak. Baltimore: Johns Hopkins University Press.

Descartes, René. 1984 [1641]. *Meditations on First Philosophy*. In *The Philosophical Writings of Descartes*, vol. 2, trans. John Cottingham, Robert Stoothoff, & Dugald Murdoch. New York: Cambridge University Press.

Descartes, René. 1985 [1644]. *Principles of Philosophy*. In *The Philosophical Writings of Descartes*, vol. 1, trans. John Cottingham, Robert Stoothoff, & Dugald Murdoch. New York: Cambridge University Press.

de Sousa, Ronald. 1987. *The Rationality of Emotion*. Cambridge, MA: MIT Press.

Di Palolo, Ezequiel A. 2005. "Autopoiesis, Adaptivity, Teleology, Agency." *Phenomenology and the Cognitive Sciences* 4: 429–452.

Dolhinow, Phyllis J. 1972. "The North Indian Langur." In Phyllis J. Dolhinow (ed), *Primate Patterns*. New York: Holt, Rinehart, & Winston, 85–124.

Dorsett, D.A. 1976. "The Structure and Function of Proprioceptors in Soft-Bodied Inverte-brates." In P.J. Mill (ed), *Structure and Function of Proprioceptors in the Invertebrates*. London: Chapman & Hall, 443–483.

Dreyfus, Hubert L. 1991. *Being-In-The-World: A Commentary on Hweidegger's Being and Time*, Division 1. Cambridge, MA: MIT Press.

Dreyfus, Hubert L. 2000. "Responses." In *Heidegger, Authenticity, and Modernity*, vol. 1: *Essays in Honor of Hubert L. Dreyfus*, ed. Mark A. Wrathall and Jeff Malpas. Cambridge, MA: MIT Press, 305–341.

Dreyfus, Hubert L. & Stuart E. Dreyfus. 1990. "Making a Mind Versus Modelling the Brain: Artificial Intelligence Back at a Branch-Point." In Margaret A. Boden (ed), *The Philosophy of Artificial Intelligence*. London: Oxford University Press, 309–333.

Dreyfus, Hubert L. & David Hoy. 1994. Directors of Summer Institute at University of Santa Cruz.

Dreyfus, Hubert L. & Paul Rabinow. 1983. *Michel Foucault: Beyond Structuralism and Herme-neutics*, 2nd ed. Chicago: University of Chicago Press.

Dundes, Alan. 1992. "Wet and Dry, the Evil Eye: An Essay in Indo-European and Semitic World-view." In Alan Dundes (ed), *The Evil Eye: A Casebook*. Madison: University of Wisconsin Press, 257–312.

Edelman, Gerald M. 1992. *Bright Air, Brilliant Fire: On the Matter of the Mind*. New York: Basic Books.

Ehrenberg, Rachel. 2010. "Eureka! Brain Makes Mental Leaps." *Science News*, June 5, 2010: 9.

Ehrenreich, Barbara. 1997. "What a Cute Universe You Have." *Time*. 25 August 1997: 82.

Eibl-Eibesfeldt, Irenäus. 1974. "The Myth of the Aggression-Free Hunter and Gatherer Society." In Ralph L. Holloway, *Primate Aggression, Territoriality, and Xenophobia*. New York: Academic Press, 435–57.

Eibl-Eibesfeldt, Irenäus. 1979. "Universals in Human Expressive Behavior." In Aaron Wolfgang (ed), Nonverbal Behavior. New York: Academic Press, 17–30.

Eimas, Peter D. 1975. "Speech Perception in Early Infancy." In L.B. Cohen & P. Salapatek (eds), *Infant Perception*. New York: Academic Press, 193–231.

Eimerl, Sarel & Irven DeVore. 1965. *The Primates*. New York: Times, Inc.

Ekman, Paul. 1989. "The Argument and Evidence about Universals in Facial Expressions of Emotion." In H. Wagner & A. Manstead (eds), *Handbook of Social Psychophysiology*. New York: John Wiley & Sons, 143–164.

Ekman, Paul. 1992. "Facial Expressions of Emotion: An Old Controversy and New Findings." *Philosophical Transactions of the Royal Society of London*, Series B 335: 1–7.

Ekman, Paul, J.J. Campos, R.J. Davidson, F.B.M. de Waal, eds. 2003. "Expression: Panel Discus-sion." In *Emotions Inside Out: 130 Years after Darwin's The Expression of the Emotions in Man and Animals. Annals of the New York Academy of Sciences*, vol. 1000. New York: New York Academy of Sciences, 266–278.

Eldredge, Niles & Ian Tattersall. 1982. *The Myths of Human Evolution*. New York: Columbia University Press.

Ellis, Ralph D. 1995. *Questioning Consciousness: The Interplay of Imagery, Cognition, and Emo-tion in the Human Brain*. Philadelphia: John Benjamins Publishing.

Emmeche, Claus. 1991. "A Semiotical Reflection on Biology, Living Signs and Artificial Life." *Biology and Philosophy* 6: 325–340.

Emmeche, Claus. 1994. "The Computational Notion of Life." *Theoria* 9(21): 1–30.

Epstein, Mark. 1995. *Thoughts Without A Thinker*. New York: Basic Books.

Eshkol, Noa & Abraham Wachmann. 1958. *Movement Notation*. London: Weidenfeld & Nicholson.

Fentress, John C. 1989. "Developmental Roots of Behavioral Order: Systemic Approaches to the Examination of Core Developmental Issues." In Megan R. Gunnar & Esther Thelen (eds), *Systems and Development*. Hillsdale, NJ: Lawrence Erlbaum Associates, 35–76.

Fields, H.L. 1976. "Crustacean Abdominal and Thoracic Muscle Receptor Organs." In P.J. Mill (ed), *Structure and Function of Proprioceptors in the Invertebrates*. London: Chapman & Hall, 65–114.

Fink, Eugen. 1978. "Operative Concepts in Husserl's Phenomenology." In Anna-Teresa Tymieniecka (ed), *The Human Being in Action: The Irreducible Element in Man*, Part II. Boston: Reidel, 56–70.

Fink, Eugen. 1981. "The Problem of the Phenomenology of Edmund Husserl," trans. Robert M. Harlan. In William McKenna, Robert M. Harlan, & Laurence E. Winters (eds), *Apriori and World: European Contributions to Husserlian Phenomenology*. The Hague: Martinus Nijhoff, 21–55.

Fink Eugen. 1995. *Sixth Cartesian Meditation*, trans. Ronald Bruzina. Bloomington: Indiana University Press.

Firth, Raymond. 1973. *Symbols: Public and Private*. Ithaca: Cornell University Press.

Flanagan, Owen. 1991. *The Science of the Mind*, 2nd ed. Cambridge, MA: Bradford Books/MIT Press.

Flanagan, Owen. 1992. *Consciousness Reconsidered*. Cambridge, MA: Bradford Books/MIT Press.

Fodor, Jerry. 1975. *The Language of Thought*. Scranton, PA: Crowell.

Foster, Mary LeCron. 1978. "The Symbolic Structure of Primordial Language." In Sherwood L. Washburn & Elizabeth R. McCown (eds), *Human Evolution: Biosocial Perspectives*. Menlo Park, CA: Benjamin/Cummings, 77–121.

Foster, Mary LeCron. 1982. "Meaning as Metaphor I." *Quaderni di Semantica* 3(1): 95–102.

Foster, Mary LeCron. 1990. "Symbolic Origins and Transitions in the Palaeolithic." In Paul Mellars (ed), *The Emergence of Modern Humans: An Archaeological Perspective*. Edinburgh: Edinburgh University Press, 517–539.

Foster, Mary LeCron. 1992. "Body Process in the Evolution of Language." In Maxine Sheets-Johnstone (ed), *Giving the Body Its Due*. Albany, NY: State University of New York Press, 208–230.

Foster, Mary LeCron. 1994a. "Symbolism: The Foundation of Culture." In Tim Ingold (ed), *The Companion Encyclopedia of Anthropology*. New York: Routledge, 366–395.

Foster, Mary LeCron. 1994b. "Language as Analogic Strategy: Suggestions for Evolutionary Research." In L.H. Rolfe, A. Jonker, & J. Wint (eds), *Studies in Language Origins*, Vol. 3. Amsterdam: John Benjamins, 179–204.

Foster, Mary LeCron. 1996. "Reconstruction of the Evolution of Human Spoken Language." In Andrew Lock & Charles Peters (eds), *Handbook of Symbolic Evolution*. Oxford: Oxford University Press, 747–772.

Foucault, Michel. 1977. "Nietzsche, Genealogy, History." In *Language, Counter-Memory, and Practice*, ed. Donald F. Bouchard, trans. Donald F. Bouchard & Sherry Simon. Ithaca: Cornell University Press, 139–64.

Foucault, Michel. 1979. *Discipline and Punish*, trans. Alan Sheridan. New York: Vintage Books.

Frayer, David W. 1981. "Body Size, Weapon Use, and Natural Selection in the European Upper Paleolithic and Mesolithic." *American Anthropologist* 83: 57–72.

Freud, Sigmund. 1935. *A General Introduction to Psycho-Analysis*, rev. ed. Joan Riviere (ed). New York: Liveright.

Freud, Sigmund. 1938. *The Basic Writings of Sigmund Freud*, trans. and ed. A.A. Brill. New York: Modern Library.

Freud, Sigmund. 1953. *Complete Psychological Works of Sigmund Freud*, 24 Vols., trans. and ed. James Strachey, Vols. 4, 5. London: Hogarth Press.

Freud, Sigmund. 1959. "The Uncanny." In *Collected Papers*, Vol. 4, ed. Ernest Jones, trans. Joan Riviere. New York: Basic Books, 368–407.

Frith, Uta. 1993. "Autism." *Scientific American* 268(6): 108–114.

Furuhjelm, Mirjam, Axel Ingelman-Sundbert, and Claes Wirsén. 1976. *A Child Is Born*, revised ed. New York: Delacourte Press.

Galilei, Galileo. 1957. *Discoveries and Opinions of Galileo*, S. Drake (trans. and ed). Garden City, NY: Doubleday.

Gallagher, Shaun. 2000. "Phenomenological and Experimental Research on Embodied Experience." Paper presented at *Atelier phénomenologie et Cognition*. December 2000. Phénomenologie et Cogntion Research Group, CREA, Paris.

Gallagher, Shaun. 2003. "Bodily Self-Awareness and Object Perception." In *Theoria et Historia Scientiarum*, vol. VII (1): 53–68.

Gallagher, Shaun. 2005a. "Dynamic Models of Body Schematic Processes." In *Body Image and Body Schema*, ed. Helena De Preester and Veroniek Knockaert. Amsterdam: John Benjamins, 233–250.

Gallagher, Shaun. 2005b. *How The Body Shapes The Mind*. Oxford: Clarendon Press/Oxford University Press.

Gallagher, Shaun. 2010. "Merleau-Ponty's *Phenomenology of Perception*." *Topoi* 29: 183–85.

Gallagher, Shaun & Jonathan Cole. 1998. "Body Image and Body Schema in a Deafferented Subject." In *Body and Flesh*, ed. Donn Welton. Oxford: Blackwell, 131–147.

Gallese, Vittorio. 2007. "Intentional Attunement. The Mirror Neuron System and Its Role in Interpersonal Relations." *Interdisciplines*. "What Do Mirror Neurons Mean?" http://www.Interdisciplines.org/mirror/papers/1

Gardner, Helen. 1948. *Art Through the Ages*. New York: Harcourt, Brace & Co.

Georgopoulos, Apostolos P. 1992. "Motor Cortex: A Changing Perspective." In R. Caminiti, P.B. Johnson, Y. Burnod (eds), *Control of Arm Movement in Space*. New York: Springer-Verlag, 175–183.

Gibbs, Raymond W. Jr. 2006. *Embodiment and Cognitive Science*. Cambridge: Cambridge University Press.

Gibson, Eleanor J. 1988. "Exploratory Behavior in the Development of Perceiving, Acting, and the Acquiring of Knowledge." *Annual Review of Psychology* 39: 1–41.

Gibson, James J. 1966. *The Senses Considered as Perceptual Systems*. Boston: Houghton Mifflin Company.

Gibson, James J. 1979. *The Ecological Approach to Visual Perception*. Boston: Houghton Mifflin Company.

Giunti, Marco. 1995. "Dynamical Models of Cognition." In Timothy van Gelder & Robert F. Port (eds), *Mind as Motion: Explorations in the Dynamics of Cognition*. Cambridge, MA: Bradford Books/MIT Press, 549–571.

Golani, Ilan. 1976. "Homeostatic Motor Processes in Mammalian Interactions: A Choreography of Display." In P.P.G. Bateson & P.H. Klopfer (eds) *Perspectives in Ethology*, Vol. 2. New York: Plenum Publishing, 69–134.

Golani, Ilan. 1981. "The Search for Invariants in Motor Behavior." In Klaus Immelman, George W. Burlow, Lewis Petrinovitch, & Mary Main (eds), *Behavioral Development*. London: Cambridge University Press, 372–90.

Goldstein, Joseph. 1983. *The Experience of Insight*. Boston/London: Shambhala.

Goldstein, Joseph & Jack Kornfield. 1987. *Seeking the Heart of Wisdom: The Path of Insight Meditation*. Boston/London: Shambhala.

Goodall, Jane. 1990. *Through a Window: My Thirty Years with Chimpanzees of Gombe*. Boston: Houghton Mifflin.

Gordon, James. 1991. "Spinal Mechanisms of Motor Coordination." In Eric R. Kandel, James H. Schwartz, & Thomas M. Jessell (eds), *Principles of Neural Science*, 3rd ed. New York: Elsevier Publishing Co., 581–595.

Gotthelf, Allan & James G. Lennox. 1987. *Philosophical Issues in Aristotle's Biology*. Cambridge: Cambridge University Press.

Gould, Stephen Jay. 1980. "Piltdown Revisited." In *The Panda's Thumb*. New York: W.W. Norton & Co.: 108–125.

Gould, Stephen Jay. 1989. *Wonderful Life*. New York: W.W. Norton & Co.

Gould, Stephen Jay. 1994. "So Near and Yet So Far." Review of *The Neandertals: Changing the Image of Mankind*, by Erik Trinkaus and Pat Shipman, and *In Search of the Neanderthals: Solving the Puzzle of Human Origins*, by Christopher Stringer & Clive Gamble. *New York Review of Books*, 20 October 1994: 24–28.

Gould, Stephen Jay. 1995a. "Evolution by Walking." *Natural History*, March 1995: 10–15.

Gould, Stephen Jay. 1995b. "Spin-Doctoring Darwin." *Natural History* 104: 6–9, 70–71.

Grammont, Franck, Dorothée Legrand, Pierre Livet, eds. 2010. *Naturalizing Intention in Action*. Cambridge, MA: Bradford Book/MIT Press.

Grammont, Franck. 2010. "Naturalizing Intention in Action: An Integrative View." In Franck Grammont, Dorothée Legrand, Pierre Livet (eds), *Naturalizing Intention in Action*, Cambridge, MA: Bradford Books/MIT Press, 3–17.

Granit, Ragnar. 1977. *The Purposive Brain*. Cambridge, MA: MIT Press.

Gray, Peter. 1991. *Psychology*. New York: Worth Publishers.

Grene, Marjorie. 1976. "Merleau-Ponty and the Renewal of Ontology." *The Review of Metaphysics* 29(4): 605–625.

Griffin, Donald R. 1984. *Animal Thinking*. Cambridge, MA: Harvard University Press.

Hadreas, Peter J. 1986. *In Place of the Flawed Diamond: An Investigation of Merleau-Ponty's Philosophy*. New York: Peter Lang.

Haldane, J.S. 1931. *The Philosophical Basis of Biology*. New York: Doubleday, Doran & Co.

Haldane, J.S. 1953. "Foreword." *Evolution (Symposia of the Society for Experimental Biology)*, No. VII. New York: Academic Press.

Hall, K.R.L. & Irven DeVore. 1972. "Baboon Social Behavior." In Phyllis Dolhinow (ed), *Primate Patterns*. New York: Holt, Rinehart & Winston, 125–80.

Hanna, Robert & Evan Thompson. 2003. "Neurophenomenology and the Spontaneity of Consciousness." In *The Problem of Consciousness: New Essays in Phenomenological Philosophy of Mind*, ed. Evan Thompson. Calgary: University of Calgary Press, 133–161.

Haraway, Donna. 1988. "Situated Knowledges: The Science Question in Feminism and the Privilege of Partial Perspective." *Feminist Studies* 14(3): 575–599.

Harding, Robert S.O. 1975. "Meat-Eating and Hunting in Baboons." In Russell H. Tuttle (ed), *Socioecology and Psychology of Primates*. The Hague: Mouton Publishers, 245–257.

Harrison, Andrew. 1978. *Making and Thinking: A Study of Intelligent Activities*. Indianapolis: Hackett Publishing.

Hart, Benjamin L. & Lynette A. Hart. Animal Behavior Society Meeting, July 1993. Reported in *Science News* 144(5) (1993): 70.

Haugeland, John. 1985. *Artificial Intelligence: The Very Idea*. Cambridge, MA: Bradford Books/ MIT Press.

Heidegger, Martin. 1961. *An Introduction to Metaphysics*, trans. Ralph Manheim. Garden City, NY: Doubleday/Anchor.

Heidegger, Martin. 1962. *Being and Time*, trans. John Macquarrie and Edward Robinson. New York: Harper & Row.

Held, Richard. 1965. "Plasticity in Sensory-Motor Systems." *Scientific American* 213(5): 84–94.

Held, Richard & Alan Hein. 1963. "Movement Produced Stimulation in the Development of Visually Guided Behavior." *Journal of Comparative and Physiological Psychology* 56: 872–876.

Hendriks-Jansen, Horst. 1996. *Catching Ourselves in the Act*. Cambridge: Bradford Books/MIT Press.

Henley, Nancy. 1977. *Body Politics: Power, Sex, and Nonverbal Communication*. Englewood Cliffs, NJ: Prentice Hall.

Hockett, Charles. 1960. "The Origin of Speech." *Scientific American* 203: 89–96.

Hoffmeyer, Jesper. 1996. *Signs of Meaning in the Universe*, trans. Barbara J. Haveland. Bloomington, IN: Indiana University Press.

Hoffmeyer, Jesper & Claus Emmeche. 1991. "Code-Duality and the Semiotics of Nature." In Myrdene Anderson & Floyd Merrell (eds), *On Semiotic Modeling*. New York: Mouton de Gruyter.

Holldobler, Bert & Edward O. Wilson. 1978. "The Multiple Recruitment Systems of the African Weaver Ant *Oecophylla longinoda* (Latreille) (Hymenoptera: Formicidae)." *Behavioral Ecology and Sociobiology* 3: 19–60.

Hommel, Bernhard. 2003. "Acquisition and Control of Voluntary Action." In Sabine Maasen, Wolfgang Prinz, & Gerhard Roth (eds), *Voluntary Action: Brains, Minds, and Sociality*. Oxford/New York: Oxford University Press, 34–48.

Horgan, John. 1995. "The New Social Darwinists." *Scientific American* 273(4): 174–181.

Howells, William. 1959. *Mankind in the Making*. New York: Doubleday & Co.

Husserl, Edmund. 1966. *The Phenomenology of Internal Time Consciousness*, ed. M. Heidegger, trans. James S. Churchill. Bloomington: Indiana University Press.

Husserl, Edmund. 1969. *Formal and Transcendental Logic*, trans. Dorion Cairns. The Hague: Martinus Nijhoff.

Husserl, Edmund. 1970a. *The Crisis of European Sciences and Transcendental Phenomenology*, trans. David Carr. Evanston, IL: Northwestern University Press.

Husserl, Edmund. 1970b. "The Origin of Geometry." In *The Crisis of European Sciences and Transcendental Phenomenology*, trans. David Carr. Evanston, IL: Northwestern University Press, 353–378.

Husserl, Edmund. 1970c. "The Vienna Lecture." In *The Crisis of European Sciences and Transcendental Phenomenology*, trans. David Carr. Evanston, IL: Northwestern University Press, 269–299.

Husserl, Edmund. 1970d. *Logical Investigations*, vol. II, trans. J.N. Findlay. London: Routledge & Kegan Paul.

Husserl, Edmund. 1973a. *Cartesian Meditations*, trans. Dorion Cairns. The Hague: Martinus Nijhoff.

Husserl, Edmund. 1973b. *Experience and Judgment*, ed. Ludwig Landgrebe, trans. James S. Churchill & Karl Ameriks. Evanston, IL: Northwestern University Press.

Husserl, Edmund. 1977. *Phenomenological Psychology*, trans. John Scanlon. The Hague: Martinus Nijhoff.

Husserl, Edmund. 1980. *Ideas Pertaining to a Pure Phenomenology and to a Phenomenological Philosophy: Book 3 (Ideas III)*, trans. Ted E. Klein & William E. Pohl. The Hague: Martinus Nijhoff.

Husserl, Edmund. 1981a. "The World of the Living Present and the Constitution of the Surrounding World External to the Organism," trans. Frederick A. Elliston & Lenore Langsdorf. In Peter McCormick & Frederick Elliston (eds), *Husserl: Shorter Works*. Notre Dame: University of Notre Dame Press, 238–250.

Husserl, Edmund. 1981b. "Foundational Investigations of the Phenomenological Origin of the Spatiality of Nature," trans. Fred Kersten. In Peter McCormick & Frederick Elliston (eds), *Husserl: Shorter Works*. Notre Dame: University of Notre Dame Press, 222–233.

Husserl, Edmund. 1983. *Ideas Pertaining to a Pure Phenomenology and to a Phenomenological Philosophy, Book I (Ideas I)*, trans. F. Kersten. The Hague: Martinus Nijhoff.

Husserl, Edmund. 1989. *Ideas Pertaining to a Pure Phenomenology and to a Phenomenological Philosophy: Book 2 (Ideas II)*, trans. R. Rojcewicz & A. Schuwer. Boston: Kluwer Academic Publishers.

Husserl, Edmund. 2001. *Analyses Concerning Passive and Active Synthesis*, trans. Anthony J. Steinbock. Dordrecht: Kluwer Academic.

Hutchinson, Ann. 1970. *Labanotation*, rev. ed. New York: Theatre Arts Books.

Jackson, Frank. 1982. "Epiphenomenal Qualia." *Philosophical Quarterly* 32: 127–136.

Jackson, Frank. 1991. "What Mary Didn't Know." In David M. Rosenthal (ed), *The Nature of Mind*. New York: Oxford University Press, 392–394. (Originally published 1986. *The Journal of Philosophy* 83(5): 291–95.)

Jackson, John Hughlings. 1915. "On Affections of Speech from Disease of the Brain." *Brain* 38: 147–174.

Jackson, John Hughlings. 1931. *Selected Writings of John Hughlings Jackson*, ed. J. Taylor. London: Hodder & Stoughton.

Jacobson, Edmund. 1967. *Biology of Emotions*. Springfield, IL: Charles C. Thomas.

Jacobson, Edmund. 1970. *Modern Treatment of Tense Patients*. Springfield, IL: Charles C. Thomas.

James, William. 1950 [1890]. *The Principles of Psychology*, 2 vols. New York: Dover Publications.

Jeannerod, Marc. 2006. *Motor Cognition: What Actions Tell the Self*. Oxford: Oxford University Press.

Johnson, Paul B. 1992. "Toward an Understanding of the Cerebral Cortex and Reaching Movements: A Review of Recent Approaches." In R. Caminiti, P.B. Johnson, & Y. Burnod (eds), *Control of Arm Movement in Space*. New York: Springer-Verlag, 199–261.

Johnstone, Albert A. 1984. "Languages and Non-Languages of Dance." In Maxine Sheets-Johnstone (ed), *Illuminating Dance: Philosophical Explorations*. Lewisburg, PA: Bucknell University Press, 167–187.

Johnstone, Albert A. 1986. "The Role of 'Ich Kann' in Husserl's Answer to Humean Skepticism." Philosophy and Phenomenological Research 46(4): 577–595.

Johnstone, Albert A. 1991. *Rationalized Epistemology: Taking Solipsism Seriously*. Albany, NY: State University of New York Press.

Johnstone, Albert A. 1992. "The Bodily Nature of the Self or What Descartes Should Have Conceded Princess Elizabeth of Bohemia." In Maxine Sheets-Johnstone (ed), *Giving the Body Its Due*. Albany, NY: State University of New York Press, 16–47.

Johnstone, Albert A. "Why Intentionality Requires Consciousness." Chapter in *Epistemic Experience*, work in progress.

Kaelin, Eugene, 1962. Personal communication.

Kauffman, Stuart A. 1993. *The Origins of Order: Self-Organization and Selection in Evolution*. New York: Oxford University Press.

Kauffman, Stuart A. 1995. *At Home in the Universe*. New York: Oxford University Press.

Kaye, K. 1982. "Organism, Apprentice and Person." In E.Z. Tronick (ed), *Social Interchange in Infancy*. Baltimore: University Park Press, 183–196.

Keeton, William T. & James L. Gould. 1986. *Biological Science*, 4th ed. New York: W.W. Norton & Co.

Keller, Evelyn Fox. 1983. *A Feeling for the Organism*. New York: W.H. Freeman.

Kelly, James P. & Jane Dodd. 1991. "Anatomical Organization of the Nervous System. In Eric R. Kandel, James H. Schwartz, & Thomas M. Jessell (eds), *Principles of Neural Science*, 3rd ed. New York: Elsevier Publishing Co., 273–282.

Kelso, J.A. Scott. 1995. *Dynamic Patterns: The Self-Organization of Brain and Behavior*. Cambridge, MA: Bradford Books/MIT Press.

Kelso, J.A. Scott. 2005. "An Essay on Understanding the Mind." Arthur S. Iberall Distinguished Lecture on Life and the Sciences of Complexity." Storrs, CT, December 2005. (A similar lecture delivered as the F.J. McGuigan Prize Lecture for Understanding the Human Mind, American Psychological Association meeting, Washington, DC, August 2005.)

Kelso, J.A. Scott. 2009. "Coordination Dynamics." In *Encyclopedia of Complexity and Systems Sciences*, ed. R.A. Meyers. Berlin: Springer-Verlag, 1537–1564.

Kelso, J.A. Scott & David A. Engstrøm. 2006. *The Complementary Nature*. Cambridge, MA: Bradford Books/MIT Press.

Kersten, Fred. 1981. "Introduction" (to Husserl's "Foundational Investigations of the Phenomenological Origin of the Spatiality of Nature"). In Peter McCormick & Frederick Elliston (eds), *Husserl: Shorter Works*. Notre Dame" University of Notre Dame Press, 213–221.

Klein, Richard G. 1989. *The Human Career: Human Biological and Cultural Origins*. Chicago: University of Chicago Press.

Konkel, Lindsey. 2009. "Ants, All for One!" URL: http://www.naturalhistorymag.com/samplings/271845/ants-all-for-one

Kuhl, Patricia K. & Andrew N. Meltzoff. 1982. "The Bimodal Perception of Speech in Infancy." *Science* 218: 1138–1141.

Kuhl, Patricia K. & Andrew N. Meltzoff. 1984. "The Intermodal Representation of Speech in Infants." *Infant Behavior and Development* 7: 361–81.

Kuhn, Steven L. 1995. *Mousterian Lithic Technology: An Ecological Perspective*. Princeton: Princeton University Press.

Laban, Rudolf. 1975. *Laban's Principles of Dance and Movement Notation*, 2nd ed., Roderyk Lange (ed). Boston: Plays.

Lacan, Jacques. 1978. *The Four Fundamental Concepts of Psycho-Analysis*, ed. Jacques-Alain Miller, trans. Alan Sheridan. New York: W.W. Norton & Co.

Laitman, Jeffrey T. 1983. "The Evolution of the Hominid Upper Respiratory System and Implications for the Origins of Speech." In Eric de Grolier (ed), *Glossogenetics*. New York: Harwood Academic Publishing, 63–90.

Lakoff, George & Mark Johnson. 1980. *Metaphors We Live By*. Chicago: University of Chicago Press.

Laing, R.D. 1963. *The Divided Self: An Existential Study in Sanity and Madness*. Baltimore: Penguin Books.

Lamarck, Jean Baptiste. 1963. *Zoological Philosophy*. Trans. Hugh Eliot. New York: Hafner.

Landgrebe, Ludwig. 1977. "Phenomenology as Transcendental Theory of History," trans. J. Huertas-Jourda & R. Feige. In Peter McCormick & Frederick Elliston (eds), *Husserl: Expositions and Appraisals*. Notre Dame, Ind.: Notre Dame University Press, 101–13.

Landis, Carney & William A. Hunt. 1939. *The Startle Pattern*. New York: Farrar & Rinehart.

Langer, Susanne K. 1948. *Philosophy in a New Key*. New York: New American Library.

Langer, Susanne K. 1953. Feeling and Form. New York: Charles Scribner's Sons.

Langer, Susanne K. 1957. *Problems of Art*. New York: Charles Scribner's Sons.

Laverack, M.S. 1976. "External Proprioceptors." In P.J. Mill (ed), *Structure and Function of Proprioceptors in the Invertebrates*. London: Chapman & Hall, 1–63.

Legrand, Dorothée. 2010. "Bodily Intention and the Unreasonable Intentional Agent." In Franck Grammont, Dorothée Legrand, Pierre Livet (eds), *Naturalizing Intention in Action*. Cambridge, MA: Bradford Books/MIT Press, 161–180.

Lennox, James G. 1997. "Material and Formal Natures in Aristotle's *De Partibus Animalium*." In Wolfgang Kullmann & Sabine Föllinger (eds), *Aristotelische Biologie*. Stuttgart: Franz Steiner Verlag, 163–181.

Lennox, James G. 1997. Personal communication.

Lemon, Roger N. 1990. "Mapping the Output Functions of the Motor Cortex." In Gerald M. Edelman, W. Einar Gall, & W. Maxwell Cowan (eds), *Signal and Sense: Local and Global Order in Perceptual Maps*. New York: Wiley-Liss, 315–355.

Leroi-Gourhan, André. 1964. *Le geste et la parole*, vol. 1. Paris: Albin Michel.

Leroi-Gourhan, André. 1971. *Préhistoire de l'art occidental*. Paris: Mazenod.

Levin, David Michael. 1988. *The Opening of Vision*. New York: Routledge.

Lewis, David. 1991. "Postscript: 'Knowing What It's Like'." In David M. Rosenthal (ed), *The Nature of Mind*. New York: Oxford University Press, 234–35.

Liberman, Alvin M. & Ignatius G. Mattingly. 1985. "The Motor Theory of Speech Perception Revised." *Cognition* 21 (1): 1–36.

Lieberman, Philip. 1983. "On the Nature and Evolution of the Biological Bases of Language." In Eric de Grolier (ed), *Glossogenetics*. New York: Harwood Academic Publishing, 91–114.

Lieberman, Philip. 1972. "Primate Vocalizations and Human Linguistic Ability." In Sherwood L. Washburn & Phyllis J. Dolhinow (eds), *Perspectives on Human Evolution, 2*. New York: Holt, Rinehart & Winston, 421–37.

Libet, Benjamin. 1985. "Subjective Antedating of a Sensory Experience and Mind-Brain Theories: Reply to Honderich (1984)." *Journal of Theoretical Biology* 114: 563–70.

Lissman, H.W. 1950. "Proprioceptors." *Physiological Mechanisms in Animal Behavior (Symposia of the Society for Experimental Biology)*, vol. 4. New York: Academic Press, 34–59.

Lloyd, Barbara & John Archer. 1985. *Sex and Gender*. New York: Cambridge University Press.

Losick, Richard & Dale Kaiser. 1997. "Why and How Bacteria Communicate." *Scientific American* 276: 68–73.

Lukacs, John. 1996. Personal communication.

Luria, Aleksandr Romanovich. 1966. *Human Brain and Psychological Processes*, trans. Basil Haigh. New York: Harper & Row.

Luria, Aleksandr Romanovich. 1973. *The Working Brain: An Introduction to Neuropsychology*, trans. Basil Haigh. Harmondsworth, England: Penguin Books.

Lyons, William. 1986. *The Disappearance of Introspection*. Cambridge: Bradford/MIT Press.

Maasen, Sabine, Wolfgang Prinz, Gerhard Roth, eds. 2003. *Voluntary Action: Brains, Minds, and Sociality*. Oxford/New York: Oxford University Press.

MacFarlane, Aidan. 1975. "Olfaction in the Development of Social Preferences in the Human Neonate." In *Parent-Infant Interaction*, Ciba Foundation Symposium 33. Amsterdam: Elsevier, 103–117.

Macnab, R.M. 1982. "Sensory Reception in Bacteria." In *Prokaryotic and Eukaryotic Flagella (Symposia of the Society for Experimental Biology* 35). Cambridge: Cambridge University Press, 77–104.

Mann, A. 1972. "Hominid and Cultural Origins." *Man* n.s. 7: 379–86.

Manton, S.M. 1953. "Locomotory Habits and the Evolution of the Larger Arthropodan Groups." In *Evolution (Symposia of the Society for Experimental Biology)*, No. VII. New York: Academic Press, 339–376.

Marler, Peter. 1975. "On the Origin of Speech from Animal Sounds." In J.F. Kavanagh & J.E. Cutting (eds), *The Role of speech in Language.* Cambridge: MIT Press, 11–37.

Marler, Peter. 1976. "An Ethological Theory of the Origin of Vocal Learning." In Stevan R. Harnad, Horst D. Steklis, & Jane B. Lancaster (eds), *Origins and Evolution of Language and Speech. Annals of the New York Academy of Sciences* 280: 386–95.

Masland, Richard L. 1972. "Some Neurological Processes Underlying Language." In S.L. Washburn & Phyllis Dolhinow (eds), *Perspectives on Human Evolution, 2.* New York: Holt, Rinehart & Winston, 421–437.

McCleary, Richard C. 1964. "Preface." *Signs.* Evanston: IL: Northwestern University Press.

McConnaughey, Bayard H. 1978. *Introduction to Marine Biology.* St Louis, MO: C.V. Mosby.

McDonald, Kim A. 1995. "Replaying 'Life's Tape'." *The Chronicle of Higher Education*, 11 August 1995, A9.

McGrew, W.C. 1992. *Chimpanzee Material Culture.* Cambridge: Cambridge University Press.

Mehler, Jacques & Emmanuel Dupoux. 1994. *What Infants Know*, trans. Patsy Southgate. Cambridge: Blackwell.

Mehler, Jacques, Peter Jusczyk, Ghislaine Lambertz, Nilofar Halsted, Hosiane Bertoncini, Claudine Amiel-Tison. No date. "A Precursor of Language Acquisition in Young Infants." Laboratoire de Sciences Cognitives and Psycholinguistique, CNRS & EHESS, 54 Bd. Raspail, 75006 Paris, France.

Mellars, Paul. 1989. "Technological Changes across the Middle-Upper Palaeolithic Transition: Economic, Social and Cognitive Perspectives." In Paul Mellars & Chris Stringer (eds), *The Human Revolution*. Princeton: Princeton University Press, 338–365.

Meltzoff, Andrew N. 1981. "Imitation, Intermodal Co-ordination and Representation in Early Infancy." In George Butterworth (ed), Infancy and Epistemology: An Evaluation of Piaget's Theory. Brighton, England: Harvester Press, 85–114.

Meltzoff, Andrew N. 1990. "Foundations for Developing a Concept of Self: The Role of Imitation in Relating Self to Other and the Value of Social Mirroring, Social Modeling, and Self Practice in Infancy." In D. Cicchetti & M. Beeghly (eds), *The Self in Transition: Infancy to Childhood*. Chicago: The University of Chicago Press, 139–164.

Meltzoff, Andrew N. 1993. "The Centrality of Motor Coordination and Proprioception in Social and Cognitive Development: From Shared Actions to Shared Minds." In G.J.P. Savelsberghin (ed), *The Development of Coordination in Infancy*. New York: Elsevier Science Publishers, 463–496.

Meltzoff, Andrew N. 1995. "Understanding the Intentions of Others: Re-Enactment of Intended Acts by 18–Month Old Children." *Developmental Psychology* 31(5): 838–50.

Meltzoff, Andrew N. & Richard W. Borton. 1979. "Intermodal Matching by Human Neonates." *Nature* 282(5737): 403–404.

Meltzoff, Andrew N. & Shaun Gallagher. 1996. "The Earliest Sense of Self and Others: Merleau-Ponty and Recent Developmental Studies." *Philosophical Psychology* 9(2): 211–233.

Meltzoff, Andrew N. & M. Keith Moore. 1977. "Imitation of Facial and Manual Gestures by Human Neonates." *Science* 198: 75–78.

Meltzoff, Andrew N. & M. Keith Moore. 1983. "Newborn Infants Imitate Adult Facial Gestures." *Child Development* 54: 702–709.

Meltzoff, Andrew N. & M. Keith Moore. 1994. "Imitation, Memory, and the Representation of Persons." *Infant Behavior and Development* 17: 83–99.

Meltzoff, Andrew N. & M. Keith Moore. 1995a. "Infants' Understanding of People and Things: From Body Imitation to Folk Psychology." In José Luis Bermúdez, Anthony Marcel, Naomi Eilan (eds), *The Body and the Self*. Cambridge: Bradford/MIT Press, 43–69.

Meltzoff, Andrew N. & M. Keith Moore. 1995b. "A Theory of the Role of Imitation in the Emergence of Self." In P. Rochat (ed), *The Self in Early Infancy*. New York: North-Holland-Elsevier Science Publishers, 73–93.

Merker, Bjorn. 2007. "Consciousness without a Cerebral Cortex: A Challenge for Neuroscience and Medicine." *Behavioral and Brain Sciences* 30/1: 63–81.

Merleau-Ponty, Maurice. 1962. *Phenomenology of Perception*, trans. Colin Smith. New York: Routledge & Kegan Paul.

Merleau-Ponty, Maurice. 1963 [1942]. *The Structure of Behavior*, trans. Alden L. Fisher. Boston: Beacon Press.

Merleau-Ponty, Maurice. 1964a. "An Unpublished Text by Maurice Merleau-Ponty: A Prospectus of His Work," trans. Arleen B. Dallery. In James M. Edie (ed), *The Primacy of Perception*. Evanston, IL: Northwestern University Press, 3–11.

Merleau-Ponty, Maurice. 1964b. "The Primacy of Perception," trans. James M. Edie. In James M. Edie (ed), *The Primacy of Perception*. Evanston, IL: Northwestern University Press, 12–42.

Merleau-Ponty, Maurice. 1964c. "Phenomenology and the Sciences of Man," trans. John Wild. In James M. Edie (ed), *The Primacy of Perception*. Evanston, IL: Northwestern University Press, 43–95.

Merleau-Ponty, Maurice. 1964d. "The Child's Relations with Others," trans. William Cobb. In James M. Edie (ed), *The Primacy of Perception*. Evanston, IL: Northwestern University Press, 96–155.

Merleau-Ponty, Maurice. 1964e. "Eye and Mind," trans. Carleton Dallery. In James M. Edie (ed), *The Primacy of Perception*. Evanston, IL: Northwestern University Press, 159–90.

Merleau-Ponty, Maurice. 1964f. "Indirect Language and the Voices of Silence." In *Signs*, trans. Richard C. McCleary. Evanston, IL: Northwestern University Press, 39–83.

Merleau-Ponty, Maurice. 1964g. "Man and Adversity." In *Signs*, trans. Richard C. McCleary. Evanston, IL: Northwestern University Press, 224–43.

Merleau-Ponty, Maurice. 1968. *The Visible and the Invisible*, ed. Claude Lefort, trans. Alphonso Lingis. Evanston, IL: Northwestern University Press.

Merleau-Ponty, Maurice. 1988. *In Praise of Philosophy and Other Essays*, trans. John Wild & James Edie. Evanston, IL: Northwestern University Press.

Mickunas, Algis. 1974. "The Primacy of Movement." *Main Currents* 31(1): 8–12.

Midgley, Mary. 2004. "Do We Ever Really Act?" In *The New Brain Sciences: Perils and Prospects*, ed. Dai Rees & Steven Rose. Cambridge: Cambridge University Press, pp. 17–33.

Milius, Susan. 2009. "Smart from the Start." *Science News,* August 15, 2009: 27–29.

Mill, P.J. (ed.). 1976. *Structure and Function of Proprioceptors in the Invertebrates*. London: Chapman & Hall.

Moerman, Daniel. 1989. Personal communication.

Montagu, Ashley. 1976. "Toolmaking, Hunting, and the Origin of Language." In Stevan R. Harnad, Horst D. Steklis, & Jane B. Lancaster (eds), *Origins and Evolution of Language and Speech, Annals of the New York Academy of Sciences* 280: 266–74.

Moran, G., J.C. Fentress, & I. Golani. 1981. "A Description of Relational Patterns of Movement During 'Ritualized Fighting' in Wolves." *Animal Behavior* 29: 1146–1165.

Morgan, Lloyd. 1930. *The Animal Mind*. New York: Longmans, Green & Co.

Moulton, Janice. 1983. "A Paradigm of Philosophy: The Adversary Method." In Sandra Harding & Merrill B. Hintikka (eds), *Discovering Reality*. Dordrecht: Reidel, 149–164.

Muller, Herbert. 1943. *Science and Criticism*. New Haven: Yale University Press.

Murdock, George Peter. 1969. "The Common Denominator of Cultures." In Richard G. Emerick (ed), *Readings in Introductory Anthropology*, vol. 1. Berkeley: McCutcheon Publishing, 323–326.

Nagel, Thomas. 1993. "The Mind Wins!" Review of *The Rediscovery of the Mind*, by John Searle. *New York Review of Books*, 4 March 1993: 37–41.

Nagel, Thomas. 1979. "What Is It Like To Be a Bat?" In *Mortal Questions*. New York: Cambridge University Press, 165–180.

Nauta, Walle H. & Michael Feirtag. 1979. "The Organization of the Brain." *Scientific American* 241(3): 88–111.

Nenon, Tom. 1994. "Connectionism and Phenomenology." In Mano Daniel & Lester Embree (eds), *Phenomenology of the Cultural Disciplines*. Dordrecht: Kluwer Academic Publishers, 115–133.

Noë, Alva. 2004. *Action in Perception*. Cambridge, MA: MIT Press.

Noë, Alva. 2009. *Out of Our Heads: Why You Are Not Your Brain, and Other Lessons from the Biology of Consciousness*. New York: Hill & Wang.

Nussbaum, Martha Craven. 1978. *Aristotle's "De Motu Animalium."* Princeton: Princeton University Press.

Nussbaum, Martha C. & Hilary Putnam. 1992. "Changing Aristotle's Mind." In Martha C. Nussbaum & Amélie Oksenberg Rorty (eds) *Essays on Aristotle's "De Anima."* Oxford: Clarendon Press, 27–56.

Olson, C.R. & S.J. Hanson. 1990. "Spatial Representation of the Body." In Stephen J. Hanson & Carl R. Olson (eds), *Connectionist Modeling and Brain Function: The Developing Interface*. Cambridge, MA: Bradford Books/MITPress, 193–239.

On the Edge (Institute for Science, Engineering and Public Policy, Portland, OR) 1(6) February 1996: 3.

O'Regan, J. Kevin & Alva Noë. 2001a. "A Sensorimotor Account of Vision and Visual Consciousness." *Brain and Behavioral Sciences* 24, no. 5: 939–973.

O'Regan, J. Kevin & Alva Noë. 2001b. "Author's Response: Acting Out Our Sensory Experience." *Behavioral and Brain Sciences* 24, no. 5: 1011–1031.

Overgaard, Søren. 2003. "The Importance of Bodily Movement to Husserl's Theory of *Fremderfahrung*." *Recherches Husserliennes* 19: 55–65.

Panksepp, Jaak. 2005. "On the Embodied Neural Nature of Core Emotional Affects." *Journal of Consciousness Studies* 12(8–10), (special issue on *Emotion Experience*, ed. Giovanna Colombetti & Evan Thompson), 158–184.

Panksepp, Jaak & Jeff Burgdorf. 2003. "'Laughing' Rats and the Evolutionary Antecedents of Human Joy?" *Physiology & Behavior* 79: 533–547.

Patočka, Jan. 1998 [1968–1969]. *Body, Community, Language, World*. Chicago: Open Court Publishing.

Penfield, Wilder. 1966. "Speech, Perception and the Cortex." In John C. Eccles (ed), Brain and Conscious Experience. New York: Springer-Verlag, 217–237.

Penfield, Wilder. 1975. *The Mystery of the Mind*. Princeton: Princeton University Press.

Penfield, Wilder & T. Rasmussen. 1950. *The Cerebral Cortex of Man: A Clinical Study of Localization of Function*. New York: Macmillan Co.

Pennisi, Elizabeth. 1993. "For Distance, Eyes See Like Ears Hear." *Science News* 144(9): 133.

Petit, Jean-Luc. 2010. "A Husserlian, Neurophenomenologic Approach to Embodiment." In *Handbook of Phenomenology and Cognitive Science*, ed. Shaun Gallagher & Daniel Schmicking. Dordrecht: Springer, 201–216.

Petitot, Jean, Francisco J. Varela, Bernard Pachoud, Jean-Michel Roy. 1999. *Naturalizing Phenomenology*. Stanford: Stanford University Press.

Piaget, Jean. 1952. *The Origin of Intelligence in Children*, trans. Margaret Cook. New York: International Universities Press.

Pickenhain, L. 1984. "Towards a Holistic Conception of Movement Control." In H.T.A. Whiting (ed), *Human Motor Actions: Bernstein Reassessed*. New York: Elsevier Science Publishing Co., 505–528.

Plato *Cratylus*

Plato *Phaedrus*

Plato *Statesman*

Plato *Theaetetus*

Portmann, Adolph. 1967. *Animal Forms and Patterns*, trans. Hella Czech. New York: Schocken Books.

Potts, Albert. 1982. *The World's Eye*. Lexington: University Press of Kentucky.

Premack, David & Guy Woodruff. 1978. "Do Chimpanzees Have a Theory of Mind." *The Behavioral and Brain Sciences* 4: 515–526.

Prinz, Wolfgang. 2003a. "Introduction—Between Motivation and Control: Psychological Accounts of Voluntary Action." In Sabine Maasen, Wolfgang Prinz, & Gerhard Roth (eds) *Voluntary Action: Brains, Minds, and Sociality*. Oxford: Oxford University Press, 17–20.

Prinz, Wolfgang. 2003b. "How Do We Know About Our Own Actions?" In Sabine Maasen, Wolfgang Prinz, & Gerhard Roth (eds) *Voluntary Actiion: Brain, Minds, and Sociality*. Oxford: Oxford University Press, 21–33.

Putnam, Hilary. 1981. *Reason, Truth and History*. New York: Cambridge University Press.

Raab, Markus, Joseph G. Johnson, Hauke R. Heekeren, eds. 2009. *Mind and Motion: The Bidirectional Link Between Thought and Action*. Volume 174 of *Progress in Brain Research*. Amsterdam/Boston: Elsevier.

Raichle, Marcus E. 2006. "The Brain's Dark Energy." *Science* 314: 1249–1250.

Rak, Yoel. 1987. "Kebara 2 Neanderthal Pelvis: First Look at a Complete Inlet." *American Journal of Physical Anthropology* 73: 227–231.

Rak, Yoel. 1993. "Morphological Variation in *Homo neanderthalensis* and *Homo sapiens* in the Levant: A Biogeographic Model." In William H. Kimbel & Lawrence B. Martin (eds), *Species, Species Concepts, and Primate Evolution*. New York: Plenum Press, 523–36.

Raloff, Janet. 1996. "How the Brain Knows When Eating Must Stop." *Science News* 150(30): 343.

Raloff, Janet. 2010. "Destination Brain." *Science News*, May 22, 2010: 16–20.

Rees, Dai & Steven Rose, eds. 2004. *The New Brain Sciences: Perils and Prospects*. Cambridge/ New York: Cambridge University Press.

Register Guard (Eugene, OR). 7 November 1989. Section B: "Myths in the Market."

Relethford, John. 1990. *The Human Species: An Introduction to Biological Anthropology*. Mountain View, CA: Mayfield Publishing.

Requin, J., A. Semjen, & M. Bonnet. 1984. "Bernstein's Purposeful Brain." In H.T.A. Whiting (ed), *Human Motor Actions: Bernstein Reassessed*. New York: Elsevier Science Publishing Co., 467–504.

Reynolds, Larry T. & Leonard Lieberman (eds). 1996. *Race and Other Misadventures: Essays in Honor of Ashley Montagu in His Ninetieth Year*. Dix Hills, NY: General Hall, Inc.

Reynolds, Peter C. 1991. *Stealing Fire*. Palo Alto, CA: Iconic Anthropology Press.

Ricoeur, Paul. 1991. "The Model of the Text: Meaningful Action Considered as a Text." In Kathleen Blamey & John B. Thompson (eds), *From Text to Action: Essays in Hermeneutics II*. Evanston, IL: Northwestern University Press, 144–167.

Ristau, Carolyn A. 1996. "Aspects of the Cognitive Ethology of an Injury-Feigning Bird, The Piping Plover." In Marc Bekoff & Dale Jamieson (eds), *Readings in Animal Cognition*. Cambridge, MA: Bradford Books/MITPress, 79–89,

Robeck, Mildred C. 1978. *Infants and Children*. New York: McGraw-Hill Book Co.

Roediger, Henry L., J. Philippe Rushton, Elizabeth Deutsch Capaldi, & Scott G. Paris. 1987. *Psychology*, 2nd ed. Boston: Little, Brown & Company.

Rojcewicz, R. & A. Schuwer. 1989. "Translators' Introduction" to Edmund Husserl's *Ideas Pertaining to a Pure Phenomenology and to a Phenomenological Philosophy, Book II*. Boston: Kluwer Academic Publishers.

Rose, Steven. 1975. *The Conscious Brain*. New York: Alfred A. Knopf.

Rose, Steven, ed. 1982a. *Towards a Liberatory Biology*. London/New York: Allison & Busby.

Rose, Steven, ed. 1982b. *Against Biological Determinism*. London/New York: Allison & Busby

Rose, Steven. 2005. *The Future of the Brain: The Promise and Perils of Tomorrow's Neuroscience*. Oxford/New York: Oxford University Press.

Rosenbaum, David. 1991. *Human Motor Control*. New York: Academic Press.

Rowell, Thelma. 1972. *Social Behavior of Monkeys*. Baltimore: Penguin Books.

Rowland, Lewis P. 1991. "Diseases of the Motor Unit." In Eric R. Kandel, James H. Schwartz, & Thomas M. Jessell (eds), *Principles of Neural Science*, 3rd ed. New York: Elsevier Publishing Co., 244–257.

Ruff, Holly. 1980. "The Development of Perception and Recognition of Objects." *Child Development* 51: 981–992.

Rumelhart, David E. 1989. "The Architecture of Mind: A Connectionist Approach." In Michael I. Posner (ed), *Foundations of Cognitive Science*. Cambridge, MA: Bradford Books/MIT Press, 133–60.

Runeson, Sverker & Gunilla Frykholm. 1981. "Visual Perception of Lifted Weight." *Human Perception and Performance* 7(4): 733–40.

Runeson, Sverker & Gunilla Frykholm. 1983. "Kinematic Specification of Dynamics as an Informational Basis for Person-and-Action Perception: Expectation, Gender Recognition, and Deceptive Intention." *Journal of Experimental Psychology* 112(4): 585–615.

Runeson, Sverker. 1994. "Perception of Biological Motion: The KSD-Principle and the Implications of a Distal vs. Proximal Approach." In Gunnar Jansson, Sten Sture Bergström, William Epstein (eds), *Perceiving Events and Objects*. Hillsdale, NJ: Lawrence Erlbaum Associates, 383–405.

Sacks, Oliver. 1993. "To See and Not See." *The New Yorker,* 10 May 1993: 59–73.

Sacks, Oliver. 1995. "A New Vision of the Mind". In John Cornwell (ed), *Nature's Imagination: The Frontiers of Scientific Vision.* Oxford: Oxford University Press, 101–121.

Sagi, Abraham & Martin L. Hoffman. 1976. "Empathetic Distress in the Newborn." *Developmental Psychology* 12: 175–76.

Sambursky, S. 1956. *The Physical World of the Greeks*, trans. Merton Dagut. Princeton: Princeton University Press.

Sanders, Laura. 2009. "Trawling the Brain: New Findings Raise Questions About Reliability of fMRI as Gauge of Neural Activity." *Science News*, December 19, 2009: 16–20.

Saroyan, William. 1960. *The Time of Your Life*. In Joseph Mersand (ed), *Three Dramas of American Realism*. New York: Washington Square Press.

Sartre, Jean-Paul. 1956. *Being and Nothingness*, trans. Hazel E. Barnes. New York: Philosophical Library.

Savage-Rumbaugh, E. Sue & R. Bakeman. 1977. "Spontaneous Gestural Communication among Conspecifics in the Pygmy Chimpanzee (*Pan paniscus*)." In G.H. Bourne (ed), *Progress in Ape Research*. New York: Academic Press, 97–116.

Savage-Rumbaugh, Sue & Roger Lewin. 1994. *Kanzi*. New York: John Wiley & Sons.

Scaife, M. & J.S. Bruner. 1975. "The Capacity for Joint Visual Attention in the Infant." *Nature* 253: 265–66.

Schmahmann, Jeremy D. (ed.). 2000. *MRI Atlas of the Human Cerebellum*. San Diego: Academic Press.

Scheerer, Eckart. 1987. "Muscle Sense and Innervation Feelings: A Chapter in the History of Perception and Action." In Herbert Heuer & Andries F. Sanders (eds), *Perspectives on Perception and Action*. Hillsdale, NJ: Lawrence Erlbaum Associates, 171–94.

Schneirla, T.C. 1959. "An Evolutionary and Developmental Theory of Biphasic Processes Underlying Approach and Withdrawal." In *Nebraska Symposium on Motivation* 7, ed. M.R. Jones. Lincoln: University of Nebraska Press, 1–42.

Schöner, G. No date. "What Can We Learn from Dynamic Models of Rhythmic Behavior in Animals and Humans?" Essay in book ms under review by Kluwer Academic, unpaginated.

Science News. 1994. "Imaging Clues to Schizophrenia." 146(18): 284.

Scott, John Paul. 1963. *Animal Behavior*. New York: Doubleday Anchor/American Museum of Natural History.

Searle, John. 1984. *Minds, Brains and Science*. Cambridge, MA: Harvard University Press.

Searle, John. 1990a. "Is the Brain a Digital Computer?" In *Proceedings and Addresses of The American Philosophical Association* 64(3): 21–37.

Searle, John. 1990b. "Consciousness, Explanatory Inversion, and Cognitive Science." *The Behavioral and Brain Sciences* 13: 585–642.

Searle, John. 1992. *The Rediscovery of the Mind*. Cambridge: Bradford Books/MIT Press.

Sellars, Wilfrid. 1963. *Science, Perception and Reality*. London: Routledge & Kegan Paul.

Sheets-Johnstone, Maxine. 1966. *The Phenomenology of Dance*. Madison: University of Wisconsin Press. (Second editions: London: Dance Books Ltd. 1979; New York: Arno Press 1980.)

Sheets-Johnstone, Maxine. 1979. "On Movement and Objects in Motion: The Phenomenology of the Visible in Dance." *Journal of Aesthetic Education* 13(2): 33–46.

Sheets-Johnstone, Maxine. 1981. "Thinking in Movement." *Journal of Aesthetics and Art Criticism* 39(4): 399–407.

Sheets-Johnstone, Maxine. 1983. "Evolutionary Residues and Uniquenesses in Human Movement." *Evolutionary Theory* 6: 205–209.

Sheets-Johnstone, Maxine. 1984. "Toward an Openly Hermeneutical Paleontology." *University of Dayton Review* 17(1): 89–96.

Sheets-Johnstone, Maxine. 1986a. "Existential Fit and Evolutionary Continuities." *Synthese* 66: 219–248.

Sheets-Johnstone, Maxine. 1986b. "Hunting and the Evolution of Human Intelligence: An Alternative View." *Midwest Quarterly* 28(1): 9–35.

Sheets-Johnstone, Maxine. 1990. *The Roots of Thinking*. Philadelphia: Temple University Press.

Sheets-Johnstone, Maxine 1992a. "The Materialization of the Body: A History of Western Medicine, A History in Process." In Maxine Sheets-Johnstone (ed), *Giving the Body Its Due*. Albany, NY: State University Of New York Press, 132–58.

Sheets-Johnstone, Maxine. 1992b. "Taking Evolution Seriously." *American Philosophical Quarterly* 29(4): 343–52.

Sheets-Johnstone, Maxine. 1994a. *The Roots of Power: Animate Form and Gendered Bodies*. Chicago: Open Court Publishing.

Sheets-Johnstone, Maxine. 1994b. "The Body as Cultural Object/The Body as Pan-Cultural Universal." In Mano Daniel and Lester Embree (eds), *Phenomenology of the Cultural Disciplines*. Dordrecht: Kluwer Academic, 85–114.

Sheets-Johnstone, Maxine. 1996a. "Taking Evolution Seriously: A Matter of Primate Intelligence." *Etica & Animali* 8: 115–130.

Sheets-Johnstone, Maxine. 1996b. "Human Versus Nonhuman: Binary Opposition as an Ordering Principle in Western Human Thought." *Between the Species* 12 (1–2): 57–63.

Sheets-Johnstone, Maxine. 1996c. "An Empirical-Phenomenological Critique of the Social Construction of Infancy." *Human Studies* 19: 1–16.

Sheets-Johnstone, Maxine. 1996d. "Tribal Lore in Present-Day Paleoanthropology: A Case Study." *Anthropology of Consciousness* 7(4): 31–50.

Sheets-Johnstone, Maxine. 1996e. "What Is It Like To Be a Mind? or Why a Brain Is Not a Body." In Larry T. Reynolds & Leonard Lieberman (eds), *Race and Other Misadventures: Essays in Honor of Ashley Montagu in His Ninetieth Year*. Dix Hills, NY: General Hall, Inc., 317–337.

Sheets-Johnstone, Maxine. 1997. "On the Significance of Animate Form." In Anna-Teresa Tymieniecka (ed), *Analecta Husserliana*, vol. LV: *Creative Virtualities in Human Self-Interpretation-in-Culture*. New York: Kluwer Academic, 225–243.

Sheets-Johnstone, Maxine. 1998a. "Consciousness: A Natural History." *Journal of Consciousness Studies* 5(3): 260–94.

Sheets-Johnstone, Maxine. 1998b. "Neandertals." *Sulfur* 43: 105–130.

Sheets-Johnstone, Maxine. 1999. "Emotions and Movement: A Beginning Empirical-Phenomenological Analysis of Their Relationship." *Journal of Consciousness Studies* 6 (11–12) (special supplementary issue on *Reclaiming Cognition*, ed. Rafael Nuñez & Walter J. Freeman), 259–277.

Sheets-Johnstone, Maxine. 2002. "Descriptive Foundations." *Interdisciplinary Studies in Literature and Environment* 9(1): 165–179.

Sheets-Johnstone, Maxine. 2003. "Kinesthetic Memory." *Theoria et Historia Scientiarum* VII(1): 69–92. Also in Sheets-Johnstone 2009: Chapter X.

Sheets-Johnstone, Maxine. 2004. "Preserving Integrity Against Colonization." *Phenomenology and the Cognitive Sciences* 3: 249–261.

Sheets-Johnstone, Maxine. 2005. "What Are We Naming?" In *Body Image and Body Schema*, ed. Helena De Preester and Veroniek Knockaert. (Originally Keynote Address at "Body Image and Body Schema Conference, Ghent Unviersity, March-April 2003.) Amsterdam: John Benjamins, 211–231.

Sheets-Johnstone, Maxine. 2006a. "Essential Clarifications of 'Self-Affection' and Husserl's 'Sphere of Ownness': First Steps toward a Pure Phenomenology of (Human) Nature." *Continental Philosophy Review* 39: 361–391.

Sheets-Johnstone, Maxine. 2006b. ""Sur la nature de la confiance." In *Les moments de la confiance*, ed. Albert Ogien and Louis Quéré. (Originally invited paper at Symposium on Trust, École des Hautes Études en Sciences Sociales, September 2003.) Paris: Economica, 23–41.

Sheets-Johnstone, Maxine. 2007a. "Finding Common Ground between Evolutionary Biology and Continental Philosophy." *Phenomenology and the Cognitive Sciences* 6: 327–348.

Sheets-Johnstone, Maxine 2007b. "Schizophrenia and the 'Comet's Tail of Nature': A Case Study in Phenomenology and Human Psycho-Pathology" (target article with commentaries and response). *Philoctetes* 1(2) (co-sponsored by NY Psychnoanalytic Institute), 5–45.

Sheets-Johnstone, Maxine. 2008. *The Roots of Morality*. University Park, PA: Pennsylvania State University Press.

Sheets-Johnstone, Maxine. 2009. *The Corporeal Turn: An Interdisciplinary Reader*. Exeter, UK: Imprint Academic.

Sheets-Johnstone, Maxine. 2010. "Why Is Movement Therapeutic?" *American Journal of Dance Therapy* 32(1): 2–15.

Sheets-Johnstone, Maxine. 2011a (forthcoming). "Fundamental and Inherently Interrelated Aspects of Animation." In *Moving Ourselves, Moving Others: The Role of (E)motion for Intersubjectivity, Consciousness, and Language*, ed. Ad Foolen, Ulrike Ludtke, Jordan Zlatev, Tim Racine. Amsterdam: John Benjamins.

Sheets-Johnstone, Maxine. 2011b (forthcoming). "On the Elusive Nature of the Human Self: Divining the Ontological Dynamics of Animate Being." In *In Search of the Self: Interdisciplinary Perspectives on Personhood*, eds. J. Wentzel van Huyssteen & Erik P. Wiebe. Grand Rapids, MI: Wm. B. Eerdmans Publishing.

Sheppard, R.Z. Book Reviews. *Time*. 16 November 1992: 101.

Sherrington, Sir Charles. 1947. *The Integrative Action of the Nervous System*. New Haven: Yale University Press.

Sherrington, Sir Charles. 1953. *Man On His Nature*. New York: Doubleday Anchor.

Siebers, Tobin. 1983. *The Mirror of Medusa*. Berkeley: University of California Press.

Simner, M.L. 1971. "Newborn's Response to the Cry of Another Infant." *Developmental Psychology* 5: 136–50.

Sinnott, Edmund W. 1963. *The Problem of Organic Form*. New Haven: Yale University Press.

Smithers, Tim. 1993. "On Behavior as Dissipative Structures in Agent-Environment System Interaction Spaces." Paper presented at meeting of "Prerational Intelligence: Phenomenology of Complexity in Systems of Simple Interacting Agents," 22–26 November 1993, *Zentrum für interdisziplinäre Forschung, Universität Bielefeld*, Germany.

Sokolowski, Robert. 1972. "Discussion." In Anna-Teresa Tymieniecka (ed), *Analecta Husserliana*, vol. 2: *The Later Husserl and the Idea of Phenomenology*. Dordrecht: D. Reidel Publishing, 64–77.

Sokolowski, Robert. 1974. *Husserlian Meditations*. Evanston, IL: Northwestern University Press.

Sorabji, Richard. 1992. "Intentionality and Physiological Processes: Aristotle's Theory of Sense-Perception." In Martha C. Nussbaum & Amélie Oksenberg Rorty (eds) *Essays on Aristotle's "De Anima."* Oxford: Clarendon Press, 195–225.

Sperry, Roger. 1939. "Action Current Study in Movement Coordination." *Journal of General Psychology* 20: 295–313.

Sperry, Roger. 1952. "Neurology and the Mind-Brain Problem." *American Scientist* 40: 291–312.

Sperry, Roger. 1990. "Forebrain Commissurotomy and Conscious Awareness." In Colwyn Trevarthen (ed), *Brain Circuits and Functions of the Mind: Essays in Honor of Roger W. Sperry.* New York: Cambridge University Press, 371–388.

Spitz, René A. 1983. *Dialogues from Infancy,* ed. Robert N. Emde. New York: International Universities Press.

Spooner, Brian. 1976. "The Evil Eye in the Middle East." In Clarence Maloney (ed), *The Evil Eye.* New York: Columbia University Press, 76–84.

Stein, Gertrude. 1926. *Composition as Explanation.* London: L. & Virginia Woolf (Hogarth: Second Series).

Stern, Daniel N. 1981. "The Development of Biologically Determined Signals of Readiness to Communicate, Which are Language 'Resistant.'" In Rachel E. Stark (ed), *Language Behavior in Infancy and Early Childhood.* New York: Elsevier/North Holland, 45–62.

Stern, Daniel N. 1985. *The Interpersonal World of the Infant: A View from Psychoanalysis and Developmental Psychology.* New York: Basic Books.

Stern, Daniel N. 1990. *Diary of a Baby.* New York: Basic Books.

Stiner, Mary C. 1994. *Honor Among Thieves: A Zooarchaeological Study of Neandertal Ecology.* Princeton: Princeton University Press.

Straus, Erwin W. 1970. "Born to See, Bound to Behold: Reflections on the Function of Upright Posture in the Esthetic Attitude." In Stuart F. Spicker (ed), *The Philosophy of the Body.* Chicago: Quadrangle Books, 334–361.

Stringer, Christopher & Clive Gamble. 1993. *In Search of the Neanderthals: Solving the Puzzle of Human Origins.* London: Thames & Hudson.

Symons, Donald. 1979. *The Evolution of Human Sexuality.* New York: Oxford University Press.

Teleki, Geza. 1974. "Chimpanzee Subsistence Technology: Materials and Skills." *Journal of Human Evolution* 3: 575–594.

Teuber, H.L. 1966. "Discussion" of "Cerebral Organization and the Conscious Control of Action," by D.M. MacKay. In John C. Eccles (ed) *Brain and Conscious Experience.* New York: Springer-Verlag, 442–445.

Thelen, Esther & Alan Fogel. 1989. "Toward an Action-Based Theory of Infant Development." In Jeffrey J. Lockman & Nancy L. Hazen (eds) *Action in Social Context.* New York: Plenum Press, 23–63.

Thelen, Esther & Linda B. Smith. 1994. *A Dynamic Systems Approach to the Development of Cognition and Action.* Cambridge: Bradford Books/MIT Press.

Thompson, Evan. 2005. "Sensorimotor Subjectivity and the Enactive Approach to Experience." *Phenomenology and the Cognitive Sciences* 4: 407–427.

Thompson, Evan. 2007. *Mind and Life: Biology, Phenomenology, and the Sciences of Mind.* Cambridge, MA: Belknap Press/Harvard University Press.

Thompson, Evan, Alva Noë, Luiz Pessoa. 1999. "Perceptual Completion: A Case Study in Phenomenology and Cognitive Science." In *Naturalizing Phenomenology,* eds. Jean Petitot, Francisco J. Varela, Bernard Pachoud, Jean-Michel Roy. Stanford: Stanford University Press, 161–195.

Thorpe, W.H. 1974. *Animal Nature and Human Nature.* Garden City, NY: Doubleday/Anchor Press.

Tinbergen, Niko. 1968. *Curious Naturalists*. New York: Doubleday Anchor/American Museum of Natural History.

Tomasello, Michael. 1990. "Cultural Transmission in the Tool Use and Communicating Signaling of Chimpanzees?" In Sue Taylor Parker & Kathleen Rita Gibson (eds), *"Language" and Intelligence*. New York: Cambridge University Press, 274–311.

Toth, Nicholas. 1987. "The First Technology." *Scientific American* 256: 112–21.

Trinkaus, Erik. 1983. *The Shanidar Neanderthals*. New York: Academic Press.

Trinkaus, Erik. 1981. "Neanderthal Limb Proportions and Cold Adaptation." In C.B. Stringer (ed), *Aspects of Human Evolution*. London: Taylor and Francis, 187–224.

Trinkaus, Erik. 1992. "Cladistics and Later Pleistocene Human Evolution." In Gunter Brauer and Fred H. Smith (eds), *Continuity or Replacement*. Rotterdam: A.A. Balkema, 1–7.

Trinkaus, Erik & Fred H. Smith. 1985. "The Fate of the Neandertals." In (ed), *Ancestors: The Hard Evidence*. New York: Alan R. Liss, 325–333.

Trinkaus, Erik & Pat Shipman. 1993. *The Neandertals: Changing the Image of Mankind*. New York: Alfred A. Knopf.

Trivers, Robert L. 1972. "Parental Investment and Sexual Selection." In Bernard Campbell (ed), *Sexual Selection and the Descent of Man 1871–1971*. Chicago: Aldine, 136–179.

Valéry, Paul. 1964a. "Philosophy of the Dance." In *Aesthetics,* trans. Ralph Manheim. New York: Pantheon Books, (Bollingen Series XLV.13), 197–211.

Valéry, Paul. 1964b. "Man and the Sea Shell." In *Aesthetics*, trans. Ralph Manheim. New York: Pantheon Books, (Bollingen Series XLV.13), 3–30.

Valéry, Paul. 1964c. "Some Simple Reflections on the Body." In *Aesthetics*, trans. Ralph Manheim. New York: Pantheon Books (Bollingen Series XLV.13), 31–40.

Valéry, Paul. 1964d. "Some Simple Reflections on the Body." In *Aesthetics,* trans. Ralph Manheim. New York: Pantheon Books (Bollingen Series XLV, 13), 31–40.

van Geert, Paul. 1993. "A Dynamic Systems Model of Cognitive Growth: Competition and Support Under Limited Resource Conditions." In Linda B. Smith & Esther Thelen (eds), *A Dynamic Systems Approach to Development: Applications*. Cambridge, MA: Bradford Books/MIT Press, 265–331.

van Gelder, Timothy & Robert F. Port, eds. 1995. *Mind as Motion: Explorations in the Dynamics of Cognition*. Cambridge, MA: Bradford Book/MIT Press.

van Gelder, Timothy & Robert F. Port. 1995. "It's about Time: An Overview of the Dynamical Approach to Cognition." In Timothy van Gelder & Robert F. Port (eds), *Mind as Motion: Explorations in the Dynamics of Cognition*. Cambridge, MA: Bradford Books/MIT Press, 1–43.

van Hooff, J.A.R.A.M. 1969. "The Facial Displays of the Catarrhine Monkeys and Apes." In Desmond Morris (ed) *Primate Ethology*. Garden City, NY: Doubleday Anchor, 9–88.

Varela, Francisco J. 1996. "Neurophenomenology: A Methodological Remedy to the Hard Prloblem." *Journal of Consciousness Studies* 3(4): 330–350.

Varela, Francisco J. 1999a. "The Specious Present: The Neurophenomenology of Time Consciousness." In *Naturalizing Phenomenology*, ed. Jean Petitot, Francisco J. Varela, Bernard Pachoud, Jean-Michel Roy. Stanford: Stanford University Press, 266–314.

Varela, Francisco J. 1999b. "Present-Time Consciousness." *Journal of Consciousness Studies* 6, No. 2–3: 111–140.

Varela, Francisco J. 1999c. "Reply to Owen and Morris." *Journal of Consciousness Studies*, vol. 6, No. 2–3: 272–273.

Varela, Francisco J. & Natalie Depraz. 2005. "At the Source of Time: Valence and the Constitutional Dynamics of Affect." *Journal of Consciousness Studies* 12(8–10) (special issue on *Emotion Experience*, ed. Giovanna Colombetti & Evan Thompson), 61–81.

Varela, Francisco J., Evan Thompson, Eleanor Rosch. 1991. *The Embodied Mind: Cognitive Science and Human Experience*. Cambridge, MA: MIT Press.

Vedeler, Dankert. 1987. "Infant Intentionality and the Attribution of Intentions to Infants." *Human Development* 30:1–17.

Vedeler, Dankert. 1991. "Infant Intentionality as Object Directedness: An Alternative to Representationalism." *Journal for the Theory of Social Behaviour* 21/4: 431–448.

von Frisch, Karl. 1964. *Bees: Their Vision, Chemical Senses, and Language*. Ithaca: Cornell University Press.

von Frisch, Karl. 1967. *The Dance Language and Orientation of Bees*. Cambridge: Harvard University Press.

von Helmholtz, Hermann. 1912 [1868]. "Recent Progress of (*sic*) the Theory of Vision." In *Popular Lectures on Scientific Subjects*, vol. 1, trans. E. Atkinson. NY: Longmans, Green, & Co.

von Helmholtz, Hermann. 1962 [1910]. *Physiological Optics*, vol. III, trans. and ed. James P.C. Southall. New York: Dover Publications.

von Helmholtz, Hermann. 1971a [1878]. "The Facts of Perception." In *Selected Writings of Hermann von Helmholtz*, ed. and trans. Russell Kahl. Middletown, CT: Wesleyan University Press, 366–408.

von Helmholtz, Hermann. 1971b [1868]. "Recent Progress in the Theory of Vision." In *Selected Writings of Hermann von Helmholtz*, ed. and trans. Russell Kahl. Middletown, CT: Wesleyan University Press, 144–222.

von Helmholtz, Hermann. 1971c [1870]. "The Origin and Meaning of Geometric Axioms (I)." In *Selected Writings of Hermann von Helmholtz*, ed. and trans. Russell Kahl. Middletown, CT: Wesleyan University Press, 246–265.

von Helmholtz, Hermann. 1971d [1878]. "The Origin and Meaning of Geometric Axioms (II) (Introduction and Section I) [1878]." In *Selected Writings of Hermann von Helmholtz*, ed. and trans. Russell Kahl. Middletown, CT: Wesleyan University Press, 360–365.

von Helmholtz, Hermann. 1971e [1862 Heidelberg lecture]. "The Relation of the Natural Sciences to Science in General." In *The Selected Writings of Hermann von Helmholtz*, ed. and trans. Russell Kahl. Middletown, CT: Wesleyan University Press, 122–143.

von Helmholtz, Hermann. 1971f [1894]. "The Origin and Correct Interpretation of Our Sense Impressions." In Selected Writings of Hermann von Helmholtz, ed. and trans. Russell Kahl. Middletown, CT: Wesleyan University Press, 501–12.

von Helmholtz, Hermann. 1977 [1878]. "The Facts in (sic) Perception." In *Hermann von Helmholtz: Epistemological Writings*, trans. Malcolm F. Lowe, eds. Robert S. Cohen & Yehuda Elkana. Dordrecht: D. Reidel, 115–163.

von Holst, Erich (with Horst Mittelstaedt). 1973. "The Reafference Principle." In *The Behavioral Physiology of Animals and Man: The Collected Papers of Erich von Holst*, vol. 1, trans. Robert Martin. Coral Gables, FL: University of Miami Press, 139–173.

von Uexküll, Jakob. 1928. *Theoretische Biologie*, 2nd ed. Berlin: Springer.

von Uexküll, Jakob. 1957 [1934]. "A Stroll Through the Worlds of Animals and Men," trans. Claire H. Schiller. In Claire H. Schiller (ed) *Instinctive Behavior*. New York: International Universities Press, 5–80.

Walker, Warren F. Jr. 1975. *Vertebrate Dissection*. Philadelphia: W.B. Saunders.

Washburn, Sherwood. 1960. "Tools and Human Evolution." *Scientific American* 203(3): 63–75.

Washburn, Sherwood L. & Shirley C. Strum. 1972. "Concluding Comments." In S.L. Washburn & Phyllis Dolhinow (eds), *Perspectives on Human Evolution, 2.* New York: Holt, Rinehart & Winston, 469–491.

Webbink, Patricia. 1986. *The Power of the Eyes.* New York: Springer Publishing.

Weiten, Wayne. 2007. *Psychology: Themes and Variations,* 7th ed. Belmont, CA: Thomson/ Wadsworth.

Wells, Martin. 1968. *Lower Animals.* New York: World University Library/McGraw-Hill Book Company.

Wells, Martin J. 1976. "Proprioception and Learning." In P.J. Mill (ed), *Structure and Function of Proprioceptors in Invertebrates.* London: Chapman & Hall, 567–604.

Whiten, A. & R.W. Byrne. 1988. "Tactical Deception in Primates." *The Behavioral and Brain Sciences* 11: 233–273.

Wickler, Wolfgang. 1969. "Socio-Sexual Signals and Their Intra-Specific Imitation among Primates." In Desmond Morris (ed), *Primate Ethology.* New York: Anchor Books, 89–189.

Wilson, E.O. 1972. "Animal Communication." *Scientific American* 227: 52–60.

Wilson, Edward O. & Bert Holldobler. 1990. *The Ants.* Cambridge, MA: Belknap Press.

Windle, William F. 1971. *Physiology of the Fetus.* Springfield, IL: Charles C. Thomas.

Wittgenstein, Ludwig. 1963. *Philosophical Investigations,* trans. G.E.M. Anscombe. Oxford: Basil Blackwell.

Wittgenstein, Ludwig. 1980. *Culture and Value,* ed. G.H. von Wright, trans. Peter Winch. Chicago: University of Chicago Press.

Wolpoff, Milford H. 1980. *Paleoanthropology.* New York: Knopf.

Wright, B.R. 1976. "Limb and Wing Receptors in Insects, Chelicerates and Myriapods." In P.J. Mill (ed), *Structure and Function of Proprioceptors in the Invertebrates.* London: Chapman & Hall, 323–386.

Youngerman, Suzanne. 1984. "Movement Notation Systems as Conceptual Frameworks: The Laban System." In Maxine Sheets-Johnstone (ed), *Illuminating Dance: Philosophical Explorations.* Lewisburg, PA: Bucknell University Press, 101–23.

Zahavi, Dan. 1999. *Self-Awareness and Alterity: A Phenomenological Investigation.* Evanston, IL: Northwestern University Press.

Zahavi, Dan. 2000. "Self and Consciousness." In *Exploring the Self: Philosophical and Psychopathological Perspectives on Self-Experience,* ed. Dan Zahavi. Amsterdam: John Benjamins: 55–74.

Zahavi, Dan. 2002. "First-Person Thoughts and Embodied Self-Awareness: Some Reflections on the Relation between Recent Analytical Philosophy and Phenomenology." *Phenomenology and the Cognitive Sciences* 1: 7–26.

Zahavi, Dan. 2005. *Subjectivity and Selfhood: Investigating the First-Person Perspective.* Cambridge, MA: Bradford Books/MIT Press.

Zaner, Richard. 1981. *The Context of Self.* Athens, OH: Ohio University Press.

Zeki, Semir. 1992. "The Visual Image in Mind and Brain." *Scientific American* 267(3): 69–76.

Zhang, Dongyang & Marcus E. Raichle. 2010. "Disease and the Brain's Dark Energy," *Neurology* 6, January 2010: 1–14.

Name index

A

Abbott, E., 190
Adams, J.A., 389
Agamben, Giorgio, 518
Altmann, Stuart A., xxviii,
    33, 330, 475
Archer, John, 307
Aristotle, xvii, xviii, xxii, xxvii, 3, 37, 68,
    77–112, 134–5, 192, 233, 280, 282, 294, 400,
    405–6, 449,
    453, 460, 484, 487–9, 501, 505, 513, 518
Asanuma, Hiroshi, 370,
    379, 389
Atkinson, E., 189

B

Bacon, Sir Francis, 308
Baerends, G.P., 443
Bakeman, R., 33
Baillargeon, Renée, 432
Barcroft, Joseph, 282
Barnes, N. Sue, 462
Bartieniess, Irmgard, 35
Beer, Randal D., 61, 192
Beesley, Simon, 523
Beethoven, Ludwig van,
    99, 148
Bell, David, xviii, xxxii
Bell, William J., 197
Benesh, Joan, 35
Benesh, Rudolf, 35
Bennett, Jonathan, 3
Bergson, Henri, 321, 421
Berkeley, George, 399
Bermúdez, José, 509
Bernstein, Douglas A.,
    396–7, 409
Bernstein, Nicolas, 365, 370
Bertenthal, Bennett I., 434
Bertollo, Maurizio, 501
Bhaerman, Steve (Swami Beyondananda), 348
Bloom, Lois, xxxi, 430–33, 474
Blumhagen, Dan W., 352–3

Bohm, David, 479–80,
    488, 492
Bonnet, M., 370
Borton, Richard W., 194, 220
Bower, Bruce, 349, 387, 394, 418, 465, 519
Bower, T. G. R., 223–5, 227, 432
Brace, C. L., 21, 386
Brentano, Franz, 479
Bruner, Jerome S.,   xxix, xxxi, 194, 321, 341–3,
    346, 434, 474
Brues, Alice, 22–3, 35
Bruzina, Ronald, 126, 134, 150
Bull, Nina, 437, 457
Burgdorf, Jeff, 478
Burnyeat, Myles, xxi, 48, 77–9, 81, 83, 89, 93–6,
    111
Butterworth, George, 219, 227–9, 245, 250, 349
Byrne, R. W., 75, 330–1

C

Calvin, William H., 385, 407, 413, 418
Caporael, Linnda R., 335
Carlson, Neil R., 393–4, 404
Carpenter, C.R., 14
Carruthers, Peter, 55, 114
Cassirer, Ernst, 74, 107,
    240–4, 249
Cézanne, Paul, 428–9
Chalmers, David, 71, 140–1, 152, 514
Churchland, Patricia S., 82–3, 281, 291, 350, 375,
    395
Churchland, Paul M., xix, 40–2, 44–6, 72, 141,
    143–4, 147–9, 396, 405, 409
Claesges, Ulrich, 150
Clark, Andy, 523
Clark, Eve V., 6
Cole, Jonathan, 512, 514
Comani, Silvia, 501
Condillac, Etienne Bonnot de, 128, 190, 197,
    333, 348
Conrad, Joseph, 301–2
Coppock, Patrick, 345
Cosmides, Leda, 82

Cotterill, Rodney M. J.,
    371, 389
Couliano, Ioan P., 319
Cowley, Geoffrey, 34
Crick, Francis, 82, 418
Crowell, Steven, 152
Cunningham, Merce, 151
Curtis, Helena, xxi, 44, 69,
    75, 291, 340, 377, 454, 462–3, 473, 507
Cutting, J. E., 345, 434

D
Dahl, Hartvig, 457
da Lentino, Giacomo, 319
Dallery, Arleen B., 310
Damasio, Antonio R., 82, 460
Damasio, Hanna, 82
Danto, Arthur, 497–8, 502
Darwin, Charles, 3, 6,
    42, 45–6, 73, 76, 79,
    188–9, 191–2, 267–8, 282,
    287, 303, 305, 320, 355–7,
    375–7, 385–6, 392, 413,
    461, 480, 494, 506–8
da Vinci, Leonardo, 99–100, 284–7, 292
Dawkins, Richard, 15
Democritus, 97
Dennett, Daniel, xxi, xxxi, 4, 38–40, 43–4,
    48–9, 51–2, 72–4, 333, 340–1, 348–9, 351, 354,
    358–61,
    363–5, 369, 371, 384, 387, 393, 395, 407,
    413–18,
    509, 517
Denny-Brown, D., 382
Depraz, Natalie, 457,
    468–71, 496
de Rivera, Joseph, 457
Derrida, Jacques, 150, 357, 388
Descartes, René, xxi, 77–9, 81, 114, 314, 349, 358,
    400, 449
De Luca, Cinzia, 501
De Preester, Helena, 509
de Sousa, Ronald, 326
DeVore, Irven, 301, 303
Di Paolo, Ezequiel, 490
Dodd, Jane, 366
Dolhinow, Phyllis J., 14
Dorsett, D.A., 56–8
Dreyfus, Hubert L., xxviii, 216, 235, 300–1, 306,
    310, 499
Dreyfus, Stuart E., 216, 235
Dundes, Alan, 308
Dupoux, Emmanuel, 434

E
Edelman, Gerald M., xxiv, 39, 187–9, 191–2, 389
Ehrenberg, Rachel, 508
Ehrenreich, Barbara, 357
Eibl-Eibesfeldt, Irenäus,
    14, 305
Eimas, Peter D., 329, 345
Eimerl, Sarel, 301, 303
Ekman, Paul, 305, 489
Eldredge, Niles, 8, 34
Ellis, Ralph D., 226–7
Emmeche, Claus, 346
Engel, J. J., 73, 399
Engstrøm, David A., 471, 483–5, 487, 492, 494,
    500, 502
Epstein, Mark, 486
Escalona, S. K., 219
Eshkol, Noa, 35

F
Feirtag, Michael, 311–2, 384
Fentress, John C., 188
Fields, H. L., 76
Fink, Eugen, 115, 126, 129–30, 133, 150, 193, 265,
    283–7, 292
Firth, Raymond, 13
Flanagan, Owen, xxxi, 68–9, 411–2, 418
Fodor, Jerry, 327, 360
Fogel, Alan, 219, 229–31
Foster, Mary LeCron, 15–16, 33, 331
Foucault, Michel, xxviii, 300, 302, 304, 306
Frayer, David W., 23
Freeman, Walter, 458
Freud, Sigmund, 15, 319, 410
Frith, Uta, 307
Frykholm, Gunilla, 198, 434
Furuhjelm, Mirjam, 133

G
Galilei, Galileo, 109, 133, 400
Gallagher, John C., 192
Gallagher, Shaun, 225, 496, 512–4, 522–3
Gallese, Vittorio, 496, 521
Gamble, Clive, 4–13, 21–22, 24–25, 33–4
Gardner, Helen, 112
Gauss, Carl Friedrich, 159
Georgopoulos, Apostolos, 384
Gibbs, Raymond W., Jr.,
    475, 496
Gibson, Eleanor J., 197
Gibson, James J., xviii, 119, 202–6,
    209, 212, 226, 228, 231
Giunti, Marco, 61

Goethe, Johann Wolfgang von, 345
Golani, I., 35, 188
Goldstein, Joseph,
Goldstein, Kurt, 241, 249, 427, 478, 485–7
Goodall, Jane, 445
Gordon, James, 366
Gotthelf, Allan, 449
Gould, James L., 46, 57, 340, 441,
     449, 461, 473
Gould, Stephen Jay, xx, 4–8,
     19, 25–26, 33, 72, 386, 438
Gowitzke, Barbara, 513
Grammont, Franck, 477, 519–20
Granit, Ragmar, 370, 383, 390
Gray, Peter, 417
Grene, Marjorie, 264
Griffin, Donald R., xxxii, 439–42
Grünbaum, A. A., 210
Guillaume, P., 245

H
Hadreas, Peter J., 277
Haldane, J.S., 13, 75, 79, 376
Hall, K.R.L., 33
Hanna, Robert, 466, 496
Hanson, S.J., 191
Haraway, Donna, 310
Harding, Robert S. O., 351, 392
Harrison, Andrew, 429, 448
Hart, Benjamin L., 375
Hart, Lynette A., 375
Haugeland, John, 283
Heekeren, Hauke R., 492
Hegel, G.W.F., 276
Heidegger, Martin, 201, 215,
     218, 238–9, 255–6, 468, 486, 512
Hein, Alan, 227
Held, Richard, 227
Hendriks-Jansen, Horst,
     194, 197
Henley, Nancy, 307
Herr, Lucien, 276
Hockett, Charles, 3
Hoffman, Martin L., 345
Hoffmeyer, Jesper, 346
Holldobler, Bert, 355–6
Hommel, Bernhard, 519
Hopkins, B., 349
Horgan, John, 82
Howells, William, 21, 316
Hoy, David, 310
Hume, David, 73, 399
Hunt, William A., 473

Husserl, Edmund, xvii–xix, xxiv, xxix, xxxii,
     51, 105, 111–22, 125–27, 129–30, 133, 136–9,
     150–2, 155–93, 195–7, 199, 204, 210–13,
     216–18, 234–5, 238–9, 243–4, 247,
     249, 252–3, 261, 269, 275–6, 305, 309, 3
     12–13, 317, 321, 325, 343, 345, 371, 414, 431,
     433, 435, 459–60, 466–7, 472–5, 479–80,
     483, 487–8, 493, 495–9, 502–6, 508–9, 511,
     514–16, 519, 521–2
Hutchinson, Ann, 35
Huxley, Thomas, xvii

I
Irwin, Bill, 99, 101

J
Jackson, Frank, 141,
     147, 149
Jackson, John Hughlings,
     243–4, 389
Jacobson, Edmund, 514
James, William, 76, 130, 286–7, 293, 421, 465,
     479–84, 495, 500
Jantzen, Kelly J., 501
Jeannerod, Marc, 477, 520
Johnson, Joseph G., 492
Johnson, Mark, 293
Johnson, Paul B., 379–80
Johnstone, Albert A., 13, 112, 171–2,
     186, 374, 388
Jonas, Hans, 460
Joos, Kurt, 294

K
Kaelin, Eugene, 248
Kaiser, Dale, 73, 76
Kant, Immanuel, 159, 190
Kauffman, Stuart A., 282
Kaye, K., 194
Keeton, William T., 46, 57, 340, 441, 449,
     461, 473
Keller, Evelyn Fox, 177
Kelly, James P., 366
Kelso, J.A. Scott, 371, 389, 406, 460, 462, 471,
     479–80, 483–5, 487, 492, 494, 500–502, 521
Kersten, Fred, 182
Klein, Richard G., 29–30, 35
Koch, Christof, 82, 418
Konkel, Lindsey, 506
Kornfield, Jack, 485–7
Krebs, J.R., 15
Kuhl, Patricia K., 221, 335
Kuhn, Steven L., 3, 28

L
Laban, Rudolf, 35
Lacan, Jacques, 244–5, 249, 271,
    276, 319, 357, 435
Laitman, Jeffrey T., 3
Lakoff, George, 293
Lamarck, Jean Baptiste, Chevalier de, 23,
    318, 488
Laing, R.D., 299, 311
Landgrebe, Ludwig, 116, 119, 128, 199–201, 204,
    215, 218
Landis, Carney, 473
Langer, Susanne K., 13, 15, 112
Laverack, M.S., 55–9, 63–4, 66–7, 75–6
Legrand, Dorothée, 477, 519
Lennox, James G., 90–1, 111–12, 449
Lemon, Roger N., 379–80, 382–3, 385, 389
Lenski, Richard E., 72
Leoncavallo, Ruggiero, 100
Leroi-Gourhan, André, 15, 388
Leucippus, 97
Levin, David Michael, 310
Lewin, Roger, 345
Lewis, David, xxx, 402–3, 405
Lewis, Dori, 35
Liberman, Alvin M., xxviii, 143, 321–4, 326–8,
    334, 404
Libet, Benjamin, 42
Lieberman, Philip, 3
Lissman, H.W., 60, 75
Livet, Pierre, 477
Lloyd, Barbara, 307
Locke, John, 399
Logothetis, Nikos, 489
Lorenz, Konrad, 267, 270
Losick, Richard, 73, 76
Lowe, M.F., 189–90
Lukacs, John, 17
Luria, Aleksandr Romanovitch, 448, 469, 487,
    491, 512, 515
Lyons, William, 166

M
McCleary, Richard C., 269
McClintock, Barbara, 177
McConnaughey, Bayard H., 58
McDonald, Kim A., 72
MacFarlane, J., 194
McGinn, Colin, 411
McGrew, W.C., 303
Maasen, Sabine, 519
MacKay, D.M., 71, 493
Macnab, R.M., 64–5

Maine de Biran, 460
Mann, A., 16
Manton, S.M., 75
Marler, Peter, 15
Masland, Richard L., 345
Mattingly, Ignatius G., 143, 321–4, 404
Mehler, Jacques, 329, 434
Mellars, Paul, 26–7, 34
Meltzoff, Andrew N., xvii, 144,
    194, 219–21, 225–7, 245,
    313, 335, 349, 371
Merker, Bjorn, 465
Merleau-Ponty, Maurice, xviii,
    xxv–xxviii, 113, 119,
    137–8, 200–4, 206–13,
    218, 234–5, 237–277,
    300–1, 303, 306, 312,
    315–17, 352, 427–8, 463,
    496, 498, 509, 515, 522
Mickunas, Algis, 113
Midgley, Mary, 499
Milius, Susan, 507
Mill, J.P., 60, 74
Milner, Morris, 513
Mitchell, Stephen A., 486
Moerman, Daniel, 98
Monet, Claude, 99, 101
Montagu, M. F. Ashley, 21, 386, 389
Moore, M. Keith, 144, 194, 221, 245, 349
Moran, G., 35, 188
Morgan, Lloyd, xxx, 329, 386
Moulton, Janice, 279–80
Muller, Herbert, 347,
    371–2
Murdock, George Peter,
    299–300

N
Nagel, Thomas, xxi,
    xxix–xxx, 37–40, 215,
    356, 370–3, 391, 411, 413,
    464, 493
Nauta, Walle H., 311–12, 384
Nenon, Tom, 182–6, 191
Newton, Isaac, 400
Noë, Alva, 473–5, 477,
    491, 496, 499, 509, 514, 519
Nussbaum, Martha Craven, 86, 95

O
Olson, C.R., 191
O'Regan, J.Kevin, 514
Overgaard, Søren, 516

P

Pachoud, Bernard, 508
Panksepp, Jaak, 460, 463,
     473, 478
Patočka, Jan, 458–9, 473
Peirce, Charles Sanders, 346
Penfield, Wilder, xvii, xxix, 328, 368–9, 373,
     377, 381, 390, 392, 417
Pennisi, Elizabeth, 392, 417
Pessoa, Luiz, 514
Petit, Jean-Luc, 522
Petitot, Jean, 508
Pfeiffer, John, 8
Piaget, Jean, 224, 227, 245, 250
Picasso, Pablo, 177, 294
Pickenhain, L., 370
Pinto, Jeanine, 434
Plato, xxvii, 97, 280, 293, 314
Port, Robert F., 61, 521
Portmann, Adolph, 33, 107–10,
     267, 270, 305, 344
Potts, Albert, 306
Premack, David, 12
Prinz, Wolfgang, 519
Proffitt, D.R., 434
Putnam, Hilary, 86, 354, 367–9, 387

R

Raab, Markus, 492
Rabinow, Paul, xxviii,
     300–1, 306
Raichle, Marcus, 465, 500
Rak, Yoel, 22
Raloff, Janet, 393, 407, 417, 490
Rasmussen, T., 328, 373,
     381, 390
Relethford, John, 386
Requin, J., 370, 389
Reynolds, Peter C., 385
Ricoeur, Paul, 334
Ristau, Carolyn A., xxxii, 439
Robeck, Mildred C., 74
Roediger, Henry L., 394
Rosch, Eleanor, 454–5,
     472, 496
Rosenbaum, David, 366, 378, 381, 383
Rose, Steven, 492–4, 500
Roth, Gerhard, 519
Rowell, Thelma, 339
Rowland, Lewis P., 366
Roy, Jean-Michel, 508
Ruff, Holly, 432
Rumelhart, David E., 192

Runeson, Sverker, 198,
     434, 448
Ryle, Gilbert, 402

S

Sacks, Oliver, 332
Sagi, Abraham, 345
Salzhauer, Amy, 34
Sambursky, S., 97–8
Sanders, Laura, 489
Saroyan, William, 318, 320
Sartre, Jean-Paul, 137, 205, 238–9, 270,
     272, 307, 314, 316, 319–20
Savage-Rumbaugh, E. Sue,
     33, 345
Scaife, M., 194
Scheerer, Eckart, 73, 190, 399–400
Schmahmann, Jeremy D., 464
Schneirla, T. C., 454
Schöner, G., 61
Scott, John Paul, xxxii,
     444, 460
Searle, John, 37–40, 45, 47, 53, 72, 214–15, 345
Sejnowski, Terrence J., 82–3, 281
Sellars, Wilfrid, 42
Semjen, A., 370
Sheets-Johnstone, Maxine, xx, 4, 14, 16, 18, 21,
     32–35, 68, 71–2, 74, 79, 107, 111–12, 116, 123,
     130, 150–1, 189–91, 195, 202, 206, 215, 226,
     234, 251, 276, 288, 299, 301, 314, 316, 319–20,
     325, 331, 338, 343, 346, 349, 351, 356–7, 376,
     386, 388, 402, 406, 416, 429, 435, 438, 446,
     448, 454, 456–7, 462, 466, 471–3, 475, 477–8,
     482–3, 486–7, 490, 494–5, 499, 502, 504,
     506–7, 511–12, 514–16, 519, 522–3
Sheppard, R.Z., 356
Sherrington, Sir Charles,
     49–50, 73, 75–6, 282, 382–3, 390, 484, 491
Shipman, Pat, 4–6, 32–33, 35
Siebers, Tobin, 307, 319
Simner, M.L., 345
Sinnott, Edmund W., 453
Smith, Fred H., 19, 21–22
Smith, J.A., 112
Smith, Linda B., 198, 206, 214–5, 219, 228–31,
     233, 406, 474, 500
Smithers, Tim, 192
Socrates, 216, 294–5, 496–7
Sokolowski, Robert, 150, 506
Sorabji, Richard, 86, 96
Spelke, Elizabeth, 432
Sperry, Roger, xvii, xxix, 371–2, 374–5, 377–8,
     384, 389, 416, 462, 491

Spitz, René A., 150, 222–5, 227, 460
Spooner, Brian, 307
Stein, Gertrude, 421, 426
Stern, Daniel N., XVII, XXXI, 73–4, 105, 136–7,
    194, 219–24, 227, 232, 234–5, 245, 313, 325,
    332, 342, 346, 349, 371, 431, 433, 435–9, 464,
    469, 471, 474, 508, 515
Stiner, Mary C., 3, 27
Straus, Erwin W., 308
Stringer, Christopher, 4–13, 21–22,
    24–25, 33–34
Strum, Shirley C., 74
Symons, Donald, 376

T
Tattersall, Ian, 34
Teleki, Geza, 375
Teuber, H. L., XVIII, XIX, 37, 71, 229
Thales, 161
Tharp, Twyla, 99, 420
Thelen, Esther, XVII, 198, 206, 214–5, 219,
    228–31, 233
Thorpe, W.H., 441
Thompson, Evan, 454–66, 468–71, 477, 490, 496,
    498–9, 509, 514
Tinbergen, Niko, XXXII,
    443–4
Tomasello, Micharl, 303
Toth, Nicholas, 16
Trinkaus, Erik, 4–6, 19, 21–23, 32–33, 35
Trivers, Robert L., 388

V
Valéry, Paul, XXVII, 110, 237, 273–5,
    277, 279, 299
van Geert, Paul, 341
van Gelder, Timothy, 61, 521
van Hooff, J. A. R. A. M., 14
van Roon, J., 443

Varela, Francisco, 454, 457, 468–72,
    494–6, 508–9
Vedeler, Dankert, 198
von Frisch, Karl, 16
von Helmholtz, Hermann, XVII, XXIII–XXIV,
    155–192, 197, 204, 325, 431, 508
von Holst, Erich, XVIII,
    229, 381
von Uexküll, Jakob, XXIX, 55, 107, 267, 270, 372,
    453, 463, 478, 503

W
Wachmann, Abraham, 35
Wallace, Alfred, 508
Wallon, H., 244–5, 249
Walker, Warren F. Jr., 391
Washburn, Sherwood L.,
    74, 386
Webbink, Patricia, 307
Weiten, Wayne, 513
Wells, Martin J., XXXII, 75, 444–5
Werner, Heinz, 221
Wertheimer, Matt, 207–8
Whiten, A., 75, 330–1
Wickler, Wolfgang, 33
Wilson, Edward O., 3, 355–6
Windle, William F., 74
Wittgenstein, Ludwig, XIX, 331, 345, 391, 419,
    428, 457, 501
Wolpoff, Milford H., 16, 335
Woodruff, Guy, 12
Wright, B.R., 56

Y
Youngerman, Suzanne, 35

Z
Zahavi, Dan, 466, 496
Zhang, Dongyang, 500

Subject index

A

action 477, 486, 493–94, 499–500, 523, note 7
action potential 146
  concept of 396–99, 400–402
  see also neural firing
adaptation 52, 445
  adaptationist explanation 6, 19, 110
  question of adaptiveness 20
adultist stance 464, 471, 474, note 10
adultist stance (perspective) 201, 210, 224
affect 231
  affective feelings of others 326–27
  affective qualities 221, 222
  see also motivation(s); vitality affects;
    wonder, affective infrastructure of
affective-kinetic-cognitive aspect
  of life 483, 487
affective/tactile-kinesthetic body 457, 464,
  483, 502–504
affective/tactile-kinesthetic body, tactile-
  kinesthetic/affective body 483, 502–504
affectivity 454, 503
  and animation 454
  and responsivity 454
  see also receptivity
afferent stimulation 366,
  367, 369
affordances 119, 203, 205
  affordant kinetic powers of organisms 205
agency 49, 65–66, 82, 200, 232, 365–69, 416, 435,
  474, 485
  and kinesthesia 125–26
  and kinetic spontaneity
    62, 119
  and living bodies 315
  and movement 218
  and perception 372
  and the core self 219,
    232, 435
  and the role of volition in perception 168
  see also agent(s); agentivity; kinesthesia, and
    self-agency
agent(s) 23, 48–49, 51, 66, 97, 117, 119, 125, 145,
  146, 165, 188, 192, 200, 307, 343,

365, 367, 369, 374, 384, 414–16, 434,
  436, 474, note 10, 492
  sense of agency 62, 65, 366–69
  see also agentivity; kinesthesia, and
    self-agency
agentivity 434–37, 444, 474, note 10
  see also agency; agent(s)
alchemy 360, 364
aliveness 116, 146, 187, 217, 229, 234, 490, 505,
  510, 521
  dynamics of 425
  see also animate, as distinct from inanimate
analogical apperception 324, 326–28, 371
  see also analogical thinking
analogical thinking 5, 13, 17, 18, 27, 29
  see also corporeal
    concepts; corporeal representation;
    symbolizing behavior
anemone(s) 57, 69, 70, 445
animate (animated) 62, 97, 105, 145, 201, 234
  animation and cognition 46, 62
  as distinct from inanimate 79, 94, 116, 222,
    300, 339, 407
  understanding the animate 41, 44, 47
  see also inanimate
animate form(s) 5, 97, 142, 145, 218, 232, 234,
    250, 312–13, 317, 318, 339, 343, 356, 370,
    376–77, 382, 384–85, 428, 442, 445–47, 463,
    475, note 12, 477–78, 487, 495–97, 502, 503,
    505, 510, 519
  and brains 408
  and readiness toward meaning 333, 335
  as topological entities 61
  makeovers of 357–58
  once-animate 288, 352
animate life (existence) 20, 56, 58, 68, 69,
    107–109, 114, 115, 182, 227, 229, 244, 267,
    329, 337, 339, 341, 356, 357, 392, 416, 419,
    420, 426, 428, 442, 445, 467, 471, 483, 490,
    495, 497, 502, 503
animate organism(s) 114–17, 133, 134, 181,
    465–70, 472, 473, note 7, 475, note 11,
    482–83, 491, 497, 499, 502, 505,
    508, 516

animate values 305–306
see also corporeal archetypes; form values
animation 97, 105, 109, 126, 128, 133, 139,
    453–75, 483, 487
    and background consciousness 463
    and brain research 465
    and life, time, affectivity, and movement 462
    and motion 105
    and physiognomies 313
    and pre-reflective
        self-awareness 457
    concept of 463
    semantics of 110
    see also animate (animated); physiognomic
        perception
animism 82, 83, 97, 406, 411
"anonymous functions,"
    246–48, 252
Anthozoa 69
anthropological linguistics 331–32
ants 506–507
arthropods (Arthropoda) 67, 70
    and vertebrates, compared 67
articulable skeleton 63, 67
articulatory gestures 214, 221, 321, 323–25,
    327–29, 331–34, 336, 337, 349, 368
    see also invariants, invariant gestures
"aspect-exhibitions," 162, 165, 179, 180
    see also "I move"; movement and perception
atomists (early Greek) 97
attentiveness 224, 257, 338, 341
    see also kinesthetic consciousness; meaning;
        responsivity
Australopithecus afarensis 115
"autonomous functions," 243, 245, 251

B
background (Background) 214–18
bacteria 44–45, 47, 52–53, 62, 64–66, 340, 473
    cognitive capacities of 46, 52, 64, 65
"bare attention," 130
bat(s) 39, 43, 51, 67, 370,
    371, 373
bees (honeybees' *Tanzsprache*) 16
    see also Hymenoptera
beetle(s) 55–56, 79, 270
behavior 477, 486, 493–94
    distinguished from movement 22, 201,
        442, 446
being a body,
    and having a body 242–43
    and learning to move ourselves 266, 487,
        499, 510, 517
    experience and 293

movement is natural mode of 428
    see also "what is it like?," to be a body
        one is not
being-toward-meaning 344
biological matrix 14–15, 18, 343, 346
    corporeal representation as 14–15, 17, 18
    readiness toward meaning as 340, 343
    see also meaning; movement and meaning
biological naturalism 39, 40, 44, 47, 53
blackbirds 442
bodies as social constructs 318
bodily dynamics 337–39, 341, 342
bodily reference point 219, 220, 223, 226
    see also emergent sense of self; kinetic
        intercorporeal attunement; kinetic bond;
        movement, as matchpoint; movement/I
        relationship
bodily semantics 343
    see also animate values; evolutionary
        semantics; form values; movement
        and meaning; spatio-temporal-energic
        semantics
body,
    as semantic template 15, 17, 27, 306, 334
    physical and lived 502
body-body problem (Danto) 497–99, 502
"body-body problem"
    (Hanna & Thompson) 466
body/brain divide 490–91
body build,
    and tool type 22, 26–27
    see also morphological-kinetic-conceptual
        schema; morphology, tool
        morphology and body morphology
"body form," 29
body image 512, 514, 522, note 3
"body schema"/
    "body-scheme," 225–26, 434, 512,
        514, note 3
botany 38
bracketing 130, 163–64, 179, 204, 205, 211, 212,
    215, 238, 239
    see also suspension of natural attitude
brain(s) 67, 489–501
    and hypothetical cerebroscope 492–93
    and living bodies 184
    and whole-body nervous system 480, 482
    as culminating perceptual organ of chordate
        nervous systems 79
    as oracle at Delphi 354, 497
    as part of "reverberating"
        neurophysiological dynamic living
        whole 482
"dark energy" of 465

experiential ascriptions to 392, 393, 395, 408,
    411, 473, note 8, 491
functional information about 395
heterophenomenological account of 393,
    395, 403, 407
homonymous 501
intrinsic activity of 465
    and phenomenology 466
intrinsic dynamics of 465
James's account of 480–81
materialist accounts of 395–96
modular conception of 480
pointillist conception of 480
research 465–66
sense organs as conduits to 79, 82
solid notion of 484
see also the brain; reductionism
brain activity 393–97, 399,
    401, 405, 407, 408, 410, 412, 416
    and neural firing 396–402
brain matter 398, 408, 411, 412
    kinetic character of
        395–96, 406, 409, 417
    see also physicalism animated
brain states 413
brains in vats 354
    brain-in-a-vat scenario (Dennett's) 358–63, 383
    brain-in-a-vat thought experiments 354, 412
breath/breathing 486–87
    see also self, contrast between spatial and
        temporal
"brutes," 144
Buddhism (Theravada),
    and nature of mind 480, 485
    and notion of self 485–87
Buddhist meditation 478

C
cardinal structures,
    cardinal temporality 135–40
    distinct from ordinal 134–36, 138
    see also kinesthetic consciousness, cardinal
        structures of; style
"Center of Narrative Gravity," 4, 43, 69
central pattern generator (CPG) 230
change 231–33, 416
    see also development
chiasm/chiasmatic solutions 463
chiasma 274–75
chimpanzees 446
    bonobos 16, 336–38, 342
cilia (ciliated) 56, 59–61, 70, 71, 75
clams 444
co-articulation 232, 321, 380

coelenterates (Coelenterata) 57, 58, 69, 70
cognition 45, 53, 116, 118, 120, 126, 128, 167, 171,
    188, 197, 198, 216, 227, 233, 242, 253, 341–42,
    349, 351, 410, 431
    "cognitive factors," 27
    connectionist modellings of 182–86
    sensory-cognitive ascriptions to the
        brain 408
    sensory-cognitive capacities 408
    sensory-cognitive experiences 408
    sensory-cognitive functions 408
    sensory-cognitive powers 408
    see also "embodied cognition"; surface
        recognition sensitivity
cognitive science 490, 492, 496
    an enactive 460
    and philosophy 477, 517–18
cognitive neuroscience 454
cognitivist (adj. or noun)/cognitivists 38, 40,
    44, 48, 187, 188, 354, 376,
    385, 407
    accounts of brain as computational
        device 375
    and neurological Mecca 354, 356, 370, 385
    assumptions 228
    computational 6, 45, 181, 322, 324, 372
    computational networks 42
    knowledge of animals 68
    notion of rules 6
    programs 68
    rise of cognitivist science 156, 181, 412
    science and hilosophy
        181–87
    vocabulary 23
    see also reductive materialism/committed
        materialists; reified neurology
cognitivist science 68
    and philosophy 181–87
    rise of 156, 181
    see also cognitivist (adj. or noun)/cognitivists;
        consciousness, computational-cognitivist
        accounts of
combinatorial explosion problem
    see degrees of freedom, problem
common denominator of being (and of
    meaning) 242, 243
common kinetic repertoire 195, 198
common natality of humans 194, 195,
    215, 217
    common evolutionary heritage 288
    common humanity 288
communal task 156–57, 182, 189, 239
communication 14–16, 230, 303, 328–31, 339–40
    nonverbal communication 229, 436

see also comsigns; intercorporeal
   sense-making; tactical deception
complementarity/complementary 480, 484–85,
   487, 491–92, 501
   conceptual 494–95
   of existential fit (physical and lived
      bodies) 502
   of mind and motion
      495–96, 501
   of phenomenology and science 502, 508–510
   of receptivity and responsivity 503, 507–508
comsigns 330–31, 475, note 11
   see also intercorporeal sense-making; kinetic
      intercorporeal attunement
concepts, learning of 142–43
connectionism 157, 182–85
   see also phenomenology, and connectionism
consciousness 460, 464, 478–80, 483
   and brain-process
      480–81, 501
   and brains 42
   and language 39, 43–44, 69, 413–14
   and the *how* question
      38–40, 42
   and unconsciousness 67
   arises in forms that are animate 39,
      47–48, 52–53
   as "inessential," 68, 69
   background 463
   bona fide evolutionary account of 64, 66
   computational-cognitivist accounts of 45
   core 464
   historical (evolutionary) perspective
   identification with matter 69
   inner time (Husserl) 466
   kinesthetic 460
   kinetic 463
   on/understandings of
      39–40, 43, 44, 68–69, 109
   see also corporeal consciousness; kinesthetic
      consciousness; meta-corporeal
      consciousness; "stream of thought"/"stream
      of consciousness" (James)
consciousness and mirrors 246
consequential relationship(s) 118, 136, 196,
   437, 474
   see also if/then relationship(s); infants,
      relational concepts
"constants of conduct," ("aprioris") 243, 261
constitution,
   a dynamic process 483
   and impermanence
      487–88
   of objects 466 133, 170, 211

and creation 132–33, 138, 139, 164
broadly defined 167
of space and time 119, 126, 127, 130–34, 139
see also kinesthetic consciousness; movement,
   creates qualities it embodies; protentions
   and retentions;
   self-movement; transcendental subjectivity
constructive phenomenology
   129, 136, 138, 155, 265, Chapter Five:
   variously specified at 200, 212, 215, 217,
   232, 273, 276
coordination dynamics 471, 480, 483–85,
   492, 495
   affective-kinetic 472
   see also complementarity/complementary;
      metastability
"coping behavior"
   see emotions, and "coping behavior"; "skillful
      coping"
core self 219, 232, 435
   see also agency, and the core self; emergent
      sense of self; self, sense of; self, unavoidably
      divided by language
corporeal archetypes 306–309
   see also animate values; form values
corporeal concepts 17, 18, 20, 21, 30, 34, 116, 118,
   119, 438–39, 515
   kinetic concepts 133, 444
   see also evolutionary semantics; infants,
      nonlinguistic concepts and/or thinking;
      kinesthetic consciousness;
      tactile-kinesthetic body; thinking
      in movement
corporeal consciousness 48, 53, 59, 62–69, 246
   and kinetic spontaneity 65, 66
   and "The Reality of
      Selves," 67
   internally structured 65, 66
   nature and evolutionary history of 63
   possibilities for elaboration in internally
      structured 65, 66
   see also animation and cognition;
      consciousness; internal sense organs,
      evolution of, from external sense organs;
      kinesthetic consciousness;
      meta-corporeal consciousness;
      proprioception, evolutionary history of
corporeal-kinetic intentionalities 471
corporeal-kinetic patternings 471
corporeal matters of fact 5, 19–21, 24, 32, 38, 47,
   53–56, 59, 61, 66, 67, 69, 141, 142, 318, 328,
   329, 351, 438
corporeal representation 13–15, 27
   as biological matrix 18

see also biological matrix
corps engagé 361, 374, 375, 381, 457
   see also intelligence in action; tactile-
      kinesthetic body
correlation 158, 161–62, 164–68
   see also consequential relationships; if/then
      relationships; movement and perception,
      correlation of; movement and perception,
      inseparability of; relational concepts
creationism,
   academic 348
   linguistic 44
"creative poverty of not yet knowing," 283,
      288–90, 295, 517
creativity as process 421
Crustacea 70
crying
   see "nonspecific behavioral arousal"
cultural (pan-human) universal 281, 300, 306,
      309, 315, 316, 318
   see also animate values; corporeal archetypes;
      form values
curiosity 195

D
Da-bewegung (kinetic-tactile-kinesthetic
      being) 218
dark energy 500
   see also intrinsic activity
Darwin III 188
Darwin machine(s) 385, 418
Darwinian bodies 79, 319
   and mental powers 375–76
Dasein 210, 218
definitions of life 38, 41, 44, 53, 69, 340
   see also responsivity
degrees of freedom 119
   problem 364, 365, 381
descent with modification 42, 62, 63
descriptive foundations 494, 495
development 197–98, 233
   see also change
diacritical erasure 46–47, 49
diacritical markings 46–47, 49, 148
   liabilities of 48
   use of, to distinguish cognitively among
      organisms 46–47
diversity of life/living bodies 41, 58, 66, 499
dynamic congruency (of affectivity and
      movement) 454, 471, 473, note 3, 478
dynamics,
   and animation 483, 510
   essentially modes of animation 483–84
   import of recognizing 482

of movement 511–12
   distinct from sensations 511–12, 522,
      note 4
   "shared" (Kelso) 492, 494
   and "translational relationship"
      (Rose) 494
   temporal and metastability 488
   the word 483, 488
   see also qualitative dynamics
dynamic systems research,
   relation to phenomenology 229–33
   see also dynamic systems researchers
dynamic systems researchers (theorists) 197,
      219, 227–33

E
efferent stimulation (efferent impulse, efferent
      system) 366–68, 370, 383
eidetic ontological phenomenology 258
"eidetic reflection"
   see reflection, "radical reflection"
eidetic science 176
eidetic truth(s) (eidetic intuition, eidetic
      insights) 133, 175, 176, 178
eliminative materialism 45, 349–54, 396
embed/embedding/embedded 463, 465, 472
"embodied cognition," 231
   see also embodiment; living body/bodies, and
      embodiment
embodied minds 501
   see also mindful body(ies)
"embodied movement"
   (Varela & Depraz; Gibbs) 470, 475, note 13
   see also "motor embodiment" (Varela &
      Depraz, Thompson)
embodiment(s) 310–13, 314, 453, 463, 471, 472,
      475, note 13 477, 478, 496, 501, 508, 512,
      520–21, 523, note 7
   a linguistic embalmer 472, 496
   see also "embodied cognition"; "lived body";
      living body/bodies, and embodiment
emergence 229–231, 233
emotion(s) 467–69,
      472–73, note 3, 473, note 7
   actual experience of 469, 471, 472
   contrast between robot and real-life 490
   and "coping behavior," 467, 469
   etymology of 455–457
   move through the body 456
   move us to move 456
enaction 454, 470, 472, note 2, 497, 512, 520–21
   "enactive emotion" Thompson) 463
   "enactive evolution" Thompson) 463
   "enactive neuroscience" (Noë) 474, note 10

"(the) enactive approach" Thompson) 455,
    470, 471
empathy 335–36, 371
empirical (observed) facts 175, 178–79, 240
empirical science 78–79, 83
    empiricist and rationalist science 78–79
entomology 356–57
epistemological gateway 67, 219, 226
    see also epistemological subjects;
        epistemology
epistemological subjects 218–19
    see also epistemological gateway;
        epistemology
epistemology 83, 95, 155,
    161, 239, 242, 253, 260, 276, 413
    20th-century 83
    and active free variation 174
    and an ontogenetic poetics of language 271
    and Merleau-Ponty's methodology 244
    and the truths of experience 179
    biased 447
    completed 143
    epistemological understandings of
        Nature 482–83
    Husserl's 238
    trans-disciplinary 156, 180, 181, 187
    Western 232
    see also epistemological gateway;
        epistemological subjects; metaphysics, in
        advance of a supportive epistemology;
        perception, proper metaphysics and
        epistemology
eukaryotic organisms 59, 60, 70
    amoeba 59, 69
    paramecia (Paramecium) 59, 70, 463
    see also surface recognition sensitivity
evolution,
    cladistic view of 25–26
    makeover of 357–58
    see also consciousness,
        bona fide evolutionary account of;
        evolution as a history of animate form;
        evolution of; evolutionary continuities;
        evolutionary discontinuities
evolution as a history of animate form 38, 53, 61,
    76, 337, 496–97, 510
evolution of,
    an evolutionary semantics 339–45
    animate form 40, 53, 59, 63, 343, 375
    consciousness 66–67
    hominids 335
    life 38, 40, 59
    living bodies 373
    mammals 391

mental powers 6
mind 188
nonhuman animals 67
proprioception 54, 58–59, 66–67
species 356
wonder 284–88
see also external sense organs; instincts;
    internal sense organs; symbolism-
    symbolization
evolutionary armchair pronouncements 68
evolutionary biology 478, 501–510
    and animate life 495, 512, 518, 519
evolutionary continuities 4, 7, 18, 59, 66, 305,
    329, 392, 473, note 7
evolutionary discontinuities 8–9, 17,
    41–43, 305
    and "mental essence" of humans 6
evolutionary semantics, 331, 339–45
    see also animate values; bodily semantics;
        form values; spatio-temporal-energic
        semantics; symbolic structure of
        primordial language
evolutionary theory 42, 267
"existential analysis," 212, 213, 241, 246, 261
"existential dissidents," 238, 239
existential fit 107, 316–17,
    446, 502
existential truths 240, 247
expansionist program (expansionist
    materialism) 395
expectation(s) 162
    see also correlation
experience 156–160, 166, 481–83, 485–87
    and behavior 155–56, 187
    and neurological happenings 491–92
    basis of all forms of gnosis 483
    breaking into parts 479
    challenge of anguaging 482, 490
    kinesthetic and/or proprioceptive 477
    kinetic 478
    of no-self 485
    sensible (experiences) 481, 482
    truths of 479, 482, 485,
        487, 490, 496, 499, 504–505, 509,
        514–15, 518–20
    unfolding dynamic nature of 482
experience and fact
    252–60, 268
    facts of experience 186
experiential dynamics 471
exploration 197
    see also curiosity; wonder
external sense organs 56, 57, 59, 63, 64, 66
    evolution of 58

see also evolution as a history of animate
form; proprioception, evolutionary
history of
eye movement,
see movement, eye
eye(s) 81
evil eye 307–309

F
façons de parler 356, 406
fact(s)/factual matters 120, 166, 168, 175,
180, 195, 203, 208, 281–85
facts and essences 175–80
factual and eidetic knowledge 176–77
see also experience and fact; fact(s)/factual
matters
familiarity 469, 471, 474, note 10
familiar dynamics 469
see also kinesthetic/kinetic melodies
feeling alive 453, 466
"feeling of being alive" (Thompson) 458–60,
464
feelings of aliveness 458
phenomenological groundings of 460
felt bodily sense (of a situation) 361–63
see also intelligence in action; kinetic bodily
logos; mindful body; movement and
meaning
"felt time," 135
fetus (fetuses) 133, 228, 434, 515
five senses 52
flagella 70, 71
flesh 266–67, 270
force,
concept of 399–400
form and matter,
intimate link between 81, 90, 98, 110
mutually constraining 90–92, 98–102
see also matter; "receiving into itself
the sensible forms of things
without the matter"
form values 107–111, 267, 305–306, 344
see also animate values; corporeal archetypes
"Fourth Body," 273–75
free variation(s) 169, 172, 180
active self-entation
172–73, 187
imaginative and active 173–75, 187
method of 252
see also freely-varied movement; laboratory
freely-varied movement 119, 122–23, 167–75
see also free variation, imaginative and active;
possible experience
functional tone (of objects) 372, 503

fundamental disposition toward meaning 14
see also meaning; readiness toward meaning

G
geometry,
axioms of 159–61, 168, 173, 175–77
origin of 160–61
gluon 290
goal-directed movement(s) 380, 382, 385

H
habitualities (dispositions) 185–86
hard-shelled animals 444
see also invertebrates
having a body 242–43
heterophenomenology/heterophenomenological
methodology 413–17
"holding sway," 51, 168
hominid(s) 5, 8, 9, 12, 13, 19, 24, 26, 28, 42
and humans 42, 66, 67
and language 3, 8, 324, 339
and tool-making 16, 17, 21, 29, 375
bodies 19, 115, 300, 315, 374
differences between Middle and Upper
Paleolithic 29
evolution of 28, 28, 29, 43, 67, 334, 343
see also Homo sapiens sapiens; metaphysical
distinctions, between "higher" and "lower"
forms of life; Neandertals
Homo habilis 42, 115
Homo sapiens sapiens,
and campsites 7, 9, 10, 17
and new habitats 7, 10, 11
and planning ahead 24–25
and settlements 7, 10, 11
and social networks 10, 24
subsistence tools of 27, 28
see also body build, and tool type;
morphology; movement dispositions;
movement possibilities
Homo televideous 356, 357
humans, as special creations 42, 44
hydrozoans (Hydrozoa) 56–59, 70
Hymenoptera 45, 70

I
"I cans" XXII, 20, 22, 62, 65,
116–18, 125, 129, 170, 172, 195, 196, 199, 233,
307, 309, 317, 472
and morphology 21, 22
and movement possibilities 20, 22
"I move" ("I do") 116–17, 119, 162, 164, 165,
168, 171–73, 179, 180, 196, 199–201, 211,
213, 218, 229, 235

if/then relationship(s) 136, 137, 162, 164, 165, 180,
    196, 433, 444
  qualitative aspect of 136
  see also consequential relationship(s); infants,
    relational concepts
imagination 168, 191, 192, 226, 227, 350, 371,
    375, 402
  see also free variation, imaginative and active;
    possible experience
imitation 225–27
impermanence,
  see Buddhism; constitution
implicate/explicate order (Bohm) 489
inanimate 94, 97, 406, 407
  see also animate (animated)
"inborn complexes," 246, 248, 252
induction (inductive conclusions) 170–72
  and random movement 172
infants/infancy 438, 464, 491, 495, 497, 500
  characterization of, by Merleau-Ponty 245, 247
infants' nonlinguistic concepts and/or
    thinking 431, 432, 474, note 10, 534
infants' physical knowledge 432–33
infants' relational concepts 433
  see also consequential relationship(s); if/then
    relationship(s)
infants' "theory (theories) of objects," 431–33
infinite task 239, 281, 290
"information,"
  kinesthetic 520
  proprioceptive 514
information pick-up 203, 205, 206, 212,
    228, 231
  see also information-processing/information
    processing machines
information-processing/information processing
    machines 181, 233, 375–76, 383, 447, 523,
    note 5
  see also information pick-up; the brain, as site
    of information-processing
initiation of movement 51, 62, 65, 367–70
  see also kinetic spontaneity; movement
    possibilities
inner time consciousness
  and "undivided wholeness in flowing
    movement" (Bohm) 488
instincts,
  evolution of, in movement 442, 454
  instinctive and learned behavior 440,
    442, 446
intelligence 41, 45, 181, 188, 242, 250
  and Middle and Upper Paleolithic
    "boundary," 32
  and worms 41, 91

as rarified mental essence of humans 18
  kinetic 424, 426, 440, 445, 446, 471
  symbols of 10
intelligence in action 442
  see also kinetic bodily logos; mindful body;
    movement and meaning
intention movements (nonverbal behaviors) 436
"intentional arc," 242, 244, 248
  intentionality/intentionalities 82, 94, 186, 217,
    218, 385, 414
  functional 247
  imputation of, to brains 82
  intentional object 212
  intrinsic and as-if 47
  "motor intentionality," 206, 209–211,
    240, 244, 245, 248–50, 266, 274
  see also corporeal consciousness;
    tactile-kinesthetic body
interchangeability of body and 372
intercorporeal dynamics 437, 515
  see also kinetic intercorporeal attunement
intercorporeal
  sense-making 329, 331, 335–36, 345,
    510, 514–15
intercorporeality,
  see intercorporeal
    sense-making
internal sense organs 63, 67
  adaptive significance of 65
  and protection from damage 63, 67
  evolution of, from external sense organs 62–67
  chordotonal organs 63, 70, 71
  see also evolution as a history of animate form;
    proprioception, evolutionary history of
internal time consciousness 487
intrinsic activity 500–501
  see also dark energy
intrinsic dynamics 214–15, 228, 500–501
  see also movement-born; non-specific
    behavior arousal; primal animation
introspection 141, 148, 149, 162–67, 174, 178–180,
    187, 249, 251, 252, 255–58, 270, 363–64, 413, 415
intuition (flash of insight) 177–78
  and invariance 177
  as a form of consciousness 178
  relationship of, to observation 175–76
  see also intuitive knowledge
intuitive knowledge 117, 170, 176–77
  see also intuition
invariants,
  and insight 177
  bodily 333
  invariant gestures (of speech) 323, 334
  invariant structures 301, 305

of experience 158, 161, 165, 175–77, 180,
224, 229, 232
spatio-temporal 444
tactile-kinesthetic invariants 219, 232, 324–26,
327, 329, 331, 334–6
invertebrates 56–58, 62, 63, 66, 69–71
and vertebrate homologies 63
modes of external proprioception in 56, 57
proprioception in
hard- and soft-bodied, compared 56–59
soft-bodied, best evidence for proprioception
in 58

J
joints,
of Nature and artificial joints 496–97
see also whole

K
Kanzi 336–339
killdeer 439
"kinestheses," 162, 165, 169, 172–73, 184, 196, 211, 249
correlated only with other kinestheses 132
kinesthesia 49, 51–52, 62–63, 69, 120–121,
125–130, 141, 147, 149, 172–73, 204–206,
209–211, 228, 250–51, 256, 265, 401, 434, 445,
459, 471, 474, note 10, 510–21
and self-agency 49–51, 125
and sense-making 510–11
and the necessity of active self-
imentation 172
disregard of 52, 141, 148
kinesthetic memory 51, 382
Merleau-Ponty's treatment of 522, note 3
neglect of 513
reduced to positional knowledge 513
see also dynamics, of movement, distinct
from sensations; kinesthetic consciousness;
proprioception
kinesthetic consciousness 113, 114, 118–121, 123,
125–28, 130–135, 138–40, 150,
200, 201, 204, 206, 209, 210, 215, 217, 218,
223, 247, 460, 499, 523, note 6
and originary experiences
of movement 129–130, 136
and speech erception 323–26
and transcendental subjectivity 120, 127–28
as ground of sense-making (constituting)
consciousness 133
as unfolding kinetic dynamic 123
cardinal epistemological structures of 130,
134, 140, 144
invariant structures of 134
phenomenology of 130–40

qualitative nature of 49, 131
see also attentiveness; constitution
(constituting consciousness); primal
animation; transcendental subjectivity
(sense-making consciousness)
kinesthetic experience 477–78, 498,
511–15, 520, 522, note 4,
523, note 6
and the practice of "naturalizing," 518–19
differentiating felt from perceptual 516–17
"insuppressibility" of 520
"kinesthetic information" (Jeannerod) 520
see also proprioception, "information"
kinesthetic/kinetic melodies 469, 487–88,
511–12, 513, 516
kinesthetic memory 512, 521
kinesthetic motivation problem,
see degrees of freedom, problem
kinetic apprenticeship and learning 129, 194,
195, 197, 201, 210, 211, 215, 216, 218,
246, 247, 256
kinetic bodily logos XXXI, XXXII, 424, 426,
440, 442–46
see also intelligence in action; mindful body;
movement and meaning
kinetic bodily pairings 135
kinetic bond 198, 211, 221, 225
see also bodily reference point; kinetic
intercorporeal attunement; movement, as
matchpoint
kinetic domains 18–20, 27
sensory-kinetic domains 317
see also movement (kinetic) dispositions
kinetic intelligence, see intelligence, kinetic;
kinetic bodily logos
kinetic intercorporeal attunement 198, 221,
224, 227
see also bodily reference point; kinetic bond;
movement, as
matchpoint
kinetic melodies 448, 469, 487, 512, 516
kinetic qualia/quality/qualities 49, 50, 126, 131,
133, 140, 141, 146, 469
aesthetic quality created by movement 102
and behavior 138
see also kinesthetic consciousness, qualitative
nature of; movement, creates qualities it
embodies; movement, qualitative character
of; qualia
kinetic spontaneity 62, 65, 66, 75, 117, 119, 128,
229, 234
"Know thyself," 48, 63, 68, 292
see also corporeal consciousness;
self-knowledge

L
laboratory,
    expanded concept of 156
    see also free variation, active
        self-experimentation
language,
    and other forms of symbolic behavior 3
    distinction between mind and brain 493, 494
    invention of 72, 324, 332–35, 348, 349
    language-tethered consciousness 349
    see also consciousness, and language;
        creationism, academic; creationism,
        linguistic; hominid(s), and language;
        language and experience; symbolic
        structure of primordial language
language and experience 224, 435, 466, 471
    languaging experience 466–70, 482, 490,
        494, 519
        challenge of 470
language of the philosopher 262, 271–72
    see also linguistically-attuned philosophy
language properly conceived as *post-kinetic*
        438, 515
    see also experience, challenge of languaging;
        intention movements; language and
        experience; movement, and language
        development; thinking and language
learning by moving 26
    see also being a body, and learning to move
        ourselves; corporeal concepts
lifeless natural science 109
like,
    see to be like something
linguistically-attuned philosophy 262
    see also language of the philosopher
"lived body," 310, 313–17,
        498, 499
    see also embodiment; living body/bodies
living body/bodies 6, 14,
        20, 40, 80, 95, 110, 120, 142, 144, 146, 147,
        149,
        162, 184–87, 210, 251, 272, 290,
        300–306, 309–311, 314, 315, 317, 324,
        328, 331, 338, 350–55, 358, 359, 361–64,
        370, 372–75, 385, 392, 399, 446, 467,
        491, 506, 517
    and Aristotle's physiology of perception 95
    and brains 372–75
    and eliminative materialism 350–54
    and embodiments
        311–13, 496
    and "lived body," 314–15
    and semantics of quality 10

connectionism and a lack of understanding
        of 184–87
    semantic specificity of 302–306
lobster(s) 43, 48, 51–52, 56, 63, 68, 70, 107
    "eating one of its own claws," 48, 49
locust(s), 55, 107, 270
    "look to see what moves," 48–53, 62
    as against proprioception and kinesthesia,
love of wisdom 295, 502, 520
"lower" animals 444–45
luminous point-figure experiments 434–35

M
magic,
    phenomenological 414–15
    phenomenological 413
matter 78, 89
    and form 78, 89
    animation of 402, 406, 409, 411
    "as physics and chemistry describe it," 77–79,
        83, 96, 103, 109
    as primitive 105, 109
    conception of 79, 90, 398, 401, 404, 409
    homonymously organic 83
    living and non-living
        409, 417
    not in and of itself explanatory of
        anything 110
    problematization of 110
    see also animism; force concept of; form
        and matter; matter-in-motion; matter-
        pure-and-simple; Meccanized (reductive)
        neurology; metaphysics; quality; "receiving
        into itself the sensible forms of things
        without the matter"; reductive materialism/
        committed materialists; reified neurology
"Matter will surely not move itself," 89, 97,
        103–104, 405
matter-in-motion 400–401, 407, 411
matter-pure-and-simple 97, 109, 395–96,
        398, 409
maxims 48, 52
    see also rules
meaning,
    a non-sensuous presence 148, 314
    acts of 134
    and a brain mechanics of cognition 184
    and animation 139
    and axioms of geometry 160, 168
    and brains 362, 380–81
    and displayer/displayed-to animals 339–40
    and dispositions 186
    and emergence 230, 233

and form values 107–108
and information 228, 231
and insight 177–78
and kinetic inter-attunement 198
and learning to move oneself 233
and natural attitude 163, 167, 200–201,
    211, 222–23
and Nature as a principle of motion 106
and neural events in brains 42
and phenomenology 162, 167, 178, 199, 209
and Sartre, Heidegger, and Merleau-
    Ponty 239
and the Background 213–14
and the philosophy of Merleau-Ponty 237, 243,
    260–61, 268–69, 271–73, 277
and thoughts 427–28
cultural 217, 424
experience and 156, 199, 229, 231,
    325, 339–40
interanimate 331
intercorporeal sense-making and 336
muddled 10
nonlinguistic 20
of the mental 49
ontic 165
sound meanings 326
structures of 134
"symbolic," 26
systematic reasonableness of 424
see also comsigns; corporeal representation;
    object as meant; semantics of quality;
    tactical deception
meaning(s) 230–31
see also animate form(s), and readiness
    toward meaning; being-toward-meaning;
    movement and meaning;
    tactile-kinesthetic body, and meaning
Meccanized (reductive) neurology 347, 355, 385
mechanisms 282–83
mechanisms/mechanics,
    of Nature 488, 489
mechanomorphism 386
medium,
    see perception, role of medium in Aristotle's
    account of; quality, perception of, in
    aesthetic and everyday experience
medium of art object 100–101
    see also perception, role of medium in
    Aristotle's account of
mental and physical,
    reduction of mental to physical 42, 183
    relationship of 37–38, 378–79
    separation of 6, 10, 11, 19, 182–87

see also mind/body dichotomy; mind/body
    problem; physical anthropology; "symbolic
    behavior," contrast of, with survival
    behavior
mental powers 6, 319, 375, 392, 408, 473
meta-corporeal consciousness 53, 59, 66, 76
    see also consciousness; corporeal
    consciousness; proprioception,
    evolutionary history of; surface recognition
    sensitivity
metaphysical distinctions
    between "higher" and "lower" (or "simpler")
        forms of life 25, 38, 46, 49, 53
    between life and death 41
    between mind and body 13, 33, 38, 182–83,
        242, 347, 372–73, 428
    between organic and inorganic 38–42, 49
    see also mental and physical, separation of;
        metaphysics; mind/body dichotomy
metaphysics 79–80, 90, 155, 311, 417, 427
    and experience 79–80
    Aristotle's holistic 90–92
    at odds with world 417
    biased 447
    continuous 41
    descriptive 47, 247
    fundamental metaphysical question 89
    homuncular 82
    in advance of a supportive epistemology 69
    in advance of a supportive natural history 69
    kinetic metaphysical primitiveness 103
    non-dualistic 78
    of aliveness 436
    of nature 110
    one at odds with experience 427
    process metaphysics 427, 439
    reigning 20th-century 79
    substantive 427–28
    Western metaphysics 233
    see also metaphysical distinctions;
        perception, proper metaphysics
        and epistemology of
metastability 483–84
    of Nature 488–89
mind 478–89
    and phenomenology 483
    approaching ultimate truths about 482
    as "flowing movement of awareness" 488
    description and explanation of 493–94
    not a solid 482
    part of Nature 488
    solid and dynamic conceptions of 482–83
    see also "solids" (James),

mind/body dichotomy 3–4, 33, 182–83, 186,
     428, 466
mind/body problem 52, 77, 79, 353–54, 358–9,
     370, 372, 374, 388, 391–92, 412, 466,
     485, 490–91
mindbody/mindbodies 79, 109
mindful body/bodies 422, 424, 426, 430, 478,
     483, 487, 488, 495, 501, 510, 521
  and embodied minds 478, 495, 521
  see also intelligence in action; kinetic bodily
     logos; movement and meaning
mindfulness 486–87
mirror neurons and embodied simulation
     521–22, note 2
molluscs (Mollusca) 57, 58, 60, 62, 108
  gastropods (Gastropoda) 58, 70
Monera 473
Morgan's canon 386
morphological semantics,
  see form values
morphological-kinetic-conceptual schema 21,
     26–29
  see also morphology, tool morphology and
     body morphology
morphology 18–20, 23, 39
  anatomical and cultural change 28–29
  and animate form 26, 29
  and technology 26–29
  hominid 3
  qualitative 108
  tool morphology and body morphology 26–28
  see also body build; morphological-kinetic-
     conceptual schema
mother tongue 195–96, 198, 223, 235, 334, 514
motivation(s) 231
  kinesthetic 62, 217–19, 364–65, 445
  see also affect
motor cortex (system) 368, 379–85, 389
"motor embodiment" (Varela & Depraz,
     Thompson) 470, 471
motorology(ies) 470–71, 496, 508
motor program(s) 197, 228, 230, 366–68, 381,
     385, 389, 410, 416, 441, 484, 508, 510, 514
  see also kinetic spontaneity
motor(s), motoric forms, motor topics 477–78, 490
movement 424
  and animation 453
  and attraction 97
  and idea of motor programs 55–56, 230–31
  and language development 430–39
  and Nature 93–5
  and perception of quality 94–95
  and quality 96
  and time 119, 133–40, 209

  as a natal phenomenon 201, 211
  as change of position 31, 123, 202–203, 208,
     211, 400
  as matchpoint 223–24
  ballistic 30–31
  cardinal structures of 209, 420, 448, 499
  concept of, as dynamic energy 401
  conceptual foundation for 402
  conceptual significance of 31–32
  creates qualities it embodies 124–27
  distinguished from behavior 23, 201, 442, 446
  distinguishing from stillness 61–62
  eye 470, 511
  felt as distinct from perceived 515–17
  Galilean-Cartesian construal of 95, 400–401
  inside and out 477, 511, 515–17, 522, note 3
  making things happen through 399
  "must itself be considered a perceptual
     system," 206
  originary significance of 116–20, 128, 133, 139
  paleoanthropological significance of 22
  preeminence of 223–24
  qualitative nature of 49–50, 119, 134, 138, 203,
     206, 252
  "sensations of," 511
  "the mother of all cognition," 118–19, 128–9
  understanding 402–403
  see also dynamic congruency; mother tongue;
     tactile-kinesthetic body
movement and meaning 105, 130, 132, 165,
     209–10, 227–9, 302–03, 331, 377, 382, 426,
     442, 504
  see also intelligence in action; kinetic bodily
     logos; meaning; mindful body; semantic
     congruency
movement and perception 113–14
  correlation of 119, 165–68, 171, 179,
     196–97, 204
  inseparability of 422, 428–29
  sensory-kinetic powers and sensitivities 317–18
  sensory-kinetic relationship 159
  sensory-kinetic worlds 317–18
movement as matchpoint 223, 334, 336
  see also kinetic bond; kinetic intercorporeal
     attunement
movement-born/born to move 117, 200–201,
     211, 217–18, 227, 234, 445
  and curiosity 195–96
  and stillborn consciousness 210
  see also primal animation
movement/I relationship (movement
     forms the I that moves before the
     I that moves forms movement) 119, 201,
     229, 233, 459

see also core self; emergent sense of self; movement, as matchpoint; primal animation; self, sense of; tactile-kinesthetic body, and kinetic bond with the world

movement notation 31

movement of objects 250–51

movement (kinetic) dispositions 20–21
and conceptual dispositions 26
and kinetic domains
19–20, 27
and terrain and climate 23
and the question of adaptiveness 20

movement (kinetic) possibilities 18–21, 23, 26, 32, 54, 58, 62, 65, 117, 170, 196, 232, 338, 344, 382, 385, 442, 445, 448, 471
and conceptual possibilities 26
and "I cans," 20
and kinetic domains 19–20
and terrain and climate 23
kinetic commonalities and 19
differences 19–20
kinetically dynamic possibilities 442
sensitivity to 55, 63, 67, 227
species-specific 62–63, 65–66
see also kinesthesia; kinesthetic consciousness; proprioception; self-movement

mysterianism/mysterians 410–13

N

naming 481
see also languaging experience; languaging experience, challenge of

narrative as primary form of discourse 434

natural attitude 80, 114, 130, 151, 163–67, 171, 173, 178, 179, 194, 200–212, 222–25, 228, 229, 234, 238, 239, 254, 414, 415, 517, 519

natural attitude view of movement 200–212, 228, 234

natural experience 268, 495

natural selection 445

nature (Nature) 90, 91, 93, 95, 114–15, 487
dynamics of 488–89
and animation 97
elemental 93
"is a principle of motion," 77, 453, 460, 487
kinetic nature of the naturally organic 102
see also movement; nature and ontology

nature and ontology 266–72

Neandertal(s) 115
bodies and movement dispositions of 19, 22, 27
bodies/morphology of 22, 23
conception of, as deficient 24, 30

front teeth of, as tools 21

subsistence tools of 27, 28

see also body build, and tool type; corporeal concepts; morphological-kinetic-conceptual schema; morphology; morphology, tool morphology and body morphology; movement dispositions; movement possibilities

Neandertal(s) and *Homo sapiens sapiens*, and stone tool-making 26–29
"boundary" between Middle and Upper Paleolithic 28
conceptual possibilities and dispositions compared 31–32
controversy about 3, 4, 33
differences between 3, 6, 27, 30–31
evolutionary relationship of 4–7
movement possibilities and dispositions compared 26

neural firing 143, 291, 350, 352, 355, 360, 396–402, 485
see also action potential

neurophenomenology 471, 509

neurophysiology 42, 141, 143, 350, 351, 353, 355, 358, 376, 382, 388, 498, 510, 512
see also cognitivist (adj. or noun)/cognitivists, and neurological Mecca; Meccanized (reductive) neurology; motor cortex; perception, physiology of/physiological explanations of; physiology

neuroscience 491
and reductionism 492

"no-gap-here" metaphysical theory 42

nonhuman animals 22, 43, 67–69, 72, 114, 115, 188, 287, 303, 329, 338, 343, 392, 408, 439, 442, 463, 473, 513

nonlinguistic concepts 17, 401, 432, 434, 515
see also concepts, learning of; corporeal concepts; infants, nonlinguistic concepts and/or thinking; meaning(s), nonlinguistic

"nonspecific behavioral arousal," 229, 230
see also intrinsic dynamics; primal animation

O

object as meant/the meant 134, 167, 170, 199

object *as such* 89, 92, 98, 101, 171
physical body, *as such* 338

object(s) in motion 93, 112, 117, 202, 206–209, 211
distinguished from movement 93, 201
see also natural attitude view of movement

object(s) of sense 78, 84, 86–89, 91, 92, 96, 99, 100, 107, 110–112

activity of, *see* perception, as dynamic process
as qualities in the world 87
power of 87, 92
see also organ(s) of sense; perception
"objective phenomenology" 356, 371, 413
one-two punch 385–386
ontogeny 495, 496
ontology,
    20th-century 83
opossum 350, 444
organisms,
    embodied, enactive, embedded, and
        animate 497, 505
    see also animate organism(s)
organ(s) of sense 78, 80, 83–89, 92, 93, 96, 99,
        100, 107, 110–112
    activity of, *see* perception, as dynamic process
    as conduit(s) to brain 79, 82
    as receptor organ(s) 81
    empirical rendering of 83
    homonymous 81, 83
    localized nature and experience of 80, 81, 83, 86
    power of 80, 92, 96
    relationship of, to object of sense 78
    see also object(s) of sense; perception
"organic bond"
    see "prelogical bond"
organic form 39, 45, 105, 108, 313

P
pain 140
paleoanthropology 5, 18, 22
    paleoanthropological data 28
    paleoanthropological reconstructions 20, 21,
        23, 24
parsimony 328, 386
passion 271, 282, 294, 295, 335, 455
passive synthesis 170, 178, 181, 244, 325, 326
pathology (as a point of departure for doing
        phenomenology) 240–44
perception,
    20th-century scientific explanations of 80
    amodal perception 220
    Aristotelian account compared to Galilean
        science account 92–98
    as dynamic process 86, 88, 92
    as preparation to respond 373, 375, 447
    as spatially localized experienced
        happening 81, 86, 92
    bottom-up account of 78, 81
    de-animation of 156, 181
    essential role of movement in 94
    experience(s) of 80, 83
    in aesthetic and everyday experience 98, 99

kinetic nature of 86, 93
moving on behalf of 81
natural history approach to 88
object-recognition account of 77, 83
of quality 92–95, 133
organ(s) of 78
phenomenological account of 164, 196
physiognomic account of 87
physiology of/physiological explanations
    of 92–95
proper metaphysics and epistemology of 81, 95
Representational Theory of 80, 87, 374
role of medium in Aristotle's account of 79,
    87, 88, 90, 92, 94, 96
spatial and qualitative nature of,
    distinguished 86, 93
subject of 94, 99
see also movement and perception; object(s)
    of sense; organ(s) of sense
"perceptual faith," 259–61, 265, 273
phenomenological
    analysis/analyses/understandings 113, 139,
        156, 164, 168, 171, 173, 194,
        196, 212, 213, 217, 257,
        312, 326, 371, 488, 506, 514, 520
phenomenological attitude 114, 179
phenomenological Ego 239
phenomenological *epoché*,
    see bracketing; suspension of the natural
        attitude
phenomenological inquiry into neuron firing
    396–402
phenomenological methodology,
    see bracketing; constructive phenomenology;
        free variation; freely-varied movement;
        suspension of the natural attitude
"phenomenological reflection"
    see reflection, "radical reflection"
phenomenologically-derived ontology 238–40,
    248, 273, 276
phenomenology 113, 115, 118, 121, 126, 129, 130, 133,
        134, 139, 155–57, 161, 162, 164, 167, 169, 172, 178,
        180, 193–235, 371, 414, 454, 457, 460,
        461, 464, 466, 470, 474–75, note 10, 483,
        501–510, 522, note 3
    and "phenomenological analysis," 196
    and "phenomenological reflection," 249
    and connectionism
        157, 182
    and descriptive psychology 180
    and evolutionary biology 501–510
    and free variation 169, 176, 178
    and improvisational dance 419
    and introspection 162, 165, 167, 179, 415

and kinesthetic consciousness 114, 121–25, 172
and Merleau-Ponty 238–39, 240, 247–49, 251,
253, 255, 260, 262, 269, 271, 273, 276, 301
and quality 130–34
and science 155, 163, 179–80, 186, 406
Danto's recognition of, in relation to lived
body 498
eidetic 176, 255
genetic 161, 199, 217, 239
of emergence/change 232–33
of quality 133–34
of time 134–40
ontological 258
static 199
task of 121
"the science of origins" 118
see also bracketing; complementarity/
complementary, of phenomenology and
science; constructive phenomenology;
free variation; freely-varied movement;
heterophenomenology; natural attitude;
natural attitude view of movement;
"objective phenom-enology";
phenomenologically-derived ontology;
psychology, "eidetic"; suspension of the
natural attitude
philosophers and laboratory coats ("The
Philosopher's White Coat") 352–54
philosophers/philosophy of mind 40, 44, 48, 156
Aristotle's 75, 76, 80, 83, 89, 93, 99, 106, 110
physical anthropology 5, 14
physical bodies *as such* 338
physicalism animated 409–410
physiognomic perception 87, 220, 221, 313, 332
and cardinal temporality 135
and invariants of movement 122
and objects in the world 89
and perception of quality 110
and qualitative change 137
and thinking in movement 433
and vitality affects 136–137, 220
Aristotle's physiognomic account of
perception 87
see also perception
physiology 78, 93–95, 188, 318, 336, 378
physiology/physiological explanations of
perception 93–95
see also motor cortex; neurophysiology
poetics of language 271, 272
polyp(s) 56–60
possible experience 168, 174, 175, 177, 252
and active free variation 174
and actual experience 172–74
possibilities of experience 174

see also free variation; freely-varied
movement
practicing philosophy close-up 292, 295, 509
predator-prey interactions 440
"prelogical bond," 262
prepersonal existence (prepersonal life,
prepersonal I) 203, 243, 245, 248, 251
pre-reflective self-awareness 461
"presentabilia," 168–170, 179
"presentations," 169, 172
primal animation 202, 211, 212, 214–216, 218,
222–230, 232, 234, 343, 430, 434, 442, 445,
447, 453, 458–460
and kinesthesia, tactile-kinesthetic
bodies 459
and kinesthetic consciousness 459
and primordial dynamism 459
see also intrinsic dynamics; kinesthetic
consciousness; movement-born;
non-specific behavior arousal
primal sensibility 117, 216, 218, 343, 503
see also primal animation; primitive/
primitiveness; "there from the start"
primitive (primitiveness) 96, 98, 103, 109
animals 57
"form of the language game"
wittgenstein) 331
infancy as primitive state of being 438
intelligence 28
matter as 109
meaning 160
motion/movement as "there from the
start," 96, 101, 107, 225, 226
notions 41
quality as "there from the start," 96
reflex 231
see also "psychological primitive"; "there from
the start"
primordial dynamism 459
and primal animation 459
primordial language, symbolic structure
of 331–32
see also analogical thinking;
symbolizing behavior
privileging,
of humankind and of language 43
of self-movement but dismissal of
kinesthesia 250
of the brain 354, 358
of the physico-chemical over the
experiential 81
of the visual 52
problem of a missing body 265
professional is personal 292, 294

profiles (of objects) 132, 136, 138, 165, 167, 470, 473–74, 495, 496, 506, 509
projection (psychological) 10, 244
prokaryotic organisms 59, 60
  see also surface recognition sensitivity
promissory note(s) of committed materialists 289, 409, 411–13
proprioception 49, 53–63, 65–67, 69, 140, 141, 147, 203–205, 219, 226, 445, 462, 464, 471, 477, 508, 512–14, 519, 523, note 6
  affective and cognitive elaboration of 67
  an epistemological gateway 67, 226
  and continuous sensitivity 60, 65, 67
  definition of 60–61
  evolutionary history of 53, 54, 56
  "information," 514
  proprioceptive ability 53
  "true proprioception," 58–59
  see also epistemological gateway; surface recognition sensitivity
protention(s) 459, 461
protentions and retentions 131, 138, 139, 483
  see also constitution
protists (Protista) 66, 71, 473
protozoa (Protozoa) 54, 59, 60, 62, 71
"psychological primitive," 225–26
  see also movement/I relationship; primal animation; primitive/primitiveness
psychology
  descriptive 180
  developmental 105, 188, 206, 219, 229, 332, 371
  eidetic 253, 255, 257
  empirical 223, 255
  experimental 230
  Gestalt psychologists 206
  "mere folk psychology," 94
  of the unconscious 15
  ontogenetical-psychological history 245
  "psychological clarification," 254–55
  psychological clinics and laboratories 249
  "psychological induction," 252, 254, 260
  see also Name Index for individual psychologists and psychiatrists; "psychological primitive"
punctuated equilibrium 5, 8, 42, 43

Q

qualia 49–51, 74, 87, 140–41, 146, 148, 149, 389, 403, 420, 448
  qualitative incommensurability 144

  see also kinesthetic consciousness, qualitative nature of; kinetic quality; movement, qualitative nature of; quality
qualitative change 137
  see also style
qualitative dynamics/qualitative kinetic dynamics 477, 486, 493–94, 499, 511–12
  see also dynamics; experience
quality/qualities 92–111, 123, 133–36, 138
  aesthetic quality 100–102
  and behavior 138
  and motion 104, 110
  and natural history 106–111
  coincidence of form, quality, and movement 102–106
  commonalities with movement as fundamental 96, 98, 100
  dually-anchored in aesthetic and everyday experience 99
  fundamentally kinetic nature of 104, 105
  of the essence of life 104, 106
  perception of, in aesthetic and everyday experience 98–102
  semantic nature of 106–109
  see also evolutionary semantics; kinetic quality; movement; perception; qualia; style

R

radical materialism 347
radula 58, 71
ratification 258–61, 263
  see also verification
rationality 426–27
reactivation 160–61
  see also self-evidence
readiness toward meaning 340, 343, 345
  see also biological matrix; movement and meaning; responsivity
"real existence" (Socrates) 497, 519
received wisdom (theory, dogma) 19, 248, 289–91
"receiving into itself the sensible forms of things without the matter," 78, 80, 81, 89, 92, 93, 96, 102, 111
  see also matter, and form; object(s) of sense; organ(s) of sense; qualia
receptivity 501–506
  and being awake and awakened 504–506
  as active 502–503, 505–506
  semantic aspect of 504
  see also movement and meaning; semantic congruency

recognition counting 135
red (color) 140, 142, 143, 146–48
reduction of body to brain 373–74
reductionism (neurological)
    480, 492–95, 500
  and cerebroscope 492–93
  interests and goals of 501
reductionist-materialist programs 43, 69, 90,
    96, 282
  see also Meccanized (reductive) neurology;
    reductive materialism/committed
    materialists; reified neurology
reductive materialism/committed
    materialists 37, 69, 82, 110, 408–414
  as alchemists 413
  reversing materialists' charges against
    mysterians 411–13
  reversing materialists' charges against
    phenomenologists 413–17
  see also eliminative materialism; Meccanized
    (reductive) neurology; reified neurology
reflection 199–201
  "hyper-reflection," 261, 262, 265
  "radical reflection," 224, 253–57
reflex behavior 444
reified neurology 410
  see also cognitivist (adj. or noun)/cognitivists,
    and neurological Mecca; motor programs;
    reductive materialism/committed
    materialists
replicators/self-replication 40, 42, 44, 53
responsivity 44, 46, 221, 223, 226, 340, 344, 377,
    406, 447, 472, 506–08
  complementarity of, with receptivity 507–08
  semantic responsivity 344
  see also evolutionary semantics; meaning;
    turning toward
retranslation 157, 159, 161, 174
  see also self-evidence
rules,
  "learning rules," 6, 17–19, 25
  owner's manual 52
  "rule-governed behaviors," 6
  see also maxims

S
sand wasps 443
scallop(s) 56, 68–70
searching behavior 197
  see also dynamic systems research
secondary qualities 77, 80, 83, 109
self,

Buddhist and metastable notions of 485–87
  contrast between spatial and
    temporal 486–87
emergent sense of 219, 222
sense of 67, 140, 219, 222, 245
"The Reality of Selves," 48, 67
unavoidably divided by language 435
see also bodily reference point; core self;
    "Know thyself"; movement/I relationship;
    primal animation; self-knowledge
self-evidence 130, 159, 164
  see also reactivation; retranslation
self-knowledge 48–53, 62
  and agency 51
  see also "Know thyself"
self-movement 113, 114, 117, 119–26, 128–36, 138,
    139, 147, 152, 168, 170, 172, 187, 188,
    194–96, 200, 201, 204, 206, 208, 209,
    212, 214, 217, 226–29, 250–52, 257, 283,
    369, 378, 399, 438, 444
  and experienced temporality 135
  constitution of 132, 133
  ephemerality of 133
  nature of consciousness of 130–34
  not an object 131, 132, 138
  originary 132–34, 136, 138, 139
  see also agency; agent(s); agentivity;
    kinesthetic consciousness; move-ment;
    tactile-kinesthetic body
self-organizing systems
  see coordination dynamics
semantic congruency 478, 504, 518
  see also movement and meaning; receptivity
semantic specificity 302–306
  see also animate values; corporeal archetypes;
    evolutionary semantics; form values
sensations,
  spatially pointillist and temporally
    punctual 511
sense-making (faculty) 119, 128, 139, 342, 382–83
  see also intercorporeal sense-making;
    meaning, intercorporeal
    sense-making and; readiness toward
    meaning;
    transcendental subjectivity
sense-making(s) 453, 461,
    466, 487, 506, 510–11
  see also intercorporeal sense-making;
    meaning, intercorporeal
    sense-making and; sense-making (faculty)
senses,
  essence of, distinguished from organ of 86

five 52, 204
    localized bodily 80
    uniform explanation of 84–86
    see also organ(s) of sense; perception
sensilla 55, 56, 63, 70, 71
sensing and moving 422
sensorimotor 471
    "sensorimotor subjectivity" Thompson) 470
    "sensorimotor profiles" (Noë) 470
sensory-kinetic 499
sensory-kinetic bodies 471
sensory-kinetic realities 471
sentience 460, 464, 466
    phenomenological groundings of 460
"skillful coping" (Varela and Depraz;
    Thompson) 469–70
"smart data bank," 403–405
"solids" (James) 484,
    "collocation of," 481, 482, 486
    distinction between solid and dynamic
        conceptions of mind 482
    "illusion of self's solidity," 485
    "solid" approach to the body 481–82
    see also self, contrast between spatial and
        temporal
somersaulting hydra 57
sound-maker(s) 143, 324–26, 328, 329, 334, 335
spatio-temporal-energic semantics 442
    see also animate values; bodily semantics;
        evolutionary semantics
spider(s) 54, 63, 70, 107, 315
spiritus (pneuma) 41
"spontaneous infant kicking"
    see "nonspecific behavioral arousal"
starfish 58, 69
static mechanics 184
Stentor 59, 71
stone tools,
    as analogues 16
    as symbols 17
    striking 23, 31
    stone tool(s), comparison of Neandertal and
        early modern
    see also Neandertal(s), body and movement
        dispositions of;
"stream of thought"/"stream of consciousness"
    (James) 479–82
style 206, 209, 233, 499, 511
    and quality 137, 138
    kinetic style 252
    see also kinetic quality; quality
subjective life/subjective experience(s) 38, 40,
    42, 130, 139, 140, 180, 220, 356, 370, 373,
    376–8, 381, 413, 415, 462, 479

subjectivity 478
subject-world relationship 495, 503, 505
sufficient similarity 215
"summum bonum of bigger brains," 5, 21, 25,
    30, 438
surface recognition sensitivity 59, 60, 62, 66,
    445, 462
    in the service of movement 59, 60, 66
    see also meta-corporeal consciousness;
        proprioception
surrounding world 55, 66, 117, 129, 433, 438, 445
suspension of the natural attitude 239, 254,
    414, 415
    see also bracketing
symbol(s) 308, 336, 342, 352
    campsite as 9
    tool as 8–10
    see also primordial language, symbolic
        structure of;
        "symbolic behavior"; symbolism/
        symbolization; symbolizing behavior
"symbolic behavior," 4, 5, 7–12, 17, 25, 27
    and art 4, 7, 8, 10–11
    and burial practices 7, 11, 17
    and campsites 7, 9–11, 17
    and language 4
    and tools 7, 9–10, 17
    contrast of, with survival behavior 9–11, 17
    see also symbol; symbolic codes; symbolism/
        symbolization; symbolizing behavior
symbolic codes 8–11
    see also symbol; "symbolic behavior";
        symbolism/symbolization; symbolizing
        behavior
symbolic structure of primordial language 332
symbolic system(s) of thought 426, 427
    see also symbolism/symbolization;
        symbolizing behavior
symbolism/symbolization 7–14, 26, 32, 308
    and art 7, 8
    and dance 424, 425, 427
    and light switches 8, 10, 16, 18, 28
    and stone tools 16–17
    anthropologists' and philosophers' view of 13
    as a form of analogical thinking 13, 17
    evolution of 13
    primary human modes of 15
    referential aspect of 13
    social aspect of 12
    tactile-kinesthetic body as focal point of 332
    see also analogical thinking; corporeal
        representation; symbol; "symbolic
        behavior"; symbolic codes; symbolizing
        behavior

symbolizing behavior 15–16
    see also analogical thinking; primordial
        language, symbolic structure of;
        symbolism/symbolization
synergies of meaningful movement 462, 467,
    478, 491, 495, 499

T
tactical deception 330, 331
    see also intercorporeal sense-making; kinetic
        intercorporeal attunement
tactile discrimination 52–53
    chemically-mediated 52–53
    relationship of, to proprioception 52–53
    see also external sense organs; proprioception
tactile-kinesthetic,
    corps engagé 361
    experience(s) 376, 378
    powers 348
    see also corps engagé; experience; invariants;
        subjective/subjective experience(s); tactile-
        kinesthetic body
tactile-kinesthetic body 378, 382–83, 459,
    510–11, 515
    and an evolutionary semantics (comsigns and
        tactical eception) 330–336
    and analogical thinking 17, 32
    and brains in vats 361
    and concept of force 399–400
    and habitualities (dispositions,
        tendencies) 186
    and imaginative kinetic free variations 169–173
    and infancy 214–215, 229
    and intentionality 209, 218, 382–83
    and kinetic bond with the world 198, 211,
        221, 225
    and meaning 231
    and motivations 218, 231, 364, 365
    and motor intentionality 211
    and movement itself as a perceptual system 228
    and natural attitude view of movement 227–28,
        233–34
    and primal animation 218
    and primordial language 331
    and speech perception 327–28, 334
    and the philosophy of Merleau-Ponty 247,
        249, 256–57, 265
    and vitality affects 222
    and "what is it like?" 215
    as constituted and constituting 218
    as "psychological primitive," 225–26
    thinking modelled on 26
    validation of, by work of Sperry and
        Penfield 377–78

    see also affective/tactile-kinesthetic body;
        affective-kinetic-cognitive aspects of life;
        analogical thinking; corporeal concepts;
        corporeal consciousness;
        kinesthetic consciousness; kinetic bodily
        logos; movement; thinking in movement
tactile-kinesthetic concepts,
    see corporeal concepts
tactile-kinesthetic invariants 471, 475, note 11
taking a stand 294
the brain 465, 467, 482, 490, 491, 495–8, 501, 518
    and the charge of animism 406–411
    and voluntary activity performance) 378
    as an organ of and for language 417
    as an organ of and for movement 371, 374,
        378, 417
    as computational device 68, 359, 375
    as oracle at Delphi 466
    as site of information-processing 403–405, 407
    computational models of 379
    experiential ascriptions to 473, note 8
    sensory-cognitive functions given to 407–408,
        411, 412
    see also information-processing/information
        processing machines; physicalism
        animated
"the great somatic sensory systems of the
    body," 328
"the mind is function of body," 3, 189,
    376–77, 506
"there from the start," 96, 101, 107, 225, 246,
    247, 341
    see also primitive; "psychological primitive"
thinking,
    kinetic nature of 421, 448
    modelled on the body 18, 26, 309, 351
    retification of 427–28
    see also analogical thinking; thinking and
        doing; thinking and language; thinking in
        movement
thinking and doing 177, 239, 294
thinking and language 426–27
thinking in movement 198, 226, 351, Chapter 12,
    variously specified at, 430–47, 519
    and thinking in words, compared 434–36
    see also corporeal concepts; kinesthetic
        consciousness; tactile-kinesthetic body
thought experiment(s) 83, 168–69
    flatland thought experiment 173
    of philosophers 140–50, 289
    see also brains in vats, brain-in-a-vat thought
        experiments
three-dimensionality 146, 149
throwing 20, 30–31

see also early modern humans, body and
movement dispositions of; stone
tool(s), comparison of Neandertal
and early modern
to be like something 466
"to the things themselves," 55, 114, 121, 156, 438, 497
things themselves 10, 78, 259, 263, 265, 266,
271, 275, 493
touch 52, 53, 84–89, 120–21, 195, 247, 257,
264, 275
as primary sense 84, 85
touched/touching 263–66
transcendental clue 139, 140, 173, 212–13, 231
"transcendental Man," 239
transcendental subjectivity (sense-making
consciousness) 119, 120, 126, 128, 139, 199,
200, 239, 483
see also constitution; kinesthetic
consciousness
transparency 468–69, 471–72
"transparency acquisition" (Varela) 469
see also familiarity
truths of experience,
being true to xix, xxiv, 151, note 8, 179, 519
turning toward 343
see also responsivity

U

Umwelt(s) 55, 61, 107, 372, 416, 445, 453, 462, 463,
473, note 6, 478
unconscious/unconsciousness 8, 9, 15, 38, 67,
168, 170, 181, 220, 325, 484
see also corporeal consciousness;
kinesthetic consciousness; meta-corporeal
consciousness
"unconscious inference," 168, 170
"undivided wholeness in flowing movement"
(Bohm) 488–89

V

verification 121, 161, 166, 196, 237, 244, 260
see also ratification; self-evidence

vertebrates 63, 66, 67, 286
and arthropods, compared 67
visual proprioception (visual kinesthesis)
203, 226
vitality affects 105, 136, 220–22, 227, 431, 469
"vitality affects" (Stern) 469
vole(s) 441
volition-perception relationship 168–69,
171, 179
see also correlation; movement and perception,
correlation of; movement and perception,
inseparability of

W

weaverbirds 441
Western science and/or philosophy,
20th-century 79, 81, 87, 89, 90,
93, 111
"What is it like?," 37, 67, 147, 215, 356, 370–71
question presupposes internally-mediated
corporeal consciousness 67
to be a body one is not 32, 44, 363, 371
"What is it like to be a bat?," 67, 370, 371, 391,
397, 417
What is it like to be a (newborn) human
infant? 215, 348
What is it like to think in movement? 198
"What it is/was like," 24, 32, 361, 397, 398
see also Chapter 11
whole body 481–82
destruction of, in artificial carvings 496–97
person 500
whole-body nervous system 480–81, 501
wonder 25, 44, 85, 97, 133, 210, 234, 239,
263, 266–67, 275, Chapter 7, 302, 349,
355, 356, 363, 369, 412
affective infrastructure of 285
shallow and deep wonder 288–89
worm(s) 69
annelids 57, 60, 62, 67–69
earthworm 55, 69
fan worms 444–45